ROME, NAPLES AND FLORENCE

ROME
NAPLES
AND
FLORENCE

BY
STENDHAL, *pseud.*

Marie Henri Beyle

Translated by
RICHARD N. COE

GEORGE BRAZILLER, Inc.

© JOHN CALDER LTD. 1959

LIBRARY OF CONGRESS CATALOG CARD NUMBER: 60-7174
PUBLISHED 1960 BY ARRANGEMENT WITH JOHN CALDER, LTD.
ALL RIGHTS RESERVED. NO PART OF THE CONTENTS OF THIS
BOOK MAY BE REPRODUCED WITHOUT THE WRITTEN CONSENT
OF THE PUBLISHERS, GEORGE BRAZILLER, INC., NEW YORK.

PRINTED IN GREAT BRITAIN

CONTENTS*

men—A city without opera—A Neapolitan
adventure—True patriotism—Backstairs patriot-
ism—Criticism in print: a form of censorship—
Lack of courtly decorum—Italian touchiness—A
new language—How to imitate Louis XIV—Eng-
lish modesty—Italian exaggeration— -issimo—
Bolognese society—How to pay an initial visit—
The language of glances—On being charming—
Dolce far niente—Mannerisms and affectations—
Mistrust—Perils of existence under Louis XVI—
Precautions—Anecdotes—The Knave of Hearts—
A Gallic tale—Misanthropy—The brightest
member of the family—Fools—Il rocolo—Lines
taken from Propertius—A precarious condition—
Honour under the Venetian government—Ber-
gamo—The cup of coffee—History of Italy—
Pride and vengeance—Thermal springs at la
Poretta—Concerning loans—The brou-brou—In-
terest at 12 per cent—Vexations of a land-owner
—Absence of dandyism—The price of a lady's
favour—The dandy: a rare phenomenon—Sense
of duty: a rarer phenomenon—Gambling with-
out affectation: a pleasing experience—The
Speaker's Platform in Paris—De Tracy's Logic in
Ravenna—Love in Italy—Guide-books—Anec-
dotes in the Italian manner—Rare occurrence of
suicides—How to make a fortune in Bologna—
Social mechanics—Rosenfeld and Frederick the
Great—Miracles—English travellers in Italy—
Wit: a social impossibility—Italian caution—
Ethical curios—Cautiousness—Wit in the Italian
manner—Contempt for threats—Parisina—
Bolognese society—The salon in Bologna—Emo-
tions—Lack of security—Moral transformation
experienced by a whole army—Absence of Logic

—Count Albareze—Anxieties—A precarious
condition—The common herd of literature—
Charlatanism—Signor Maio, Librarian to the
Vatican—Intrigue at the *Institute*—Florentine
pretentiousness—Impossibility of translating cer-
tain ideas—Supremacy of Florence in the year
1400—A literary *soirée*—Ariosto and Catullus—
Moral superiority of certain Italian men of let-
ters—Count Perticari—Signor Pietro Giordani—
Concerning the immorality of certain artists—
Death in the Visconti family—Concerning the
French *bourgeoisie*—The tomb of Machiavelli—
Wit: an unintelligible mystery—Concerning the
four categories of love—Countess Valamara—
Paris as seen through foreign eyes—The *marchese*
Pepoli—The Bentivoglio family—Attempts to
establish a constitution—Santi Bentivoglio—
How a monarchy may seduce the people—
Political disturbances in the XIIIth, XIVth and
XVth centuries—Bulls published by Pope Inno-
cent VI—Giovanni Auguto—Problem of the
Bolognese Ambassadors in Rome—Cheese-
paring among the aristocrac᷉—The younger
nobility—A disappointment—*La Montagnola*—
His Eminence Cardinal Spina

The highroad to Florence—Panorama of the
Apennines—Ignorance is bliss—Robbers in the
High Apennine

Santa Croce—Semi-Gothic arcades—Danger in
the streets—The *Palazzo Vecchio*—Harshness of
the Florentine dialect—Rossini—The Tuscan
character—The Florentine character—The
peasants of Tuscany—Tuscan philosophy—A

capons'—St Peter's—*Chalmer's Dictionary*—The
Roman mob—Fixed bayonets in church—*Il
Teatro Argentina*—Trajan's Column—*Il Teatro
Valle:* draconian police regulations—The consol-
ation of music—Busts of famous men in exile—
A minister devoid of hypocrisy—Protestantism
and art—Fragments rejected by my printer—The
marriage of North and South—Roman women
in love—More marionettes—Cassandrino—The
Princess Santa Valle

Appendices

Translator's Foreword

THE 'Italian Journey' in the eighteenth and early nineteenth centuries was an adventure which few who possessed the means and the leisure were tempted to refuse. Italy, so accessible, yet at the same time so remote and (in Calabria at least) so primitive, was heir to such a wealth of traditions, that every traveller might find there something to satisfy his curiosity. For Gibbon or Montesquieu, there were the vestiges of Rome, the still-visible evidence of her power and of the grandeur or weakness of her political institutions. Pompei and Herculaneum had only recently come to light, to arouse the learned speculations of a Winckelmann, and at the same time to fill the coffers of the King of Naples. Misson, the protestant pastor, had travelled in search of art and culture, the learned Dr Burney in search of music, de Brosses in search of that whole heritage of courtiership and splendour which still lingered on from the flamboyant epoch of the Renaissance. And if the poets—Goethe, Byron, Shelley, to name only the greatest—found in Italy the incarnation of that new sweetness and sensuality which was to invade the literary consciousness of Europe in the age of Romanticism, the ordinary educated Englishman, Frenchman or German might walk the fields of Mantua or contemplate Lake Trasimene, and there discover, with an emotion no less real for being more traditional, the haunting echo of verses or the distant ring of battles familiar to him from the school-room.

Yet for Henri Beyle—known to us as Stendhal—Italy was more than an adventure, an excursion, or even a theory: Italy was the deepest and most powerful experience of his life; it was an ideal, a touchstone which he employed to test the value of every personality and of every institution; it was the symbol of all his aspirations, in music as in art, in politics no less than in love, but above all in that all-embracing sphere of activities, philosophical, social and sentimental, which he entitled *la chasse au bonheur*—the Pursuit of Happiness. For the greater part of his life, Stendhal could conceive of no perfect happiness outside the land of Italy.

Among those nations of Europe who had long felt the power and attraction of Italy, England, in the early years of the nineteenth century, was at the greatest disadvantage; for the wars of the French Revolution and of the Napoleonic era had closed the frontiers, and many a projected 'Grand Tour' had had to be cancelled or postponed. (Indeed, the few eager travellers who had rashly taken advantage of the ephemeral Peace of Amiens to journey abroad had sometimes suffered heavily for their presumption, and —like Joseph Forsyth—had written their 'Journeys' and 'Memoirs' in the enforced idleness of a Napoleonic gaol.) In consequence, when peace was at last restored, there was a headlong rush to cross the Alps. Milan and Florence, Rome and Naples were thronged with English tourists, while hard upon their heels came Russians, Poles and others who had suffered from the twenty-year blockade; and the period 1815-1830 may well be called the Golden Age of travel in Italy.

Stendhal, on the other hand, had profited not a little from those very calamities which had so frustrated the enquiring or the restless spirits of St Petersburg and London. Born in Grenoble on January 23rd, 1783, he had come to Paris in search of adventure and experience a few weeks before the turn of the century—in fact, the first news which greeted him upon his arrival was that Napoleon had overthrown the disintegrating power of the *Directoire*, and had taken into his own hands the government of France. From the outset, Stendhal conceived an admiration for the First Consul which, though highly critical at times, was never wholly lost; and indeed, for the next fifteen years, the fortunes of the two men were to be closely, if indirectly, linked. None the less, Stendhal's first taste of Paris was one of bitter disappointment. He was friendless, almost penniless; worse still, disconcerted and bored. He lodged in a decrepit attic in the rue du Bac, with little food and no heating. Never of the strongest constitution, he soon contracted pleurisy; and that, indeed, might have been the end of Henri Beyle, but for the intervention of a distant cousin, Noël Daru, sometime secretary to the comte de Saint-Priest in Montpellier. Noël Daru was seventy years of age, and comparatively wealthy; he promptly rescued Henri Beyle from his perilous situation, installed him in his own comfortable house in the rue de Lille, and there introduced him to his sons Pierre and Martial.

Pierre Daru—later one of Napoleon's greatest civil administrators—was already an influential figure in the War Office, and, as soon as Beyle was recovered, the rising 'chef de la première division' used his power to obtain for his young cousin a post in his own department. But by this date, France stood already on the eve of the battle of Marengo; Napoleon had thrown the vanguard of his army across the Great Saint Bernard, and Daru was ordered to follow. And so, on the 7th of May, 1800, we find Henri Beyle, seventeen years of age and perched with desperate insecurity astride a bay horse, engulfed in the baggage-train of that extraordinary army. For the first time, Stendhal was headed southward into Italy.

A few days later, having come under fire from the guns of the Fort du Bard, and feeling like some hero out of Ariosto in spite of his ignominious civilian costume, Henri Beyle struggled into Ivrea. Having nothing better to do, and being filled to overflowing with curiosity, he went to the opera; and there, in that third-rate theatre, with its creaking stage, its down-at-heel players and its patchy orchestra, came the blinding, almost mystic revelation. 'J'éprouvai un bonheur *divin*', he wrote, many years later, to his sister

Pauline Beyle. It was the discovery of *music* (the opera performed was
Cimarosa's *Matrimonio segreto*, and Cimarosa, from that instant onward,
was to rank for him as one of the sublimest artists of all time); but it was the
discovery of much more—of a freedom, a release, a welling-up of unknown
emotions, a *happiness* so wholly unsuspected in the desiccating atmosphere
of Grenoble or amid the disenchantments of Paris, that henceforward he
knew, as if by some inner prompting, that there was no life possible for
him, save southward of the Alps.

In consequence, much of the story of Stendhal's life for the next forty
years is the tale of his attempts to escape from the routine of his occupations
and responsibilities in France, and to recapture the intoxication of this land
of enchantment. This first visit—he soon abandoned his civilian clothes for
the uniform of a second-lieutenant in the 6th Regiment of Dragoons—
lasted some eighteen months. He visited Mantua, Bergamo, Verona; took
part, not without distinction, in the battle at the crossing of the Mincio;
and was later stationed at Bra, in the region of Alessandria. None the less,
the true core of this early experience was the discovery of Milan. Here, he
had a foretaste of that all-possessing love for the city which was to haunt
him for so long, of the freedom and informality of its manners, of the magic
of its women. On the one hand, *la Scala*; on the other, Angela Pietragrua,
that majestic, raven-haired, generous and faithless creature who was to
torment him almost to the verge of suicide. By the end of the first year, he
was already, subconsciously at least, that *Arrigo Beyle, Milanese*, whom he
describes with such lucidity and affection in the *Souvenirs d'Égotisme*. For all
that, however, Beyle was suited to any life rather than that of the professional
soldier. In November 1801, he asked for, and was granted, leave of absence
from his regiment; and in fact it was to be ten years before he saw the skies
of Italy again.

During the following decade, he tried his hand, with greater or lesser
success, at commerce in Marseilles, at literature in Paris and at administration
in Germany. Pierre Daru was still his superior in the Napoleonic service.
At first, relations between the two cousins had been fairly strained; but after
some years, Daru had learned how to get the best out of his somewhat
unmanageable subordinate, and, in August 1811, as a mark of his satisfaction,
he was prevailed upon to grant him two months leave. Thus it came about
that, at eight o'clock on the morning of August 29th, Beyle managed to
shake off the snivelling Angelina Bereyter, his mistress from the Italian
Opera in Paris, and set forth in the stage coach for Milan.

As he drew near to the city, all the old fever of love was reawakened.
Even 'une certaine odeur de fumier particulière à ses rues' could move him
almost to tears—how much more, then, the visit which he was to pay,
trembling with shyness, to Angela Pietragrua, last seen in 1801. But if
Angela had not changed, Henri Beyle had: if she was still the same magnificent coquette, he was no longer quite the same blushing second-lieutenant,
content to admire from afar. There were several skirmishes, 'une grande

bataille', and Angela was conquered . . . for a while. Yet the presence of such a romantic lover, to one of her temperament and inclinations, was decidedly an embarrassment; and she it was who, within a day or two of her 'defeat', persuaded him to leave Milan and set out upon a tour of Italy— Mantua, Florence, Rome, Naples, Ancona—of which he kept a diary, and of which not a few reminiscences have passed into *Rome, Naples and Florence*. All the while, however, his heart was in Milan; each stage of his journey was hurried and abbreviated, that he might return to Lombardy without delay; and so, by October 22nd, he was back again in the Albergo della Città—only to find that Angela had left some days earlier for Varese. Here he followed her, only to catch her in an evil temper, and to be violently snubbed for his pains. Disconsolate, he made his way back into Milan, and the remaining three weeks of his freedom (he had long overstayed his leave, besides committing other indiscretions which were not calculated to please Daru!) were spent in alternate quarrels and reconciliations—a series of up-heavals which awoke in him an intensity of emotion of which he had never before suspected himself capable. Five-and-twenty years later, he still recalled these weeks as among the most tormented and yet the happiest of his life.

Upon his return to Paris, he had to face the anger of Daru, and there ensued a scene which still rankled as late as 1826. But the following months were destined to be so eventful that his immediate disgrace was forgotten. Once more abandoning the exasperatingly faithful Angelina Bereyter, he set off for Moscow with despatches, arrived in time to see the fire and the beginning of the retreat, survived the terrible road from Smolensk to Vilna and the passage of the Berëzina, and was no sooner back in Paris than he was off on a new mission, this time to Bautzen and Sagan. In 1813, there was precious little leisure allowed to a Napoleonic administrator; but in Sagan, finally, his health gave way, and in August of that same year, he was once again accorded leave—and once more took the highroad to Milan.

'I am destined once again', he wrote to Pauline, 'to see my beloved land of Italy. Italy is my true home. Not that I bear a disproportionate fondness for this object or for that; it is simply that the country as a whole *matches my temperament.*'

This third Italian journey was in many ways an echo of the second, two years earlier. The scenes with Angela were repeated; there were the same 'victories', the same jealousies, the same reconciliations. This time, however, it was to Monza that Angela escaped to avoid his importunities, while Beyle set foot for the first time on the soil of Venice. In the latter days of his leave, however, there came a calmer period, a few weeks of autumnal happiness which seem to centre about one particular event: for, on October 12th, Beyle and his mistress spent the evening at *la Scala*, and there, for the first time, he watched a ballet—*Prometeo*—by Salvatore Viganò. Henceforward, Viganò—'the Shakespeare of the ballet'—was to rank with Cimarosa and Canova among the greatest geniuses of the century—the very incarnation of *la mia cara Italia*.

On this occasion, Beyle was careful not to overstay his leave; for nothing in the world would he have quarrelled *now* with Pierre Daru, for he had hopes—promises even—of a permanent post in Italy, the ultimate goal of all his desires. But alas! the great collapse was already at hand. The allied armies were advancing upon Paris, and the Napoleonic epic was all but ended. And Beyle, an efficient, albeit a minor cog in the administrative machine, was gravely compromised, in the eyes of the Bourbon restoration, by his all-too-enthusiastic support of the previous régime. At one stroke, he lost his rank, his salary and all the benefits of his accumulated service; moreover, the very prospect of France under Louis XVIII and the 'Jesuits' he found too nauseating to be borne. Less than nine months, therefore, after his return to Paris, we find him cutting loose once and for all from poor Angelina Bereyter; and by August 10th, 1814, he was back again in Italy—not as a tourist this time, still less, as he had fondly hoped, as an administrator under Prince Eugène, but pitifully, as a *refugee*.

This, his fourth 'visit' to Milan, was to last the better part of seven years. He had nothing but the most inadequate private income to meet his needs; he was friendless and politically suspect, his health was still only partially restored. Moreover, his relationship with Angela was now more of a torture than a joy. The moments of reconciliation grew ever rarer; she sent him off successively to Genoa, to Leghorn, to Florence, to Venice and to Padua; but eventually her infidelities became so flagrant, that not even so willingly blind an idealist as Henri Beyle could deny himself the truth any longer. Towards the end of 1815, he broke with her for good, yet not without the cruellest suffering. 'C'était une catin', he wrote of Angela much later, 'mais une catin sublime.'

All in all, these first two years were years of misery; yet, for all that, Italy was still Italy; there was still music at *la Scala*, there were still paintings in the Brera; furthermore, to while away the time and to distract his thoughts, Beyle was beginning to write—no longer those ever-deferred, ideal comedies and tragedies which had for so long been destined (in his own mind) to win him immortality, but works of a more pedestrian nature: the *Lives of Haydn, Mozart and Metastasio* (cribbed largely from Carpani and various others), a *History of Painting in Italy*; and finally, towards 1816, a book simply *about* Italy, to meet the needs of that ever-growing stream of travellers now pouring south across the Alps. This plain 'travelogue' (yet how personal, how delightfully inaccurate, how tendentious, in a word, how *Stendhalian!*) was destined to be the primitive version of *Rome, Naples and Florence*, and it appeared in Paris in September, 1817.[1] On the surface, it was simply the factual account of a journey; but facts, for Henri Beyle—now for the first first time appearing before the public as *M. de Stendhal, Officier de Cavalerie*

---

1 *Rome, Naples et Florence en 1817*, par M. de Stendhal, officier de cavalerie. Paris (Delaunay), 1817. In-8,° 366 pp. The book sold well, and in fact represents Beyle's first success as an author. In October 1817, the French text was re-issued in London, with some minor alterations: *Rome, Naples et Florence en 1817, ou Esquisses sur l'état actuel de la société, des moeurs, des arts, de la littérature, etc., de ces villes célèbres.* Londres (Colburn), 1817. In-8°, pp. xii+353.

—were never more than an excuse. Just as he had used his *History of Painting* to propound a *theory of beauty*; just as he was to use his *Life of Rossini* to suggest a *theory of music*; so likewise the factual background to *Rome, Naples and Florence in 1817* was just so much necessary camouflage to disguise, or evidence to justify, a *theory of Italy*—a theory which is complex, involving love and art no less than history and politics, and which, in point of fact, is nothing less substantial than a far-reaching exploration of *la chasse au bonheur*.

Meanwhile, however, the grimmest days of his Italian exile were over. By July 1816 he had recovered from his infatuation for Angela—an infatuation so obsessive that Napoleon's return from Elba, and indeed all the campaign which ended in the disaster of Waterloo, seem to have left him indifferent—and gradually the circle of his friends was widening. In particular, Ludovico di Breme, from 1816 until his death in 1820 the recognised leader of intellectual life in Milan, had been curious to know this timid and somewhat unprepossessing refugee, whose reputation, despite his passion for anonymity, had been gradually infiltrating across the frontier; and, having met him, had introduced him to the whole of that carbonarist *élite* which gathered nightly at *la Scala*.

Napoleon, it must be remembered, had left his mark upon Italian politics, not merely by the administrative reforms which he had introduced to supersede the older, *laissez-faire* imperium of Austria, but above all by his promise, formulated soon after Marengo, of an independent, *united* Italy. With the return of Lombardy under Austrian dominion—a dominion which, at first, had not proved exceedingly repressive—a group of intellectuals had come rapidly to the fore, under the vague and perhaps misleading title of *carbonari*, whose primary object it was to bring about the longed-for unification of the whole Peninsula. To this group (whose organ was to be the periodical *il Conciliatore*) belonged, more or less actively, the poet Silvio Pellico, the philosopher Melchiorre Gioja, the critics Borsieri and Ermes Visconti, not to mention such minor figures as Carlo Guasco and Giuseppe Vismara.

It was the last of these new-found friends who, in the first weeks of 1818, introduced Beyle to one of the 'guardian angels' of the group, Mathilde Viscontini-Dembowski, the Milanese wife of a dissolute and drunken Polish officer. Mathilde's marriage was desperately unhappy; she found consolation, however, partly in her unflagging political activity, partly in her sincere and lasting affection for the poet Ugo Foscolo. This meeting was the prelude to the greatest emotional crisis of Stendhal's life—'la grande phrase musicale', as he himself was to call it—which began on the 4th of March, 1818, and ended only with the death of 'Métilde' in 1825. If Italy was the incarnation of all that Henri Beyle loved, or ever desired to love, then 'Métilde' was the incarnation of Italy—of *Lombardy* in particular, with all that singular beauty 'tinged with melancholy' which Beyle had ever admired above all else in Lombard women.

But no sooner had Beyle grown aware of the depth and extent of his own love (beside which his fifteen-year-long passion for Angela Pietragrua

appeared now as a kind of adolescent infatuation) than he grew aware also
that Mathilde was deliberately avoiding him. Here, once again, politics had
intervened. Mathilde had a cousin, signora Traversi, who was hand-in-glove
with the most reactionary elements in Milan, and who had directly provoked the assassination of Count Prina. Beyle, ever a 'liberal', had pointedly
and publicly refused to be introduced to her. For such a patent insult, la
Traversi had vowed him an undying hatred; and this hatred—or at least an
echo of it—had been transmitted to Mathilde.

The remaining three years of Beyle's life in Milan were wholly overshadowed by this love he had for a woman who never once gave him the
least sign of encouragement. Unlike Angela, Mathilde had not the minutest
trace of the coquette in her character; she seems to have been serious almost
to the verge of pedantry, and circumspect almost to the point of prudishness.
Moreover, at grips with such a far-reaching storm of passion within himself,
Beyle was once more overwhelmed with that frightening timidity and
gaucheness which had ruined so many of his earlier love-affairs. His diaries
and jottings of this period tell us part at least of this anguished and yet
boundlessly happy episode in his life; yet he has left us no coherent portrait
of 'Métilde' herself. Rather, if we are to understand her, we should turn
to his heroines: for each in turn of these creatures who dominate his novels
—Armance de Zohiloff, Mathilde de la Mole, Madame de Chasteller,
Clélia Conti—owes something at least (if not her very existence) to the
memory of 'la grande phrase musicale'.

The seven years in Italy, however, were now drawing to a close. The
political situation had deteriorated rapidly. Abortive revolutions in Naples
and Piedmont had disturbed the Austrian authorities in Lombardy; the
carbonari were arrested and imprisoned or executed; di Breme was dead;
Beyle himself was grown more than suspect to the government and the
police, but the Austrians, rather than risk an international incident by
deporting him, resorted to the ingenious scheme of spreading the rumour
among the remaining 'liberals' of the city that Beyle was a French royalist
agent provocateur, deliberately cultivating their acquaintance in order to
betray them. Gradually, salon after salon began to be shut against him. For
good measure, the police themselves began to make his life progressively
more uncomfortable. At long last, in the summer of 1821, Beyle's situation
became untenable; an object of suspicion to friends and enemies alike, he
realised that all he loved and treasured in Milan was lost to him for good.
On June 6th, he said farewell to Mathilde for the last time (he was never to
see her again), and on the 13th, took the coach for Paris.

This date marks an essential turning-point in Beyle's life. The long period
of formation was over at last; the period of creation was about to begin.
Henceforward, his love for Italy, like his love for Mathilde, changes
character. He was not yet done with the Peninsula; in 1823-4 (Lombardy
being still barred against him) he spent some five months in Florence and
Rome, and in 1830 he received the post he had so eagerly coveted some
twenty years earlier—a consular appointment, first in Trieste, later in

Civitavecchia. But, although he was to keep it until the end of his life, it had come too late; and when it was his, he no longer really wanted it. For, in effect, the book of Italy was closed to him in 1821; and what new discoveries the country had still to offer were destined to come, no longer from the present, but rather from the remote past—from those countless histories of the Mediaeval Republics which he was soon to read and re-read with such childlike eagerness.

From his earliest youth, Beyle—like Proust—had been obsessed with the problem of *reliving the past*. For the first twenty years of the century, he had lived a life so full, so passionately occupied, that this problem had, to some extent, been pushed into the background; but, now that the present stood enveloped in a sudden emptiness, the past began to occupy more and more of his thoughts. This past—*his* past—must not be allowed to vanish; to be re-lived, it must be *re-created*; and so, out of Beyle the administrator, Beyle the exile, Beyle the lover, there begins slowly to emerge Stendhal the writer. Two things above all had most imperatively to be recovered, salvaged from the waste-land of 'remembered facts': 'Métilde' and Italy. At first, his mind began to work analytically: he dissected his own sensations (*De l'Amour*), dissected his reactions to literature (*Racine et Shakespeare*), dissected the music he had once heard and still remembered (*Vie de Rossini*). But dissection was no real substitute for creation. There was a whole world to be created—a world whose centre was Milan. By 1826, this half-remembered, half-imagined world of Italy was so vividly present within his soul, that he took down the old, now half-forgotten travelogue of nine years earlier, determined to resurrect it in a new shape. In a remarkably short space of time, he had discarded from it what now seemed ephemeral or unimportant, swelled it to twice its original size with material which had long lain in his notes or in his mind—and thus was born the present volume, still with its old but now misleading title, *Rome, Naples et Florence*.

No sooner was the manuscript off his table and away to the publisher, than he was deeply committed to *Armance*—the first work of purely imaginative fiction which he had attempted. Nor is this mere chance. The processes of analysis and memory were slowly yielding to the unifying force of imagination; and *Rome, Naples et Florence* is already the portrait of an *imaginary* rather than of a real Italy: it is a first sketch, a glimpse of that miraculous country, in the midst of which is set *la Chartreuse*. From Milan to Parma is but a step. In between, admittedly, there come the novels set in France: *Armance, le Rouge et le Noir, Lucien Leuwen*. In 1826, Stendhal had still much to learn about the *techniques* of imaginative creation; but little or nothing to add to what he wanted to write about. Successively, Mathilde was transformed, from novel to novel; successively, through the *Promenades dans Rome* and the *Chroniques Italiennes*, Italy was transformed likewise—all as a prelude to the greatest transformation of all, the *Charterhouse of Parma*. Dictated from start to finish in a spell of two-and-fifty days, the *Charterhouse* was the final culmination of a life not merely fully *lived*, but already fully *relived*, through art and imagination, until memory seemed more real, more obsessive, than even the original experience itself. In the dream-fantasy of Parma, Italy and Mathilde—even Angela—are brought finally together, and the vision of an ideal land of beauty, where love and art alike are 'a promise of happiness'—the vision conceived prophetically in that flea-bitten opera-house in Ivrea thirty-nine years earlier—is given its perfect and eternal form.

*　　*　　*

So much is it necessary for the reader to know as a background to *Rome, Naples and Florence*. *Rome, Naples and Florence* is not a *factual* guide to Italy; it is an idealised *vision* of Italy by one of the most subtle and romantic spirits of all time. It is also, in its context (nor should the fact be overlooked or forgotten), a *pamphlet*—a political pamphlet written by an ardent, liberal-minded intellectual who had been both morally nauseated and physically victimised by the period of stupidity, meanness and reaction in which he lived. It is generally recognised that Stendhal, in *le Rouge et le Noir*, created the first great *political* novel of our epoch. But in this field as in others, much of the essential work of preparation had been done earlier. *Rome, Naples and Florence*, by the very fact that it is a work about Italy written by a French-man, is doubly political in its implications: it offers *positive* criticism of the actual state of affairs in Italy, and a positive solution to the evils which, from 1815 onwards, had afflicted the Peninsula; but it also suggests a *negative* criticism of the régime which held sway in France, by contrasting French society, as contemporaries knew it, with life as it was—or might be—lived in that idealised land beyond the Alps.

Stendhal's vision of Italy is far from simple. Italy represents a kind of Utopia (perhaps Maxime Leroy was not entirely wrong when he classed Stendhal among the 'Utopian socialists' of the nineteenth century), where aristocratic *sensibility* and plebeian *energy* contrive by some miracle to exist side by side, neither quality sapping nor devouring the other. It is a land of leisure, where love is fed by passion, yet still cultivated as an art (another Utopian contradiction); where, in fact, art and love are all but synonymous, being but different manifestations of the same dynamic force. It is a country of moral freedom, where the sham conventions of society are powerless against the natural ardour of men and women born without hypocrisy, and yet where men and women, despite the inhuman government under which they exist, still contrive to retain sufficient dignity to prevent their liberty ever degenerating into licence. It is a land of informality, and yet of natural grace and manners; of rational cynicism, and yet of decent respect towards the established superstitions; of an ignorant and vicious despotism, and yet (for such is the fertile nature of the Italian mind) of a despotism which itself breeds heroes out of slaves and conjures up painters, sculptors and musicians by the very restraint which it imposes upon all more direct and forceful means of expression. But above all, Italy, for Stendhal, is the homeland of Angela Pietragrua and of Mathilde Viscontini; and so, with all its defects, its vices, its preposterous absurdities and anachronisms, it is a land singled out by nature and blessed above all others; a land where 'the love of art and

the art of love' have been brought to a higher pitch of perfection than anywhere else upon the surface of the globe.

*   *   *

The present translation is based upon the critical edition by Daniel Muller
(2 vols., Champion, 1919), which is included in the *Oeuvres Complètes de
Stendhal*, published under the general editorship of Paul Arbelet and
Edouard Champion. Occasional verifications have been introduced from
the text presented by the late Henri Martineau (*Le Divan*, 1927) and from
other recent editions.

The primitive version of Stendhal's 'Journey', *Rome, Naples et Florence en
1817*, has previously appeared in English[1] although the translation has been
out of print for well over a century, and is inaccurate into the bargain; the
much fuller, and indeed almost completely different text of 1826[2] is now
appearing in English for the first time. In France, it was customary for
many years to add the discarded portions of the 1817 text as an appendix
to that of 1826; but recent critical studies—notably by MM. Martineau,
Bardèche and del Litto—have convincingly demonstrated that the 1817
edition is an important book in its own right, and consequently, that to
present it thus in fragmentary form is to do it a very real disservice. I have
confined myself, therefore, to indicating in the notes those passages which
have survived from the earlier version.

All Stendhal's writings—not excluding the novels—are rich in references
to contemporary events and personalities—so rich that, in order to avoid
losing the original text altogether in a grotesque labyrinth of footnotes
(Stendhal's *and* my own), I have preferred to compile an *Index* at the end,
which gives a certain minimum of necessary information. Such few footnotes of my own as have seemed indispensable are signed (*Trans.*); all the
others are Stendhal's own additions in the original French. However, since
some of these footnotes were added in 1826, whereas others belong to the
earlier edition, the date has been indicated in each case in square brackets.
For the section at the end headed *Notes* (to which references are indicated by
an asterisk * in the text), I am heavily indebted to Daniel Muller, and also
to the important annotated edition of *Rome, Naples et Florence en 1817*,
published in 1956 by Henri Martineau. I also gratefully acknowledge my
indebtedness to Mr Philip McNair for his valuable suggestions in the field
of Italian geography, history and politics, and to Mademoiselle Marie-Louise
Thyss for her numerous and ingenious elucidations of Stendhal's somewhat
idiosyncratic French.

RICHARD N. COE,
Leeds, May 1959

1 *Rome, Naples and Florence in* 1817: *sketches of the present state of Society, Manners, Arts,
    Literature, etc., in these celebrated cities*, by the Count de Stendhal. London (Colburn)
    1818, pp. xii + 339.
2 Of the original 1817 edition, Stendhal preserved rather less than one third (107
    pages out of 353). The 1826 edition, which is in the same format, has a total of 652
    pages; consequently, just over five-sixths of the revised version is made up of
    new material.

PREFACE*

A LONDON bookseller has already done me the honour of printing a second edition* of this pamphlet. For, in all truth, it has no claim to be called a book. The Author freely confesses that he has given never so much as a second glance to the larger part of those notes, from which the first edition was taken. In those days I entertained a fierce aversion to any form of literary affectation, and I was stoutly resolved to make no concessions to the critics of the press merely in order to win some renown as a man of letters in Paris. Indeed, I never foresaw that I should take up my abode in this *Capital of the World* for longer than one month in every two years, and then, merely that I might observe what was newly come to light, whether in the theatre, or in the broader realm of manners. I was persuaded that an Author may in no way deserve the approbation of his readers, save inasmuch as he remains true to himself; and further, that he may never hope to win a reputation in Paris, save in so far as he should make it his chief concern *to be like others*. In a word, I was as arrogant as a man may be who has just known six full months of happiness.

In this third edition, it is my pleasure to place before the reader the contents of my *Journal* more or less in their entirety; for, in 1817, caution had obliged me to refrain from printing many passages, innocent enough and indeed trivial enough in all conscience, yet which might have brought unwelcome attentions upon certain persons in Italy, whom I hold dear to my heart. These motives for reticence no longer exist. In the space of seven years, what sweeping changes may overtake *Fashionable Society**—the only society which can afford pleasure to the enquiring mind!

What interest may there be sought today in a portrait of
the land of Italy as it was in the year 1817? I have myself on
not a few occasions replied with this self-same query to those
obliging persons who would have persuaded me to print a new
edition. 'Other travellers, without exception, are wont to
confine their descriptions of Italy to the realm of the *inanimate*;
their portraits concern only the monuments, the sites, the
sublime manifestations of nature in that happy land. Whereas
you', I have been told, 'prefer to trace, to the limits of your
modest ability, the *manners* of the inhabitants and the *contours
of Italian Society*—that aggregate of singular and ingrained
preferences for love, for pleasure, for solitude, for plain
speaking, and so forth, whence, even now, there may chance to
spring a genius, a Canova or a Rossini. Whereas in England or
in France, the burden of *affectation*, without which there is
neither prospect of *success* nor hope of *esteem*, reduces all
artists to the status of waxen *dolls*. The majority of French
travellers who post towards Rome for the purpose of enjoying
the beauties of Italy, and of affording themselves a year of pure
enchantment, take the road homeward half-dead of boredom,
without having addressed a word to so many as three women
of fashion in the whole course of their excursion; and indeed,
the happiest instant of their entire journey comes when they
return at last to their favourite table at the *café Tortoni*.'

These notes were jotted down in 1817, nor have I altered
so much as twenty lines of them. At that epoch, I was happy;
and there is nothing in all the world to which I render such
sincere homage as to *happiness*. I propose to tender no excuses
to the public for making it the gift of an indifferent book.
After these last two pages which I have written, even that
reader who is least attuned to my own peculiar *nuances* of
feeling must know full well what manner of book he is to
expect. If it should prove boring, none will read it: it needs
no metaphysical argument to show that in such a case it were
as though it had never existed. There might be *imposture*, did

I but count a friend or two among that band of *literary critics* who wield the press. But never yet have I deserved the most meagre of reviews. Indeed, a certain bookseller, who has undertaken to dispose of a volume of mine entitled *de l'Amour*, writes to me the following letter, which I, being engaged in correcting the proofs of this very page before your eyes, have received at this very instant:

Paris, 3rd April 1824

Sir,

I could heartily wish that the moment were at hand, when I might submit to you an account of the profits that I hoped to reap from the sale of your volume *de l'Amour*; I begin to fear, however, that that day may never come; I have not yet managed to sell so many as forty copies of this book; indeed, I would be tempted to apply to your production a phrase which referred originally to Lefranc de Pompignan's *Sacred Poems*: 'Sacred they are indeed, for none will lay a hand on them.'

I remain, Sir, yours, etc.

F. MONGIE, senior,

BOOKSELLER*

Were all my 'productions' destined to remain 'sacred' (as M. Mongie so elegantly turns the phrase), this baleful circumstance would none the less, in *my* eyes, appear less humiliating than the obligation to crawl upon my hands and knees up to the editorial offices of *le Constitutionnel*, there to beg the favour of a review. I am well aware that he who follows these principles of mine runs little risk of covering himself with what passes in France for glory. But if ever I found myself in a mood to beg favours, I would rather set off post-haste for Rome, there to solicit the office of a *monsignore*, which is, if truth be told, the only one that I desire. Despite all that common gossip may allege—in speech and in print—against Italy, the individual who deliberately cultivates affectation is as rare a bird in

Roman or in Milanese society as the man who behaves with natural simplicity in Paris. 'But', cries the herd, 'in Rome it is not the practice to rail against religion!'—no more, indeed, than it is the custom for a man of breeding to utter coarse obscenities in a drawing-room.

You are persuaded that the Italian is a hypocrite through and through, for ever lying and dissembling; yet, if the truth were known, he is the most *natural* creature in the whole continent of Europe. *You* would have him the wiliest of schemers, a model of consummate prudence, a very Machiavelli incarnate; yet do but consider the trusting, childlike *naïveté* of those unhappy conspirators in Piedmont and in Naples.

MONTMORENCY, 30TH JULY 1824

ROME, NAPLES AND FLORENCE

BERLIN, 2nd September 1816. Four months' leave! I have just read the letter . . . my heart is thudding with the joy, the ecstasy of it! Twenty-six years old, and still such an impassioned ass! So I *shall* see the fair land of Italy. . . . But not a hint of all this emotional turmoil to His Excellency. The Eunuchs are unrelenting in the black rage of their hearts against the poor libertines. And even when I reach home again, I must steel myself against the prospect of two months' sullen, silent *displeasure.* Yet joy in the dream of the journey overrides all else; *and who knows where the world may be three weeks from now* ?*

ULM, 12th September. Utter emotional sterility. A wind from the North, which withers the promise of pleasure. The Black Forest—most aptly descriptive!—is melancholy and impressive. The sombre green of the fir-trees makes a spectacular contrast with the blinding whiteness of the snow. But the retreat from Moscow has left me curiously indifferent to the thrill of snow among the forests.

MUNICH, 15th September. This evening, M. le comte de *** introduced me to signora Catalani. I found the salon of the celebrated *prima donna* stuffed to bursting-point with ambassadors and half the big-wigs under heaven; the rainbow-glitter of ribbons and decorations was alone enough to set one's head in a whirl. His Majesty is indeed a very gallant gentleman. Yesterday being Sunday, signora Catalani, who is a desperately pious creature, betook herself to the Chapel Royal, and sat herself down most unblushingly in the minute private gallery exclusively reserved for the King's daughters. A court chamberlain, who, scared well out of his wits by the audacity of the thing, had attempted to advise her of the error of her ways, was repulsed with heavy losses. *She* (so she claimed), being *honoured* with the *devotion* of innumerable *Crowned Heads*, was fully *entitled* to sit . . . *etc.*, *etc.* His Majesty King Maximilian accepted the situation with all the gallantry of a man who has spent twenty years of his life a Colonel in the honourable service of France. In many another petty principality in the land, where court etiquette is the whip and scourge of society, a *faux pas* of such calamitous magnitude might well have led signora Catalani straight into the common gaol* !

MILAN, 24th September. It was seven o'clock in the evening when I arrived; I was limp with exhaustion; but I dragged myself straight off to *la Scala* . . . and there, at one stroke, lay all the justification of my journey. My senses were so utterly weary that they were beyond the furthest reaches of pleasure. Yet all the fantasy that the most exotic intricacy of an oriental imagination may evolve, all that is most baroque and most bizarre, all that is most sumptuous in architectural devising, all that can be made to live and breathe through the soft brilliance of draperies, all that can be coaxed into reality through the symbolism of characters who have not merely the costume, but the very faces and gestures of their make-believe and alien lands . . . all this and more have I seen tonight.

25th September. No time wasted: another visit to the finest opera-house in the world; another performance of *la Testa di Bronzo*. I had time now to give full rein to my admiration. The scene is set in Hungary; never was there a Prince in that country prouder or more imperious, more generous or more warlike than Galli. He is one of the finest actors I have ever met with, and he possesses the noblest bass voice that I have ever heard; the very corridors of this gigantic theatre are set humming with the echoes of it.[1]

And what a masterly handling of colour in the distribution of costume! It was as though I beheld, constantly evolving before my eyes, a series of most exquisite paintings by Paolo Veronese. There stood Galli, a Prince of Hungary in the national uniform of a hussar, with all its traditional brilliance of red, white and gold; and beside him his Chancellor of State, clad from head to foot wholly in black velvet, having no hint of glitter or ornament about him, save the insignia of his Order; while the Prince's ward (the entrancing mademoiselle Fabre) flaunted a cape of sky-blue and silver, with a white plume flown bravely in her shako. The whole stage of *la Scala* is afire with wealth and magnificence; the crowd of singers and actors rarely numbers less than a hundred at any given moment; and one and all are costumed with a splendour which, in France, would be reserved most severely for the star performers. One of the more recent ballets given on the stage here required one hundred and eighty-five specially-designed costumes of velvet or satin. The production expenses are immense. *La Scala* is the focal point of the entire city; it is the universal *salon*, the hub of society, which is here, and here *only*; not one open house in the whole of the town. *Rendez-vous at la Scala*— such is the accepted convention for all manner of business. The first experience is literally intoxicating. I am in a feverish daze as I write this.

26th September. I have recaptured the summer; this is the most stirring of all seasons in the fair land of Italy. There is a sort of drunkenness in my soul. I drove out to Desio*, a charming land-scape garden ten miles north of Milan, at the foot of the Alps.

And now I am just back from *la Scala*. Dear God! My enthusiasm is still screwed to the same pitch as before! I called

[1] It is scarcely likely that words which may have been true of a voice in 1816 should still hold good a decade or so later [1826].

la Scala the finest opera-house in the world, because no other on earth can conjure up so much pure pleasure through the medium of music. There is not a single chandelier in the whole of the auditorium; all the illumination there is comes from the fan of light reflected from the stage. Imagination itself can conceive of nothing more grandiose, more magnificent, more impressive or more original than the *décor*, with its profoundly architectural rhythm. During this evening's performance alone there were eleven changes of scenery. Henceforward and for evermore, I am doomed to contemplate our own theatres with unalleviated disgust; this is the real price and penalty of journeying to Italy.

A box in the third tier costs me the sum of one *sequin* for each evening, on the understanding that I shall continue to reserve it for the entire duration of my stay. In spite of the almost total darkness in the auditorium, I managed perfectly well to pick out different people as they made their way into the pit. It is quite customary to give and acknowledge greetings from box to box across the theatre; I have a footing now in seven or eight different boxes, in each of which there may be five or six persons, and conversation firmly established, as in a *salon*. The tone of society is utterly *natural*, gay without being boisterous, and ruthlessly stripped of *gravity*.

In music, there is only one device for the measuring of beauty: a thermometer to record the fever-heat enchantment of the fire within our souls; whereas in painting, I may stand ice-cold and unmoved before a canvas by Guido Reni* and pronounce: *This is superlatively beautiful.*

27th September. A Duke of Hungary (the librettist *had* to make it a Duke, for, here in Milan, the police-censorship would never tolerate a *King* upon the stage, were there the remotest chance of preventing it—I might quote some curious instances); a Duke, then, let it be; a Duke of Pressburg, in love with his own ward; and she, meanwhile, secretly married to a young officer (played by Bonoldi), who chances to be a *protégé* of the Chancellor of the Realm. This young officer has never known his parents; in fact, however, he is an illegitimate son of the Duke himself, and it is the Chancellor's ambition to engineer a public recognition. At the first hint which reaches him that his sovereign has designs upon his wife, the noble youth, abandoning his garrison, rides headlong to appeal to his protector, who, in sudden alarm, conceals him in a secret chamber underneath the Castle. This underground hiding-place has but one issue, whose access lies hidden in the pedestal of a statue which decorates the great hall of the Castle—a statue made in the likeness of a brazen head. This head, with all the signal-code required to operate the secret door, gives rise to the most rare and romanesque imbroglio . . . as in the *finale* of Act I when (the Duke being now at the very instant of leading his ward towards the altar-steps), the scene begins with a series of mighty thumpings delivered by a chicken-hearted lackey interred by mischance in the cellarage, and banging at the pedestal which holds the head in a desperate appeal for exhumation.

At long last, the Chancellor reveals to the Duke the secret of the young hero's birth; but he, meanwhile, has been pursued into the mountains as a deserter, captured and condemned to death. At the very climax of joy, as the sovereign exults in his new-discovered fatherhood, there come the echoes of a firing-squad: the sentence has been carried out. The quartet which opens with this sinister rattle of rifle-fire, the sudden metamorphosis of comedy into tragedy—all this would be counted a triumph, even if the score had borne the signature of a Mozart; judge then of the achievement, when it is that of a beginner at his first attempt! Signor Solliva, who is a pupil of the Milan *Conservatoire*, founded by Prince Eugène, is twenty-five years old. His music is more assured, more intense and more dramatic than any that I have heard for years. Never for an instant does his invention slacken. Is he a genius . . . or simply an expert *plagiarist*? In recent months, Milan has seen two if not three Mozart operas in rapid succession, for Mozart is just beginning to find an audience south of the Alps; and Solliva's music is a perpetual reminiscence of Mozart. Is it a brilliant *pastiche*? Or is it truly a work of genius?

28th September. It *is* genius* ! There is a warmth about the music, an inward dramatic ferment, a stamp of assurance about each and every twist of style, that most plainly do not stem from Mozart. But Solliva is young still; dazed by the intensity of his own admiration for Mozart, he has learned to speak with the self-same accents of his hero. If Cimarosa were still the idol of his generation, he would have been heard to echo the voice of Cimarosa.

Dugazon used to tell me, when I still lived in Paris, that every new aspirant who joined his drama class* was a little would-be Talma. It used to take six months to strip away the borrowed plumes and to discover whether there was any genuine core of individuality underneath.

Among painters, the most accomplished by far in the portrayal of *dynamic activity* in his subjects is Tintoretto. Similarly, Solliva is unrivalled in the portrayal of dramatic tension. There is very little straightforward melody in his work. Bonoldi's *aria* in the first act is a failure. Where Solliva comes into his own is in passages of a very different character—in the *ensembles*, of course, but also in certain sections of accompanied recitative, which provide the ideal medium for psychological analysis. No art of description can convey the impact of Galli's entry in Act I, when he appears immersed in heated argument with his Chancellor. Such is the profusion of luxuriance that the eyes are dazzled; such is the power of sound, so virile in mood and yet so natural in expression, that the ear is overwhelmed; such is the total effect that the soul is swept irresistibly away by the action unfolding before it: this is indeed *sublime*. The finest tragedies in the world are dead and dreary

by comparison. Solliva, like Correggio, understands the value
of *density*; his music never flags for a second; if a thematic
development contains no element of surprise, it will be ruthlessly abridged*; ideas are condensed and massed into compact-
ness; and the eventual outcome is as fine as a symphony by
Haydn in his most dynamic vein.

1st October.   I have just learnt that *la Testa di Bronzo* is based
upon a French melodrama. In Paris, it was a dismal failure;
in Milan—thanks to the music—a triumph, a masterpiece;
for the music brings depth and delicacy to the raw material of
emotion. 'Yet how is it', I enquired of signor Porta, 'how is it
that no *Italian* librettist seems capable of inventing the sort of
tale, the rich proliferation of dramatic incident, which opera
demands?'

'In Italy', came the answer, 'all thought is dangerous, and
writing the epitome of indiscretion. Today is the first of
October; yet did you notice the wind?—how soft, how
sweetly sensuous, how languidly pervasive of the air. Would
you have us risk a threat of exile among the snows of Munich,
the icy reaches of Berlin, amidst a race of sad, uncivil folk who
dream of nothing but the insignia of their orders and the
sixteen quarterings upon their coat-of-arms? Our climate is
the fairest jewel in all our heritage.'

And so Italy can hold no hope for literature until she shall
first have won herself a constitutional government, with an
Upper and a Lower House*; until the time of such an event, all
culture is but a sham, all literature academic pedantry. In such
a boundless desert of universal commonplaceness a true genius
may yet find scope; but it is the fate of an *Alfieri* to work blindly
in the dark; he must despair of any guidance from a *real* public.
Free men who loathe oppression will laud him to the skies,
while parasites who live by tyranny will pelt his name with
mud and execration. And yet such is the degree of idleness,
ignorance and hedonism among the younger generation of

B

Italians, that fully a century must certainly elapse before Italy shall have earned her constitution. Napoleon had set her on the right road, perhaps even without realising whither it led. He had already revived the tradition of individual courage among the peoples of Lombardy and the Romagna. The battle of Raab, in 1809, was won by Italians.

Such weary subjects are better left alone; instead, let us rather talk music. For here, south of the Alps, music is the only art which still retains a hold on life. With the exception of one solitary genius, the artists and the sculptors of Italy are of the same persuasion as the artists and the sculptors of Paris or London: honest folk who think in terms of *cash*. Whereas music still nourishes a belated spark of that creative fire which has burned unbroken from century to century, feeding the successive inspirations of a Dante or a Raphael; first poetry, then painting, then finally the music of a Pergolesi or a Cimarosa. In the beginning of things, this divine spark was first touched off by *liberty* and by the heroic cast of life which held sway under the mediaeval republics. In music, there are two paths which lead alike to the ultimate goal, two dissimilar styles which give promise of a similar delight—the way of Haydn and the way of Cimarosa: *harmony*, with its transcendent beauty, *melody* with its enchantment of delight. The style of Cimarosa is ideally suited to the peoples of the South, and defies the plodding mimicry of fools. It was towards the year 1780 that melody scaled the loftiest heights of glory; but ever since, the character of music has undergone a gradual transformation; harmony has usurped the throne, while melody wanes plaintively away. Painting is dead and buried. In sculpture, destiny has conjured up a Canova, a genius born to pierce the crust of mediocrity by the sheer power of vegetative growth that the soul of man possesses beneath these cloudless skies; yet Canova, like Alfieri, is a freak; he has no peers and no posterity; and all in all, sculpture is likewise as dead in Italy as the art of Correggio and his generation. Engraving still flourishes well enough; but then, engraving is scarcely more than a trade for artisans.

Music alone still keeps a hold on life in Italy; and the only sensible *activity*, in all this fair land, is the art of *love*; no other pleasure of the soul may thrive unhindered, and melancholy frustration is the sole reward of a social conscience. Friendship is smothered by mistrust; but in compensation, *love* under such skies is a pure delight; no other land knows aught but the palest *imitation*.

I have just come away from a box at the opera, where I was introduced to a tall and handsomely-proportioned woman, whose age, at a guess, would be about thirty-two. She is still beautiful, with that rare style of beauty which is never met with north of the Alps. All about her bears the stamp of great wealth and luxury, yet her whole being radiates an aura of the profoundest melancholy. As I was leaving the box, a mutual friend who had brought us together addressed me, saying: 'I must tell you a story'.

There is nothing rarer, here in Milan, than to fall in with an Italian eager to embark upon a narrative with none for audience but another of his own sex. The effort is usually reserved for the company of some more tender feminine acquaintance, or at best, for an occasion when the narrator is well established in the reassuring luxury of a *poltrona* (easy-chair). The tale my new friend told me was enriched with a wealth of picturesque circumstance, more often than not described in gesture; I pass it on in an abridged version.

'Some sixteen years since, a man of great estate, by name Zilietti, a banker from Milan, arrived one evening in Brescia. His first act was to visit the theatre; and there, in a box, his attention was captured by the striking features and the extreme youth of an unknown woman. Now Zilietti was forty years old, and had recently been amassing wealth to the tune of millions; indeed, one might have suspected that he had no care in all the world save money. Moreover, his journey to Brescia concerned some business matter, whose successful issue depended upon a prompt return to Milan. In an instant, every thought of money had flown from his head. With some difficulty, he managed to find an instant to whisper a word or two in the young enchantress' ear. You know her, of course: her name is Gina, and she was the wife of a man of noble birth and high fortune. In the end, Zilietti succeeded in persuading her to elope with him. And for sixteen years now he has adored her; yet, for that her husband is still alive, he has never been able to make her his wife.

'Six months ago, Gina's lover fell ill—for you must know that for some two years now, she has taken herself a lover, the poet Malaspina*—that excessively handsome fellow whom you met recently in the *salon* of la Bibin Catena. Zilietti, whose love is not a whit diminished since that first encounter, was desperately jealous. Every instant of his time which was not spent among his ledgers was passed with Gina. She meanwhile, distracted with the knowledge that her lover lay in danger of his life, yet well aware that every servant about her person was salaried with gold to spy and straightway report upon her every step, ordered her coachman to set her down by the Cathedral porch; and thence, making her way secretly through the crypts and passages beneath the nave, she emerged upon the further side, where the Archbishop has his residence, found the shop of an old-clothes'-merchant, and equipped herself with male attire and a set of ropes. Not knowing how else to reach home safely with her purchases, she bundled the garments out of sight beneath the folds of her own dress, and regained her carriage without further incident. No sooner was she inside her own front door than she asserted that she felt unwell, and locked herself alone in the privacy of her bedroom. At the first hour after midnight, having knotted her ropes into the rough semblance of a ladder, she fastened one end of it to her balcony and clambered silently down into the street. Her apartment, incidentally, was a *piano nobile* (first floor) at some considerable distance from the ground. At half past one in the morning, disguised as a man, she reached her lover's bedside. Malaspina was in the seventh heaven of delight; if he had felt sorrow at the oncoming of death, it was only because he had despaired of a last glimpse of his beloved. "Yet come no more, sweet Gina", said he, when at length, towards three in the morning, she found the courage to tear herself from his side. "The doorkeeper of this house is in the pay and service of Zilietti; I am poor, nor are you richer than I am; yet wealth and luxury are woven into the pattern of your life, and I should die in despair if I should know myself the occasion of a rift between yourself and Zilietti."

'Gina tore herself out of his arms. Yet at two o'clock in the morning of the day following, there came a tapping at the window of Malaspina's apartment, which, like Gina's, was situated on the first floor, and looked out upon one of those great stone balconies which are so frequent in Italy. It was Gina, who, having climbed out of her own window with the aid of a rope-ladder, had then hoisted herself up to that of her lover by the same means. Yet when she found him, he was lost in a delirium, and could say no word but her name, nor speak of anything, save of his passion for her. And for thirteen nights without respite the same expedition took place, until at length Malaspina was well out of danger.'

To the good ladies of Paris, no adventure imaginable could bear a stronger taint of absurdity; and I, for being rash enough to retail such madcap escapades, am now well placed to receive *my* portion of the ridicule. I offer no moral justification for such manners; nevertheless, my soul is stirred within me and moved to exaltation. Tomorrow, when I meet Gina anew, I shall be compelled to treat her with the deepest reverence; there will be a turmoil in my heart as though I were once again but a callow lad of twenty. And *that* is an experience which I no longer enjoy in Paris.

Had I but dared, I could dearly have embraced the acquaintance who told me this tale. I made him spin it out an hour or more in the telling. How can I check an impulse of deep affection towards him?

2nd October. Solliva is a meagre little fellow with all the stunted and unprepossessing appearance of *genius*. I am taking grave risks with my reputation by such unguarded assertions based on a first work; it would be wiser to wait for the second. If the Mozartian influence proliferates at the expense of *inward dramatic life*, then we must prepare to face the inevitable conclusion: here was yet another composer (and they are all too common in the field of music) whose talent ran to *one* opera only. Two operas, or maybe three—that is the best we may look for from our young hopefuls; after which there is nothing but repetition in a worked-out vein: look at Berton in France.

Galli, who is thirty years old and uncommonly handsome, is unquestionably the pillar and strength of *la Testa di Bronzo*. Some critics have preferred Remorini who, in the part of the Chancellor, is likewise a first-class bass with an extremely flexible voice, trained to a degree which is rarely met with among basses; yet, all in all, it is nothing more than a *mechanical instrument*, perfect of its kind, yet monotonous, with scarcely a hint of the human heart which inspires it. There is one little passage in this opera, in all not more than twenty bars in length:

O fortunato istante!

which has been universally acknowledged. It is a cry welling up from the heart; yet the composer has somehow caught the authentic echo of nature, and the audience set no bounds to the enthusiasm of its applause.

Mademoiselle Fabre, a young French singer born in Milan, actually within the walls of the Royal Palace, and brought up as a *protégée* of the vice-reine, possesses an extraordinarily fine voice, whose quality has improved notably since she took to living under the same roof as Velluti, the celebrated male soprano. Her performance is utterly bewitching in certain passages of intense emotion; yet she would be heard to still greater advantage in a smaller theatre. In her private life, rumour would have it that she is in love with Love. Personally, I have no doubts whatsoever on the matter, ever since I watched her in Act II of *la Testa*, singing

Stringerlo al petto . . .

in the scene where she suddenly discovers that her husband, whose death she had heard in the echoes of the firing squad, is in fact still safe and sound. One of the Chancellor's most trusted agents had arranged for the soldiers to be issued with blank cartridges. The whole scene is both melodramatic and moving; and at this evening's performance, the entire audience was held in rapt attention.[1] Yet on other occasions, when Mademoiselle Fabre is inattentive or over-tired, then there is nothing drearier; such talents as she still possesses would bring her high repute in a harem, but hardly elsewhere. She is twenty years old, and even on her off days I find her infinitely preferable to such soulless songstresses as mademoiselle Cinti, for instance.

Bassi is superb: nothing frigid or mechanical *there*! What a supreme *buffo*, had God but favoured him with the gift of a voice! What ardour and energy in a spirit steeped to the last degree in the essential reality of his part! For forty nights on end, never missing an evening, he has performed in this *Testa di Bronzo*; yet never a glance into the audience; from first to last he *is* the part he plays—the cowardly yet mawkish lackey of the Duke of Hungary. In France, any man of such intelligence (Bassi also writes attractive little comedies of his own) who took his acting so seriously, and let his part absorb him so completely, even when there was no one there to listen, must surely dread to seem absurd. I propounded this objection to

---

[1] The widow of Marshal Ney* was in the theatre on this occasion [1817]. Just before the moment when the crash of rifle-fire is heard from the platoon which is carrying out the sentence, friends managed to lead her away from the audience [1826].

him this very evening, and this was his answer: 'I act well because it pleases *me* to do so. My interpretation is modelled upon a certain cringing lackey of my own imagination. When first I came to play the part, I could *visualise* this creature. Now, as soon as I step into the footlights, I *am* this same sneaking footman whom once I only *saw*, and this gives me intense pleasure. If I were to watch the audience, I should be bored to tears; and in all probability, my mind would go blank. And besides, even with all the voice I can muster, there is not much to boast of; if it were not redeemed by competent acting, what would there be left?'

Perfect tonal quality in the voice, like perfect harmony in a woman's features, is only achieved at the price of a frigid temperament.

By a kind of instinctive reflex, which I observed tonight in the reactions of a German acquaintance, Baron Koenigsfeld, such characters as Bassi, who are entirely the creatures of their own emotions, produce an incontestable *shock* upon a certain category of not particularly intelligent aristocrats: lofty breeding prefers a more *calculated* talent; primitive *inspiration* seems coarse and overdone. Only yesterday, this same punctilious nobleman stormed himself blue in the face at a waiter in the restaurant for having mis-spelt his aristocratic surname upon his place-card.

3rd October. The orchestra at *la Scala*, for all its exquisite interpretation of *legato* passages, is somewhat lacking in *brio* in the more powerful sections of the score. There is a suspicion of timidity in the way the instruments attack the note.

The orchestra at the *Théâtre Favart* suffers from a contrary distemper, being mainly concerned to make life as awkward as possible for the singer, and to create as much noise as it can. In the *ideal* orchestra, the string section would be French; the wind, German; and the rest, Italian—including the conductor.

At *la Scala*, this post, where co-operation with the singers is so essential, is held by the celebrated Alessandro Rolla, who had to be requested by the police to give up performing on the viola, on account of the number of nervous breakdowns produced in the female portion of the audience.

For a Frenchman newly-arrived in Milan, the following comparison might prove instructive: in the field of music, Molière is represented by Cimarosa, and Corneille by Mozart, while Mayr, Winter, etc., are the equivalents of Marmontel and company. The prose of La Fontaine, with all its limpid innocence (as in *les Amours de Psyché*), is paralleled in music by Paisiello.

4th October. Today, I went to see the frescoes by Luini at Saronno, which are most moving; and I visited the Charter-house at Carignano, with more frescoes, this time by Daniele Crespi, a most remarkable painter who had modelled his vision upon the brothers Carracci, and his sensibility upon Correggio. I caught a glimpse of Castelazzo; but I was extremely disappointed with a certain castle at Montebello, which owes its fame to the fact that Napoleon stayed there in 1797. Acting in accordance with the well-worn precept: *major e longinquo reverentia*, from that time forward Bonaparte steadily avoided taking up his residence in cities, where he would have been too easily accessible. By contrast, Leinate, which is a garden full of architecture and belonging to Antonio Litta, a Duke of the Empire, I found delightful. Litta is one of the few members of the Napoleonic court who have not played turncoat since 1814, and he has held out his ground most stoutly against the *Tedeschi*. It is worth noting, moreover, that Napoleon promoted him to the rank of High Chamberlain *without his asking*. Antonio Litta has written a book, printed in one single edition comprising one solitary copy, which he has every intention of consigning to the flames before his death. He is said to enjoy an income of some seven or eight hundred thousand *livres* a year. In one of the avenues of Leinate, I caught a distant glimpse of the wife of his nephew, *il duchino*; she is numbered among the dozen loveliest women of Milan. She reminded me of some old Spanish portrait, with her air of fine disdain. It is exceedingly unwise to go walking alone in the gardens of Leinate; the park is mined with concealed spouts and fountains*, expressly fashioned to produce a fine soaking for the unwary visitor. As soon as I placed my foot upon the lowest step of a certain staircase, no fewer than six jets of water were set off in a great spurt between my legs.

It was Italy that provided the model and inspiration for French architects in the days of Louis XIV, and gave them a taste for gardens like those of Versailles and the Tuileries, where architecture and trees merge to form an essential unity.

In the *Gergnetto*, a villa belonging to His Most Militant Piety Giacomo Mellerio, I found some sculpture by Canova. I paid another visit to Desio, a landscape-garden in the plain English style situated to the north of Milan, which still seems the finest of them all. It affords a clear view of the mountains, quite close, and of the *Rezegon di Lek**. Here, the air is healthier and more bracing than in Milan. Napoleon had ordered the rice-fields and the *marciti* meadows (which are under perpetual irrigation, and yield eight crops a year) to be removed five miles beyond the confines of Milan. Unwisely, however, he allowed the peasants a fixed term of delay in order to change to a new type of cultivation. The advantages of rice as a staple crop in this part of the country are immense; consequently, the landowners found ways and means to bribe the vigilance of the police; and now, westward of Milan, towards the Porta Vercelli, I discovered rice-fields within a cannon-shot of the town itself. As for robbers on the highway, scarcely a night passes without meeting a band or two within gunshot-range. The police here bears a remarkable resemblance to that of Paris: most of its energies are dissipated in politics, and (to show no ill-feeling) it carries out the most barbarous pruning-operations on all the trees planted by Napoleon, thereby claiming the immemorial *right of faggots*.

But in the last resort, here in Italy, even the *agents provocateurs* are Italians, and share Italian tastes; and so this police, for all its corruption, has driven the citizens of Milan to work wonders for the improvement of their city. For instance, in the fiercest of downpours, the traveller may walk close beneath the walls of the houses without getting drenched. Tin-plate guttering carries the spill of water from the roofs directly into the main drain which runs beneath the level of every street; and as the cornices jut out from the wall to some considerable distance, and the balconies likewise, there is comparative shelter to be found in keeping close to the houses, even when the rain is at its heaviest.

The reader would deem me an enthusiastic ass, were I simple-minded enough to set down word for word all that I wrote on the 4th of October 1816, on the road home from Desio. This delightful villa, incidentally, belongs to the *marchese* Cusani, who, under the Napoleonic *régime*, once sought to outrival the luxury of Antonio Litta.

Galli has a bad cold. *La Scala* has revived *Elena*, an opera by Mayr, which had been running before the *première* of *la Testa di Bronzo*. Dear God, how *dull* it seems!

Yet what wild enthusiasm still survived to greet the *sextet** in Act II! This is the kind of music I used to hear so often in Bohemia: a *nocturne*, the very quintessence of melancholy, sweet and deeply moving. There is genius in such a passage; old Mayr must have saved it up from the days of his youth, or else pilfered it where he chanced to light upon it. Alone, this passage rescued the entire opera from disaster. Here you have the hall-mark of a nation born with an innate feeling for *beauty*: a whole opera, two hours long, saved from the depths by one single passage of scarce six minutes' duration; the crowds come flocking in from fifty miles' radius just to hear this one sextet sung by Mlle Fabre, by Remorini, Bassi,

Bonoldi, etc.; and night after night for forty performances on end, these same six minutes will win forgiveness for an hour or more of boredom. There is nothing *shocking* in the rest of the opera; there is merely *nothing*. . . . And so, from the two hundred miniature *salons* which go by the name of boxes, each with its curtain-draped window giving a view across the vastness of the auditorium, there arises a lively buzz of conversation. A box costs eighty *sequins*; only six years ago, during the Golden Age of Italy (the Napoleonic *régime*, 1805-1814), the same box would have cost two hundred or two hundred and fifty. In France, Napoleon brought back the Jesuits, and left the land in mourning for that liberty which, in the year 1800, she had still enjoyed; in Italy, he appeared as the scourge of corruption and the protector of true merit. Given twenty years' experience of rational despotism under so great a man, the people of Italy might perhaps have grown to deserve the high honour of bicameral government.

There are eight or ten boxes now, where I know I shall be made welcome; and I know of nothing more charming, more sympathetic, more truly and unreservedly admirable than the manners and customs of society in Milan. Nothing could be further removed from the life that is lived in England; never a hint of a withered heart or a countenance of despair. As a general rule, every woman is escorted by her lover; mild sallies of wit there may be, even lively arguments and wild bursts of laughter; but solemnity and self-importance have been banished from the earth. At the root of the matter lies the fact that Milan is a republic goaded into perpetual irritation by the presence of three regiments of Teutons, and compelled to furnish three millions in levies to the Emperor of Austria. Our own especial air of standing on our dignity (which the Italians call *sostenuto*), our noble art of *pretentiousness*, without which no man may be judged worthy of his salt, would appear in Italy the *nec plus ultra* of intolerable weariness. Once your spirit has grasped the fascination of this happy-go-lucky existence in Milanese society, there is no escaping from its spell. Many a Frenchman of the great Napoleonic generation came hither to embrace those fetters which he wore about him until his dying day.

Of all the cities in Europe, none has better-planned streets*, nor finer courtyards behind the façades of its houses, than Milan. These courtyards are square, and, as was the fashion in ancient Greece, are surrounded by a portico supported by granite columns of extraordinary beauty. In all Milan there must be some twenty thousand granite columns; the stone is quarried in Baveno, beside Lake Maggiore, and is ferried down towards the city along the famous canal which links the Adda to the Ticino. Leonardo da Vinci was concerned with the construction of this canal in 1496, when we in France, as indeed throughout the North, were as yet no better than uncouth barbarians.

Only two nights ago, the owner of one of these proud mansions, finding himself unable to sleep, was strolling up and down beneath the porticos at five o'clock in the morning, while the dawn lay hidden in a steady fall of warm rain. All at once his eye was caught by a figure emerging from a side entrance on the ground floor, and he recognised one of his acquaintances, who was, as it chanced, an exceedingly hand-some young man. Putting two and two together, he quickly concluded that the stranger had passed the night unbidden beneath his roof. Knowing that the young man had a genuine interest in agriculture, and using the rain as a pretext for conversation, the husband, without interrupting his sheltered stroll beneath the portico, kept his rival for two whole hours standing there in the downpour while he plied him with endless questions on farms and farming. Not until eight o'clock had struck, and the rain showing no signs of abating, did the husband most gallantly take leave of his acquaintance and return within the house.

The good people of Milan combine two rarely compatible

qualities which I have never before observed so closely united
in any national character: shrewdness and generosity. In
argument, the Milanese is as sparing of words as Tacitus; in
sharp contrast to his English opposite, at least half the sense of
his discourse is conveyed by glance and gesture; yet as soon as
he comes to set pen to paper, he succumbs in an instant to the
glamour of a fine flow of Tuscan rhetoric, and spins words
faster than Cicero.

Signora Catalani is come to town with the promise of four
recitals. The tickets are to cost ten francs each, and the whole
of Milan holds up its hands in horror. It is scarcely credible.
I have seen an entire box-full of people, one and all blessed
with a fortune of eighty or a hundred thousand *livres* a year,
and quite prepared, should the need arise, to lay out thrice that
sum on the construction of a *palazzo*, object furiously to this
'extravagance' of ten francs. In Milan, to all intents and purposes,
theatre-going costs nothing. The price of a seat at *la Scala*, on a
regular subscription, is precisely six-and-thirty *centimes*. For
this absurd sum, the spectator may sit through the first act of
an opera (a full hour's entertainment in itself: the whole
performance is timed to begin at half-past seven in winter; in
summer, at half-past eight), followed by a full-length serious
ballet, lasting an hour and a half; after the ballet comes the
second act of the opera, say three-quarters of an hour; and the
evening finally closes with a short comic ballet, usually exquisite,
which is designed to see you off the premises in a gale of
laughter towards half-past twelve or one o'clock in the morning.
The purchase of an ordinary ticket (two francs for occasional
visitors, thirty-six *centimes* for regular subscribers) entitles you
to a seat in the pit, which is equipped with benches comfortably
upholstered and with a good back to lean against. The pit can
seat about nine hundred persons. If you happen to enjoy the
privilege of a box, it is normal to arrive there early so as to
receive visitors. A box at *la Scala* is treated as freehold property,
like a house, and may change hands for as much as twenty-five

thousand francs. The Government grants an annual subsidy of two hundred thousand francs to the *impresario*, who exercises, in addition, the right of leasehold over all the boxes in the fifth and sixth tiers, bringing in a further hundred thousand francs. The balance of his assets is made up from the sale of tickets. Under the Napoleonic *régime*, the management also controlled a Casino, and the profits from the bank, to the tune of some six hundred thousand francs a year, made possible the engagement of front-rank dancers and singers. *La Scala* can seat an audience of some three thousand five hundred persons; but the pit is rarely more than half full, which is one of its greatest advantages*.

Half-way through the evening, it is the normal duty of the escorting gallant to regale his mistress with ices, which are served in the box. There is invariably some wager afoot, and the stake is always the same: *sorbets*, or water-ices. These *sorbets* are divine; they may be of three kinds, *gelati*, *crepè* and *pezzi duri*; and no one should fail to make so rewarding an acquaintance. I am still undecided which of the three species is the most exquisite; and so, every evening, I resort to experiment.

6th October.   And so, at last—after so many fanfares—the much-heralded recital by signora Catalani *has* eventually taken place*. It was held in the *Conservatoire*, and the hall was half-empty. I doubt whether there were more than four hundred people in the audience, all in all. The musical taste of the Milanese is instinctive and unerring. Everyone who heard her concurs in the verdict: for pure vocal quality, signora Catalani has had no rival within living memory. La Banti, la Correa, Mrs Billington, Marchesi, Crivelli—not one of them can hold a candle to her. Even in the most brilliant of *coloratura* arias she creates the effect of *singing in a grotto*; every note has a *silvery reverberation*. . . .

What marvels, then, were it our fortune to witness, had nature but seen fit to bestow upon her the gift of a *soul*! But, alas! in the event, she sang every single aria on the programme *in exactly the same style.* In anticipation, the aria

Frenar vorrei le lacrime . . .,

so gentle and so persuasive, was to have been the climax of the evening. Yet she sang it with the same profusion of tinkling and cascading *fioriture* as she had employed in the variations on the theme

Nel cor più non mi sento. . . .

In actual fact, signora Catalani's total *repertoire* comprises no more than a dozen items; with so slender an equipment does she tour the capital cities of Europe[1]!

'One must hear her once, if only to experience the exquisite

---

[1] This evening's recital consisted of the following items:

Della tromba il suon guerriero . . ., by Portogallo
Frenar vorrei le lacrime . . ., by Portogallo
Nel cor più non mi sento . . ., by Paisiello

For the second recital, in Milan, the following items:

Deh! frenate le lacrime . . ., by Puccita
Ombra adorata, aspetta . . ., by Crescentini
Nel cor più non mi sento . . ., by Paisiello

For the third recital, the following items:

Della tromba il suon guerriero . . ., by Portogallo
Per queste amare lacrime . . ., by***
Oh! dolce contento . . ., by Mozart

For the fourth recital, the following items:

Son regina . . ., by Portogallo
Dolce tranquillità . . . Signora Catalani sings this aria in a trio with Galli and with her pupil, Signorina Cori.
Oh cara d'amore!, by Guglielmi, also sung with Galli.
Sul margine d'un rio . . ., by Millico
Che momento non pensato . . ., a *terzetto* by Puccita, sung together with Galli and Remorini. In the event, Galli's voice completely eclipsed that of the peerless *prima donna.*

For the fifth recital, the following items:

Quelle pupille tenere . . ., by Cimarosa
Che soave zefiretto . . ., by Mozart
Stanca di pascolare . . ., by Millico
Frenar vorrei la lacrime . . ., by Portogallo
Là ci darem la mano . . ., by Mozart
Dolce tranquillità . . ., by***

[1817]

nostalgia for what *might have been*, had nature not disdained to bestow a hint of sensibility in the neighbourhood of so astonishing a larynx. . . .'

'It is fully eighteen years now since signora Catalani first came to Milan and sang

> *Ho perduto il figlio amato,*

and she has not made an iota of progress!'

'What does the composer matter? There *is* only one aria as far as signora Catalani is concerned—the one which *she* sings: an embroidered sequence of *fioriture*, nine-tenths of it in appalling taste. Since the day she left Italy, she has failed to find a single competent teacher. . . .'

This is a sample of the comments that I could hear exchanged all around me. And there is truth in every word of it. Yet, for all that, we shall scarcely hear the like again, as long as we live. She can sing ascending and descending chromatic scales better even than Marchesi, who was pointed out to me among the audience. He is still passably young, and enviably wealthy; and he still gives occasional concerts before a favoured company of friends; in this, he follows the practice of his rival Pacchiarotti in Padua. In his early days, Marchesi contrived to make himself the hero of a quantity of entertaining sentimental escapades.

This evening I heard the oddest tale, concerning a certain highly-respectable citizen of this province, whose misfortune it was to be afflicted with an unusually high-pitched voice. One night, just as he was about to pay a visit to a certain lady, no less notorious for the pettiness of her vanity than for the magnificence of her fortune, our squeaky-voiced friend was greeted with a hail of cudgel-blows about his person; the more he called for help, the higher his voice squeaked; and the higher he squeaked, the thicker the blows fell about him. 'How now, hog of a *soprano*, that'll learn you to come a-courting!' The point is that the assailant was a priest, who was avenging a brother's injuries upon the shoulders of our friend the highly-respectable citizen, under the delusion that his victim was Marchesi. When the anecdote reached the ears of the *soprano* himself, he not merely dined out on it for half a year, but drew a timely moral from it for his own governance, and thenceforward steered his path very clear of this particular wealthy *bourgeoise*.

On the stage, signora Catalani, who must be thirty-four or thirty-five years old, still retains a remarkable degree of beauty; I could dearly wish to see her in *opera buffa*, where the contrast between the majesty of her features and the magnificence of her voice on the one hand, and the frivolity of the *rôle* on the other, must be profoundly striking. Whereas she will never grasp the first thing about *opera seria*. She is a creature of desiccated sensibility.

All in all, I was disappointed. I would gladly have journeyed ninety miles to hear such a programme; it was my good fortune to be actually in Milan. As soon as the recital was over, I whipped up the horses into a great gallop, to pay a call on Signora Bina R***; yet, by the time I arrived, I found I had already been forestalled by three or four *habitués*, who had run full tilt all the way from the *Conservatoire* so as to give the company, pessimistically chary of squandering its ten francs, a first-hand account of the evening. The distance involved was something over a mile and a half; nor was it therefore wholly surprising to observe a certain breathlessness about the conversation. I waited, by my watch, a full three-quarters of an hour, during which time not one single person managed to finish a sentence.

Naples is no longer the capital of the world of music; that pre-eminence is now usurped by Milan, at least in so far as music is a direct emanation of the passions. Give your Neapolitan audience a fine voice, and it is satisfied; Naples lies too close to Africa to appreciate the artistry which may portray the rarer shades of sensibility. Such, at least, is the picture I have just had painted for me by Signor de Breme.

7th October. I was forgetting to record the most striking impression of all at yesterday's recital by Signora Catalani; for several moments on end I was struck motionless with wonderment, for I had glimpsed the fairest countenance that ever I set eyes on. Its possessor is Lady Fanny Harley. *Raphaël, ubi es?* There is not one among the whole swarm of our wretched present-day artists, for all their load of trappings and titles, who can boast the technique to set on canvas such a face; their interpretation would forcibly be *modelled on classical antiquity*; it would *have style* (as they say in Paris)—in other words, it would impose an expression of strength and serenity upon features which owe their fascination precisely to the *complete absence of strength of any kind.* This apparent propensity to easy emotion, this expression of unsophisticated *naïveté* and gentle grace, is one of the most significant characteristics of certain modern faces, and the one which gives them so marked an ascendancy over the antique. But no contemporary artist could so much as begin to grasp the logic of this argument. How fortunate we might count ourselves, could we but set the clock back and return to the age of Ghirlandajo or Giorgione (1490)! In such an epoch, our artists might at least prove capable of executing a faithful copy of Nature, *as in a mirror*; and what a jewel beyond price would be a mirror wherein there dwelt an unfading portrait of Lady Fanny Harley, clad in all this evening's radiance!

8th October. I have no idea why the sight of supreme beauty threw me last night into such a maze of metaphysical notions. O, the pity of it, that the concept of *ideal beauty*, in relation to the form of the human head, should have gained currency in the world only *after* the death of Raphael! The burning sensibility of this great artist alone could have worked the perfect fusion of abstract idealism with natural reality. The pretty, sophisticated wit of our socially-lionised painters never reaches within a thousand leagues of the problem. If only they could bring themselves, just once in a while, to condescend to make a faithful drawing from the life, without the inevitable *stiffening* (however devoutly borrowed from the Greeks), they might yet achieve greatness *all unawares*. Fra Lippo Lippi, now, or Fra Angelico of Fiesole, if nature had offered them a glimpse of a head so angelic as that of Lady Fanny Harley, would have asked for nothing better than to copy it faithfully. This is the reward and fascination of studying painting in the second half of the fifteenth century. I can fully appreciate what force urged Herr Cornelius and other artists of the German school to model themselves on this period. Indeed, who would *not* prefer Ghirlandajo to Girodet?

20th October.   Unless I manage to leave here within three days, I shall never make my tour of Italy; not that I am entangled in any sentimental adventure, but merely that I am now on such footing of familiarity in four or five boxes at *la Scala*, that I am received as though I were a friend of ten years' standing. Nobody gets up when I come in, and the conversation continues as though none had entered save the footman. 'And *that's* something to be proud of, I'm sure!' I can hear the scandalised voice of my Parisian acquaintances. 'Gross discourtesy, in *our* opinion!' It may be so, indeed; yet, in my estimation, it is the sweetest reward in all the world for the two years I once spent learning, not merely the classical Italian of Tuscany, but the dialects of Milan as well, and of Piedmont, Venice, Naples and the rest. Beyond the frontiers of Italy, even the names of these dialects are unfamiliar, and they are spoken exclusively within the boundaries of the principality whose name they bear. Nevertheless, if you are deaf to the niceties of Milanese, the people among whom you have elected to travel are fated to remain both intellectually and emotionally invisible. The overbearing chatter and the brash impertinence which characterise the young blades of a *Certain Nation* inspire nothing but a shudder of revulsion in Milan. By a whim of chance, I genuinely prefer listening to talking; and this constitutes a positive advantage, which sometimes redeems even my rarely disguised inability to suffer fools gladly. When I was in Paris (and this is a further confession I owe to the reader), a lady of fashion and intelligence once confided to me in a letter that there was something *rustic* about me. In all likelihood, it is this same taint of character which explains how it came about that the plainspoken informality of Italy so promptly won me heart and soul. What unspoilt simplicity! How directly words convey what each one is feeling or inwardly thinking *at the instant*! And how plainly it is apparent that no one is trying to *imitate* anyone else. Once, when I was in London, an Englishman said to me, referring to the mistress who was the idol of his heart: 'In all she is or does, there is never a hint of *vulgarity*'. It would take me a week to explain the meaning of this exclamation to a Milanese; but once he had grasped the elusive core of it, the joke would set him laughing for hours on end. I should be forced to begin by explaining that England, unlike Milan, is a land where men are penned and segregated into *castes*, as in India . . . etc., etc.

'The *informality of Italy*!'—I can hear the sneer of my friends from the Faubourg Poissonnière—'Did you ever hear such nonsense?' Yet the art of being natural, or simple, or candidly impassioned (if I dare use the phrase), is a *nuance* which attaches to every action that a man may perform; and consequently, I ought by rights to digress at this point with a description twenty pages long of the divers and manifold aspects of behaviour of which I have lately been witness. Such a description, contrived with due attention to style, and with all that scrupulous exactitude of detail which is my particular pride, would take a considerable time in the writing, and the clock in the tower of *San Fedele* has just struck the third hour after midnight. And besides, three out of every four of my readers would dismiss any such description as the purest fantasy. I shall therefore content myself with a plain statement of fact: there *is* something here that is most singularly worth seeing, and which *can* be seen, by all who have eyes to see; but to make an invisible world visible, a sound knowledge of Milanese dialect is essential. If ever Béranger, the great poet, passes this way, *he* will understand what I mean. But Saint-Lambert, the poet of *les Saisons*, the court-parasite of King Stanislas, the only-too-favoured lover of Madame du Châtelet—Saint-Lambert would have found this land a torture and a desolation.

25th October. This very evening, signora Bibin Catena, a woman radiant with beauty, intelligence and *joie de vivre*, condescended to teach me the gentle art of playing *tarocchi**. This is one of the most obsessive preoccupations of the Milanese. It is a game which requires a full pack of fifty-two cards, each one three times the size of our own familiar variety. A score or more have attributes similar to the aces in an ordinary pack, and can beat any other card; they are beautifully designed, moreover, with symbols representing the Pope, Pope-Joan, the Jester, the Hanged Man, the Lovers, Fortune, Death, etc. There are, however, four suits (*bastoni*, *danari*, *spade*, *coppe*) just as in other games, pictured respectively by staves, coins, swords and goblets. Signor Reina, one of the friends whose acquaintance I owe in the first place to the kindness of signora G***, told me that this game was originally invented by Michelangelo. This same Signor Reina has brought together one of the finest libraries in Europe; he is, moreover, of an extremely generous disposition—an uncommon phenomenon, and one which I never before recall having discovered in alliance with a passion for books. He was among those deported to the Delta of the Cattaro in 1799.

If there be indeed a grain of truth in the claim that it was Michelangelo who invented the game of *tarocchi*, that moment of inspiration has proved an abundant source of quarrels ever since among the Milanese, and fair grounds for scandal in the eyes of such vain and mettlesome Frenchmen as deign to visit the city. I met one of the latter breed this evening, in whose opinion the Italians were the unmanliest of creatures for failing to draw swords a score of times at least in the course of a game of *tarocchi*. And indeed, having been created, in an evil hour, almost totally bereft of vanity, the Milanese set no bounds to the uninhibited ferocity of the quarrels which arise among them over cards. In other words, they enjoy *tarocchi* as the occasion for the liveliest outbursts of emotion. This very evening, there came an instant when I was convinced that all four players in the box where I sat were about to grab handfuls of each other's hair; as it was, the game came to a standstill for a full ten minutes. The pit began to lose patience, calling out: '*Zitti! zitti!*' and to tell the truth, since the box was no further removed than the second tier, the whole performance on the stage was, to all intents and purposes, being interrupted by the quarrel. '*Va a farti buzzarare!*' shouted one of the card-players. '*Ti te sei un gran cojononon!*' retorted another, his eyes afire with fury and screaming at the top of his voice. The twist of inflexion which fell upon the word *cojononon* struck me as a masterpiece of comic realism. Such storms of anger may seem excessive; yet they leave so little trace of their passage that I noticed, as we all left the box, that none of the parties to the quarrel seemed to feel the slightest need to apologise, or to smooth the matter over with his erstwhile antagonists. If the truth were told, the Italian who is genuinely angry is, so I believe, silent and self-controlled; and whatever tonight's manifestation may have implied, it was assuredly not anger. Rather call it *impatience*—the essential, comic, whirlwind impatience of two staid citizens quarrelling over a toy, and delighted to recapture a fleeting instant of childhood in the process.

Against the background of this lying and hypocritical generation ('this age of cant*', says Lord Byron), such wild displays of primitive and unsophisticated behaviour in the midst of the wealthiest and most aristocratic *élite* of Milanese society left so indelible an impression on my mind, that I conceived the notion of coming to settle in Italy for good. Happiness is contagious.

My compatriot, devil take him! whom I could devoutly have wished at the bottom of the sea, came to pester me again later in the *Caffè dell' Accademia*, in front of *la Scala*. 'The vulgarity of it!' he exclaimed. '*Cojononon!* And the *shouting*! Come now, can you honestly claim that such a race has any refinement of sensibility? Or that their musical ear is offended by the slightest of discords?' Obviously, I *deserved* to see all my ideas desecrated by the tongue of a fool; it was my own fault for having talked unguardedly to him in the first place.

For it was *I* who first engaged in conversation with this Monsieur Mal***; and how bitterly have I lived since to regret it! I must tell the truth, though *National Honour* shall disown me for it, and cast me out for ever: when I am in Italy, the mere presence of a Frenchman spells the instant and unfailing annihilation of all my happiness. I am strolling in the gardens of Paradise, drowsy with the taste of dreams, enchanted with the folly and sweetness of make-belief; there comes a tug at my sleeve, and there he stands beside me, reminding me that it is cold and raining and well past midnight, that there are no lamps in the street where we are walking, and that we shall probably get lost and fail to find our way back to the inn where we are staying, and maybe fall in with robbers into the bargain. This is precisely what happened to me this evening: the very neighbourhood of a compatriot is death to the life within me.

Is there any way of explaining this instinctive nervous reaction, or of analysing the charming propensity for destroying aesthetic delight which seems to emanate from the 'charm' of the average Frenchman? Could it be that this very 'charm' is jealous of a pleasure in which, through impotence, it has no share? Or is it not rather that it finds the whole thing merely affected and absurd*?

27th October. Signora Marini has managed to secure me a ticket for the ball which is being held this evening by the merchant guilds, in their own private *Casin' di San-Paolo*. No enterprise could have required more ingenuity. Armed with my ticket, and talking with the clipped accent of the Milanese, I have just managed to induce the doorkeeper to let me take a look over the premises. My tone of easy familiarity, which is indispensable here, taken together with the fact that I was a Frenchman, was in the end a more palpable inducement than the *mancia* (the tip).

The wealthy merchant-bankers of Milan, whose staid common-sense and attachment to the tangible advantages of luxury shorn of vain display suggest a temperament akin to that of the Dutch, recently opened a common fund, with some four hundred subscribers, with the object of acquiring premises in the *via San-Paolo*—a building of the type known in Italy as a *palazzo*, which they purchased at bargain price. It is an imposing mansion, built of age-darkened stone. The façade is not, as it would be in Paris, simply a flat wall-face. At street-level there is a pattern of arches in the Etruscan manner, surmounted by a row of pilasters about the first floor. The whole effect is not unlike that building known in Paris as the *Palais de la Chambre des Pairs*. As a result of the refacing operations which have recently been carried out on this latter edifice, the architecture has been ruthlessly denuded of all the glamour of its ancient memories—a most *tactful* procedure to have adopted in respect of a seat of aristocratic government! If ever the merchant-princes of Milan were to entertain the foolhardy notion of perpetrating such an outrage upon their own *Casin' di San-Paolo*, the plebian throng of cobblers and joiners whose shops crowd the remaining portions of the street, which is one of the busiest thoroughfares in the city, would have licked its lips in gloating anticipation.

The municipal authority of Milan includes a standing committee *di ornato*; this committee comprises four or five citizens of outstanding reputation as connoisseurs of art, together with two recognised architects, and exercises its functions on an honorary basis. Whenever a householder proposes to remodel the façade of his property, he is required to submit his design to the municipality, which hands it over to the *commissione di ornato*. The committee considers the plan and reports back. If the landlord is proposing to erect something devastatingly ugly,[1] the members of the *commissione di ornato*, who are all persons of rank and consideration, make a point of pouring down scorn and ridicule upon the offender in every conversation. In such a society, amidst a people gifted with an *innate sense of beauty*, yet where the subject of politics is fraught with constant danger or despair, there is matter enough in the façade of a new building to sustain conversation for a month, before its precise degree of beauty is established to within a fraction. The ethical traditions of Milan are intensely republican; indeed, the whole of Italy today is nothing but an extension of the Middle Ages. There is more solid consideration attached to a fine *palazzo* in the heart of the city than to untold millions in banknotes. If the building has any pretensions to beauty, it will immediately be baptised with the name of its owner. Hence, if you ask the way, you will be told: 'The Law-Courts are in such-and-such a street, in the *casa Clerici*'.

In Milan, the true patent of nobilty is conferred by the building of a fine *palazzo*. Ever since the days of Philip II, the Milanese have looked upon the *Government* as a species of predatory vermin, exclusively concerned with plundering the city of some fifteen to twenty millions a year; anyone who attempted a rational apologia for its authority would be treated as a lunatic; even the theoretical principles which might motivate any such apologia must necessarily seem incomprehensible and absurd. The Government weighs not so much as

---

1 For instance, that wooden, bronze-lacquered façade behind the pillars of the *Théâtre Favart* [1826].

a featherweight with public opinion. I need hardly mention that there was a notable exception to this general rule under Napoleon, from 1796 until 1806, this latter being the date when the Emperor dissolved the Legislative Assembly for having refused to ratify his *Legal Stamp Duty*. But thereafter, from 1806 until 1814, Napoleon drew his support exclusively from the aristocracy and the wealthier sections of the *bourgeoisie*. On one occasion, so the tale goes, a certain signora Bignami, the wife of a prosperous banker, refused to accept a post as Lady-in-Waiting, on the grounds that Prince Eugène (a true and typical French *marquis*, with his handsome person, his bravado and his empty-headed vanity) plainly was prepared to honour no quality other than *birth*, and was constantly *aristocratising* the decrees of his stepfather. Honest old Marshal Davoust was the man for Italy, the ideal Viceroy. He had in full measure the Italian gift of *caution*.

It is an impression I have, that architecture is more of a living art in Italy than either painting or sculpture. A Milanese banker will willingly live the life of a miser for half a century, simply in order to enjoy the eventual pleasure of building himself a *palazzo*, whose façade will cost him a hundred thousand francs more than it need have done, had he been content with a plain wall. The secret ambition of every citizen in Milan is to build a house of his own, or at the very least, to remodel the façade of the one which was handed down to him in the family inheritance.

Yet it should be remembered that Milanese architecture was nothing short of pitiful as late as 1778, when Piermarini was designing *la Scala*, which is indeed a model of perfection as far as interior decoration is concerned, but still leaves a formidable amount to be desired respecting its two façades. The modern tendency is rather towards classical simplicity. An extraordinarily graceful discovery, characteristic of the Milanese tradition, is the exact relation between *plain* and *decorated* surfaces over the whole area of a façade. Two architects in particular have achieved renown: the *marchese* Cagnola, who designed the *Porta Marengo*; and signor Canonica, who is responsible for a number of fine theatres, including the *teatro Carcano*, which is the most *armonico* (resonant) of all, the *teatro Rè*, etc.

I have been introduced to more than one prosperous Milanese, fortunate enough to have building work actually in hand at this present hour. When I went to call on these acquaintances I would find them perched on ladders at the scene of operations, as absorbed as generals in the heat of battle. I have even started climbing ladders myself.

I have discovered the masons to be a remarkably intelligent race of men. Not one but has his distinct views upon the design of the façade adopted by the architect. Once *inside* the building, however, I have found the structural planning of these Italian houses much inferior to that of equivalent dwellings in Paris. Italian architects are still copying the interior arrangements of those mediaeval *palazzi* which were constructed in Florence in 1350 or thereabouts, and later decorated by Palladio and his school (c. 1560). The architecture of that period was designed to meet certain social requirements which in fact no longer exist. The only feature of an Italian residence which seems to me worth preserving is the bedrooms, which are lofty, salubrious, and in every respect the contrary of our own.

The four hundred part-owners of the *Casin' di San-Paolo* have in these latter days subscribed a positively fantastic sum for the decoration of their *palazzo*. The ballroom, which is brand-new and of unsurpassed magnificence, struck me as being probably on a greater scale than even the principal gallery of the *Musée du Louvre*. For the ornamentation of the ceiling, they employed the finest artists in the land—not that that means a great deal, however. On the other hand, some of the decorative work in wood and *papier-mâché*, which is moulded in imitation of marble, is conceived in the most exquisite taste, and is quite strikingly beautiful. When Napoleon ruled in Milan, he established a *collegio dell' ornato*, as well as a school of engraving, both of which have amply fulfilled the aims of their great sovereign and founder.

The Italian *ideal of beauty* reduces *detail* to a minimum, and consequently implies *grandeur of outline*. (At this point I have preferred to delete some four pages of philosophical speculation, largely unintelligible to any save those with an overmastering passion for painting.)

The immediate impression produced upon my own mind by the *Casin' di San-Paolo* is one of *awe*. The residences of our own Ministers of State have that over-gilt, rococo effect of a boudoir or of a fashionable shop. Admittedly, nothing could be more appropriate, when the Minister is a Robert Walpole, purchasing boroughs and paying out in sinecures. This *physical* impact produced by the architecture of a building, and evoking an emotional response exactly corresponding to the purpose for which the building itself is intended, is called *style*. And since the majority of buildings are designed to inspire awe, if not sheer terror (a Catholic church, for instance, or the palace of a despot, etc.), more often than not, when an Italian pronounces: 'That building *has style*', the real meaning of the verdict is simply: 'That building *inspires respect*'. Whereas the pedants, as soon as *they* start preaching about style, mean plainly: 'This particular architecture is classical, it is modelled on the Greek, or at least upon certain specific *nuances* of gallicised hellenism, in the same way as Racine's *Iphigénie* is modelled on Euripides.'

A phrase you might hear: 'The *via dei Nobili*, in Milan is a fine architectural conception'. Understand by this that it is atrociously mournful and gloomy. If *I* lived in the *Palazzo Arconati*, I doubt whether I should manage to smile once in a week.

These *palazzi* fill me continually with memories of the Middle Ages, with echoes of the bloody conspiracies of the Visconti (1301), with visions of the gigantic passions of the fourteenth century. But I am alone with these my dreams. The actual owners of these grandiose structures sigh for nothing so deeply as for a snug little apartment in Paris, looking out upon the *boulevard de Gand*. The only section of the population of Milan which really has anything in common with France is the very wealthiest. Over and above our own vices, however, they are afflicted with avarice, which is one of the commonest faults of the Milanese, and which conflicts most entertainingly with a powerful dose of petty vanity. The only extravagance among such people is their horses; I have seen beasts which cost three, four, or even five thousand francs. A Milanese dandy posturing in the saddle is a sight not easily forgotten. I was forgetting to mention that, any day you please, at two in the afternoon, you may witness the *Corso*, when the whole of society takes the air, whether in its carriage or on horseback. In Milan, the *Corso* is held upon the rampart-walk, between the *Porta Rense* and the *Porta Nuova*; but in the majority of Italian cities the main street is the arena for the *Corso*. The *Corso* and the opera are the two events which no Italian will ever willingly miss.

Nowadays, in Lombardy, the majority of noble families spend scarcely a third of their income, whereas, prior to the Revolution of 1796, they would make free with twice as much. Two or three of these Milanese aristocrats saw service under Napoleon. Their manners are most realistically described in a series of little occasional poems in Milanese dialect, by Carline Porta.

28th October, at 5 o'clock in the morning, after the ball. In four hours' time I am due to leave for Desio, which I am impatient to explore again at leisure. So, unless I write now, I shall never write at all. I am struggling to achieve a calmer frame of mind, so as to pen something more solid than a mere lyric effusion which will sound ridiculous in three days' time. And since there is always the chance that my papers may be seized by the Austrian police, I shall write nothing of the manifold secret intrigues into which I was initiated by my various acquaintances, for all that these intrigues are a matter of common gossip. I should sink into the blackest regions of despair if I were to prove *traitor* to this charming Italian *élite* which has deigned to talk as freely in my presence as though I were a tried and trusted friend. On the other hand, the Austrian police takes no official cognisance of anything unless it can discover it *in writing*. There is a certain praiseworthy moderation in this principle.

I am just home from the *Casin' di San-Paolo*. Never in all my life have I beheld so much radiance gathered together under one roof, nor such beauty: beauty so intense that I was fearful to gaze upon it. To a French observer it was a species of beauty that seemed haughty and sombre, promising distant felicity beyond the storms of passion, rather than the transient pleasures of wit, gallantry and gay flirtation. For beauty—this I believe—is nothing but a *promise of happiness*.

Notwithstanding its hint of sad severity, a disfigurement deep-engraved by the glum and cantankerous pride of English husbands, deeper still by the rigours of that grim English law named *Propriety*, the English style of feminine beauty harmonises much more naturally with the atmosphere of a ballroom.[1] A peerless, sparkling freshness, illumined by the sweet smile of childhood, animates their fine features, which are incapable of inspiring fear, and seem from the outset to promise ungrudging and absolute submission to the will and whim of the man whom they are destined to love. But such unqualified subservience sows the seeds of a suspicion of *ennui*, whereas the fires that flash in Italian eyes spell instant annihilation even to the earliest dawning hint of that sentiment, which is the most implacable enemy of consummated love. I am convinced that, in Italy, even in the arms of the most venial of mistresses,

1 Miss Bathurst, Rome, 1824. [1826]

no man need go in fear of boredom. *Caprice* is ever on the watch, armed to affright the monster.

The men at the ball tonight would have furnished superb models for any sculptor, such as Danneker or Chantrey, who specialised in portrait-busts. But a painter might well have proved less satisfied. Those fine eyes so exquisitely drawn seem now and then to betray a certain dullness of intellect; the glint of pride, the gleam of acumen, the tantalising flicker of humour—these qualities come but rarely to trouble the still waters.

By contrast, the faces of the women time and again betrayed a passionate intelligence embodied in forms and features of the rarest beauty. Their hair and eyebrows tend to a deep, magnificent auburn; their faces may at first seem sombre and reserved—yet wait a while, until some deep disturbance in the soul should rise up to breathe a sudden animation into the sleeping surface. But it is a waste of time to hope to find those soft, rose-petal complexions of English girls or children. In any case, this secret hint of sadness most likely passed unnoticed by all the company tonight save one—myself. I broached the matter with signora G***, one of the most brilliant women in all the Duchy, who, by her answers, gave me to understand that the victorious mask of *laughing self-confidence*, which women flaunt so frequently on gala-nights in France, would here brand the wearer as a grinning ape. No jokes were spared at the expense of a small group of middle-rank *bourgeoises*, whose artfully glittering glances sought to prove the ecstasy of their enjoyment. I have a suspicion, none the less, that even the haughtiest of Milanese beauties would not disdain to don this glittering mask, were her appearance amid the dancers fixed by decree to last no more than fifteen minutes. For the danger is that, after a short while, any expression that a woman may assume *artificially* upon her features will inevitably degenerate into a *grimace*; and, in a land corrupted by mistrust, there can be no more glaring instance of bad taste. When the spirit is untroubled by the faintest breath or edge of passion, then let the expression drift into a state of *natural relaxation*, if I may be permitted the phrase. These were the instants when I, a foreigner, found something sombre, almost menacing, in the fine features of these Italian women. General Bubna, who has lived in France, and who enjoys the current reputation of a brilliant and epigrammatic wit, remarked this evening: 'In France, women watch each other; in Italy, they watch the men.' Bubna is a remarkably shrewd individual who has somehow discovered how to make himself welcome and appreciated, notwithstanding his position as Governor-General representing the tyranny of an occupying power.

Until the ball tonight, I had never observed the least display of vanity in Italy. The sequence of dances normally includes a waltz, a *monférine* and a French quadrille. The guests began to arrive at ten o'clock; and from that moment until midnight, *vanity* reigned undisputed among the company. One fair face alone escaped contagion: that of signora ***, whose husband, so I heard, had declared point-blank that if a certain signor Frascani were to make an appearance at the dance, he would drag her off forcibly to spend the entire duration of the Carnival among his wild and primitive estates at Trezzo. (It is now two years since Frascani and signora *** first found favour in each other's eyes; yet her husband still does her the honour of treating her lover as a rival.) Signora *** had passed word to Frascani, who was not seen all the evening. It was striking eleven when I was told this story; and it was two in the morning when at length she found the courage to leave the ball; and not once, I am prepared to swear, in all this time, did any hint of merriment or pleasure, or even simple animation, disturb the fixed despair of that fair countenance.

'Is jealousy, then, of such frequent occurrence among the husbands of Milan?' I enquired of signor Cavaletti, sometime equerry in the service of Napoleon. 'At the very most, during the first two years of marriage', came the reply, 'but even that

C

is rare. A fine way of spending one's time, indeed!—being jealous of a wife with whom one is no longer in love. Of course, a mistress is a different matter altogether.'

Thanks to this acquaintance of long standing, and to the good offices of two or three other persons, to whom Cavaletti introduced me as *a Frenchman who is only stopping here three weeks, and in whose presence no reticence is needed* (these were his very words), soon all the faces dropped their anonymity of masks, and the ball lost its alien insignificance. I began to learn names; soon I could trace the undercurrents of intrigue.

As the hour drew on towards midnight, and every dress had been flaunted, scrutinised and passed (the majority, to tell the truth, were showy rather than elegant), gradually the icy and disdainful mask of vanity was shed in favour of more attractive preoccupations. In Italy, it is the height of absurdity for a pretty woman to have no object for the affections of her heart. There is nothing ephemeral about these *liaisons*; they may last eight or ten years, perhaps as long as life itself. All this was told to me, with as little circumlocution as I am using in the writing of it, by signora M***. If, after a year of marriage, when a woman may be assumed to be no longer in love with her husband, she shows no sign of interest elsewhere, the young men merely shrug their shoulders, saying: '*E una sciocca*' ('She is a goose'); and henceforward, at dances, the *beaux* are wont to relegate her to the shameful status of wallflower. In the course of this evening, I observed (or thought I observed) every shade and *nuance* of attachment. For instance, the handsome features of young Count Botta, as his gaze strayed towards signora R***, were a perfect study in the dawning phases of love, before the crisis of declaration. There is a saying in France that a happy lover cuts a poor figure at a ball; if his soul can register the least hint of passion, every other man present is instantly transformed into a rival. But in Milan there is only one hour in all the evening when love fades into oblivion, and that is during the scrutiny of the dresses.

Such is the inadequacy of the French language that nothing short of ten full lines will suffice to praise a woman with due tact and delicacy. Silence alone, therefore, shall portray the manifold graces of signora Bibin Catena, whose epigrammatic turn of mind may fear no comparison even with that of General de Narbonne. Towards two in the morning, signora C*** made me observe signs of jealousy in more than one face. Count N*** was so deep in despair that he abandoned the ball. The mistress whose gallant he was (*che serve*) sought him distractedly through gallery after gallery, first through the gaming-rooms, of which there were eight or ten, then through the sitting-out rooms, by the dim half-light which fell from the lamps of alabaster, until at length the splendour of beauty deserted her features, which froze by degrees into a still mask of sadness; all around her seemed to grow stale and unprofit-able; and ultimately (since she would be required to give an account of her evening), she seated herself disconsolately beside a gaming-table, amid a throng of strangers, all recognised *per avere altre amicizie* (to have other attachments). In Italy, the word *amore* is rarely uttered. I find it the most frustrating business in the world to invent a turn of phrase in French which may adequately embody the observations which were forced upon me by the events of the night. Our language simply has not the vocabulary to incarnate such concepts which, in France, remain unspoken, and besides, in all probability, hardly ever arise. But here, there is no other topic of conversa-tion. Consequently, in Italy, when conversation languishes and dies, the cause is never boredom, but merely prudence.

The Italians are not fond of dancing. By one o'clock in the morning, the only couples left on the floor were foreigners or stray eccentrics with no *liaison* to keep them more happily employed. Three or four handsome German officers, blond as Adonis, continued waltzing to the bitter end; at the outset, the grace of their movements was wondrously admired; but by the end, their crimson faces and their stevedore-like display of brawn and energy (*di facchino*) had become the joke of the evening. These wretched young men, who are received nowhere save in one or two excessively wearisome and reactionary families, are forced into making a display of their physical vitality as their only hope of winning themselves a mistress. And on the day following you may observe them, rigid as mummies, in the pit of *la Scala*, their gaze glassily riveted, four hours without blinking, upon some pretty woman with whom they had chanced to dance the night before; on Sundays, they will bow to her in church after Mass; and every evening, at the hour of the *Corso*, they will cavort on horseback beside the door of her carriage.

Among the twelve most handsome women at the ball, there numbered one most attractive Frenchwoman, madame la comtesse Ag[osti]. Other claimants for this high honour include *le signore* Litta, Rughetta, Ruga, Maïnoni, Ghirlanda (from Varese), la contessa C*** (from Mantua), and a beautiful Spaniard, Señora Carmelita L[echi].

It is the fashion here for young men to wear their hair very thick and long, and their cravats looped into enormous bows. There is a sweeping grandeur about their attire which betrays a race daily accustomed to the sight of paintings in fresco, which are normally on a colossal scale. Signor Izimbardi drew my attention to the fact that, among the highest sections of the aristocracy, the women affect a drawling, nasal type of speech*.

I was honoured with an introduction to an artist of genius —signor Peregò, the creator of the *décor* at *la Scala* which made so deep an impression upon my mind. He is also responsible for sections of the ornamentation of the magnificent *Casin' di San-Paolo*, amongst which, all in all, I spent seven whole hours in such a transport of delight. At this same ball I was introduced likewise to signor Romagnosi and to signor Tommaso Grossi. I further caught a glimpse of Vincenzo Monti. Signor Manzoni was not present—prevented (so rumour goes) by his extreme piety from making an appearance.

At the moment he is engaged upon a translation of M. de Lamennais' *Essai sur l'Indifférence en Matière de Religion*; due allowance being made for this lapse, however, his talent as a lyric poet falls little short of Lord Byron's.

30th October.   I can say nothing about the ethical conventions of Italy, nor of the traditional code which prevails in the pursuit of happiness, save that which I have gathered at second hand; and the evidence that has come to my notice may well be misleading. 'To have eyes and to see' (as Napoleon used to say) is not enough in such a matter. Imagine for a moment, as you sit in your study, that the wall which divides you from the house next door should grow suddenly transparent—what would you behold? A scene with three actors, one woman and two men—yet, as it stands, utterly meaningless, stripped of the dullest spark of interest. What are the *relationships* between these people? Yet they must have a history; the play must have passed through many scenes of exposition and development to build up this latest climax surprised through the transparency of the wall; and once the background is known, *then* the dialogue makes sense, may even perchance prove deeply moving to the invisible onlooker.

I have likewise been 'watching scenes'; in such a fashion precisely, neither more nor less; yet I freely confess that I have nothing but second-hand narratives to help me fill in the all-important background, which is the very key to any essential intelligence of the present action. The average bird-witted tourist, who never exchanges a word save with the occasional waiter or guide, with the old woman down at the laundry, and (in the course of the one dinner which he gets out of him) with his banker, will be accusing me here and now of exaggeration, of downright lying . . . etc. I would strongly urge him to close this book.

The secret of invulnerability—as other travellers have all too readily discovered—is to stick to plain figures. How many

pictures in *this gallery*? How many columns in *that* portico?
And if, in addition, the traveller should cultivate a handy
talent for chopping up this kind of statistical inventory into
palatable hunks by means of adolescent text-book platitudes
couched in reverberating academic periods, concerning the
origins and subsequent history of divers notable buildings, not
forgetting the *evolutionary transition* of civilisation from Egypt
to Etruria and from Etruria to Rome . . . then no more is
needed, and the bird-wits will pronounce it *admirable*!

By contrast, what perils await the author who talks of the
manners of a country he has visited! For the hare-brained idiot
who has made the Grand Tour will say: 'It is not true, for *I*
was in Venice, and stayed there two-and-fifty days, and never
saw the like'; while the blunt-minded idiot who has never
ventured further than his own front door will counter: 'It is
indecent, sir! For no one behaves like that in the *rue Mouffetard*.'

An English traveller, by name John Scott, a man of sharp,
satirical intelligence, was killed the other day in a duel, on
account of a certain paragraph which he had published. This
was a true tragedy; for Scott had a foot firmly set upon the
ladder which leads to the highest honour and distinction in the
realm of English letters, and indeed had but recently won the
homage of all his crusty-livered, atrabilious countrymen with a
book of travels, in which the land of France and all things
French are smeared with mud and obloquy. But John Scott,
dying, left heirs and successors, and they have played him a
truly knavish trick; for what should they do, but publish the
Diary of a journey to Milan, upon which he was working at
the time. This *Diary* is as yet unadorned by the faintest breath
of invention; it is the rock-bed of *fact*, naked and undefiled,
upon which the future travelogue should stand. And here we
find the truth without disguise: for who *were* John Scott's
acquaintances in Milan? A café-waiter here and there, a dominie
to teach Italian, and some poor, threadbare *Custodian of
Ancient Monuments*.

Similarly, reverting to our friends the column-counting statisticians* (instances to be drawn only from among the dead), go to the library, and hunt up Millin's *Voyage dans le Milanais*. Monsieur Millin was in Rome once—the year, if I remember right, about 1806—and returned one evening to his lodgings in despair. 'What is the matter?' enquired a friend (by chance a scholar) who happened to be there. 'The matter? The matter, say you? Do you know who is here? Denon! And do you know how much he spends? *Five hundred francs a day!* I am finished, ruined for ever! What will Rome think of me now?'

2nd November. Signora M*** V***, who, for pure beauty, echoes the enchantment of Leonardo da Vinci's wondrous *Herodias**, and in whose soul I have sensed an unrivalled understanding of art, said to me yesterday, at one o'clock in the morning: 'The moonlight is perfect; I tell you, therefore, go and look at *il Duomo*; but you must stand on the *Palazzo Regio* side.'

I went; and there I discovered a miracle of silence. Pyramids of white marble, tapering into gothic infinity, aspiring eternally towards Heaven; cut as of paper against the unfathomable blue of a southern sky strewn with the glitter of stars—in all the world I know no spectacle to equal it. The very firmament, moreover, seemed to be woven out of velvet, designed as a setting for the still silver of moonlight. A warm wind frolicked gently in that narrow labyrinth of alleys which, on certain sides, enricles and hedges the massive vastness of *il Duomo*. An instant of sheer delight!

The semi-gothic façade and the pinnacles (*guglie*) of the southern side, towards the *Palazzo Regio*, owe their origin to Napoleon (1805-1810). The open-work tower, wrought wholly in a filigree of milk-white marble, which is a landmark for many miles around, and which carries the gigantic carving of the Madonna, was built in the reign of Maria-Theresa.

It was Gian Galeazzo Visconti, Duke of Milan—the same

who, having defeated in battle and taken captive his own
uncle Bernabò, caused him to die by poison in the picturesque
castle of Trezzo—who laid the foundations of the great
Cathedral of Milan; perhaps hoping thereby to placate the
wrath of the Blessèd Virgin. He it was likewise who began
that frivolous and undignified marble *bonbonnière* known as the
Charterhouse of Pavia.

We are deeply indebted to signor Franchetti, sometime
Auditeur au Conseil d'Etat, for an excellent work on the subject
of Milan Cathedral. Count Pompeo Litta, who, under the
somewhat antiquated title of *Famiglie celebri italiane*, is responsible for a most scholarly publication, with engravings of
excellent workmanship embodied in a descriptive text strangely
free of inaccuracies (deliberate or otherwise), has reproduced a
beautiful illustration of the tomb of the Gian Iacopo de' Medici,
designed by Michelangelo and placed in the Cathedral. In the
fourteenth century, craftsmen set to work on the exterior
columns of this gigantic mass of gothic masonry, and chiselled
out more than two thousand niches of varying dimensions,
later destined to be occupied by an equivalent number of
statues. Some of these statues, perched a hundred feet and more
above the ground, are yet less than thirty inches high. Behind
the High Altar, the great windows of the apse are sixty feet in
height and thirty broad. But in the body of the church, the
five naves lie bathed eternally in that dim and stainèd gloom
of coloured glass which so well becomes a religion built upon
the doctrine of an ever-burning Hell.

In the neighbourhood of the High Altar, on the southern
side, there is an underground passage, open to the public, which
begins inside the Cathedral and emerges beneath the portico
in the courtyard of the Archbishop's residence. It is a fine place
for thwarted lovers to meet 'by chance', while the coachman
and the lackey, who, in all probability, may be spies, are left
to cool their heels in the doorway of the church. Close beside
this passage-way, the eternal *cicerone* loves to point to a statue

of St Bartholomew, flayed alive from head to foot, yet bravely
sporting his own hide across his shoulders like a bandolier—
which gruesome effigy enjoys a splendid popularity among the
masses, and might indeed figure to better advantage in the
lecture-theatre of some hospital, were not the anatomy so
structurally inaccurate. I hinted as much this evening to
signora F***, as we sat together in her box; and there was a
hush of silence. I realised immediately that I had breathed a
deadly insult against the spirit of *backstairs patriotism**; and in a
flurry of precipitation I took my leave. As a general rule, in
Italy, even among the most enlightened sections of society, it is
wisest to behave as though one were at Court, and never to
speak disparagement against the meanest object, so long as that
object belongs to *Italy*.

3rd November. Tomorrow is the festival of St Charles, who,
together with, if not with precedence over, the Madonna, is the
true deity of the Milanese; and endless preparations are afoot.
The pedestals of the enormous gothic pillars of the Cathedral
are all draped in red damask; while at a height of thirty feet or
so above the flagstones are being hung huge paintings representing the central episodes in the life of the Saint. I spent two
hours idling among the workmen, and listening to their gossip
and conversation. For each spark of adoration touched off by
St Charles, there is another to match it inspired by Napoleon.
These two are the twin patrons of Milan.

Feeling in a mood to go and explore churches, I set off to
view the famous Church of the Madonna which stands close
to the *Porta San-Celso*. Architecturally, this is a most curious
construction, reminiscent of the most primitive form of
Christian sanctuary, now very largely forgotten. Inside, as in a
modern theatre, the seating would have been divided into five
or six different blocks or categories, each answering a corresponding need or quality in the souls of the faithful. I found

much to admire in the church, in particular its tiny interior portico, and the four pendentives in fresco, the work of Appiani.

On the way home, I stopped to look at the magnificent antique columns of *San-Lorenzo*, of which, in all, there are sixteen. Corinthian and fluted, they stand in a straight line and rise to a height of twenty-five to thirty feet. But, if they are to be truly appreciated, the eye must already have acquired some skill in sifting the ruins of a genuinely venerable antiquity from the host of petty, senseless accretions which the puerile tastelessness of our own age has foisted upon them. Ideally, a ruin should be surrounded by a low iron railing, as are the flower beds in the gardens of the *Tuileries*; if it shows signs of collapsing, it should be reinforced with iron staples, or else buttressed with brickwork painted dark green, as, so I am informed, has been practised in the case of the Colosseum at Rome. The church of *San-Lorenzo*, which stands in the shelter of these sixteen antique columns, made me smile by the unexpectedness of its design.

Among various people pointed out to me, there was a little hunchbacked creature who possesses, I suspect, quite undeniable talents as an architect. The *Porta Marengo* (now re-christened under pressure from the local reactionaries) is a fine conception, yet shows no slavish imitation of antiquity; whereas the building in Paris which houses the *Exchange*, is not, nor ever will be, anything but a pedestrian copy of a Grecian temple. Yet the plain fact is that in Greece eleven months out of the twelve are dry and sunlit, whereas in Paris, it rains fully two hundred days in every year. In literature, this blind and submissive aping of antiquity is called *classicism*; dare one hope that at least *architecture* may, in the end, find the strength to struggle free and be herself? Yet hear the argument: 'Our climate is essentially wet; and any architect who was asked to design an Exchange specifically adapted to meet the require-ments of such a climate would *of necessity* produce a building which was ugly; consequently, why not design something which, however inappropriate, is at least *beautiful*?'

To keep the rain off effectively, the columns which support the porticos of the Exchange should rise no higher than fifteen feet, at the very most; in addition, it would be essential to provide an immense covered vehicle-park for waiting carriages.

To end my day's excursion, I went to see Leonardo da Vinci's *Last Supper* at the Convent *delle Grazie*, where I spent two whole hours. Later this evening, at the *Caffè dell' Accademia*, signor Izimbardi remarked: 'Who, I wonder, was the genius—the *priest* of genius—who, one day in the hidden mists of the past, decreed the eating of chick-peas on St Charles' Day, November 4th? Every four-year-old in the whole of the city remembers this, if nothing else; and all the days of its life adores St Charles!' Signor Melchior Gioja, on the other hand, is convinced that the custom of eating chick-peas is a relic of paganism. Personally, I am insufficiently acquainted with the problem to offer an opinion. Tomorrow, however, I shall go myself and consume chick-peas at the personal invitation of signora C***. The invitation, I confess, is unexpected, for the Milanese never invite guests to dinner. The notion which they entertain of the magnificence which must be displayed upon such rare occasions is positively *Spanish*!

5th November. Every evening, during these last few days, I have strolled out, towards one o'clock in the morning, to gaze at *il Duomo*. Bathed in the silver radiance of moonlight, Milan Cathedral is a thing of such ravishing beauty that all the world cannot contain its equal.

Never before have I been so deeply impressed by the pure quality of architecture. This structure of white marble worked in filigree obviously *lacks* certain qualities: it has, for instance, none of the magnificence and none of the solidity of St Paul's Cathedral in London. But if I had to explain to someone endowed with a certain degree of artistic sensitivity, I might suggest the following ideas: 'The splendour of such architecture derives from the fact that it is gothic *stripped of the obsession with death*; it is joy sprung from a heart profoundly tinged with melancholy; and further, since it is supremely irrational, and constructed apparently out of the instability of a whim, it is an echo of the wildest capriciousness of *love*. Yet imagine all this snowy radiance of marble transmuted for an instant into grey granite—nothing more is needed to replunge the observer among all the dreary intimations of mortality.' But such speculations are nothing but a web of words to the uninitiated, and a source of irritation. In Italy, such philistines are rare; but in France they constitute an overwhelming majority.

The semi-gothic façade of *il Duomo* is not strictly beautiful, but it achieves a certain measure of *prettiness*. To see it at its best, you should catch it reddening in the reflections of the setting sun. I am told that *il Duomo* is the vastest church in all the world, after St Peter's; not excepting even the Cathedral of St Sophia.

I hired a *sediola* and drove out to Melegnano, the site of the glorious battle fought by François I, on the road to Lodi. The *sediola* consists of a seat balanced upon an axle-shaft between two enormous wheels. We made about nine miles an hour. On the return journey, there was a superb view of Milan Cathedral, whose mass of white marble towers high above the roof-tops of the city and stands out vividly against the background of the Alps above Bergamo, giving the illusion of being actually set hard against the mountain, although, in reality, there are some thirty miles of plain which stretch between the two. Seen from this distance, *il Duomo* is pure white, of the whiteness of virgin snow. The complexity of human endeavour, the forest of marble pinnacles and spires, seems to strengthen the effect of nature and to echo the wondrous contours of the Alps, whose ridges stand in jagged outline against the empty sky.

I know of nothing in all the world more beautiful than this panorama of snow-capped summits forming a horizon sixty miles distant, while the lesser peaks lie hidden in a soft and sensuous obscurity.

6th November.   Coming home from *la Scala* by way of the *via San-Giovanni alle Case rotte*, there is a view of one angle of the church of *San-Fedele* (designed by Pellegrini) which is superb; but the style of beauty is distinctly Hellenic: it is at once cheerful and dignified; it holds no hint of *terror*.

This hidden corner of Milan is fascinating for any traveller with an eye to appreciate the characteristic *expressiveness* of stones well-ordered by the hand of man. The *via San-Giuseppe*, the *teatro alla Scala*, the church of *San-Fedele*, the *Palazzo Belgiojoso*, the *Casa degli Omenoni*—all these are crowded together in the narrowest compass. The great hall of the Customs-House, which, in these days, is piled ceiling-high with bales, is enduring proof of the *solidity* of that type of ornamentation which became traditional in the *salons* of the sixteenth century. The *Galerie de Diane*, in the *Tuileries*, is a poor and flimsy thing by comparison.

The *Piazza San-Fedele* was widened recently by the demolition of the house belonging to Count Prina, who was Minister of Finance under Napoleon, and who was assassinated on the 20th April 1814 at the instigation of the pro-Austrian faction, aided and abetted by a small group of Italian liberals—the latter (so at least runs the popular version of the story) being now desperately repentant of their share in the crime. The priest of the church of *San-Giovanni*, past which we were walking only this evening, refused point-blank to unlock the gates of the rood-screen and thus give sanctuary to Count Prina; for the unhappy Minister, who had already been dragged feet foremost about the streets of Milan by the mob, but who was not yet mortally wounded, might then have been carried to the altar-steps and saved. As it was, the long-drawn agony of the unhappy victim lasted for three mortal hours. According to report, the professional assassins who directed the attack, being

resolved to compromise the mob, caused Prina finally to be
battered to death with an umbrella. France has never produced
a genius worthy to rival this Piedmontese in the art of extorting
and spending public money wholly at the beck and bidding of
a despot. The establishments he left behind him at his death
were a reflexion of his innate obsession with grandeur. The
piazza San-Fedele, which was swept clear after his death, is
flanked on one side by the façade of the *Palazzo Marini* (1555),
an edifice more remarkable for its sheer mass than for its
beauty. Prina's ambition was a Dukedom; to which end, he
slaved relentlessly day and night at his desk: not by depreda-
tion (or very little), but by *work* he aimed to reach his goal.
In March 1815, a certain Police Commissioner, named (if I
remember rightly) Villa, was cashiered from the service; for
he had the misfortune to be an honest man, and had passed
in reports which left no serious doubts as to the identity of the
murderers. Signor Villa had already collected three rooms-full
of effects and valuables which had been plundered from the
Residence of the unfortunate Minister, and later had been
restored by the culprits, who, at the moment of making
restitution, had betrayed the names of those who had paid
them to do what they did.

7th November.   Various people have wanted to show me many
different things in Milan; but finally I have made up my mind:
I refuse to visit the sights and wonders of the city unless I am
absolutely alone. The guide-chatter of the *ciceroni* (and not of the
professional variety alone) should be reserved to titillate the
apathetic sensibility of tourists from beyond the Rhine.
Nothing is more nauseating to the sort of person who, one day,
might develop into a *connoisseur*; it merely breeds an attitude of
blasé superiority towards everything that falls short of pure
perfection. In Milan, the *patriotic instinct* is so overwhelming
that the most honest and upright of citizens yet bred under
heaven will burst himself with extolling the absurdest of

palazzi, with nothing to plead in its favour but its size! This is a phenomenon I have observed repeatedly during these latter days in the *salon* of signor Reina, a patriotic revolutionary of 1799, since honoured by persecution. Incidentally, signor Reina has just lent me a most curious little work: the *History* of the Lombard revolutionaries who were deported to the Delta of the Cattaro. The author was a hunchback, signor Apostoli, who, as a wit, falls scarcely short of Chamfort. Nothing could be less common in Italy, where the dry succinctness of *wit* in the manner of France is smothered in *prolixity*.

In later years, the frustration of poverty drove poor Apostoli into accepting the salary of an informer in the service of Austria. He would confess as much frankly among his friends gathered together in the *Caffè di Padua*; and the stigma of infamy passed him by. This hunchback, with all his brilliant gifts, eventually died—so I am told—of starvation. His book is called *Lettere sirmiensi*; and it is a record of the truth, even when the truth tells against his fellow-deportees. He never succumbs to that over-riding passion for *sententiousness* and *generalities*, which no Frenchman in a similar situation could for a moment have withheld from a narrative of this description.

The sights of Milan which have left me *genuinely* lost in admiration include the view of the cupola of the Cathedral riding high above the trees in the gardens of the *Villa Belgiojoso*; the frescoes by Appiani which are housed in this same villa; and the *Apotheosis of Napoleon*, by the same artist, which is in the *Palazzo Regio*. In none of these things can France produce a single serious rival. The beauty that is theirs by right does not depend upon *argument*; it simply pleases the eye. Without this sensual and instantaneous pleasure, which is in some measure instinctive, or at least *irrational*, there is neither painting nor music. And yet, for all this, I have known good folk of Koenigsberg find pleasure in art through sheer persistence of argument. The North judges rationally, building a structure of logic upon a basis of earlier experience; the South judges physically, in direct response to a stimulus of sensual delight.

8th November. High up among the bastions of the fortress, now transmuted into terraces and walks, and richly shaded with plane-trees which, in this fertile soil of Italy, within ten years of planting have topped a height of fifty feet, rises the *Circus*—another of Napoleon's notable achievements. The floor of the Circus can be flooded with water, and only three days ago I witnessed some thirty thousand spectators gathered together at one time to cheer a 'naval engagement', whose contesting crews were recruited from among the boatmen from Lake Como. The previous day, in honour of the advent of some Austrian archduke, I had watched the horse-racing enthusiasts, mounted in antique chariots (*bighe*), drive four times round the *spina*,[1] in furious contest for the fastest time. The Milanese mob grows delirious with excitement at this sport, which, I confess, leaves me curiously unenthusiastic. In fact, I was frankly growing bored, when the *bighe*-races eventually gave place to the fantastic and hideous spectacle of six-and-thirty dwarfs, the tallest no more than forty inches high, all bundled up to the neck in sacks, from which their heads alone emerged, and racing for dear life by hopping on two feet, like frogs. The falls and antics of these wretched freaks sent all the common people into fits of laughter; and in this land of shameless sensuality no one is too highly born or bred to escape the common touch—not even the lovely signora Formigini.

This evening, as I sat in the box of a woman universally renowned for her sympathy, her *disinvoltura* and her learning, I made complaint of this callous inhumanity. 'In Italy', came the answer, 'dwarfs, as a rule, are a cheerful race—think, for instance, of the flower-seller in the *foyer* of *la Scala*, with his bouquets for the ladies: his tongue is sharp, his humour caustic.' Within the walls of Milan alone, there must be a thousand or

1 A straight line set along the major axis of the ellipse. [1826]

more of the inhabitants who have never grown above three feet in height. At the root of the trouble lies the dampness of the climate, to which must be added *la panera* (the excellent local cream, the like of which is unknown outside the Duchy —even in Switzerland).

The Archduke, in whose honour such festivities are organised at the instigation of those Milanese ultra-reactionaries who pack the seats of the Municipality, is a cold, reasonable, ill-dressed creature with a cumbrous baggage of erudition in the fields of statistics, botany and geology. But in feminine company he is tongue-tied and dumb. I have seen him myself, parading up and down along the *Corso*, in a pair of boots which my own footman would disdain to wear. 'The essence of sovereignty', retorted someone (I forget who) to Louis XVI, 'is *ceremonial*.' The Milanese look back regretfully to the days of Prince Eugène, with his easy charms and his peacock vanity, which furnished him with a compliment for every lady's ear. In Paris, the Viceroy had seemed flat and uninspiring; in Milan, he glittered, he was radiant, and even created the illusion that he was a man of amiable character. In this particular field of talent, the French are unrivalled. On the 31st of December there is to be a solemn procession and ceremony: the long-heralded entry of the Emperor Francis II. It will be a *fiasco*. The Milanese have no bent for spontaneous enthusiasm. In Paris, no one is too dreary or insignificant to provoke a flutter of handkerchiefs; and, as the procession passes, the acclaim is almost genuine—for the moment. But in Milan, by the time a lad reaches the age of seventeen, the tenor of his life is silent and oppressed with melancholy; not a trace of wildness or high spirits. In all Italy there is nothing rarer than *hilarity*—for I refuse to accommodate under this title the joy which derives from passion finally consummated.

10th November. I have travelled for nine miles in a *sediola* about the ramparts of Milan; the *corso* rides along the top of the walls, which rise thirty feet above the plain—a considerable height in this land of unbroken flatness. The fertility of the soil is so astonishing that the expanse of the plain is transmuted into a kind of forest, limiting the vista to a hundred paces. Today is the 10th of November; yet all the trees still keep the full richness of their foliage. The shades of red and bistre are indescribable. From the height of the rampart which stretches from the bastion of the *Porta Nuova* to the Marengo Gate, there is a view of the distant Alps which is nothing short of sublime. In all the days I have spent in Milan, I have scarcely seen anything more magnificent. Among other peaks, my guides pointed out the *Rezegon di Lek* and the *Monte Rosa*. Seen thus across the fertile luxuriance of the plain, these peaks offer a pattern of beauty which is overwhelming, yet at the same time *reassuring*, like Greek architecture. In Switzerland, by contrast, the mountains never fail to hint at the insignificance of man, to suggest the fate of some poor devil of a traveller swept into eternity by an avalanche. In all probability, such bleak forebodings are no more than my own personal reaction. The retreat from Moscow has left me plainly suspicious of the attributes of snow; not on account of the dangers to which I was myself exposed, but as a result of the hideous sight of horror, suffering and the extinction of pity. At Vilna, breaches in the walls of the hospital were blocked with frozen portions of human corpses*. This picture is never far from my memory; is it a wonder, then, that I have little pleasure in the prospect of snow?

I left my *sediola* finally to make my way towards the *foyer* of *la Scala*, where I listened to a rehearsal of *Maometto secondo*, an opera by Herr Winter, a celebrated German composer. It contains a *Prayer Scene*, most notably interpreted by Galli, signora Festa and signora Bassi. Milan lives in expectation of Rossini, who is to work on a libretto entitled *la Gazza Ladra*, in an Italian version arranged by signor Gherardini. In my own private estimation it is a dismal subject, and grossly unsuited

to musical treatment*. Rossini is the target of much unfavourable gossip—he is idle, he cheats his own *impresari*, he even
cheats himself . . . etc., etc. Perhaps so; yet I know so many
virtuous composers who bore me to tears!

Yesterday, at Mass in the *chiesa dei Servi di Maria*, the organist
gave a most divine recital of cantilenas by Rossini and Mozart
at their most passionate: *cantare pares*.

What a mob of people there is who make it their business to
spread the most infamous scandal about a man of genius* who
refuses to give a tinker's curse for all the customary precedences
of the social hierarchy! Is it unfair to conclude that, in this
century of ours, with its blight of venial adulation, gossip
and cheap journalism, the only certain evidence of genuine
talent is *envy*?

11th November. An evening passed in the company of the
charming Bianca Milesi. Among those present a blatant fool
with pretensions to knowledge in matters musical tried his
utmost to persuade us that Rossini was nothing more or less
than a common murderer! When jealousy is raised to such a
pitch of fanaticism, I find it most entertaining. On his last
visit (this seems to be the one fact established) Rossini was rash
enough to sit in the *caffè dell' Accademia*—where informers lurk
in the very tiling of the floor—and boast of his rapid promotion in the favours of la contessa B***. I can well believe it;
Rossini is singularly handsome, and is anything rather than
shy of his own emotions. Taking him as a genius, this lack of
emotional reticence is perhaps his only weakness; yet, taking
him as a man, it is a sure passport to success.

This morning, I climbed for a second time to the summit of
the *guglia del Duomo*. Bergamo, a picturesque little township
nestling in the rising foothills of the Alps some thirty miles
distant, is clearly visible. Likewise, the tiny chapels of the
famous *Madonna del Monte*, in the neighbourhood of Varese
and similarly some thirty miles distant, were no less distinct.

From this lonely station of mine, islanded thus in the upper air at the very point of this needle worked in white filigree, the ridges of the Alps seem to dance for joy.

Architecturally, the *Porta Nuova*—yet another of Napoleon's creations—suggests the dry and sterile execution of a *miniature*. As an instance of bad taste it is rivalled only by the theatres of Paris. In art, the surest road to *pettiness* lies through a *super-abundance of detail* and an over-conscientious preoccupation with its treatment.

The most impressive features of the *Palazzo di Brera*, at least if you approach the building from the north, are a flight of steps and a courtyard. Later, perhaps, after I have visited Rome, I may think differently. The whole edifice is on the tiniest scale, yet far more beautiful than the *Louvre*, excepting only the western façade; and even that owes such beauty as it possesses exclusively to the carvings.

The *Collegio di Brera* was founded by St Charles Borromeo in 1572. This extraordinary man had some spark of the genius of a Napoleon,[1] that is to say, an intellect without meanness and a determination which never lost sight of its goal. In serving the cause of tyranny and religion, he annihilated whatever *strength* had hitherto resided in the character of the Milanese. In 1533, the fencing-schools were widely frequented; and Castiglione could find the courage to insult Maraviglia, a diplomatic spy in the service of François I. But St Charles lured this people away from the practice of swordsmanship and set it about telling its beads instead. At the *Brera*, I noticed a bust over a doorway, with an inscription informing me that a certain Friar of the Order of the *Umiliati*, driven desperate by the severity of St Charles, who insisted (and there is no doubt here about the sincerity of his convictions) upon a thorough-going moral reform among the clergy, had drawn a bolt at

---

[1] St Charles was born at Arona, hard by the colossus, in 1538, and died in Milan in 1584. He won his claim to immortality during the plague of 1576. [1826]

him from a crossbow—and missed. Donato Farina was the name of the would-be assassin; the incident took place in 1569. Yet, since the days of St Charles no less than before, the priests of the Duchy have kept mistresses. Nothing could seem more natural: no one would dream of condemning them. The explanation given is a model of logical simplicity: 'You see, they aren't married.' I myself, one Sunday morning, was witness to the fret and anxiety of a certain great lady, lest she be late for a Mass which was being celebrated by the priest who was her lover. In all this, moreover, there is nothing contrary to the Declarations of the Council of Trent, which decreed categorically that, if the Devil himself were to robe himself as a priest to administer a Sacrament, that Sacrament would none the less be valid.

In later life—usually at about fifty—the priests of the Duchy take either to drink, or else to religion—the latter normally consequent upon the death of one of their mistresses; and when *that* happens, they voluntarily take upon themselves the most fantastic penances, and find relief in an attempt to persecute their younger colleagues. The customary reward is a fine display of public contempt and hatred. In 1792, when the *émigré* priests from France began to flood into Italy, Italian priests throughout the land were profoundly shocked by the restraint and the sobriety of their existence.

The Brera Museum attracts me constantly. There is a picture by Raphael, in his first manner, the *Marriage of the Virgin*, which is of interest to connoisseurs. As a painting, it gives me a sensation similar to that produced by Rossini's opera *Tancredi*. The emotions which inspire it, although lacking in power, have a certain integrity. None of the characters is vulgar, all have the essential quality which makes them worthy of love—all of which is in diametrical contrast to Titian.

There is also an *Agar*, by Guercino—a miracle of art created to melt the hardest of hearts, and to soften the most inveterate of misers or the most brazen of sycophants.

Among other treasures, one may remark the frescoes by
Bernardino Luini, the artist whose work I so greatly admired
at Saronno. They were transferred here into the Museum
complete with the section of wall upon which they were
originally executed. As a painter, Luini acquires an especial
virtue in our eyes, by contrast with the pseudo-emotionalism
and the affectation of contemporary artists. By temperament,
he may well be frigid; but there is a divine splendour in the
faces he has drawn; like Leonardo, he tempers the sweetness
of grace with a certain *calm* which derives from within. It was
Napoleon who ordered the finest paintings from the Zampieri
gallery in Bologna to be transferred to the Brera; and among
them, a number of masterpieces by the Carracci brothers, who
towards 1590, were responsible for the rebirth of painting in
Italy. Before they appeared, the Italians had been painting in
the same style as the French were writing in the days of Dorat,
Voiture or Marchangy. In France, in our own time, David
has brought about a parallel revolution. Carlo Malvasia, who
was himself a contemporary of Guido Reni and of the latest
surviving masters of this school (1641), has written the lives of
the brothers Carracci in his *Felsina Pittrice*, with a commendable lack of squeamishness in the face of details which, in his
own epoch, must have seemed frankly ignoble, but which,
today, are curiously fascinating.

12th November.   One morning about a month ago, my friend
Guasco walked into my room, accompanied by a tall young
man, who, in spite of his extreme emaciation and his black
clothes, contrived to produce a most distinguished appearance.
This visitor turned out to be signor Ludovico di Breme,
sometime Chaplain to His Majesty Napoleon I, King of Italy,
and son of His Majesty's Minister of the Interior.

And now I am a daily visitor to signor di Breme's box at
la Scala. The company there assembled consists entirely of men
of letters. No woman ever passes the threshold. Signor di

Breme is a man of great education and intelligence, well acquainted with the ways of society. He is a passionate devotee of madame de Staël, and a great patron of literature. A certain coldness has fallen between us, since the occasion when I ventured to remark that all the works of madame de Staël might be summarised as *one* work: *L'Esprit des Lois de la Société**. In any case, all she ever did was to write up, in a glittering and flamboyant style, ideas which she had heard other people formulate in her own *salon*. When this outrageous bluestocking—who had the most brilliant talent for improvisation in all the land of France—arrived in Auxerre, whither she had been exiled, she embarked upon her career in the charming *salon* of Madame de la Bergerie by providing her own panegyric for a week on end without interruption. For instance, on the fifth day, her conversation ran upon one theme only: the beauty of her own arms. Yet those who heard her were never bored.

However, since signor di Breme is a model of politeness, I rarely fail to make an appearance, evening by evening, in his box. My contribution to the circle takes the form of news from France, spiced with anecdotes of the retreat from Moscow, of Napoleon, of the Bourbons; and, in return, I listen to news from Italy. Here, quite frequently, I meet Monti, the greatest of all poets now alive, yet singularly defective in logic. As soon as he is worked up into a rage about something, his eloquence is sublime. Monti is fifty-five years of age, and still remarkably handsome. He was kind enough to show me his portrait, which is by Andrea Appiani, and incontestably the latter's masterpiece. Monti is the very soul of Dante resuscitated in the eighteenth century. Like Dante, he formed his genius upon the model of Virgil, and he has nothing but contempt for the *monarchical* super-subtleties of a Racine, etc. But this is a subject which would lead us too far astray.

In general, the literary eloquence of Italy feels no repugnance towards that sort of language, whose very violence and energy may cause offence to more delicate ears.[1] At every turn there is evidence that this is a country which, for five hundred years, has escaped the contemptuous despotism of a Court like that of Louis XIV or Louis XV. In Italy, passion never takes refuge in *elegance*. And indeed, what poor sort of a thing *is* passion, if it can find leisure to remember the existence of anything that is not *itself*?

Silvio Pellico*, a man of sound sense and solid education, perhaps may scarcely hope to rival Monti in the power and luxuriance of his style. But, in literature, stylistic *power* is synonymous with *effect*, with *influence* upon the reader, with *merit*. Signor Pellico is extremely young still; yet it is his unhappy fate to be precisely in the position of a man destitute of every means of fortune, upon whom the cruel hand of Destiny has chosen to bestow, not the brazen insensitivity of an intriguer, but the boundless generosity of a tender heart. His reaction to calumny is simple despair. 'And yet', I asked him, 'how else do you *expect* a fool to hunt for his revenge?' His answer came back immediately: 'The happiest day of my life will be the day of my death!'[2] There is a sublime portrayal of love in his tragedy *Francesca da Rimini*.

When I am together with signor di Breme in his box, a frequent visitor is signor Borsieri, a man of Gallic intelligence, vivacious as quicksilver and sparkling with audacity. There is also *il marchese* Ermes Visconti, whose notions appear sensible, sound and even tolerably precise, notwithstanding his profound admiration for Kant.

If you were to enquire after the foremost philosopher in modern Italy, I would suspect the choice to lie between signor Visconti and signor Gioja, the author of ten fine quarto volumes, above whose head, day and night, hangs the relentless

---

[1] Or might, if the words in question were translated into French. [1826]
[2] Signor Pellico is due to be released from the fortress of Spielberg at the end of 1826. During his imprisonment, it is reported that he has composed some eight or ten tragedies. [1826]

menace of arrest and imprisonment. However, there is at Naples—at least, according to signora Belmonte—another school of philosophy, of a highly individualistic tendency. But I should be hard put to it to commend the intelligence of any subject of the Kingdom of Naples who should have the temerity to publish a metaphysical treatise containing an explanation of Man and of Nature. Certain persons in Naples have already seized the initiative: they have furnished *their* explanation, and caused it to be promulgated *officially*, and would be only too delighted to send our unwise metaphysician to the gallows! It is still not seventeen years since these same 'official' philosophers, strong in the backing of Admiral Nelson, found themselves able to afford the joy of hanging every single creature of worth and intellect within the boundaries of the Two Kingdoms. Did ever a French admiral play so despicable a rôle as this *Nelson*—in whose memory there now stands a column on the heights above Edinburgh, the *Capital of Reason and of Humanity*? Above and beyond all else, one virtue stands singled out for admiration by the peoples of the North: that of risking one's life; for this alone among virtues offers no scope for hypocrisy, while the meanest among mankind can respond to its appeal.

It is precisely certain truths of this order—plain, unvarnished —which do me so much harm in particular circles, where, for all the high-sounding pretensions to *philosophy* which echo about the room, there are still a certain number of *lies* to which homage must be paid. All in all, I am more at ease in feminine society, where a man may be witty or platitudinous in his opinions, but never *hateful*.

Signor Confalonieri, a man of staunch courage and a true patriot, is a regular visitor to the box belonging to signor di Breme. There is also signor Grisostomo Berchet, who has taken a certain number of poems by Bürger and published them in an excellent Italian translation. He is a minor official (*e un impiegato*); but his treatment of Italian verse, the very metre of which seems dazed at the unfamiliar prospect of embodying a genuine *idea*, is so disrespectful, and he twists so hard at the measure in order to wring into it some semblance of rationality, that I suspect he will soon be dismissed from his post. Every now and then our literary arguments are enlivened by the good-humoured presence of signor Trechi, a most charming man, whose cast of mind is more reminiscent of France than in the case of any other of my Italian acquaintance.

I know of nothing in all Paris which compares with this box, where, every evening of the week, the host will receive some fifteen or twenty visitors, each in his own field a distinguished man; and when the conversation flags, there is always the music.

Both before and after my visits to signor di Breme, I have calls to pay in five or six other boxes, where the conversation is apt to turn on any subject under the sun rather than on philosophical speculation. In Paris, not all the wealth of a millionaire could evoke the fascination of such an evening. The streets outside *la Scala* are bleak and choked with rain and snow; yet what does it matter? *La Scala* has two hundred and four boxes in all; and perhaps a hundred and eighty of these are sufficient to contain all that is of worth and value in Milanese society. The most charming of all these miniature *salons* (I use the word *charming* in its French sense: alive, gay, glittering, all that is the diametrical opposite of *boring*) is perhaps that of signora Nina Viganò, daughter of the living genius who created *Mirra*. Signora Nina—or, to adopt the current Italian usage, which applies to all women, duchesses not excepted, both in their presence and in reference to them in other company: *la Nina**—has a singing voice of quite unique enchantment, and specialises in Venetian melodies written by signor Perruchini, together with a certain type of highly-emotional *aria*, which signor Caraffa, in days gone by, used to compose especially for her. Besides this, *la Nina* is a painter in miniature; and, in the limited field of her art, displays a talent far richer than that of many a celebrated painter in oils.

This delightful personality is at home every Friday, this
being the only day of the week when there is no performance
at *la Scala*; and there is nothing so momentous could befall,
that it should make me decline the pleasure of her invitation.
Towards one o'clock in the morning, when all the company
has dispersed save eight or ten, there will be invariably some
guest in a mood to tell the most entertaining tales of life in
Venice, as life was lived there in the 'nineties of the last century.
From 1740 until 1796, I suspect Venice of having been the
gayest city in all the world, the happiest, the least stricken by
that plague of feudal and superstitious imbecility which, even
in our own time, lies like a blight across the rest of Europe, and
destroys the face of North America. Everything that London
is, Venice was the opposite; above all, the asinine insanity of
being *solemn* was as rare, uncommon and out of fashion (save
in the rites and ceremonies of politics) as hilarity among a
congregation of Trappist monks. Yesterday, *la Nina* told us
anecdotes of Venice which would fill a book . . . of how
signora B[enzoni] made a call upon the Patriarch, and begged
upon her knees for the life of some poor wretch, who was to
be dragged forth to execution on the morrow—who, when
the morrow came, was indeed duly dragged forth and executed,
while the Patriarch, in honour of his humble suppliant, made
a special point of being there to watch . . . of how a somewhat
addle-pated foreigner, being upon the point of leaving Venice,
did boast in the presence of signor R***: "Fore God, Sir, as I
travel homeward from Venice, no man can count himself
happier than I; for there is one woman in this city who is
more beautiful than all the rest, and *her* have I had to be my
mistress!'—whereupon, next morning, signor R*** (and, close
upon his heels, a lackey staggering beneath the burden of an
immense case of pistols) did call upon the unwary foreigner,
and did challenge him to a duel. For signor R*** himself had a
mistress—yet she was fifty years old, and past her best. . . . Ah,
indeed! Venice was the happiest of cities; yet justice in the

civil courts was a corrupt and broken reed, and justice in the criminal courts was unknown.

As soon as some absurdity saw the light of day in Venice, the morrow would witness the circulation of a score of sonnets. The enchanting Nina knows them all by heart; yet it takes the most patient pleading to induce her to recite.

If ever I disbelieved her estimate of the charm and fascination of the Venetian character, I was finally convinced when signora C*** introduced me to Colonel Corner. Striking *simplicity* of this prepossessing young man, whose medals reveal each a chronicle of gallantry under fire, whose ancestors were Doges before the . . . . had so much as shaken off their plebeian dust, and whose brief career has already made inroads upon his fortune to the tune of a couple of million crowns! In no other land could such a personality pass for anything but a vain and impertinent rake.

It was he, yesterday, who was responsible for an impromptu picnic, in which we all took part, at the *Cascina di Pom'* *; for entertainment, there was poetry to charm the ear, and conversation to delight the mind, and in both, a complete absence of affectation. Signor Ancillo, an apothecary from Venice and a most entertaining companion, recited to the company an antique sonnet of aristocratic source concerning the birth of Christ. Voltairian satire makes too strenuous a demand upon the intellect; Venetian satire is more sensual and less exacting; its themes are platitudinous, but it handles them with infinite subtlety and grace. Signor Ancillo is also fond of reciting certain poems by Buratti; which, if they are not perfection in the absolute degree, yet assuredly they run it very close.

It was at Nina's, this evening, that I caught a glimpse of Count Saurau, the Governor-General of Milan. He seems to be a man of considerable education, and, I surmise, of lively intelligence; but I have a suspicion that he is not of noble birth —a misfortune which robs him of the right to wield authority with a light heart. Yet, from a remark or two that he let fall

concerning *Coriolano* (a ballet by Viganò), I observed that he
possesses all that exquisite sensibility for art which no man of
letters in France (and least of all a *Voltaire*) can achieve in the
experience of a lifetime.

13th November. I have not the courage to set down here the
tales of love that I have heard. In Brescia, towards the year
1786, there lived a certain Count Vitelleschi*, a man of singular
character, whose abounding energy seems to ring with echoes
of the Middle Ages. All that I have heard concerning him
betrays an individuality of the stamp of Castruccio Castracani.
Since he held no rank or office in the State, his wild ambition
could find no outlet save in the dissipation of his fortune
through new and curious extravagances, in the feverish violence
of his escapades in honour of the woman he loved, and ultimately in the assassination of his rivals. A stranger chanced one
day to gaze upon his mistress, at the instant when he was about
to offer her his arm. 'Look at the ground!' shouted Vitelleschi.
The stranger continued to stare unwinking, and Vitelleschi
blew his brains out. A venial slip or two of this nature was no
more than the merest peccadillo when the offender was a
wealthy patrician; but came the day when Vitelleschi chanced
to murder the distant cousin of a Bragadino (an aristocratic
Venetian family of most ancient lineage), and was arrested,
brought to Venice and thrown into the notorious prison-
fortress beside the *Ponte dei Sospiri*. Vitelleschi was handsome
as the Prince of Darkness, and his tongue was of pure honey.
The gaoler had a wife, whom Vitelleschi made motions to
seduce; but the gaoler got wind of the affair, and finding here
the excuse for some light relief or variation in the exercise of
his calling (such as, for instance, loading his prisoner with
chains), he went to call on Vitelleschi. The latter seized his
chance and spoke to the man; and thus, word by word in the
lonely depths of his dungeon, and laden with fetters, Vitelleschi
won over and seduced his own tormentor, who, day in, day

out, would visit the prisoner of his own accord, for the joy of two hours' simple conversation. 'Yet the worm which eats my heart', said Vitelleschi, 'is *honour*. For I, like you, am a man of honour. And while I lie here rotting in these chains, my enemy goes free in Brescia, and struts the highways in the insolence of his pride. Ah! Let me but kill him—then would I die content!' Such proud purpose at length began to melt the gaoler's heart, and he made him a proposal: 'For a period of one hundred hours I will lend you back your freedom.' In his joy, Vitelleschi embraced his keeper. It was a Friday night when he crept out of the prison; a gondola lay ready to carry him to Mestre, where he found a *sediola* prepared and harnessed, and relays waiting for him by the road. When he reached Brescia, it was the third hour past the stroke of noon; he took up guard in the doorway of the church; and as his enemy stepped out into the sunlight after Vespers, he killed him then and there, in the very centre of the congregation, with a shot from a carbine. But *he* is Count Vitelleschi; no one dreams of making his arrest; and so he takes his seat once more in the waiting *sediola*, and by Tuesday night is back again in prison.

Yet soon enough, reports of this new outrage began to assail the ears of the *Signoria* of Venice; and promptly the August Council summoned into its presence Count Vitelleschi, who came before his judges scarcely able to drag one foot behind the other, so weak and fleshless had he grown. The accusation was read aloud in his hearing. 'How many are the witnesses who have signed this latest calumny?' asked Vitelleschi in a voice like a sepulchral echo. 'More than ten score,' came the reply. 'Yet Your Excellencies are aware that on Sunday last, which is the day of the assassination, I lay here, *here* in this very same accursèd prison. Conceive, then, the number of my enemies!' Among the more venerable judges there were some who, beneath the weight of this argument, began to grow less fully certain of his guilt; while the younger members of the Court were already prepossessed in Vitelleschi's favour on account of the very singularity of his character; and so, after a short delay, the eventual outcome of this new murder was the release from prison of the murderer. A year passed; and then, one day, the gaoler received a visit from a priest, who handed him the sum of 180,000 *lire venete* (90,000 fr.)—the precise sum derived from the sale of a small estate, which had been the last of all his lands remaining unmortgaged in the hands of Vitelleschi. He was brave, passionate and unpredictable; the story of his life would fill a volume; when he died, he had reached a ripe old age, and still contrived to keep his neighbours in a state of terror. He left behind him two daughters and four sons, one and all remarkable for a rare degree of beauty. There is a tale told, how once he took up voluntary residence in a chimney, and lived there fifteen days on end to spy upon his mistress, who, to her honour and his nameless joy and happiness, proved faithful to her love. For she had been granting secret assignations to a young man of great wealth who was passionately in love with her—yet all in order to win him as a husband for her daughter. Vitelleschi, convinced at last of his mistress' innocence, let suddenly go his hold half-way up the chimney where he had been crouching, came slithering into the fireplace, and burst with laughter at the stupefaction of the young gallant. 'A narrow escape you had, sir, indeed! Now see the profit in dealing with a man of honour! Any other in my case would have killed you first, and argued the wherefore of the matter later!' Count Vitelleschi was invariably of a gay disposition; he was a stranger to misanthropy, and his sallies were not without grace. It is of him that the story is told, how, one day in the Sacred Season before Easter, he disguised himself as a priest, and acted confessor to this same mistress who had held his constant love for fifteen years. The true confessor had been lured out early in the morning by one of the Count's *buli*, who lay at home and pretended to be at death's very door; and there he was drugged with opium. As soon as he was soundly asleep, Vitelleschi proceeded to strip him of his habit, and with solemn step did march devoutly to the confessional.

If I were to relate further anecdotes, requiring even greater wealth of detail, I must fall into the same absurdity as did that English traveller who spent his days describing *ice* to the King of the Coasts of Guinea. Yet the point of all these tales is never in doubt; for one and all go to prove that the only idea which may never occur to an intelligent Italian is that he should *fashion himself upon a model*. Any young man in Italy, five-and-twenty years of age and master of his fortune, once he has cast off the shyness of adolescence, is the undisputed slave of *immediate sensation*; it fills him to the exclusion of all else. All that is not either the enemy he hates or the mistress he adores is vanity to him. Only among the aristocracy you may discover an occasional bird-witted dandy cut on the pattern of France; but such exceptions, like the young nobles from the Court of the Tsars, are half a century behind the times and still aping the vanished age of Louis XV. Their appearances in public, particularly on horseback, are outrageously absurd.

Yesterday, in the *Giardini*, towards one o'clock, there was a most agreeable concert. Many German regimental bands have eighty or more players. The audience consisted of a hundred women, all of surpassing beauty; and the music was sublime. These Teutonic bandsmen gave us the finest selection of Mozart, and of a young man named Rossini; a hundred and fifty wind-players, each *perfectly* master of his instrument, somehow imbued these melodies with a unique tinge and flavour of melancholy. Compared with such a performance, our own military bands are no more than the clumsy footgear of an old fishwife set against the rapture of some tiny ballet-slipper of white satin whose enchantment invites your gaze this very evening*.

14th November. Della Bianca, the youngest of all my new acquaintances, usually sits, wrapped from shoulder to toe in

his cloak and immersed in silence inviolate, in the first row of
the pit; but tonight, when I questioned him concerning the
marchesina D***, whose gaze lay riveted upon her lover below
her, exiled by the jealousy of a husband from the box where
his mistress remained, he, instead of giving a direct answer,
spoke as follows:

'Music satisfies, when, by night, it allows the soul to relive
those moments of ecstasy which *love* has afforded it by day*.'

Who could conceive a nobler simplicity of language,
corresponding to a similar directness of experience? I made no
reply, and left my companion to himself. When music acts
upon a man with such intensity, the best of friends is a rash
intruder.

15th November. Rain in torrents; for three days now, a
ceaseless downpour, with rarely so much as ten minutes'
respite. In Paris, two whole months could scarce suffice to
witness such a deluge—which is the reason why, in France,
the climate is perpetually damp. Yet here it is hot. I have
spent all day at the Brera, in the Museum, contemplating
plaster-casts of sculpture by Michelangelo and Canova. The
vision of Michelangelo is constantly swayed by the stark
imminence of Hell; that of Canova is compounded of sensuality and sweetness. The colossal head of Pope Rezzonico
imploring pardon of God for the sin of his father, a rich
Venetian banker who had paid a good round sum in cash to
secure his son a Cardinal's hat, is a masterpiece of naturalistic
interpretation. It has none of those *ignoble* qualities which may
be remarked in comparable 'colossal' sculptures in the Paris
museum. Canova had the courage to avoid a slavish imitation
of the Greeks; instead, he rivalled the achievement of the
Greeks themselves, and invented an original conception of
beauty, thus spreading dismay and mortification among the
monstrous regiment of pedants. Pedantry, in consequence,
will still be hurling insults at his head when he is dead and gone

D

for fifty years, and the daystar of his glory will but rise the faster. Canova, the genius who, at the age of twenty, had never learned to spell, left at his death a hundred statues, thirty of which will live for ever; whereas Michelangelo, in all his life, left but one statue truly worthy of the genius that was his —the *Moses*, which is to be seen in Rome.

Michelangelo was as familiar with the Greeks as Dante was with Virgil. Both gave admiration where admiration was due; neither imitated*; and so both have won a reputation which lives on undiminished through the centuries. Respectively they may be called the sculptor and the poet of the Holy Roman Catholic and Apostolic Church, and such they will remain; for it must be remembered that, in the year 1300, when the religion of Rome was strong in the radiance of its dawning manhood, it had none of those gentle graces with which it stands endowed by the author of *le Génie du Christianisme*. For proof, take the massacre of Cesena.[1]

In France, our own artists, who are all pupils of David and worthy compatriots of La Harpe, pass judgment on Michelangelo in accordance with the canons of Greek sculpture—or rather, to be more precise, according to what they imagine those canons to have been. But, however implacable their rage against Michelangelo, it burns still fiercer against Canova, who, first and foremost, has not yet acquired the honour of being three centuries dead, and who, more unforgivably still, having enjoyed the most signal good fortune to be born a contemporary of M. David, did yet somehow neglect to profit from this gift of Destiny, and failed to become his disciple. Among Frenchmen, few are more charming than M. Denon; yet a score of times I have heard him declare that

[1] The reader should be acquainted with the first three volumes of Pignotti's excellent *History of Tuscany*, which is a far better work than that of Sismondi. Pignotti is as accurate as he is vivid. For the History of the Church in Italy, I recommend the veracious de Potter and signor Tamburini's *Vera Idea della Santa Sede*. Satire, however ingenious, is not history, and Voltaire's writings on the Church are valueless. [1826]

Canova never learnt how to draw. Michelangelo and Canova might pass for the blackest criminals in the world, were it not for the fact that a conscienceless rogue named Correggio has the insolence to sell his paintings, no bigger than a sheet of drawing-paper, for the sum of one hundred thousand francs apiece (and that beneath our very eyes!), while the noble products of the Master's own illustrious brush, each as big as a gallery in itself, languish in pained seclusion in the Luxembourg.[1] Incidentally, the mention of Correggio reminds me that Signor Reina took me once on a visit to poor Appiani, who, since his last stroke, has lost his memory, and sits crying quietly to himself; and on the way home, in a spasm of generosity unprecedented in a bibliophile, *lent me a book!* The work in question proved to be the *Memoirs of Correggio*, by Father Affò, s.j., a highly curious composition, even though sadly overburdened with *minutiae*. Father Affò is to render a similar service on behalf of Raphael, to which end he proposes to spend four years researching in Urbino.

Signor Cattaneo, Curator of the Numismatical Collection at the Brera, received me in a vein of politeness which was wholly French. True, I was the only reader in the whole of his library. I went there to study the cyclopean monuments which I am to visit at Volterra. This library was founded by Count Prina, as were also the bonded warehouses for salt and tobacco, and the powder-arsenal; he further built up the personnel of the Customs Inspectorate, which, as a body, is less vile a set of scoundrels today than it was before 1796.

18th November. It was, if I am not mistaken, under Napoleon that the Milanese discovered a particular and graceful style of architecture to apply to their private residences. An excellent

---

[1] I pay my sincerest respects to the personal character of M. David*; unlike a mere man of letters, he steadfastly refused to sell his soul. But, as an artist, his paintings fail to please the eye; perhaps in more northerly latitudes—say in Stockholm—they might at last come into their own. [1826]

example of this manner is to be seen in the façade of the *contrada Santa Margarita*, which, since the police have chosen it for their headquarters, every traveller has only too frequent occasion to visit. The spacing of the windows is graceful and without a trace of heaviness; the relationship between plain and decorated surfaces is perfect; and the cornices jut out unashamedly over the street.

The *via degli Orefici* still bears traces of life as it was in by-gone days, under the mediaeval republics, for there are still to be seen here a hundred goldsmiths' shops set side by side. In the fourteenth century, at the first threat of danger to their street, all the goldsmiths would rush to arms and muster their own defence against marauders. I should imagine, too, that there would have been chains drawn across the thoroughfare at either end. One *History of Milan* which I read with constant delight is that by Verri, the friend of Beccaria, who writes with all the plainspoken informality of a typical Milanese, and yet with all the dark mistrust of a typical Italian. I am spared that aura of solemn *vagueness* and affectation which so often proves more than I can stomach in French writings of our own century. Count Verri has all the resplendent common-sense of our own historians towards the year 1550; his style is on all occasions bold and natural. It is plain that his fear of the *police* has ousted and vanquished his fear of the *critics*.

The history of Milan is as fascinating as a novel by Walter Scott, beginning with the year 1063, when the priests shamelessly provoked a civil war in order to avoid the strictures of the law of celibacy which Rome was seeking to impose upon them, until the year 1515, when François I triumphed at the battle of Melegnano. If I insist upon this exact period of four hundred and fifty-two years, it is for the especial benefit of popular historians; for there is material here for two fine octavo volumes *of compelling interest* (as the saying goes): conspiracies; love, ambition and revenge, each with its own tale of assassination; great enterprises to the advancement of the commonwealth; a dozen popular uprisings reminiscent of the assault upon the Bastille in 1789—all this, and nothing more recondite required than a touch of simplicity in the telling of it, to make the liveliest of narratives. Even our own dull chronicles of the same epoch, where nothing ever rises to the surface save the gross and boorish passions of churls with never a spark in their breasts save dreams of food and plunder, have been transmuted into sagas of real interest.

The murder of the Grand-Duke Lucchino Visconti by his wife Isabella da Fiesco (1349) is by a long chalk more enthralling than the tale of Vaurus and his elm-tree. The episodes which I have in mind would plainly have to be grouped together under the conventional title: *Gems from the History of Milan*; but I would suggest as a sub-title: *Introduction to the Study of the Human Heart*. The gigantic passions of the Middle Ages break through at every chapter in the undimmed effulgence of their ferocious energy, and the mask of affectation is stripped away*. The ardent spirits of the age had neither time nor place for affectation; and the historians who have served them have proved not unworthy of their heroes, for they have shown no tendency to share with M. de Fontanes his implacable academic hatred towards any language which describes the thing it sees.

Is it possible to conceive a sequence of events more picturesque than the annals of the Visconti?

Matteo Visconti, being determined to overthrow the Republic and make himself king in Milan, uncovers a conspiracy and punishes the conspirators.

Antiochia Visconti Crivelli, wife to one of the conspirators, gathers an army ten thousand strong, and flings it against the usurper (1301).

Matteo II Visconti dies poisoned by his own brothers (1355).

Gian Galeazzo Visconti poisons his uncle (1385); but in compensation he builds the Cathedral of Milan. *Giammaria Visconti* is assassinated by a band of conspirators (1412); Milan is declared a republic (1447); *Francesco Sforza* (1450) proceeds to handle this new republic as Bonaparte was later to handle our own; but his son *Galeazzo* is assassinated in the Church of *Santo-Stefano* (1476).

Lodovico il Moro gives his name to the mulberry-trees (*moroni*), whose cultivation he introduced into the Duchy; yet it is he who flings open the gates of Italy to King Charles VIII, and poisons his own nephew in the hope of reaping the succession. This very morning I was shown a most interesting and brilliantly executed painting by signor Palagi, who had the commission from Count Alari: it depicts the unhappy *Galeazzo Maria*, weakened already by the working of a slow poison, yet raising himself by a supreme effort upon his bed of pain to receive a ceremonial visit from Charles VIII; while *Galeazzo Maria's* young wife stands by, seeking to read the future in the eyes of the King of France, and to discover whether he will lend them aid in their revenge against the murderers. I cannot but suspect that a subject of this character offers more pertinent interest to a Milanese than some conventional *Wrath of Achilles*. Count Alari, a sometime equerry in the service of Napoleon, has indeed proved worthy to add his contribution to the moral resurgence of Italy. During these latter days, the whole of the city has made the pilgrimage *alla casa Alari*, to see a painting entitled *Francesca da Rimini*, by a young Florentine artist. Personally, I found the picture somewhat commonplace, devoid of *power*, *sine ictu*; and, being rash enough to say so, found myself accused of hating every painter ever bred in Italy. In any skirmish with *Patriotic Sentiment* there is only one sure weapon of defence, which is *a downright lie*; and in this I am of one mind with M. de Goury, for, when I start to lie, I start to yawn. . . . But the plain fact remains: *Francesca da Rimini* will never come within a hundred leagues of M. Guérin's *Didon*.

Signora P*** has been advising me to go to Monza and look at the *Iron Crown*; I, seemingly, being in need of further inducement, she added that I should find in Monza a superb

game-preserve full of pheasants—a prospect which I find less
attractive still*. 'And finally', she added, 'you may glance at the
Cathedral, with its splendid tower housing a peal of eight
bells, all perfectly *intuonate*.' It was this final phrase which at
last caught my wandering interest, for it is so typically Italian;
indeed, what are church bells, if not a part and parcel of the
art of music? This remark was something of a revelation, for
it showed me that, having once mastered my original feeling
of astonishment, I have grown to be curiously fond of the
strange campanological traditions of Milan. This tradition goes
back, I believe, to St Ambrose, to whom belongs the further
merit of having extended the Carnival by four days. Lent, in
Milan, is not deemed to start until the Sunday following what
elsewhere is known as Ash Wednesday; and on the evening
of this latter occasion, people of means and fortune come
pouring into Milan from every village and township within a
hundred miles' radius—for this is the great season of the
Carnovolone.

19th November. Sitting this evening as the guest of signora
Foscarini in her box, I was told of the following adventure,
which dates from the Carnival of 1814.

At this time there lived a Milanese lady, who enjoyed a
profound attachment to a certain French officer. This *liaison*
had continued ever since the year 1806. Now, in Milan, it is
traditional for all major revolutions *nelle amicizie* to take place
during the Carnival. The cause is not far to seek, for it lies in
the unwonted liberty which accompanies the season of masked
balls. These are attended by the whole of *Society*—that is, by
every person of birth and consequence in the city; no one would
miss one for the world, and indeed they are enchanting. I have
heard of ten people banding together in an organised mas-
querade, for which the masks and costumes cost each actor
not a penny less than eighty *sequins*. Such escapades as this,
obviously, belong to 1810; for ever since the Austrian occupation

and the presence of *i Tedesch'*, all pleasure has taken wing and vanished. On such gala occasions, all the boxes in the theatre are illuminated, and laid for supper at two in the morning; and truly, there is a kind of madness abroad in the night. The opera begins at seven o'clock, which is the hour when the guests assemble; but at midnight, men precariously perched on seventy-foot ladders, which are themselves balanced upon the shoulders of other men standing on the floor of the pit, make the circuit of the auditorium, lighting the six candles which have been placed in front of each box; and half an hour later, the ball is opened.

And thus it happened, in the course of the last ball but one of the Carnival of 1814, that Teodolinda R*** became suddenly aware that Colonel Malclerc had plainly broken the pledges of their attachment. It was five o'clock in the morning before this gallant officer retired to his lodgings; but scarcely had he passed the threshold, when he was handed a letter written in abominable French, which demanded satisfaction of him for some unspecified offence. He was convened, upon his honour as a gentleman, to equip himself with pistols, and to repair straightway, in the company of one friend, to the *Cascina di Pom'*, which is the *Bois de Boulogne* of Milan. The Colonel promptly went and roused up an acquaintance; and, by the first light of dawn, in spite of the snow and the biting cold, both gentlemen were duly present at the appointed spot. Here they discovered that the principal actor was to be an oddly undersized individual heavily enveloped in furs; he refused to give his name, and his second proved equally uncommunicative. But this was neither here nor there; the pistols were loaded, and the opponents duly measured out their dozen paces. Yet, at the very instant of firing, the undersized individual was obliged to take a step forward; and Malclerc, who was consumed with curiosity, managed for the first time to look hard at him . . . and recognised his own mistress, Teodolinda R***. He tried to laugh the matter off; but she

crushed him with the bitterness of her contempt and the brutal
logic of her argument. He made a move to close the gap
between them, but she cried out: 'Not a step nearer, or I fire!'
and her second had the greatest difficulty in convincing her
that, by doing so, she would be going beyond her rights.
Immediately she turned on her own second: 'Is it my fault
if he refuses to fire?'; then back to Malclerc: 'Ungrateful
wretch! You have done me the greatest wrong that ever man
can do to woman! The duel is fair and equally contested, for
all your protestations to the contrary . . . yet if you insist, one
pistol shall be charged, the other empty, and we will fire at
three paces' distance. . . . *I* have no intention of returning
alive to Milan, unless I know and see that *you* are dead; and
then I should drive post-haste to the *principessa* N***, and
announce in person that you have ceased to be. . . . If I were
simply to have you assassinated—and I have *buli*[1] in my service,
who would think nothing simpler—you might complain that
we Italians are nothing, one and all, save murderers at heart.
So *fight*, then, I charge you—or are you merely a coward
when it comes to anything more manly than insulting the
honour of others?' This episode was told me actually in the
presence of the man who had played the part of second to
signora R***. 'It was always my belief', he added, 'that *la
Teodolinda* was quite determined to die.' And the fact is there
for all to observe, that in spite of her youth and the exquisite
cast of her enchanting beauty, she has remained for three whole
years disconsolate—which is a phenomenon of no little rarity
in the land of Italy, where *vanity* counts for nothing in the

---

[1]The *buli*, a bold and skilful race, were professional assassins, who,
as late as 1775, would hire out their services as required. See the *Lettres
d'Italie*, by M. Roland, the famous Minister of the Interior. I am told
that, should the need arise, there are still a few remnants of the breed to
be found and used, in the neighbourhood of Brescia. I have myself once
heard a young man quite seriously intimidate his enemy with the threat
of assassination at the hands of his *buli*. But the wider activities of these
worthy gentry were gravely curtailed by Napoleon. [1826]

constancy of a resolution. Her whole occupation has been the learning of Latin and of English, that she herself might supervise the education of her daughters. When the man who had played second at the duel had left the box, I was told that, at the time of the encounter, he was himself a rejected suitor of *la Teodolinda*; and that he had even proposed so to deal with Malclerc, that the Colonel could find no further pretext in the difference between his sex and hers, on condition that she would take him for her lover; which offer she refused.

I confess that I have no certain evidence of all these details; nor can I hope for further confirmation until signor P***, who has been settling his children in the Pension Fellenberg, returns from Switzerland in three months' time—if, by then, I am still here. I adore *strength*, but only of one kind: the kind of strength which lies as readily within the compass of an ant as of an elephant.

A certain traveller (of the order of those who wander across Europe guide-book in hand, armed with a pin to prick holes in the margins of the book against the sights that they have seen) once remarked in my hearing to a charming old gentleman who had published an account of a journey to Zürich:[1] 'But hearken sir! I am but recently returned from Zürich, and *I* saw nothing of all the things you mention.' 'Sir', came the retort, 'I mentioned nothing save that which is rare and uncommon. Aspects of life in Zürich which in no wise differ from the equivalent aspects of life in Frankfurt scarcely impressed me as deserving description; but true originality is rare, and must be discerned with a certain penetration of mind.'

Teodolinda R*** suffered no dishonour from this escapade, which stirred up a fearsome storm of public comment. *E una matta* was the general verdict. In Milan, public opinion is as lenient towards women in the matter of love as in Paris it is

---

1 *Voyage de Zürich à Zürich*, by the author of the concluding volumes of Grimm. [1826]

lenient towards men in the matter of political integrity. Everyone sells his little soul to the Ministry in office, everyone haggles and bargains to his own particular advantage—and should fortune prove on his side, society will fight for invitations to his table, and the guests will rise and wipe their lips, and cry: 'There's no one like old so-and-so for knowing on which side his bread is buttered!' Which is the more immoral, for a woman to have a lover, or for a man to sell his vote in order to promulgate an unjust law, or see his enemy hanged? Society is daily witness to the homage paid to men who think nothing of such peccadilloes.

In Milan, if a woman be both pretty and pious, public opinion will respect in her the victim of an overmastering passion: *the Fear of Hell*. Signora Annoni, one of the loveliest women in all the city, is in this case. By contrast, a silly creature who has no lover of her own, or none but others' cast-offs (*spiantati*), is greeted on every hand with undisguised contempt. For the rest, any woman may pick her lover where she will; no invitation will exclude her recognised admirer. On more than one occasion, at a Friday *soirée*, I have observed a woman arrive as guest with a lover upon her arm as yet unknown to the mistress of the house; nevertheless, the normal practice is for the woman to drop word privately in a note, giving the name of her *cavaliere servente*, who later leaves his card in a formal visit, and thereafter will be invited by name.

As soon as a woman gives reason to suspect that her choice of lover is in the minutest degree influenced by financial considerations, there is no limit to the contempt to which she will be exposed. If there are grounds for believing that she entertains several lovers at once, she will cease to be invited. Even so, such severities are new, and date only from the days of Napoleon, who, in his passion for law and order, and in the interests of his own despotic authority, restored to Italy a glimpse of moral conscience. The most beneficial influence, in this respect, has derived from the divers *Academies for Young*

Ladies which he founded, one at Verona, and one at Milan, under the direction of Madame Delort, a pupil or at least a disciple of Madame Campan. It has been observed that nowadays such scandals as there are originate unfailingly, either among women who have already reached middle age, or else who were educated in convents. In Milan, public opinion had no existence before 1796; and it follows logically therefore, that any woman whose character was formed before that date, or who was born into the type of family which failed to keep abreast of the times, can scarcely be expected to model her behaviour upon the dictates of an arbiter of morals, of whose existence she is not even aware.

20th November. It is not uncommon for a woman, upon marriage, to bring her husband a dowry of five hundred thousand francs—which, in terms of current values in Milan, represents some eight hundred thousand in Paris. Out of this, she may receive an allowance of some two thousand for her personal needs. Kitchen and household accounts fall entirely within the province of her husband; the wife has no concern in all the world, save the laying-out of her allowance, to the tune of one hundred and seventy-five francs a month. She has her carriage, her box at the opera, a rope of diamonds and half a score of servants—and she may count herself lucky if she has five francs in her pocket. The wealthiest woman in Milan will be content, in spring, to buy herself half a dozen dresses in plain English dimity at twenty francs apiece, and throughout the year will change her costume only as a man may change his cravat—for variation rather than for effect. At the onset of winter, she may make three or four further dresses for the cold season, costing maybe as much as thirty francs. The silken garments of her wedding-trousseau are precious and to be preserved with meticulous care, and will still be worn some eight or ten years hence, on gala occasions—for first nights at *la Scala,* or at *feste di ballo* during the Carnival. Everyone is known for what they are, so where lies the sense in elaborate clothes?

It is this extreme poverty, even among the wealthiest of women, which explains the delight with which they will accept the gift of six pairs of shoes from Paris, and attach no consequence to their acceptance. It is perfectly in order for a woman to make public use of her lover's box at *la Scala*, and even of his carriage: no shame is implied, other than that of avowed penury. At mid-day, it is customary for a woman to receive one favoured guest alone in private familiarity; between two and four, she will welcome friends of her own sex in an intimate circle; and, between eight in the evening and half an hour after midnight, she will be at home in her box to her more casual acquaintances. Each box holds some ten or a dozen seats; and when these are filled, it is incumbent upon the earliest arrivals to take their leave and make way for late-comers as they appear. The first visitor of the evening may claim a seat next to his hostess, hard against the balcony of the box; and as he takes his leave, there will follow immediately a general reshuffle among the guests remaining, each moving up one seat nearer to the balcony, while the newcomer occupies the now-vacant seat nearest the door. In this fashion, every visitor may eventually come in turn to occupy the seat of honour beside his hostess. I have even had occasion to observe a particularly shy young man actually rise and take his leave as soon as this ladder of seniority began to threaten him with the proximity of the lady of the house; for he was in love with her; and since she returned his love, the whole situation, to a disinterested outsider, was fascinating.

The *foyer* (*l'atrio*) of *la Scala* serves as a general club and *rendez-vous* for all the rakes and dandies in Milan; it is a hive of gossip which can make or mar a woman's reputation. Every lady who accepts a gentleman's arm upon the *Great Staircase* may rest assured that he will be credited to her as a lover—particularly at *premières*, when the gesture is irrevocable.

Nothing but dishonour awaits the woman of whom it may be suspected that she entertains a lover, whom she dare not summon to offer his arm at the critical hour of half-past eight, as she mounts the staircase to her box. Only yesterday, I overheard a man most hotly disclaiming his right to render this insignificant service to a lady of his acquaintance. '*Mia cara*', he protested at the end, 'unhappily I do not enjoy the favours which would entitle me by right to offer you my arm; and I have no wish to lend countenance to the suspicion that I am sharing the honour with signor F***.' The lady proceeded to deny vigorously that signor F*** was her lover, but the other persisted in his refusal. In the confirmed absence of any lover, a woman may expect her husband to escort her. Upon occasions I have heard a young and notably handsome husband make shameless complaint against this nuisance. It implies plain dishonour for the husband, moreover, if he is suspected of having to escort his wife because *she* has failed to to persuade her lover to make the gesture of giving her his arm across the *atrio*. All these formalities touched the height of their observance in the years before 1796; nowadays, the conventions are less rigid, and more than one young woman has had the audacity to climb the *Great Staircase* escorted by no one save her servant—a quirk of behaviour which, in the eyes of many a high-born dowager, is nothing short of *scandalous*.

Yesterday, as I stood talking in the *atrio* with a group of dandies of my acquaintance, they drew my attention to a fine-looking, sunburnt young man with an expression of unrelieved dejection, who stood motionless with his back against the wall of the *foyer*; his stance was suggestive of a duty conscientiously performed; and indeed, it proved to be an English gentleman with an income of some twenty-two thousand guineas a year. Moroseness in conjunction with such a fortune seemed nothing less than monstrous to my new acquaintance. 'This unhappy Englishman', I explained, 'is suffering from the ravages of *thought*.' (For in Italy, the essence of any man below the age of thirty is pure *sensation*.) What a contrast with your German, who, in the same period of his life, is a thorough-going *Kantian*, even at his mistress' knees!

I have a leaning towards the company of older men, of forty years and upward. I find them stuffed with prejudice, inade-quately educated, and infinitely more *natural* than the present all-too-literate generation which has been at school since 1796. I am constantly aware that my younger friends, by suppressing a detail of behaviour here and there, are determined to give me a false impression; whereas the others, finding nothing to be ashamed of, are just as frank as I could wish. The majority of the older generation have a firm belief in the Blessèd Virgin, together with a certain element of *respect* towards God (since God may also wield a conceivable influence, and no wise man should neglect precautions). In Italy, as indeed everywhere, a child learns its religion from its nursery-maid, who is invariably a peasant. The aristocracy of Milan is markedly less well-mannered (*scial*) than are the other classes of society, because the parents see far less of their own children when they are young. There is a delightful poem in Milanese dialect by Carline Porta, which lists the qualities considered necessary in an aspirant who seeks to be tutor to the heir-presumptive of a noble line.[1] As for the genuine Italian paterfamilias rising fifty, you may discover his portrait limned with genius in the comedy: *l'Ajo nell' imbarazzo*, by the celebrated Count Giraùd.

I drove a quarter of a league out of Milan to hear the echo at la Simonetta*, and fired the customary pistol-shot with its fifty-fold reverberation. Architecturally, this country manor, with its belvedere supported by columns at the level of the second storey, impressed me most agreeably.

[1]   *Alla marchesa Paola Travasa,*
        Vuna di primm damazz di Lombardia . . .
        LA NOMINA DELL CAPELLAN   [1826]

22nd November. An English sea-captain, driven by opposing currents upon the coasts of Guinea, once so far forgot his common-sense as to appear before a princeling of the country, and to speak of *snow* and *ice*. For the *Great Chief*, upon hearing that there existed a land where water was as hard as stone, was so overcome with laughter that there seemed to be no way in which the fit might properly be cured.

This intoxication of mirth is an experience which I feel no urge to inflict upon my readers; in consequence, I shall forbear to transcribe those passages of my *Journal*, in which I have attempted to record the rare and remarkable sensation I received from *Mirra*, a ballet by Salvatore Viganò*. I have been watching it this evening for the eighth, or perhaps even the tenth time, and my excitement has not yet subsided.

In the realm of tragic emotions, the most fervent satisfaction I had yet experienced before my journey to Milan I owed originally to Monvel, whom I saw again later as the Emperor Augustus in *Cinna*. Talma, with his dislocated wrist and his unnatural voice, always gave me a secret desire to laugh; still today, these same characteristics make it impossible for me to appreciate this great actor at his proper worth. Many years after I had last watched Monvel, I travelled to London and saw Kean* in *Othello* and in *Richard III*; and then indeed I *did* believe that the theatre had no more vivifying experience to offer; yet the finest tragedy that Shakespeare ever wrote can scarcely move me half as much as a ballet by Viganò. He is a genius whose art will die with him, and be forgotten; and he has neither peer nor parallel in France. Conceive, then, the folly of trying to evoke a picture of such an art; inevitably, the reader will find his imagination fettered by misleading recollections of Gardel.[1]

It is a dangerous undertaking to describe a journey, not as a series of objects seen, but rather as a tale of sensations experi-

[1] Signorina Pallerini, who dances the part of Mirra, invites comparison with Madame Pasta*. [1826]

enced. Any tendency to praise is sure to kindle a furnace of hatred in every heart whose reactions are at variance with mine. In such a *Journal* as this, what infinite matter for mockery, should its readers prove to be men of *fortune* and *recognised merit*. Yet there is this also, that for whomsoever I may be writing, it is surely not for people such as these. *Merit* is all very well; but merit, to be *recognised*, must tread the deadly social mill a thousand times—and I would not waste so much as a hundred evenings so!

The only account of a *Journey to Italy* which could worthily hope for general applause would need to be composed, on terms of mutual equality, by Mrs Radcliffe (to describe the beauties of nature and the handiwork of man) and by the Président de Brosses (to delineate the manners of the time). I am only too well aware that such a *Journey* would prove infinitely superior to all its rivals; but it would occupy scarcely less than eight volumes. As for the technique of dry and philosophical description, we have already a notable master-piece in such a style: the *Statistical Analysis of the Department of Montenotte*, by monsieur de Chabrol, *Préfet de la Seine*.[1]

23rd November. I have been fortunate enough to secure an introduction to one of the most respectable citizens of Milan, signor Rocco Marliani. This upright and honourable man is one of the Conscript Fathers of the city, which is still, beneath all the contradictions of appearance, so essentially republican at heart. The Sovereign, be he Spanish or Austrian, has come, by centuries-old tradition, to be considered as the public enemy of the city. To enter his service is *excusable*, for it is he who holds the purse-strings; but to do so with eagerness is *infamous*, for is he not, today as in the past, an enemy? Signor Marliani said nothing to me of all this; but talked at length

[1] For any discussion of the religious question, see de Potter's *Vie de Scipion Ricci*. As an historian, M. de Potter is accurate beyond reproach or criticism. I have also relied upon signor Litta's *Famiglie illustri*. [1826]

instead of Carlo Verri and of Beccaria*.[1] These inestimable citizens, through the publication of their celebrated periodical *il Caffè* (1764-1765), made Milan the centre of a new school of philosophy. In marked contrast to their contemporaries in France, these philosopher-reformers were profoundly indifferent to the titillations of style, or to their fame and reputation in the *salons*. The leadership of society (of a society whose preoccupation lay in the experience of passion rather than in the petty triumphs of vanity) having been thrust upon them by their fortune, by the lustre of the civic dignities they held, and by their birth, neither Verri nor Beccaria had any use for successes of so brittle and flimsy a type. Beccaria, for instance, the author of the famous treatise: *dei Delitti e delle Pene*, was received with open arms by Parisian society, and was on the threshold of a career of celebrity likely to rival that of Hume, when without warning he disappeared from all this glitter of success, and came galloping homeward towards Milan—for he feared lest his mistress might be soon forgetting him!

By contrast with d'Alembert, d'Holbach and Voltaire, Verri and Beccaria escaped the tyrannical necessity of employing sarcasm to rend asunder the veil of prejudice and ignorance which lay upon their country. In Italy, the native haunt of passion, mockery is but a form of relaxation. For, by definition, every creature of passion:

(1) Is fully occupied and feels no need to be entertained. No lack of amusement can ever threaten to send him toppling headlong into the abyss of *boredom*, as was the case with madame du Deffand (*Letters* to Horace Walpole, *passim*).

(2) However unintelligent you may suppose him, nevertheless he cannot fail to have observed, at divers times, his own ironical attitude towards the present objects of his passion. For him, in consequence, the foremost truth extracted from experience is that no sword of irony is sharp enough to pierce and change the real heart of things.

[1] Born in 1735, died in 1795. [1826]

(3) No Italian (with the exception of those who are either absurdly rich or else exceedingly aristocratic) would give two pins for his neighbour's good opinion. If he deigns to bend his thoughts at all upon his neighbour, his only rational motives can be hatred or mistrust. Since mediaeval times, every city has pursued its neighbour with unabated loathing; and the ingrained habit of such civic discord cannot but sound an echo of mistrust between one individual and the next. Indeed, Italy owes everything she is to this, her mediaeval heritage; but these *Middle Ages* which formed her character have likewise poisoned it with hatred; and the fair land of Italy is quite as much the native home of *hatred* as of love.

Signor Marliani has been telling me a host of anecdotes concerning Verri and Beccaria. These philosophers never needed to waste their energy on keeping their readers amused; their only concern was to *convince* their fellow-citizens by a body of water-tight arguments lucidly and exhaustively set out. The Empress Maria-Theresa, who never wholly grasped what the whole disturbance was about, learning that one of them (Beccaria, I believe) had received an invitation from a foreign Court, in the same fashion as the renowned M. Lagrange was summoned from Turin to Berlin, resolved in a sudden fit of vanity, to keep him in Milan. Signor Marliani was also a close friend of Parini, the virtuous and celebrated author of *il Giorno* (a satire which has a tone and colour of its own, reminiscent neither of Horace nor of Juvenal). Parini, a great poet who lived in extreme poverty, having been finally appointed to the Chair of Literature by the Austrian Government, proceeded to use the cloak of 'literature' to inculcate the precepts of virtue and rationalism among the nobler classes of Milan. Parini, whose portrait signor Marliani showed me, had one of the finest heads it has ever been my pleasure to behold.

Thus, when Napoleon came with the crash of cannon at Lodi to awaken Italy from her age-old slumbers, and subsequently, in fourteen years of government (1800-1814), to tear

up by the roots that strangling crop of anti-social practices
which choked her life, he found the land already partly
fertilised with a strong dose of rationalism, thanks to the
enlightened genius of Beccaria, Verri and Parini. These
outstanding figures had on the whole been patronised rather
than persecuted by Maria Theresa, by the Emperor Joseph II,
and by Count Firmian, the Governor of the Duchy.

When Bonaparte marched into Milan in 1796, His Excellency
the Archduke, Governor of the City, was relieving the boredom of his office by exploiting a most profitable monopoly of
the grain trade; no one seemed shocked. 'He has a fine job, and
makes the best of it by peculation—what could be plainer?
Sarebbe ben matto di far altrimenti!' I have heard this verdict
pronounced with my own ears, although, admittedly, its
formulator belonged to the older generation.

25th November. I have a great taste for driving about in
a *sediola*; now and then the traveller may get a soaking in the
rain, as happened to me today; but willy-nilly he sees the
country, and in my experience, this is the way to make it live
in the memory. My current excursion took me to the *Pian
d'Erba*, by the shores of Lake Pusiano, to see the *Villa Amalia*,
which is the property of signor Marliani. The grounds have
been laid out as a landscape garden, and I explored the rides of
this romantic wilderness armed with an umbrella against the
driving rain. This prosaic implement may spoil the pleasure,
but the tourist can hardly do without it on occasion.

But to return to my Milanese philosophers, Verri, Beccaria
and Parini, who might indeed have proved worthy disciples of
Socrates (which does *not* mean that they shared the bombastic
rhetoric of Plato), and who, if they were tolerated by the civil
authorities, owed this unexpected immunity to the jealous
rivalry of Church and State. For before turning their rage
against Beccaria, the priests had intrigued for the dismissal of
the notorious Count Firmian, Governor, or rather *Sovereign*

of the Duchy from 1759 until 1782. It is scarcely to be credited, yet the fact is true, that, even today (1816) and despite the Holy Alliance, the Imperial House of Austria has still not plainly understood that there is neither hope nor possibility of reviving the ancient glories of despotism, save with the help of the Jesuits; and thus, in its blindness, it sends the good and reverend Fathers packing. The intrigues of the Roman Court are watched with eagle-eyed, unwavering suspicion in Lombardy, and the Government will contemplate no candidate for a bishopric unless he be at daggers drawn with Rome (as is precisely the case with Monsignor Farina, recently appointed to the See of Padua). Professor Tamburini, of Pavia, an energetic old man of lively intellect and impetuous temper, not unlike the *abbé* de Pradt, basks in the warm sunlight of governmental favour; for he has published thirty volumes in octavo, and every one a blow against the Pope.[1]

This one factor alone—a priesthood constrained to behave decently, and not to degrade itself by intrigues and espionage —is enough to guarantee that, in the long run, the Metternich *régime* in Milan will prove less odious than the Milanese in general are inclined to predict.

Count von Metternich has adopted the *status quo* of Milan, as it had been in 1760 (a period, maintains Beccaria, when, amid all the one hundred and twenty thousand inhabitants of Milan, there were scarce forty who had learned to savour the delights of reason; for the remainder, there were no gods, save of the table, nor goddesses, save of the bed). But this great Austrian statesman had been better advised to adopt the *status quo* as it was in 1795, on the eve of the Napoleonic invasion, and to perpetuate the political state of Lombardy as it was then fashioned. Moreover, he had at the time at his disposal a group of admirable administrators for the fulfilment of such a project

---

1 See, for instance, his work entitled *Vera Idea della Santa Sede*, in two volumes. Personally, I find it admirable. A second edition has just been published in Milan. [1826]

—the Maréchal de Bellegarde, General Klenau, His Excellency Count Saurau, the Governor-General.

But in the place of this moderate ideal, whose realisation might have been considerably smoothed by promoting all noted liberals to the rank of Chamberlain,[1] the Government has resorted instead to persecution, and in a year or two there will have arisen a barrier of implacable hatred between Austrians and Milanese. In consequence of which, at some crisis yet to come, the Milanese will seal an alliance with the Hungarians, and force a future Emperor, caught in a moment of weakness, to concede a bicameral parliament. As things are today, every citizen who retains a spark of generosity in his soul has retired into rustic solitude to manage his estates, there to escape the sight of Austrian uniforms. The only truly valid patent of nobility is that conferred by Napoleon through the *Order of the Iron Crown*. In the civil division, out of every ten persons who were awarded this honour, nine had truly merited it. If Napoleon had thought to decree that such persons *alone* should enjoy the privilege of aristocracy, he would have conferred upon the Lombards, as near as may be, the exact degree of liberty which they have as yet the experience to manage. I have been told of a mayor in some provincial township, whose name had already been included in the Honours List for the award of the Iron Crown. Whereupon, however, the Viceroy was apprised, through a series of anonymous letters, of some long-forgotten infamy imputed to the mayor, although by now the proofs were no longer to hand; but even this mere suspicion was enough; the mayor received, in secret, a consolation prize of twenty thousand francs, and lost his Iron Crown. Urged on by this example, provincial administration began to acquire an unfamiliar taste of honesty.

Through the intermediary of a feminine acquaintance, General Klenau once persuaded me to lend him my copy of

1 Reading between the lines: not one of those with whom I have the honour of being acquainted would have accepted. [1826]

Cabanis' treatise: *des Rapports du physique et du moral*; and, while he lived, I never once betrayed this fatal secret.

This evening, in the course of conversation among the guests assembled in the box of signora N***, the following remark emerged: 'Whatever else may be the faults of this Austrian army of occupation which has settled here in the midst of us, we can hardly complain of its *insolence*. The troops behave like an army of mendicant friars; and besides, the Maréchal de Bellegarde has proved an eminently reasonable individual.'

'And in the old days', I asked, 'what about the French, when *they* occupied the town? You know you need make no bones about your answer: *vengo adesso di Cosmopoli**.'

'A French garrison commandant', replied one of my friends, 'might manage to dun some three hundred francs a month out of his paymaster, but he would cheerfully keep open board to the tune of four hundred in the nearest *osteria*, drinking and dining among a host of new acquaintances from the city. Whereas your German officer receives nothing but a beggarly two-and-forty francs a month in subsistence allowance, and even these he hides miser-fashion in the innermost recesses of a triple nest of leathern wallets, and ties the top with string; merely to see one walking down the street is enough to set a body yawning! On the other hand, the sheer *insolence* of the French soldiery was unspeakable. You should persuade someone to recite you one of the most masterly of all poems in the dialect literature of Milan: *Giovanin Bongee*.'[1]

---

1   *Desgrazi di Giovanin Bongee.*

De già, lustrissem, che semm sul descors
De quij prepotentoni di Frances . . .

[*The Misfortunes of Giovanni Bongee*. Your excellency, since the conversation has fallen upon the topic of these insolent Frenchmen . . . etc.]

It was Carline Porta himself—a most charming individual—who recited me this little poem. The original can be found in the first volume of his *Works* (Carline Porta was born in Milan in 1776 and died in 1821); but the editors have not had the courage to print some of the more pointed passages*. The Austrian censorship, which is left in the hands of

27th November. Death from laughter is not a common occurrence, otherwise I should surely have died this very evening while listening to the tenor Ronconi giving a recital of *arie buffe*. The occasion was a *soirée* given by signora Foscarini, whither I was introduced by signor Pin, a Councillor of the Municipality, the most original and wittiest of men. Ronconi sang us the famous aria *Con gran pompa e maestà* from Paisiello's *Rè Teodoro*. Dear God, what music! What genius in pure simplicity!

The young composer Paccini was at the piano. He has, in common with Ronconi, a particular talent for delicate and vivacious rather than energetic interpretation.

The finest pair of eyes that ever I beheld in all my life likewise made their mark upon me at this same gathering. Signora Z*** is from Brescia; and her eyes are assuredly as fine as those of signora Tealdi, the mistress of General Masséna, while their expression is less of this world.

Signor Locatelli yielded finally to our insistence, and gave a rendering of that wondrous dramatic monologue where the Venetian senator lies sick upon his bed. The effort left him all but dead with exhaustion; yet, immediately afterwards, with the onlookers laughing until the tears rolled down their cheeks, and begging him to continue, he retired once more behind his screen and performed *la Figlia di San Raffaele*.

Thanks to Ronconi with his *arie buffe*, and later to the willing complaisance of signor Locatelli, it was fully midnight before the ball began; and by one o'clock, the company had already quitted the *salon*, for the Milanese have little love for dancing. We strolled down in a party of eight or ten to the *caffè dei Servi*, and drank cups of coffee *con panera*, while signor

renegade Italians, is atrociously severe. If you wish to buy Italian books, the best place is in Lugano. The *Landmann* of the Canton of Ticino receives every year more than one well-furnished casket from His Imperial and Royal Majesty. I have heard some capital tales concerning the financial administration in the districts of Bellinzona and Lugano. [1826]

Locatelli, the hero of the evening, produced from his repertoire two further little monologues. Different people then recited sonnets, some eight or ten in all, and for the most part, if the plain truth be told, somewhat indecent in content. The waiters were laughing as unashamedly as ourselves, and stood around, afraid to miss a word, scarcely a pace or two from us. In England, birthplace of the *Dignity of Man*, such undue familiarity would have had us all seething with indignation. From nine o'clock at night until two in the morning, I was laughing without respite; and during those five hours, if my eyes were blinded once with tears of mirth, they were blinded a dozen times. Again and again we were forced to implore signor Locatelli to call a halt, for the laughter was more than we could bear. An evening such as this, unthinkable in England, is hard enough to imagine even in France. Italian lightheartedness knows neither bounds nor restraint. The Milanese rarely laugh from any sense of obligation; and this evening, two or three persons who felt themselves in melancholy mood rose quietly and abandoned *la brigata*.

28th November. This morning I revisited *Sant' Ambrogio* (*Sant Ambreuze*), on account of the mosaics in the vaulting of the choir. I have also made another excursion to see the charming façade of the *Madonna di San Celso*, which is the work of the architect Alessi. The portico, which, in some unfathomable and mysterious fashion, seems to combine a hint of classical simplicity with a sigh of melancholy drawn from the Middle Ages, is by Bramante, the uncle of Raphael. Architecturally, the most pleasing aspect of Milan is the inner courtyards of the *palazzi*. Every one is a forest of columns; and for me, columns are to architecture what melody is to music.

This being the occasion of some festival or other undetermined, the superb portico of the *Ospedale grande* now houses an exhibition, consisting entirely of the portraits of its benefactors —full-length for those whose gifts to charity have reached the

sum of one hundred thousand *lire* (66,000 fr.), and half-length
only for those who have contributed lesser amounts. Charity
on a large scale was, in olden days, the prerogative of aristocratic murderers; nowadays, it belongs rather to the province
of the superannuated courtesan. These paintings, belonging to
the seventeenth and eighteenth centuries, achieve an over-all
degree of badness inconceivable in France; few are so much
as tolerable; one alone has any claim to art, and that is a recent
work by signor Hayez, a young Venetian painter with some
sense of *chiaroscuro*, a notion of colour, and all in all a style of
individual power. I was impressed by his painting entitled
Count Carmagnola, which shows the general's wife and daughter
begging him not to repair to Venice, whither he had been
summoned by the Senate, and where in fact he was beheaded
in 1432. The daughter is seen from behind, prostrate at her
father's knees; her attitude is deeply moving, because the
artist has caught a genuinely *natural* position.

After spending a while in the courtyard of the *Ospedale
grande*, I revisited the one belonging to the *casa Diotti* (the
palazzo which houses the present seat of government), and
at the same time, I took another look at the *chiesa della Passione*,
which stands close by. My stay in Milan is drawing to a close—
a prospect which causes me no little distress; I am in fact seeing
all these buildings for the last time. (As for paintings, I had
rather spare my reader the boredom of descriptions, which are
so dead and meaningless for anyone who has never seen the
originals; yet, at the time, I took pleasure in the writing of
them*.)

It would have been wiser to have planned my arrival in
Milan for the 1st of September; in such a fashion I should have
escaped this constant tropical downpour. Above all, I should
have confined my visit strictly to six weeks. These last days,
among the many masterpieces at whose altars I have returned
to *worship* (to use a typical Milanese expression), I would
recall Guido Reni's *Saint Peter* and Guercino's *Agar* (both at the

Brera), the great Correggio which hangs in the *Palazzo Litta*, and another painting by the same artist belonging to signor Frigerio, a surgeon who lives near the *Corso di Porta Romana*.

My recapitulatory round of visits included a pretty little octagonal cemetery on the top of the rampart; and the morning concluded with a session at the *Institute*. Such members as remain receive their customary little pensions from the Austrian Government with commendable punctuality; but when one dies, his place is left vacant. The nation is too wakeful, and must be lulled back into slumber.

On this occasion, I was introduced to Count Moscati, the famous physician, who holds the *Grand Cordon de la Légion d'Honneur*. Later, in the evening, I met him again; signor Moscati must be ninety years old; and, in the *salon* where I enjoyed the honour of his conversation, he appeared in the full crimson glory of his *Grand Cordon*, with a little green velvet skull-cap perched on the top of his head. He is a sharp-witted, agile old man, without a hint of complaining. His curious manner of spending his nights arouses a good deal of amused comment here; yet he protests that nothing could be healthier in extreme old age. 'Cheerless contemplation is the bane and poison of declining years. Was it not Montesquieu who maintained that the failings of the climate should be corrected by the wisdom of the law? I can assure you that few households in Milan are less crotchety or dismal than my own.'

The *healing art*, as it is here entitled, can nowhere boast so distinguished a gathering of practitioners as i signori Scarpa, Rasori, Borda and Paletta.

I had some conversation about painting with signor Scarpa. The intelligentsia of this country has not time for platitudes; its members have the forthright courage of their own individual opinions, and they would be bored to death at the prospect of echoing someone else's ideas. Signor Scarpa maintains that the sort of pompous *Lives* of Titian, Raphael, etc., which are published by asinine pedants, actually *prevent* young artists from producing any work of value. Instead of pursuing the vision of happiness through their brushes and chisels, they dream of awards and honours. Raphael refused a Cardinal's Hat—and this, in 1512, when there was no greater dignity in all the earth—for occasionally he would feel the itch to wonder what *we* would be saying about him in 1816! O that the soul of man were made immortal, and that he might listen to us now!

29th November.   I was guest today at a picnic whose whole charm lay in its frank and friendly informality; yet never could a gathering have been merrier. There was no affectation, save just that touch required to enliven conversation and to inflame the desire to please; and indeed, from the second course onward (leaving aside one plainly ridiculous creature), we all enjoyed the illusion of intimate acquaintance. Our party was made up of seven women and ten men, including my courageous and delightful friend Dr. Rasori. To furnish the table, the organisers had selected Vieillard*, a French caterer who is incontestably the finest in the Duchy. His wife, madame Vieillard, formerly lady's-maid to madame de Bonténard, who was driven hither by the tempests of emigration, began her career by catering for her master and mistress; and it was this devoted loyalty which first set her in the eye of fashion. She is a mine of witty and spirited invention and of pertinent remarks, and she favours her customers with her original epigrams. She is responsible for the nicknames of three or four notorious dandies about the town, who hold her in awe and trembling. Towards the conclusion of our picnic, she came to visit us; and everyone stopped talking to listen to what she had to say. The women addressed her as an equal; madame Vieillard is tiny and must be at least a hundred years old, but she is a neat and decent old soul.

This sudden shower of Gallic aphorisms forced me to marvel at the immensity of distance that separated our picnic from some formal dinner in France. This distance was infinite, immeasurable . . . and there is nothing more to say.

I attempted in vain today to secure an introduction to the renowned Melzi d'Eril, Duke of Lodi, who is the Milanese counterpart of Cardinal Consalvi. Generally speaking, few great houses are more difficult of access than those of Milan; as soon as the walls enclose a tolerably pretty woman, her lover will set his face most resolutely against introductions. Were it not for the financial and ethical difficulties involved, the surest plan were to keep as mistress the handsomest singer that a man might lay his hands on; and every Friday, to give a splendid dinner for four guests—no more—followed by an evening of punch. Thus the *cavalieri serventi* would come at last to shed their fears of you. A further refinement would consist in daily parading up and down the *Corso*. This part of the programme —the only one which might lie within my present compass—I have never had the singleness of purpose to adopt. Every day in summer, at the hour of the *Ave Maria*, as they say in Milan, when dinner is finished and dusk is falling, every carriage in the Duchy will foregather at the *Bastione di Porta Rense*, where the road rides thirty feet above the plain. Viewed from such an eminence, the whole countryside seems nothing but a dense and trackless forest; but the horizon is ringed with the snowy summits of the Alps. Assuredly this is one of the noblest panoramas that may be vouchsafed to the eye of man. In the opposite direction, towards the city, the traveller's gaze lights first upon the verdant meadows belonging to Herr Krammer; and beyond, sailing high above the treetops of the *villa Belgiojoso*, floats the spire of the Cathedral. The whole picture is entrancing; yet it is with no sense of aesthetic contemplation that carriage after carriage comes creaking to a halt for half an hour upon the *Corso*. Rather is it a sort of ceremonial review of polite society. Any woman not on parade may expect the inquisitive to wonder at the reasons for her absence. Dandies cavort up and down in the saddle, on mounts that may have cost them a couple of hundred guineas apiece; while young men of lesser fortune, together with their seniors in middle age, will follow the throng on foot. On Sundays, the entire populace will turn out, man and boy, to gaze upon *its* aristocracy, and to admire the carriages. I have frequently found occasion to be astonished at this fond loyalty on the lips of the common people. The joiners and locksmiths employed about the house will always have a friendly nod to greet the footman who, for twenty years and more, has mounted behind the carriage on the *casa Dugnani*; and if the master himself should chance to catch sight of the *marangone de casa* (the household carpenter), he will never fail to nod in amiable condescension. A pretty woman in her carriage is invariably escorted by half the fops and dandies of the town; but a lady of noble birth will rarely admit her more plebian admirers to pay her homage thus in the public view. Dowagers rely for entertainment upon a most singular form of conversation with their footmen, whose post, as soon as the carriage is halted, is by the step, at hand to open the door should milady care to take a turn on foot (an eventuality not realised once in ten years); and thus respectfully positioned, two paces distant from the carriage door, nor ever drawing nearer, the footman will reply to each observation that his superannuated *padrona* may care to formulate deep in the hidden recesses of her coach. It was in the course of one such conversation that I overheard the oddest accusation ever levelled against the Simplon route (constructed by *quel maladett Bonapart*); for this (and nothing else) must be the cause of all those strangely early autumn frosts which, *since the Revolution*, have marred the face of Lombardy! Since there is nothing in all Milan so utterly and invincibly ignorant as a lady of good family,[1] she invariably pictures the chain of the Alps, visible in every detail from the *Corso*, as a kind of

[1] Ceaselessly surrounded by flattery from the tender age of three. Let the reader call to mind the *blue minuet*, in the education of *Mesdames de France* (*vide* the *Mémoires de Madame Campan*). [1826]

wall, built into a barrier against the chill winds from the North —a wall now breached by Bonaparte, that abominable *bête noire* of her confessor, in the process of blasting out the route across the Simplon Pass.

In winter, the *Corso* is held before dinner, between two and four in the afternoon. Not a town in Italy but has its *Corso*, or general ceremonial inspection of polite society. Could it be a tradition of Spanish origin, like that of the *cavalieri serventi*? The Milanese are intensely proud of the number of carriages which decorate their *Corso*. On one occasion, a High Festival by brilliant sunlight, I observed four lines of carriages drawn up on either side of the broad causeway, while down the centre crept two further lines of vehicles in motion, the whole being disciplined and ordered by ten Austrian hussars; the din was ushered to its climax by the presence of two hundred young *beaux* on horseback and three thousand miscellaneous spectators on foot; while the latter complimented one another proudly: *Three thousand carriages! Imagine! Almost as fine a sight as Paris!* This insistent pandemonium gives me nothing but a headache; I find no pleasure in it. But, to win the hearts of the Milanese, a foreigner must hire the finest carriage in town and parade his mistress up and down the *Corso*.

In summer, driving homeward from this ceremony, it is the custom to stop in the *Corsia dei Servi* and eat ices; then home for ten minutes, and *en route* promptly for *la Scala*! I am told that these ten minutes are by tradition the hour for assignations; and that a secret signal given at the *Corso*, such as the placing of a hand against a carriage-door, may convey the intelligence to a lover on the alert, whether the coast is clear that night or no.

30th November. A brilliant Spanish officer, one don Pedro Lormea, once told me in Altona: 'As soon as I first set foot in an unknown city, I ask a friend (assuming I have made one) to

name me the dozen wealthiest men, the dozen prettiest women
and the one most scandalous villain in all the town; after which,
with the help of fortune, I begin to cultivate acquaintance—
first with the scandalous villain, next with the pretty women,
last of all with the millionaires.'

As I find myself today, having adopted more or less this wise
advice, there is no pleasanter occupation that I know than
walking aimlessly about Milan. Here follows, for the benefit
of such readers as are making, or have already made, this
delightful excursion, the plan of campaign which I have come
to relish. Setting out from *la Scala*, I follow first the *via Santa
Margherita*, passing with due reverence before that Commissariat of Police which exercises such a sway upon my destiny
and can, for instance, if it has a mind to, send me packing out
of Italy within an hour or two—yet which has so far always
proved most courteous. (I should indeed record my thanks to
don Giulio P[agani].) Hard beside this awe-inspiring *palazzo*
stand numerous print-shops, and here I linger awhile, appraising
the latest engravings. If there should chance to be something
by Anderloni or Garavaglia, I am hard put to it to resist the
temptation of buying. Then I stroll towards the *piazza de'
Mercanti*, which dates back to the distant Middle Ages; and my
gaze falls now upon the empty niche from which a wave of
revolutionary frenzy once hurled the statue of that infamous
sovereign, Philip II. Next, the *piazza del Duomo*. My awareness
of visual beauty has already been sharpened by the engravings;
and now, after letting my eyes dwell fondly upon this marble
castle, my path leads me onward, down the *via degli Orefici*,
where the living beauties of the town would fain distract me
from the rarer loveliness of art. Nevertheless, the sight of the
Cathedral and the contemplation of the engravings have left
my sense of beauty so enhanced, and all other senses so
radically diminished, that money, interest and other dis-
enchanting, wearying ideas seem to have lost all power and
meaning. One thing is certain, that with such a life a man might

live next door to paradise on two hundred guineas a year. And so onward again, past the doors of the post-office, where women come to fetch their mail in person, since every servant in the house is a creature in the pay of someone else, be it husband, lover or mother-in-law. The way home takes me once more through the *piazza del Duomo*, this time to the *Corsia dei Servi*, where, towards midday, it is unheard of not to find at least one, perhaps more, of the dozen loveliest women in Milan. It has been in the course of many an aimless outing such as this, that I have managed to formulate a clear idea of the characteristic style of Lombard beauty, whose qualities are deeply stirring, yet which has never found a painter great enough to grant it immortality, as Correggio did for that beauty which is characteristic of the Romagna, and Andrea del Sarto for that of Florence. If the latter holds a blemish, it must lie in a hint of *virile rationality*, which is never seen among the women of Milan; *they* are women through and through, although, at first encounter, they may seem *terrifying* to the poor foreigner newly-ventured from Berlin, or else *naïve* and *unsophisticated* to any tourist fresh from the *salons* of Paris. Appiani drew little inspiration from the features of the Milanese; but there a few unmistakable traces in the various portraits of *Herodias* by Leonardi da Vinci.

Yesterday, at long last, I found someone to show me the studio of signor Carloni, a portrait-painter with a true instinct for a likeness. He specialises in large-ish miniatures in red and black crayon. Signor Carloni has been sensible enough to keep copies of the portraits of every woman of note who ever sat for him. His collection contains some fifty items; and of all that I have seen, nothing has ever tempted me so violently; most assuredly, had I been rich, I would not have let it go. However, for all that I lack a fortune, I have at least the satisfaction of vanity—(dare I speak it?) of *artistic*[1] vanity—for I could console myself that, even before I had set foot in this

[1] Promising joys yet to come. [1826]

E

delightful studio, I had, unprompted, divined the genius of Lombard beauty.

The French language in its present state of evolution makes it almost impossible to praise a woman without offence, save by resorting to three or four complex sentences, the whole making a total of not less than a dozen lines. The essential formulae are always negative. I am well aware of this, yet I am short of breath to deal in such subtleties. Let me state plainly, then, with no more refinement than some rough Danubian peasant, that what struck me above all, as I explored signor Carloni's collection, was the pure beauty (Roman in its basic structure, yet Lombard by the sweetness and the melancholy of the expression) of a woman of true genius, la contessa Aresi. If ever the painter's art could render the perfection of charm, devoid alike of affectation and of triteness, together with the stamp of a mind that possesses alertness, brilliance, originality and a never-flagging fertility in invention, and all this cast in the most exquisite and most alluring mould of beauty, then surely this alloy of all the qualities should nowhere else be found, save in the portrait of signora Bibin Catena.

Could there be anything more striking than the *beltà folgorante* of signora R[uga], or the stirring lovelinesss of signora Marini, hinting as it does with unmistakable evidence of some sharp struggle between religion and sensibility? Could there be anything more fascinating than the *beltà guidesca* of signora Ghirlan[da], with its echoes of some Madonna by Guido Reni, and recalling, if less directly, certain heads of *Niobe*? All the purity of the various *Madonnas* by Sassoferrato is incarnate in the portrait of the pious signora A[nnoni]. And could there be anything more original than the portrait of signora N****, with its plain tale of youth and energy displayed in the service of a tempestuous and impassioned soul, as familiar with the machinations of intrigue as the Cardinal de Retz himself, who understood neither caution nor restraint? This head, so fine yet bearing not a trace of the antique, seems to follow you to every corner of the painter's studio, with those vivacious, brilliant eyes which Homer bestows upon the goddess Minerva.

And, in glaring contrast, it is the consummate prudence of a madame de Tencin which forms the dominant note in the features of the attractive signora L[amberti], whose romantic career began when she took an Emperor to be her lover. There is no secret of flattery which she does not practise, and yet she never allows herself to seem insincere.

Yet how should I describe the aura of enchantment mingled with awe which, in the next portrait, seems to emanate from the angelic serenity and the exquisite calm of a face set in that mould of noble tenderness so beloved of Leonardo da Vinci? If her thoughts were turned towards you, there could be no telling the infinite wealth of kindness, justice and untroubled innocence with which these features would be filled; yet she seems to be withdrawn in contemplation of some happiness now vanished. The colour of her hair, the contour of her forehead, the set of her eyes—all these are characteristic of Lombard beauty. This portrait, whose first excellence as a work of art is to evoke no hint of suggestion of the antique heads of Greece, awakes in me the rarest of all response inspired by the achievement of an artist: I can imagine *nothing* to surpass its pure perfection*. The whole face lives and breathes in a world of purity and mystic devotion, where no taint of vulgarity has ever touched: signora M***, so the story runs, has known long years of misery.

If I have a dream of happiness, it is to meet with this extraordinary woman in the fastness of some lonely gothic castle, where—as at Trezzo—the turrets overhang a noble ravine, and the walls are girded by a raging torrent. She is a woman whose sensibility has left her no stranger to the mark of passion, yet whose soul has never forfeited its maiden purity. Against this, however, no charms could offer a greater contrast than those which infuse the exquisite features of the beautiful contessina

R***. Oh, why can I find no words to explain that *her* prettiness
has not a feature in common with *French* prettiness? Both are
fascinating; yet the one is not, nor ever will be, the other; and
it is we who profit from the difference. More and more I feel
the truth of a remark once made to me by a man of great
perspicacity, to the effect that a woman whose portrait one
beholds *in miniature* comes so close to the beholder that upon
the instant she seems an intimate friend; whereas the same
portrait *in oils* has the very contrary effect, imposing an immensity of distance between subject and viewer, a distance
made all the greater by the barriers of social convention.

1st December.   Signor Reina has allowed me to glance at a
considerable collection of Beccaria's letters; oh, the simplicity,
the *plainness* of the man! Could anything offer a more glaring
contrast to the *abbé* Morellet, who translated his writings into
French? And how Beccaria must have *loathed* Paris! Had it not
been for the partisan spirit of the age, not a soul in France but
would, in all sincerity, have proclaimed him an *ass*. In one of his
letters he writes: 'I was twenty-two years old when I began to
think, after I had forfeited the favours of the contessa C***;
and when I had in some manner recovered from my despair,
being at my uncle's house in the country, I proceeded to
examine my own heart, and found there:

(i)   A great compassion toward the wretched state of man-
      kind, the slave of so infinite a quantity of errors;

(ii) A desire for fame in the world of letters;

(iii) The love of Freedom;

(iv) The masterpiece that I admired above all else in the world
      at that time was *les Lettres persanes*; therefore, to
      remedy my grief, I set about composing the treatise
      dei Delitti e delle Pene.'

In another letter, composed much later, Cesare Beccaria
says: 'When I began to write, I was firmly persuaded that the
mere existence of a manuscript of this character in the recesses

of my desk might well be the direct occasion of my imprisonment, or at least, of my exile. At that time, I was convinced
that life beyond the confines of Milan was in no way distinguishable from death; and against the menace of such a fate, I felt
my resolution turn to water. And when there came rumours
of a warrant of execution, it was as though my heart was
pierced. I trembled to see my book in print. I may truthfully
claim that, during the whole space of a year, I could not sleep
for fear of learning, hour by hour, of my exile from Milan. I
had no illusions concerning the "justice" of my native land; the
most upright of judges would have pronounced my condemnation, and that *all in good faith*, since I had received no commission
from the Government to consider the character of crime nor
the nature of its punishment. And when at length the clergy
did begin to weave intrigues about my head, I was already
more dead than alive. It was Count Firmian who saved me; as
a duly-appointed Professor, I might breathe at last; but I
vowed to my wife never to write another word.'

This correspondence of Beccaria amply deserves publication,
were it not that it might cause political embarrassment to the
marchese's heirs and successors. I have uncovered an excellent
portrait of this worthy philosopher, in many ways so similar
to Fénelon, in some ways better (*vide* Saint-Simon).

Signor Bettoni, the printer—a man of countless activities—
has published a set of one hundred portraits of famous Italians.
The reproductions are admirable, the commentaries beneath
contempt; the likenesses of Boccaccio, of Pope Leo X, and of
Michelangelo are masterpieces of the engraver's art. The
portrait of Carlo Verri, which is of little artistic value, reveals
an individual with far more of the Frenchman about him than
ever was the case with Beccaria. Alessandro Verri, the brother
of Carlo, is still alive in Rome; but he is nothing better than a
black reactionary, a man who abominates Napoleon, not on
account of his unseemly passion for a crown and sceptre, but
rather for the reforms he undertook in the cause of civilisation.

This is the theme which guides all Alessandro's writings, the *Notti Romane al Sepolcro degli Scipione, Erostrate*, etc. Compared with the bombast of these *Roman Nights*, even *le Génie du Christianisme* is a model of simplicity. This was not the style of Carlo Verri; but then *he* wrote of what he believed.

3rd December. I spent the evening at the *teatro Filodrammatico*, the name now imposed by the reactionaries upon the old *teatro Patriottico*, which was founded in the Era of Liberty, in 1797 or thereabouts, and subsidised with superb generosity by the citizens of Milan. Occupying the premises of what was originally a church, this theatre offers many grounds for official condemnation. The actors are amateurs, all young people drawn from business circles: last Friday, signor Lucca gave an excellent performance in the title-part of Alfieri's *Agide*; but his outstanding triumph is in the rôle of the *Major* in Schiller's *Kabale und Liebe*. Signorina Gioja interprets the *ingénue* parts in a style which is purely Italian, and which owes nothing to any famous model. Signora Monti, one of the most lovely women in the whole land of Italy, has succeeded beyond belief in the leading parts of a number of tragedies by Alfieri, not to mention her own husband's *Aristodemo*. The *teatro Patriottico* has cost enormous sums to the society which originally founded it, and which ever since has kept it in being, in the teeth of the unpublished resolve of the Austrian police.

My ticket for this evening's performance was presented to me by signor Locatelli, a young and infinitely talented young actor with a genius for comedy. He was playing the title-rôle in *Achille in Barlassina*. The *protagonista* (as they call the hero in Milan) is a *castrato* straight from *la Scala*, who, having flouted the Governor of Milan by carrying off the latter's pet *prima donna*, has fled headlong from the threat of vengeance, and taken refuge, disguised as a woman, in Barlassina, a village on the outskirts of the city. Yet scarcely has he reached safety,

when, in one of those incredible outbursts of vanity so peculiar
to the *castrati*, he feels irresistibly impelled to talk about opera,
and to hint at his triumphs in this town and in that. And so,
before you can turn round, one of the local *dilettanti* is head
over ears in love with our *soprano*; and (what is far more to the
point) distinctly enterprising. His 'lady', moreover, is five foot
ten inches high, and struts about the village in the heroic attire
of Achilles, somewhat sketchily veiled by a dress of printed
calico which he had hastily borrowed from a lady's-maid in the
service of the *prima donna* his mistress; for so terrible was the
jealousy of the Governor-General of Milan, that he was forced
to take to his heels in the very middle of a performance of
Metastasio's *Achille*. Signor Locatelli[1] gave an inspired interpretation, couched in a vein of unrestrained absurdity, in the
part of the *soprano*, whose every stratagem is shattered into
fragments by his own conceit and foolishness; he even sang a
full-scale *aria*! Ultimately, the *soprano*, by surrendering the
prima donna, in whom he has already quite lost interest,
manages to extract a pardon from the Governor. And at the
dénouement, when he achieves his final ambition (which by now
was engrossing all his thoughts) of dazzling the whole population of Barlassina, and in particular his 'lover', the unfortunate
dilettante, by appearing once more in the *complete* costume of
Achilles, and rid at last of his wretched print calico dress, it
was a good five minutes before the gusts and gales of laughter
which rocked the audience would allow the actors to continue.

All *castrati* are afflicted with a sort of butterfly-mentality,
which makes them chop and change their inclinations like
children. Signor Locatelli showed a masterly appreciation of
this characteristic eccentricity. He is, moreover, himself the
author of this delightful little farce, which might well be
worthy of Potier at the *Gymnase-Dramatique*, but for the fact
that our own audience has not the slightest conception of the

---

1 I never discuss politics with any of my friends; most of them, in fact, still
believe me to be *persona grata* with the Government*. [1826]

special brand of silliness peculiar to a *castrato*, nor of the *prepotenza* of an Italian *governatore* of the old *régime*.

In Italy, laughter among the audience is never anything but genuine; it is never a weapon of self-deception, nor a means of proving to one's neighbour that one is familiar with the foibles and mannerisms of polite society. This evening, the audience followed every word of the play with rapt attention. The opening scenes must be of pellucid clarity—at least half the charming sketches of M. Scribe would be quite unintelligible, here in Italy, owing to the haphazard nature of the exposition. On the other hand, once the initial situation has been well and truly grasped, no multiplicity of telling detail is ever too realistic or boring for an Italian audience. In Milan, the primary, if not the exclusive source of comedy lies in observing the antics of a man who has lost his way among the labyrinthine paths which lead to the object of his heart's desire.

I have myself known, in society, lovers who took the oddest, the most ridiculous precautions in the matter of cloaks and footgear. The surreptitious exit from their mistress' house might need full fifteen minutes of ingenious preparation; yet, to the woman who stood by and watched all this paraphernalia, it never seemed absurd.

In Italy, youth, as such, holds no fascination, and reckless bravado, still less; the younger generation is serious and uncommunicative, yet rarely sad. Bravado assumes one form only, *la disinvoltura*—a contempt for convention and gossip.

As I see it, the average Italian is less afraid of the reality of misadventures or of future ills than he is of the fearful *visions* of calamity which spring to life in his imagination. Once face to face (*al tu per tu*) with the *fact* of disaster, he is a creature of boundless resource, as indeed became apparent in the retreat across Russia (remember Widemann, captain of the Guard of Honour, in Moscow). I never cease to wonder at such *circumspection* in a land where the climate is so favourable to man. In Poland, for six months out of twelve, should a man remain so much as one night exposed to the inclemency of the weather, he will die; but here in Lombardy, I would wager there are not fifteen nights in all the year equal in severity to any single night in Poland from the first of October to the first of May. At *la Tramezzina*, upon the shores of Lake Como, close to the fine villa owned by signor Sommariva, there grows an orange-tree which, so I am assured, has flourished winter and summer unprotected for sixteen years.

So it can only be supposed that the harshness of tyranny has proved fair compensation for the mildness of nature.[1] Watch any regiment at the march past, observe the preponderance of the *bilious* or *melancholic* temperament, which is striking by the monotony of its recurrence and the depth of its scars. Since all the established regiments of Italy have been exiled to Hungary, I have been reduced to keeping my eyes open after Mass, standing in the porch of some fashionable church (*San-Giovanni alle case rotte*, or *la chiesa dei Servi*). The easy laughter of the *sanguine* temperament, or of the people of southern France, is all but unknown in Italy. Perhaps I may light upon some trace of it still in Venice; but in Milan, even the pupils at dancing-class—lasses between the age of twelve and sixteen—are fascinating for the very gravity of their demeanour. I have watched them, now and then, on the stage, a *corps de ballet* thirty or more strong, rehearsing some ballet by Viganò, at which the great man in his kindness has allowed me to be present.[2] Thirty is the age at which the average Italian begins to talk and have ideas.—But let me return to the *teatro Patriottico*.

1 *Cf.*, for instance, the character of Cosimo de' Medici, who became Duke of Florence in 1537, Duke of Sienna in 1555 and Grand-Duke of Tuscany in 1569; and who died in 1574, after the land of Tuscany had groaned for seven-and-thirty years beneath the weight of his oppression. What a superb object-lesson, flaunted in the face of an entire people, to vaunt the recompense of evil-doing! [1826]

2 He refuses, none the less, to accept the box which I have offered him in the theatre, for fear of jeopardising his reputation with the Authorities; for the police have refused point-blank to allow him to handle the magnificent theme of the *Ebrea di Toledo**. [1826]

During the first play (Kotzebue's *Two Portfolios*), I subjected all the boxes in the theatre to a most careful scrutiny. The first fact that I noted was that a great number of women are to be seen here who do not appear at *la Scala*.

It is not at all uncommon for a young woman, disillusioned by the rupture of a first *liaison*, which may well have endured until she had reached the age of six- or eight-and-twenty, to resolve to pass the rest of her unhappy life in solitude. Milanese society has no approval to bestow upon such resolutions, nor upon the constancy with which they are maintained; for in Italy, there is no tradition of hypocritical piety which a woman may assume to hide the peccadilloes of her youth. These victims of unhappy love, by the willing isolation of their lives, are a fine source of scandal to their elders, whose entry upon the world of gallantry dates from before the fateful year of 1796. Hard as it may seem to believe, these same nun-like creatures who while away their lives between the piano and the works of Lord Byron are actually branded as *immoral*!

A woman's reputation depends upon the voice of other women; this voice belongs in the last resort to the *majority*; and the majority is always at the beck and call of *fashion*. I can envisage nothing more instructive, to an apprentice in the speculations of philosophy, than the sight of a young creature charged with immorality for no reason beyond the steadfastness of her refusal to take a second lover, once the first had shown himself unworthy of her affection.

Yet such is the case, verified this evening by my own enquiries; and this reproach fell constantly from the lips of women who had never been slow to profit—as some might think, excessively—from the privileged laxity of morals which reigned in the years before 1796.[1] In those times, the ascendancy of a chosen lover might often fail to endure from one Carnival

[1]   *Molti averne,*
         Un goderne,
         E cambiar spesso . . . [1826]

to the next; whereas nowadays the majority of *liaisons* last for seven or eight years. I have known of more than one which has lasted ever since the day when the Patriots marched home from Marengo, and that was sixteen years ago.

A *marchesa*, by birth and breeding second to none, may seek and hold the friendship of a simple drawing-mistress. Friendship, in Italy, disdains to recognise the barriers of rank; for vanity is held to be no more than one passion among a host of others, and is very far from wielding the despotic sceptre which it holds in France, rearing its head where least expected, in little girls of three and in old men of eighty. I have come at last to understand what Johann von Müller used to tell us in Cassel*, that the French have *less sense of drama* than any race on earth: for, to begin with, no Frenchman has a grasp of any passion save his own, which is vanity; and secondly, he has so fondly interwoven this particular passion with all the cardinal acts in the life of the animal known as man (death, sexual inclination, etc.), that when he is shown these same cardinal acts in the context of another race, he is *unable* to recognize them. From which observation, Johann von Müller used to conclude that, to a Frenchman, Voltaire must inevitably appear the greatest of all tragic dramatists, for the very reason that he seems plainly the absurdest to anyone outside France. For eight years, this idea has stuck in my mind as a mere paradox; and had it not been for the great reputation of its author, I should have forgotten it altogether. Yet the fact is that the German, instead of judging everything in terms of himself, invariably adopts the standards of others. If he reads a *History of Assyria*, he becomes an Assyrian; and the *Adventures of Cortez* transform him turn and turn about into a Mexican or a Spaniard. As soon as he begins to reflect, he discovers that everybody is right— which is why he will dream away his life for twenty years on end, and as likely as not fail to reach any conclusion.[1] Whereas

[1] The Author is better aware than anyone, how little right he has to offer *categorical* solutions to problems of such magnitude. Yet he desires to be

the Frenchman is more expeditious, and needs no more than a minute to judge a whole people and to pronounce upon the entire complex of its physical and ethical traditions. 'Does *this* or *that* conform to pattern? No?—then it is plainly intolerable.' And so he passes on to something else.

An Italian will spend years in studying the quirks and oddities of an alien race, and the peculiar idiosyncrasies it may have contracted in the pursuit of its own happiness, and will understand them to perfection. No creature in pursuit of its own happiness, whatever form this happiness may take, strikes him as ridiculous merely on account of the unusual object of the quest; absurdity dwells only in the mistaken efforts it may make to reach its avowed goal. This is the key to Machiavelli's *Mandragola*, to the *Ajo nell' imbarazzo*, and to all other genuinely Italian comedies (by *genuinely Italian*, I mean all comedies which are not imitated from the French). I would give a great deal to be allowed to see the reports sent home by Venetian ambassadors and Papal nuncios at divers foreign Courts; I have found matter enough for astonishment even in the tales of plain merchants—for instance, signor Torti, with his relation concerning the heroic probity of the Turks, and their general customs: how the Turkish women in Constantinople affect to display their figure to the gaze of foreigners, by drawing their costume which envelops every part of them save their eyes, close about their bodies; how they feign the vapours like any Parisian *coquette*, and shed their pretty slippers with studied negligence.

As a general rule, none but the most phlegmatic among the inhabitants of Italy has the least conception of vanity. In this

clear and concise. If he were to resort to all the paraphernalia of modesty, and parry criticism by wrapping his argument in all manner of cautious and dubitative forms, this *Journey* would run into three volumes, and would be six times as wearisome. Nowadays, *brevity* is the only token of respect which the public will acknowledge in its Authors. Moreover, I do not claim to portray things *as they are*; I am concerned to describe the *impression* which they made upon myself. [1826]

respect, I trust never to meet any *Gascon* so fully absurd as the little priest I fell in with tonight in a certain *salon* after the performance at the *teatro Patriottico*. He had come to inherit a princely annuity from the late *marchese* d'Adda, recently deceased. Now the devouring obsession of the *marchese's* life had been his abject terror of the Devil. Firmly persuaded of the truth of certain doctrines which the Papacy has but recently abandoned, he used to live in imminent distress, lest the Devil should take possession of his body by way of some orifice; in consequence of which, the little priest was never absent from his side. At dawn, it was his duty to pronounce a blessing over the *marchese's* mouth before the latter dared to open it . . . the rest of the tale is plainly unrepeatable in French, for all that there is nothing shocking about it in Milanese. But the essence of the jest, which served to torment the little priest, lay in reminding him *now*, in the heart of his present opulence and in spite of his violet stockings, of one or two among his erstwhile offices in the service of the late *marchese* d'Adda. Tonight, the self-appointed torturer-in-chief was signor Guasco, who acquitted himself of his delicate mission with a subtlety of touch and an air of *sang-froid* which lay altogether beyond reproach. At the end of the evening, we all assembled beneath the carriage-gate, and surrendered heart and soul to the irrepressible surge of laughter which was choking us.[1]

---

1 There is an Italian proverb which runs as follows: *A priest starts black, turns violet first, then red, and finishes white.* A priest's uniform is seen upon his legs. When first he arrives in Rome, his stockings are black; and he exchanges black for violet only when he is promoted *monsignore*, like our friend this evening. Red stockings are the emblem of a cardinal, while white stockings are the symbol of the Pope. In Italy, where priests are wealthy, and as fond of laughter as they are of women, there is no absurdity attached to this condition. Since ethics and dogma have been brought to a point of complete separation, they have none of the lugubrious characteristics of their protestant brethren. They only become mournful towards the age of sixty, when the fear of the *Devil* once more begins to loom large. [1826]

5th December. I have just come home from the Mint (*la Zecca*). It was Napoleon who summoned to Milan signor Moruzzi, an artisan from Florence, who transformed the *zecca* of the Duchy into an institution far transcending anything that I have seen in Paris. However, since our lords and masters, the big industrialists*, will assuredly not do me the honour of reading so frivolous a *Journey*, I will abstain from further description.

Il cavaliere Moruzzi informed me that there was a new street in the making, at present actually under construction: the *contrada dei due Muri*. I lost no time in hurrying to the spot. In Milan, the making of a street begins with the digging of a trench four foot deep along the centre of the roadway, into which the various drainage-pipes carrying rainwater from the roof-tops into the street eventually discharge. The frontages of the houses being built of brick, the drain-pipes are often concealed *inside* the brickwork of the façade. As soon as the sewerage has been completed, the street surface is paved with four strips of granite and three of cobbles, thus:

$$ \llcorner \quad \underset{G}{C} \quad \underset{G}{\text{oOo}} \quad \underset{G}{C} \quad \underset{G}{\text{oOo}} \quad \underset{G}{C} \quad \text{oOo} \quad \lrcorner $$

Here you have two granite pavements, three feet wide, running the length of the houses, and two further lanes of granite set to provide a smooth carriageway for the wheels of vehicles; while the rest of the street is surfaced with small, pointed cobbles.

Since vehicles never drive other than along the two central lanes of granite, and since pedestrians invariably keep to the pavements on either side, accidents are extremely rare. Furthermore, since the architectural convention of the buildings allows for broadly overhanging cornices, together with jutting balconies at the level of every floor, the pedestrian has only to hug the pavement on the wind-sheltered side of the street to remain dry even in a sudden downpour of rain. As for the monsoon-weather of recent weeks, however, there is no escape, and a man has only to venture twenty paces down the street to be wetter than if he had jumped into the canal. The twin causeways of granite which carry the wheels of divers traffic along the streets are laid on top of the four-foot containing walls of the underground channel which follows the centre of the roadway; and at every hundred paces there is a pierced flagstone, through which all the rainwater which has fallen upon the surface of the road may drain away into the dyke below. This explains how it comes about that the streets of Milan are the best-designed in all the world, and always clean. For many centuries now, in Italy, rulers have given thought to the needs of the ordinary citizen.

In the year 1179, the Milanese undertook to build a ship canal to link their city with Lake Maggiore and Lake Como, *via* the Ticino and the Adda. This canal cuts across the town along a line similar to that which, in Paris, is occupied by the great Boulevard which runs from the Bastille to the Madeleine. In the year 1179, we in France were still no better than serfs, and our feudal lords were bound for the Crusade, in the wake of Louis VII; whereas Milan was already a republic, where no one went to war, save that he had a mind to and fully understood what he meant to gain by it. Hence it arises that today, in 1816, *our* streets are still such a menace to the unhappy pedestrian . . . but hush! What of the voice of *Patriotic Sentiment*? *Our* rue des Petits-Champs (as all *True Patriots* always say) is in a class by itself, compared with these Milanese *alleyways* which I have just been describing . . . such idiotic vanity is but another streak of primitive barbarism!

6th December.   This evening, the rain came down in torrents; *la Scala* was deserted; the all-pervading gloom disposed the mind to philosophic speculation. I discovered signor Cavaletti alone in his box. 'Will you do me the favour', he began, 'not to let your mind be seduced by the manifold denunciations against the Church, the Aristocracy and the Sovereign Princes of Italy, which you hear at every hand? Instead, enquire philosophically, and consider the six focal centres of activity which control the destiny of the eighteen million inhabitants of Italy: Turin, Milan, Modena, Florence, Rome and Naples.[1] You do not need telling that these different peoples are very far from forming a homogeneous nation. Bergamo detests Milan, which is likewise execrated by Novara and Pavia; whereas your Milanese himself, being fully preoccupied with keeping a good table and acquiring a warm *pastran* (overcoat) against the winter, hates nobody; for hatred would merely disturb the unruffled serenity of his pleasures. Florence, which in days gone by so bitterly abhorred Sienna, now is so reduced to impotence that she has no strength for loathing left; yet, allowing for these two exceptions, I search in vain to discover a third; each city detests its neighbours, and is mortally detested in return. It follows therefore that our rulers have no difficulty in the fulfilment of their aim: *divide ut imperes.*

'This unhappy people, shattered by hatred into fragments fine as dust, is governed by the several courts of Vienna, Turin, Modena, Florence, Rome and Naples.

'Modena and Turin are as clay in the hands of the Jesuits. Piedmont is the most monarchical country in Europe. The ruling oligarchy in Austria has still not progressed a step beyond the notions of a Joseph II, who, for want of anything better, passes in Vienna for a great man; it constrains the priesthood to respect the laws and to abstain from intrigue; but, in all other respects, it treats us as a colony.

'Bologna, and indeed the whole of the Romagna, are a constant nightmare to the Court of Rome; so Consalvi sends a Cardinal to govern the country, with orders to make himself beloved—and he obeys! Consalvi, who wields unchallenged

[1] See Gorani, *Mémoires secrets des Cours d'Italie* (c. 1796). Gorani was an ultra-liberal. [1826]

authority as Minister in Rome, is an ignoramus blessed with mother-wit and a sense of moderation; and he is well aware that, in Bologna, as indeed throughout the Romagna, the Italian people have preserved some traces of that ancient energy inherited from the Middle Ages. In the Romagna, when a mayor proves too consummate a scoundrel, he is assassinated; and no single witness will ever be brought to light to testify against the murderer. Such brutal behaviour in the Bolognese is abhorrent to their nearest neighbours, the citizens of Florence. The celebrated government of the Grand-Duke Leopold, successor to the appalling despotism of the Medici, has transformed the Florentines into a race of holy-minded *castrati*. All passion is extinct within their souls, save a love of handsome liveries and a taste for the prettiness of religious processions. Their Grand-Duke adores money and women, and behaves like a father to his children. At bottom, he is as indifferent towards them as they are towards him; but they need only cast a glance at what is happening in the world outside to view each other with rational affection. The Tuscan peasant is a singular creature; this race of uncultured husbandmen forms what is perhaps the most agreeable society in Europe; and I find it infinitely more attractive than the urban population.

'In Italy, the extreme outposts of civilisation follow the course of the Tiber. Southward of this river, you may discover all the energy and all the happiness of a race of savages. In the Papal State, the only law in force is that of the Catholic faith, which means the *performance of ritual*. Of its quality, you may judge by its effects. Under its authority, all moral philosophy is forbidden, as favouring a *spirit of individual enquiry*.

'The Kingdom of Naples is confined to this one city, which alone among all the towns of Italy has the tone and the bustle of a true capital.

'Its government is an absurd monarchy in the style of Philip II, which yet manages to preserve a few rags and tatters

of administrative discipline, a legacy from the French occupation. It is impossible to imagine any form of government of
more abysmal insignificance, or with less influence to wield
upon the populace. The one thing which is admirable and
worthy of your notice is the character of the *lazzarone*, who
knows no law save *fear* and the cult of the One God—*San
Gennaro*!

'That state of spiritual dedication, which here goes by the
name of love, has never penetrated so far south as Naples; it
has been routed and put to flight by the obsessive violence of
immediate sensation, that rude tyrant of the southern races. In
Naples, if a pretty woman should chance to have lodgings
across the street from your own, be sure to make a sign. . . .

'Even if you might suspect a touch of the *African* in such,
and other, manners of the city, at least remember that you are
not an Englishman, and refrain from loud-lamenting indignation. If you are elderly or melancholic, avert your gaze, and
bear in mind always that the main objective of your stay in
Naples is the *lazzaroni*. Even your own illustrious Montesquieu
once said a very foolish thing about the *lazzaroni*.[1] Yet observe
well, before you leap to a conclusion. A *sense of duty* (which
sense is neither more nor less than the *public hangman* of the
North) has no hold on the heart of the *lazzarone*. If, in a blind
fit of anger, he should chance to kill his best friend, yet still his
God, *San Gennaro*, will grant him forgiveness, on condition
that he treat himself to the additional pleasure of going and
chattering about his fit of temper at the feet of the Friar appointed
his confessor. Nature, who, in her bounty, has poured plente-
ously forth about the Bay of Naples every gift which in her
lieth to bestow upon man, has named the *lazzarone* to be her

---

[1] *The* lazzarone, *the most wretched offspring of the human race, trembles in
terror, should Mount Vesuvius chance to throw out a stream of lava. What,
I beseech you tell me, have they, who dwell in such a state of misery, still left
to lose?* (I am quoting from memory.) Montesquieu, *Oeuvres Diverses**
[1826]

eldest son. The Scot, for all his civilisation, and for all that his race will hardly furnish a capital indictment once in half a dozen years, is worth no better than a younger son who, by dint of unremitting labour, has made a fortune. Do but compare the fate of the half-naked *lazzarone* with that of the Scottish peasant who, by the very asperity of the air in which he lives and breathes, is forced to *think*, and think with strictest logic, or else *Death* will ambush him on every hand not a hundred paces from his croft. Naples is the land *par excellence* where the advantages of despotism, in the Napoleonic sense, swell to immense proportions. Try to make friends with some vine-grower in Ischia or Capri, who will treat you as a boon companion from the second day of your acquaintance, should you but chance to catch his fancy! For want of half a century of Napoleonic despotism, no form of republican government will ever succeed in taking root among the populace of Naples. The Neapolitans even stretch absurdity so far as to hurl abuse at General [Manhès], who, for eighteen mortal months, eradicated daylight robbery and murder from the wild regions to the south of the city. Had Marshal Davoust, now, been King of Naples, the very frontiers of European civilisation would have been pushed back against encroaching Africa. Whenever I hear an Englishman complain that he risks being murdered at every step he takes, my only reaction is to laugh. Whose fault is *that*? In 1802, Napoleon brought civilisation to Piedmont at the cost of a thousand executions, which put paid to ten thousand murders. I would never deny that, in Louisiana for instance, where the populace is rational, passionless and phlegmatic, it *may* be possible to abolish the penalty of death. But in Italy (excepting only the city of Milan) a death sentence stands as preface to every chapter in the history of civilisation. These imbecile Teutons, who think they know how to govern us, refuse to hang a murderer unless he first confess his crime. Instead, they keep the unhappy outcasts cooped up in Mantua, and when the feeding of them starts to strain their avarice, they take advantage of the *Imperial Birthday*, which falls on February the twelfth, to let them loose once more upon society. Yet, by the very fact of being cooped up there together, these brutes grow envious of each other's crimes, and so become a species of raging beast, who, to take an instance, will come across a peasant fallen asleep in the fields, and pour molten lead into his ear, simply for the pleasure of watching his face as he dies.'

After this solemn and depressing conversation, I escaped to visit the *contessina* C***, where we laughed and played at faro until three in the morning. Of all games, faro is the one most admirably suited to the temperament of Italy; each player may holds his cards, and yet dream what dreams he pleases. To hold a hand at faro opposite a mistress whom one worships heart and soul, yet who is spied on by the eye of jealousy—this is the most wondrous experience that the game can offer*. *Almen così si dice.*

8th December.   In Milan, a woman who is two-and-thirty years of age, a mother, yet still beautiful, feels no reticence at displaying her passions, her fiercest despairs and ecstasies of love, in the presence of her own daughters—maidens of twelve or fifteen, and by no means obtuse. I had an instance of such imprudent behaviour before my eyes this very morning and could not but disapprove of what I saw. An aphorism of Montesquieu sprang immediately to my mind: *No child will learn from its parents to emulate their intelligence, but every child may learn to imitate their passions.*

The rôle which a woman enjoys in Italian society is very different from the part she is allowed to play in France. The Italian woman is constantly escorted by one or two men *of her own choosing*, who, should they happen to incur their mistress' disfavour, may be punished by the least bearable of all misfortunes. By the age of fifteen, a girl may already be beautiful, and therefore be of consequence in society; nor is it by any means uncommon to observe a woman continue her conquests until well past the age of fifty. 'What does *age* matter?' I found myself addressed one day by Count Fantozzi, who is desperately in love with signora M***, notwithstanding her five-and-fifty years. 'What does *age* matter, while beauty, exuberance, and best of all *sensibility* remain unimpaired?'

In the course of a conversation about Lampugnani, I have heard signora L*** say openly in the hearing of her daughter, the beautiful Camilla: 'Ah! There was a man who *understood* the art of love! We were made for each other, he and I.' This absorbing revelation, not a word of which was lost on the daughter, continued unbroken for an hour or more. Am I to be accused of sanctioning such behaviour, merely for having described it?—I, whose most constant article of faith it is, that *modesty* is the mainspring of all true passion in the business of love? Yet, to savour revenge in all its sweetness, I have only to look beyond the calumny and visualise the *lives* of those who utter it! I often regret the existence of some cabbalistic language, whose mysteries are known only to the initiated; for *them*, an honest man might talk at liberty, safe in the knowledge that none but his own kind would fathom his meaning. Nevertheless, however awkward my subject may prove, I refuse to shrink before it. I will even confess that signora Z***, in the course of a formal reception after Mass last Sunday, seized the occasion of the presence of her two daughters and of a pair of visitors of the opposite sex who never in all their lives had made but this one call upon her, to propound a series of far-reaching aphorisms concerning the art of love. In corroboration of her maxims, she drew freely upon instances known to them all (that, for example, of la Belintani, who is at this very moment in Spain, in the company of her lover), illustrating the precise instant at which it behoves to resort to infidelity in order to punish a lover whose behaviour falls short of the ideal. Here in Italy, girls are watched over with a severity which is truly Spanish. Whenever the mother leaves the house, her place is taken by some elderly and hawk-eyed relative, who acts the part of a duenna. I have heard that it is not uncommon for a girl to have her young gallant, with whom she will as likely as not have no contact, save for an occasional encounter in the street—the whole affair amounting to no more than a few signs exchanged, a glance or two in church of a Sunday, and a dance two or three times in the year at the outside. Yet not infrequently so simple an intrigue may run company with the deepest of emotions. I shall never forget the remarks I heard from the lips of a little lass of fourteen, at a performance of *la Vestale* (the entrancing ballet by Viganò). Her whole commentary was imbued with a perspicacity and a profundity which were truly frightening.

Any notions which a girl in Italy may formulate concerning her life in prospect is based upon a composite legend, made up of secrets divulged in unguarded moments, of facts related second-hand, and of the divers motions of joy and sadness which she may have observed in those about her; never upon the irresponsible chatter of books. There is no reading of novels, for the admirable reason that none exist. I know of one heavy-handed imitation of Werther, entitled *le lettere di Iacopo Ortiz*, and two or three unreadable productions from the pen of the *abate* Chiari. As for our own French novels in Italian translation, the only impression they create is that of a diatribe *against* love. In Italy, any *paterfamilias* with a brood of daughters to keep watch upon will brutally make a bonfire out of any novel he may happen to discover in the house.[1] This total dearth of reading-matter, other than the severest of historical volumes, provides one of the strongest elements in

[1] A few years after the occasion of this *Journey*, when I was in Paris, I witnessed a fierce discussion, which took place in the hearing of seven or eight adolescent girls, and involved all the many possible explanations of the high fortune and favour of madame la marquise Octavie, whose situation, at that time, was beginning to attract public notice. The argument lasted some five-and-forty minutes. [1826]

my most vivid admiration for the conversation of the women of
Italy. In countries where novels abound—in Germany, in
France, etc.—the most romantic of women, even in the most
passionate instants of self-oblivion, can never wholly escape the
contagion of *la Nouvelle Héloïse*, or of whatever novel may have
chanced to catch the eye of fashion; for the utmost longing of a
woman's heart is to please her lover; and since she herself has
found such ecstasy in the reading of the novel, unfailingly her
own utterance will echo a phrase or two of the tale which drew
tears from her eyes and seemed to her to touch the loftiest
heights. Inevitably, therefore, in any land of novels, the
spontaneous beauty of natural expression is contaminated and
debased. A man has need of many years' experience of life
before he can forgive all this tinsel and trimming, discern the
veritable essence of the passion and stave off the frigidity which
emanates from the shell of empty rhetoric in which it is contained. It is common knowledge that the love-letters, and
frequently even the conversation, of women with a *penchant*
for literature, are nothing better than an anthology of their
favourite novels. Could this explain why they somehow seem
less womanly than other women, why they sound so absurd?
In Italy, on the other hand, a woman, from the first instant
that she may inspire love in the breast of another, or experience
it in her own, knows no passion more absorbing than this in
all her life; in the eyes of such a creature, the literary bent is
nothing save an ornament to her existence, a means of
offering additional delight to the heart of the man she loves.
I doubt not for one instant but that any woman in Italy, upon
reaching the last page of a novel, or of a *Garland of Sonnets*,
would gladly and unhesitatingly fling the book upon the fire,
were her lover to ask it of her in a certain manner. The average
love-letter (to judge by those which were offered me for
inspection by a certain jealous lover, the *marchese* B***) lays
no claims to literary excellence—or, in other words, makes no
effort to appeal to the *indifferent* reader. The same ideas recur

in endless repetition. To grasp a notion of the style, glance at the *Lettres d'une Religieuse portugaise*.[1]

10th December. I accompanied Radael to the stage-coach which leaves from the *via Monte Napoleone* and carries him to Mantua in three-and-twenty hours; for, in order to reach Bologna, the traveller must pass through the native fields of Virgil. The Duke of Modena has refused to allow the stage-coach to cut across his estates, on the grounds that 'all travellers are *Jacobins*'. His Royal Highness' argument is undoubtedly valid: his Chief of Police, Besini, confirms it amply in a series of faithful reports. The average Italian reads but little, and that with the gravest mistrust; and therefore, if he learns at all, he learns through travel. *This world is naught but a Vale of Weeping*—so runs the Collect which is learnt in Modena—*and by burning*...
....
................*is there any service more valuable that the Church may render unto their souls?*........................
....
......*either this, or else acknowledge the doctrine which is preached by the Jesuits of Modena**.................................
....
Nothing, in such a context, is more rational than persecution and the recital of the *auto-da-fé*; nothing could be more absurd than toleration.

I know of no more entertaining sport in all the world than to observe an Italian take his seat aboard a stage-coach. His faculties of *concentration*, which, in this peninsula, are rarely called upon, save at the behest of some overmastering passion, are ill-equipped for rapid exercise. No Italian, at that fatal instant when the coach awaits his pleasure, was ever seen

[1] The reader is referred to an excellent edition published by Firmin Didot, Paris 1824, complete with the original Portuguese text. [1826]

unless half-dead with fright at the thought of having overlooked a single one among a hundred-odd precautions—
precautions against cold, against damp, against highwaymen,
against some cavalier reception at an inn, etc., etc. The more
things he must keep an eye upon at once, the worse embroiled
and bewildered he becomes, and his boundless despair at the
least oversight must be witnessed to be credited. The least of
all things, in his eyes, is the grotesque figure he may cut in the
estimation of that crowd of idlers which ever gathers about a
stage-coach at departure-time. He would willingly sacrifice a
full score of onlookers, if by such means he might recover the
one thing which had slipped his mind—the black silk doffing-
cap which custom bids him place upon his head the moment he
sets foot in the pit of some theatre, where, to the mortal
inconvenience of the audience, *Royalty* should chance to occupy
its box, thereby condemning the audience aforementioned to
have upon its head a cap to doff.[1]

There is nothing more wondrous, nor more exasperating to
an Italian (depending upon the general trend of his reactions)
than the intellectual acrobatics of some dandified French wit,
who, in an hour's conversation, can dart back and forth
from Homer to political economy, from Bolivar to Raphael,
from chemistry to Mr Canning, from trade-routes under the
Roman Empire to the eruption of Vesuvius, from Alexander
the Emperor to Erasmus the philosopher, and from Paisiello
to Humphry Davy, by way of a hundred other topics in

1 Acting upon the principle that there is no such thing as perfection outside
France, the Napoleonic authorities in Milan forbade Italian audiences at
la Scala to remain covered in the pit. in the vastness of this cavernous
auditorium a man might well be apprehensive of a chill; yet should you
have yielded to the urge to cover your head, a pair of police officials,
instantly alert, and indeed posted there with no other concern save this
alone, would place a formal, warning hand upon your elbow. Among a
thousand edicts issued by the Napoleonic administration, none perhaps
caused greater vexation among the Milanese than this one insignificant
regulation. Prince Eugène was strangely devoid of tact in such matters.
[1826]

between. By the time the conversation draws finally to a halt, your poor Italian, who has been lashing his mental processes into a gallop in order to reflect deeply upon each and every one of these divers topics as they hover dragonfly-wise about the lips of this Gallic word-spinner, is left with nothing but a raging headache.

Any Frenchman who can bring himself to strip his conversation bare of lingering literary reminiscences, and who can sternly confine that extraordinary vivacity which is his by brilliant privilege of birth to depicting the *outward and visible* circumstances of the excursion or picnic upon which he, the one foreigner in a society of Italians, may happen to be engaged, stands every chance of seeming a very marvel of marvels in the eyes of some pretty woman. But, for this, he must make it a rule to break off pat, the moment he observes that his listener has ceased to follow the thread of his discourse; and he must constrain himself to silence for ten mortal minutes in every hour. Should he once give grounds to the dire suspicion that he is a *chatterer*, then all is lost beyond redemption; whereas there is never so much as a hint of danger in silence. Any ignorant second-lieutenant from the South of France, to whom La Harpe is but an unopened book, stands much nearer to the promise of reaping adoring glances from soft Italian eyes than the most exquisite young ornament of Parisian society, for all that he may be prop and pillar to the *Society for the Propagation of Christian Ethics*, and author of a pair of fascinating poems (already printed!) besides.

12th December. This evening, as I sat in *la Scala*, some forlorn and heart-broken creature, forsaken now by his mistress, signora Violantina R***, for a full year, chose *me* as confidant to the tale of all his woes. I came upon him towards eleven o'clock, alone in that waste of benches which fills the pit. He had sat there since seven, gazing from afar at that distant box whose reigning sovereign he once had been. He is young still, hand-

some as Apollo, noble and wealthy; yet, for twelve weary
months, he has known nothing but despair, nor sought to hide
his state from the inquisitive glances of the whole city.
Astounded by the note of tragic gravity with which this poor,
ill-fated lover told his secrets, I suspected at first that he had
some trifling favour to ask of me. Yet the truth was otherwise:
all he wanted was to *talk*, to talk of the woman he had loved
for eight long years, and whom, even now, with yet another
year gone by since the fatal quarrel intervened, he adores more
than ever he did before. And what a quarrel! None more
humiliating in all the world! He told me of it *in extenso*:
how, for six months on end, a German officer, 'an ugly brute'
(this was untrue: the officer in question is a charming and
handsome lad, but decidedly *vain*), would sit in the pit, 'just
at this very spot', and gaze through glasses at his mistress in
the box above. 'I was jealous', he went on, 'and further, I was
fool enough to hint as much to Violantina: not the slightest
doubt but that it was *my complaining* which first incited her to
switch her thoughts to this damned soldier, Graf von Keller.
With no object other than my own discomfiture, she took to
glancing night by night in his direction, as we came to leave
the theatre. Von Keller, encouraged by this response, leased a
small apartment, whose windows afforded him a view of the
balcony of the house in which she lived. He screwed up all his
courage, and wrote to her. This mutual flirtation had been in
progress for some three weeks, when her lady's-maid, whom
I had recommended, had a quarrel with her mistress, and in the
upshot handed me a letter which von Keller had addressed to
Violantina. In order to awaken a sting of jealousy in Violantina,
I pretended to pay court to Fulvia C***. The long evenings in
la Fulvia's box left me half-dead with boredom, save only at
those instants when I might hope to be observed by Violantina.
One day, I thought to send Fulvia a magnificent bouquet of
flowers gathered from my garden at Quarto; and from such
insignificant beginnings there sprang a quarrel which led to

hard and decisive words. In desperation, I shouted at her: *von Keller or myself—choose between us!* And with this sentence, I stalked out of the room, slamming the door hard behind me. The very next day I received a note from her, couched in these exact phrases: *Set out on your travels, my dear: for there is no longer anything between us save friendship. Spend a month at la Battaglia, and drink the waters.* . . . And *that,* my dear S***, after eight years! Who could have foretold it?'

And at this point, the *marchese* N*** settled down to tell me, hour by hour, the history of his love, from the very day when he had first set eyes on Violantina. I have a boundless passion for tales of this character, which betray with such a telling wealth of detail the hidden workings of the human heart: at once I was all ears. As for *il marchese,* he cared for few things less than to study the degree of attention in his listener; all *he* needed was to speak of Violantina; yet for all that, the emotion shining in my own eyes brought him a sort of consolation. And thus it came about that, by half an hour past midnight, when the final curtain fell on the little ballet, *The Pupil of Nature,* his flood of words was still far from exhausted. We sought refuge in a deserted coffee-house, the *Casin' dei Nobili,* where our sudden entry startled a lover and his mistress who had picked upon this public yet solitary spot for a tryst. Here we settled; and when the clock struck two, *il marchese* was still talking. The coffee-house closed its doors: he insisted upon seeing me to my lodgings. In the street, where the absence of lights removed the final barriers of restraint, tears coursed freely down his cheeks while he told me of a happiness that was his no longer. For a full fifteen minutes he nailed me to the spot beneath the porch of *la bella Venezia,* the inn where I was staying. And the clock on the church of *San-Fedele* was chiming a quarter to three when finally I sat down to write these pages. If only I had a secretary, I would stay up all night long, dictating the tale of *il marchese* N*** and of his love for Violantina. I know of nothing which gives a truer nor a profounder picture of the inner, secret life of Italy. The tale held maybe as many as thirty incidents—one and all quite incomprehensible in France. A Frenchman would feel nothing but anger at adventures which delighted the *marchese*, and *vice versa*.[1]

This tale had held my attention for three and three-quarter hours without a break. My own contribution to the dialogue amounted to less, perhaps, than a hundred words in all; yet my interest never wavered. 'It is inconceivable', I reflected, 'that any man so deeply involved in such a tide of emotion should find the strength of mind to tell a lie, save here and there, perchance, where the details were too humiliating to bear utterance in words.' Repeatedly, *il marchese* N*** would retrace the manner of some happening afresh, lest I should fail to see some circumstance in its clearest light. La Violantina, he told me, had a false tooth—a flaw of which I had hitherto been unaware. 'And *now*', he went on, 'how will she manage to have it renewed, the next time it comes loose? In the past, it was *I* who took her all the way to Turin, to visit Fonzi, who is a personal friend of mine. I introduced her to Fonzi as the unhappy *marchesina* C***, my own sister; and, as a result of these precautions, not a single person in all Milan suspected the existence of this false tooth. For a woman of four-and-twenty, which is her age, a false tooth is a most bitter humiliation. Do you suppose that von Keller could show such tact and ingenuity? *Ah! It is her own reputation that she will be murdering!*' he added gravely.

This poor, love-lorn wretch has by now entrusted the same tale to perhaps a score of listeners. His despair is the common gossip of every *salon* in Milan. On one occasion, he journeyed to Venice to take his mind off his misfortunes; but the sombre melancholy of his demeanour marked him down as a man apart, wherefore the Venetians taunted him unmercifully, and soon enough he was telling his tale anew. Yet he is very far from being a fool, nor yet is he a man of feeble constitution.

[1] *Cf.* the *Memoirs* of Casanova. [1826]

It is the hardest thing in all the world, I find, to set this sketch of his adventures down in French. The dialect of Milan is rich in words and proper phrases to convey exactly every circumstance of his love. My own periphrases in French are strangely imprecise, suggesting here too much and there too little. Yet how should *we* possess an idiom to express conceptions to which we never allude?

12th December.   I have consulted with signor Izimbardi, my private oracle, concerning the endless confidence which kept me from my bed this morning until four o'clock. 'Nothing more normal, here in Milan', was his reply. 'Ah! You should have seen C***, at the period when his quarrel with *la Luizina* had brought him to the brink of despair; or P***, when he resolved to make an end of his *liaison* with *la R****, into whose apartments he had blundered at an inconvenient hour.' And upon the instant he recited a dozen names, amongst which I recognised those of several of my recent Milanese acquaintances, whom I had hitherto thought of as men of unusual deliberation and gravity. 'And as for the women. . . !' he went on. 'Would you wish me to tell you of *la Ghita*, and of her despair when she discovered that P***, so far from loving her, had merely desired to add another victim to his list of conquests? For close on a year, she wanted even the strength of will to dress; she would appear at *la Scala*, even at *prime recite* and on gala-nights, in an old red calico dressing-gown buttoned up to her chin; for a month at least she sat at home in solitude, receiving not a single visitor, save perchance old Father S***, an aged Friar, who, I suspect, acted as courier between herself and P***. During all these days, she never once was seen in her box; and when, at last, some six weeks later, she did eventually return, it was solely with the fixed desire to catch a glimpse, however distant, of P***, the idol of society. You must consider the torment of a broken heart as the exact Milanese equivalent or emotional counterpart of *smallpox*:

a disease which, sooner or later, one and all must catch. Our great-grandmothers, who lived a seraglio-like existence scarcely distinguishable from that of the Grand Turk, were less afflicted by this malady. In Italy', added signor Izimbardi, 'it is a property of the imagination that, once having yielded to this characteristic passion, it knows of no conceivable happiness, save in the presence of the beloved.'

At this point, we embarked upon an excursion into the uppermost regions of metaphysics, which the reader shall be spared. Following upon a long dialogue on the subject of *love*, during the course of which it fell to me to interrupt signor Izimbardi's conclusions with a series of reiterated denials, so as to provoke him into illustrating his theories with searching anecdotes (the leading actors of which were forthwith identified by name and title) to prove the truth of his assertions: following, as I have said, upon such a dialogue, which took place in an ill-lit and deserted corner of the *caffè dell' Accademia*, we discovered, all unawares, that we had resolved the thorniest questions in the field of art, music, etc.; illuminating answers and ultimate truths sprang light as laughter to the mind. Signor Izimbardi continued: 'Whenever a young man who has **never** done a rash nor senseless thing in all his life, but merely filled his head with reading, dares to talk to me about art, I laugh out loud, to his very face! *First learn to use your eyes*, I tell him; *later, we can talk*. On the other hand, whenever a man who, like your acquaintance of yesterday, is known to be a prey to some enduring despair, should resolve to beard me on the subject of art, it is my habit to guide our conversation towards the memory of those men of talent whom he may have known between the age of eighteen, say, and twenty; and in particular, to dwell upon their weaknesses and foibles. I poke fun at their absurdities and mannerisms, both of mind and of body, with the specific object of forcing my acquaintance to confess whether, in that first upsurge of his youth, he was ever aware of these oddities, and furthermore whether he *enjoyed* them as a kind of consolation to set against his own inferiority; or whether he did not rather *worship* them as an added symbol of perfection, and seek to emulate them in himself. No man yet born alive, unless he should, in the eighteenth year of his age, have hero-worshipped some great model with an intensity sufficient to make his very weaknesses adorable, is fit to talk of art with me. A spirit compounded of wild unreason, dreams, and depths stirred at a feather's touch is a far sounder qualification even than a superior intellect, if a man is to dare so much as to open his mouth in judgment on those statues sculpted by Canova, to visit which the whole city of Milan is presently to go on pilgrimage to *la Cadenabbia,* beside the Lake of Como, where they stand in signor Sommariva's villa.' I was about to comment, jokingly, upon the multitude of geniuses required, before each young man might find one for himself, and so fit himself for the test; but I recalled in time that nothing is better calculated than this particular brand of flippancy, devised to engender a so-called *witticism,* to fall like frost upon Italian hearts, and seal Italian lips swifter than lightning.

I was shown this morning a delightful sonnet by Carline Porta upon the death of the painter Giuseppe Bossi, a noted, much-dandified creature, who enjoys something of a local reputation as a genius:

> *L'è mort el pittor Boss. Jesus per lù!* . . .

In any literature which admits both truth and realism to so marked a degree, the desiccated bleating of the blunt-minded is hushed into silence by the very nature of things. During the course of the day, I have read and re-read this same sonnet it may be a dozen times. A sonnet having but fourteen lines, a man may boldly embark upon the opening quatrain with little to fear from the threat of final boredom; it is a verse-form I adore without reserve. Italian literature holds some eight or ten sonnets which may be numbered among the highest achievements of the spirit of man. Carline Porta is particularly brilliant in his caricatures of the Milanese *aristocrat* attempting to speak in the classical idiom of Tuscany by adding random inflexions to the truncated dialect of his native city—as, for instance, in *la Preghiera*:

> *Donna Fabia, Fabron di Fabrian*
> ....
> *Oramai anche mi', don Sigismond,*
> *Convengo appien ne la di lei paura . . .*[1]

Unfortunately, however, the finest works of all by this charming poet are hardly suited to ladies' ears; and this is a disadvantage which he shares with both Buratti and Baffò. All three are poets who have sublimated the common idiom of every-day conversation; and in every art the outcome of such a transmutation is to isolate and clarify its essential patterns.

The sonnet which follows is another which I have been re-reading with untold delight, for it holds the seeds of truth, and, being true, makes some form of revolution inevitable, sooner or later, in the land of Italy:

> *Sissignor, sur Marches, lù l'è marches*
> ....
> *D'ess saludaa da on asen come lù . . .* *

Monti apart, I would gladly sacrifice the entire output of Italian verse published here during the past half-century for this one sonnet and *el dì d'incœu*:

> *El pover meritt che l'è minga don*
> *Te me l'hann costringiuu là in d'on canton . . .* *

Strength, simplicity, naturalism without a hint of that frigid and academic patina of *classical imitation* so beloved of our MM. Fontanes and Villemain—these are the qualities which lend such distinction to the dialect poetry of Italy. It is a *genre* where mediocrity is neither tolerable nor tolerated; yet this advantage is the first which *la poesia dialettale* would lose, the moment it fell into the toils of *Academies* and *Literary Gazettes.*

1 There exists a Milanese-Italian dictionary, 2 vols. in octavo, published by the Royal Stationery Office, and impeccably printed. The key to the language of the Milanese is the word *minga*, meaning *not at all*. [1826]

F

At home, the *Académie Française* has bestowed upon us nothing but the gift of *pedantry*; and French literature has never produced a single masterpiece, save at those rare intervals when the asinine brood chose to consider it 'unworthy of notice' (1673). No man on earth is plainer, nor less affected, than the average Italian poet: Grossi, Pellico, Porta, Manzoni and even Monti, despite the flattering temptations of repeated success. But even so, the vernacular poets are invariably less pedantic and more charming than all the rest. Oh, how drab are those waste-lands of the spirit that we call *literary criticism, literary reviews, histories of literature*, etc.!—a great jumble of pedantic rubbish fit only to nauseate any creature with a hint of sensibility, and make him sick of poetry for ever. If you would keep some semblance of pleasure in our northern poetry, it is fatal to have known the poet; for all you will discover is a little, puffed-up jackanapes forever solemnly invoking *his muse*! By contrast, my personal acquaintance with Porto and Grossi has left me an ever more ardent admirer of their charming verses.

BELGIOJOSO, 14th December. This morning, as I set out from Milan by way of the Pavia Gate, and passed beneath the triumphal archway erected to commemorate the battle of Marengo, but now defiled by some libellous inscription thought up by the obscurantist faction in the city, my eyes were filled with tears. I found myself murmuring, with the kind of mechanical pleasure that springs from frequent repetition, these beautiful lines by Monti:

> *Mossi al fine, e quei colli, ove si sente*
> *Tutto il bel di natura, abbandonai,*
> *L'orme segnando al cor contrarie e lente . . .*[1]

[1] From the fifth canto of *la Mascheroniana*, written by Monti on the occasion of the death of Lorenzo Mascheroni. The poet employs his genius to describe a year in the life of Napoleon. In another poem, entitled *la Bassvilliana*, he had embarked upon a history of the French Revolution. It is a tragedy that he never exploited the whole of this noble subject.

Signor Izimbardi, a man of enlightened views, and one of my newly-founded acquaintance, was full of insistence that he should be allowed to show me the sights of Lake Como. 'Tell me', he enquired yesterday evening, as we sat in the *caffè dell' Accademia*, 'what you expect to discover in Rome? The *sublime*? The *beautiful*? Well enough! But Lake Como—*our* Lake Como —is nature's counterpart of the ruins of the Colosseum in architecture, or of Correggio's *Saint Jerome* in painting.' 'Yet', I replied, 'were I to follow nothing but my *inclination*, I should never set foot outside Milan. Not a day of all my leave, but should be spent within the city. I have never encountered a race of men that were so closely fashioned after my own heart. No sooner am I in Milanese company, and conversing in the accents of Milan, than the very memory of human wickedness fades and vanishes from my mind, while all the evil in my own soul falls instantly asleep!'

I shall never forget the fine cast of Monti's features, as I watched him in the *salon* of signora Bianca Milesi, declaiming the famous passage in which Dante speaks of Hugues Capet*. A spell was cast, and I had fallen beneath it.

I have been favoured with a distant glimpse of signor Manzoni, a young man with a markedly religious turn of mind, who is rival to Lord Byron for the honour of being the greatest lyric poet now alive. He has composed two or three *Odes* which move me to the very depths of my soul; nor is there a single line of them to put me in mind of the *Fontanes* school of versifiers, one and all busy scratching their skulls in a stern determination to be *sublime*, or else rushing off hot-foot to pay a call upon the Minister and have their names set down then and there upon the *Honours List*. If the true measure

Monti is as susceptible to influence as a child, and in the course of his life has switched allegiance not less than five or six times; in *la Bassvilliana* he was a fanatical reactionary, whereas nowadays he is a patriotic liberal; but the one grace which saves him from contempt is that never once in all his career has he changed sides for *money*. *Cf.* Mr Southey. [1826]

of greatness in a poet should be adjudged to lie in the *average level of emotional intensity* which he is able to excite, then, to my mind, the anonymous author of *la Prineide* or of *la Visione del dì d'incœu* is the greatest of all living Italian poets. Signor Tommaso Grossi is no more than a humble attorney's clerk; yet his greatness as a poet suffers from one disability: the language in which he writes is no more comprehensible than Turkish a score of miles or so outside Milan, while Paris, Philadelphia and London are blithely unaware that such a tongue exists. Who suffers? The ignorant denizens of London and Philadelphia, not *I*! How should *their* blindness detract from *my* pleasure? The world of letters recognises more than one *genre*, whose present enchantment is not to be denied, yet which, three or four centuries hence, will be nought but dust and ashes. Lucian is as boring today as *Candide* may likely be in the year 2200 A.D. And still the academic mind insists that literary merit must be judged, not by the *intensity* of the pleasure it affords, but by its mere *persistence*.

I have already mentioned a young man who writes in the purest tongue of Ariosto and Alfieri, and whose dawning genius gives promise of yet another major poet to enrich the heritage of Italy, *si fata sinant*: Silvio Pellico. A dominie by trade (unhappy race of men!), he is hard put to it to scrape together a meagre twelve hundred francs a year, and so was neither rich enough nor vain enough to publish his writings; and indeed his tragedy *Francesca da Rimini* remained in manuscript until signor Ludovico di Breme himself undertook the expenses of printing. Signor Pellico has entrusted me with the MSS of three further tragedies, which, in my opinion, are less elegiac, more strictly *tragic*, than *Francesca*. I once heard signorina Marchioni, the finest tragic actress in the land, announce to signor Pellico that *Francesca* had recently enjoyed no less than five consecutive performances in Bologna— a record probably unequalled for at least a century. Signor Pellico is far more skilled at portraying the mystery of love

than Alfieri, although even this is not saying a great deal; in
Italy, love is expressed, not through literature, but rather
through *music*. In Paris, so I am informed, there lives an ingenious young man* whose brittle little comedies are rewarding
him to the tune of three thousand francs a month. Yet the
author of *Francesca* wears out his days construing Latin with a
parcel of brats, and may count himself lucky if he earns
twelve hundred francs a year; the publication and production
of his play have brought him not a groat!

Here lies the contrast between France and Italy in their
respective attitudes toward the arts. In Italy, the artist may
easily starve; and yet, for a month on end, the whole great
city of Milan was talking of *Francesca*. In the instance of this
particular young poet, the lack of financial encouragement is
disastrous; yet nothing could be healthier for art as such. Art
in Italy will never degenerate into a vile and mercenary calling,
duly rewarded by the *Villèles* of this world with seats in the
Académie and offices in the Censorship! Even Monti, each
volume of whose immortal poetry may run into something
like thirty editions, once whispered to me that he is invariably
out of pocket on the deal. When *la Mascheroniana* was published in Milan, not a week had passed before pirated editions
began to flood from *foreign* presses—from presses, that is to
say, in Turin, Florence, Bologna, Genoa, Lugano, etc.

Yet, if I miss Milan, the reason lies not so much in these
exceptional men whose names my pen has just been tracing,
but rather in the whole tenor of existence which pervades the
city, in its *informality*, in the natural unsophistication of its
manners and in the supreme art of *happiness*, which here is
practised with an added grace, for that the honest townsfolk
have not an inkling that it is an art at all, still less that it is the
least accessible of any. For me, the *style* of Milanese society
echoes and reflects the style of La Fontaine in poetry. Since
it is the custom for a woman of charm and distinction to
receive the same acquaintance in her box night after night for

perhaps ten years on end, there reigns an atmosphere of perfect comprehension; all know each other intimately, all intimately understand each other's thoughts, and a hint half-spoken suffices. Herein, I suspect, lies the secret enchantment of so much wit and laughter; for what sense is there in making hypocritical pretence among friends encountered three hundred times a year ten years on end?

This intimate knowledge that each man possesses of his neighbour makes for a social climate where the unfortunate who struggles along as best he can on fifteen hundred francs a year may converse without embarrassment and as an *equal* with his neighbour, who may enjoy an annual income of five or six million—a phenomenon which, in England, would plainly appear *incredible*. I have frequently wondered at this sight. If the millionaire one day should take it into his head to play the condescending plutocrat, or if the poor man should think to stand upon his dignity, the rest of the company would dissolve into fits of uncontrollable laughter, and the roar of mirth would last, without disguising its object, for a week. The cock-of-the-roost vanity of some ministerial jack-in-office, strutting amid the burghers and burghesses of Paris, would appear quite unintelligible in Milan: a full hour's explanation would be needed before the light could hope to dawn. If a Milanese falls so far into poverty as to be forced to accept employment under the Austrians, he is looked upon with genuine commiseration; no one doubts but that his situation may require him now and then to play the informer; certain topics will therefore not be discussed in his presence. *Poverino, è impiegato!*—such is the common verdict, pronounced with a shrug of the shoulders, a gesture of pitying sympathy which I had not hitherto encountered.

In Paris, almost invariably, should you think to call upon an intimate acquaintance, it will prove necessary, at each recurrent visit, to chip away a narrow crust of ice, formed during the four or five days which have elapsed since the last meeting; and when at length this infinitely delicate operation is brought to a successful conclusion, and you are back once more on the old footing of intimacy and tranquil content, firmly ensconced in the warmth and luxury of friendship, then midnight strikes its jarring note, whereupon the mistress of the household promptly sends you packing once again. But in Milan, when we chanced to hit upon an evening when all was happy and hilarious, we would begin by remaining snugly settled in the theatre, in the box of signora L***, until past one o'clock in the morning; with the lights still brightly burning, we would linger on about the faro-table, long after the auditorium had grown dark and all the spectators were gone home. And when eventually the stage-door keeper would come and remind us that one o'clock had struck some while ago, we, for no better reason than that we were loath to separate, would make our way to supper at Battistino's, the theatre's own coffee-house which caters expressly for such a situation, and before we finally went our different ways, it would be dawn. I was not in love; nor might I even count particular friends among the company; and yet those nights of informal, unaffected pleasure will never lose their freshness in my memory.

PAVIA, 15th December. Fourteen years of despotism under the aegis of a genius rudely transformed Milan, a great city hitherto renowned for nothing save over-eating, into the intellectual capital of Italy. Still today, in 1816, despite the interference of the Austrian police, Milan publishes ten times more books in a year than Florence, for all that the Duke of Florence makes a great parade of liberalism.

Even at this late hour, in the streets of Milan, you may meet with three or four hundred *enlightened* individuals, the intellectual cream of all the land of Italy, recruited by Napoleon from Domodossola to Fermo, from la Pontebba to Modena, to hold high office in his Italian Kingdom. These sometime

Civil Servants—hallmarked by their greying hair and quizzical expressions—are kept in Milan, partly by their passion for the life of a capital city, partly by their fear of persecution elsewhere.[1] Politically, they are the counterparts of our own *Bonapartists*; and they maintain that, before Italy may hope to be ready for a system of bicameral government, the country has need of some twenty years of Napoleonic despotism. Towards the year 1808, it became positively 'fashionable' for administrative officials in the Kingdom of Italy to *read books*. In France, by contrast, the Napoleonic dictatorship was more lethal in its effect; for the Tyrant was afraid of books, and feared to stir up old memories of the Republic, which are, even today, the only memories still to remain alive in popular imagination; he lived in terror of the old enthusiasm of the *Jacobins*. But in Italy, the local brand of Jacobin had trailed limping and hobbling in the wake of Napoleon's own victories, nor had such as they ever saved the country in its hour of danger, as had Danton or Carnot. The old mediaeval Italian virtues of *subtlety* and *forcefulness* have vanished without trace; the new Italian hagiology, presided over by St Charles Borromeo, has stifled these inestimable qualities for ever. Today's Italian knows no more of conspiracy than he may read in Machiavelli. Signor Bettoni, the bookseller, made his fortune by perceiving this sudden fashion for books; no sooner did the symptoms become apparent, than he published an edition of Alfieri in forty-two octavo volumes. The list of subscribers corresponded almost exactly to the roll of Civil Servants—those *enlightened intellectuals*—hand-picked by Count Prina and Napoleon. These, as a class, were distinguished, not so much by any impassioned strain of genius or enthusiasm, as by their *systematic approach* and their *tireless activity*—both qualities which are markedly uncommon among so passionate

---

1 All this has changed since 1820; today, a sort of *Terror* reigns in Milan, and the Duchy is treated as a colony of disaffected natives at the point of imminent revolt. [1826]

a nation, ever slave to the sensation of the moment. Boundless devotion or frenzied bursts of energy—qualities which rarely characterise the French official class, as was only too glaringly apparent in the face of the advancing Cossacks*—were never rare in Italy. Napoleon has asserted that it was here that he discovered his most faithful administrators; but then, he had not stolen away their freedom, nor brought back among them a tyranny which they had abolished. It is the sons of these sometime administrators who now form the *élite* of the younger generation, which, born about 1800, is already displaying its remarkable qualities.

The citizen of Milan is strangely devoid of any serious malice; in respect of which, he offers the one valid guarantee: *his own happiness*. All the foregoing is self-evident; the explanation which follows, however, is merely hypothetical.

Out of every hundred and fifty actions, great or small, important or otherwise, which fill out the space of an average day, the Milanese performs at least one hundred and twenty *solely because they appeal to him at a given instant*.

Out of these same hundred and fifty actions, no more than thirty are motivated by any sense of *duty*—i.e., by a force which runs counter to present inclination, and which draws its sanction from the *threat of retribution* which must necessarily follow in the wake of disobedience.

In England, this monstrous Leviathan, *Duty*, sanctioned by the prospect of literal starvation in the streets, intrudes maybe in one hundred and twenty out of every hundred and fifty actions.[1] Here you have the origin of that blight of melancholy afflicting the life of a race which, otherwise, is neither unenlightened nor deprived of sound traditions having the force of common-law. But the most fatal legacy of this sickness is that, among the wealthier classes, this same sense of *duty*, now sanctioned by the fear of *Hell*, as preached by Mr Irving, or

[1] During my stay in England, in 1821, no less than seven poor brutes were found *dead of starvation* in the streets of London. [1826]

else by the fear of *ostracism*, should the cut of your coat chance
to be the merest shade unfashionable, accounts perhaps for no
less than one hundred and forty out of the one hundred and
fifty actions which go to make a day. I am firmly persuaded
that there exist in England certain Great Personages—aye,
more than a few, and Peers of the Realm at that, and millionaires into the bargain—who, seated in solitary state before
their hearths, are afraid to cross their legs, for fear of being
vulgar![1]

Yet the oddest thing of all is that no one—not even the
poor counting-house clerk, slaving away from seven in the
morning until nine o'clock at night, day in and day out, for
a paltry two hundred pounds a year—is exempt from this same
terror of *appearing vulgar*. Not one Englishman in a hundred
has the courage to be himself; whereas not one Italian in ten
can so much as conceive the possibility of being otherwise. In
England, a man is lucky if he encounters a genuine emotional
experience once in a month; but in Italy, the same phenomenon
occurs three times a day.

In France, where strength of character is unknown (individual devil-may-care courage is not strength of character:
look at our current elections, and the *terrors* they awaken!);
in France, you may look to find no more remarkable society of

---

1 For evidence, see the admirable *Memoirs* of Miss Wilson; also the novels
Matilda and *Tremaine*.

Any book such as this is of its very nature so ephemeral, that now, ten
years after the original *Journal* was composed, I discover innumerable
tiny allusions and turns of phrase which need to be replaced by some more
up-to-date equivalent. In 1816, I used to keep my *Journal* regularly every
evening; but now, in 1826, I am resolved to publish only those extracts
which still appear true and valid. I have been living in Italy for six years,
ever since 1820*; and these six years of constant journeying throughout
the length and breadth of a country which the majority of travellers are
content to visit in a mere six months, represent the only title I may claim
to exact my reader's confidence; may it perhaps redeem my lack of
erudition, and even my lack of *style*. I have dared to tell the truth; and this
alone may account for the vitriolic torrents of abuse which have been
hurled at me by the *Literary Reviews* of Italy! [1826]

men than among the convicts in the galleys. These outcasts
possess that one major virtue, in which their fellow-countrymen are so singularly deficient: *forcefulness of character*. But
in Italy, where a complete surrender to the sensation of the
moment is no rarity, and the strength of character which
results directly from this spontaneity is just as common,[1] the
very institution of the convict-galleys appears as nothing less
than an abomination, physical and moral. If the Honourable
Representatives who sit in our *Two Chambers* could find time
to deal with this outrage, decreeing instead that convicts
should be transported to one of the Cape Verde Islands, and
there interned under strong guard and beneath the governor-
ship of M. Appert, then these unhappy outcasts might at least
rediscover some useful function. One threat only appals a true
Frenchman—the threat of *ridicule*. North of the Loire, not a
single man dare brave this fearful peril, and the grave Senator
in his fifties is no bolder than the fledgling lawyer of eighteen.
Hence the rarity of *civic* courage, which lacks that sacred code
of *ceremonial*, whence military valour draws its strength.

PAVIA, 16th December.   From Milan to where I am at present,
the highway cuts through some of the richest farming-land in
Europe. At every turning, the traveller beholds dykes of
running water, spreading fertility on either hand; his road
hugs the banks of the deep-water canal which forms the
shipping-link between Milan and Venice and gives access by
sea to the Americas; on the other hand, however, he may as
likely as not find himself set upon by highwaymen under the
very glare of noon. All the resources of Austrian despotism
have failed against this plague. Yet the solution is simple
enough: one militiaman stationed in every village to watch
for sudden and unwonted spending, and to demand a

---

[1] This *strength* has its roots in *admiration*—admiration for the feats a man has
  dared to perform in the sudden tempests of his own passion. The result is
  self-confidence. [1826]

satisfactory explanation from the peasant concerned: *Where did you get all that money?*

I shall say nothing of Pavia, of which you may discover accounts and to spare in the texts of countless descriptive-minded travellers.[1] Be grateful to me at least for having spared you a twenty-page report cataloguing that remarkable institution, the *Museum of Natural History*.

Such wonders belong, for me, to the same province as astronomy; I marvel at them; I even grasp their meaning now and then; but tomorrow it is as though they had never been. Truths of this complexion demand a mind set in a like mould to themselves—a mind dispassionate and mathematical, concerned *exclusively* with *proven facts*. The moral sciences show so much evil in this creature known as man—or rather (which comes to the same thing) it is so pleasant and so tempting to think of him as being better than he is—that the imagination can but rarely find a taste of happiness unless it take flight into a world remote from reality. Bréguet can devise a watch which will keep time unerringly for twenty years; whereas the gimcrack mechanism through which we live breaks down and gives pain seldom less than once a week. This notion invariably sets me dreaming of utopias, whenever any genius, such as Dr Scarpa, embarks upon the theme of natural history. Irrational as it is, this idea has haunted me throughout the day. If you believe in miracles, then tell me this: why, when one man kills another, does the murderer not fall dead beside his victim?

All in all, then, I am so ill-equipped to feel the spell of dispassionate knowledge, or of any science which takes heed of naught save of *verified data*, that nothing all day long has caught my fancy so much as that strange description of the *Natural History Museum* in Pavia which appears in the poem *l'Invito a Lesbia*. The poet was that same Lorenzo Mascheroni

---

[1] *Cf.* the *Voyage* by our friend M. Millin, member of such a multitude of Academies*. [1826]

whom Monti has made immortal through the portrait of his
death, described in the most haunting lines the nineteenth
century has yet produced. Mascheroni was a geometrician;
and the following lines will answer better than I could ever
hope to do myself for that descriptive sketch, which, seeing
that I have dated this letter of mine from Pavia*, I surely owe
you:

> Quanto nell' Alpe e nelle aeree rupi
> Natura metallifera nasconde;
> Quanto respira in aria, e quanto in terra,
> E quanto guizza negli acquosi regni
> Ti fia schierato all' occhio: in ricchi scrigni
> Con avveduta man l'ordin dispose
> Di tre regni le spoglie. Imita il ferro
> Cristoliti e rubin; sprizza dal sasso
> Il liquido mercurio; arde funesto
> L'arsenico; traluce ai sguardi avari
> Dalla sabbia nativa il pallid' oro.
> Che se ami più dell' eritrea marina
> Le tornite conchiglie, inclita ninfa,
> Di che vivi color, di quante forme
> Trassele il bruno pescator dall' onda!
> L'aurora forse le spruzzò de' misti
> Raggi, e godè talora andar torcendo
> Con la rosata man lor cave spire.
> Una del collo tuo le perle in seno
> Educò, verginella; all' altra il labbro
> Della sanguigna porpora ministro
> Splende; di questa la rugosa scorza
> Stette con l'or su la bilancia e vinse . . . etc.[1]

[1] All that Nature did purpose to keep hidden within the bosom of the
Alps, or in the heart of the uttermost rocks; all that breathes in the air or
upon the land, or sports in the depths of the waters; all this and more hath
a cunning hand set forth before thine eyes in these sumptuous galleries.
Here, *Iron* apes the crysolite and the ruby; liquid *Mercury* spurts from the
rock where it was engendered; deadly *Arsenic* glitters with dark fires,

I came to Pavia with the intention of observing the young
Lombards whose University this is, the most renowned for
learning in all Italy, and I am overjoyed with what I have seen.
Some half a dozen ladies of Milan, aware that I purposed to
break my journey in Pavia, entrusted me with commissions for
their sons. These young men, with whom, before long, I was
talking of Napoleon and of Moscow, were eager enough to
accept a dinner at my inn, and to fill the seats in a box which
I have taken at the *teatro dei Quattro Cavalieri*.

Do but compare these lads with the *Burschen* of Göttingen[1]
—there are no words adequate to describe the difference! The
students who throng the streets of Pavia are a far cry from
those fresh-complexioned Teutonic scholars; *their* eyes betray
no gentle contemplation, no vague meandering in the land of
make-belief. They are mistrustful, silent, untamed; immense
locks of black or dark-brown hair frame a countenance whose
pale and sallow tints speak of total unfamiliarity with that
facile happiness and thoughtless amiability which characterise
the young Frenchman. However, let but a woman appear in the
street, and in an instant, all the sombre gravity of these young
patriots is transmuted into a new and startling expression. *Our*
pretty little dressed-up dolls, arriving here fresh from Paris,
would be scared out of their silly wits, convinced that every
one of these honest students was a desperate brigand. Yet that
is precisely the reason why I like them. They make no pretence
at gentle manners, at hilarity, still less at nonchalance. Any
young man who prides himself on being *blasé* and cynical

while the covetous glance of man discerns amid his native sands the
scarce-yellowing dust which shall furnish him with *Gold* . . . etc. (It
might almost be Latin pentameters that I have been translating!) [1826]
[1] Concerning the *Burschen*, I can add nothing to the excellent description
already furnished by Mr Russell, of Edinburgh, in his *German Journey*.
The duelling rites of these German students afford ample evidence, how
little-valued in their native land is the factor of *present sensation*. It is a
bizarre experience to visit, within a space of six months, both Göttingen
and Pavia—not to mention the pit of the *Théâtre Italien* in Paris! [1826]

stands condemned (in my eyes) as a self-confessed eunuch of the seraglio, glorying in his own abasement. Here, among the students of Pavia, *hatred* may reach to monstrous heights of fury—hatred of the *Tedesch'*. The hero of the hour is he who, venturing by night into an unfrequented street, has managed to thrash the life out of some young Teuton, and make him 'show his heels', as they like to put it. The reader will readily understand that I personally was witness to no such escapades; but I listened by the hour to tales of similar adventures, endlessly repeated yet never boring; for *I*, meanwhile, found leisure to observe the features of the teller. These lads can recite the whole of Petrarch off by heart, while half at least write sonnets of their own. What stirs them to the depths is that impassioned flood of sensibility which Petrarch, for all his veneer of metaphysical, Platonic pathos, yet cannot succeed in keeping hidden throughout. One such among my student friends chose, quite unbidden, to recite the first of the Petrarchan *canzoniere*, which is the loveliest sonnet ever written in all the world:

> *Voi ch'ascoltate in rime sparse il suono*
> *Di quei sospiri ond' io nudriva il core,*
> *In sul mio primo giovenile errore,*
> *Quand' era in parte altr'uom da quel ch' i' sono;*

> *Del vario stile in ch' io piango e ragiono*
> *Fra le vane speranze e'l van dolore,*
> *Ove sia chi per prova intenda amore,*
> *Spero trovar pietà, non che perdono.*

> *Ma ben veggi' or, si come al popol tutto*
> *Favola fui gran tempo; onde sovente*
> *Di me medesmo meco mi vergogno:*

E del mio vaneggiar vergogna e'l frutto,
E'l pentirsi, e'l conoscer chiaramente,
Che quanto piace al mondo è breve sogno.[1]

The southern regions of France—Toulouse in particular—bear a striking resemblance to Italy; in religion, for instance, or in music. A young man in these parts is less petrified with terror at the thought of going 'against the fashion' than are his fellow-countrymen north of the Loire; I have even observed quite a substantial element of solid *enjoyment* of life among the younger generation in Avignon. Happiness, one might almost suspect, seems to flourish in alliance with the accents of the South, and to evaporate with them. On the other hand, the young, working-class Parisian, born to poverty, and conse-

---

[1] At this point, I have preferred to cut out a lengthy passage of analysis concerning the younger generation in Italy. Any such metaphysical excursions, which are, after all, nothing but *the juice squeezed from a hundred anecdotes*, need to be read, if they are to sound anything but intolerably pompous, beside the banks of the Ticino. Generalisations of this nature are apt to seem risky and ill-founded anywhere outside Italy, and to spark off all manner of municipal vanities. On the other hand, should the reader perchance be *already* afoot in Italy, then this day-to-day record of my *Journey* may perhaps seem less of a wilful paradox. Often, in my notes, a single word is the clue to a whole adventure; and were I to set down *all* the tales that I have heard, and whose quintessence inspires me with my moral conclusions, four solid quarto volumes would hardly give the space I need. I would refer my readers to those documents, published in 1825, which give the story of the student rebellion in Pavia. Observe (i) the death of young Guerra; (ii) the incidents which followed hard upon his funeral. The procedure employed by the police on that fatal day will not be forgotten twenty years from now, and year by year the tales of their infamous barbarity will grow and be exaggerated. If it be a question of *courage*—or rather, of danger submerged in a tidal-wave of *anger*—then the students of Pavia may perhaps claim sovereignty over those of any other university in the world. Nothing but the actual imminence of death—of death in its most sordid manifestation—could stem the onrush of ten thousand Italian students; grape-shot alone could save the day, ripping limb from limb and spraying the stones with human entrails, repeating the scenes which accompanied the death of General Lacuée. [1826]

quently goaded into *action*, driven to pit himself against people who have no urge to make life a bed of roses for him, will be less sickly and more satisfied than his gentlemanly counterpart, forever haunting the ballrooms of the Faubourg Saint-Honoré. And if, in the case of the aforementioned young *muscadin*, high breeding should find alliance with high fortune, the ultimate destiny of his present character must lead him, by relentless logic, into a Trappist monastery. Labour, combined with the fruitful experience that follows hard upon action directed at others, will save our young proletarian from the risk of stopping dead in his tracks three times a day to observe, calculate and measure his present degree of happiness. An Italian of the same age, ceaselessly active in pursuit of objects to satisfy his most futile of desires (which all too easily may burgeon into passions), has no thought save of women, no idea in his head, save to find a solution to this or that age-old predicament. Suggest to him that he stop and *weigh the quantity of religious emotion in his soul*—he will merely take you for a lunatic. Temperamental he may be, and uncivil; but his style of argument is honest, untainted by deceit; he will readily rant and storm about the room; yet no fear of being out-manoeuvred in dialectic will ever reduce him to the base subterfuge of pretending to have lost the thread in his opponent's argument through some ellipsis in the train of logic. Infinitely nearer, in my opinion, to true happiness than his French contemporary, his expression, none the less, is far more sombre. A day in the life of any young Frenchman is taken up with a score or so of trifling, meaningless sensations; the Italian is enslaved body and soul by two or three; the Englishman may meet with one in every six weeks, and finds the interval a thing of infinite weariness; while the German has no knowledge of sensation whatsoever, unless it be filtered through the all-enveloping mists of *reverie*. Is there sunshine in his soul? . . . then the fall of a leaf or of an Empire is all one to his impervious serenity.

Youth is the season of courage; we are all braver at twenty than we are at thirty.[1] Yet, oddly enough, in respect of that special brand of courage which dares to fly in the face of ridicule, the very contrary is true. Could it be that, unknown even to themselves, our young Parisians, seemingly sacrificing all basic ideals upon the altar of *transcendental metaphysics*, yet cherish in their heart of hearts a dream of fair women?

I sought in vain beneath the walls of Pavia for traces of that ancient battlefield, from which Du Bellay has drawn us so exquisite a portrait of the misfortunes of François I (1525). There is one admirable street in Pavia, laid out on the pattern which is traditional in Milan, with its four-fold, parallel causeways of Baveno granite. Of granite likewise are the guard-rail posts, set at twenty-foot intervals on either side of the central thoroughfare. The local word for these is *paracarri*—a word which, in good time, was to become the popular nickname for all French troops. *Ah! poveri paracarri!* I heard the phrase often enough while I was in Milan, uttered with a sigh of nostalgia; whereas, prior to 1814, the word was never spoken, save with a thrill of hatred. No race loves another unless it hates a third more bitterly still.

Two miles out of Pavia, coming from the direction of Milan, one may observe a quantity of slender brickwork towers rising high above the roof-tops. It was customary, at the court of any sovereign prince in Lombardy, or duke of the House of Visconti, for every great vassal to build a refuge-tower for his personal safety, lest some rival courtier should feel tempted to come and assassinate him. I was delighted with the architecture of the *collegio Borromeo*; the artist responsible was Pellegrini, architect likewise of the church at Rhô, on the highroad out of Milan towards the Simplon.

It was in 1362 that Galeazzo II Visconti founded the

[1] By the age of thirty, a man has lost all that fine flower of courage which stems from *anger*. [1826]

flourishing University of Pavia. He established faculties of
civil and canon law, of medicine and physics, and of that art
which so scared the soul out of Napoleon, nor has it lost its
terrors for the multitude today—*logic*! This same sovereign,
Galeazzo II, it was, who further devised a notably ingenious
system for inflicting unimaginable tortures upon a prisoner for
one-and-forty days without respite, yet never letting life
depart for good. A surgeon stood at hand to tend the victim,
in order that, upon the last day of the forty-one, he might yet
survive to die a cruel death.[1] Bernabò, the brother of Galeazzo,
was meanwhile devising measures still more inhuman in Milan.
A young Milanese once told how he had dreamed that he
was stabbing a wild boar; Bernabò promptly chopped off
one of his hands and gouged out one of his eyes, as a lesson in
discretion. Princes of such a stamp as these, assuming that they
fail to reduce all things to one common level of degradation
and brutishness, may conjure up among their subjects some
singularly forceful characters, as indeed many can be found in
Italy during the sixteenth century. Even today, in occasional
circumstances of *private life*, such characters may now and
then be met with; their first concern, however, is to remain
undetected; in our own epoch, *love* is almost the only passion
which can prick them into betraying their true colours. One
art alone, the art of *music*, can probe deep enough into the
recesses of the human soul to portray the subterranean stirrings
of spirits such as these; we must allow, however, that they are
ill-equipped to fashion sly and witty little entertainments such
as *Candide* or the *Mémoires contre Gœzman*. In the eyes of
cultured travellers, such as M. Creuzé de Lesser[2], they might
indeed seem even *stupid*.

---

[1] *Chronicon Petri Azarii*, p. 301. This author has preserved for us a faithful
description of the tortures to which I allude: *Intentio domini est . . .*, etc.
Many hapless wretches perished thus in 1372 and 1373. [1826]

[2] *Vide* a certain *Voyage en Italie*, a handsomely-produced volume published
by P. Didot, *c.* 1806. [1826]

PIACENZA, 18th December. This morning, as I drove out
of Pavia on the road to Piacenza, soon after crossing the
Ticino by a covered bridge, I found myself embarked upon
one of the loveliest highways that I have known in all my life.
It runs through Stradella and San Giovanni, and follows the
line of foothills which form the southern boundary of the
valley of the Po. A priest, who chanced to be my travelling-
companion, saw to it that our baggage passed unmolested
through the customs at Stradella; the excise-officers refused
our little offering, and treated us with courtesy. Here and
there, the road rises slightly to climb a promontory of the
foothills, affording a view to northward which is both start-
lingly beautiful and strange. If it is like this on the 18th of
December, what must it be in autumn? Between San Giovanni
and Piacenza, I was shown some human bones—unlovely
relics of the battle of Trebbia in 1799. These same fields likewise witnessed the discomfiture of the Roman legions before
the onslaught of Hannibal.

Piacenza boasts a pair of equestrian statues still more absurd
than those of Paris, for all that neither of them exhibits the
crowning anachronism of a great Prince in a full-bottomed
wig and with naked legs*. Piacenza is a city of but five-and-
twenty thousand souls; yet its theatre is superior in design to
any in the whole realm of France. For two centuries and more,
every one of a hundred petty townships in Italy has had its
own theatre; it stands to reason, therefore, that by dint of trial
and error, architects should have come eventually to settle
for the most appropriate structure. Even in Paris, is it not a
fact that each new theatre, rebuilt upon the ruins of the old,
is a marked improvement upon its predecessor? Since a stifling
atmosphere and insufficient oxygen are fatal to the voice,
Italian theatres are a century at least ahead of ours for ventila-
tion. To even matters out, however, the peasantry about
Piacenza is a good two hundred years behind our own for
common-sense and kindliness of heart—two qualities which

make of France the foremost nation in the world. By contrast,
the Placentine peasant is still today no better than an evil-
minded brute, fashioned thus by four centuries of despotic
government, whose cowardice defies belief;[1] furthermore, the
very climate of the land gives added scope to his proclivities.
Leisure is not lacking; sensual enjoyment—thanks to the
generosity of nature, which scatters this and other bounties
with a lavish hand, even among the poorest of the poor—may
be had for the asking; and in consequence, these peasants are
not, as might be the subjects of some petty German princeling,
just simply bestial and vicious; they rise above the primal
elements of evil to a rare sophistication of ferocity and vengeance. The perversity of your petty *Margrave* is aided and
abetted by the rigours of the climate; the Hessian peasant,
driven forth from his hovel into the wastes of winter, is by this
alone condemned to death. I have collected two or three tales
of the *banditti* which are enough to make the blood run cold,
if one dwells merely upon the refinements of cruelty involved;
but which, to the bold philosopher who dares contemplate the
genius and the remorseless daring of such folk, are meat for
heroes and food for admiration. They put me in mind of
la Roche-Guinard, and of old Cervantes' Spanish brigands.
Maïno, the Alessandrian marauder, was one of the most
remarkable individuals of this our century; all he lacks is four
full pages in the *National Biography*, which chance has granted
to the dullest of provincial administrators. But what is the
empty vanity of human nomenclature against the strong reality
of natural, existing *fact*? Our rude forefathers were incapable
of *seeing* electricity; yet did electricity *exist* the less for that?
A day will come when we shall admit, admire, *historicise* true

1 From 1300 to 1400, bestialities of the Visconti; in 1758, death of Giannone
in the dungeons of the Citadel of Turin; in 1799, mass tortures in Naples.
At a still later date, nothing but the progress of *philosophic enlightenment*
and the fear of *public opinion* has held in check the impetuous wish to
follow certain uncompromising counsels! (Rome, 1814, C. Alb*.) [1826]

strength of character whenever and wherever we may find it. Maïno, like other robbers of his kin, will still be hanged; yet public opinion will grant him in the end more courage, daring and sheer military genius than many a well-brevetted Captain who never turned his face toward danger unless he had a thousand stiff-drilled men behind his back, and who at last is bravely laid to rest in *Père Lachaise*, to the braying of much hypocrisy and falsehood.

Ever since the fifteenth century, when Italy rid herself of her plague of petty tyrants, every ten years or so there has appeared some noted robber, whose wild, adventurous career has set the heart of every listener beating a full score of years after his inevitable and violent death. In Piacenza, among the populace, when a girl first begins to think about her future lover, the heroism of the robber is never far to seek among the elements that build her dream. Ghino di Tacco was a notorious member of the clan; yet he received his knighthood at the bidding of the Pope himself, so greatly did His Holiness admire the robber's courage.

REGGIO, 19th December.   I was held in Parma (which, in all other respects, is a commonplace and uninteresting little township) by the wondrous frescoes of Correggio.

The *Madonna blessed by Jesus*, which is to be seen in the Library, moved me literally to tears. I bribed a lad in charge of the gallery to leave me in solitude for fifteen minutes, perched on top of my ladder. I shall never forget the downcast glance of the Virgin, nor the impassioned grace of her stance, nor the simplicity of her dress. And what am I to say about the frescoes in the *Convento di San-Paolo*? Perhaps only this: that he who has never beheld them can have no conception of the ultimate powers of painting as an art. Raphael's figures have their rivals in antique sculpture; but feminine love being unknown to antiquity, Correggio stands unchallenged. Yet, if the beholder is to have earned the privilege of understanding such an artist, he must himself have proved guilty of the highest absurdities in the service of the passion of love. After examining the frescoes, which are always of far deeper significance to me than any pictures, I paid a visit to the new Museum built by the Grand-Duchess Maria-Luisa in order to renew my acquaintance with *Saint Jerome* and other masterpieces which formerly used to hang in Paris.

Being a conscientious traveller, my duty bade me pay a call upon signor Bodoni, the celebrated printer. I found a pleasant surprise in store for me, for there was not a hint of vanity about this Piedmontese craftsman, but rather a deep and genuine passion for his art. I was allowed to inspect all his French authors; whereupon he enquired of me which I most admired, his *Télémaque*, his Racine or his Boileau. I confessed that all three appeared to me equally fine.

'But, sir, do you not observe the *title* of the Boileau?'

Thus adjured, I considered it at length, and was at last obliged to confess that I could remark nothing more exquisite in this particular title than in all the others.

'Ah, good sir!' cried Bodoni, '*Boileau Despréaux*, in one single line of capitals! Six whole months, sir, I spent in vain research, before I could hit upon the perfect type-face!'

And indeed, the title is set out thus upon the page:

ŒUVRES

DE

BOILEAU DESPRÉAUX

To such lengths of absurdity may our passions lead us—an absurdity which, I confess, in this present era of artificiality, scarcely merits belief.[1]

In the honourable field of *patriotism*, Reggio is to Italy what Alsace is to France. The lively enthusiasm and the courage of its inhabitants are widely celebrated. The ideal season for a

---

1 Anecdote concerning the tragedy of *Annibal**; Bodoni's admiration for the *characters* of the play—in particular for the *Capitals*! [1826]

visit would lie in the spring, in the time of the annual Fair. There are three Italian cities which require to be seen in the season of the Fair: Padua, Bergamo and Reggio. I attempted—unhappily without success—to obtain an introduction to Count Paradisi, sometime President of the Senate under Napoleon, and one of the most noted personalities of our time; a man of glacial disposition, but with a clear and deep-searching mind. I am told that he is engaged upon his *Memoirs*. Entrusted to a hand such as his, the *History of Italy* between 1795 and 1815 might well prove an enduring masterpiece;[1] but he is reputed to be distinctly lazy.

SAMOGGIA, 20th December. I have picked up one or two curious details concerning the Jesuit College at Modena, and the skill and subtlety which are employed by the Reverend Fathers to quench the tiniest spark of generosity in the hearts of their pupils, and to foment the most sordid spirit of egoism. My information dates back to the year 1800, when signor de' Fortis, at present one of the Superiors of his Order, was on the staff of the College at Modena. Every boy was encouraged to play the informer against his comrades, and the *tale-bearer* was held up to the admiration of his fellows as an ideal pupil. 'Do whatever takes your fancy', a Reverend Father once admonished one of his pupils. 'Afterwards, go away and recite a *Deo gratias*, and all will be sanctified.' Here in the town, there is one street which boasts a delightful arcade supported by an elegant series of columns. In days gone by, Correggio's *Night* used to hang in Modena; but Augustus, Elector of Saxony and King of Poland, paid out the sum of one million two hundred thousand francs for a hundred pictures from the Modena gallery, and so I had to visit Dresden before I might

1 Signor Botta has since managed to desecrate and defile this noble subject. The blind hatred which he bears towards Bonaparte has induced signor Botta simply to *deny* the whole Lonato affair. Signor Paradisi has pointed out some of the major blunders of this miserable historian—who is, I confess, in all other respects, a most honourable individual. [1826]

allow my astonished gaze to dwell upon those noble master-pieces—*Saint Mary Magdalene*, *Night*, *Saint George*, etc. Yesterday I stepped aside from the main highroad in order to glance at the village of Correggio. Here, in the year 1494, was born the man whose mastery of colour taught him to portray those rarest shades of emotion which lie forever beyond the range and scope of poetry, and which, in a later age, only Cimarosa and Mozart did learn at last to capture and to preserve in musical notation. As I walked about the streets of Correggio, I caught glimpses of women whose features still echoed the *Madonnas* of this great painter.

My mind still occupied with these moving reflections, I drove through Rubiera, whose stronghold does service as a prison for the victims of the Jesuit Congregation, the un-challenged sovereign of Modena. This association of ideas robbed me suddenly of all the delight that had hitherto possessed me; I could not bring myself to sleep the night in Modena, but pushed on rather to Samoggia, where I arrived at four o'clock in the morning. From Parma onwards, the panorama of the Apennines upon the right is a constant pleasure.

Extremes meet: on the one hand, the courage and patriotism of Reggio; and hard against it, Modena, with its Jesuitry and its government of . . . . !

BOLOGNA, 27th December. For a week now I have been in no mood for scribbling. My mind is still obsessed with Milan. Events have overtaken, overwhelmed me—the insignificant events of the traveller's busy life, which are nothing but physical sensation, and which leave no trace on the morrow to be preserved. I can only suppose that my acquaintance in Milan must have written the most unusual letters of introduction on my behalf; for a good half of my period of probation in Bologna—the novitiate imposed by *mistrust*—seems to have been remitted.

I have visited a whole series of superb galleries: the *Marescalchi*, the *Tanari*, the *Ercolani*, the *Fava*, the *Zambeccari*, the *Aldrovandi*, the *Magnani*, and finally the *Municipal Museum*. In a different mood, I might have spent a score of mornings in unqualified delight; but there come days when the most glorious of paintings is nothing but a source of irritation. Let me hasten to assure my reader's vanity that, if I have recorded this misadventure, it is not for the selfish and empty pleasure of talking about myself, but rather because this is the sort of misfortune which eludes the wariest of calculations. Imagine! to have precisely four-and-twenty hours to spend in some dreary little township, and in all this space of time, to find oneself bereft of the littlest ounce of sensibility in respect of that very form of beauty for whose sake alone one visited the place! I am chronically susceptible to this strange distemper.

I fell a victim to it, for instance, standing before that exquisite, full-length *Madonna* by Guido Reni, which hangs in the *Palazzo Tanari*. That morning, my mind would dwell upon anything, rather than on painting. I left the gallery feeling as surly as an old bull-mastiff—a humour which even the fine copy (fine, that is to say, inasmuch as it reflects the beauty of the original) of Domenichino's *Saint Andrew* failed signally to mellow. The original fresco, so sublime yet so utterly despised by those disciples of David who form our school of art at home in France, can be seen at *San Gregorio* in Rome. In Bologna, when a French squadron was billeted one day by chance at the *Palazzo Tanari*, the troops saw fit to while away the time by jabbing bayonets through this gigantic canvas. One of the young Counts of Tanari was complaining to me bitterly of this incident, when by good fortune I noticed that he was holding in his hand a copy of Destutt de Tracy's *Commentaire sur l'Esprit des Lois*. 'And yet, sir', I retorted, 'had it not been for *us*, would *you* have known that Montesquieu existed?'

28th December.   The city of Bologna nestles against a ridge of hills which look towards the north, much as Bergamo reclines against a similar range of hills which face the south. Between the two there stretches the proud *Vale of Lombardy*, the most extensive cultivated valley in all the civilised world. In Bologna there is a villa built high up on the hillside, whose façade and columns in the manner of a Grecian temple can be seen from twenty points of vantage within the city, and form a prospect to delight the eye. The mountain-slopes which support this 'temple', and which seem to advance like some great promontory into the very multitude of houses, are flecked with wooded groves and copses, just as some artist might have conceived the landscape on his canvas. But for the rest, Bologna shows a barren, frowning aspect—an impression whose roots lie in the fact that every street has arcades which run *on either side*. Ideally, arcades should shelter one side only, as at Modena; such will be the rule in Paris two centuries from now. All in all, the arcades of Bologna are far from possessing the elegance of those in the *rue Castiglione*; but on the other hand, they are infinitely more convenient, and broad enough to give shelter from the heaviest downpour, such as that which greeted me on the day of my arrival and which resumed its torrential activities this morning. My first action upon setting foot in the city was to seek out the famous *Leaning Tower*; I had already observed it a mile away on the road. It is called *la Garisenda*, and is said to be one hundred and forty feet high; it deviates from the perpendicular by as much as nine feet. A native of Bologna, abroad in alien lands, feels homesick at the memory of this tower.

Of all the cities I know, Bologna is among those which offers the least encouragement to hypocrisy. In the time of the Papal conquest, after the fall of the Bentivoglio dynasty (1506), His Holiness set about the ruthless extermination of all republican traditions; in retaliation for which, the townsfolk schooled themselves to a high degree of proficiency in the art of detecting ecclesiastical absurdities. Furthermore, for centuries on end, Bologna occupied in the field of natural science the same position of eminence which is now occupied by Paris; and the Popes having failed to invent that supreme absurdity, which consists in transmuting famous scientists into *Barons**, science steadfastly retained the right to speak its mind. The priesthood in Bologna perforce turns a blind eye on the traditional *libertinage* of the city; otherwise relentless lampooning would prevent the Church from enjoying these same privileges herself. Lambertini, before his translation to the Holy See, was the merriest and the most free-spoken of prelates; on this point we have the evidence of the Président de Brosses*, that *Voltaire* among travellers in the land of Italy (1739).

My courier took me, as soon as we had arrived, to the Palazzo Caprara, then showed me the façade of the *Palazzo Ranuzzi*, and finally, at my request, led me to the church of *San Domenico*, wherein repose the mortal remains of him who was the *Catholic among Catholics**. My excursion to *San Domenico* was well rewarded: a vault decorated with frescoes by Guido Reni, including a series of charming small-scale figures; two miniature statues by Michelangelo, belonging to the period when this greatest of all artists was still in his first youth, before his style had acquired its permanent stamp of *terror*; and a painting by Tiarini, which is the very incarnation of a mother's joy when her child is brought to life before her eyes.

The whole city is instinct with the glory of the brothers Carracci; their name is everywhere. This morning, my own bootmaker gave me their history almost as accurately as Malvasia. He told me that Lodovico had died of shame and grief as the result of an error of draughtsmanship in the figure of the *Angel of the Annunciation*—a fresco which may be seen at *San Pietro*. I promptly retraced my steps towards *San Pietro*, the Cathedral of Bologna, accompanied by my little bootmaker, who was all eagerness to have me take him as guide. In Paris, your bootmaker may have every comfort in his home; he may even be able to furnish his apartment with ebony; but

just try to start a conversation with him about M. Gérard's
Psyche!

The brothers Carracci were almost as remarkable for their
strength of character as for the vitality of their genius. Imagine
some young writer in Paris at the moment, bubbling with
ideas, poised upon the very threshold of his career, and yet
possessed of the supreme courage to write *as simply as Voltaire*,
without so much as a hint of *passages throbbing with contemporary
significance*, without a glance at the *imperative needs of the
century, deep-rooted in historical inevitability*, etc., etc.—he would
strike a note as absurd as a woman who dared risk showing
her own complexion in a *salon* where every other woman
present was wearing rouge. No one would read his book;
some indescribable sensation of *chill* and *catastrophe* would
emanate from its pages. By contrast, let him but ape the style
of *le Génie du Christianisme*, say, or of M. Guizot; and if he
has so much as the outline of an idea in his head, fame may be
his for the asking. This comparison may serve to illustrate the
full extent of the violence which Lodovico Carracci and his two
cousins, Agostino and the immortal Annibale, dared fling in
the face of their century. Yet their whole livelihood depended
upon their brushes. More than once they were sorely tempted
to abandon the natural simplicity of their native style in order
to pander to the fashionable affectations of the day. The
dramatic narrative of the councils which they summoned
among themselves to discuss the problem, in circumstances
always overshadowed by their extreme poverty, lends an
uncanny interest to certain passages in the *Felsina Pittrice*. The
brothers Carracci,[1] as everyone knows, were the masters of
Domenichino, Guido Reni, Lanfrano, and of a host of competent painters of secondary stature, who would have shone
forth in splendour unrivalled had they lived in our own time.

1 Lodovico Carracci, born in 1555, died in 1619.
  Annibale Carracci, born in 1560, died in 1609.
  Agostino Carracci, born in 1558, died in 1601. [1826]

Caring for nothing in the world save art, they earned no more than the equivalent of fifteen hundred or two thousand francs in all their lives, and died in poverty—greatly different in this from their illustrious successors. Yet now, two centuries after their death, their names are still mentioned with reverence, and here and there some solitary romantic spirit will contemplate their paintings and weep for joy.

The civic vanity of Bologna finds especial pride in its *cemetery*—an old Charterhouse some quarter of a league without the city walls. A few third-rate sculptors may eke a living out of the demand for tombstones. Two hundred years ago, if I remember right, the Bolognese decided to construct a covered causeway from the valley-floor to the heights of *la Madonna di San Luca*—a double colonnade of some six hundred and fifty arches. All the domestic servants of the city leagued together in a *guild*, and bought four arches; all the beggars formed a *guild*, and bought two more. By way of this still-standing colonnade, three miles in length, I climbed the hill myself—and there at the summit, studying the paintings which hang within the church, I caught my inevitable cold. This is the third time that I have fallen victim to this exasperating ailment; an Italian would have taken the wiser precaution of wearing a black silken cap. The character of the common people I have met with is frank and merry, very much alert; they goad each other with practical jokes whenever they meet in the street; and when they separate, it is with a song on their lips.

29th December. I have just been introduced to the *abate* Mezzofante, who speaks two-and-twenty languages just as readily as you and I speak each our own; and yet, in spite of all this learning, there is nothing stupid about him. I attacked him concerning the *abbé* de Pradt's book, *le Congrès de Vienne*; for I had spotted a copy of it in the public library, for which institution he is responsible. 'Such a book *here!*', I taunted him.

'Why, if a man reads that, he may develop an *enquiring mind*; it spells death to the authority of the Pope; death to the *Unity of the Faith*!' Everyone in Bologna is well aware that Cardinal Consalvi's successor is bound to be a rabid reactionary, and Pius VII is very old indeed; nevertheless, under the Papal *régime*, no government official can ever be sacked from his post; and this security permits a degree of independence which would make our own poor Civil Servants rub their eyes in disbelief.[1]

Mr Bysshe-Shelley*, that great poet, that man of such extraordinary qualities, at once so good and so unspeakably maligned, who permitted me to share the honour of his company on this visit, assured me that signor Mezzofante speaks English as faultlessly as he speaks French. At present, my daily pilgrimage takes me to the *Municipal Museum*, where I stand and gaze in wonder at Raphael's *Santa Cecilia*, at a Francia or two, and at eight or ten masterpieces from the brush of Domenichino and Guido Reni. There are some quite astounding *colour-effects* in the *Death of St Peter Martyr*, who, after he himself had perpetrated numberless atrocities, was struck down on the 6th of April 1252, near Barlassina. But I should find twenty pages scarce sufficient were I to pay adequate tribute to this admirable Bolognese school, which, for some reason that I cannot fathom, is out of fashion with our present arbiters of taste. When a noble genius is dead, and thus embarked at last upon posterity, what cares *he* for these half-century fluctuations, which alternately set him high upon the peak of fashion, only to leave him floundering and mis-understood? Not forty years ago, even the great Dante, today adored throughout the length and breadth of Italy, was esteemed no better than a bore and a barbarian; and what is there to show that by the year 2000 A.D. he may not be doomed to another century or two of neglect? This evening, in the charming company which gathers about signor degli Antonj,

1 *Cf.* M. Delandine, at Lyon. [1826]

I became aware that my particular taste for the Bolognese school was highly gratifying to the *municipal vanity* of the region. I had resolved, if necessary, to brazen it out with bare-faced lying, lest I make myself a host of enemies, as in Milan; yet it was a mighty relief to find that lies are not required. I chattered on and on about art like a magpie; and it was only when I had been at it for an hour or so that I observed that my companion and listener was an ecclesiastic, *ma di quelli fatti per il cappello.* Yet, all in all, he seemed not ill-pleased with me; he is *aide-de-camp* to Cardinal Lante, who is Papal Legate in Bologna, or in other terms, the *Grand Pasha* himself! Amongst other matters, which elsewhere in Italy might smack of liberty and danger, my prelate said to me:

'Pius VI *knew how to rule.* Called to exercise the sovereign authority over a State which is of necessity pacific and immune from threat of war, he knew how to discern the one over-mastering passion which possessed his subjects during that portion of the century which chance had allotted to furnish him the intoxicating delights of power.'

'True enough', added someone else, 'yet not one among the present sovereigns in the land can boast so much intelligence. They snap their fingers, one and all, at their heirs and successors; yet they invite the jeers of the crowd, and sacrifice their own popularity to a future which they themselves are incapable of foreseeing and whose course they cannot hope to alter.'

'In spite of all his pettiness and vanity', pursued my *monsignore*, 'in spite of the ecstasy with which he would contemplate his own well-moulded leg; in spite of the notorious embezzlement of the Lepri inheritance; in spite, finally, of the eighteen thousand murders which disfigured a reign of five-and-twenty years—ah yes! in spite of these, Pius VI *knew how to rule.*'

'Consalvi likewise *knows how to rule*; but God alone knows what lies in store for us after Pius VII!'

'We shall be worse off than in Spain', interposed a lawyer, a man of ardent temper and of the most original cast of mind, coming up to join our circle.

'If one could only fall asleep, like Epimenides, for eighty years or so', added an author, 'then, when at last one woke up, one would surely find every nation in Europe governed like America—the sober government of *economics*.'

'I love to listen to you word-spinners', concluded my *monsignore* in a burst of laughter, 'prophesying *democracy* and yearning for universal suffrage—when the first undoubted act of such a government would be to cast into the fire all ideologies devised before its coming!'

Such, in Bologna, is the tone of conversation; ideas are bandied back and forth as boldly and as freely as in London— but with this difference, that what is philosophical and flat beside the Thames is entertaining in Bologna. Moreover, many a doubtfully aristocratic observation which passes muster in Bologna would cause no common scandal amidst the well-bred company of Portland Place.

The Italian still retains an antique passion for Latin quotations; French is unknown south of the Apennine. Signora Lambertini embarked freely and in my hearing upon the whole saga which ended in the elevation of Pope Pius VII, and upon the sequence of coincidences which embraced a simple Friar and set him on the throne of the Vatican. I would be glad to relate the whole adventure, which redounds not a little to the credit of the Sovereign concerned, were I sure that my publisher dare print it. The trick of fortune which brought Cardinal Chiaramonte into the gardens of *San Giorgio* in Venice at the precise moment when Cardinals Albano and Mattei chanced to be strolling there together, and thus led him directly to the Triple Tiara, is a tale to console the ambitions of every humble priest.

Here, at least, is the story of the Lepri affair, as it was reported to me by *il cavaliere* Tambroni.

Signora Lepri was renowned as one of the loveliest women in Rome. Now, about this time, it came to pass that her

G

husband, the *marchese* Lepri, died; and she, upon the instant that the news was brought to her, declared that she was pregnant. The infant daughter to whom, nine months to the day after her husband's death, she gave birth, was her first-born child. Now the *marchese* Lepri had a younger brother, who, finding himself cheated of an enormous fortune by the singular circumstances attending on the birth of this child, let it be rumoured that the *marchesa* had entertained a lover, yet never, while her husband had remained alive, had wholly forgotten her duty and obedience. Such pacts are not uncommon in the land of Italy. Whatever the truth of the matter may have been, young Lepri, out of pure spite and fury, entered the Church, and by a solemn deed and covenant made over to Pope Pius VI all rights which might devolve upon himself in the matter of his brother's inheritance. The world then beheld the edifying spectacle of Pope Pius VI in person disputing, before a tribunal of his own judges, the inheritance of the *marchesa*'s infant daughter. One or two among those courtiers devoted to his better interests made so bold as to suggest to him that malicious tongues might perchance make capital out of such procedure; but nobly came the Pope's retort: '*Five million isn't made for spitting at!*' Unfortunately, it had slipped his memory that the *avvocati rotari* cast their votes in secret. A majority of Judges on the tribunal had kept sufficient rags of conscience to let the verdict go against their Sovereign; but the Papal police soon ferreted out the names of those whose honesty was inconvenient; and they promptly received injunctions nevermore to show their faces in the Law Courts—a ban which was indeed no trifling matter, since the senior Judge on this tribunal might normally expect to receive a Cardinal's Hat. The *Hat* is the life-blood and hope of every ecclesiastic in Rome; his credit wanes or waxes in the world, accordingly as his chances of preferment are seen to increase or to diminish. After this notable instance of severity, the Pope appealed to a second tribunal, which proved less rigid in integrity than the *Rota*. A portion of the *marchese* Lepri's property fell to the lot of Prince Braschi, Pope Pius' nephew, whom we beheld in Paris about 1810; Napoleon had made him a *Baron of the Empire*. It is rumoured that the Lepri family is likely soon to be empowered to recover its estates. In physical appearance, Pope Pius VI was not a whit less noble than in moral stature: handsome but *vulgar*. Not even Canova could endow that head with an aura of nobility, for all that, by this time, it had been sanctified by misfortune.[1] None the less, Pope Pius VI *knew how to rule*; and so his passing is regretted.

30th December. Bitter indeed is the scorn which the humble *bourgeois* inspires in the heart of the Piedmontese aristocrat. In Milan, this contempt lies dormant, yet ever darkly smouldering; in Bologna, however, it is all but extinct, for after all, the poorest of cobbler's sons may enter the Church, and climb in the footsteps of Pope Pius VII to the heights of St Peter's throne.

The papacy being a *lottery*, this chance of power appeals to the populace and reconciles it to the papal rule, which, by rights, should be the most detested government in Europe. In its *moderation* lies its only hope of survival. In the eyes of the average Italian priest, as indeed in the belief of all the lower orders of society, each and every phenomenon in this world of ours is a miraculous effect of Providence; nothing depends upon the natural interplay of elements, nothing springs from the logical pattern of secondary causes. When a convent-full of little girls lie sick of poisoning, from having eaten food out of faultily-galvanised copper dishes, does anyone dream of calling in a doctor? Instead, the inmates fall a-praying. Not an iota of power here escapes from the hands of the priests. Laymen, be they dukes or princes, are as nothing in the land.

1 See the statue of Pius VI, which stands before the High Altar of St Peter's, Rome. Raphael Mengs has introduced a portrait of signora Lepri among the figures which throng his mediocre fresco entitled *Parnassus*, at the *villa Albani*. [1826]

Well, imagine then, some peasant lad, some cobbler's son, not over-bright perhaps, even in the first instance, who by-and-by becomes a student in theology, and spends ten mortal years in learning to manipulate a load of *words* to answer every question under the sun—what mind ever created could emerge un-warped from such a schooling? My own private wonder is not that they are mad, but that they are not madder. Assuming our scholar to be an honest man and a true believer, with no propensities for intrigue, he remains a harmless ignoramus all his life, But one day, along comes a Cardinal Consalvi, scouring the land for ignorance allied with virtue—and so our oaf becomes a Cardinal himself, and next a Papal Legate, or in other words a despot with unlimited command. He is bound to respect no one, obey no authority, save only the Bishop or Archbishop of his Province, neither of whom may likely prove to be a whit less ignorant than himself. In Bologna, the Vice-Legate of the region is one Monsignor Pandolfi, whose un-sullied virtue and unspeakable imbecility are the common gossip of the town.

Without the saving grace of moderation, all would be lost. Monsignor *** may be a doddering moron; but he lets things take their natural course; and indeed, the fell disease which, for two centuries past, has gradually been dilapidating and depopulating the Papal States is nothing more contagious than chronic *stagnation*. Happy the Province whose Legate is an energetic scoundrel! He may harbour a multitude of vicious caprices; he may be a thief; he may blatantly defy the laws, in order to crush his private enemies; but at the same time his ever-active mind may spur him on to build a causeway, construct a bridge, or enact a decree which his subjects have been clamouring for in vain for half a century.

The spiritual collapse which follows hard upon physical degeneration has been staved off, for a while at least, by the efforts of the good citizens of Bologna, who, by nature being gifted with nimble minds and a quick intelligence, were able to grasp the import of Napoleon's unique abilities—for all that they caught no more than distant glimpses of the genius of this great commander, whose brilliance was often dimmed by the incapacity of his administrators. By dint of their own incompetence, the latter eventually goaded the Bolognese into open rebellion—an event which happened in the year 1809, unless I am mistaken. A blunder of such magnitude deserved to occasion a hundred resounding dismissals from the service; but Napoleon was in Vienna at the time, fully preoccupied with the battle of Wagram, which he was to win *by the skin of his teeth*; Spain was giving rise to anxiety; there was Hungary to be handed over to the Archduke Charles, etc. . . .

The Bolognese, as far as I can judge, have far more intelligence, more enthusiasm and more originality than the Milanese; above all, they are far less mistrustful. I have been here no more than a fortnight; yet in this short season I have already been granted the freedom of more *salons* in which to spend an evening than I would have acquired by living in Milan for three whole years. But the laws of love are not the laws of reason; my soul has been enslaved by the gentle and informal manners of Milan. Here, every gesture and every anecdote is a sharp reminder of the perversity of the human race; in Milan, I had forgotten that such perversity existed. I doubt whether, in all Milan, there exists a woman with such a brilliant gift of repartee as that which distinguishes Princess Lambertini; yet more than one has given a rarer gift of happiness to her lover. And *this*—with due apologies to all our fair philosophers and mystics—this, within the bounds of virtue, is the only true thermometer to test a woman's worth.

The spirit of Venice is too brittle, too heartless and too *flippant*. Bologna offers a warmth of sympathy and a wealth of imagination in ideal proportions—the perfect blend, as I believe, to produce the rare quintessence of *wit*. Yet I, most likely, am a biased judge: I think too contemptuously of that style of wit which may be learnt by heart.

31st December. I am still suffering from a heavy surfeit of ecclesiastical pomp and circumstance. On the first day of the Carnival, which falls on December 26th, even the smallest of Italian cities may boast its own opera; yet in Bologna, the priesthood, which once upon a time, in 1740 or thereabouts, was so unstinting in its patronage of music, has been transformed, ever since the day Napoleon appeared to prod the land of Italy into wakefulness, into a congregation of pleasure-hating puritans, in consequence of whose machinations the city, under one pretext or another, *still* awaits its promised opera. The *première*, so they say, will take place within eight or ten days. I am thirsting for music; an evening without music is somehow, to me, a thing of desiccated weariness. Admittedly, there are charming concerts here every Sunday morning down at the *Casino*; but I have always sensed something *pretentious* about concerts*; the mere mastery of technical difficulties seems to me a shabby sort of triumph. The true concert-goer should be a man who, at will, can tune his own soul to seven or eight varying pitches of emotion, like an actor.

The only serious musical experience I have yet encountered in Bologna came to me through the entrancing voice of signor Trentanove, a young sculptor whom I met in the house of signora Filicori, a woman of uncommon intelligence and still more uncommon beauty: on which occasion, alone and unaided, he sang a duet.

I have recently had forwarded to me from Berlin a manuscript which contains a score of anecdotes about Napoleon—all true, all appositely chosen, and not a one written by the sort of flunkey who composes the abject, servile stuff that finds its way into print. I sent off for this manuscript in order that I might have it by me to lend out upon occasion, after a suitable amount of cajoling. This manner of flirtation with Italian women affords me unparalleled delight. A born intriguer, so the saying goes, is a man who loves intrigue for its own sweet sake, regardless of the object to be gained. In this same vein of disinterestedness I adore to meddle in the secrets of Italian women, who are the most uniquely feminine of all the fair sex under heaven, and poles apart from those desiccated males-in-miniature who throng the streets of Paris. After a whole week of pretty supplications, and with many dark hints as to the dangers with which my compliance might be fraught, I eventually lent the precious manuscript to signora Ottofredi. Unfortunately, however, this tiny volume with its exquisite binding encloses three or four passages so badly written as to be illegible; and, to add to the disaster, these tortuous hiero-glyphics occur towards the end, at the climax of the most fascinating anecdotes. Thus it occurred that I found myself summoned in person to decipher the recalcitrant script; and so I had the pleasure of finding myself deep in the *sancta sanctorum*, in a secret conclave of eight Italian women, no lover being present and only one husband to keep watch. The general curiosity knew no bounds, and so I allowed myself to be beguiled into telling of two curious adventures so secret and so fraught with danger that I dare not keep them about me in any written form. . . . The third day after the curtain had gone up upon this private comedy of mine, in which I played the villain with impertinent delight, signora Ottofredi con-fided to me: 'I must show you a letter which I once received from a relative of mine, who lives not far from Naples.' What follows now is an abridged translation of this private document:

Lucera, 12th May 1816

Signora Marchesina, my own very dear Cousin,

Here is a tale to amuse you; Heaven alone knows when I may discover means to post it to you, but chance will find a way. I am still deeply affected by the emotions which possess the hero of this adventure; and even I myself, *debolmente*, had a part allotted to me in the drama. This morning, at half past three, as I was strolling homeward—as luck would have it, alone—in the first faint light of dawn, I chanced to find myself in a position to render signal service to don Niccola S***, of whom you have already heard. He is a young aristocrat, the most notable in all the Two Sicilies, handsome and eloquent; but this morning he was too upset to reserve even the more intimate circumstances of his situation to himself.

There is in Naples a noble household known to all the realm—known likewise to yourself, *carissima marchesina*— no less for its estate than for its lineage. The family consists of an old man of seventy, yet still active, full of vigour and severity; his wife, a lady of astute, suspicious mind, prouder than a queen of her noble rank, once beautiful, now pious as a nun; and finally, their daughter, an exquisite child of some seventeen or eighteen summers, the living image of the *Madonna* owned by the *marchese* Rinucci. I often speak with her. In all the Kingdom, there is no creature of more resplendent beauty; but the ruling character of her mind, which lends a stamp of strange and, in this land, most *rare* enchantment to her features, is an expression of peerless serenity, even to the point of loving-kindness. This is a phenomenon which I have never observed in Rome. Often in conversation with donna Fulvia, a close friend of the family, I expressed wonder that Lauretta, being now eighteen and still unmarried, should have no lover—for eighteen, here in Naples, makes four-and-twenty in Bologna. A week ago perhaps, or rather less, when friends were gathered for the evening in the *salon* of Lauretta's father, Prince C***lo, this same donna Fulvia remarked to me:

'You can hardly fail to be aware that Prince C***lo is a man to stand no nonsense. Observe that he keeps in his house no fewer than *five* of his nephews, all of whom were actively involved in the varied course of our Revolution. One and all are valiant patriots, great swashbuckling bravos, rarely missing a day in the fencing-school, always loud in praise of their own prowess. These five brothers are desperately boorish in normal company; but to a would-be lover they might prove decidedly inconvenient. They are ardent admirers of their uncle's attitude and spirit; and they have appointed themselves, in their own interests, the watch-dogs of their fair cousin, who makes malicious sport of them from dawn to dusk. They are fully persuaded that the bright honour of their noble race would be forever tarnished, should she take herself a lover.'

I have observed, *ornatissima marchesina*, that such an attitude is extremely common among the aristocracy of Naples, which, in this, is very different from our own, and seemingly rooted in barbarism. Donna Fulvia reminded me that donna Lauretta's five strapping cousins had each an apartment within the walls of her father's *palazzo*; and that any rash suitor who was bold enough to set foot inside the fortress would surely leave his life behind; he would find five swords arrayed against him; six maybe, since it was quite in character for old Prince C***lo to draw his sword against the intruder himself, or, if the weight of years lay too heavily upon his shoulders, to have the unhappy lover brutally beaten to death, particularly if the victim were less noble than himself. Yet, in spite of all these arguments brought forward by a woman of such intelligence, whose sharp observation let nothing escape her, I confess that I placed little faith in her assurance. The laws of nature may not be defied with impunity, particularly in a region such as this, whose shores lie close to Africa. The serenity and contentment which greeted me in the girl's expression were ill-assorted with some inward conflict. In this uncertainty, and seeing that my age afforded me protection from her cousins' jealousy, I have for some months past made an open bid for each occasion to talk with donna Lauretta. She, with her lively, curious and most original turn of mind, would keep my plied with endless questions about England, and about that city of Paris which she loved, while I would lend her the novels of Walter Scott—in brief, we fell not short of matter for conversation. She never lacked some original observation to impart to me, some pertinent comment on the books that she had been reading. I am a fervent admirer of her beauty, and make no secret of it to myself. And so it came about that this morning, towards three o'clock, as I was strolling homeward—alone, as fortune would have it—I was accosted by don Niccola so brusquely that for an instant I thought it was a robber. All day long I have been running errands for him; I have paid a score of visits; for the essential business lay in discovering what ripples had been stirred in the common gossip of this little town of ours by one particular incident the night before.

Now here is the tale which don Niccola told me, in order to enlighten my ignorance—the narrative being enhanced by such a spate of burning words and such a wealth of picturesque gesture as to be decidedly comic. We stood talking by the early light of dawn, in the secrecy of my private garden; he was pale, and indeed looked quite extraordinarily handsome. He bears some slight resemblance to Mazzochi, the notorious chieftain of the *banditti*.

'From the very first day which marked the enslavement of my soul', he began, 'now more than two years since, I was persuaded beyond doubt that my love for Lauretta would end in disaster. She is watched over by her cousins and her father with unparalleled severity, and more closely than your wildest imaginings could ever conceive. On two or three occasions, I sensed a sudden iciness between Prince C***lo and myself, he suspecting that I had cast glances at his daughter; for, as you know, I am so poor that marriage with so wealthy an heiress is not to be dreamed of; yet Lauretta's mother, to whom I have the honour to be distantly related, has always been gracious enough to take my part. A further factor is that I alone can boast sufficient skill at the chess-board to be a fitting opponent for the Prince. Donna Lauretta is pious, and has never been known to miss a single office of devotion; I, therefore, saw fit to feign political ambitions. I allowed all my acquaintance to suspect that I was determined to obtain some diplomatic employment in the service of the Court, that I was tired of living in my native land; and so, in view of such ambitions, it was to be expected that I should spend my days haunting the precincts of divers churches.

'The Prince, as you are aware, holds his receptions in a lofty marble *salon* presided over by the statue of Philip II. To reach this room, the visitor must first cross a lesser Antechamber, and then pass through the great Antechamber of Honour, with its frieze of sculptures—those Spanish Admirals and Viceroys who dignify the illustrious family tree. In this lesser Antechamber, a cupboard has been hollowed out in the thickness of the wall, which servants use to stack their sweeping-brooms. Leading out from the right-hand wall of the greater Antechamber with its statues, and exactly facing the doorway to the marble *salon*, one finds two further rooms whose doors are never fastened, and which communicate eventually with the bedchamber of the Prince and Princess. This latter room leads directly into that in which their daughter sleeps. Now every night, an ancient waiting-woman belonging to the Princess enters the bedchamber when her mistress is in bed with her husband, shifts an immense ivory Crucifix four-and-a-half feet tall towards the bed-foot, double-locks the chamber door, removes the key and places it beneath the Prince's pillow, sprinkles a few drops of Holy Water on the bed, and retires finally to her own abode, which lies next door to donna Lauretta's bedroom. Some eighteen months ago, one special gala evening, when a great reception was being held as a welcome to the officers of some Austrian regiment which

had been newly transferred from Naples, I seized a favourable instant to whisper in the ear of donna Lauretta:

'*Tonight, I propose to hide in the broom-cupboard; as soon
as your father is asleep, I shall scratch at the door of his chamber;
you must steal the key from underneath his pillow and let me in.*'

'*Don't you dare. . . !*'

'*I shall be waiting at the door towards one o'clock.*'

'Time allowed me no further conversation. I doubt
whether I had spoken to her of my love more than four
times in all; yet I had observed that she seemed not ill-
inclined to listen to my protestations, and that she was still
more deeply impressed by the eminent sacrifice which I had
made in giving out that I was ambitious to seek service
with the infamous Court of His Majesty King F***d—a
sacrifice involving all my pride and honour, for, as you are
aware, I would rather serve Death itself.

'Be this as it may, that evening I left the reception earlier
than all the guests, and succeeded without difficulty in
concealing myself in the broom-cupboard. If ever you were
in love yourself, imagine the fit of trembling which seized
me in every limb as, towards one o'clock in the morning,
when every creak within the house had long been stilled,
I screwed up my courage and crept towards that awesome
bedchamber—where the aged Prince C***lo might, or
might *not*, be sound asleep—with every intention of scratching at the door. *The key of his chamber-door must be immense*,
I muttered to myself when I reached the spot; for the key-
hole of the antique lock was so vast that I could plainly
observe everything that happened inside the room. Moreover, to my unspeakable amazement and terror, I realised
that the chamber was not dark; a night-light had been left
burning at the foot of the great Crucifix. For an eternity
I remained undecided. At long last, my passion for Lauretta
overcame my fears; I persuaded myself that I had detected
a snore coming from the Prince, and I began to tap gently

against the door. The bedchamber where Lauretta's parents slept was of huge proportions; Lauretta's own room lay infinitely distant. For fully half an hour I persevered; until finally, just when I was on the point of abandoning my ungrateful Lauretta, and of bidding an eternal farewell to the land where I was born, I was vouchsafed the unbearable happiness of seeing her appear. She was in her night-clothes, barefooted and with her hair unloosed, and a thousand, thousand times more beautiful than I had dared imagine. She crept softly towards her father's bed, to make sure that he was sleeping soundly; and I, observing that her progress was more halt than motion, made bold to risk another series of taps. Gentle as they were, each sound reverberated in my heart. I feared desperately lest I should fall to the ground in a faint. At long last, I watched Lauretta move towards the door; she put her lips close to the hole in the lock, and whispered:

'*Are you mad, then? Go away!*'

'*How should I go away?*' I answered. '*I cannot escape from this house. Would you refuse to speak to me? For three mortal weeks I have been unable to exchange a word with you. All I ask is fifteen minutes' conversation, whether here in the Antechamber, or else with you in your bedroom.*' I spent fully half an hour persuading her; but finally she resolved to go and steal the key from where it lay beneath her father's pillow. I whispered her a warning:

'*If the Prince awakens, he will kill you.*'

'*Perhaps not*', she answered as she moved away.

'When she came back, the key was in her hand; but the door was double-locked, and the lock itself was of an antique pattern, stiff with rust. At each revolution of the key, the echoes seemed so monstrous that I expected to die of fright. Were it not that you have already honoured me with compliments concerning my behaviour in this morning's alarm, I would not dare impart to you such details, lest you should

take me for a plain coward. But at last the door was opened;
I slipped inside the bedchamber. The harsh features of the
Prince lay uncovered on the pillow, and his face lay turned
towards me as I tip-toed across the floor. Lauretta remained
behind, relocked the door and replaced the key. No one
who is not himself in love—in love actually here and now—
can conceive the boundless terror which I felt at each of these
minute disturbances; to be adrift at sea in a rowing-boat at
the heart of a raging storm could convey no more than the
faintest echo of the sensations which possessed me. Discovery
probably meant that nevermore in all my life should I be
allowed a glimpse of Lauretta. Safe at last in her room, I
bowed my head before a torrent of reproaches; once more
I stood in danger of losing her for ever, of leaving both my
mistress and my native land. We argued bitterly until the
first light of dawn; yet in her heart she loved me.

'There was an altar in Lauretta's room, enclosed by two
tall portals, like an alcove; here she hid me. Towards noon,
after the footmen had swept out all the rooms, I, hearing no
further noise, slipped softly back along the way I had come
the night before, until I reached the greater Antechamber.
Here I changed my gait to one of boldly-ringing footsteps,
and went to pay a call upon one of the cousins.

'On several nights I came to her by this perilous route;
but shortly afterwards, Lauretta, whose love was growing
daily stronger, having gazed too intently at me across the
church, there was imminent danger that her family, stung
to jealousy, would request me never to cross their threshold
again.

'At this juncture it occurred to us that I might ascend by
way of the balcony which lay outside her window. The
first consideration was secrecy: in such a god-forsaken little
town, where everybody knew his neighbour's business, and
where the police were busy trying to catch me, there was
no one to be trusted. I journeyed twenty miles to buy a

length of rope from a fisherman; but instead of making it into a proper ladder, I merely set knots at intervals throughout its length, and left it at that. Lauretta's window was set fully fifty feet above the ground; choosing a moonless night, I appeared beneath the balcony an hour after midnight; Lauretta threw down a thread for me to catch, pulled the rope up to the balcony and made it fast; and I began to climb.

'But this balcony, which formed part of a marvellously ornate façade, was heavily decorated with carvings, and jutted out much further from the perpendicular plane of the wall than I had anticipated. Every time I attempted to get purchase against the wall with my feet, I found myself swung outwards, and hung helpless in the air for minutes on end. I could feel my muscles weakening, and I was conscious of an appalling pain between my shoulder-blades. By this time, I was all of forty feet above the ground. *I shall slip*, I thought to myself. *My body will be shattered by the fall; I shall never manage to drag myself away; tomorrow I shall be found beneath Lauretta's window; our love is already half-suspected; she will be eternally dishonoured.* It was a fearful instant. She was leaning over the balustrade, looking down at me from the balcony; I called out to her softly: '*My strength is gone, I can climb no higher.*'

'*Courage! You must have courage!*' she answered.

'I managed three more knots; then suddenly my strength gave way completely; I was done for. '*Just one more knot!*' she cried out to me, leaning so far out over the rail of the balcony that I could feel the warmth of her breath upon my cheek. I believe that it was this sensation which gave me strength; by a miracle, I ascended this one last knot. My shoulders were splitting open with the agony of it. And in the instant while I rested after this supreme effort, and realised once and for all that this was the end of my endeavours, I felt a hand entwined in the hair of my head; and Lauretta, with a strength unthinkable in a mere girl of eighteen, hauled me bodily to safety on the balcony. At this moment in time, she had a greater strength than any man. But plainly the ascent was too risky, and we never used this route again; instead, I resorted to my old, familiar hiding-place in the broom-cupboard. One evening, one of the guests having dropped a water-ice upon the floor of the *salon*, don Cecchino, one of the cousins, came out to fetch a broom. In the darkness, the first object that he seized upon was my arm; and by what miracle he failed to notice that what he held was not a wooden handle, I have never been able to discover. His sweeping-up completed, he started back towards the cupboard; but on this occasion he had a candle with him. *This time it really* is *the end*, I thought, trying to occupy as small a space as possible; but at that instant, chancing to encounter one of his brothers, he turned to talk to him; and all the while, with the candle-stick held in one hand, he was stacking the broom back in the cupboard with the other.

'This same don Cecchino took a passionate fancy to music, and night after night he would sit up until two o'clock, massacring Cimarosa on the English piano in the great reception-room. It was three o'clock before Lauretta dared open up the door; and since the month was June, by four o'clock it was already light. Eventually, after a dragging month of hints and insinuations, we managed to persuade the Princess that her favourite piano was steadily being ruined by the thumping fists of don Cecchino.'

'And did you frequently venture on these risky assignations?' I enquired of don Niccola.

'At first, no more than once a week; later on, as frequently as three days hard on end, or at the worst, not seldomer than every other day. Towards the last, our whole lives lay sacrificed to these clandestine meetings; our love left no room for any alien thoughts, and the very proximity of death seemed to add new lustre to our joy.'

'And every time, that same door with its creaking double-lock to be unlatched, scarcely twenty paces from her parents' bed?'

'Invariably. In fact, we grew so bold that we would walk together through the room as nonchalantly as though we were alone. Once, for all her protests, I managed to kiss her then and there, right in the middle of the chamber, and in the act, knocked over the great ivory Crucifix. On another occasion, one of her waiting-women came to fetch some undergarment from somewhere in her chest-of-drawers—the same which formed the base of the private altar that stood within her room. And all the while, there was I, perched on top of it, stiff and motionless, against the blackened altar-piece which hung behind; it is true that I was dressed in black; yet how the woman could fail to lift her glance and see me, completely passes my comprehension. Perhaps, since donna Lauretta is universally adored in this stiff-necked, unrelenting household, the waiting-woman had grown *deliberately* blind. Who knows, but that the Princess herself had spotted us as we crept across her room at night; and yet, pondering upon the double tragedy which inevitably must follow if she voiced her doubts, had deemed it wiser to keep silent?—whatever the truth may be, her gaze when she meets me is a fathomless well of deep, repressed hatred. And yet invariably all went well, until this morning, when I was as good as lost . . .'

(I should do a grave disservice to my book, were I to publish the conclusion of this tale.)

1st January 1817.   I, who had grown firmly convinced of the high intelligence of the Bolognese, now find myself in imminent peril of having to eat my own words. For ninety unrelenting minutes I have been subjected to an eruption of *backstairs patriotism* of the most imbecile variety—and in the best of company at that! This is indeed the besetting sin of Italy, and the defeats of Murat seem only to have aggravated the disease. The fact is that in Naples, as in Spain, the distance which separates *Society* from the lower classes is inordinately great, whereas, by contrast with Spain, the *hoi-polloi* of Naples, pampered by the serenity of the climate, is not of fighting stock; for (so the people argue), 'if I am in the right, *San Gennaro cannot fail to slay the hosts of them that contemn me*'. Signor Filangieri and a hundred like-tempered officers may be paragons of valour; but to what effect? Their own troops sprayed them with musket-shot through the door of their room, because they tried to prevent their regiments from turning tail in the face of the enemy.[1]

You may remember that, in the year 1763 or thereabouts, a tragedy entitled *le Siège de Calais* enjoyed a wild, unparalleled, most *patriotic* success. The dramatist, du Belloy, was visited by the lucrative inspiration, since exploited by many another, of flattering his fellow-citizens. The duc d'Ayen, having dared one day to cast aspersions on this piece of bombast, was soundly rebuked for his impertinence by the King himself:

'Are you ashamed to be known as *French*, my lord?' demanded Louis XV.

'Please God, Sire, that our poet's tragic verse might feel as little shame as I* !'

It was the philosophic Turgot, a man who loved his country, and considered flattery to be 'a form of intercourse between a knave and a fool', who once coined the phrase *backstairs patriot-*

---

1 There is no country, no army in the world, whose honour had not acquired a brighter lustre from the life and death of signor di Santa-Rosa. Shortly after his heroic martyrdom, I made a first attempt*, within the measure of my own feeble powers, to prophesy how this great man would stand in general repute a hundred years from now. If the present work had proved less paradoxical and more portentous, I should gladly have dedicated it to the memory of this illustrious son of Italy. It is my sincere wish that those among his compatriots who share his ideals, yet whom I dare not name for fear of compromising them, may find in these lines a token of my heart-felt veneration. All honour to the land whose sons include a Santa-Rosa and a Rossarol* ! [1826]

ism* to describe the infatuation of those who stood and gaped in wonderment before the crudely-fashioned compliments of Sieur du Belloy.

Bonaparte himself numbered among du Belloy's disciples, when, having designs to fasten chains of servitude upon the land of France, he addressed the French as a *mighty nation*—a gambit of whose adroitness he was inordinately proud. He was of the opinion that it was *shameful* for an historian to admit the reverses of his own nation, or the injustices of which it had been guilty.[1]

In Italy, no talent, however slender, need lie beyond the protecting wing of some form of regional patriotism; for, after all, no pedant is so dull, but that he must have been born *somewhere*. Whereas, in France, if a prophet is without honour, it is above all in his own country.

In Bologna, it would take more courage than I possess to hint that Mr Astley (of Bond Street) makes better boots than signor Ronchetti—a well-known shoe-maker of the city, renowned for his love of paintings no less than for his dauntless stand against Murat. Murat had ventured to observe that no one outside Paris understood how to make a pair of boots fit to be worn; in revenge, Ronchetti refused point-blank to make him a complete pair. The *King of Naples*, having approved one boot by trying it on, demanded its fellow. 'Have it made in *Paris*, Sire!' retorted Ronchetti.

The least breath of *published* criticism against his local poet or sculptor will set any Italian in a towering rage—a fury whose expression outstrips the most elementary bounds of decency. Italy is the garden of Europe, while her frontiers enclose the ruins of all the grandeur that was Rome; in consequence, not

---

1 The theory of *backstairs patriotism*, as we see it daily applied in practice respecting any *prima donna** born outside the frontiers of France, can be found, complete down to the last detail, in Virgil:

> . . . *Pallas quas condidit arces*
> *Ipsa colat: nobis placeant ante omnia silvae* . . .
>
> *Eclogues II.* [1826]

a year passes without witnessing the publication of eight or ten more or less dubious travelogues in Paris, London or Leipzig—each separately destined to prove a new thorn in the ticklish side of local patriotism. Yet this anger is perhaps not as absurd as might appear at first. In a country where the dreariest of *Almanachs* is subjected to five or six forms of censorship, any man who is censured *in print* may be assumed to have *forfeited the favour of the Pasha*. Henceforward, he is doomed; the lowest of the low may heap coals of fire upon his head. The truth or falsehood of the accusation is irrelevant: provided that it appear *in print*, the damage has been done.

In England or in France, any such frenzied resentment of criticism is inconceivable. In both these countries, the *Pasha* is nothing more fearful than a *Préfet* or a *Sheriff*; the citizens ensure their own protection; and since each day gives birth to a hundred libels, since *Whigs* and *Tories* greet each other with constant and reciprocal broadsides of libel, no mere accusation is dangerous, unless it be also *satirical*, in the devastating vein of Voltaire in pursuit of Larcher, or of Beaumarchais in full cry after Marin the Censor, 'drawn in his coach-and-four along the highroad to Versailles'.

Vanity being non-existent in Italy, a *marchese* finds outlet for his anger in more or less the same language as his lackey.

This is the darker side of the picture, the reverse effect of that conspicuous good fortune which has enriched the land of Italy with a *natural* and *powerful* poetic tradition. Italy has escaped the burden of a century and a half of tyranny exercised by a disdainful oligarchy—a *Court* established by a man deep-versed in the art of vanity. Louis XIV stole away the *judgment* of his subjects, and put it in his pocket; instead, he gave each class a *model* fit for it to emulate; Molière created comedy out of anyone so bold as to defy the despotism of convention; *originality* became synonymous with *boorishness*.

The Court of Louis XIV outlawed as *bad taste* any expression whose earthy precision gained it general currency, 'purified' and impoverished the language, refused point-blank to call a spade a spade; in the end, M. l'abbé Delille was reduced to writing exclusively in riddles. The popular *grands boulevards* are incontestably the finest walks in Paris; but unhappily there is no restriction upon who may use them. *We*, therefore, thanks to Louis XIV, whose living law still governs us today, may not enjoy them, but only visit now and then, for a quick dip into the shops. The hand of the Great Monarch, whose weight is felt in Russia and in Germany no less than in England, has left no traces of its presence in Italy. No *Italian* despot has ever succeeded in dictating the laws of taste; hence the thousand advantages that Italy is heir to; but hence also the darker side of the picture—the wrathful *marchese* mouthing foul indecencies, the boors whose boorishness is more insufferable than anywhere else on earth. Hence also the fearsome barriers which obstruct the doors of Milanese society; for, should the intruder prove a *boor*, how is he to be got rid of?

My own private advice to the reader, should he resolve to journey on the road to Rome, is *never to criticise anything*, and to establish clearly that he suffers from sudden and unpredictable headaches. Thus, as soon as he espies a threat of *backstairs patriotism*, his head may begin to ache, and he can vanish. I have encountered no woman of rarer beauty, loftier mind or more luminous intelligence than signora M***; yet even she was not a stranger to this fault*. Utterly devoid of petty vanity on her own account, she was nevertheless sensitive about the locality where she was born; the least breath of criticism involving her beloved birth-place would set her blushing. I fell into this most impolitic of blunders myself on one occasion; whereupon, as an experiment, I altered tactics and ventured, with a frankness scarcely usual in a mere acquaintance, to offer criticism of herself; she answered my rebukes with truth and candour, yet without the slightest deepening of colour to mar the most peerless complexion I have seen in all the land of Italy.

The army which was built up by Napoleon brought together in the same company the sober citizen of Reggio and the carefree *busecon* of Milan, the frowning Novarese and the devil-may-care Venetian; from which confusion of races and temperaments there emerged two consequences:

(i) The creation of a new language: the bravest troops having been recruited (so I am assured) from the Romagna, *romagnol* dialect forms began to outweigh the rest.

(ii) The internecine rivalries and the outbursts of *backstairs patriotism*, which for centuries had kept each city estranged from its neighbours, were rapidly beginning to evaporate in the ranks of the army. This was told me for a fact by my friend, the valiant Colonel Wideman, scion of a noble family in Venice.

2nd January. I mentioned my reflections concerning Louis XIV to Count K***, the most attractive Pole I have ever met, and that is saying a good deal. 'It is no longer Philip II', I added, 'but rather Louis XIV who furnishes the pattern upon which every petty German princeling desires to *model* his behaviour—not to mention every English duke!'

'*Model* is certainly the correct word', replied Count K***. 'A wealthy landowner, whose estates lie not a hundred leagues from Riga, has recently built on to his already considerable residence an immense projecting block, whose square contours exactly ape the garden façade of the *Château de Versailles*. His mistress rejoices in the title of *Madame de Maintenon*—not once have I heard her referred to by any other form of address. His dinner is announced by a pair of *Chamberlains*, who serve him in splendid isolation at a tiny table, where no other company is ever admitted, save only *Madame de Maintenon*. On Sundays, he holds a gala-ball; on Tuesdays, a grand banquet—the routine is invariable, week in, week out. On gala-nights, two score well-favoured peasant-lads, together with a like number of wenches, selected by rota from among his *serfs*, arrive during the morning at the *Château de Versailles*, ready to be washed and costumed, the men in period court brocades worth a hundred guineas apiece, the women in sumptuous gowns; after which, the whole cast is kept dancing until daybreak, while a quartet of *Chamberlains* order the ceremonial, and watch for any breach of etiquette, lest it appear unseemly at the Court of the *Roi Soleil*. The master of the house, decked in the full regalia of his Orders, makes a tour of the ballroom, exchanging a gracious word with every guest; after which, *Madame de Maintenon* gives permission to strike up the opening quadrille.

'A similar ritual is observed on Tuesdays, on the occasion of the weekly Grand Banquet: the guests at these remarkable functions include a dozen peasants with their wenches, all got up once again in silken finery; and often, in addition, a batch of inquisitve visitors from the nearby garrison. The dinner-plate is of exquisite workmanship; *His Majesty* and *Madame de Maintenon* are served beneath a canopy. The upkeep of such a 'Court' probably costs its master a million francs a year, and my land-owner has the pleasure of living in replica, detail for detail, the life of Louis XIV, in an apartment hung about with Gobelin tapestry.'

I have just emerged from the studio of a painter to whom I had been introducing a group of English visitors. Three young Italian women were already present in the room, who, after persuasion, consented to allow the artist to uncover a certain canvas, previously shrouded in a green dust-sheet, whose subject was admittedly not all that strictest decency could hope for. Unfortunately, the sight of this picture, far from provoking an outburst of moral indignation, set all our fair Italians smiling. The brunt of moral indignation was borne by one of the Englishmen, who confided to us, as we left the studio, that he felt literally, physically sick. Do not believe that I am so unrealistic as to blame a man for *what he feels*. Suffice it that I record the facts. If your uncle gets a sight of this my letter*, he will assert that I am engaged in protecting every cut-throat in the Romagna who thinks it his business to rid the world of an unscrupulous *podestà*. Without modesty, love, the purest passion of the human heart, is inconceivable.

3rd January. This morning, doubtless, you received a letter, and the letter was signed: *Your very humble and most obedient servant*. Your eyes, assuredly, travelled over these words without reading them; it never occurred to you to imagine that the person who penned these sentiments would subsequently offer to brush your suit for you, or clean your boots. Yet a Persian or a Brahmin, having but small acquaintance with the language and none at all with the manners and customs of our nation, could reach no other possible conclusion.

Similarly, the whole range of epithets in -*issimo*, such as *veneratissimo*, *illustrissimo*, etc., must of necessity, in any book printed south of the Alps, be conferred, firstly, upon all dignitaries of greater or lesser standing responsible for governing the Province where the work is published; and secondly, upon every crowned head whose legitimate authority ensures the happiness of some corner of the European continent, or whose erstwhile majesty, within the last century or so, has ascended into Paradise, there to receive the reward of all his virtues.[1] At many levels of society, the absence of this embroidery in -*issimo* is felt besides to be evidence of bad taste and of ill-mannered contempt—as though yourself, this morning, in the letter you were reading, had found a plain and unadorned *Farewell* above the signature.

The -*issimo* formula, in epithets such as *vastissimo*, *mirabilissimo*, is likewise obligatory in referring to the *palazzo*, gardens, paintings and so forth of any member of the aristocracy whose domains lie within a radius of fifty leagues of the locality where the book is published. The residence of every nobleman is a *palazzo*. Every doctor is automatically *chiarissimo*,

---

[1] *Vide* the *History of Milan*, by Pietro Verri. [1826]

or at the very least *egregio*. In a land where the heart knows no
passion so deep as vengeance, why should some poor devil of
an author, already, by the very act of publication, grown
darkly suspect to the powers that be, deliberately attract about
his head a swarm of *new* enemies? Marivaux used to nourish
an implacable hatred of Marmontel, for no better reason than
that the latter had once misquoted one of Marivaux' own
lyrics. Instead of writing: *O Heavens! How beautiful she was*,
Marmontel had shamefully dropped the *O!*, and written:
Heavens! How beautiful she was!

Even twenty years ago, it was impossible to quote a line
without referring to the writer of it, not simply as the *aforementioned author*, but specifically as *il sullodato autore*, implying
as a matter of course that it was inconceivable to allude to
him without praise. Such exaggerations, which, for a century
and a half have formed the matter of perennial reproach against
Italy in the accounts of foreign travellers, are of no deeper
significance than the *most humble and obedient servant* of our
own letters. I have heard a certain aristocratic property
described as *un miserabilissimo palazzo dove non si danno tre
camere senza acqua*.[1] The word *palazzo* ('palace') has completely
lost the sense which we would normally ascribe to it. Are we
really to accuse the poor Italians of so much *obsequious servility*,
merely because their colloquial idiom takes no account of the
conventions of another tongue? The Italian courtier is an
ungainly creature as he revolves in his appointed orbit about
his Prince: granted as much—yet what words can describe
the posturing of those dowager Duchesses at the *levee* of the
King of England? What are we to think of the notorious
scopelott' (box on the ears) given by Graf von Saurau, the
Minister of the Emperor Francis I, to some poor, absent-
minded *dilettante* who had forgotten to remove his hat in the
pit of *la Scala*, one evening when the Royal Patron was in

[1] A wretched hovel of a *palazzo* without so many as three rooms free of
rainwater. [1826]

the theatre? The subtlest arts of courtiership belonged by privilege to that generation which flourished in France in 1780 or thereabouts: 'No one else understands the secrets of service', Napoleon used to say, alluding to the smiling courtesy of General de Narbonne*.

No writers have surpassed those of France in the skills of *graceful* flattery—think for an instant of *la Famille du Jura*, by a present Comptroller of the Censorship. Written in Italian, such a work would be literally nauseating.

4th January.   His Excellency the Senator of Bologna holds a reception every Monday; Her Highness Princess Ercolani, every Friday. The remaining days are so arranged that the same people meet in company every evening of the week.

I had just written that I had been received *most graciously* in Bolognese society; this epithet, the first which springs to a Frenchman's mind when his welcome is such as to flatter his susceptibilities, I have now scratched out. *Graciousness*, as I understand the term, consists in welcoming the stranger who turns up on your doorstep armed with a formal letter of introduction as though he were in some measure a familiar member of your own circle, and with all the polite expressions of exaggerated friendliness which you would naturally employ towards a person of breeding. In Italy, to begin with, exaggeration bears no part in any form of social intercourse. The Italian refers to his house as a *palazzo*, and to the dreariest of daubs as though it were a masterpiece by Raphael; but you have only to pay a first formal call on some unfamiliar household to realise with startling clarity that your entertainment implies a painful sacrifice on the part of your host, who has been wrenched away with brutal violence from the intimacy of his accustomed circle, or torn from the haunting visions of a melancholy heart, or interrupted in the passionate concentration of study. The irritation and dismay involved in having to welcome a guest and make polite conversation are all too clearly betrayed; the awkwardness and embarrassment of the host are apparent in his every act, no less plainly than his unmistakable relief as you rise to take your leave. Travellers accustomed to the engaging courtesies of Parisian society, and ungifted by nature with any inquisitive responses to the unfamiliar, may well emerge from such a visit with outrage in their hearts. The experience is in no sense *gracious*; but the aim of travel is to discover contact with the unfamiliar, and to observe mankind for what it is. If your soul is satisfied with the polished surface of an unvarying sophistication, what need to venture away from the *boulevard de Gand*? And a further point to bear in mind: the reactions which you may observe upon the *first* occasion when your Italian hostess invites you to cross the threshold of her *salon* are not immutable and fixed for ever, as might be the case in Holland; a second or a third visit may already show a distinct improvement—but, of course, the visitor must find in his heart the courage needed to persist. If you make a sincere resolve never to interrupt a question with its answer; if you make an effort to temper the *furia francese*; if you reserve your stock of anecdotes until the company most earnestly requests the pleasure, and then—and *only* then—find an amusing tale to tell; if you stem the urge to make *witty observations*; if you firmly deny yourself the intellectual fireworks of a would-be glittering, semi-literary dialogue; and if, finally, as from the first instant of your arrival, you fight against the strong temptation to parade your infatuation for the prettiest woman in the room, then the decidedly reluctant courtesy which greeted your original appearance will be transformed by leaps and bounds into a very different attitude; for, after all, you are a strange and fascinating animal, you come from *Paris*. But never forget this: those rapier-like displays of wit which so delight the French, merely embarrass the Italians. Fifty years ago, I suspect, wit merely seemed beneath contempt in Italy; but nowadays, conscious of his lack of talent for ready repartee, the Italian

feels a sense of shame which rudely shatters those gentle
musings upon the inward sensations of his soul, that *reverie*
which forms the habitual preoccupation of the majority of his
countrymen. Moreover, there is a whole code of conventions
expressed in *glances*, which it imports most scrupulously to
observe. The brash upstart who flouts this sacred code is held
guilty of the most coarse and inexcusable breach of manners.
In Italy, it must be realised, a peasant is scarcely less punctilious
than a *marchese* in this strict observance of the glance and its
conventions; it is a sort of sixth sense, inborn among this race
whose heritage is Beauty and the art of Love. If I mention it at
all, it is only because I have been witness to such flagrant
infringements of the code.

   If you speak the language of the country, and if you truly
and earnestly endeavour to *make yourself small*, then in less
than a fortnight the embarrassment of your strangeness will
have melted into air. A Frenchman is so rare, so highly-prized
an animal that, as from this instant, you will become the target
of a boundless curiosity; you will have kindled a spark of
genuine interest in the hearts of these melancholy creatures
who, at the outset, could only glower at you with such tragic
intensity. And *this* is the moment, neither earlier nor later,
mark you, but *now* (should your desires and talents point that
way), to tempt your fortune and find favour in the eyes of
one of the fair *habituées* of this society: *only one*, be it clearly
understood. Yet here again, I find I have used a word which
ill expresses my thought: *to find favour*, in Italy, implies a
display of qualities quite diametrically opposed to those which
the phrase might signify in Paris. At first, for instance, confine
your desire to the language of glances, avoiding the slightest
hint of impudence; great intervals of silence are to be observed,
and when words come, tenderness and depth will more
advance your cause than ingenuity. A sincere allusion to the
delightful portrayal of love in the opening duet of *il Matrimonio segreto** will win you more esteem than the most satirical

of witticisms. The mental effort and the degree of alertness which are required to meet your sally with an appropriate rejoinder induce a state of mind which is fatal, if the woman is to prove susceptible to your advances. The unfailing effect of wit, in Italy, is to wither the conversation. It takes no great effort of the imagination to perceive that an art which resides wholly in the ingenuity of its form and the subtlety of its understatements is utterly barren in its appeal to a race which talks only of what interests it deeply, yet, given such a subject, talks seriously, lengthily and with an inordinate wealth of impassioned and picturesque detail. Every Italian having a touch of the primitive savage in his make-up, having a tendency to alternate retreats of silence with outbursts of frenzy, and being passionately involved in a small number of topics that lie close to his heart, it is plain that no one need seek to generate an artificial heat in conversation, or to engender spurious emotion. The commonplace passions of Italy—hate, love, gaming, avarice, pride, etc.—are *only too apt* to furnish experiences of harrowing dramatic interest and inconvenient intensity. Conversation here is nothing but a *vehicle* of emotional expression; it is extremely rare to find it enjoying consideration for its own sake. What I have here assembled is no more than a handful of truths; yet, in my experience, no traveller out of France has yet managed to assimilate their meaning.

The Italian, accustomed as he is from earliest childhood to observe his fellows—those whom he adores as much as those whom he detests—and to estimate the sincerity of their language, is withered by the lightest breath of *affectation*, which produces in him a great strain and weariness of spirit, a world removed from the ideal of *dolce far niente*. This famous phrase, *dolce far niente*, should always be understood to imply the delights of voluptuous contemplation inspired by those sensations which possess his soul. If one day *leisure* should forsake the shores of Italy, if ever Italy should have to work like England, then farewell half her happiness!

Few Italians possess a thorough knowledge of French, fewer still an adequate familiarity with the manners of our nation; and so the tragic part of the dilemma is this, that the most harmless formula of conventional politeness, which to us is as indispensable in conversation as it is meaningless in effect, will jar on Italian ears as *mere French affectation* and irritate the listener to a frenzy. In such a situation, an Italian who may, perhaps, be chary of arousing your contempt, precisely because he cannot pay you back in the same currency, will answer you with a wry, uncertain smile, and never speak to you again.

Affectation, in the special context of Italian society, recoils with such lethal effect upon the one who employs it, that a certain acquaintance of mine*, returning to France after ten years spent abroad, caught himself out in a thousand minor infringements of the social code: for instance, he would march boldly up to a door and walk through it first, without stopping to bother about that senseless ritual whose effect is merely to hold up the progress of the whole company; at dinner, he would shamelessly help himself before passing the dish to his neighbour; walking in the company of two acquaintances, he would confine his conversation to the one whom he happened to find amusing on that particular day, etc.

The whole complex ritual which takes place in France, whenever there is a wing of pheasant to be passed or taken, strikes your Italian as an unconscionable waste of time and energy, as a veritable *seccatura*. Transplant him to Paris, on the other hand, and his ignorance of a hundred instances of petty ceremonial will brand him for ever an unredeemed *barbarian* in the eyes of the *Faubourg Saint-Germain*. Ten years from now, the situation may have changed; in France, social conventions, no less certainly than literary style, are tending to adopt a swifter rhythm.

The prevailing climate of acute suspicion—inevitable reaction to the swarm of spies and host of petty tyrants cut from the cloth of Philip II, who, ever since the year 1530, have battened like a plague of locusts upon the land—means that the average Italian is scared to death of the least untoward happening. If something, no matter how insignificant, occurs to upset him—the intrusion, say, of a puppy he dislikes—he will sulk indefinitely in forbidding and melancholy silence, while his eyes, escaping the control which subdues the remainder of his features, will gaze at you with devouring intensity. Consequently, there is no pleasure to be had with strangers; no familiarity, no joy to be expected; no true social companionship to be conceived unless with friends of ten years' standing. A harsh word spoken to an Italian will drive him back into his shell for a twelvemonth. Even a doubtful jest at the expense of some woman or painting that he loves will do the trick; and ever afterwards, recalling the pain which he was made to suffer from the jest, he will confide in you his judgment on the joker: *È un porco!*

In the days of Louis XV and Louis XVI, what power on earth need a Frenchman have feared? Upon mature reflection, one might answer: to cross the path of some powerful nobleman at the theatre.[1]

---

[1] Grimm, *Correspondence*, January 1783:

'M. le comte de Chabr★★★, Hereditary Captain of the *Gardes de Monsieur*, being angered at finding no seat left vacant in the balcony at the occasion of the opening of the new Playhouse, did most ill-advisedly find cause to pick a quarrel with a certain honest attorney, and to seize his place. The latter, Maître Pernot, declining to yield up his rightful seat, the Count adjured him loudly:

"You have stolen my seat!"

"On the contrary, my lord, I am *keeping* my own!"

"And who may you be?"

"*I*, my lord, am *monsieur six-francs*" (this being the price of the seats concerned). Thence the dispute proceeded to sharper words, to insults, to a flailing of elbows. In the end, Count Chabr★★★ proved so far lacking in wisdom as to cry *Thief*! at the wretched quill-pusher, and eventually, of his own responsibility, commanded the Sergeant of the Guard to seize his person and to lodge him with the Watch. Maître Pernot submitted to this arrest with commendable dignity, and no sooner was the order granted for his release, than he did straightway enter the

Bologna keeps far closer ties with mediaeval Italy than does Milan; the former city has suffered no hand of a St Charles Borromeo to tame its native character and harness it to a *monarchy*.

Wiser now by dint of bitter experience, I have managed to eschew the errors which occasioned me such harm in Milan. Not for anything in the world would I be seen to pay greater attention to the trio of divine beauties whom I met in recent company than to any other woman in Bologna. My attentiveness towards each of my fair acquaintance has been graded in strict and unvarying proportion to the measure of curiosity which I have observed in her eyes—curiosity to provoke *questo forestiere* into speech. Signor Izimbardi had previously given me a valuable piece of advice: 'In Rome and in Bologna, never cast open glances at a pretty woman unless you should have spent the previous week in cultivating a firm friendship with her lover; then pretend that any attentions you may accord to *her* are due exclusively to your esteem for *him*.

office of a Public Prosecutor, and there made his complaint. That redoubtable Guild, to which it was his honour to belong, steadfastly refused to allow him to withdraw it after the first occasion of its making. The case recently appeared for trial before the *Parlement*. The court brought a verdict against the comte de Chabr***, condemning him, that he should suffer all the expenses of the trial, that he should make amends to the attorney, that he should pay him the sum of two thousand crowns for interest and damages, the aforesaid moneys, with the plaintiff's free consent, to be directed to the use of the Poor Prisoners in the *Conciergerie*; in addition to which, the court did lay a most express injunction upon the afore-mentioned Count, that he should nevermore allege the Royal Command as pretext to disturb the Play, etc. This affair has given cause to much rumour; many great Interests did mingle in the quarrel; every Lawyer in the land did think it a grievous hurt done unto himself, by way of the insult offered to a member of his Guild, etc., etc. M. de Chabr***, to free his mind from this adventure, is gone to seek a palm of laurels at the Siege of Saint-Roch. "He could scarce find better employment", says the tongue of malice, "for there is no doubt but that he has a singular talent for *carrying places by direct assault*.'" (Grimm, Part III, Vol. II, p. 102.)*

But imagine some poor devil without connections, instead of Maître Pernot! [1826]

Granted a moderate degree of stupidity in the lover, and no less a measure of skill on your own part, there is a fair chance that he will fall into the trap. If the lover and his mistress should both address you at the same instant, pretend to have heard only *him*. A glance will merit your forgiveness from *her*, and if she finds you in the least attractive, she will be grateful to you for such considerate attention. Always remember to speak as though your visit to the city were due to end much earlier than in reality.'

I have been studious to relate my choicest Napoleonic anecdotes (which will afford the liveliest interest, even now in 1817) to the lover of each of the three women whose heavenly radiance I found so overwhelming. I like to contemplate them as I would contemplate some diamond of fabulous price; assuredly I should never dream of possessing it; yet the very sight of such beauty is a delight to the eye.

I was at special pains to produce my anecdotes in as lucid a version as possible, so that each listener, coming subsequently to retail them in other company, might acquit himself thereof with honour. Far from endangering my own stock of social credit, this precaution has paid notable dividends. Several persons desired to hear the same tales in the original, eye-witness version (for such was mine deemed to be). Italians can never reckon too much lucidity in the presentation of any subject which interests them; the reason being that they are little skilled in *rapid* feats of reasoning, and that they look for satisfaction, not only of their intellectual curiosity, but likewise of the yearnings of their heart. In Bologna, and still more so in Milan, the same narrative will be heard with pleasure some five or six times in succession; and if it falls flat at first telling, this is invariably because our over-riding Gallic passion for satirical effect is too often achieved at the expense of lucidity.

Second only to the history of the tragic incidents between Napoleon and Maréchal Ney, the tale that earned the greatest applause was that concerning the comte de Canaples and the

H

Knave of Hearts.[1] The happy reception of this anecdote is understandable; the matter of the narrative—consummate prudence outwitted beyond redemption by a wild freak of coincidence—might have been expressly calculated to appeal to the particular genius of Italy. I have been called upon to tell this same story a score of times at least, until finally I have begun to grow bored with it myself. By contrast, another

---

1 I ask forgiveness for setting down a story which is already so well-known, and which M. de Boufflers used to tell so neatly.

In the days before the Revolution, many persons used to gather for cards at the house of madame la duchesse de Poitiers*; her *salon* was the very hub of the fashionable universe. A frequent visitor was the comte de Canaples, whose assiduity—so it was rumoured in certain quarters—was not wholly unrelated to the fact that madame de Luz, a young creature but recently married, was wont to resort thither regularly of an evening. On one occasion, the Count having alluded to a complaint from which he suffered, in consequence of which his slumbers were broken three or four times a night with a most disturbing abruptness, a German physician, who had been entertaining by his presence this aristocratic company, addressed the sufferer thus: '*I* shall cure you, M. le comte; and my instrument shall be a simple playing-card; you are to roll it into a tube, *thus*; and you are to place it like a pipe-stem in the corner of your mouth, *thus*, before you go to sleep.' That same evening, after the last game had been concluded, while M. de Canaples, still shuffling the cards absent-mindedly in his hands, was regaling the company with anecdotes, madame de Poitiers said to him: 'Wait, Count—take this *Knave of Hearts*; he shall cure you tonight of your complaint!' The following evening at the same hour, play being concluded and a similar company being assembled about the tables, in whose midst the onlooker might observe the charming madame de Luz, the gathering was increased by the arrival of her husband, the baron de Luz, newly-returned from Versailles. After relating the most recent news from the Court, the Baron added: 'I am early tonight; but yesterday, it was five o'clock in the morning before I reached home. Incidentally, dear Duchess, you are infecting my wife with dangerous vices; she is growing to be obsessed with cards and gaming; guess what I discovered in her bed—a *Knave of Hearts*!' Whereupon the Baron drew from his pocket the now-familiar *Knave*, and displayed it to the petrified assembly. The stupefaction was so general, that even the Baron himself began to grow aware of the sensation which his anecdote had created; fortunately, however, the duchesse de Poitiers had the presence of mind to draw him aside into a window-alcove, and to keep him thus apart for some considerable while, under pretext of discussing certain matters of business which were to be debated at Versailles. [1826]

anecdote (the abbé de Voisenon at midnight, with the duc and duchesse de Sône)[1] fell flatter than the feeblest of inanities: whether it is that the actual incidents appear wholly incredible, or whether it is that the duc de Sône seems merely fit for bedlam, and his imbecility, therefore, an object worthier of compassion than of laughter, I have failed to establish. Since Italians will never laugh for mere politeness' sake, it is of greater consequence here than in France that the degree of humour contained in each anecdote, or rather, the degree of imaginative co-operation and temporary suspension of disbelief which each requires, should be exactly proportioned to the degree of merriment and general *brio* which prevails in any given *salon*.

[1] Since M. le duc de Sône* was never wont to call upon his wife in the evening, she was accustomed to receive visits from the abbé de Voisenon. Suddenly, one night, when the Duchess and the *abbé* lay alone together, he in a singularly compromising disorder of attire, the footsteps of the Duke were heard approaching. 'All is lost!' cried Madame de Sône. 'All is saved!' retorted our little *abbé*, never turning a hair. 'Just pretend to be asleep.' Whereupon the *abbé* settled quietly and began to read. In a moment, the Duke stood upon the threshold of the door; the *abbé* placed his finger to his lips, bade the visitor speak no word, and motioned him silently towards the bed. 'You are witness, my lord Duke', whispered the *abbé*, as soon as the other had drawn close. 'The Duchess and I have a wager; and I have won. Your wife, who is forever complaining of insomnia, defied me earlier this evening to creep into her room at the first hour past midnight; I accepted the challenge, and wagered, not merely that I could make my way into her room without awakening her, but that I could actually place myself beside her in the bed. See, here I am!'
'But surely', replied the husband, 'it cannot yet have struck one?' Whereupon he promptly vanished into an adjoining room to consult a clock. Upon his return, the *abbé*, still observing the strictest of silences, left the bed, put on his clothes, and quitted the room in the company of M. de Sône. . . .
'Who, one hour later, drove the point of a dagger deep into the traitor's heart?' added an Italian hopefully.
'Not a bit of it.'
This final conclusion is greeted with a smile of bland and impenetrable disbelief. [1826]

I have just read all the preceding paragraphs to signor Gherardi, who swears that I am utterly mistaken; that my analysis is nothing but the wildest of fictions; and that nothing in the world bears less resemblance to the manners of Bologna.

So what is the hapless traveller to do?—leave the passage as it stands, and let the reader heed the warning. Can I feel otherwise than as I do? 'Is there anything in what I have written', I asked my mentor, 'that reflects upon the honour of the city?'

'I am aware of nothing', he answered, 'save that which reflects upon the sanctity of truth.' Encouraged by this reply, I am now resolved to publish these same paragraphs, ten years after they were written. Madame de Puisieux used to say that we all could recognise our own features, yet that never a one of us knew his own face.

Monsignor F*** was saying to me this evening: 'I wonder whether even the Gauls or the Iberians under Nero were as badly off as Lombardy under Francis II of Austria? A fine example, indeed, which proves the absurdity of domestic virtues in a King—more especially when a hireling press would persuade us to accept these private qualities in lieu of the virtues proper to his calling! Ah, God grant us a Napoleon—even if he *should* allow himself the monthly satisfaction of striking the heads off two or three of his courtiers with his own hand!'

Monsignor F*** then added: 'Unless I actually have mankind before my eyes, my misanthropic soul exaggerates the wickedness of the human race; my windows should preferably face the street, rather than look out on a garden. Having despaired of lighting upon true merit', he went on, 'I now leave my choice of friends to the impartiality of chance.'

Monsignor F*** has lent me a very singular volume, Gregorio Letis' *Conclavi de' Pontefici Romani*. There are notes in the margin a hundred years old, and written in ink now faded and yellow, which point out that Gregorio lacked the courage to tabulate *all* the merry pranks in which poison was a primary ingredient. This view of the Conclaves is filtered through rose-coloured spectacles, just as Voltaire observed the century of Louis XIV, denying that the poisoning of *Madame* had ever taken place.

Today being wet, I was glancing through my *Journal*, trying to discover a date, when I realised that, if ever these letters with which I have been bombarding my friends (lest they forget me altogether) should fall into the hands of some scion of that race of barren intellects, brittle minds and fashionable platitudes, some champion idolised by this generation of prudes, I shall afford him the greatest satisfaction—much to my own regret. For, with a little help supplied from the imagination, it is possible to deduce from what I have written that every Italian (excepting only the humble priest) is a man of polished and sophisticated wit.

Yet nothing could be further from the truth. From Bologna even unto the remotest regions of Calabria, if a man shows symptoms of wit and intellect, it is *he* who will be destined for Holy Orders; for, after all, what better fortune than to have a Pope in the family? Not forgetting that Pope Sixtus V began life as a swineherd. By right and privilege, the brother of a Pope becomes a Prince; and as for his nephews. . . ! Consider *Duke* Braschi, for a start!

The plain fact is that I have sought neither the friendship nor the conversation of anyone, except of those who attracted me personally. Yet there is perhaps no country in the world where the common fool is quite so boorish and ill-bred. He is impervious to any quantity of thrashing; for the physical discomfort inflicted by an ashplant is not particularly acute.

An English fool is perhaps less hard to bear with than a fool of any other race; but in a realm where *nature* rules supreme, in Italy, where there is no common stamp of uniformity imposed on every mind by the decorum of civilisation, what riotous luxuriance of foolishness may grow unchecked! The *naïveté* of an Italian fool expounding the history of his own inconceivable degradation is comic at the first experience, later merely nauseating. The cretinous inquisitiveness with which he battens leech-like upon unwary strangers can be supremely embarrassing; yet, if you get rid of him with a snub, you may be deemed to have insulted the society to whose generous hospitality you owe so much. A fool infatuated with some pretty woman, who treats him with the deepest contempt, yet, for some dark reasons of family politics, dare not send him packing altogether, is a creature so noisome, so venomous and so degraded that the very sight of him will breed most fertile schemes of murder; for he will survive the heartiest beating with his vanity unimpaired, and emerge to spy with ever craftier ingenuity on behalf of the husband. Such, at least, is the picture drawn for me by my ever-delightful Valsantini; for I, alas, have had no personal experience in the tangled diplomacy of seduction. Either I am the unluckiest traveller who ever rode abroad in Italy; or else all the rest are arrant liars.

The Neapolitans are noted swordsmen; moreover, the degree of culture attained by the upper classes is often surprisingly high (I have met young Neapolitan aristocrats not a whit inferior to Englishmen in this respect). These two factors combine to make the importunate fool a rarer bird in Naples than elsewhere in the peninsular. In Rome, the fool is ostracised by common consent, and banished from the *salon* to the coffee-house. The more I think of it, the more clearly I realise that I have never met a single genuine fool in Holy Orders—excluding, obviously, the humble parish priests from the country villages. In society, it is a favourite sport to entertain a country priest to supper, and make him drunk; yet even such as these, as likely as not, are skilled exponents of the secret art of catching blackbirds *al rocolo*. This is one of the most popular pastimes in Lombardy. The women have a passion for *uzei colla polenta*. Towards the end of autumn, huge numbers of small birds (*uzei*) are caught in nets, then roasted and served up on a dish of freshly-made *polenta*—a yellow dough compounded of maize-flour and boiling water. This *polenta* is the staple food, winter and summer alike, of the Lombard peasant. Some of my happiest memories are of mornings spent *al rocolo*, on the estates of signor Cavaletti, at Monticello, in the company of my host and three priests. The tang of early freshness in the air gives a wonderful sense of *animal exhilaration*. In the evening, the sheer joy and pleasure of a supper whose ingredients are *ucelletti*, *polenta* and *joie de vivre*, seem to extend the very frontiers of experience in the domain of animal satisfaction—the intensest field of sensation. I should dearly love to see some English *methodist* transported into the climax of such an orgy: either he would call down fire and brimstone, or else he must assuredly go and hang himself (see Eustace on the subject of *pleasure* in Italy). On the other hand, the plain, rollicking merriment of a German or a Swiss would feel perfectly at home in such an atmosphere; quite a number of Haydn symphonies, for instance, depict this brand of hilarity. Had I but the talents of a Mrs Radcliffe, what a description I could furnish of Monticello (near Monte Vecchio, northward of Monza)! The physical sensation of beauty is wafted at you from every side, like puffs of wind.[1]

---

[1] Ideally, the public for this book of mine should be confined to a maximum of two score readers*; but by what art of divination might they be discovered? Even Madame Roland probably passed for nothing but a desiccated blue-stocking in the eyes of her contemporaries, who were deeply shocked by the sentiments that she uttered. The trouble is that one is only too acutely conscious of the type of person by whom one would prefer *not* to be read; one is anxious to shield one's sensibility from those withering blasts of irony which can corrupt it utterly and for ever; and therefore, by paradoxical consequence, the very existence of beings at the farthest extremity of the moral scale from ourselves nevertheless exerts a palpable influence upon us. Nay, more: for the very nausea which such creatures inspire may cause us on occasion to speak with a specifically harsh and caustic accent, thus giving offence to more sensitive temperaments. Hence we find that the obsequiousness and the vulgarity of our daily press, whose sole object is to flatter the current fashion of petty *nationalism*, will now and then provoke a sharp reaction, and inspire a

There are a couple of lines from Propertius which I forgot to quote when I was discussing the question of love in Italy:

Heu! male nunc artes miseras haec secula tractant,
Jam tener assuevit munera velle puer.

Yet where is that nation to which they might *not* apply? Physical love leads straight to the bitter moral truth which this sentence embodies; love whose roots lie deep in the passions alone offers a way of escape. Generally speaking, it takes two or three years, in Italy, for a woman to realise that a man may be handsomer than Apollo, and still a fool for all that— just as, in Paris, it takes two or three years for society to realise that an intelligent man who dresses badly and moves clumsily need not therefore *of necessity* be a moron.

The whole climate of intellectual awareness which prevails in Bologna depends upon the good-will of the Legate; if his successor should prove a hidebound reactionary, in six months' time the whole Province may easily be reduced to a wilderness of boredom and abomination. My own impression is that the city owes a greater debt of homage than it is accustomed to pay to Cardinal Consalvi and to that worthy pontiff, Pope Pius VII, who cares for nothing but art and the elevation of Bishops. I have assumed the part of His Holiness' busy apologist—a rôle not wholly devoid of risk: for was it not just such another *foreign liberal* as myself who filled every dungeon in Mantua? The average Italian, so darkly mistrustful as a private citizen, grows credulous to the point of simple-mindedness as soon as he gets his fingers in a *plot*![1]

6th January. There used to be in Napoleon's armies a certain tone of swashbuckling *bravado* which was indispensable to

relentless enumeration of all the *dis*advantages which beset the realm of France. [1826]

[1] *Cf.* the secret society known as the *Regenerators* in Switzerland, under the Ministry of M. Pasquier*. [1826]

success, and which was known as *gasconading*; the majority of Italian officers, however, have remained uncontaminated by this malady. Captain Radichi, for instance, for all his youth and good looks, is as frank and as natural in his behaviour as though he had never handled a sabre in his life, still less won medals on the field of battle. Only at the rarest intervals does his manner betray that he has a temper and, if you provoke him far enough, might lose it. Such homely and unassuming simplicity puts me in mind, unless my memory misleads me, of that courageous American, Commodore Morris. I am always happy to share the company of Captain Radichi; and he is well aware of the delight he affords me whenever he is good enough to share his reminiscences. Last night, as we were making our way homewards some two hours after midnight, he said:

'My uncle, Count Radichi, was the mildest of men. One day, in Bergamo (which is my home), a *gend'arme* treated him to a stare of fixed intensity as he walked past him in the road. *'Fore Heaven!* said my uncle, *What a devilish ugly brute!* The very next day, at the *Casin' dei Nobili*, he observed that his acquaintances were behaving rather oddly towards him, adopting a queer, somewhat *sostenuto* tone in their remarks. Finally, some three days later, one of them enquired casually:

"Oh, by the way, what about that *gend'arme*? When's the thing going to be settled?"

"What thing?"

"Deuce take it!" retorted his acquaintance, gazing sternly upon him. "You don't mean to let it pass?"

"Let *what* pass?"

"The infernal insolence of that fellow's stare!"

"Whose? You mean that *gend'arme* fellow the other day?"

"Precisely."

"I had thought no more of it."

"*We* have been doing your thinking for you!"

'And so, finally, the mildest of men was obliged to walk about the town for three days on end armed with a double-barrelled shotgun loaded with the heaviest charge it could carry. At long last, on the third day, his path crossed that of the wretched *sbirro* who had stared at him so discourteously; whereupon my uncle laid him dead at his feet, then and there, in the middle of the road, by discharging both barrels straight into his body. This incident took place about 1770. My uncle forthwith crossed the frontier, spent six weeks in Switzerland, and then returned unmolested to Bergamo. Being a man of mild and humane disposition, he contributed freely to help the *sbirro's* family, but only beneath the seal of deepest secrecy; for, had anyone had the slightest reason to suspect that he was afraid of a *vendetta*, and was seeking to forestall it by generosity towards his enemies, he would have been forever dishonoured and expelled from the *Casin' dei Nobili*. If Count Radichi had refused to murder his *sbirro*, his position would have been identical with that of a man who, in more northerly climates, pockets an insult in public*.'

Count Corner, at that time Governor of Bergamo and Attorney-General of the Province—a proud Venetian aristocrat who ordered his life on a princely scale of lavishness—thought no differently from the remainder of society, and would have shut his doors against Count Radichi if the latter had refused to commit his assassination. This Venetian Count was the gayest of mortals; he would play at faro every night until four in the morning at his mistress' apartment, where he would openly receive the whole of society; he held the most fantastic routs and galas, consuming yearly some three or four hundred thousand francs of his private fortune; and he would have been singularly amazed withal had anyone proposed to him to clap a nobleman into irons for having killed a mere *gend'arme*.[1]

---

[1] Names, places, dates—I have altered everything; nothing remains of literal truth, save the marrow and moral substance of the incidents. Ten years have elapsed; the reader is a stranger to the events related, six hundred miles distant from the place where they occurred; of what conceivable import is it to him, then, that the hero of a given anecdote should be called Albizzi or Traversari? Consider, I beg you, each separate

Milan, which lies no more than thirty miles from Bergamo, traditionally showed a marked distaste for shooting-matches in the streets. Consequently, the aristocracy of Bergamo would feel an inexpressible contempt for the peaceable ways of the Milanese, and would invade the masked balls held at *la Scala*, firmly purposing to offer provocation to anyone they met. 'Let's go to Milan and smack a few faces!' was a common cry in Bergamot society—at least, so I have learned from Captain Radichi. Since those days, however, Napoleon has intervened to refashion all these divers regional idiosyncrasies, and the gentlemen of Milan, whether on the field of Raab or in the Peninsular War, fought fully as valiantly as their brother-officers from Bergamo or Reggio.[1] In the ranks of the Italian army, the courage of the common soldier springs more directly from *uncontrollable anger* than from any desire to impress his comrades, or from the promptings of vanity. Joking is unknown on the battlefield.

7th January. 'Do you ever stroll round after dinner to pay a call on la D***?', enquired one of my new acquaintances, chancing to encounter me one of these latter evenings.

'No,' I answered.

'A mistake, sir! You should call at six o'clock: *qualche volta si busca una tazza di caffè*[2]'. This remark kept me amused for three whole days. Subsequently, to mortify my foreign and standoffish prejudice, I have taken to becoming a frequent after-dinner visitor at the house of signora D***; and indeed, by this assiduity, I have more than once saved myself the price of a cup of coffee. I was present in this *salon* last night, when the conversation fell upon the politic ingenuity of the priest-hood.

anecdote as the purest figment of imagination, as a simple fable. The scenes described above took place—why not?—in Treviso. [1826]

1 General Bertoletti, an officer of such notable valour, is, I believe, a native of Milan. Pino was to prove as dauntless as Lechi or Zucchi. [1826]

2 Occasionally you may land a free cup of coffee. [1826]

I added my own contribution to the argument, deliberately adducing false evidence in the hope of provoking the truth, and doubtless talking infinite nonsense; for in the end, signora D*** lost patience, and, first drawing me aside, addressed me thus:

'I propose to trust you on your word of honour; swear to me that, while Monsignor Codronchi lives, you will never breathe a word concerning the manuscript which I intend to entrust into your keeping tomorrow morning at ten o'clock.'

For nothing in the world would I have failed at this appointment, for all that there was no free cup of coffee to be 'landed'. When I retraced my steps homeward, I was bearing a precious burden—a small, square quarto volume of manuscript, written in yellowish ink; for Italy has no notion how to manufacture ink, but every notion how to use it. It is impossible to conceive a greater artistry (more especially in the avoidance of useless *padding*) than that employed by the author of this anecdotic *Life of Monsignor Codronchi*, Grand Almoner of the Kingdom of Italy under Napoleon. Never an imprecise phrase, no hint of those eternally-wearisome *universal generalisations*, which represent the cruel price our own flimsy little historians make us pay for the pleasure of having produced a quantity of men of genius. In all the four hundred pages of this manuscript, I found never so much as a single *verily* or *furthermore*, without its purpose being clearly apparent from the context. From my perusal, I have drawn two conclusions:

(i) that, outside Italy, no one is ever destined to possess the slightest insight into the art known as *politics*;[1]

(ii) that no man, unless he have patience and remain in control of his temper, can truly style himself a *politician*. Napoleon fell far short of perfection in this respect. He had enough Italian blood in his veins to conceive the casuistic subtleties of statecraft, but he was incapable of putting them

---

[1] The art of bringing others to do what suits ourselves, in cases where neither force nor bribery can be employed. [1826]

into practice. He was also deficient in a second quality essential
to political genius: he wanted the skill to grasp those fleeting
opportunities which, in a few hours, are usually gone for ever.
For instance, in 1809, why not have presented the Kingdom of
Hungary to Archduke Charles? Or in 1813, why not have
given Count Metternich the ten million he wanted? This *Life*
of Monsignor Codronchi, who, for the last thirty years, has
been Archbishop of Ravenna, might have rivalled the finest
portraits ever furnished by the duc de Saint-Simon, if only the
author were in the least concerned to coin a few elegant
maxims. Far from such preoccupations, however, he no more
strives to condemn vice than to approve virtue. From beginning
to end, his account is supremely indifferent to *stylistic effects*; on
the other hand, not a single sentence requires toning down. His
narrative is simply a *mirror* to reality. The only conceit in his
whole work lies in the very idea of committing such details to
writing in the first place. If ever the Malvasia episode* should
appear in print, the world would be astonished.[1] Incidentally,
I found the perusal of this biography extremely exhausting:
the author makes not the slightest effort to amuse his reader.

Following the counsel of signor Izimbardi, I have just
invested in something like a hundred-and-fifty volumes of
mediaeval Italian history by contemporary historians; and
further, to lead me through this tangled labyrinth, I have
adopted three guides: Pignotti, who, in his *History of Tuscany*,
is obliged to discuss the affairs of the whole Peninsula; Carlo
Verri*; and finally, for the dogmatic aspects of Papal history, de
Potter's *Esprit de l'Eglise*. On days of spleen (*di luna*), or when

---

[1] I steadfastly observed my promise of silence made to signora D***,
breaking it only upon one occasion, at the instance of Lord Byron.
In the heat of an argument, being desperate to furnish proof in support of
a certain theory of moral behaviour, I was unwise enough to bring the
Malvasia episode to the ears of this great poet. He swore to me that he
would turn it into rhyme; I have searched for it in *Don Juan*, but without
success. Monsignor Codronchi, a man of outstanding qualities, has died
only recently. [1826]

the weather is wet, I set myself to explore a period of some forty
to fifty years, following the sequence of events simultaneously
in each of my three guides; subsequently, I ferret about among
my hundred-and-fifty volumes, and dig up anything that may
have a bearing upon the period in question. It is an all-
absorbing occupation, and offers a refreshing contrast to the
highly-externalised existence of the tourist. I have abandoned
Sismondi; his ultra-liberal attitudes make him over-tendentious;
and besides, he is incapable of observing in the massive canvas
of history those particular episodes which reveal the inner
secrets of human motivation—which episodes are precisely
those which interest me. It cost me a greater struggle to set
aside Muratori; but there is no denying the brutal fact that he
was a priest, and I have sworn an oath never to believe any
priest who takes to meddling in history, whatever faith he may
profess. As a result of this research into the chronicles of the
Middle Ages, every town and almost every village through
which I pass becomes a thing of boundless interest.

I have just returned from the *salon* of signora Filicori, where
the company spent all evening relating tales of *revenge*. One
narrative in particular took my fancy; I transcribe it now,
since it is to be discovered only in a volume which is little read.
Nothing could be more exactly true to life:

'In Piedmont, chance appointed me involuntary witness to a
singular adventure; but at that time, the details of the affair
escaped my knowledge. I had been sent with five-and-twenty
dragoons (the narrator here is a certain Captain Boroni) into
the woods which spread about the banks of the Sesia, in order
to prevent the passage of contraband; it was dusk when we
reached this wild and deserted region; but there, among the
trees, I espied the ruins of an ancient castle. Riding closer, I
perceived to my astonishment that it was inhabited. Within
doors, I discovered a gentleman of local birth, a man of noble
blood and sinister appearance, about forty years of age and
fully six feet tall; he received me ungraciously, but finally

permitted me to occupy two rooms. Here, in the company of my squadron sergeant-major, we would make music of an evening. After we had lived thus for a week, we observed that our host was playing gaoler to a woman, whom we nicknamed jokingly *Camilla**; far from us then lay any suspicion of the terrible truth. Some six weeks later, *Camilla* died. I was possessed of a melancholy curiosity to see her in her coffin; I bribed a Friar who was watching beside the bier, and so it came to pass that at midnight, under pretext of sprinkling the corpse with Holy Water, he introduced me secretly within the Chapel. I beheld one of those magnificent countenances which keep their beauty even in the cold embrace of death; she had a powerful, aquiline nose whose proud and sensitive contours will remain forever engraved in my memory. Soon I left this mournful spot; but five years later, a detachment of my regiment having been detailed to accompany the Emperor on the occasion of his Coronation as *King of Italy*, I managed to unravel the whole truth of the adventure. The jealous husband, so I learned, was a certain Count ***, who, one morning, had discovered hanging from the head of his wife's bed a watch of English manufacture, the property of a young gentleman belonging to the little town in which they lived. That same day, he carried off his wife and immured her in the ruined castle, deep in the woods which border the Sesia. In all the while, he uttered not a single word. If she dared approach him with a prayer, he would silently draw forth the English watch, which never left his person, and permit her eyes to rest upon it. Thus for little short of three whole years he lived beside her. At long length she died, in the very flower of her age, of sheer despair. Her husband subsequently made a move to assassinate the owner of the watch, but his dagger missed its mark; whereupon he set out for Genoa, embarked aboard a ship, and was never heard of more in the land of Italy.' (*De l'Amour*, vol. I, p. 129*.)

I am but lately come back from an excursion to the Baths at

la Poretta. I have gathered a whole store of miracles and anecdotes; but my publisher flatly declines to print the pithier items from the collection.

No traveller can ever hope to understand this country unless he should perceive the truth of this quotation from Alfieri:

Che più? La moderna Italia, nell' apice della sua viltà e nullità, mi manifesta e dimostra ancora (e il deggio pur dire?) agli enormi e sublimi delitti che tutto dì vi si van commettendo, ch'ella, anche adesso, più che ogni altra contrada d'Europa abbonda di caldi e ferocissimi spiriti a cui nulla manca per far alte cose, che il campo e i mezzi.[1]

(*Il Principe e le Lettere*, p. 325.)

In Italy, the road to *eternal salvation* is deemed to lie, not through actions which may to a greater or lesser degree prove useful to mankind, but through a strict obedience to ritual. The Italian learns, through faith and experience alike, that terrestrial happiness is achieved through the passions and their satisfaction, while celestial felicity is the reward of scrupulous attention to religious rites. Begging *Friars* form the conscience of the lower orders; and the lower orders furnish that contingent of lackeys and chamber-maids who mould in turn the conscience of the aristocracy. Fortunate indeed are those families whose poverty obliges the one servant to live together with her master and mistress, and where she is in any case too busy about the house

---

[1] '*What shall I add? Modern Italy, having reached the nadir of her insignificance and her degradation, yet reveals to me (dear God! am I obliged to state this?) through those crimes, at once so abominable and so sublime, which daily come to light, that she abounds, even in our own time, and more richly than any other nation in Europe, in ardent spirits whose courage dwells far beyond the base regions of fear, and who lack nothing to win immortal fame, save only a battle-field and scope for action.*'

Note the interminable *length* of this sentence; this is the weakness of Italian prose, which was fashioned by Boccaccio, taking the prose of Cicero as his model. Elsewhere, Alfieri remarks: *la pianta uomo nasce più robusta qui che altrove* ('the human plant springs up more vigorously in Italy than in any other land'). Nothing is closer to the truth. Give the Romans a Napoleon for twenty years, and see the results! [1826]

to stay and gossip with the children. A true philosopher in Italy, who, having children of his own, yet entertains the extravagant hope that his mind may escape the anguish of discovering their inanity by the time they reach the age of eighteen, must staff his house with German servants, or at least with *Laghisti* (peasants from the shores about Lakes Como and Maggiore). Crime is as rare in Pallanza or Bellagio as it is in Scotland; moreover, prejudices communicated by such honest Teutons, being different from the current superstitions of the region, will obtain less ascendancy over the child's mind.

Some two weeks since, in a village not far from la Poretta, the entire population was literally petrified by a 'dark spectre' which rode through the upper air. The francophile, rationalist minority denied the existence of this phantasm, and was promptly branded impious and atheistical—an unholy crew whose mad depravity would bring catastrophe upon the land; yet the irony of the situation was that they themselves were worse than lukewarm in their denials of the apparition. The vast majority was scared to death—a circumstance of which the Church took prompt advantage to drop a hint or two about the Day of Judgement. The wretched parishioners, whose minds were warped and moulded by the begging Friars, stood on the very brink of panic; one further nudge, and they would have grown hysterical. The peasant no longer ploughed his fields save with his face upturned to Heaven, lest the Devil should swoop down out of the blue and carry him off. Countless were the Masses that were said; innumerable were the scapularies that were worn by woodcutters—for this estimable profession, so it appeared, was more directly threatened by the spectre than any other. Thanks to the hospitality of signor R***, I met and spoke with two of these woodcutters, who proved to be a pair of wily old rascals; no doubt, when it came to driving a sharp bargain, these fellows understood practical psychology a hundred times better than our own peasants at home in France. But for six centuries now, the whole mentality of the race has been relentlessly poisoned by the begging Friars. In Bologna, when a young woman meets a Friar, she stops in the street to kiss his hand! I have witnessed the sight a hundred times, and observed the glitter in the Holy Brother's eyes . . . but to return to our phantom, which, having furnished the occasion for a hundred or more Masses, was finally brought down with a shotgun; for it proved to be nothing more spectral than a gigantic eagle circling the skies in search of a stray kid. My woodcutters, for all their experience and wiles, had not even managed to recognise an eagle!

I am afraid for the future of Italy. The nation will continue to bring forth philosophers like Beccaria, poets like Alfieri, soldiers like Santa-Rosa; but the trouble is that these illustrious individuals are too isolated from the masses of the people. Before the present state of affairs can resolve itself at long last into a popular democracy, Italy urgently requires a Napoleon. But where is he to spring from?

Count Metternich is right—right for barbaric reasons, if you will have it so, but indisputably *right* for all that—when he maintains that popular democracy or bicameral government is not a *genuine requirement* for Italy: the need is felt only by a handful of generous-minded individuals who have journeyed abroad, or else read books on foreign travel. And even such sensitive minds as these, faced with the need for *getting down to brass tacks*, waste all their energy in hot air and idealistic sentiment, like the *Girondins*, and are frankly incapable of any positive action. I can see no promise of a Mirabeau, a Danton or a Carnot.

Though I have absolutely no *vocation* for calculating in terms of political economy, I record the following fact for what it is worth.

A merchant company has recently negotiated an advance purchase of certain commodities, whose nature I may not here more specifically disclose, belonging to the Papal government.

The company paid the sum of one million three hundred thousand francs; and in point of fact, the whole transaction represents a *loan* raised by the Papal administration in Bologna. But the curious part of the business is the actual history of the loan itself, which is more romantic than any tale of love and seduction. Five or six staid and wary citizens were corrupted, not by their recognised paramours, but by young ladies without a speck of influence, who, one would have sworn, had never spoken more than two dozen words to them in all their lives! It was the astuteness of the banking-houses which brought the whole business to light. My own source of information is signor Gherardi; the details which he has furnished are, to me, extremely entertaining, *I* being acquainted with the actors in the drama; there is a comedy there to be had for the asking—a fine, spanking comedy in five acts ingeniously elaborated, full of characters never before presented on the stage, and free from the insipidity of *romantic interest*! All that is missing is some dramatist with the courage to set the thing down on paper; but I should urge this same dramatist, whoever he may be, to remain strictly anonymous.

Together, signor Gherardi and myself worked out the various rates of commission, discount and brokerage to which a certain associate of the company is entitled: all of which, added to the declared interest on the loan, work out to a total of *14 per cent per annum*! Signor Gherardi strongly suspects that not one of the priests who have a direct interest in the transaction—for all their shrewdness in other fields of conduct—knows enough arithmetic to attempt this calculation, which took us precisely ten minutes.

There is a whole host of small capitalists in the Province who make a living by loaning cash against securities to silk-worm breeders at harvest-time. Three months later, or it may be only seven weeks, the peasants return the loan with an added interest of *nine* per cent.

In Milanese dialect, the term for money-lenders of this type is *brou-brou*. They have feathered their nests most comfortably and skilfully in the shelter of the Napoleonic *Code Civil* and beneath the jurisdiction of the Austrian occupation. In Bologna, if the worst comes to the worst, should you fall victim to an intolerably sharp piece of double-dealing, your confessor will normally secure you an interview with the Cardinal-Legate or the Archbishop. You may then throw yourself at the feet of this *eminentissimo* prelate; after which, he will proceed to scare the life out of the *brou-brou* (the Bolognese presumably have their own term for the nasty little brutes, but I have not discovered it). Runaway marriages are dealt with in similar fashion: the Archbishop thunders, invokes the dread name of *scandal*, and puts the fear of God into the young man's father. The local traditions are not unlike those of Gretna Green. A pair of lovers has only to tip a country priest ten crowns to wed them in some village church, and nothing can invalidate the marriage; for, however low the standing of the priest officiating, *the dignity of the Sacrament has been invoked*. (Fortunately, the present Archbishop and Legate are both models of virtue, and immune to the blandishments of the fair sex.)

Among my Milanese acquaintances, I know a *brou-brou* who was positively delighted when the Austrian civil jurisdiction came into force. The Teutonic statute-book bears the clear imprint of the land where it was fashioned; it is steeped in a sort of guileless *naïveté*, which is fair game for the scheming subtlety of the Italians. Before the death-penalty can be inflicted —even in the case of a notorious bandit such as Gerini—the accused must *make his own confession*.

I have been in correspondence with a landlord who has some property for sale, situated between Bologna and Ferrara. This property includes a charming house, and the estate brings in a clear annual income of 18,000 francs, tax deducted*. The declared price is 180,000 francs, but he would willingly let it go for 150,000. Yet the landlord's lot is not entirely enviable: who could enumerate the vexations to which he is subjected?[1] In Italy, one needs a title and a resounding name; otherwise there is little sense in owning property.

8th January.   Very little here by way of musical enjoyment; all the good singers are elsewhere. Consequently, my whole energy has been devoted to painting and to society. Profiting by good advice, I have been at pains to confine my first circle of friendships to *men* alone. My proudest conquest to date has been that of Monsignor Lante, Cardinal-Legate of Bologna—in plainer terms, all-powerful Viceroy of the Province. Hitherto, in all my life, I had no experience of Cardinals, save in conversation with Monsignor ***, who had struck me as coarse and frequently crude. Cardinal Lante, on the other hand, is a gentleman of birth and breeding, whose black vestments trimmed with scarlet braid alone impose a light restraint upon his utterance—a deference to his own condition, whose inconvenience is rarely felt more than once or twice in an evening's conversation. Inevitably, in my own mind, comparisons arise between this high-born Italian aristocrat and —for instance—the ever-obliging General de Narbonne, who was killed at Wittenberg, or many another stiff-starched lordship who would haunt the antechambers of the Napoleonic Court. What natural grace, what easy unrestraint in the manners of Cardinal Lante! His brother is a Duke in Rome, while he is the very seat of authority in Bologna.

To my considerable disappointment, I have met with an almost complete dearth of *dandies*. It is decidedly vexing when my acquaintance includes no reputable dandy to whom I may display my *dressing-case*—that weighty portmanteau whose sole function is to impress strangers whenever I travel abroad. The

1 *Cf.* the *Journal des Débats*, 28th March 1826, which gives a frightening picture of the petty pricks and vexations inflicted on a landowner whose estates lie a good 150 miles distant from Paris*; I leave the reader to imagine the state of affairs that must pertain not a score of miles from Ferrara! [1826]

race of dandies, English and French, whose whole existence turns about such niceties as the *cut* of a coat, the *style* of a gallop on horseback, the *fashionableness* of appearing in circles approved by good taste, has so far failed to migrate southward of the river Po. In the Lands of Vanity, a man may perchance deserve honour by recounting his conquests; but in Bologna, such indiscretion would damn him for ever. Bolognese dialect, as far as I can discover, has no word for *dandy*. The local variety of the species differs in no wise from that which is found among peasants in all countries alike: he is a handsome fellow, proud of the outward appearance which Heaven has given him, and strutting like a turkey-cock, head thrown back and pleased as Punch, whenever a pretty woman appears on the horizon. The women of Bologna are remarkably frank in talking about love, and in discussing the type of masculine beauty which attracts them. But the instant one of these Adonis-like creatures moves towards the group, they will withdraw behind a screen of the haughtiest reserve—so sensitive is their feminine instinct touching the value of the least familiarity. Nothing could be further from the truth than to suppose that favours are showered upon all and sundry with unthinking liberality; the women of Bologna are a thousand times less generous than those of France. Little is vouchsafed: and the value of that little is precisely known and calculated.

I have felt occasionally that there is something almost *indecent* in this trick of sudden withdrawal. In the middle of an argument, where the whole distinction between the sexes might seem to be laid aside, it furnishes an abrupt reminder that, in fact, this difference is the over-riding concern.

The least don-Juanesque of Italians—a middle-aged professor, say—is instinctively aware, as though by some unerring sixth sense, of his standing in the eyes of a girl of eighteen whom he has probably never met on more than half a dozen occasions.

There are three or four well-favoured young fellows in Bologna who could pass muster as dandies; but, observing them, I have noticed that the infinite niceties of fashionable attire, which furnish the darling preoccupation of our vain, phlegmatic northern peacocks, are nothing, here, but a tiresome piece of drudgery. Yesterday evening, towards eight o'clock, I accompanied one such creature home to his lodgings —his intention being to get dressed, so as to accompany me on a visit to madame B***, a charming Frenchwoman, who is now blind. Yet in the end, he could never muster the strength of purpose to do what he proposed; and eventually I went with him directly to his own mistress' house, and there left him, rejoining him an hour later, after my visit. The first concern of your Bond Street *beau* is to tack some shred of affectation even to the most commonplace of actions; and if the action is in itself significant, then to deck it with an affectation of disdain. South of Milan, this style of dandyism seems unheard-of. The young gallants of Bologna will jump a dyke on horseback; but they will disguise neither the joy nor the importance of jumping well.[1]

[1] An Italian never degrades himself so far as to be *circumspect*, save when travelling, or in imminent peril of mishap; but when he *does* condescend to caution, then there is no question of his cautiousness distracting him from his habitual state of reverie or passion: *it becomes a passion in its own right*. The Author craves the indulgence of his reader; for often he will be convicted of flagrant contradiction with himself, as here, and even of more serious offences. The Author, as he came to sketch these rapid observations, had not six volumes at his disposal. Moreover, he has but little memory for facts; this *Journey*, therefore, is but an *Anthology of Sensations*, wherein the erudite may discover a thousand errors and mis-statements. The Author's baggage has been inspected on no less than twenty-one or twenty-two separate occasions. The very sight of a *book* acts as a form of goad or irritant to customs-house clerks, who are officially reputed to know how to read, and who are regularly, two or three times a month, hauled over the coals for having let slip through their fingers a *Compère Mathieu* disguised as a *Life of St Ambrose*. At the customs-house at Mendrisio, I astonished the poor official by making him a present of all my books. In every city I visit, I buy some seven or eight volumes, which I lodge with the inn-keeper when I come to take my leave.

Italian books which are *published in Italy* travel by general carrier in a separate packing-case, and, up to the date of writing, have never been held up. [1826]

I have never encountered in Italy those *habitually sour-tempered* females, such as I have met with in the North, in Geneva, for instance.[1] Here, the majority of women follow that pattern of conduct which they sincerely believe to be the direct road to happiness. No—this statement could hardly be more absurd! It is flatly untrue. Plainly, the author of it was bred in the North! None the less, I shall leave it as it stands, as a sign and a warning against those bottomless abysses which gape at me on every hand. For no woman in Italy would so much as dream of following a *pattern of conduct*. The very phrase reeks of Protestantism and dismality—you can smell it a mile off! Whether she have a lover or whether she have none, every woman in Italy, from the age of sixteen to the age of fifty, will be wholly possessed by a series of obsessions, eight or ten in all, each one of which will haunt her night and day for some eighteen months or two years. These passions hold her in unrelenting subjection, fill her whole being, body and soul, and blind her to the running-out of time. Any *habitually sour-tempered* woman would soon find herself alone in a desert land, no matter how great the fortune whose disposal might lie in the caprice of her *Last Will and Testament*. At best she might have priests for company, prompt at dinner-time. Eighteen times out of twenty, if you ask an Italian: 'Why are you no longer to be seen in such-and-such company?', the answer will come pat:

'*Mi secco!*'[2]

Excepting only among certain official *contractors*, at present all as busy as ants exploiting the Papal Administration and advancing loans to the Government *at eighteen per cent per annum*, 'duty-visiting' (as far as I have observed) is unknown in Bologna. Why, what a monstrous servitude of boredom fair Italy escapes, compares with France!

1 *Prim-faced women**. [1826]
2 'I am bored!'

'You used to visit such-and-such a *salon* every day'—so might one address an Italian—'How comes it that you never appear there now?'

'Since the daughter died', he might reply, 'the mother is grown all piety and priests, *e mi secco.*' Once the account is closed, say the Bolognese, then that's that; when visits turn to boredom, then visits cease. Gratitude—as witnessed by such behaviour—may hardly count among the cardinal virtues of Bologna; yet, all in all, the total sum of boredom which oppresses a given population is thereby diminished. The first consideration, if you wish for company, is to remove any trace of sour complaining. In Paris, when a *salon* basks in the bright favour of fashion, the company may stifle for want of air; in Bologna, the money-proud citizen who dared to offer such an orgy of stifling discomfort would find his *salon*, the very day following, deserted and solitary. For lack of oxygen will infect a whole evening with ill-humour; and here, the value of an evening is known and counted. Gaming is a true pleasure in Bologna, because politeness goes by the board: players lose their temper, pocket their winnings and stalk out into the night. Wealthy citizens, without a trace of avarice in their character, will run wild with delight full fifteen minutes on end, leaping for joy at having won four pretty golden *sequins*; they will promptly quit the tables and spend the next ten minutes cradling the coins in the palm of their hands, examining the stamp and the date of *their sequins*, making rude sport of the sovereign whose head adorns the gold. Only yesterday I overheard an *elegy for Napoleon*, inspired by the sight of a fine, newly-minted, golden double-napoleon won at the tables: '*Quel povero matto! ci ha rovinati ed ha rovinato lui.*' Dare I suggest that the 'proprieties' of the gaming-table are but conventions, after all? If no one behaves 'sportingly', then no one is 'unsporting'. Since everyone pockets his winnings *con gran gusto*, and promptly quits the game, fortune deals with all alike, *e di più v' è il gusto**.

9th January. This evening I had the privilege of a prolonged conversation with His Eminence Monsignor Lante, the Cardinal-Legate. Could his intention have been to sound me? Yet, upon reflection, I fail to see to what purpose. Whatever hidden causes may serve to explain this signal condescension, His Eminence' demeanour in serious debate has much in common with that of a State-Councillor under Napoleon. His Eminence is perhaps less pompous, more brilliant, more freely given to gesticulation. Whenever the discussion veers towards some *politic untruth*, the very ghost of a sly smile gives warning that, temporarily, the argument is addressed to the gallery. Our acquaintance was but a week old when he remarked to me:

'I have observed, sir, that any Frenchman who, without being a soldier by profession, has none the less served in the wars, is fated, by some necessary law, to relate how, one dark night, venturing into the depths of a barn, he had the experience of *sleeping upon a corpse* which lay hid and buried in the straw that served him for his bedding. In similar vein, whenever a Frenchman meets a Cardinal, he is destined unfailingly to relate how this Prince of the Church, having first, by way of introduction, let loose a volley of two or three prime atheistical aphorisms, did then proceed straightway to consume ices in the company of his mistress, from whose society, during the remainder of the evening, he was not once to be parted. . . .'

'To discover a Cardinal who would speak ill of God, Your Eminence, is hardly more probable than to meet a Napoleonic State-Councillor who would condemn the Continental System!'

Throughout the Papal States, the authority of a Cardinal's Hat lies so far beyond threat or challenge, that, unless the wearer be counted among the vilest and basest of human-kind, he can afford to be condescending. On at least two or three occasions in the course of his life, a Cardinal will be king-maker in the land; besides which, he may treat the law with the contempt that it deserves. It was my proud distinction to call up in Cardinal Lante a communicative humour. I being a foreigner, he felt impelled, partly out of sheer imprudence, partly from a need to *sfogarsi*,[1] to confide in me opinions whose mention he would have avoided with any native inhabitant of Bologna. His most persistent questions dealt with certain categories of anachronism, the description of which, were it to be discovered among my papers, would cause me untold embarrassment. Yesterday, after speaking for an hour on such matters, he suddenly addressed me, saying:

'Come, sir; if this is not to be robbery, there must be fair exchange. I have regaled you with anecdotes of Rome; you, in justice, must repay me with tales of Paris. For instance, tell me, what sort of a man is he, this *Monsieur I-o-bez-dou-i-ou-ra?*'

At this, I was considerably taken aback; for I understood not a word, whereas the Cardinal was mightily complacent about his own French accent. I sought vainly for some apt reply, by which I might escape from this embarrassment, my confusion meanwhile growing plain for all to see; and during this hiatus, the Cardinal repeated two or three times: '*Monsieur I-o-bez-dou-i-ou-ra*'.

'He must be a strangely important figure in the land', he added finally, 'if you find my question so embarrassing to answer.'

For want of anything better to say, I protested somewhat faintly that I was no more than moderately terrified of *Monsieur I-o-bez-dou-i-ou-ra.*

'In any case', pursued the Cardinal, 'he gave your War Minister a pretty thorough mauling!' This clue suddenly restored me to the possession of my faculties: I perceived that the subject of discussion was none other than M. Jobez du Jura. After I had satisfied his curiosity, the Cardinal sighed deeply, and added:

'Ah! Paris—Paris is in truth the capital of the world. A man has only to take his stand in the Speaker's Tribune, and his name will echo in every corner of Europe.'

1 *To give vent to his passions**.

'Your Eminence', I answered, 'Rome has on two occasions risen to be mistress of the world, once under Augustus, and again under Leo X; and I confess that I admire the second dominion infinitely more than the first.'

If I bother to record so *naïve* a rejoinder, it is because it is always essential to flatter a Roman about Rome, just as the cruder sort of Frenchman demands to have his ears stuffed with nonsense about our *glorious* armies, immortal *victories*, etc. A dreamy look appeared in the Cardinal's eye.

'True, true', he went on. 'Yet if you Frenchmen continue to direct the tide of public opinion, what fate may lie in store for Rome a hundred years from now?'

The Cardinal's *aide-de-camp* informed me (merely stating the plain fact, without a hint of praise or condemnation—a subtle characteristic which is typical of the Roman higher clergy), that the city of Ravenna, a small community of some twelve thousand souls, had recently purchased *sixty-two* copies of Destutt de Tracy's *Logic*, translated by that brilliant intellect, signor Compagnoni, of Ancona. Signor Compagnoni is one of the most notable representatives of that host of talent recruited by Napoleon; the Emperor, having heard him speak once, promoted him to membership of the Council of State without further ado.

It was this same ecclesiastical *aide-de-camp* who proffered a suggestion which has been haunting me ever since the death of Maréchal Ney, but which I have been too wary to formulate in so many words—namely, that one of the great and signal blessings granted to the Realm of France was to have lost the battle of Waterloo. For in point of fact, Waterloo was lost, *not* by France, but by the Royal House of Bourbon.

Among the company present this evening, there was a fair creature whose lover died some six months ago, and who is therefore melancholy—that is, secretly pondering the destiny of man; and she it was who, at the end of a long conversation, remarked to me:

'No Italian woman will ever compare her lover with some imaginary *ideal*. When she and he are come to terms of intimate acquaintance, he will tell her in detail of the oddest fancies that occupy his mind, concerning his business, his health, his toilet —no matter; nothing will persuade her to judge him singular, eccentric or absurd. How, indeed, should she come by such a notion? If she keeps him by her, if she chose him in the first place, it can be for one reason only—that she loves him; and the very notion of comparing him with some *ideal lover* must seem to her as queer and as outlandish as that of watching to see if her neighbour laughs, before she may judge whether *she* is amused. His eccentricities are a constant source of enchantment to her heart; and if she observes him, it can only be to read in his eyes some special, present shade of love for her.'

'About a year ago', said I, 'I recall some Frenchwoman writing: *One thing above all that I dread to find in my lover is eccentricity.*'

'Even assuming', replied signora T***, 'that a woman of Italy could so much as conceive the notion of *eccentricity*, her very love would make her forever blind to its existence in her lover.'

—O, fortunate unawareness! Such, I would maintain without a doubt, is the very root and source of happiness, here in this fair land of Italy![1]

I omit some thirty pages of pictorial description of Bologna; these may be found, executed with a delicacy of touch which I may forever despair of rivalling, at the end of the first volume of the Président de Brosses' *Lettres d'Italie* (p. 350*). M. de Lalande, the atheist, spent some eight months in Italy; but every Jesuit in the land was under orders to furnish him a

---

[1] Murder is common enough here, granted—that is to say, tatterdemalion vagabonds beyond the pale of society may set upon each other, daggers drawn; on the other hand, compare Italy with France, where three-quarters of the wealthier classes (6,000 francs a year and upward) are *paid to tell lies*. In 1770, who, even in France, was *paid to lie*? No one. Hence the *gaiety* of the period. [1826]

sheaf of notes relating to his own particular province; which material eventually gave rise to this author's pedestrian *Voyage*, in nine volumes. He is unable to look at anything, save through dim, Jesuitical spectacles; nevertheless, as a factual guide-book, the work has its value. De Lalande gives a twist of dwarfish insignificance to every person of distinction alive at the time (1776); this is a well-established practice among the Reverend Fathers, nothing being better calculated to preserve the *status quo*. The best extant *Itinerary* is that which is published in Milan by Vallardi, who has just recently brought out a fifteenth edition. It includes descriptive articles generously furnished by *i signori* Reina, Bossi, de' Cristoforis, Compagnoni and other Milanese scholars. I can recommend the Protestant traveller Misson, and also Forsyth: the former journey dates from 1688, the latter from 1802. The reader may also consult Montaigne (1580) and Duclos (1760).

10th January.   I seem to have become a kind of favourite with the Cardinal. He is a man of impetuous temperament who often steps beyond the bounds of caution, particularly towards the end of an evening, when the wind is warm and his ailments give him respite. Lest I fall victim to the restraints imposed by my own privileged position, I am hereby resolved to confront him point-blank with questions about women. If he sees fit to climb up on his ecclesiastical high horse, then farewell, my pretty Cardinal! What lucrative sinecure for *me* lies in his gift?[1] Up till now, His Eminence has replied by sketching biographies in a vein of high comedy; that is to say, the biographies were markedly bizarre in themselves, for he never goes straining

---

[1] Says the place-seeker to the *Liberal*: 'If you pretend to set the common interest above your own private advantage, that is only because you have no hope of acquiring a good solid slice off the budget for yourself!'
    I foresee this objection, and therefore, to counter it, I have deliberately credited myself with the least worthy of motives. [1826]

deliberately after comic effect. An Italian never twists his portrait into caricature; consequently, his comic figures escape that fearful *sameness* which mars the creations of our popular *raconteurs*. The inventions of the latter are always decorously conventional, like characters in a comedy by Picard—in other words, never *individual*. The French *raconteur* never portrays from the life; rather, he *constructs figures* out of contemporary philosophic elements (my metaphor is borrowed from the mathematical sciences), and consequently has nothing to teach the true philosopher. His anecdotic material is the diametric opposite of *il Pecorone* or of the *Life of Benvenuto Cellini*. This last is the book *par excellence* for anyone who genuinely seeks an insight into the Italian character. Cardinal Lante is a man of lucid intelligence; yet I have frequently remarked that his anecdotes tend merely to peter out without making any neat or ingenious point. In Italy, it is often sufficient for an anecdote to sketch a vivid portrait of some *nuance* of emotion; but the sketch must be accurate, never exaggerated.

Had I but an amanuensis beside me this evening, I might dictate a whole volume, filled from cover to cover with His Eminence's characteristic aphorisms concerning the various women who intrigue me by their beauty or by their expressions[1] —for instance, *la marchesina* Nella, the only woman whose lover resisted my every attempt to tame his fierce, suspicious nature. There was a man who was desperately in love with her, a Genoese attorney who had recently handled a considerable law-suit in her interest, taken it through the Courts and won the case, which had dragged on for six whole months, during which time he had seen her every day. At long length, however, this star-crossed lover, after a thousand excuses and delays, was forced to return to Genoa: but the day before he took his final leave, being utterly given over to despair, he sat alone in the great drawing-room, weeping silently over his lost love,

---

[1] Cardinal Lante was the last representative of his order who allowed his conversation to depart from the strictest protocols of *gravity*. [1826]

when la Nella, seizing a torch and calling: 'Follow me',...
(Trials and tribulations of the unhappy victim.)

There is perhaps no single woman of parts in the whole city
of Bologna who has failed to bring some touch of individuality
to her manner of loving. One of the handsomest, whose lover
had cast her off in favour of some high-born Princess of Mus-
covy, poisoned herself all but fatally, and was saved only
because her house caught fire that very same night. She was
discovered, deeply unconscious, on the floor of her room
which was already filled with the fumes of carbon monoxide.
A canary which hung in a cage was already quite dead—an
incident which, upon the day following, gave rise to a topical
sonnet in Bolognese dialect. Save only in money-matters, the
blandest unconcern with the future is an outstanding characteristic of Italy; every waking thought is taken up with the present
instant. A woman will remain faithful to her lover fully
eighteen months or two years, while he is travelling abroad;
but he *must* write to her. Should he meet his death, she is
plunged into despair, not for any thought of future anguish,
but overwhelmed by instantaneous sorrow. This immediacy
of sensation explains the rarity of lovers' suicides. There is a
saying among lovers, that if a man is called upon to live several
months parted from his mistress, he should bid her farewell on
the verge of a quarrel. In Bologna, love and gaming are the
current passions; music and painting, the accepted recreations;
politics and (under Napoleon) personal ambition, the refuge of
those who are crossed in love. But the evidence to support all
these assertions lies in a wealth of heterogeneous anecdotes,
which I, being inquisitive by nature, find endlessly fascinating,
but which, north of the Alps, would sound merely pointless
and unprofitable. Their doubtful merit lies in portraying with
accuracy a whole gallery of eccentricities; but to *us*, eccentricity
is the one sin for which there can be no forgiveness. By way
of initial protest, I should be bluntly accused of inventing my
data; and as an afterthought it would be added, in tones of

shrill horror, that there was a strong suspicion of *bad taste* in the relating of such abominations. Parisian society is wont to label *bad taste* anything which goes against its own interests; and to describe the manners and customs of another civilisation without *criticising* them is nicely calculated to make a man doubt the *perfection* of his own.

Bolognese society is much less *frenchified* than that of Milan; to use an English expression, it is far more deeply imbued with the native *raciness** of Italy; I have an impression of greater liveliness and greater impetuosity; of a more tenacious and elaborate obstinacy in the pursuit of its own ends; of a sharper intelligence and of a profounder spirit of mistrust.

Yet, with all this, I believe verily that I shall never, to my dying day, fall out of love with Milan, nor with the informal simplicity of its fortunate inhabitants. It was here that I first sensed the fact that happiness is contagious. Following this principle, I am now busy working out the average standard of happiness which prevails among the working masses of Bologna. I have struck up an acquaintance with a priest from one of the city parishes, who deigns to answer my questions because he has seen me in conversation with the Cardinal-Legate. Doubtless he takes me for a *secret agent* of one sort or another.

In Milan, even before 1796, there was already a dawning awareness of such concepts as *strict impartiality* and *justice*. South of the Apennine, however, in spite of all the Napoleonic reforms, these notions have never managed to penetrate (Tuscany obviously excepted). In Rome, in the days of Pius VI, the unspeakable rascality (*e.g.*, the Lepri affair) which was common practice among successive Ministers of State, their favourites and their favourites' favourites, supplies a whole arsenal of anecdotic material which, in Bologna, is always at hand to nourish the conversation. No young man, making, at the age of eighteen, his first appearance in the world, can hope to escape with his native honesty untarnished by this corrupting host of anecdotes; for such constitute the matter of his second

J

education. The ignorant populace—witness my friend the salami-merchant[1]—still lives in the moral climate of the seventeenth century, whose anecdotes are more disquieting still. In Bologna, all success depends upon currying favour with Authority *in its current incarnation*; not by amusing it, but by rendering it some tangible service. Consequently, it is essential to be able to recognise whatever passion overshadows the rest in the heart of him who wields the sceptre; and as likely as not, he will deny the very existence of this passion; for, while he is a man, he is also a *priest*. Logically, therefore, the art of divining the secrets of the human heart is infinitely more developed in the Papal States than in New York, where (I imagine) the majority of transactions are carried out legally and honestly. Either way, however, it is assuredly less vital in New York to ferret out the dominant passion of the *Sheriff*, which, in any case, is invariably the same—to make a fortune without breaking the law. The profound psychological insight which the Italian must necessarily possess is anything but a delight to the possessor; rather is it a kind of premature old age; hence the Italians' dislike for *comedy of character*; hence likewise their passion for music, which lifts them high above the sordidness of reality and sets them free to wander in a world of tender fantasy. In one European country which I might name, a man may qualify for an appointment worth twelve thousand a year, merely by telling *eight deliberate lies per day* over a period of three years. What, in such a society, must necessarily be the highest intellectual achievement? Obviously, the art of talking.

1 This friend of mine—since the truth will out—is a pork-butcher with a shop in the *piazza San Petronio*. In Milan, I would often fall into conversation with one signor Veronese, keeper of a coffee-house on the *piazza del Duomo*. Signor Veronese, having made a fortune out of the French Occupation, promptly graduated to the rank of art-collector. In Milan, everyone collects pictures, even the little tailor whom I patronised, and who used to collect the magnificent engravings of signor Anderloni. If you feel any tendency to irritation when people refer to Italy as the *Homeland of Art*, just try scouring Paris for the equivalents of i signori Ronchetti, Veronese, or of my own little tailor! [1826]

Inevitably, therefore, such-and-such a Minister will universally be acknowledged a *brilliant statesman*, for no better reason than that he has learned to talk two hours on end on any subject under Heaven, elegantly, and with a total absence of meaning.

The great benefactor of Upper Italy was the abbé Raynal; the Emperor Joseph II, having stumbled by chance upon one of his books, read it; and ever since his reign, the influence of the priesthood has been properly restrained within the Austrian provinces. In Venice, since the days of the immortal Fra Paolo, the authority of the Church has been still more ingeniously circumscribed.

This fact alone suffices to explain the phenomenon that now, in 1817, the vast majority of the populace is happier in Milan or in Verona than in Bologna or in Ferrara. By contrast, the wealthier strata of society—individuals possessed of a private income of a hundred guineas a year and upward—are subject to vexations both more arbitrary in character and more visibly apparent in Milan or in Venice. The latter tyranny bears hardest upon pamphlets smuggled in from Paris, upon unguarded conversation in the coffee-house, upon gatherings of 'disaffected' persons; in compensation, however, most village presbyteries are comparatively uncorrupt, instead of forming nests of libidinous intrigue, often of nameless immorality, whose orgies scatter the seeds of profound distress and *impotent rage*, followed in most cases by outbreaks of criminal violence, through half the households of the little community. Here we have the secondary cause of that vast multitude of bloodthirsty *banditti* which infests the Papal States. The primary cause is that nothing is so ill-rewarded as patient industry. Say you wish to amass a fortune: it is wholly unavailing to wear out the year in diligent labour, and at the end of it, to set by a hundred crowns, carefully accumulated; rather, you must take to yourself a pretty wife and buy the favours of some Friar. Moreover, these infamous practices are no mere effect of modern decadence; they have held sway in the land for the last three centuries and more, ever since Pope Alexander VI and his son Cesare Borgia employed the subtleties of poison to bring to heel Count Astore and other petty tyrants who ruled in the cities of the Romagna (1493-1503). We have seen already that, barring a resounding name and title, it is decidedly unwise to purchase an estate in Papal territory. In Bologna today, in this year of grace 1817, the social mechanism of the city is identical point for point with what it was in 1717; not a single new economic interest has arisen; manners alone have grown more sophisticated. The oligarchs of the Province no longer take delight in sheer cruelty; they are content with a modicum of embezzlement and double-dealing, and with the satisfaction of their own sensual pleasures. Among them, there are not a few whose piety is sincere; but either they are deceived by their subordinates, or else they deliberately connive at certain abuses.[1] Signor Tambroni, a Bolognese gentleman with a shrewd eye for detail, has furnished me with much curious material concerning this melancholy subject. However, I shall not do my reader the disservice of forcing him to make personal acquaintance with this data. If his rank and position forbid him to place faith in such assertions, he will not believe them any the more willingly upon *my* unsupported evidence. Napoleon, who had a whole militia *ot* his beck and call, and who allowed the Church to feel the iron hand of his inexorable justice, did manage to do away with the *banditti*; and little by little his *sous-préfets* banished infamy from the villages. But even today, any peasant from the Romagna *expects* dishonesty,

---

[1] Recall, for instance, the convent practices which used to find tolerance in the eyes of the Bishop of Pistoia, *circa* 1780— practices which had been in vogue, moreover, since time immemorial (*Vie de Scipion Ricci*, by the veracious de Potter: Brussels edition).

If my reader were truly aware of the extent to which everything published in Italy pays tribute to *official fallacies*, or of the sacrifices which are rendered imperative in any publisher by a justifiable sense of caution, he would forgive me these frequent references to works which, being published abroad, find courage to tell the truth complete and unabridged. [1826]

simply as a matter of course. 'If I *had* money', he will put his *naïve* question, 'where should I hide it?' He is convinced that any robber who discovered it would have almost as much right to the possession of it as himself.

Among my acquaintance this evening, there was a notorious gallant, a Prince whose domain lies in Cremona. I found his conversation most diverting; *this*, surely, is how men must have lived and thought in the year 1600. Cremona, so he told me, is an opulent, superstitious and obscurantist township; and here it was, in 1809 or thereabouts, that a feminine conspiracy some forty strong, composed of ladies all of whom were excessively aristocratic, exceedingly wealthy, and some uncommonly pretty, did undertake deliberately to oppose every governmental edict, to protect and shelter refractory conscripts, to favour their escape, to vilify the *préfet*, etc., etc.; the organiser of this distaff opposition was a Friar, the handsomest man in all the city, still respectably young. Napoleon sent this tonsured Adonis into exile at Melegnano, near Milan, some sixty miles distant from Cremona. Seven years later (1816), the fair conspirators still bewail his absence, and have recently importuned the Austrian authorities to sanction his return—which favour the Government, being a stout believer in the *status quo*, has refused to grant.

To requite this anecdote, I told the story of Rosenfeld, which was so widely current in Berlin. Towards the year 1760, Rosenfeld, a handsome young man with the face of a *Christ* by Lucas Cranach, took to preaching that he was the Messiah; that Our Saviour had been nothing but a *false prophet*; but, in compensation, that King Frederick the Great was *Satan* in person. In this Teutonic realm of fantasy and visions, Rosenfeld soon found himself equipped with a numerous train of disciples. Choosing from among them seven maidens of exceptional beauty, he persuaded their parents to deliver them into his keeping; his purpose, so he explained, being to lift the Seven Seals of which it is spoken in the *Apocalypse*. Meanwhile,

in anticipation of the happy outcome of this grandiose undertaking, Rosenfeld lived in most harmonious concord with his
seven wives. Six would spend their days at the spinning-wheel,
and enabled him to make an honourable living from the
produce of this small-scale industry; while the seventh, chosen
by lot every month, was responsible for the service of his
person. After some ten or twelve years of this idyllic existence,
during which time he continued to preach the new gospel, one
of his disciples, whom he had won to his cause with many
promises of miracles, weary at length of waiting, betrayed him
to Frederick. But what amused the King was that never for an
instant did the renegade doubt that Rosenfeld was truly the
Christ; it was simply that he believed further that Frederick,
being himself Satan, or, in other words, an alternative properly-
constituted Authority, would necessarily possess the power to
compel the Messiah to perform the miracles he had promised.
Frederick responded by sending the poor Messiah to prison
until such time as his supernatural abilities might be made
manifest.

The supreme powers of the Celestial Hierarchy never inter-
vene actively in Italian affairs; by doing so, they would merit
the patent displeasure of the Inquisition; nevertheless, every
four or five years, in some inaccessible village, some *madonna*
or other will shift her glance or wobble her head—an incontestable miracle, judged by its effect, which is to shower a
fortune into the lap of the nearest tavern-keeper. For all this,
however, the priests of Our Lady of Loretto are fierce in
persecution of such rustic *madonnas*.

Here, in this land of *physical sensation*, it is imperative that a
miracle should be *visible*; a *madonna*, say, whose divine-radiant
features are copied straight from Guido Reni, must shift her
glance, and a beggar (who, for the past twelvemonth, has been
bribed to the tune of one bowl of soup and one bottle of wine
per diem to play cripple) must be made resplendently whole
before witnesses. Normally a month or two is permitted to

elapse between the first rumours of this new *Madonna of the Miracles* and the eventual healing. Northwards, in the realm of fantasy and false reasoning, the mere preaching of the gospel by some new Messiah will be deemed sufficient, or else a recovery at the hands of His Highness Monsignor Prince von H[ohenlohe], without visibly miraculous evidence.[1]

11th January. This evening, we discovered a company of nine English travellers at the Cardinal's; seven never uttered a word; the remaining two, however, amply made up for the silence of the others. They consistently reviled both the Italians and Bonaparte.[2] Among other piquant observations, they claimed that the demoralising invasion of 1796 brought civilisation to a standstill in Italy, just at the moment when the Duke of Parma, hand in glove with Austria, stood poised to give it his most serious consideration. One of the pair spoke highly of Italian literature, using it primarily as a stick with which to beat the literature of France. These two provided a fascinating exhibition for the Cardinal and his Court. His Eminence commented later, alluding to their performance: 'Never did I behold so much gravity allied with so little logic!' I have observed that, in Italy, ever since the notorious betrayal of the Genoese by the English (Bentinck's signed proclamation), no virtue in an Englishman rates higher than blatant hypocrisy.

'Personally', remarked my ecclesiastical friend, the Cardinal's *aide-de-camp*, 'I would compare the English nation to a man who is born with some disease of the spine. He is slightly crook-backed; for many years his normal process of growth has been retarded by this congenital malformation; but at long

1 When may we expect the publication of a *History of Credulity*, conceived in the same spirit of scientific detachment as a *History of Yellow Fever*? [1826]
2 There is an unhappy association between the name of Bonaparte and that of Sir Hudson Lowe. To have used such a man to such a purpose, and with such notable success, is as inglorious an episode in the national memory as that of the pontoons of 1810. [1826]

last, and in spite of his deformity, a number of his limbs have
managed to reach a stage of strong and healthy development—
a stage, indeed, which outstrips the progress of every nation in
Europe. If ever—say by 1840 or thereabouts—the *Charter of
Liberties* should pass into the Statute-Books of France, then
France may liken herself to some handsome adolescent, some
slender, well-knit fifteen-year-old; while beside her stands
England, a bull-necked hunchback of thirty, energetic and
immensely powerful in spite of his deformity.'

'By 1840', I added, 'America—that ever-fresh broadsheet
directed against political abuses—will have reformed the
aristocracy, dealt away with entails, and bridled the Bishops,
whose influence so jeopardises the courage of the British
people that they have to be driven into battle with a stick
across their shoulders.'

'You forget, sir, that it was the Bishops who persecuted
Locke, and that all study of logic is severely—and rightly—
proscribed by the prevailing aristocractic philosophy. At
Oxford, the undergraduate studies nothing save the *quantities*
of certain Greek words included in the Sapphic metre.'[1]

In Bologna, if you allude to someone as 'a man of intelligence',
the individual so designated will commonly be expected to
furnish proof of the quality ascribed to him, not in words, but
in deeds. Has he made a couple of million in the last six months?
Did he, in spite of his years, manage to carry off the prettiest
woman in the Province? Mere brilliance in repartee is heartily
despised and labelled 'chattering' (*è un chiacchierone*). The social
mechanism responsible for this verdict is simple enough to

[1] In Parliament, on the 13th April, 1826. Mr Abercrombie demanded a
reform in the parliamentary representation of the city of Edinburgh.
This city boasts a population of one hundred thousand persons; yet its
Members are nominated by a Civic Council composed of three-
and-thirty Aldermen, of whom nineteen may designate their own
successors. Mr Canning replied that nothing could shake his indomitable
purpose to resist reform, from whatsoever quarter . . . etc., etc. The
electoral system at Lyons shows no trace of this crippling defect. [1826]

follow. If your *brilliant intellect* had any real depth, its unhappy possessor would soon be flung to rot in the dungeons of San Leo, whose walls, rising high out of the Apennine, fifty miles distant, enclose that same fortress which formerly witnessed the strangling of Cagliostro. Passers-by along the high-road heard his screams, a good two hundred paces from the castle-walls. On the other hand, mere brilliance without depth can never lead to anything more positive than satire, whether gentle or biting; whereas those who make fortunes or carry off beautiful women, and whose ill-concealed happiness, by and large, makes them the obvious target for any would-be satirical wit, will promptly form a defensive coalition amongst themselves to discredit the wretched satirist and see that he receives no further invitation. Aphorisms are diamonds forged amid an intolerable deal of chatter. But an intolerable deal of chatter implies an intolerable deal of listening, which no one born in Italy is prepared to grant. Consequently, a man of intelligence prefers to use his gifts to conquer, rather than to dazzle, his fellows.

Only the other evening, as we were taking leave of signora Pinalverde, Frascobaldi turned to me and said:

'I pray you excuse me from dining with you tomorrow at the *San-Michele* (a tavern in Bologna); this evening, you must know, in conversation with don Paolo, I was unwary enough to let slip an aphorism or two; I allowed my satirical tongue to run away with me; I fear I may have made myself conspicuous.'[1]

Compare this reaction to that of any Frenchman who has the good fortune to be a millionaire at the age of thirty-six. Frascobaldi has both these advantages; moreover, nothing could be further from the truth than to describe him as shy or uncouth; born with a small private income of twelve hundred francs a year, he made his fortune here, in the fair land of

---

[1] Sharp eyes are ever on the watch; and to *make oneself conspicuous* is always equally dangerous, whether the watchers belong to the police, or are simply rivals in the same fashionable circles. [1826]

Italy, and knows the country like the back of his own hand. Is it not true that the enquiring mind, ever-curious to fathom the mysteries of the human spirit, may reap greater profit from a journey to Italy than from fabulous travels to the Islands of Cochin-China or to the State of Cincinnati? Savage or primitive communities can teach us no secrets touching the heart of man, save only universal maxims whose truth has for centuries been generally acknowledged by all save imbeciles and Jesuits. This chance remark of Frascobaldi's shed a sudden, vivid light upon the problem of my own happiness; as a direct result of his observation, I was able to control my temper when I discovered that the words which I had traced three days ago in the layer of dust which had settled on the marble surfaces of the furniture in my room, were still there, visible and undisturbed, today.

With this same Frascobaldi for company, I was strolling idly beneath the long arcade which forms the southern boundary of the *piazza San Petronio* (the *grand boulevard* of Bologna), when, having stopped to glance at a display of engravings in a print-shop, I chanced to mutter:

'God in Heaven! What atrocious stuff!'

'Ah! What a typically French attitude!' retorted Frascobaldi, who happened that morning to be in a talkative—even argumentative—mood, a decidedly rare occurrence. 'Those engravings are sold for six *paoli* (3 fr. 18) apiece; they are designed to appeal to the cruder taste; would you expect to find everyone as sophisticated as yourself? If all the earth were covered with mountains as lofty as Mont Blanc, then all the earth would be a dreary plain. It is an ingrained French habit to take offence at anything which strikes you as disagreeable in any walk of life; the object irritates you, so you must crush it with an epigram; whereas in Italy, our instinct is simply to look the other way; and so *immediate* is this reflex that it might well be claimed that we simply *fail to notice* anything distasteful—even the brash vulgarity of self-conceit;

for, at bottom, our minds are far more sensitive than yours. Whenever I am forced, even momentarily, into contact with vulgarity, the sight of it nauseates me, and the poison endures until the moral revolution which follows the next meal; but in France, the vulgarity of a fool is an essential ingredient in life, for without it, there would be nothing to furnish matter for an epigram. *Tanto meglio per voi*', he concluded icily. 'The whole of Europe is agreed that you in France possess more brilliant intellects than we in Italy.'

'In the streets of Bologna', Frascobaldi observed to me yesterday, 'when you meet a stranger, it is customary never to let your glance stray higher than his chest: such depths of corruption and inanity lie hidden in the human eye! Speaking personally, I never allow my gaze to roam upwards towards an unknown face, unless I have first discovered an *Iron Cross* attached to its owner's coat.'

Deliberately, to provoke his comment, I sang the praises of some brilliant talker:

'If this fellow has some intelligence (*qualche talento*)', came the retort, 'how do you explain the fact that he has no paramour, no pretty mistress? Or else why is he not scrambling after contracts with the Government, which could turn him in a fortune of thirty thousand *scudi* (=159,300 fr.) in a year?— there is nothing unusual in such a profit *con questi matti di preti*.'

The profession of *wit* or social satirist (a hobby which is rare enough in all conscience) is the special province of a small group of delightful but venerable figures—greybeards whose lack of more active interest in life makes them immune from the vengeance of their victims; but in any case, their brand of humour owes much less to Voltaire than to Ariosto; it borrows little from the spirit of irony, much from a fantastical imagination and a tenacious memory for eccentricities.

To speak openly and ironically of the Government represents a gross lapse of taste in Italy; among the *bourgeoisie*, it is considered positively dangerous, and may indeed prove to be so; in aristocratic circles, where the police dare not claim their victims,[1] it is felt to be alarmingly senseless, since it excites in the listener a feeling of *impotent hatred*, which can breed nothing but eventual distress. In every walk of society, the prevailing philosophy is simply to *enjoy life as it comes*— or rather, this is less a philosophy than an ancient custom in the land, adopted and obeyed without discussion. It would be characteristic of the Italian attitude to confront some popular spinner of words with the following vexatious dilemma: 'Sir, since you talk so finely, let us see you *act*: tomorrow, as luck would have it, there is a perfect occasion to demonstrate your talents. . . .'

In a country where *vengeance* used to be a passion universally acknowledged, whose practice lasted right down to the latter years of the seventeenth century—after which period, the nation's energy and character fell to so low an ebb that today even vengeance demands too great a feat of will—nothing excites a more profound contempt than *spoken threats*.[2] Duelling is unknown in Italy; and consequently, threats achieve no purpose, save that of setting your enemy upon his guard.

Bolognese society is far less provincial than that of Milan; the *salons* in which one foregathers are planned on a much grander scale. Its members, moreover, entertain far closer relations with Authority. It is quite customary, for instance, for the Cardinal-Legate to join the company at signor degli

---

1 From 1820 onwards, ever since the *Terror* was introduced to crush the *carbonari*, the old, aristocratic immunity has been suppressed: at Modena, in 1821 or thereabouts, a priest of noble birth was sent to the scaffold. By such measures, the monarchy has shown itself guilty of an enormous blunder, which portends nothing less than the unification of all classes in Italy, and the elimination of that persistent hatred with which the *bourgeois* normally answers the contempt of the aristocrat. [1826]

2 Allow me, yet once again, to quote in evidence of my assertions the fascinating *Memoirs* of Benvenuto Cellini. This, above all others, is the book which every traveller should read, who purposes to turn his steps towards Italy; second only in importance comes the Président de Brosses. [1826]

Antonj's, to participate a while in the conversation and then to slip away, without attracting a jot more attention than any other inconspicuous citizen.

I shall not attempt to describe (for who should dare?) the radiant hours which we have spent this evening, in company of signora M [artinetti]; let it suffice (lest I forget) to record the date and the fact. Together, we read the poem *Parisina*, newly-composed by Lord Byron, of which a copy has been sent to our hostess by an obliging fellow-countryman of the poet, now resident in Leghorn. What intensity! What a fresh and won-drous range of colouring! About half-way through the poem, when we came to the lines:

> *Till Parisina's fatal charms*
> *Again attracted every eye . . .*

we were obliged to pause a while in the reading, so deeply were we affected by the excess and sheer exhaustion of delight. Our very souls were so over-filled, that to give ear to further beauties, however exquisite, would have been an exercise too laborious to perform; we preferred to weave a fantasy of dreams about the impressions that occupied our hearts.

At long last, after divers fruitless efforts to turn to other topics, followed by a silence that endured no little while, we returned once more to the less impassioned sections of the poem. What a superb description of that instant, so bewitching throughout the length and breadth of Italy, the hour of the *Ave Maria*! As the daylight fades, so bells far and near begin to sound the *Angelus*; work is laid aside until the morrow, and pleasure awaits . . .

> *It is the hour when from the boughs*
> *The nightingale's high note is heard;*
> *It is the hour when lovers' vows*
> *Seem sweet in every whispered word;*
> *And gentle winds, and waters near,*
> *Make music to the lonely ear.*
> *Each flower the dews have lightly wet,*

And in the sky the stars are met,
And on the wave is deeper blue,
And on the leaf a browner hue,
And in the heaven that clear obscure,
So softly dark, and darkly pure,
Which follows the decline of day,
As twilight melts beneath the moon away.

In the space of three whole hours, I can swear that I detected not the faintest breath of affectation, nor yet—still greater wonder—the least suspicion of exaggeration; rather, the company seemed frozen into silence, not for want of feeling, but because the very intensity of feeling outstripped the power of words. We were eleven, of whom three had but a sketchy knowledge of English. For nothing on earth would I have dared make comment or offer criticism; firstly, for that I myself preferred to drift with the tide of my own sensations; secondly, because any observations of mine would have struck a discordant note; yet *now* I may speak my thoughts, averring that the taste of Italy might well have endured—and consequently welcomed—a developed analysis of the dawn of Parisina's passion for Hugo.[1]

12th January. I was in danger of forgetting the most essential chapter of these considerations, which is to examine the condition of a stranger on the occasion of his first visit to an Italian *salon.* After an hour or so, each woman in the company will gradually have manoeuvred herself into the centre of a group, engaging in conversation with the particular man of her choice, along with two or three other acquaintances who

[1] It is perhaps unnecessary to remind the reader of the historical incident upon which Lord Byron's poem is based. Niccolo III d'Este, the ruler of Ferrara, was apprised by one of his spies that his wife Parisina was indulging in a *liaison* with Hugo, the handsomest ornament of his Court, and his own bastard son. The Prince insisted upon learning the truth with his own eyes, and afterwards struck off the heads of his wife and son alike. [1826]

have no impulse to disturb this relationship. The dowagers, meanwhile, together with such unfortunates whose current humiliation it is to have no lover, will be at the tables. The poor foreigner will find himself reduced to the society of those would-be lovers who have yielded before the onslaught of a husband's jealousy, and who now stand dismally bunched in the centre of the room, attempting, by some pretence at conversation, to mask a remote exchange of glances with the estranged beloved. Each is concerned exclusively with himself; and if he turn his thoughts an instant to his neighbour, it is at best to eye him with suspicion, more probably to treat him as an open enemy. Not infrequently, the group about signora A*** may engage in a laughing exchange of banter with the group whose centre is signora B***; but even here, there is no place for the poor outsider. The tiers of boxes at *la Scala* are far more propitious to his interests, for there, in Milan, conversation is general, while the stranger, seated in shrouding darkness, may behave naturally and without self-consciousness.

Countless French travellers, cut to the quick by the thankless rôle to which their vanity has been reduced in some Italian *salon*, have gone posting homeward on the morrow, only to spent the remainder of their lives in fierce disparagement of this alien society, goaded thereto by all the perfidy of wounded self-esteem. They flatly refuse to understand that vanity *attracts no bidders* on the Italian market. Seekers in pursuit of happiness direct their footsteps resolutely towards the realms of *sensibility*, and turn their backs on epigrams, on witty anecdotes and piquant incidents. If foreigners *must* recite their pretty sonnets, there are always the *Academies*, where (as they may easily discover) a welcome of the most exquisite politeness awaits the dismallest of poets; for vanity has gone to earth in its original headquarters—the arid ranks of pedantry!

If I have made my meaning plain, by now the reader must grasp as clearly as myself the reason why *Gallic wit* can find no place in an Italian *salon*. The common pastime amid such company is musing reverie; and the musing mind, it stands to reason, remains impervious to the neatest anecdote, the choicest shaft of wit. In Italy, if you tell a story, I have observed on countless occasions that the listener is primarily concerned to *grasp the moral*, or else to consider the light which the narrative may shed upon the dark recesses of the human soul, rather than to appreciate the nice absurdities of a situation or to laugh at the victim's subsequent discomfiture. Had we the power of looking deep into the heart of man, we should discover, here in Italy, more *happiness* than *pleasure*; we should observe that the Italian lives by his heart more frequently than by his head; whereas your traveller from Paris, who, but two days since, had not yet crossed the Alps, can only hope to entertain the *mind*.

If you would gather together in one room a group of thirty persons, unlinked by any tie of interest or affection, in the faint hope that they should not merely entertain one another, but further should provide amusement for the onlooker, then it is imperative to pick these your guests from Paris or the neighbouring provinces.

Prince Leopold of Tuscany (1780), that worthy monarch, whose reign, in the far-off days of the Enlightenment, was heralded as such a piece of philosophic virtue—forming, as the landscape-painters say, *a strong piece of foreground*—maintained a spy in every family; the reader may imagine, then, the atmosphere engendered by the present generation of rulers, who live in greater daily fear of losing their thrones than the least secure of *préfets* to lose his office. For further evidence, simply count up the thousands of prisoners relegated to those tiny island-fortresses off the coasts of Sicily, not forgetting those who lie in irons in the prisons of Venice, nor those who languish in the grim strongholds of Austria—a total, all in all, says signor Angeloni, of some thirty thousand.

An Englishman, stranded abroad amid company to which he has not been introduced, will die rather than utter a syllable;

for perchance his neighbour may belong to a *caste* inferior to his own—in which circumstance, consider the vexation should this stranger dare presume upon such chance acquaintance to accost him later upon his native London pavements! I have frequently observed that a stranger's gaze is nothing less than torture to that excessive shyness which is the bane of English life; a woman is capable of journeying from Edinburgh to London without once daring to step down from her carriage.

In France, since the emergence of the *Société de la Vierge**— under whose auspices John Noakes may cock a snook at the noblest escutcheon in the land—there is no little risk attending the pleasure of condescension towards strangers; for, over and above the literal dangers involved, you may well chance to hear your own opinions most infamously labelled, *viz.*: *the man must be a rabid Jacobin to say such things*; or else: *none but a dirty, sneaking Jesuit could maintain . . .*

In the present state of Europe—I call upon experienced travellers to bear me out—Germany alone might perhaps afford a situation where thirty guests, all strangers to each other, might engage in conversation with a maximum of heartiness and a minimum of suspicion; although, of course, no German[1] should be expected to enliven the conversation with that spice of wit and leaven of charm which is the peculiar gift of any Frenchman of birth and breeding, whose puppy vanity has been partly tempered by the passage of thirty or thirty-five summers. In Paris, in days gone by, no true devotee of the more exclusive society had *leisure* to be affected by any circumstance. In Italy on the other hand, where *insecurity*—a menace unknown in France for generations—is a chronic malady to be endured, society has received the stamp of a very different character; for, in a land where the individual lives wholly upon his emotions, society embraces a far narrower range of activities, and makes fewer demands in time and in

---

[1] Read what Germany thinks of France in the *Mercure du Rhin*, one of the fashionable gazettes of 1816. [1826]

attention upon the lives of its separate members. In 1633, Galileo was flung into prison; in 1758, Giannone was murdered in his cell; and what a countless host of other victims, equally unfortunate if only less illustrious, having perished in their grisly dungeons?[1] Conversation having been transformed by threat of spies and prisons into the unsafest of pleasures, the very habit of it has been lost; and *vanity*, which ever thrives on manifold, reiterated outbursts of applause, was stifled before it could be truly born. What profit, here in Bologna, is there to be had from influencing the lives of others? Grant me, patient reader, an instant's reflection upon the lives of all those illustrious sons of France whose intellectual *brilliance* persists untarnished down to our present day and age: in every case, we find a life of daring and adventure. It was Beaumarchais who remarked: 'My life is a battle without end'; and similarly Voltaire, Descartes and Bayle waged ceaseless spiritual warfare against their epoch, not without imminent peril to themselves. But in Italy, they would have been swallowed up before they had so much as donned their armour by the dungeons of the petty tyrants in the land.

It may be, however, that in Italy—even granting a tolerable measure of security—the energy which is generated beneath this southern sky by various other passions would in any case have prevented *vanity* from attaining to those gigantic proportions which it has reached today in France and England. The Italian who, daily upon the stroke of two, abandons every occupation to hurry beneath his mistress' window—aware that at this hour her husband may sometimes leave her to go riding —is little concerned with the impropriety of appearing before

---

[1] Silvio Pellico, that unhappy poet to whose pen we owe *Francesca da Rimini*, lies at this very moment (May 1826) in prison, loaded with two hundredweight of chains. The brief spells which Marmontel, Voltaire, etc., spent in the Bastille bear no comparison to these atrocious and solitary confinements; they merely go to prove that the first rumours of liberty were already stirring as early as 1758. But in Italy, no Prince in any century did ever cherish the illusion that he was *loved*. [1826]

her attired in an ill-becoming shirt-frill; whoever notices this *fault*, it will not be *she*. Yet this is not all; for this same Italian, hastening full tilt towards that door which is the goal of all his dreams, yet dreading still to find it barred against him, is supremely indifferent to the whispering of those whom he may meet upon the way, those acquaintances from his own little circle with their scandalised astonishment: 'Merciful Heaven! *Did* you see signor ***? Was he not a sight indeed?' For the last three hours he has sat alone in his room, weaving dreams about his mistress' eyes, instead of adjusting the set of his shirt. In Italy, the instinct of vanity may lie dormant hours on end—an assertion which may well appear fantastic to a race amidst whom its longest eclipse is never known to last a dozen minutes. One phenomenon is most assuredly vouched for, namely, that the very *climate* of Italy, unaided by any other circumstance, may be calculated to produce a strange, inexplicable transformation in foreign nervous systems. In 1806, when the Army Corps under Marshal Marmont arrived in Friuli, in the Province of Venezia Giulia, after having embarked originally on the Texel and crossed the length and breadth of Germany, a new spirit did verily seem to take possession of these fifteen thousand French troops; the sourest individuals began to smile; happiness could be felt on every hand; the grip of winter was relaxed, and their hearts were filled with the sudden breath of spring.[1]

---

1 I am truly ashamed to offer such superficial analyses of certain problems: the current fashion for pedantry creates an unbridled enthusiasm for vague generalisations about that science which is popularly known as philosophy; but the public is less indulgent in respect of more positive, factual assertions. In deference to local susceptibilities, I have resolved, at this point in my manuscript, to omit a reasoned parallel between the character of the Bolognese and that of the good folk of Milan. A couple of hundred minute and specialised studies of this type might in due course furnish the material for some great philosopher, such as Aristotle, to draw a comparison between the contrasting mentalities of the northern and southern races. *Begin at the beginning*—such was Diderot's recipe for this method of analysis. If we are eventually to acquire a true knowledge

The Italian, for whom the pleasures of society on a grand scale are prohibited, while the attractions of a *salon* are likewise forbidden fruit, brings to his individual relationships a proportionately greater measure of ardour[1] and susceptibility; yet it must be confessed that the average French visitor—I remember more especially a certain guest of the Senator of Bologna, who, when I last saw him, was standing lonely as a monolith in the very centre of the *salon*—remains outside the circle of these particular intimacies. The foreigner here remains featureless and forgotten until, by hook or by crook, he succeeds in arousing some form of curiosity.

During the first days which followed my arrival, before His Eminence the Cardinal-Legate had condescended to ply me with his innumerable questions, and when the acquaintance who was my guide amid this alien society had temporarily left me to my own devices (he, meanwhile, being engrossed in conversation with his mistress), it was my customary resource, in such moments of unwanted leisure, to discover a seat in the vicinity of some notable picture, which I would then proceed to examine as though I were in a museum. In course of time,

of mankind, it can only be achieved through a series of monographs, each dealing with one particular passion; but *if and when* the final analysis is made, then the grotesque and shapeless lucubrations of Kant and of all the other *great transcendentalist philosophers* will become the laughing-stock of Europe. The science of metaphysics is so pitifully undeveloped among us, that we, even in our own day and age, still put our faith in *a-priori systems*; yet look at the progress made in the realm of physics and chemistry, since scientists resolved finally to leave this *a-priori* stuff to MM. Azaïs and Bernardin de Saint-Pierre. Considered as exponents of logic, the young hopefuls who have invaded the *salons* of Paris since the days of the Restoration have lost considerable ground, compared with the generation which was reared under Napoleon and bred in the *Écoles Centrales*. Our first step, once we have overthrown the tyranny of the Jesuits, must be to restore the *Écoles Centrales* to their former glory. [1826]

[1] We learn from Cabanis that the human constitution can furnish no more than a strictly limited quantity of that still little-known substance, the *nervous fluid*, for daily consumption. No man can spend his income in two ways at once: consequently, he who is delightful in company will necessarily be less so in the society of his intimate acquaintance. [1826]

this innocent occupation earned me the acquaintance of a
young man of six-and-twenty or thereabouts, whose features
are the purest image of a noble mind; he is the very mould and
pattern of energy and valour, while his eyes betray the anguished
perturbation of his heart. Some three months since, this same
Count Albareze began to doubt the constancy of his mistress,
who seemed, on every count bar one, to live as the very mirror
to his soul; and yet (for so a spy informed him) every Thursday
she would make her way to a certain outlying house and
disappear within its doors. One Sunday, Albareze stated his
intention of leaving for the country; discreetly, he penetrated
the interior of this mysterious house, crept up the first flight
of stairs, and there, having first unlocked the door by means
of a twisted wire, proceeded to hide himself in an empty room,
where he remained four days and nights in strict concealment,
never venturing to touch the door, never making more noise
than a mouse, sustaining himself frugally on a pocket-full of
provisions he had brought with him, reading Petrarch and
composing sonnets of his own. From this retreat, he was able
to observe all the inmates of the house, while he himself
remained quite unsuspected. At long last, on the Thursday,
towards eleven o'clock in the morning, his anguished gaze
beheld his mistress' arrival; rapidly she mounted the stairs to
the second floor, whilst he, abandoning his hiding-place,
followed hard behind her, and stood at length before the door
through which she herself had vanished but an instant previously. Thus posted, he could hear the voice of his rival, who,
it seems, had reached the house by way of a neighbouring roof-
top, *via* a building which fronted on some other street. Some
few hours later, when at last his mistress left the fatal chamber,
she discovered Albareze unconscious on the threshold of the
door; life seemed extinct, nor was it indeed recalled save by
unrelenting effort. He had to be carried back to his own
lodgings, where he remained for a whole month, hovering on
the very brink of insanity. All his friends paid calls upon him

to commiserate with him in his misfortune, which still today
is all the rage and gossip of the town. I have observed that no
blame attaches to the lady, save for her lack of candour; also
that the notion of a duel between the happy lover and his
unsuccessful rival is one which has never, to the best of my
belief, occurred to the mind of a single person in all the busy
city of Bologna. And rightly so; for, in the first place, the rival
was but doing his natural duty; and in the second, a duel, in
the course of which the injured party may be killed, is bound
to seem a feeble method of revenge in a land where, less than a
century ago, the laws of vengeance worked by surer means.

13th January. A friend of mine here, a generous *Liberal*
with whom, a week ago, I was not even acquainted, has offered
to take charge of all my notes, thus relieving me of a constant
source of anxiety—an anxiety which must surely seem absurd
to gentlemen whose most extensive travels have taken them
no further than from Paris to Saint-Cloud*!

Once beyond the Apennine, so I am told, the common
feature of all subordinate officials is a total lack of rudimentary
common-sense and generosity, together with a fierce desire to
cause a maximum of annoyance to travellers of every nation,
British citizens excepted. The English are rarely occupied with
politics;[1] further, it is the passionate ambition of every wealthy
Englishman to be admitted to the *Royal Levee* of the local
Italian princeling; while further still, the English have Embassies
which *protect their own countrymen*—a rare enough phenomenon
as things go nowadays: just enquire of Monsieur ***. Finally,
Cardinal Consalvi makes no attempt to conceal his partiality
for England. A *reactionary* remarked to me with spite the other
day: 'You there—you Frenchmen—it wouldn't help *you*
much to look for protection from your Embassy!'

---

[1] Any man who disturbs the *caste structure* of society may be suspected of
desiring to mount above his proper and appointed station; which desire
is *unspeakably vulgar.* [1826]

'Plain proof, your Excellency, if proof is needed', said I, 'that the *Revolution* is not yet over and done with!'

Were I myself to make complaint, however, it would be rank injustice; should ever *I* venture south beyond the Apennine, I should reckon it a clear and additional pleasure *not* to be able to rely on any measure of protection from the Minister whom I, through the taxes levied on my own poor property, still contribute to maintain. This reflection will enable me to suffer with a light heart the sorriest vexations which the divers petty tyrants of Italy, with all their train of mean officials, may see fit to inflict upon me. I have heard it said that one and all are eaten up with fear; that more than one sleeps every night in a different room, like Pygmalion, the tyrant in *Télémaque**. This I refuse to believe; yet I know it for a fact that, when the King of *** goes hunting, a peasant hidden in a wood and beating upon the great wooden percussion-box that serves for drum in local music-making—beating one stroke with a drumstick to greet the royal passage through the forest —can turn him pale with terror for two mortal hours. Yet never has the most brutal *gend'arme* in their service made *me* pale for an instant; consequently, in the sport they seek to have with me, it is surely not *I* who am likely to be the loser. I only trust that my present precarious position—a position which is more positively *liberal* than are my real opinions— will not single me out for active discrimination. I have forborne to mention a certain Vice-Legate, whose authority controls a district near Bologna, and who is responsible for some repulsive incidents*.

14th January. This evening, the Cardinal was in an evil temper. The reason, I am told, lies in a letter brought by courier from Rome last night; he fears the dismissal of Cardinal Consalvi, the *Decazes* of Italy, whose favour prevents or hinders many untoward happenings. During the course of the evening, Cardinal Lante talked bookishly of books and nothing else, and drew the substance of it from his memory, for all the world like some ageing *intellectual*. Capital, say I!—books, I suppose, must have their turn; and so, provided it come but once a year or seldomer, here's to literature! For the first time tonight, I felt the burden of decorum; these endless literary arguments prevented me from seeking the society of certain ladies, whose sparkling eyes had filled me with wonder from afar; I am just beginning to make a suspicion of headway in the promise of their favour; and at this hour, their lovers had still not joined the company. Literature is most assuredly *not* my forte; the *Immortals* of the *Académie Française* are, in my own private estimation, no more than ordinary Civil Servants, the equivalent in grade to a *sous-préfet*, say, or to an Inspector of Inland Revenue; what has Voltaire in common with a *membre de l'Académie*? If I had my way, I should choose my friends exclusively among men of genius: Monti, Canova, Rossini, Viganò; what have *I* to do with all the rabble and *hoi polloi* of literature? I might observe them now and then, with detached and scientific curiosity—poor, simple-minded, solitary creatures that they are, pipes firmly clenched betwixt their teeth, forever pacing the sanded floor of their studies, for all the world like penniless German literary hacks; I might even ask them a question or two concerning that dusty cubby-hole of knowledge in which they have spent the whole span of their industrious lives. Here, in Italy, the Grub Street rabble finds no refuge in the hierarchy of officialdom, as it does in France; in the whole country, I doubt whether there are a dozen scribblers in 'official positions', however insignificant; on the other hand, the charlatanism of the breed reaches to heights undreamed of: 'This is how *we* write tragedies, Alfieri and I', claims the first poet you may happen to meet.

'Apparently', I remarked to an artist whom I know, 'no one has yet succeeded in painting a tolerable portrait of signora Florenzi?'

'The reason, sir, is plain', he retorted without so much as

turning a hair. '*I* have not yet attempted the commission.'

Ever since M. Courier* proved so wittily that signor Furia, that learned hellenist of Florence, who had recently published a treatise concerning a certain manuscript by Longus, had in actual fact never, at any time, been in a position to read this document,[1] my veneration for Italian scholarship has been decidedly lukewarm. Once a man is recognised as the leading antiquarian, or the outstanding poet, of the little township where he lives, why should he force himself to new and greater efforts? Municipal vanity will shield his reputation until his dying day. An Italian scholar can scarcely wait for the formal ceremonies of introduction to be over and done with, before he will regale you with interpretations of some obscure passage from Cicero's *pro Scauro*, interlarded with references to that genius among geniuses, Monsignor Maio. Monsignor Maio's 'genius' consists in having thought to take a magnifying-glass to certain parchments which the monks of some mediaeval cloister had scratched clean and later used again to scribble their own ecclesiastical imbecilities. Here and there, where the parchment has worn thin, it is possible to decipher the original passage of Cicero which the monks had scratched out. *This* is the epoch-making discovery of the *palimpsests*!

Over and above all this, Monsignor Maio may go down to posterity as the most disobliging librarian in Europe; for, at the Vatican library, of which he is custodian, he resolutely denies all access to the manuscripts in his keeping—even to the most innocent, to wit, a *Virgil*. This boundless zeal for the diffusion of knowledge will doubtless earn him a Cardinal's Hat. To which let it be added that the features of this same Monsignor Maio are quite surprisingly handsome—I observed them carefully beneath the onslaught of his insolence. This would seem to be one further fact to invalidate the 'physiognomical science' of Lavater.

[1] The reader is referred directly to this highly entertaining little essay by M. Courier (*Complete Works*, Brussels, p. 49). [1826]

I have been ruthlessly taunted by Italian scholars concerning certain Latin inscriptions which our own *Académie des Inscriptions* has recently provided for a statue of Henri IV: from beginning to end, so these scholars claim, they are riddled with solecisms and grammatical howlers which would earn any schoolboy a thorough whipping. A sound knowledge of Latin is the one quality which I am unreservedly prepared to allow to all Italian scholars; in any event, they could hardly know *less* than MM. Langlès and Gail. The delightful letter addressed by M. Courier to the *Académie de Inscriptions* has so far remained unanswered. At the *Institut Français*, the energies of every member are wholly absorbed in private rivalries; all genuine learning has taken refuge in the *Académie des Sciences*.[1]

When, after a series of deliberate and sharp manoeuvres, some adventurer reaps a peerage and a fortune as the end of his ambition, *I* have no complaint to make; society is predestined to endure such creatures; but that a man* should wallow in the mire for the paltry sum of twenty guineas a month. . . ! And all the while my mind lay in the grip of such *literary* notions, His Eminence was holding forth about some scribblers' clique in Florence. Yet what have *I* to do with the pretensions and the vanity of such a crowd? Like specimens flourish no less richly in the native soil of France; and so, a week or two from now, the names of these 'illustrious Florentines' will mean no more to me than do those of our own most eminent *Immortals* to anyone who chances to live some fifty miles beyond the walls of Paris.

'In Florence', pursued the Cardinal, 'everyone has literary pretensions of one sort or another. *The rest of you*, says the Florentine to his compatriots from other Provinces, *may show a glimmer of intelligence now and then; but Florence alone has learnt the art of letters; Florence, birth-place of Dante, is not merely*

---

[1] A friend informs me by letter that there are, in spite of everything, still three or four members of the *Académie des Inscriptions* whose erudition makes them worthy colleagues of scholars such as Coray and Haase. [1826]

the fountain-head of literature; but there is no literature outside Florence. However', went on the Cardinal, 'for half a century at least, not one single original idea has wormed its way through the defences of these thick Florentine skulls; they know but one concern, which is to model their prose upon the style of writing which held sway in Florence in the year 1400 or thereabouts. Yet, at that period, two-thirds of the notions which hold the centre of our stage today were still unborn: legitimist politics, printing, representative government, political economy, America, the influence of ministerial credit in the business of floating a loan or purchasing a majority, etc., etc.—all matters such as these lay shrouded in the hidden womb of time. Yet still today, your worthy Florentine insists upon discussing all this boundless wealth of new ideas, not only in the language but even in the *style* devised by his Tuscan ancestors in the fifteenth century. In France, if a man erupts suddenly and violently into a drawing-room full of company, there is a phrase ready-made to describe the occurrence: *il est arrivé comme une bombe.* In the year 1400, however, this simile was unknown: either the parallel had not been observed, or else the manner of expression was completely different. Yet this is what the narrow, academic mind of Florence can never hope to grasp. In Milan, in the time of the Empire, when Napoleon created the posts of *First Sea Lord* and *Chief Commissioner of Police*, the Italian language never managed to decorate these officials with appropriate titles: *Ministro della Marina* means 'Minister of the Sea-Coast', while *Direttor di Polizia* means 'Director of Property'. Words change their meaning, and in the examples I have chosen, this change is unmistakable; but I would readily wager', added His Eminence, 'that, if you were to analyse every expression which has been used in this room tonight, I doubt whether you would find fifty isolated instances whose original purity has remained uncontaminated by some trace of modern thought evolved since the year 1400. Well now, gentlemen! Take any one of these expressions which, however obscurely, reflect the progress of the human mind over the last four centuries; give it to a Florentine and let him set it down on paper; and observe, without exception, the nonsense which results. To his dying day, your Florentine *stylist* will be cudgelling his brains, not to evolve a logical argument, nor to cast new light upon ancient problems, but simply to perform an impossible exercise in translation. How could you hope to describe the elaborate ceremonial of the Court of Louis XIV in the rude dialect of some rug-headed Irish kern?

'You, sir, being a foreigner in Italy, will never fathom the full depths of this absurdity—this *pretentiousness*, forever puffing its own merits vaingloriously from the housetops, and forever doomed to ignominious discomfiture. A Florentine cannot so much as ask the date of the latest newspapers arrived from Paris without making a plain ass of himself; not merely does he fail to convey his meaning, but he uses words whose sense is positively different from that which he attributes to them, and often richly comic. The deeper our knowledge of the original tongue of Dante—who, of all Italian poets, has remained the most truly individual, and consequently the most stirring—the more uncontrollable our laughter. The self-conceit of Florence is a standing offence to my own vanity; but my own vanity is constantly being flattered and delighted by the sight of Florentine self-conceit tripping up and breaking its neck (*quella pretenzione rompersi il collo*). If, having been born and bred beside the Arno, you wished to allude to the northern territories of San-Domingo, you would speak in tones of solemn gravity of *le parti deretane dell' isola . . .*'.

(At this point, the Cardinal's diatribe was interrupted by shouts of laughter from the room, for, in modern Italian, these words mean the *backside* of the island. Whereupon the speaker quoted seven or eight examples which make wonderful telling, but which, translated into French and set down in solemn black and white, would merely seem indecent.)

'There is no richer sport', continued the Cardinal, 'than some young spark of a Florentine, some educated puppy playing truant from his native haunts and arriving here in Bologna; if ever fortune sends your way a specimen of this rare literary jackass, I advise you earnestly, for your own delight, to lure him on towards the subtler refinements of sentimental analysis. His ideas may be the very incarnation of banality; but his vocabulary will astonish you. Those old Florentine merchants in that far-off year 1400, with their massive wealth, their passion for architecture and their obsessive hatred of the aristocracy, little guessed, it must be acknowledged, what subtle disquisitions would arise in after years to fill the pages of Madame de Staël's *Corinne*, of Marivaux' novels, and of all those witty letters in which Mademoiselle d'Aïssé and divers other pretty creatures of the age of Louis XV undertook to dissect and probe the heart of man. The Florentines of the first years of the fifteenth century were probably the most advanced and civilised product of their age—so true indeed is this claim, that in many respects they have never been surpassed. They reconciled two qualities which normally destroy each other: intelligence and strength of character. Immortal Dante—whose immortality derives precisely from the possession of these two warring gifts—would doubtless have grasped the super-subtle probings which fill that singular novel which its author, M. Benjamin Constant, has entitled *Adolphe*—always assuming that, in his own day and age, such spineless and star-crossed beings as Adolphe existed at all; but, had he ever felt the urge to express such emotions, he would have been forced to extend the very frontiers of his language. The vocabulary which he did in fact bequeath us is no more capable of translating *Adolphe* or *les Souvenirs de Félicie* than the title of *Chief Commissioner of Police*. You, sir—since France now has a *budget*—have stepped across the waters into England, where the thing already existed, in order to borrow an appropriate term to describe it; similarly, you now talk about *sinecures* and *precedents*; but this is a procedure which the puerile vanity of our Florentine *purists* would never condescend to adopt; rather would they have striven to prove that such-and-such an antique vocable in Guicciardini did in fact mean *budget*. Here, in the last analysis, you have the root and cause of all that argument which, under the fearful name of *Romanticism**, sets all our writers by the ears: the Florentines, with their passion for archaic words, are *classics*; the Lombards are *romantics* through and through. *I signori* di Breme, Borsieri, Berchet, Visconti, Pellico,[1] etc., claim:

'(i) that the first requirement of style is *clarity*: in forming his sentences, the writer should normally give preference to the most straightforward constructions. Should the Italians eschew lucidity, merely because the French have favoured it?

'(ii) that it behoves the writer to resist to the uttermost the beguiling temptation of hatching sentences twenty lines long.

'(iii) that the writer should set out to discover a new vocabulary for all concepts which have emerged since the fifteenth century.'[2]

This topic was still far from exhausted. In answer to a sharp challenge from His Eminence, I was obliged to hold forth concerning the French interpretation of *Romanticism*. Happily, in France, the fundamental problem of language has been resolved for generations; everyone is agreed that the tongue of Voltaire or of Pascal is a suitable medium for literature. But in Italy, there is not even this measure of agreement; judge then the distance to be covered before the Italian stage may hope

---

1 See *il Conciliatore**, a romantic journal published in Milan, *circa* 1818. [1826]

2 If the reader should still entertain serious doubts in the matter, I adjure him to glance at an amusing little comedy by Albergati, entitled *il Pomo*; he will there make the acquaintance of one don Tiberio Cruscati, *marchese*, whose entire conversation is uttered in purest Tuscan—an extravagance which renders it, not merely totally unintelligible, but likewise supremely absurd to the worthy townsfolk of Bologna, whose city lies not two-and-twenty leagues from Florence. [1826]

to witness tragedies where *interest* is made significant by *truth*.[1]

By the time this point in the argument had been reached, the missing lovers had arrived, and each had taken up his post beside his mistress; nor could I, without abrupt discourtesy, abandon the man whose noble condescension towards me had been so pronounced. Furthermore, the company having been swelled meanwhile by the arrival of a rabble of god-forsaken *literary critics*, the conversation veered (if I recall aright) towards an appraisal of the merits of some French poet—this, plainly, in my honour. And ye gods! *What* a poet! M. Jacques Gohorry!

The business on hand lay in deciding between M. Jacques Gohorry and Ariosto, for the honour of being considered the better imitator of Catullus. I, plunging an unhesitant dagger straight into the heart of *Patriotic Sentiment*, declared promptly in favour of Ariosto; but this in no wise suited the books of the *literary* element, which was eagerly panting for an occasion to show off its brilliance. Each listened with ill-concealed impatience while the other spoke; retorts grew sharper; in brief, I was treated to all the delights of a literary *soirée*. Had I been at home in France, wild horses could not have dragged a word from my lips; but a traveller abroad must always vouch the price of his admission; I too, therefore, held forth in the same vein; and I knew the joy of feeling sharp retorts and rank near-discourtesies come welling up inside me likewise. By contrast, in Milan, my spirit learned a new degree of exaltation and serenity whenever Monti, Porta or signor Pellico would grant me the honour of discussing poetry.

Here is a specimen from the poetic repertoire of Jacques Gohorry, who died in Paris on the 15th day of March, 1576. Immediately following I shall transcribe Catullus' original hexameters, and finally, the charming octaves of Ariosto, which first appeared in print in 1516, four years before the death of Raphael. What a century was this for Italy, among

---

[1] *Cf. Nabucco,* tragedy in five acts, cast in noble metre, by signor Giambattista Niccolini: the plot is an anti-Napoleonic allegory. [1826]

whose living figures there were numbered Leonardo da Vinci, Titian, Correggio, Michelangelo, Andrea del Sarto, Fra Bartolomeo di San Marco, Giulio Romano, Machiavelli, Pope Leo X, Giovanni de' Medici the great Captain, Cardano, etc., etc.

But let me set down these same lines, each syllable of which gave rise to dreary hours of argument:

> *La jeune vierge est semblable à la rose,*
> *Au beau jardin, sur l'épine naïve;*
> *Tandis que sure et seulette repose,*
> *Sans que troupeau ni berger y arrive:*
> *L'air doux l'échauffe et l'aurore l'arrose;*
> *La terre, l'eau par sa faveur l'avive;*
> *Mais jeunes gens et dames amoureuses*
> *De la cueillir ont les mains envieuses.*
> *La terre et l'air, qui la souloient nourrir,*
> *La quittent lors et la laissent flétrir.*
>
> *Ut flos in septis secretus nascitur hortis*
> *Ignotus pecori, nullo contusus aratro,*
> *Quem mulcent aurae, firmat sol, educat imber;*
> *Multi illum pueri, multae cupiere puellae;*
> *Idem cum tenui carptus defloruit ungui,*
> *Nulli illum pueri, nullae cupiere puellae;*
> *Sic virgo, dum intacta manet, dum cara suis: sed*
> *Cum castum amisit polluto corpore florem,*
> *Nec pueris jucunda manet, nec cara puellis.*
>
> *La verginella è simile alla rosa,*
> *Che in bel giardin su la nativa spina*
> *Mentre sola e sicura si riposa,*
> *Nè gregge nè pastor se le avviccina;*
> *L'aura soave e l'alba rugiadosa,*
> *L'acqua e la terra al suo favor s'inchina,*
> *Giovani vaghi e donne innamorate*
> *Amano averne e seni e tempie ornate.*

Ma non sì tosto dal materno stelo
Rimossa viene e dal suo ceppo verde,
Chè quanto avea dagli uomini e dal cielo,
Favor, grazia, bellezza, tutto perde:
La vergine, che il fior, di che più zelo
Che della vita e de' begli occhi aver dè,
Lascia altrui corre, il pregio, che avea innanti,
Perde nel cor di tutti gli altri amanti.

With the exception of the last four lines, whose hint of diffuseness springs from the need to fill out the octave, I prefer Ariosto to Catullus.

15th January. I have just finished reading the preceding pages aloud to Count Radichi.

'What!' he exclaimed, when I announced my intention. 'Do you wield a pen, sir? Then take care lest you find yourself in prison!'

'Your observations, sir, are only too exact', he remarked later. 'In Italy, the writer is concerned exclusively with *forms*, never with *ideas*. This weakness notwithstanding, I would judge our men of letters in two ways superior to your own: firstly, they refuse to sell their souls to the government in power; secondly, they do not, each time their latest book appears, themselves commit a dozen articles in the press discoursing upon its merits*. To begin with, no editor—setting aside two or three salaried agents, who, in certain provinces, hold the monopoly of the *Gazette*, a privilege which may be valued at some thirty thousand francs a year—would accept such shameless scraps of self-advertisement. We, in literature, have no *provincials* to be *gulled*; our divers principalities are so minute that every citizen is acquainted with his neighbour. Excepting only a handful of renegades, all our writers are scrupulous and honourable men; but the least touch of genius is warning enough to shun the urge to publish, whether for fear of exile and imprisonment, or whether simply from disgust

K

at the antics of the censorship. Nothing could be simpler—this I grant you—than to invent a pseudonym and to publish the book in Brussels; but such deceits are modern innovations, unknown as yet in Italy.'

'And so it comes to pass', I answered, 'that a nation eighteen million strong, comprising the most ingenious race in Europe lives out its days in silence. Name me, since 1814, *one* Italian book', I ended, 'which has been translated into French?'

Count Perticari, of Pesaro, is at present the leading figure in Italian literature—which, I grant you in all conscience, is not saying much. Here, as an instance, is what he writes of his native city—that little township which gave the world its illustrious *Rossini*, who was born in Pesaro, his father having migrated thither from Lugo (both towns lie in the vicinity of Bologna):

'Buono sia ai colti Pesaresi che, ancora con pubblico monumento dedicato, donarono della loro cittadinanza l'Orfeo de' giorni nostri; nato, egli è vero, nel 1792 a Pesaro di madre Pesarese, ma generato di padre Lughese, che venne agli stipendi di quel comune in qualità di *tubatore*, dilungandosi dal luogo nativo, dov'ebbe ed ha tuttavia il suo tetto avito. Nè per ciò sia diminuita a Lugo la gloria di essere *patria di Gioacchino Rossini*. Imperocchè sebbene gli scrittori di filologia e di storia abbiano lasciato incerto, se la patria si nomini dal luogo dove si nasce, o da quello onde si è oriondi, o finalmente da quello stirpe istessa della madre (come si raccoglie da un luogo di Livio, *lib.* XXIV, *c.* vi, e da un altro di Virgilio, *Aen.*, VIII, *v.* 510-511), niente di meno per giusta ragione di etimologia, et per antico dettato di legge è manifesto che *patria* si dice *a patre* (*lib. I, C. ubi pet. tut.-l. nullus C. de decurionibus*). E non è patria ogni terra natale, ma quella sola nella quale è nato il padre naturale; quella onde si e *oriondi*. Quindi Cicerone (*de Leg.* xi, 2, *ap. Cujac.*, vol. IV, p. 790 E): *germana patria est ea ex qua pater naturalis naturalem originem suam duxit*. Il che è confermato dalla legge 3, *Cod. de munic. et orig.*, e dal voto del gravissimo Cujaccio, che conchiude (*loc. cit.*): *Itaque natus Lutetiae, si pater sit oriundus a Roma, non Lutetiam, sed Romam habet patriam; Romanus nuncupatur, nisi et ipse pater Lutetiae natus sit.* E così fermamente esser debbe: altrimenti chi nasce in mare non avrebbe patria, e il diritto pubblico sarebbe assai poco determinato nella parte dei pesi civili comuni.'

(*Opere del Conte Giulio Perticari*, vol. III, p. 181.)

It seems scarcely credible to record that Florence has accused Count Perticari of being *too lucid* and *too French*.

Considering, on the one hand, this gross, misshapen prose, and on the other, the fresh and unsuspected field of emotional experience which this land affords, my conclusion follows with remorseless logic: one should read English literature (*The Corsair*; *Childe Harold*; Mr Moore and Mr Crabbe), and one should travel in Italy. It is distinctly vexing that I cannot for the moment lay my hands on a copy of the *Napoleone legislatore, panegirico*, by signor Pietro Giordani, another figure of illustrious renown, more especially in Piacenza. Lest my reader should feel too constantly obliged to take my word for everything, I should be happy to quote a page or two—as a *literary masterpiece* it is quite as barren of critical penetration, and quite as richly steeped in the rigours of *logic*, as is the *jewelled prose* of Count Perticari. It must be these peculiar qualities—I can surmise no different—which have elevated this pair to such a notable position of eminence amid the present generation of Italian writers. I suspect also that there must be a vast wealth of fourteenth-century archaisms which are most cunningly cut to fit the pattern of their thought; further, there is the fact that they write in *maxims*. To use that style of speech which they themselves affect, I might conclude by saying that the *noble periods* of both these gentry put me in mind of 'oceans of words and deserts of ideas'. Not thus, alas! not thus wrote Benvenuto Cellini and Neri Capponi.

Let me hasten to add, however, that both Count Perticari

and signor Pietro Giordani enjoy an enviable reputation throughout the peninsular as men of honour and high principle; *my* criticism is directed exclusively at their *literary* attainments; and this, I fancy, is a privilege which any man may purchase over the counter of the nearest bookshop.

Michelangelo di Caravaggio was, in all likelihood, a common murderer; yet I prefer his paintings, and the abounding energy which they reveal, to those sorry daubs of M. Greuze, despite the artist's many moral virtues. Why should I give a brass farthing for a man's virtues, when his trade is patently to *amuse* me, be it by his poetry, his music, his palette or his prose? Under the lash of public derision, the writer invariably reacts by protesting that *his honour is at stake.* 'A fig!' say I. 'What care *I*, sir, for your *honour*? Entertain me, if you can; instruct me, if you are able; and let the rest go hang!' Incidentally, allow me to take this opportunity to make a solemn declaration that I cast no aspersions upon the personal qualities, still less upon the civic virtues, of any of those mediocre artists whose writings (may the liberty be forgiven me) I have treated with such gross irreverence.

The Italian reads but rarely; but when he does, it is with earnest faith and a singular degree of concentration. He will lock himself in his room to open a pamphlet; all his faculties and all his attention lie ready at the service of the writer. He cannot conceive our enthusiasm for a Voltaire or a La Bruyère; hints and insinuations mean nothing to him, in a book; for he has never had the experience of a *Court*, where conversation was the art *par excellence*, the key to everything. He has never known the pleasures nor shared the pastimes of that multitude of petty tyrants who, ever since the collapse of the mediaeval republics, have sought to reduce him to utter degradation. Between his sovereign and himself there has existed since time immemorial a relationship which admits of no departure from tradition: on the one side, deep mistrust; on the other, remorseless hatred—witness the catalogue of conspiracies and assassinations. Italy has endured half a hundred petty princelings, whose very names are unknown in France;[1] the reputation of the Visconti, on the other hand, *has* travelled northward beyond the Alps; so here, as a sample, is a summary of the career of the divers princes of this dynasty: *Matteo I*, the founder of the line, who first seized the crown, died of despair occasioned by a series of Papal excommunications; *Galeazzo I*, his son, perished as a result of the cruelties which he endured in prison; poison was the instrument that made an end of *Stefano*; *Marco* was flung out of a window; *Lucchino* was a second victim of poison, administered in this case by his wife; *Matteo II* fell beneath the daggers of his own brothers; a third dose of poison was reserved for *Bernabò*, who died in his own dungeon at Trezzo; while *Giammaria* was pierced with many wounds on his way to church. This catalogue of assassinations covers the career of *one* reigning family, and all within the span of a single century. As for the abominable cruelties which served to avenge their dark suspicions, the tale is but too grimly familiar; the memory is still green, in that unhappy province which endured his reign, of the mastiff-packs employed by *Giammaria* to tear his wretched subjects limb from limb—those same Milanese who, at long last, scotched the monster, once and for all, in 1412. I earnestly beseech my reader's pardon for having dared to cite such grisly incidents, merely in order to substantiate a literary theory; but we in France, over the last twenty years or so, have bit by bit accepted the belief that courage flowers nowhere, save in the shade of a fine pair of military whiskers, while deep learning grows only in the arid fields of pedantry. Pedantry, mark you, is a gainful occupation; and none requires less effort in the mastery.

By contrast to that fathomless gulf of mutual suspicion which, since the dawn of time itself, has lain like an abyss between the Italian prince and his grovelling subjects, we in

---

[1] Which reader has ever heard of the Benzoni, sovereigns of Crema, or of the Dukes of Malatesta, rulers in Ravenna? [1826]

France, ever since the rise of the *bourgeoisie*, have observed the true affection with which the merchant-companies of Paris have beheld the King; for in days gone by, beginning with the reign of Louis the Fat, it was the King who protected them against the feudal aristocracy. In centuries nearer our own, the *bourgeoisie* adored the King, regardless of his attributes or merits, in imitation of the *Great Lords of the Land*, whose unfailing protests of adulation conspired to smooth the path for the exercise of their normal courtier's profession: begging, grabbing and begging for more*. But in Italy, at no single period in all her history, has the like of this been seen; and signor Foscolo indeed awoke an echo in every heart, when, alluding to Machiavelli, he wrote in *i Sepolcri*:

> *Te beata, gridai . . .*
> *. . . quando il monumento*
> *Vidi ove posa il corpo di quel grande*
> *Che temprando lo scettro a' regnatori*
> *Gli allôr ne sfronda, ed alle genti svela*
> *Di che lagrime grondi, e di che sangue.*[1]

In our own time, Italian prose can never be too wordy; the reader wants the *meaning* made clear, no matter what the cost; this is what makes it so abominably difficult, when the weather is at all warm, to read any serious Italian author. Italians, on the other hand, simply lack the *instinct* to grapple with Voltaire, Montesquieu or Courier, with their petty little conceits and allusions and their whole range of what one might entitle *monarchic insinuations*. This mastery of a feather-weight stylistic touch the Frenchman owes to his longstanding traditions of elegant flirtation—nowadays so grotesquely out of fashion. But here, in the South, love is a desperately serious business, and no woman of Italy, at the first lapse from gravity in your advances, will respond other than by anger or by silence.

---

[1] Machiavelli lies buried in the Church of *Santa Croce*, in Florence, beside the tombs of Michelangelo, Alfieri and Galileo. [1826]

If you are resolved to seize the first favourable opportunity which the evening may offer to whisper a word or two close to her heart, then you must steadfastly set watch upon your tongue, lest it betray you into merriment; you must even set your face against the hilarity of others, and gaze upon her with inflexible melancholy.

For an Italian, brevity, far from being the very soul of wit, is merely *unintelligible*. Ellipsis is excused solely by the intensity of passion; the heart of Italy responds to *Parisina* and *The Corsair* not a whit less warmly than that of England; but the mind of Italy, even at this late hour, still fails to grasp *les Lettres persanes*. Yet, in spite of such proliferating verbiage, Italian prose, as it is written today, is anything but lucid. Oh, the coals of fire that shall be heaped upon my head for this unwary pronouncement! I shall be *bue, stivale e somaro*.

16th January. Here, in Italy, the art of love is treated with imponderable gravity, discussed with no less earnestness than are stocks and shares in Paris. For instance, this very evening, signora Gherardi, the loveliest creature, I dare aver, that ever sprang from the rich soil of Brescia, where beauty without peer or parallel resides in women's eyes, was saying to me:

'There are four distinct categories of love:

(i) *Desire*, which is the province of brute beasts, savages and Europeans who are no better than either.

(ii) *Passion*, which is the love that Eloisa bore to Abelard, or Julie d'Etange to Saint-Preux.

(iii) *Inclination*, which was the constant delight of France throughout the eighteenth century, and which Marivaux, Crébillon, Duclos and Madame d'Epinay have portrayed with such incomparable delicacy.

(iv) *Self-Esteem*—the sort of love which prompted your own duchesse de Chaulnes, as she granted her noble hand to M. de Giac, to observe: *A Duchess, in the eyes of a bourgeois, can never seem more than thirty**.'

That strange, illogical revolution, which stage by stage condemns the lover to behold all perfection in his mistress' eyes, is referred to, in signora Gherardi's circle, as the process of *crystallisation*.

Tonight, for once, this delightful being was fallen into an argumentative mood. But true love is rare in France, being stifled by vanity, along with all other passions of any intensity: consequently I should merely bore my reader if I related all I heard. A score of illustrations were advanced to bear out this or that particular theory; one single instance I may perhaps relate, having first abridged it in the telling, if only because the heroine was both a relation and a friend of signora Gherardi herself. You must know that, in Italy, women wield far greater influence than in any other land, but they may be chastised with a corresponding increase of severity and with never a fear of public outcry. Courage may *perform* what it dare not *print*: hence the failure of the novel as a *genre* in Italy.

Count Valamara, a fair-haired, foppish creature of exquisitely gentle lineaments, being wounded in his self-esteem by jealousy of Cardinal Z***, in whose company his wife was wont to spend her evenings (nor could he discover means to prevent her from so doing), did first fill the town with rumours of a distant journey he must make to Paris, and did then proceed to abduct his wife, conveying her secretly to a castle situated amid the insalubrious marshes of the Po, not far from Ponte-Lagoscuro. There he lived with her, to all outward appearances in harmony and concord, yet never addressing a single word to her, no more than to the pair of aged and sinister retainers whom he had brought hither with him from the city. To tell the truth, however, this young creature who was his wife, and whose nervous temperament went hand in hand with an un-bridled and romantic sensibility, far from languishing on behalf of Cardinal Z***, was passionately enamoured of Gardinghi, the famous lawyer, who loved her in return, yet who had never received from her the least sign of encouragement; rather did she treat him more harshly than any other. Gardinghi had been reduced to a state where he might gaze at her from afar, yet never dare address a single word to her. Some months after her sudden disappearance, disquieting rumours began to fly about the streets of Bologna. Gardinghi embarked upon a search; after many efforts, he discovered the castle hard by Ponte-Lagoscuro, but unhappily lacked the courage to penetrate within the walls, lest he deserve the anger of this woman who had never acknowledged that she loved him save by the implication of her glance. At long last, however, after a space of some fifteen or twenty days spent lurking in disguise in a nearby village, having chosen for his lodging a mean tavern, to which, on rare occasions, one of the grim-faced domestics from the castle was wont to resort for a glass of wine, he overheard the fellow say: '*Il signor conte* treats the poor *contessina* how he will; *è un signore* (*i.e.*, *he*, being of noble birth, stands well above the law); while *we* are likely to end our days as galley-slaves.' Terrified by what he had heard, Gardinghi overcame his hesitation; the very next morning, with a pistol in his hand, he forced his way into the presence of Count Valamara, claiming, for form's sake, to be an emissary from the Vice-Legate. Once within the walls, he made his way towards the bed where lay the *contessina*; but already the power of speech had passed from her. Hurriedly summoning two peasant women to attend her, he settled beside her; nor did he ever again abandon the woman whom he loved, and who had still three days to live: she was not yet four-and-twenty years of age. The Count's behaviour by now was bordering on insanity; he seemed to be imploring mercy from Gardinghi, and left him master of the castle. Differing versions of the tale relate, however, that he tried to kill him, seizing a gun and firing it at him; but the lawyer himself has steadily denied the truth of this assertion. Today, the Count is believed to be in America; the lawyer, from that very hour, deserted the company of his friends and showed himself no more in society;

since which time, he has accumulated that stupendous fortune which makes his name sound so familiar to you. He still keeps in his service the two aged retainers of the Count; and they maintain that, every now and then, he speaks to them of the unhappy *contessina*. It is generally conjectured that she was murdered by a simple process of mental cruelty, without resort to poison or stiletto.

17th January. Tonight I was privileged to receive an invitation to attend a supper-party arranged in honour of the return of don Tommaso Bentivoglio, who arrived home yesterday from Paris. The company hung eagerly upon his words; I suspect that my own presence may have been a deliberate move to check the extravagance of his imagination. Be that as it may, here is *Paris* seen through the eyes of a foreigner, of a man who is primarily a pleasure-seeker, yet a shrewd observer none the less. In spite of the filthiness of the streets—which is due to nothing so much as to sheer *stupidity*[1]—and to the vexations of the police,[2] Paris is the universal dream of every nation in Europe. The ladies plied poor don Tommaso with a host of questions; I must confine myself to recording only a small sample of the replies.

'The Parisian', said don Tommaso, 'is the very incarnation of kindliness; he is good-natured, sweet-tempered, obliging, trusting towards strangers; he never exacts an eye for an eye nor a tooth for a tooth; and even when he appears as plaintiff before the Judge, he sincerely tries to temper the bitterness of his complaint. Compared to the native of Berlin, London or Vienna, he is a shining angel; for all his ugliness, it is a pleasure to look at him. Anyone who is victimised by his Bishop or

[1] It is the *Government* which opposes the formation of that *General Trust Company*, whose function would be to finance, by means of loans, all branches of industry; one of these branches was to have been a *Sanitation Company*, undertaking to cleanse the city of Paris by removing the mire from the streets. The powers-that-be will neither act themselves, nor permit anyone else to act instead of them—a charming disposition! [1826]
[2] Expulsion of Lady Oxford. [1826]

his local *sous-préfet* automatically takes refuge in Paris. The accumulation of more than eight hundred thousand inhabitants in one city constrains the Government to behave generously: not for any lack of *will* to do harm, but for lack of means—*it simply has not the leisure to persecute the individual.*'

A passing allusion by don Tommaso to the subject of *society* provoked an instantaneous response: 'But tell us', enquired signora Filicori, one of the most remarkable women in all the land of Italy, 'tell us, my dear don Tommaso, what exactly *is* this *Parisian Society*, which has such a universal reputation?'

'Polite society *par excellence*', replied don Tommaso, 'is the company one meets in a *salon*, where the master of the house enjoys an income of one hundred thousand *livres* a year and can trace his ancestry back to the Knights of the Crusade.

'In millionaire banking circles', he went on, 'there is likewise, I grant you, something which passes for *society*—of a sort; but generally speaking, individuals of this class can talk of nothing but money, and will never forgive you for *existing* on six thousand francs a year. In England, at an equivalent level, the first consideration is that everything should be *as expensive as possible*; a man calculates the greater or lesser degree of consideration due to his neighbour by totting up the cost of each separate item on his dinner-menu. Whenever I was invited, whether in France or in England, to go among *nouveau-riche* families, where my name would convey none but the haziest of notions (the Bentivogli, in fact, were Lords of Bologna in the fifteenth century), I rapidly discovered that, if I stuck a five-hundred-guinea diamond in my cravat, my stock would rise quite appreciably. An industrial *milieu* gives your average Frenchman something to work for; he *enjoys* work, consequently he is happy; an aristocratic *milieu*, on the contrary, would leave him stranded like a fish out of water, the sorriest creature in the world; yet personally I must confess that I would rather live among folk who talk now and then about the Crusades. In the last analysis, perhaps, there is just as much insolence among the ancient landed gentry as there is among the millionaire bankers; but at least it is inbred in the family, it is not out to exact its pound of flesh for every insult swallowed in the course of a humble childhood; furthermore, even allowing the one to be as insolent as the other, I still appreciate that extra touch of good breeding, sometimes even of intelligence, which is the prerogative of the aristocracy. Taking the good times with the bad, a man who bears one of the illustrious names of history will, on an average, be content to remind me of his ancestry, say, one in two months; whereas a self-made manufacturer who has amassed a million with his own hands will glance at me at least three times during the course of an evening, so much as to say: *You must be no end of a dolt, young man. Look at you: thirty years old, and not made your fortune yet? Why, at your age, young fellow, I was already worth a hundred thousand; and on top of that, I owned an eighth share in V*** and Co. People like you, now—don't think I don't know you! Once a month or so, you let the money go hang and take a cab—now, don't you?* Economy, *my boy, that's the secret—economy. That's the only way to get what you want in the end. When you're enjoying a hundred thousand a year—all right, let's be fair, we'll say fifty thousand, then, just for argument's sake—well now, that's a different matter altogether, isn't it? Take me, now. I bought a horse yesterday: seven thousand—just like that! And took a box at the Opera, second row and all—you couldn't see right, not out of the old one, proper uncomfortable it was, too. Which reminds me, I must pass the word round among all the lads to come and give themselves a night out— save 'em no end of money, it will. Couldn't you* do *with a box at the Opera, eh? No, no, a pleasure, I'm sure . . . oh, by the by, just let me have your card, will you? Might forget your face otherwise, eh?* Whereupon my manufacturer plunges his hand into his pocket, and pulls out a fist-full of gold, and studies it.'

(Yet that same man owns three factories, and pays a living wage to fifteen hundred workers; consequently, granting *social utility* to be the only rational basis for reckoning merit, he is worth a hundred times more in terms of consideration than his neighbour, the Marquis of ***. M. le marquis, very fortunately, wields not a scrap of influence anywhere; for if he did, there would soon enough be civil war in France, and when the shooting started, *I* should enlist on the side of the manufacturers. Add to this, that every time I go to dine with M. le marquis, I am confronted with pretty sorry fare; yet for all that, I find him amiable and good-natured, I take pleasure in contributing to the conversation; and after all, what does it cost me, once a month or so, to slip in, seemingly by chance, a swift allusion to Philippe de Commines, and to mention the name of one of his illustrious ancestors, captain over a hundred men-at-arms, who fell at the battle of Montlhéry? *Roots in the past*—this is his *idée fixe*.) (These reflections are my own.)

'That class of society', continued don Tommaso Bentivoglio, 'which ought, logically, since the Restoration, to be the gayest, turns out, in my experience, to be the most melancholy: a young man of noble birth reads advanced literature; he admires America; and yet he remains, immutably, a *Marquis*. This is indeed a sorry paradox for a man of honour—to drag out one's weary life a *Marquis* and a *Liberal*, yet never to be wholly a Liberal, nor yet fully a Marquis! Your young scion of a noble house is affected with a pang of regret whenever he chances to meet his old school-friend, plain *Monsieur* Michel, who has opened a clothier's establishment, married him a pretty wife, grown prosperous, taken his open stand as a pillar of Liberalism —and, on top of all, is solidly contented. None the less, there is a certain compensating sweetness, whenever some plebeian upstart shows more intelligence than yourself—eclipsing, by his very presence, the mediocre glitter of your conversation— to bear down upon him with the sheer weight of your accumulated ancestry, and, with infinite good breeding, to show him up for what he is—an ill-bred tyke! But, long before the sweetness of this little triumph has even been fully savoured, in blunders some imbecile, some bone-headed, reactionary *ci-devant*, advocating a policy which would be infamous were it not so patently absurd; and is it not distressing for a man of principle to find himself so placed, that he dare not voice the logical arguments which *prove* the absurdity of this die-hard ignoramus and his 'policies', even on occasions to be forced to applaud him, and finally to see this nincompoop with his ridiculous proposals reap greater honour than yourself in the opinion of all the company assembled? One single word would set the world to right, restore the situation: but this word *may not be spoken*, for it would destroy the whole elaborate fabric of your position*.'

These observations, as don Tommaso presented them, were freely interlarded with anecdotes so hoary and so well-known that I am ashamed to record them. One instance must suffice. When M. Roland was appointed *Minister of the Interior*, a certain courtier, who chanced to witness his arrival at Versailles, exclaimed aghast:

'Merciful Heaven! Do you see? *No buckles on his shoes!*'

'Ah!' retorted General Dumouriez. 'Then all is lost!'

'Now', commented don Tommaso, 'the reasoning process here involved is one which *society* shows no intention of relinquishing, even today; every public figure of any stature who has been thrown up by the events of the last forty years has been judged by this same rule-of-thumb.

'In 1790, Murat—the same who was later to be Napoleon's general—being at this time regimental baggage-master to *Royal-Cravate**, employed some passably discourteous tactics against the noble Marquis who commanded the regiment; and *this* is the sin which *society* has never yet forgiven him. If this singular individual had chanced to be born a Prince of ancient lineage, the very least among his countless deeds of valour would have sufficed to win him high and lasting renown. Take, for instance, the occasion when an English frigate lay offshore, bombarding Naples. What does Murat do, but dress himself up in all his property-box regalia, and take his stand on board a dismasted vessel within easy range of the English ship? But the powder supplied to the Neapolitan gunners was such sorry stuff that their broadsides could be seen to drop harmlessly into the sea, many fathoms short of the enemy man-of-war, while the English salvoes were busy among the houses in Pizzo Falcone, smashing window-panes two good cable-lengths behind the flagship of the *King of Naples*. Yet the hero of this courageous venture, and of a hundred others no less valorous, being no better than a 'passably discourteous' rascal, his achievements rank no higher than *splendid transgressions*, as the theologians like to say.

'There is no shrewder judge', pursued don Tommaso, 'of the wealth of absurdities attending an intrigue, nor of any other such miniature facet of existence; but from the moment when the circumstances under review take on the gigantic proportions of heroism, then *Parisian society* is left floundering in the deepest of waters. The instrument by which it measures its values is not designed to cope with *magnitude* in any form— much as one might conceive a pair of compasses which may not extend beyond a given angle.'

I shall pass in rapid silence over don Tommaso's impression of the *features* of the average Parisian, whom he portrayed as 'ugly to the point of clownishness'; for I myself have heard the noblest features in Italy described as 'unsightly and grotesque' by French travellers. This violent antipathy— inevitably mutual—belongs to the irrational domain of instinct.

'But tell me, sir', interposed signor Tambroni, 'when France at last sees fit to arouse herself from her present stupor, will she fling herself into a carefree orgy of self-indulgence, as happened in the time of the Regency, in fierce revolt against that black hypocrisy which marred the latter days of Louis XIV? Or will not rather her weakness for *political economy* and for pragmatic government on the American pattern engulf her in that mystic, melancholy temperament which casts its shadow over Philadelphia?'

'Personally', replied don Tommaso, 'I had rather see the orgies. What nation, having frontiers so vulnerable as those of France from Dunkirk southward to Antibes, can afford to indulge in a greater degree of liberty than her neighbours? If ever, to the lasting misfortune of Italy, the pent-up hatred of Jesuitism, together with the refusal of the Sacraments, should drive France into the arms of Protestantism, Paris would soon grow as gay as Geneva!'[1]

However, just as the conversation hung undecided on the brink of politics, we were saved by the entry of Crescentini, the celebrated *castrato*, who promptly favoured us with two or three anecdotes which it would take thirty pages to record. 'At midnight', observed the famous singer, 'when the final curtain has fallen, and the audience leaves the theatre to stroll beneath the stars, each individual, as he wends his way homewards, sings snatches of melody under his breath: the ordinary run of mortals hum tunes they *know*; but the man whose heart was truly fashioned for music sings tunes which well up from the depths of his own creative imagination. These miniature arias of his are but the roughest sketches of what they might become; but they echo none the less the momentary *nuance* of his sensibility. It is more than twenty years now since I first entrusted this secret trick of mind-reading to la Lambertini, who, at the time, was beside herself with jealousy on account of her lover, the *marchese* Pepoli, that delightful character who used to whip his horses up into a gallop along the banks of the Brenta, and then, balanced high above the water in his careering chariot (*biga*), would perform a back-dive (*salto ribaltato*) straight into the river.'

Since I have already been speaking of one scion of the house of Bentivoglio, I cannot withstand the urge to record one or

---

[1] Love of beauty, allied with the art of love itself, are the enduring bulwarks which shelter Italy from any threat of puritan dreariness or methodist solemnity. I would surmise that here, south of the Alps, the very existence of art is linked with Popery. [1826]

two of the notions which came crowding into my head at the sight of don Tommaso; this, notwithstanding the fact that I had most solemnly resolved within myself to eschew the manner descriptive or historical.

By the end of the fourteenth century, we observe a Bentivoglio in all the major offices of state; the Italian republics, however, having granted full honour to the *useful* occupations of the city, the Bentivogli maintained their old allegiance to the *Guild of Butchers*. But from 1390 onwards, the spirit of republicanism entered into a rapid decline, and a few years later, in 1401, Giovanni Bentivoglio, leader of the *Scacchiera* faction (the *Liberals* of those far-off days), bade his followers proclaim him Lord of Bologna. Surprised by the famous Gian Galeazzo Visconti, Duke of Milan, whose levies were marching rapidly to the conquest of the whole peninsular, his army was routed on the field of Casalecchio, and the very next day, Giovanni Bentivoglio was assassinated by the rebellious mob (1402). Henceforward, the Holy See was to instigate a series of plots against the independence of Bologna—plots whose fruition was delayed for a span of one hundred and six years, when at long last the perseverance of the instigators was rewarded. After the death of Giovanni, Antonio, his son, spent many weary years in exile; until at last, in 1435, he received permission to return to the land of his birth; but on the 23rd of December of that same year, Pope Eugenio IV, jealous of the popular favour which clung about his name, laid hands on him as he left the shelter of his Palace, and ordered his head to be struck off then and there, without so much as the semblance of a trial. Simultaneously with this venture, Tommaso Zambeccari, whose influence in Bologna was second only to that of Bentivoglio, was seized and hanged from the windows of the Palace. In 1438, the generals in the service of the Duke of Milan captured the city, and established Annibale Bentivoglio, the son of Antonio, in the seat of government. The new ruler received in marriage a bastard daughter of the Duke himself, but soon enough fell victim to the dark suspicions of his father-in-law, the Tiberius of modern times, and was thrown into prison (1442). In the following year, however, he escaped from this duress, and made his way back into Bologna. The populace flew to arms and drove out the troops belonging to the Duke of Milan; and Annibale, holding no particular title and filling no specific office in the state, continued none the less to wield the sword of government.

At this time, the Bolognese, having failed, in spite of some fifteen or twenty abortive attempts at constitution-making, to discover a form of government propitious to every warring interest alike, were none the less weary of that precarious mode of life which, for want of a more accurate designation, we describe by the term *Republic*. Yet it is precisely this *precarious existence* which has moulded the primal character of Italy as we know it today. The three centuries of Spanish despotism which since have ground this character into degradation should not blind us to the fact that no other nation has such an abundance of pure republican blood in its veins. Scarcely half a century has elapsed since true republicanism was reborn in the world, under the guidance of Washington and Franklin; but it requires a full century and a half before *law* becomes *instinct*. Yet the most curious feature of the situation is that the Italian character is utterly devoid of that steadfast patience and stability of temperament which flourish on the northern slopes of their own Alps, and which have enabled the Swiss to preserve at least the semblance of a republic.

On the 24th of June, 1455, as Annibale Bentivoglio was leaving the church of San Giovanni Battista, he fell to the ground, transfixed by one mortal thrust from the sword of Baldassare Canedoli, who straightway ran through the streets of Bologna, crying: *Viva il popolo!* The populace did indeed rise up in anger, as he had expected; but it rose against the murderer, massacring his accomplices and destroying their houses.[1] No general outcry had clamoured for the life of Annibale; nor was he a tyrant.

His only heir was a child, six years of age and incapable of holding the reins of government. Count Poppi, chancing to be in Bologna at that time, drew the attention of the mob to the existence of a bastard son of Ercole Bentivoglio by the wife of Agnolo da Cascese, a Florentine merchant. Santi—the same who was later to be celebrated under the illustrious name of Santi Bentivoglio—entertained no suspicions concerning the mystery of his birth; and after the death of him whom he sincerely believed to be his father, he continued to reside in Florence, following the trade of wool-merchant which the latter had always plied. He was but two-and-twenty years of age when Cosimo de' Medici, being appraised of the situation in a letter sent by the *Signoria* of Bologna, summoned him into his presence, and with the following words, embarked upon one of the most singular dialogues which the pen of history has ever seen fit to record:

Weigh well, young man, this matter which you must consider: Wherein resideth, to the philosophic mind, the greater advantage— in the delights of a private citizen's estate, or in the pleasures which the government of a city may afford . . .? Having learned both who he was, and also of the great office to which he was called, Santi at first hesitated; but by the advice of Neri Capponi, in that season the first statesman in Florence, he was prevailed upon to accept. History does indeed appear, on this occasion, to have borrowed her material directly from the *Arabian Nights*.

Santi, welcomed with enthusiasm by the Bolognese, proved worthy of his elevation, and, for the space of sixteen years, governed the city with energetic and impartial justice. Upon his death, in 1462, Giovanni II, the son of Annibale, took from

[1] *Cronic. di Bolog.* Simonetta, Neri Capponi. Observe the singularly infamous episode in the career of General Ciarpelone, undertaken for a gain of four hundred florins. [1826]

his hands the helm of the republic. In a spirit similar to that of Lorenzo de' Medici in Florence, Giovanni II exploited every form of lure and enticement to *monarchise* his fellow-citizens. One family, however, remained impervious to the seduction of his courtly manners: the Malvezzi, a noble and influential clan, who conspired to overthrow him, but were delivered up by treachery (1488). Twenty members of the clan perished, by order of Giovanni II, upon the scaffold, while every living being who bore the name Malvezzi, regardless of whether or not he had had a hand in the conspiracy, was banished from the realm, and his estates made forfeit to the Prince. It was Giovanni II who, observing in the Bolognese a boundless passion for *beauty*, embellished their city with sumptuous buildings. Painters, sculptors, poets, scholars—all that generation of artists whose genius was the glory of Italy—were summoned to Bologna and rewarded with princely magnificence for their labours. Giovanni II enriched his native city with the most noble collection of statues, paintings, manuscripts and books. Furthermore, he maintained in his service a fine regiment of *assassins*, whose employment it was to remove (*scannare*), throughout the length and breadth of Italy, not only those who had offended him, but their sons and brothers likewise, lest they should feel the call of vengeance. This prince had reigned for four-and-forty years, during which time his one concern had been to transform the free citizens of a republic into a race of devoted *subjects*, when the impetuous genius of Julius II, one of the most skilful commanders whom chance has ever seen fit to place upon the Throne of St Peter, inspired him to lay siege to the city of Bologna (1506). Giovanni II, abandoning a people who bore no love towards him, took his treasure with him in his flight, and died an exile in an alien land.

On the 21st of May 1511, the French restored the ancient line of sovereignty in Bologna, in the persons of Annibale and Ermes, sons of Giovanni II; but their reign was hard put to it to survive a single year, and they were finally expelled from the territories of the republic when Bologna surrendered to the Pope. Since that fatal day, numerous scions of the house of Bentivoglio have earned renown and reputation by notable courage in the field, allied with a remarkable gift for poetry: for instance, Ippolito Bentivoglio, who died in 1585. The North but rarely affords the sight of this bright alliance between a deep skill in learning and a contemptuous disregard for life. Ippolito composed tragedies which enjoyed the widest success; music and architecture fell alike within his province; he knew Greek, and possessed every living tongue.

The history of the thirteenth, fourteenth and fifteenth centuries is the tale of those countless vain attempts to *evolve a system of sound government* which harassed the peninsula. We in our own generation, happier in this at least than our fore-fathers in theirs, have learned that any government composed of *two Houses* and a *President*, or King, is tolerable; but at the same time, we should take care lest we delude ourselves; for this most *eminently reasonable* government is (one may suspect) just as eminently unfavourable to genius and originality in any form; and no period in history can ever hope to rival the fascination of the Middle Ages. Hence the eternal, insoluble argument which is due to break out at any moment between the poets and the philosophers*.

Imagine that in the year 1455 or thereabouts—the steady rule of Santi having then endured for some nine years—some genius were to have published a treatise in three fine quarto volumes, enunciating (with appropriate commentary) these *Four Commandments*:

(i) The thirty wealthiest citizens of Bologna shall form, for the duration of their natural lives, a *Council* for the deliberation of affairs of state.

(ii) Fifty citizens, chosen by ballot every third year, shall form a second Chamber.

(iii) These two bodies, at the expiration of every tenth

year, shall elect a *podestà*; and Santi Bentivoglio shall be the first to hold this office.

(iv) All laws shall be enacted by these three powers in conjunction with each other, and the *podestà* shall appoint his nominees to every office of state, subject to the approval of the *Thirty*.

If this had been set out and acted on, then Bologna might have realised her heart's desire. The city had needed to endure some thirty years of revolution; but when at last, by the relentless operation of the laws of nature, every citizen who was thirty years old or more on the day when that famous quarto treatise saw the light had vanished from the scene of human affairs, then Bologna would have weathered the storm, and come safe to rest in the haven of her felicity. It is unlikely that her renown would have suffered much harm from this pacific existence; in all probability, she would still have produced Domenichino, the brothers Carracci and Guido Reni, the only men of genius who have adorned her reputation since 1455.

If I have pursued this fancy for a space, it is because it applies no less aptly to Florence, or indeed to any of the republics of Italy. But alas! the time was not yet ripe. In Florence, at twenty-year intervals, thirty picked citizens were granted the *balìa*, or in other words, the power to devise a new constitution and to put it into practice. Whereupon, promptly enough, there ensued another spate of terror and banishments. Whenever a nation has a *precise* idea of the type of government it desires, it has no need to commit atrocities.[1]

If we observe what boundless dominion the Popes may wield, even in this latter age in which we live, I have no need to stress the almost infinite respect which they commanded in the fourteenth century. Notwithstanding this vast authority, however, on one occasion (in 1361), Pope Innocent VI having dispatched a pair of emissaries to the Court of that same

[1] The *Terror* of 1793 will never be resurrected. [1826]

Bernabò Visconti, Duke of Milan, whose name is already so familiar to the reader of these pages, the Nuncios chanced to come upon the Duke some miles outside his capital, upon a bridge which spanned a narrow stream known as the Lambro. Bernabò demanded to be informed without delay what matter the Bulls might contain; whereupon, judging the style of address contained therein to be unbecoming, he turned to the emissaries with the words: *Scegliete, o mangiare o bere* ('Choose whether you would rather eat or drink'). The significance of this laconic threat was not lost upon the two ambassadors: the choice was offered them, whether they would rather eat the Bulls, wax seals, leaden seals, parchment, braid and all, or else be flung headlong into the Lambro. They opted for the first alternative, and the meal was served and eaten then and there, upon that very bridge whose hump-backed arch may still be seen today. Some few months later, one of the two Nuncios, whose surname was Guillaume, himself ascended the Throne of St Peter, taking the name of Urban V.[1]

Under a rational scheme of government, defiance of the Pope takes the form of pamphleteering rather than of practical jokes. I must forbear to mention the splendid valour and the prudent cruelties which characterised the age: the illustrations are too numerous. Florence having embarked upon a maritime campaign against the Pisans (1405), her fleet was blockading the mouth of the Arno. Upon a certain occasion, when the Florentine galleys were giving hot pursuit to a Pisan vessel laden with corn, the quarry sought refuge in the lee of the Tower of Vada, beneath the protection of whose mortars she might heave to in safety. Whereupon a certain citizen of Florence, by name Pietro Marenghi, resolved to swim towards the enemy; and thus, bearing in one hand, which he held high and dry above the waves, a burning fire-brand, he set forth, beneath a hail of projectiles of every description, and at last

1 *Annal. Mediol.*, p. 799; Verri, vol. I, p. 381; Gattari, *Storia Padovana.*
[1826]

succeeded in setting fire to the Pisan ship. Pietro Marenghi was fortunate enough to regain his own vessel.

Giovanni Auguto*, the noted military commander—that same who, having been born in England, was finally laid to rest, with much due pomp and ceremony, in *Santa Maria del Fiore*, the cathedral church of Florence, and upon whose tomb there may be seen one of the earliest masterpieces of the painter's art, *viz.*, his likeness, seated on horseback, portrayed in colossal dimensions by Paolo Uccello—having ordered his troops to sack the city of Faenza (1371), two of his officers had forced their way into a convent, and there, among the pupils whose education was confided to the Order, had discovered a damsel of rare and exquisite beauty; whereupon, each claiming to possess her, a furious quarrel broke out, and swords were drawn. At this moment, Auguto himself broke in upon the scene; and he, fearing lest he should lose either one or the other of his valiant henchmen, drew his dagger and plunged it into the breast of the lovely maiden, who fell dead at his feet. (*Superb subject for a painting:* the dying maiden, Auguto in the act of stabbing her, the two brawling men-at-arms, one of whom has not seen her fall and still threatens his companion with his sword, the blade of it trembling with fury, while the other, so placed that he has witnessed his general's act, stands transfixed with horror; in the distant background, a glimpse of nuns fleeing before the licentious soldiery.) In the course of another campaign, two begging Friars approached Auguto in a deputation, and greeted him with the words: '*May the Lord grant you His peace!*' To which the English captain replied with icy disdain: '*May the Lord destroy the alms by which you live!*' No little affrighted, the Friars asked him what these words might signify. 'Is their meaning not plain enough?' he retorted. 'By *war* I live; by *peace* (which you would wish upon me) I must starve!'

18th January. 'What!' demanded a Bolognese, vibrant with

anger. 'Just because France chanced to throw up a Mirabeau and a Danton, now *Mexico* is to be free, while it is decreed that Bologna should forget what she was in 1500, and revive the *status quo* of 1790! *No, per Dio!* Let the Pope grant us at least a half-way freedom of the press; let the College of Cardinals be confined within its ancient, constitutional functions, as His Holiness' *necessary* adviser; or else, *per Dio! nascerà qualche disordine!*'

'Doubtless', I argued, 'and then you will wake up to discover thirty thousand Russian troops upon the soil of Italy. The enemy to be overthrown is not the Pope, but rather the Tsar.'

'You, sir, are nothing but a damned, ill-bred upstart!'

I was forgetting to mention that Bologna has forfeited her Embassy in Rome. The privilege, which was granted in 1512, was not restored after 1814. By this manoeuvre, precisely at a time when the clamour for liberty is increasing within the city, the powers in their wisdom have seen fit to remove the one piece of stage-property which might have fostered the necessary illusion. O powers of logic! The authorities are determined to provoke a landslide, rather than accept a gradual declivity. Signor degli Antonj, one of the leading citizens of Bologna, is at present engaged upon a memorandum touching this matter and destined for the cognisance of the Pope. Cardinal Consalvi, a genuine seventeenth-century aristocrat, is equipped with a subtle mastery of the art of seduction, a delicate instinct for Court intrigue, together with the most sensitive appreciation of the finer qualities which constitute the excellence of an *opera buffa*; consequently, the memorandum composed by signor degli Antonj, which is the wonder of all Bologna, is fated to strike his intelligence as nothing more than a tedious wilderness of paper. Do you recall the *Archbishop of Lisbon* in Lemercier's *Pinto*? Here you have an exquisite portrait of the modern administrator.

And yet, if Cardinal Consalvi were all things that, by virtue of his office, he *ought* to be, then at all costs I should decline to meet His Eminence; for his society would be as aridly wearisome as that of a President of the United States.

From Turin in the west to Venice in the east, from Bassano in the north to Ancona in the south, Napoleon's victories, by lightening the burden which lay on the people, instilled a mortal fear into the nobility; promptly (1796) vain luxury was banished from the state; order appeared in the body politic; economy reigned, debts were paid off; retreat to country solitudes became a necessary fashion. Between 1796 and 1814, the personal fortunes of the aristocracy were doubled. In the face of this common enemy, the nobles renounced their age-old rivalry of pomp and splendour, vying with each other now in a novel contest of prudence and economy. Profligate expenditure soon grew to be the hallmark of the self-made man of humble origins. In certain provinces—in Piedmont, for instance—the aristocracy received official intimation of the shape of things to come, when the French, no sooner had they occupied the country, exacted tribute in the shape of a compulsory war-levy. Thus, living on their own estates, far from the amusements of the great cities, they turned to husbandry as a resource against the inroads of boredom. Among their offspring, the generation which, by 1796, was already in its twenties, was affected by the enthusiasm of the times, enlisted in the service of the French and gained experience. Those children who were but four or five years old at the period of their parents' enforced retirement received their schooling at the hands of some local village priest, and thus were prevented from acquiring any ideas whatsoever, bar the smattering of rational notions which fell eventually to their lot in 1809 or thereabouts, when they enrolled as Guards of Honour or as Auditors (thus we find signor di Santa-Rosa exercising the functions of *sous-préfet* on the Genoese littoral). By contrast, that whole generation which first saw the light of day in the neighbourhood of 1810 now languishes in the hands of the

Jesuits of Modena, or in other words, is being brought up in at atmosphere of servile flattery from the age of eight, and by 1827 will have developed into a race of irredeemable morons. The whole pedagogic system of the Jesuit order rests on a basis of egoism and reciprocal denunciation.[1]   must not fail, however, to append one significant and valuable truth: *there are exceptions*. A number of children, born of wealthy families towards 1800, have been entrusted to the care of M. de Fellenberg, in his Academy near Bern, at which establishment, in spite of its aristocratic tone, not to mention its tendency to breed a consciousness of *caste*, the education provided is less absurd—and consequently a *greater danger to civilisation*—than that offered by the Jesuits. Impoverished nobles send their sons to the University of Pavia; it was one of these young gentlemen who found occasion to observe to me: 'In time of war, the peasantry should be authorised by law to kill every man they meet who does not speak Italian.' The Austrians have declared that all persons educated outside the territories of their own dominion shall automatically be disqualified from taking service with the state; the only exception to this decree being made in favour of the colleges of Tuscany, whence the pupils emerge as wise as greybeards, and wholly as incapable of any generous response.

The average Italian of 1830—similar in this to his mediaeval forbears—is destined to experience a passionate love of liberty, without the faintest notion of the means by which his dream may be fulfilled. His first step, inevitable in the circumstances, will be to set up a spate of revolutionary governments; but he will never discover the secret of dislodging the latter in favour of a steady constitutional authority: his innate self-conceit will never allow him to copy the formula evolved in France.[2]

[1] *Vide: Les Constitutions des Jésuites* (Prague edition).
[2] In 1822, in Naples no less than in Spain, it was customary to deride the 'rash temerity' of the French, whose bid for freedom had achieved but half its object, while even this moderate degree of liberty might be maintained only by imposing a burden of taxation twice as heavy as in 1789. [1826]

Alas, I must soon bid farewell to Bologna, this fair city whose symbol is *intelligence*. During the fortnight I have lived here I have discovered a style of life most aptly suited, both to my own natural tastes and also to such pleasures as the province may afford; and this indeed is a quality not lightly to be dismissed. No journey is likely to prove so constantly agreeable that the traveller never encounters that fatal instant when his thoughts revert nostalgically towards the intimate satisfactions of his own familiar circle. This sense of disappointment is the more acute, in that it is common to suppose that a tour of Italy must of necessity be an uninterrupted succession of ecstatic delights. Yet, to bring home a good bag of partridges, it is not enough that the coverts should be abundantly stocked; it is further necessary to carry a gun. Three out of every four travellers appreciate no pleasures save those of *polite society*, and are wholly impervious to the delights of art. There is, moreover, a certain breed of wealthy manufacturer who can grasp neither the one nor the other; the only satisfaction *he* can know is that afforded by a private circle of parasites. Many an English traveller, at each successive halt, is content to read such descriptions of the place as may be extant in the works of the Latin poets; whereupon he resumes his itinerary, railing bitterly against the manners and customs of the land of Italy, of which manners and customs his experience has been gathered exclusively through contact with the vilest classes of society. Now, there exists in all the world but one despotism which has suffered the lower orders to retain a scrupulous degree of honesty, and that is *Turkey*.

Since I have been in Bologna, I have become an *Associate* of the City Museum, having paid my subscription to the Curator. Thus, whenever I find myself with half an hour in hand, devoid alike of visits and excursions, it has become my habit to climb the steps of this Museum, intending, in all likelihood, to confine my attention to one solitary painting: Raphael's *Santa Cecilia*, for instance, or the *Self-Portrait* by

Guido Reni, or Domenichino's *Sant 'Agnese*. Almost every morning, I wend my way towards Casalecchio, making a picturesque excursion to the Falls of the *Reno* (the Bolognese equivalent of the *Bois de Boulogne*); or, failing this, I turn my steps towards *la Montagnola*, where the *Corso* of the city may be witnessed. Here you may discover an *Esplanade* as broad as the gardens of the *Tuileries*, tastefully planted by Napoleon with ornamental trees, and elevated by some thirty feet above the level of that far-stretching plain which unrolls from the very foot of *la Montagnola*; for let your eyes but travel northwards, the nearest eminence to interrupt the view is the hill above Vicenza, some two-and-seventy miles from where you stand. The remainder of my day is spent in visits, or else dawdled away beneath the portico of *San Petronio*. When it rains, I have recourse to my beloved mediaeval historians: Giovanni, Matteo and Filippo Villani; Ammirato; Velluti; the *Chronicles* of Pisa, Sienna and Bologna; the *Life* of the famous Minister Acciajoli, by Matteo Palmieri; the *Annals* of Pistoia, by Tronci; Malevolti, Poggio, Capponi, Bruni, Buoninsegni, Malespini, Corio, Soldo, Sanuto, Dei, Buonaccorsi, Nardi, Nerli—all honest folk amongst whom the talent for historical narrative has not been corrupted and destroyed by the sham 'culture' of our Academies*. But I have no ambition to dictate a daily schedule for other travellers; in such matters, each man is captain of his soul; I am merely describing my *own* routine.

Among the women of Bologna, I have observed two or three varieties of beauty or species of intelligence, of whose very existence I was previously unsuspecting. I had never encountered such melting beauty in alliance with such a provocative originality of mind, as I perceived in signora Gherardi.[1]

---

[1] Despite the icy fear which grips the rulers of Italy, and which, since 1801, has been hardening into tyranny or crystallising in a spate of executions, a wealth of new buildings is constantly being erected in Bologna, as indeed in every city in the land; this activity is symptomatic of the rich harvest of prosperity and culture whose seeds were sown in

PIETRA MALA, *19th January*. At first, as it strikes out from
Bologna to cross the Apennine, the highroad to Florence
follows the almost level bottom of a charming valley. For the
space of an hour, we hugged the course of the torrent; then,
gradually, we began to climb among the clumps of chestnut-
trees which border the road. At Loiano, we halted, and,
glancing back northwards, we discovered a magnificent view:
the eye strikes diagonally across the celebrated plain of Lombardy, which attains to a hundred and twenty miles in breadth,

Italy by Napoleon, and whose tenacity, having survived the fall of the
militias, continues to resist the worst efforts of the obscurantists to destroy
it. None the less, Bologna, in this year of grace 1827, is in a sorry plight;
and it is the consequent fear of compromising certain people with the
authorities which alone prevents me naming those many intelligent and
charming friends who welcomed me with such indulgent hospitality.
The same consideration forbids me to print certain anecdotes whose
subject-matter is too plainly indicative of the personalities concerned.
After the death of Cardinal Lante, Bologna was most admirably administered by His Eminence Cardinal Spina, whom we in Paris have beheld
as Grand Almoner to Her Highness the Princess Borghese. It was purely
on account of the respect which the city bore towards this Legate that
Bologna refused to rise in support of the *Constitutionalists* in Naples.
But alas! Cardinal Spina was recalled by Pope Leo XII, and replaced by
His Eminence Cardinal Albano. Let me assure the idle traveller that the
project of writing in no way entered into the original purpose of my
journey; but since the circumstances of a tourist's existence are so designed
as to shatter all the trammels of *habit*, the sojourner in a strange land must
of necessity have occasional recourse to the *Universal Fountainhead of
Happiness*—in plainer language, he must *work*, lest he begin to regret that
he ever left Paris. He scribbles notes in pencil at odd moments, while
waiting for the post-horses, *etc.*; in summer, he sits in some church and
jots down observations, for churches offer a pleasantly cool retreat;
their very dimness is agreeable, while they are free of insects and offer
silence in exchange for the noise without. During the course of my
travels, I noted down scarcely the tenth part of the host of distinct
sensations which I experienced. Yet today I remember nothing, save
that which I recorded at the time; indeed, quite frequently, as I re-read
these notes, which have slumbered for the last ten years in the inviolate
secrecy of a sealed packet—in which precise state, to tell the truth, they
were conveyed to Paris by the special carrier in the service of N***and
Co.—I seem to be perusing the work of some unknown, but contemporary traveller. [1826]

and which, in length, extends from Turin to Venice. These measurements—I confess it openly—derive from memory rather than from observation; nevertheless, with such a wealth of famous cities at one's feet, there is a fascination in trying to discover them in the midst of this infinite expanse of plain, whose floor is carpeted with trees as though it were a forest. Every Italian loves to play the *cicerone*; the master of the post-station at Loiano was resolved to convince me that I could espy the Adriatic (fifty-seven miles distant); but I must decline to acknowledge the honour. Upon the left, the horizon stands much nearer to the eye; and countless summits of the Apennine offer the singular aspect of an *ocean of mountains* retiring in a succession of watery crests towards the skyline.

Praise Heaven, indeed, that I am *not* a scientist: this massy pile of rocks heaped each upon the other afforded me this morning a not unimpressive experience (for is it not indeed a species of *Beauty*?); whereas my companion, a most learned geologist, can still perceive nothing in all this stirring panorama but an array of arguments to confirm the hypotheses of his compatriot, signor Scipione Breislak, and to confound the theories of certain French and English scholars. Signor Breislak, a Roman by birth, maintains that everything which we behold upon the surface of the globe, mountains and valleys alike, was formed originally by *fire*. To take another instance, were I in the least versed in the science of meteorology, I could surely never know so keen a thrill of pleasure on certain days, as I stand and watch the clouds go scudding across the sky, or else take wild delight in the proud castles and monstrous dragons which they conjure up in my imagination. Once, among the chalets of Switzerland, I watched a shepherd stand motionless for three whole hours, his arms folded across his breast, gazing at the snow-covered summit of the Jungfrau. Such, for him, was the very stuff of *music*. My ignorance not infrequently allows me within hailing distance of the spiritual state of that old shepherd.

Ten minutes' stroll brought us to a sink-hole choked with small stones, whence there rises a vapour of some description, almost perpetually ignited. We flung a bottle of water over these stones, and promptly the fire blazed twice as fiercely. This phenomenon earned me a full hour's lecture on the subject, to which I steadfastly refused to listen, lest it should threaten to transform a noble mountain into a chemical laboratory. At long last, however, my scientist friend fell silent; and thus was I enabled to strike up a conversation with the group of peasants who stood clustered about the fireside in this mountain inn; a far cry, indeed, from the charming *salon* of signora Martinetti, where we had foregathered no later than yesterday evening! I here set down a tale which I have just heard told beneath the cavernous inglenook of the inn at Pietra Mala.

Some two years since, it began to be perceived, both in Bologna and in Florence, that travellers who took the road upon which we were now embarked showed a strange tendency to vanish. The enquiries which were set on foot by the two spineless governments concerned succeeded only in establishing one fact beyond dispute, namely, that no trace of human remains was ever discovered among the ridges of the Apennine. One evening, a Spanish traveller and his wife were obliged by the raging snow-storm which had overtaken them to seek the shelter of an ill-famed tavern in Pietra Mala —this same village where we now find ourselves. It would be hard to conceive a more squalid and unprepossessing hovel; yet the hostess, so the travellers remarked, wore diamond rings, which ill-accorded with her ogre-ish appearance. This woman told the travellers that she would send a servant to borrow white bed-linen from the priest, whose dwelling lay some three miles distant from the inn. The Spaniard's young wife being scared almost to death by the sinister aspect of the tavern, her husband, pretexting that he desired to fetch a handkerchief from the coach outside, made signs to the *vetturino*, and managed, without being observed from within the building, to hold a certain conversation with him; incidentally, this fellow too, who had heard rumours and to spare concerning travellers who had vanished, was in no better state, if not in a worse, than his passengers. Rapidly, they agreed together upon a plan. In the full hearing of the hostess, the Spaniard advised the *vetturino* that he and his wife should be awakened at an hour not later than five o'clock the following morning; after which, having let it be understood that they both felt unwell, the travelling couple ate no more than a few mouthfuls at the supper-table, and retired immediately to their room; here they waited, half expiring with terror and straining their ears for the least noise, until every sound within the house had ceased; and so at last, about an hour after midnight, they made their escape and fled to join the *vetturino*, who was already waiting at the appointed place, the better part of a mile from the tavern, with his horses and his coach.

Upon his safe return to Florence, the *vetturino* poured out the tale of his alarms to his own master, signor Polastro, a man of scrupulous honour. Urged on by the insistence of the latter, the police made strenuous efforts, and after many failures, arrested a certain vagabond creature who was observed to haunt this particular tavern in Pietra Mala. Under the threat of immediate execution, he revealed to his captors that the priest—a man named Biondi, the same to whom the hostess was accustomed to send out to borrow white bed-linen—was the chief among this band of brigands, whose practice it was to descend upon the inn towards two o'clock in the morning, at which hour it might be expected that the travellers would be sound asleep in their beds. There was always a grain or two of opium in the wine which was served at supper. The rule of the gang was to murder both the travellers and the *vetturino*; after which deed, the robbers would stow the corpses away once more inside their own carriage, harness the horses, and drag it to some deserted spot among the high peaks of the

L

Apennine. Once this chosen place was reached, the horses likewise would be slaughtered, while the coach, the travellers, and all their private effects would be destroyed in one grim funeral pyre; nothing, strictly *nothing*, would be preserved, save only gold, silver and precious stones. The corpses and the charred remnants of the vehicle would be buried with meticulous care, while watches and jewellery would be sold in distant Genoa. Alerted at long last by this confession, the police managed to entrap the whole gang as its members sat all unawares about a sumptuous banquet laid for them in the presbytery and presided over by Biondi; only that worthy lady, the hostess of the tavern, was not present; and she, whose task it was, by sending out for sheets, to warn the gang that travellers worthy of attention had recently descended at the inn, was discovered at home in her own lair.

Judging by all reports that I have heard, I perceive that I shall have little good to say of the present-day inhabitants of Florence. Be that as it may, at least I can avoid betraying the laws of hospitality; consequently I have just this minute consigned to the flames some seventeen letters of introduction destined for the city beside the Arno.

FLORENCE, 22nd January. The day before yesterday, as I descended upon Florence from the high ridges of the Apennine, my heart was leaping wildly within me. What utterly childish excitement! At long last, at a sudden bend in the road, my gaze plunged downward into the heart of the plain, and there, in the far distance, like some darkling mass, I could distinguish the sombre pile of *Santa Maria del Fiore* with its famous Dome, the masterpiece of Brunelleschi.

'Behold the home of Dante, of Michelangelo, of Leonardo da Vinci', I mused within my heart. 'Behold then this noble city, the Queen of mediaeval Europe! Here, within these walls, the civilisation of mankind was born anew; here it was, that Lorenzo de' Medici so brilliantly sustained the part of Kingship, and established a Court at which, for the first time since the reign of Augustus, military prowess was reduced to a secondary role.' As the minutes passed, so these memories came crowding and jostling one against the other within my soul, and soon I found myself grown incapable of rational thought, but rather surrendered to the sweet turbulence of fancy, as in the presence of some beloved object. Upon approaching the *San-Gallo* gate, with its unbeautiful Triumphal Arch, I could gladly have embraced the first inhabitants of Florence whom I encountered.

At the risk of losing all that multitude of personal belongings which a man accumulates about him on his travels, immediately the ceremony of the *passport* had, with fitting ritual, been observed, I abandoned my conveyance. So often have I studied views of Florence, that I was familiar with the city before I ever set foot within its walls; I found that I could thread my way through the streets without a guide. Turning to the left, I passed before a bookseller's shop, where I bought a couple of descriptive surveys of the town (*guide*). Twice only was I forced to enquire my way of passers-by, who answered me with a politeness which was wholly French and with a most singular accent; and at last I found myself before the façade of *Santa Crocce*.

Within, upon the right of the doorway, rises the tomb of Michelangelo; beyond, lo! there stands Canova's effigy of Alfieri; I needed no *cicerone* to recognise the features of the great Italian writer. Further still, I discovered the tomb of Machiavelli; while facing Michelangelo lies Galileo. What a race of men! And to these already named, Tuscany might further add Dante, Boccaccio and Petrarch. What a fantastic gathering! The tide of emotion which overwhelmed me flowed so deep that it scarce was to be distinguished from religious awe. The mystic dimness which filled the church, its plain, timbered roof, its unfinished façade—all these things spoke volumes to my soul. Ah! could I but forget. . . ! A Friar

moved silently towards me; and I, in the place of that sense of
revulsion all but bordering on physical horror which usually
possesses me in such circumstances, discovered in my heart a
feeling which was almost friendship. Was not he likewise a
Friar, Fra Bartolomeo di San Marco, that great painter who
invented the art of *chiaroscuro*, and showed it to Raphael, and
was the forefather of Correggio? I spoke to my tonsured acquaintance, and found in him an exquisite degree of politeness.
Indeed, he was delighted to meet a Frenchman. I begged him
to unlock for me the chapel in the north-east corner of the
church, where are preserved the frescoes of Volterrano. He
introduced me to the place, then left me to my own devices.
There, seated upon the step of a faldstool, with my head
thrown back to rest upon the desk, so that I might let my gaze
dwell on the ceiling, I underwent, through the medium of
Volterrano's *Sybils*, the profoundest experience of ecstasy that,
as far as I am aware, I ever encountered through the painter's
art. My soul, affected by the very notion of being in Florence,
and by the proximity of those great men whose tombs I had
just beheld, was already in a state of trance. Absorbed in the
contemplation of *sublime beauty*, I could perceive its very
essence close at hand; I could, as it were, feel the stuff of it
beneath my fingertips. I had attained to that supreme degree
of sensibility where the *divine intimations* of art merge with the
impassioned sensuality of emotion. As I emerged from the
porch of *Santa Croce*, I was seized with a fierce palpitation of
the heart (that same symptom which, in Berlin, is referred to
as an *attack of nerves*); the well-spring of life was dried up
within me, and I walked in constant fear of falling to the ground.

   I sat down on one of the benches which line the *piazza di
Santa Croce*; in my wallet, I discovered the following lines by
Ugo Foscolo, which I re-read now with a great surge of pleasure; I could find no fault with such poetry; I desperately
needed to hear the voice of a friend who shared my own
emotion:

. . . . . . *Io quando il monumento*
Vidi ove posa il corpo di quel grande
Che temprando lo scettro a'regnatori
Gli allôr ne sfronda, ed alle genti svela
Di che lagrime grondi e di che sangue:
E l' arca di colui che nuovo Olimpo
Alzò in Roma a' Celesti; e di chi vide
Sotto l' etereo padiglion rotarsi
Più mondi, e il Sole irradiarli immoto,
Onde all' Anglo che tanta ala vi stese
Sgombrò primo le vie del firmamento;
Te beata, gridai, per le felici
Aure pregne di vita e pe' lavacri
Che da suoi gioghi a te versa Apennino!
Lieta dell' aer tuo veste la Luna
Di luce limpidissima i tuoi colli
Per vendemmia festanti; e le convalli
Popolate di case e d' oliveti
Mille di fiori al ciel mandano incensi:
E tu prima, Firenze, udivi il carme
Che allegrò l'ira al Ghibellin fuggiasco,
E tu i cari parenti e l'idïoma
Desti a quel dolce di Calliope labbro
Che Amore in Grecia nudo e nudo in Roma
D'un velo candidissimo adornando,
Rendea nel grembo a Venere Celeste:
Ma più beata chè in un tempio accolte
Serbi l' Itale glorie, uniche forse,
Da che le mal vietate Alpi e l'alterna
Omnipotenza delle umane sorti
Armi e sostanze t' invadeano ed are
E patria e, tranne la memoria, tutto.
. . . .
. . . . *E a questi marmi*
Venne spesso Vittorio ad ispirarsi.

Irato a' patrii Numi, errava muto
Ove Arno è più deserto, i campi e il cielo
Desïoso mirando; e poi che nullo
Vivente aspetto gli molcea la cura,
Qui posava l' austero, e avea sul volto
Il pallor della morte e la speranza.
Con questi grandi abita eterno: e l' ossa
*Fremono amor di patria. . . . ***

Two days later, the memory of this experience touched off a most impertinent train of thought: for is it not a surer guarantee of happiness (so I reflected) to possess a heart so fashioned, than to strut about in the coveted regalia of a *Knight of the Order of the Holy Ghost*?

23rd January.   Yesterday, all the live-long day, I roamed about in a sort of melancholy, historical abstraction. My first excursion led me to the church of *Santa Maria del Carmine*, which contains the Masaccio frescoes; after which, feeling myself ill-disposed properly to appreciate the oil-paintings of the *Palazzo Pitti* or of the *Uffizi*, I decided rather to visit the tombs of the Medici at *San Lorenzo*, together with the *Michelangelo Chapel*, so called on account of the sculptures executed by this great man. Emerging from *San Lorenzo*, I began to wander aimlessly about the streets, contemplating, from the wordless depths of my own emotion (with my eyes wide-staring, and the power of speech utterly gone from me), those massive *palazzi*—those veritable fortresses and castle-keeps—built towards the year 1300 by the merchants of Florence. On the perimeter of that vast *piazza*, whose centre is occupied by the Cathedral of *Santa Maria del Fiore* (built in 1293), my glance lighted upon those long arcades, whose arches, with their distant hint of gothic inspiration, rise to an elegant apex formed by the junction of two curves (similar to the upper section of the *fleur-de-lis* design which you may find engraved upon a five-franc piece). This style of design is found repeated above the door of every house in Florence; but a modern generation has built a wall to block the ancient arcades which used to encircle the immensity of that open space, in the midst of which, in splendid isolation, rises the mass of *Santa Maria del Fiore*.

I experienced a great joy for knowing no one, for having no fear of being forced to make conversation. The power of this mediaeval architecture took undisputed possession of all my faculties; I could believe that *Dante* was the companion of my steps. Today, since waking, I doubt whether so many as a dozen thoughts have crossed my mind for which I might not find a ready formulation in the lines of this great poet. I feel ashamed of these observations, which will surely earn me the reputation of an *egoist*.

As it is only too plain from the solid structure of these *palazzi*, put together out of great, rude blocks of stone left rough and rugged on the side which affronts the street, *danger* has all too often stalked the streets of Florence. Yet it is precisely the absence of danger in our own thoroughfares which makes us all so insignificant. I have just returned from spending a whole hour, alone and motionless, in the centre of the dark little courtyard of the *palazzo* erected in the *via Larga* by that Cosimo de' Medici, whom fools revere as the *Father of his Country*. The fewer efforts this architecture makes to imitate a Grecian temple—or in other words, the more directly it echoes the character of the men who built it, and their needs —the more I find it fascinating. However, in order to preserve this sombre illusion which, throughout the day, has peopled my fancy with such figures as Castruccio Castracani, Uguccione della Fagiola, etc., as though I might come upon them face to face at the corner of each street, I must resolutely avert my gaze, lest it fall upon the featureless, insignificant creatures who throng the streets today—those sublime streets still redolent of the passionate energies of the Middle Ages!

For alas! the present-day citizen of Florence is ignorant of the very semblance of passion. Even his avarice is not a passion; it is nothing but a convention—one among many—resulting from a marriage between intense vanity and extreme poverty.

Florence, whose thoroughfares are paved with massive blocks of white granite, irregular in shape, is of a cleanliness rarely encountered elsewhere; her streets are perfumed with a curious and characteristic odour. With the unique exception of one or two townships in the Low Countries, Florence bids fair to be acclaimed the cleanest city in the universe; and undoubtedly she is to be numbered among the most elegant. Her græco-gothic architecture has all the clean finish and the consummate artistry of a perfect miniature. Happily for the tangible beauty of Florence, her citizens, at the same instant when they forfeited their liberty, did likewise forfeit the *energy* which inspires the building of such massive structures. Consequently, those shameful façades in the style of *Piermarini* are nowhere found to shock the eye of the beholder; nor does anything disturb the exquisite harmony of these streets, instinct with the *Ideal Beauty* of the Middle Ages. There are a score of odd corners in Florence—for instance, as you come down from the *Ponte della Trinità* to pass before the *palazzo Strozzi*— where the traveller may well believe himself to be living in the year 1500.

Yet, despite the rare beauty of these countless streets, so richly steeped in grandeur and in melancholy, there is nothing which bears comparison to the *Palazzo Vecchio*. This fortress, built in 1298 by the freely-offered contributions of the merchant guilds, surges upwards, with its brickwork battlements and its fantastically towering walls, not in some solitary and deserted spot, but in the very centre of the finest *piazza* in Florence. Southward, it looks down upon Vasari's noble *Gallery*; northward, it is set off by an equestrian statue of one of the Medici; while in a cluster about its foot stand Michelangelo's *David* and Benvenuto Cellini's *Perseus*, together with the charming *Loggia dei Lanzi*—in a word, all the artistic masterpieces of Florence and all the activity of her civilisation. By a fortunate circumstance, this *piazza* has grown to be the *boulevard de Gand* of the city, the constant thoroughfare for all and sundry. What monument of Grecian architecture could tell so many tales of men and deeds as this grim mediaeval fortress, rough-hewn, implacable and energetic as the century which gave it birth? 'Up there', observed my *cicerone*, 'from that high window on the northern face, they hanged Archbishop Pazzi in all his solemn pontifical attire.'

My mind harks back to the *Palais du Louvre*, and I find myself regretting its ancient tower. The neo-classical architecture which has usurped its place has no surpassing qualities of beauty to stir the echoes in my soul as might have done that antique bastion built by Philippe-Auguste. (I have added this comparison as an afterthought, to explain the idea which is in my mind; for, when first I trod the streets of Florence, I had thoughts for nothing save what lay before my eyes; the *Louvre* held no more place in my imagination than did the far Kamchatka).

In Florence, the *Palazzo Vecchio*—this stark, contrasting incarnation of the stern realities of mediaeval times set square amid the artistic glories of the past and the insignificant throng of modern *marchesini*—creates an impression of unparalleled grandeur and truth. Here, for the instruction of the philosophic mind, stand the masterpieces of those arts, whose genius was fired by the violence of passion and bore fruit, only to wither in a later century and fade, becoming petty, insignificant and misshapen when the tempest of desire ceased to swell the sails by which alone that frail craft, the human soul, so impotent when passion falters and evaporates, leaving it bereft alike of vice and virtue, is driven across the stormy seas of life.

This evening, seated on a cane chair in front of the coffee-house in the centre of the great *piazza* facing the *Palazzo*

Vecchio, neither the crowd nor the cold—the one as inconsiderable as the other—could prevent my eye from beholding the whole tapestry of incident which had been unfolded upon this same *piazza*. Here, on these very stones, Florence had risen a score of times in the name of *liberty*, while blood had flowed in the cause of an unworkable constitution. And now the rising moon, by imperceptible degrees, began to print the massive shadow of the *Palazzo Vecchio* upon the scoured flagstones of the *piazza*, and to lend her magic touch of mystery to the colonnades of the *Uffizi*, beneath whose arches gleamed the lights of houses, distant beyond the Arno.

Seven strokes rang out across the city from the belfry of the *Signoria*; fear lest I should arrive too late to find a seat at the theatre alone had force to drag me away from this awe-inspiring sight; for I was, so to speak, a spectator who gazed upon the very tragedy of history. I flew like the wind to the *Hhohhomero**, for such is the local pronunciation of the name of that Florentine theatre, *il Cocomero*. I am resentful to the point of outrage against the dialect of Florence, so renowned throughout the land. At first it seemed to me that the tongue I heard was *Arabic*; and it is impossible to pronounce it with any speed.

The overture began, and, to my delight, I found myself yet once again in the society of that charming old friend of mine, Rossini. By the end of the third bar, I had recognised his presence. To confirm my supposition, I wandered down into the pit and enquired; and indeed, as I had surmised, the *Barbiere di Siviglia* which stood on the programme *was* his, not Paisiello's. With all the temerity of true genius he has dared to weave new melodies about that same *libretto** which has already won such reputation for his rival. The part of Rosina was played tonight by signora Giorgi, whose husband, in the days of the French occupation, was an erstwhile judge on some tribunal. While I was in Bologna, there was pointed out to me a young cavalry officer who is not ashamed to play *primo buffo* parts*. In Italy, no stigma attaches to any reasonable action; in other words, the country has suffered less corruption from that artificial principle of 'honour' inculcated by Louis XIV.

Rossini's *Barber* has all the characteristics of a painting by Guido Reni; its very negligence reveals the Master's hand; there is never a hint of effort or conscientious drudgery. Rossini is a man of infinite ideas and no education. Imagine a *Beethoven* endowed with such a boundless inspiration: what miracles might there not result! Tonight's music struck me as being somewhat too closely borrowed from Cimarosa. The only passage of indisputably authentic Rossini was the trio of the second-act *finale**, sung by Rosina, Almaviva and Figaro, of which the only criticism I have to make is that such music is misapplied to the unravelling of a complex intrigue, and should belong rather to a situation where the text suggests energetic characterisation and rank obstinacy.

When danger is imminent, when a single minute can make or mar all, it is an insult to reason to listen to the same words repeated ten times over.[1] Yet this so-called *necessary absurdity* in music can easily be remedied. During the last three or four years, Rossini has been turning out operas which rarely contain more than one, or at the most two isolated passages worthy of the composer of *Tancredi* or of *l'Italiana in Algeri*. I was suggesting tonight a plan whereby all these scattered master-touches should be gathered together in one single score. It would give me greater satsfaction to have composed this single trio from the *Barbiere di Siviglia* than that whole monstrous rigmarole of an opera by Solliva, which delighted me so hugely in Milan.

24th January. My admiration for *il Barbiere* increases day by day. A young English composer, whom I suspect of being flatly devoid of genius, declared himself to be *profoundly*

1 This does not apply to the *music*, which embodies ten different inventions.
[1817]

shocked by Rossini's temerity*. The impudence of the fellow—
how *dare* he lay hands on a work by Paisiello? This same
scandalised young man told me an anecdote which is typical
of Rossini's devil-may-care attitude. No passage in the score
of his Neapolitan rival is more deservedly famous than the
Romance: *io son Lindoro*. A certain Spanish tenor (Garcia,
I believe) suggested to Rossini a well-known serenade which
lovers frequently sing beneath their mistress' windows in
Spain; idle by nature, the composer lost no time in appro-
priating this gift from the gods; the result is a monument of
frigidity—a piece of factual *reportage* set in the midst of an
historical pageant*.

Poverty is the bedevilling feature of the Florentine opera:
costumes, *décor*, singers—nothing is exempt; the atmosphere
reminds me of some third-rate French provincial town. Ballets
are unheard-of, save during the Carnival. All in all, Florence,
set in a narrow valley amid a wilderness of bare mountains,
offers little to justify its reputation. I would a hundred times
rather choose Bologna, even for its paintings; in addition to
which, Bologna has both intelligence and individuality; while
Florence offers nothing but fine liveries and interminable
phrases. Bologna and Florence mark the extreme limits of
French influence in Italy.

In my experience, the temper most seldom to be observed
among young Italians is that which distinguishes the family of
Parson Primrose: *They had but one character, that of being all
equally generous, credulous, simple and inoffensive**. Such families
are not uncommon in England. The moral climate beyond
the channel is singularly apt to fashion young ladies of angelic
disposition; and I myself have been honoured with the
acquaintance of creatures not a whit less idyllic in their perfection than the daughters of the good Vicar of Wakefield; but a
nation must first have its *Habeas Corpus Act*, and, if not the
statutes, then at least the traditions of English life, before it may
furnish its poets with the living models of such a temperament.

In the lowering atmosphere of Italy, any such *simple and inoffensive* being would soon be destroyed utterly. Yet, if there be any refuge south of the Alps, where such English *naïveté* may look for shelter and solace, then that refuge is surely in the bosom of some Florentine family living in the retired isolation of its country estate. In Milan, the passions of love would all too soon appear to animate this *naïveté* and to afford it a greater charm—yet a charm belonging to a totally different order of things.

Basing my conclusions upon the expressions I have remarked and upon observations gathered *à l'anglaise*, that is, around the *table d'hôte* provided by signora Imbert, at the coffee-house and in the theatre, I would aver that the Florentine is the politest of mortals, the most meticulous, the most obedient to his painstaking calculations of prosperity and economy. In the street, his aspect is that of a clerk, employed at a salary of eighteen hundred francs a year, who, having just brushed his suit with careful affection and polished his own boots, is now hurrying off to his counting-house, so as to be punctual to the minute at his desk; nor has he forgotten his umbrella, for the weather is decidedly unsettled, and nothing ruins a good hat so readily as a heavy shower of rain.

How should the traveller, newly-arrived, with the memory of Bologna, that city of ardent passions, still fresh in his mind, escape the impression that something *narrow* and *arid* dwells in the common mould of all these features?[1] But in revenge, where should he hope to encounter a beauty more radiant than that of signora Paz*** or of signora Mozz***?

[1] Here I am resolved to set aside not a few pages of manuscript: for in all things touching the knowledge of the human heart, or concerning that subject which is vulgarly entitled *philosophy*, I am only too well aware that this present year of grace 1826 (being wholly absorbed in the *Critique of Pure Reason* and pre-occupied with the dethronement of Condillac) is visited by a marked distaste for plain, unsentimentalised *facts*. The shrewder heads conceive them frankly as a *threat*, while the hot-headed younger generation dismisses them out of hand as being insufficiently conducive to mysticism and spirituality. [1826]

28th January.   It was my musical instinct which warned me
from the first of something *staid* and *prosaic* in all these faces;
consequently, I was in no way shocked to observe, that very
same night of my arrival, the sober, decent, *Florentine* reaction
to the *Barber of Seville.* Yet it could scarcely be avowed that
sobriety and *decency* were the most commendable qualities of
that notorious ballad: *la Cetra spermaceutica*, which was
declaimed last year at Carnival-time, in the presence of those
very persons, whose heroic prowess beneath the Sign of
Venus was therein made immortal. This is the apotheosis of
physical desire. So strange a spectacle would incline me to
believe that the true passion of *love* is a rare enough phenomenon
among the worthy citizens of Florence. So much the worse for
them: they know but a sorry substitute; yet one which, all in
all, has the supreme advantage of never leading its devotees
astray into the wilderness of unreason. Here are the opening
stanzas of Count Giraùd's ballad:

> *Nel dì che bollono*
> *D'amor le tresche*
> *Sotto le tuniche*
> *Carnovalesche;*
>
> *Nume d'Arcadia,*
> *Io non t'invoco,*
> *Che i versi abbondano*
> *Ben d'altro foco.*
>
> *Sul Pindo piangono*
> *Le nove Ancelle*
> *Che teco vivono*
> *Sempre zitelle*.*

I strongly urge every tourist to obtain a copy of this admirable
ballad, and to profit from his visit to the *Cascine* or to the
Opera to learn to recognise those fair Florentines whose

presence graced the original reading, and who, one and all, are mentioned by name in the Count's miniature epic. Recently, eight of these ladies were confined to their residence under supervision by order of the Grand-Duke Ferdinand III, and thereby hangs a tale indeed; but *I* dare not tell it.

The necessary counterpart to these social traditions, which in my own opinion, are so little conducive to happiness, is the overweening power of *Popery*. Sooner or later, no one in Florence can hope to go scot-free without a *confessional certificate*, duly signed and sealed. The local free-thinking brotherhood is still aghast at the audacity of this or that jibe against His unmentionable Holiness which fell from the pen of Dante *only five hundred and ten years ago*. As for the *Liberals* in this land, I might freely compare them with certain Noble Lords beyond the Channel—most honourable gentlemen, mark you—who are firmly convinced that it is their solemn right and duty to govern the remainder of the nation to their own personal advantage (*Corn Laws*). I should have detected this sophism even before America had appeared upon the scene to demonstrate that an aristocracy is not an indispensable condition of human happiness. Not, of course, that I would deny this error its agreeable quality; what could be more flattering than to marry the tangible advantages of egoism with the spiritual satisfaction of generosity?

Among the *Liberal* faction of Florence, as I understand the matter, there reigns a stout belief that the fact of noble birth conveys rights of a different order from those of a simple plebeian; its adherents would gladly join with our own Ministers in France in urging laws to protect the strong. A young Russian (of noble blood, it goes without saying) pointed out to me today that Cimabue, Michelangelo, Dante, Petrarch, Galileo and Machiavelli were all descended from patrician stock; and indeed, if such be the literal truth, then my Muscovite acquaintance may well be proud of his distinction. For these are the six most illustrious sons of this mercantile province, of whom two at least may number among those eight or ten exalted figures whose Olympian genius is the surpassing glory of the human race. Michelangelo had talent enough to furnish the reputation of a considerable poet, besides the abilities of a first-rate sculptor, architect and painter.

Seated without the Leghorn Gate, where I am wont to idle away many a long hour, it has been my pastime to observe the peasant women, and to note the rare degree of beauty in their eyes; yet there is no trace in their expression of that dreamy sensuality, no sign of that *susceptibility to passion* which characterises the women of Lombardy. Here, in Tuscany, the one quality which you may never discover is that strange *capacity for exaltation*; instead, by way of compensation, you may discern no lack of mental alertness, of pride, of rational intelligence, together with an elusive hint of provocative malice. I know of nothing so captivating as the glance of these handsome peasant-women, beneath their delicious head-dress with its black plume nodding and curtseying above their mannish hats. Yet I sense in such sharp and glittering eyes a deeper power of criticism than of adoration. I can never mistake that rational, speculative glint, nor discern in their look the potential *irrationality* of love. These madonna-eyes flash with the mocking light of battle rather than with the softer fires of passion.

The country-folk of Tuscany, as I will most readily believe, form the oddest and the wittiest peasantry in Italy. They may well be accounted, within the bounds of their condition, the most civilised race in all the world. They look upon religion much rather as a social convention, whose ill-observance would constitute *a breach of good manners*, than as a *Faith*; and Hell holds few terrors for such as they.

If you would weigh them in the scale of *moral values*, you would find them infinitely superior to all that horde of honest *bourgeois* folk, those worthy citizens with four thousand a year and minds narrower than a needle's eye, who throng the *salon* of each *sous-préfecture* in France; with this difference, that, among ourselves, *conscription* excited not one tenth part of the despair which reigned throughout the length and breadth of Tuscany. Mothers would follow their sons, wailing and weeping, right into the very streets of Florence—a hideous spectacle. By contrast, it was a truly comic sight to witness the severity of the *préfet*, M. Franchet, who, with one stern word, confounded all that meticulous ingenuity displayed by the Chamberlains of the Court of Princess Elisa with the sole object of earning absolution from the duty of *reproducing their kind*.

In painting, the great masters of the Florentine school have gradually led me, by a different path, to an identical verdict concerning the national character. Those old citizens of Florence, as they are portrayed by Masaccio and Ghirlandaio, would seem like figures out of Bedlam were they to tread the earth today and invade the fashionable coffee-house which flourishes in the shadow of *Santa Maria del Fiore*; yet, compared with the figures depicted by Paolo Veronese or by Tintoretto (I have deliberately chosen two painters who never *idealise* their subjects), the frost seems already to have bitten deep into their souls; their features reflect a hint of desiccation, of narrowness, of pedestrian rationality, of squeamish decorousness; in a word, not one but seems to lack that finer capacity for EXALTATION. They stand much closer in spirit to the true meaning of civilisation, yet infinitely further removed from those qualities which alone awaken my interest in any individual member of the human race. Bernardino Luini, the undisputed master of Milanese portraiture (do you recall his frescoes at Saronno?), is anything but an emotional painter; yet such is his romanticism, that every figure he created seems a miniature *Werther* beside that gallery of level-headed folk who stalk through the frescoes of Andrea del Sarto's masterpiece, *la Nunziata*. It was the wish of Heaven that Italy should furnish each degree of contrast; and so it was decreed that she should harbour a race to whom the very concept of passion was but a word devoid of meaning: such is the people of *Florence*. I have scoured the history-books in vain to discover, in all the century preceding ours, one single scene of passion enacted on the stage of Tuscany. Yet do but restore to this breed a tincture of the old unreasoning madness, and you may behold anew some Pietro Marenghi breasting the waves to fire the enemy's ship. Who could have guessed, in 1815, that the Greeks, so docile and so obsequious to the will of their Turkish masters, stood poised upon the very brink of heroism?

Milan is a riverless city, circular in shape, set in the centre of a plain, whose level expanse, devoid of undulation, is threaded by a hundred streamlets of fresh-running water. Florence, by contrast, lies in the hollow of a narrowish valley cut deep in the contours of high and barren ranges, and set hard against the rampart of hills which flank it on the south. This latter city, which, by the pattern of her streets, is in some ways reminiscent of Paris, is set astride the Arno much as Paris is built astride the Seine. Likewise the Arno—a mere mountain torrent, artificially swollen, by means of a transverse causeway constructed to work a mill-wheel, to the dimensions of a self-respecting river beneath the bridges of Florence—flows from east to west. If you mount the southern hillside, climbing through the gardens of the *Palazzo Pitti* and from thence embarking upon a circuit of the walls as far as the highroad to Arezzo, you may gain some notion of the countless multitude of little hills which compose the domain of Tuscany; carpeted with olive-groves, with vineyards and with narrow strips of cereal, the undulating surface of the land is cultivated like a garden. And indeed, agriculture is a pursuit most admirably suited to the placid, pacific, husbanding genius of the Tuscan race.

The landscape—just as we may observe it in paintings by Leonardo or by Raphael in his early manner—often terminates in a perspective of dark foliage against the clear blue of a cloudless sky.

The famous *Cascine*—the common *rendez-vous* whither all resort, to see or to be seen—are situated much as the *Champs-Elysées* in relation to Paris. The displeasing aspect of these gardens, as far as I am concerned, is that I find them constantly encumbered with some six hundred or so foreign visitors, English and Russian predominating. Florence is nothing better than a vast museum full of foreign tourists; and each nationality brings with it its own manners and customs. The English, with their rigid *caste-system*, their meticulous observance of it and their firm resolve never to depart from it, even by a hair's-breadth, provide the material for countless satirical anecdotes. It is by such tales that the impoverished nobility of Florence, which gathers nightly at the apartments of the Countess of Albany, widow of the *Pretender* and sometime mistress of Alfieri, takes its revenge against the gilded luxury of Albion. M. Fabre (of Montpellier), to whom posterity will be indebted for his portraits of the great tragic dramatist, showed me, among a multitude of other treasures, some very curious *objets d'art*. I am deeply obliged to a Brother of *San Marco* for a glimpse of the wondrous frescoes which Fra Bartolomeo left upon the walls of his cell. This divine genius abandoned his art for four whole years, as an act of Christian humility, and even then only resumed his brush in response to the command of his Superior. Some two weeks since, a painter of my acquaintance undertook a series of studies, using as model the charming head of a girl who, by trade, was a straw-braider for the making of hats. Now this painter is an exceedingly decorous German, surely not a day under forty; moreover, the sessions took place in the presence of the girl's entire family, who were delighted at the addition of a few *paoli* to their exiguous weekly budget. Yet the local priest was shocked to the remotest fibre of his being by such flagrant immorality: 'If the girl continues with these sessions', he thundered, 'I shall castigate her by name in my sermon, and she will be publicly dishonoured.' In the Papal States, no priest would dare usurp such authority; here you have indeed the bitter fruits of inexhaustible long-suffering and of egoism.

If you are susceptible to the thunderous power engendered when the creative energy of thought is cast in the noble mould of language, remember to ask for copies of the sonnets *Berta non sazia* . . . and *l'Urna di Berta*; not forgetting likewise the epigrams:

> *Berta condotta al fonte da piccina* . . .
> *Di Berta lo scrivano diceva al sor pievano* . . .
> *Mentre un gustoso piatto Berta scrocca* . . .
> *Dissi a Berta: devi esser obbligata* . . .
> *Si sentiron suonar dei Francesconi* . . .
> *Per cavalcare un buon caval da sella* . . .
> *La Mezzi m'ha in secreto ricercato* . . .
> *In mezzo ai Birri armati di pugnali* . . .

During the few hours that I have had these turbulent lines in my possession, I must have read them ten times over. I must add a warning, however, that no mother would knowingly recommend these poems for her daughter's chosen reading; let it be said also that they are more commendable for their energy than for their delicacy. . . .

Little by little, I sense that my heart is grown inconstant towards the art and beauty of Bologna. Having no commerce save only with Dante—and yet what loving commerce withal! —my whole mind is peopled with those figures who stalked down the years of the twelfth century, so splendid in their stern simplicity, so sublime at least in the violence of their passions and in the power of their intelligence. The elegance of the Bolognese school, the *Hellenic*, rather than *Italian* beauty of those heads by Guido Reni, begins to shock my soul as a sort of profanation. I cannot conceal the truth from my own heart: *I am in love with mediaeval Italy.*[1]

---

[1] I have omitted all the descriptions I had attempted of various paintings. The Président de Brosses has performed the task a hundred times better than ever *I* could hope to achieve it (vol. II, pp. 11-67). The

29th January. The city of Florence possesses four fine bridges, which span the Arno at more or less regular intervals; and these, in juxtaposition to the quays of the embankment and the hill-slopes to the south, with their frieze of cypresses cut out sharply against the sky, form a most pleasing prospect. The scene admits of less grandeur than the setting of the famous bridge at Dresden; but the effect is infinitely more charming. The second of these Florentine bridges (following the current of the Arno) is overbuilt with goldsmiths' shops. Here it was, this morning, that I renewed my acquaintance with a dealer in precious stones, a Jew in whose company, once, in days gone by, I ran most imminent danger of drowning. This Nathan, besides being a fervent devotee of his persuasion, has perfected to an astonishing degree a sort of philosophy of impassivity, together with the most useful art of paying as little as possible for all his daily needs. The accident of our encounter afforded us sincere delight on either side. Upon the instant,

unwavering sureness of taste which is shown by this contemporary of Voltaire never ceases to amaze me*. As for signor Benvenuti and other members of the artistic fraternity who have appeared upon the scene since 1740, I would say only this: that even the daubs of M. Girodet and of the rest of *immortal* David's talented disciples are a positive pleasure to the eye, compared with *la Morte di Cesare*, with *le Fatiche d'Ercole* or with *la Giuditta*, as conceived by signor Benvenuti. Since the women of Florence are infinitely more beautiful than their sisters who have the misfortune to be born in Paris, it is inevitable that one should discern, here and there within these dreary acres of canvas, a head or two of pleasing delineation. But the deep-seated reason for the pallid insipidity of modern art lies in the fact that the Government insists upon commissioning paintings of the *Miracle of St**** from artists whose religious fervour is perhaps not screwed exactly to the pitch of a Fra Bartolomeo. If the artist is to have a chance of achieving anything worth while, he must live, or paint, or write *to the immediate dictation of the passions.* Judging as nearly as possible by results, the present generation of Florentine painters is far too level-headed to surrender to those inconvenient and expensive urges. In this respect, the artists of Florence are the most eminently *respectable* people. In all the range of contemporary Italian painting, while I have noted an occasional rival to the *celestial grace* of M. Prud'hon, I have seen nothing even distantly reminiscent of M. le baron Guérin's head of *Dido*, or of Gros' picture of the *Plague at Jaffa*. [1826 fearing to lose my company, he promoted me to the status of a business associate, and bade me follow him to the house of a client, to whom he proceeded to sell, for the sum of ten *louis*, an exquisite engraved stone by Pickler. No less than three-quarters of an hour was spent in bargaining; yet to me the time seemed short. Except for the actual formulation of an offer, not one single word was uttered of those which a Frenchman would have employed in similar circumstances. The Italian who buys a ring is concerned to inaugurate a collection for his descendants; having purchased an engraving for the sum of thirty francs, he will willingly lay out a further fifty in order to transmit it to his grandchildren in a frame of untold magnificence. Once, in Paris, I overheard M. le baron de S*** remark, as he acquired a rare volume: *This should fetch a good fifty francs when it comes to the sale* (*i.e.*, to the sale of effects following his own demise). But the Italians have not yet realised that nothing which a rich man may accomplish will survive him by so much as a dozen years. And indeed, in nearly all instances, the country houses where it has been my privilege to be received have remained in the same family for a century at least, if not for two.

Tonight, Nathan introduced me into the society of a group of wealthy merchants and their wives—the pretext being that he desired me to witness a play performed by marionettes in their own charming little theatre. This delightful miniature stage measures no more than five feet across the proscenium arch, and yet affords an exact copy of the *teatro alla Scala*. Before the curtain rose, all lights were extinguished in the drawing-room where the performance was to take place; and indeed, the *décor* was most impressive, for the reason that, in spite of its lilliputian scale, it was not treated *as a miniature*, but rather conceived in the sweeping, decorative style of a *Lanfranco* (it had in fact been designed by a pupil of signor Peregò, of Milan). There were tiny lamps proportionate to all the rest, and each change of set was carried out rapidly, neatly and by means exactly copied from *la Scala*; I can conceive of nothing more enchanting. A company of four-and-twenty marionettes, each eight inches tall, equipped with leaden legs and costing a *sequin* apiece, performed a delicious, if somewhat indelicate comedy which proved to be an abridged version of Machiavelli's *Mandragola*. Subsequently, these same marionettes proceeded to dance a miniature ballet, with considerable style and elegance.

But the experience which afforded me still greater delight than the puppet-show was the genial manner and polished intelligence of the conversation which reigned amid this Florentine assembly, the tone of unforced politeness which characterised the welcome which they deigned to accord to myself. Here was a change indeed from Bologna! In Florence the aura of curiosity which surrounds a newcomer carries the battle by storm against the opposing preoccupations of love. Besides, is there not all the time in the world to talk to one's lover?

It was my privilege tonight to behold the solid structure of reason enhanced with all that subtle charm which is the fruit of long experience; civilised urbanity and worldly wisdom were the qualities which gave the talk its special savour, rather than natural freedom or vivacity; the darting stings of irony, which flashed out only at rare intervals, were tempered into moderation. The general impression was so pleasing to my mind that for an instant I regretted having consigned to the fire my letters of recommendation; for the company tonight included two of those to whom I bore an introduction. My action, notwithstanding, was no less than honour demanded; for, until now, I have spoken nothing but ill of the citizens of Florence, such as they have been fashioned by Cosimo III and Leopold. Yet it were unjust to shut my eyes to their amiable qualities, which, in Paris, would ride the very crest of fashion—as opposed to those charms peculiar to Bologna, which would seem a very echo of Bedlam, or at least

would scare all beholders by their off-hand familiarity. By a
fortunate chance, the conversation touched scarcely at all upon
literature—at most, a passing allusion to *Old Mortality*, a novel
by Walter Scott, which has newly made its appearance in
signor Molini's reading-rooms. For my benefit, one of the
guests declaimed some eight or ten lines by signor J.-B.
Niccolini, which truly seemed to me to echo some of the
proud grandiloquence of Racine. The company was numerous,
and I distinguished among those present some five or six women
of not inconsiderable beauty, yet so profoundly steeped in
reason that they seemed scarcely women at all in my eyes; such
rational creatures must surely be incapable of grasping any
but the most material aspect of love.

I was forgetting to mention that this morning I hired a
sediola in order to visit the famous Charterhouse which lies
some two miles distant from the walls of Florence. This
consecrated building stands upon a hill-top beside the highway
to Rome; at first glance you might well mistake it for a *palazzo*
or a gothic stronghold. As a structure, the mass is imposing;
yet the impression is very different from that which is left upon
the mind by the *Grande Chartreuse*, near Grenoble. There is
nothing *holy* about this edifice; nothing sublime, nothing to
exalt the spirit, nothing to fill the soul with involuntary
religious awe; rather is this a satire against religion itself; the
mind dwells willy-nilly upon the limitless treasuries of gold
poured out in order to afford some eighteen *fakirs* the grim
satisfaction of mortifying the flesh. It would be simpler, all in
all, merely to lock them away in a dungeon cell, and to convert
this Charterhouse into a common gaol to serve the whole of
Tuscany. And even so, with this new attribution, it might well
still number no more than eighteen inmates, so dispassionately
do these people affect to calculate their interests, and so little
swayed are they by those surging tempests of the heart which
may send the most upright among men toppling headlong into
the abyss.

A poor Corsican domestic, named Cosimo, has, in these latter days, inspired a scandal which has re-echoed through the length and breadth of Florence. Having been apprised that his sister, whom he had not seen for twenty years, had allowed herself to be seduced, among the desolate mountains of Corsica, by a man belonging to an enemy clan, and had eventually eloped with her seducer, he first proceeded to set his master's affairs in the most meticulous order; and having done so, betook himself to a forest some three miles distant, and there blew out his brains. Acts which are pre-eminently reasonable have not that strong resilience to satisfy the needs of art; a philosophical republican from beyond the Atlantic may command my admiration, yet, a few days hence, I shall have forgotten that he ever lived. But never shall I manage to forget poor Cosimo. Could it be (you, gentle reader, not *I*, shall furnish the answer) that this cult of unreason in myself is nothing but a personal idiosyncrasy? Assuredly I find nothing to blame, yet nothing to attract me either, among these level-headed Tuscan folk. For instance, they have neither the heart nor the will to distinguish between the *right to be free* on the one hand, and on the other, a tolerant authority which *permits them to do as they please*; for it is this latter privilege which they presently enjoy beneath the ægis of a Prince (Ferdinand III) to whom exile has taught the way of wisdom; yet this same Prince it was who, some years since, arraigned nine thousand of his subjects upon nine thousand separate indictments of 'jacobin proclivities' (*sic dicitur*).

The wise burgesses of Tuscany, by nature of a timid disposition, are content to enjoy the prosperous and untroubled times; they labour to build their fortunes; they even struggle, without undue exertion, to improve their minds; but never are they visited by the disquieting notion that they should insist upon a share in the direction of the state. This very suggestion, which would distract them from their penny-wise preoccupations, half-scares the wits out of their sober heads, while foreign nations who make such matters their concern appear to them no better than a howling throng of lunatics.

For my own purposes, I like to picture the Tuscans as a living symbol of the *bourgeoisie* in Europe at that point in time when the epoch of violence which we call the Middle Ages had recently faded and died. They argue endlessly about *language*; they argue no less about the price of various oils; and for the rest, so obsessive is their fear of turbulence, even when the goal of it might be liberty, that, were some new Cola di Rienzi to incite them to revolt, I suspect that they would turn their arms against him, preferring to defend the existing despotism. To men of such a temper, what is there to be said? *Gaudeant bene nati.* Who knows but what this state of torpor might not have been the common destiny of Europe, or at least, of the larger part of it, had *we* endured a soporific government like that of Tuscany? Grand-Duke Ferdinand, realising full well that he could command neither enough soldiers nor enough courtiers to live a happy life surrounded by the general execration of his subjects, has chosen rather to become a most *familiar* monarch, and you may meet him strolling unaccompanied through the streets of Florence. His Highness the Grand-Duke has three Ministers, of whom one, Prince Neri Corsini, is a dyed-in-the-wool reactionary, whilst the other two, signor Fossombroni, a geometer of noted reputation, and signor Frullani, are very reasonable beings; His Highness foregathers with them but once a week, and in fact takes little or no hand in the government of his domain. Year by year it is his habit to commission some thirty thousand francs' worth of pictures from the studios of those excruciating painters whom the public (which admires them) sees fit to designate for such an honour; likewise, year by year, he purchases a fine estate or two. Granted only that Heaven sees fit to preserve this supremely *reasonable* being, whom it has thus pleased her to bestow upon the Duchy, I am convinced that, in the end, he will propose to undertake the government

of his Tuscan subjects *free and for nothing*. The voice of opinion
rings loud in praise of his Consort, a Princess of Saxony; likewise of the latter's sister, who has married the Prince Royal.[1]
Were it not for the constant intrigues and the ever-present
blight of *Popery* which infects the scattered townships of the
realm, urban life in Tuscany would be exceedingly agreeable,
for the populace elects its own Mayors and municipal officers
(*anziani*). But, in the last analysis, all this is *theoretical*, like the
invitation issued by the Emperor Leopold in 1790 to the Senate
of Milan, requesting it to *deliberate upon whatever matters might
be of utility to the commonwealth*. No one in his senses takes this
sort of humbug seriously, save only Mr Roscoe and other such
illustrious English historians.

Madame la maréchale de Rochefort once remarked to
Duclos, the celebrated philosopher: 'Why, what have *I* to do
with *your* paradise? A bit of bread and cheese, and the first
wench you pick off the streets—and there you are, happy as a
sandboy!' Patient reader, do *you* admit no higher dream of bliss?
Would *you* not rather aspire to the impassioned, unreasoning
despair of a Rousseau or a Byron?[2]

During the course of my visit to *la Certosa*, there was placed
in my hands that massive *Register*, whose yellow pages are
thick as cardboard, and in which a large proportion among
those who visit the spot have inscribed some feeble inanity to
record their passage. Yet how great was my astonishment to
discover, amid such ill-favoured company, a soaring and
inspired sonnet on *Death*! I read it ten times over. This evening,
however, when I alluded to my 'discovery', the whole company burst out laughing. 'What?' demanded many accusing
voices. 'Did you never hear the poet Monti's *Sonnet on Death*?'
To which I would add a warning, *sotto voce*: 'Let no traveller

1 Now the reigning Grand-Duke. [1826]
2 Lord Byron, the English Rousseau, was by alternate phases dandy, mad-
  man and poetic genius. *Cf.* his visit to Father Paul of Ivrea, the Franciscan
  monk of Athens: *vide* H. Lauvergne, *la Grèce en* 1825. [1826]

ever delude himself that he has nothing left to learn about his neighbours' literature!'

LA MORTE

Sonetto

Morte, che sei tu mai? Primo dei danni
L' alma vile e la rea ti crede e teme;
E vendetta del ciel scendi ai tiranni,
Che il vigile tuo braccio incalza e preme.

Ma l'infelice, a cui de' lunghi affanni
Grave è l'incarco, e morta in cor la speme,
Quel ferro implora troncator degli anni,
E ride all'appressar dell' ore estreme.

Fra la polve di Marte, e le vicende,
Ti sfida il forte che ne' rischi indura;
E il saggio senza impallidir ti attende.

Morte, che se' tu dunque? Un ombra oscura,
Un bene, un male, che diversa prende
Dagli affetti dell uom forma e natura.

Nathan stoutly confirms my intuitive estimate of the Florentine character—which character, moreover, he heartily approves of; for indeed, he is so utterly mistrustful of fortune's favour, that he considers every passion a catastrophe; only with supreme reluctance will he admit to one exception, which is hunting. He is, besides, a fervent advocate of that inner wisdom which Lormea used to preach to me in Hamburg: *Have ready a courteous answer and a merry one to greet all men; for the rest, consider their words as sounding brass or a tinkling cymbal; beware, lest they should stir the least movement of response within your soul, save only in the case of imminent peril, as might be:* Draw back! Here comes a bolting horse! *Only if the words are spoken from the heart of an intimate friend—assuming you are fond enough to believe in existence of such a being—may you make this exception: consign to writing the counsel which is offered, and, on that very day a full year hence, consider what is written.*

For lack of this philosophy (urges Nathan), three men out of four vow their souls to perdition for sins which they do not even find pleasure in committing; whereas, by the grace of it, men of but limited abilities have come to know happiness. With a little practice, it will soon deliver a man from the torment of entertaining contradictory desires.

VOLTERRA, 31st January. Like all towns belonging to that ancient Kingdom of Etruria, whose civilisation, a true model of liberal attainment for the time, was overthrown and destroyed utterly by the dawning power of Rome, Volterra stands perched on the loftiest point of a high hill, in a situation similar to that of Langres. I discovered that the *Patriotic Sentiment* of the town was in high dudgeon on account of some treatise or other from the pen of a Swiss traveller, who had asserted that the *aria cattiva* of the locality annually decimates the population of Volterra. This traveller, M. Lullin, accords the highest praise to the agricultural economy of Tuscany, which he designates by the term *Canite,* in honour of the Wedding-Feast of Cana; let me confess, moreover, that the style of Genevan prose is rich in a sort of *puritanical bombast,* which invariably tickles my sense of humour. The honest townsfolk of Volterra accuse this M. Lullin of having made a slip of a mere handful of millions, in that passage where he attempts to calculate the profit accruing to the national exchequer from the export of those straw hats which form the staple industry of Tuscany. 'Yet', I protested, 'since we in the North, year in and year out, see fit to print and publish some eight or ten volumes touching these native haunts of *Beauty,* were it not better simply to accept this votive offering as a rightful homage due to the land of Italy? What have *you* to do with our nonsensical ravings? The true catastrophe would come, if no one bothered to mention you at all, and if Volterra were to fare no better, say, than Nuremberg.' Pen in hand, I visited the Cyclopean ramparts, which formed the object of my journey; I examined an immense quantity of small alabaster tombs; and finally I spent a fascinating evening amid the *Calasanctians*—in plainer language, in a company of *Monks*. Who could have foreseen it, not three months since?

I cannot but deem myself flattered by the truly exquisite courtesy shown me by the *marchese* Guarnacci, Knight of St Stephen, who was gracious enough to allow me to inspect his Cabinet of Antiquities, and later introduced me to divers members of the Ricciarelli family, a patrician clan of Volterra, in whose possession there hangs a painting by their illustrious ancestor, Daniele Ricciarelli, one of the notable imitators of Michelangelo.

(Refreshing tidiness observed in a small factory which turns out alabaster vases and statuettes; peculiar charm of some of these figurines.

Impudent glances of a group of Capuchins whom I encountered in procession; striking contrast with the humility of their bearing.)

The total population of Volterra numbers some four thousand souls; the Bishop commands an annual income of some forty thousand *livres*.

I have detected a fair number of discrepancies and exaggerations in the plates which signor Micali, in his book *l'Italia avanti il Dominio dei Romani*, has devoted to Volterra. Among Italian scholars, even the most erudite, one vital quality is lacking (setting aside the question of *lucidity*): the gentle art of not considering as already proven whatever fact is vital to the thesis in question; in this respect, the manner of argument employed defies belief! Observe, however, that M. Raoul-Rochette has none the less managed to *spoil* this volume in the

French translation for which he is responsible. Herr Niebuhr would be infinitely superior to all this rank ineptitude, were it not for the damned philosophic genius of Germany, which flings a veil of haziness and distortion over the very brightest inspirations of this learned gentleman from Berlin. Indulgent reader, will you permit me a gastronomic comparison? Everyone knows M. Berchoux's line:

Et le turbot fut mis à la sauce piquante*.

In Paris, it is customary to serve the turbot on one dish, and the *sauce piquante* in another. I could most sincerely wish that our Teutonic historians might mark and note and inwardly assimilate this soundest of culinary practices; might they then not be prevailed upon to offer the public, *in one dish* the facts which their research has yielded, *and in another* their philosophical reflections? This separation would allow the reader to profit directly from the history, and to defer until a more propitious occasion his perusal of *the Author's Cogitations upon the Absolute*. In the present state of confusion which reigns between these two choice ingredients, there is some difficulty involved in savouring the element preferred.

CASTELFIORENTINO, 1st February, at two o'clock in the morning. This evening at six o'clock, returning from Volterra, I found my way into this village, which lies some score of miles south-west of Florence. Harnessed to my *sediola* I had the leanest and swiftest nag in all the province; yet I chose deliberately to check his speed, so as to be *forced* (such, at least, being the pretext) to ask for hospitality in some cottage in Castelfiorentino, half-way between Volterra and Empoli. Here I came upon a trio of those Tuscan peasant-wenches, so handsome and in every way so superior (by common report) to the fine ladies of the towns. About them I found gathered a group of peasants, some seven or eight in number. I defy you flatly to guess at the occupation of this rustic company: each, by turn about, was engaged in improvising a tale in prose, in the

style of the *Arabian Nights*. I spent the whole evening enraptured, from seven until midnight, listening to these inventions. At the outset, my hosts were grouped about the fireside,
while I sat apart at my appointed table, eating my supper;
but gradually, as they became aware of my growing interest,
they began to address their words to me. Since there is invariably an *Enchanter* among the *dramatis personae* of these tales, I
deduce that they are probably Arabian in origin. One in
particular among those I heard created so vivid an impression
in my mind that I could dearly wish to write it down, had I but
someone at call to take dictation. But how should I find the
courage to embark upon thirty pages in my own hand? The
wildest supernatural fancies were here employed to bring
about a series of events which led in turn to the profoundest
and most startling interplay of human passions. The listening
imagination was dumbfounded by the audacity of the fictions,
and at the same time entranced by the freshness of the imagery.
There was a *Lover*, who had hid himself among the branches
of a tree, that he might behold his mistress bathing in the waters
of a little lake; the *Enchanter*, his rival, was gone from thence;
yet this wizard, notwithstanding the many leagues which lay
between him and his enemy, grew instantly aware of what was
taking place by the sharp discomfort engendered by a ring
upon his finger; he uttered a spell; whereupon, in swift
succession, the arms, the legs and finally the head of the unhappy lover fell from the tree where he had made his perch,
and vanished beneath the waters of the lake. During this cruel
chastisement, the story-teller related the dialogue between the
lover and his mistress, together with the latter's rejoinders—as
when, for instance, the lover's trunk was severed from him,
and no part of him survived the execution save his head, etc.
This strange alloy of fantasy and pathetic truth left me spell-
bound; there were instants, as I listened to these tales, when I
could fully believe myself to be living in the fifteenth century.
The evening ended with an improvised dance. During the

previous conversation, I had succeeded so well in *making myself small* that the peasants felt no pang of jealousy to see me join with them and their trio of handsome lasses; and so we trod a measure, they and I, which lasted until one o'clock in the morning. In sharp contrast, however, when I ventured to comment upon the beauty of the landscape (which might, I hinted, oblige me to pass the whole of the morrow in Castel-fiorentino), this tentative gambit fell upon unsympathetic ears. 'The beauty of the landscape on the first day of *February*?' retorted one of the peasants. 'Hark at the pretty compliments the gentleman is paying us now!' etc., etc. Yet the reason which led me thus to voice this indirect proposal was simply that I was reluctant to let such fortune slip between my fingers. It would have been too senseless to suppose that I might ever persuade these peasants to accept the *truth—viz.*, that it was indeed the ingenuity of their inventive minds, together with the untutored yet perfect courtesy of their manners, and not (as they suspected) some melodramatic designs upon their women, which tempted me, in spite of the atrocious, piercing, gusty *tramontana*, to remain for the space of two whole days in such a drab and windswept hole as Castelfiorentino. I will forbear to attempt any further description of my evening; I am but too keenly aware that the only manner to convey its quality would be to transcribe from beginning to end the enchanting tales which gave it such peculiar charm. *Charm*! How feeble the word is grown! How rank a sin to have abused it so! This evening's six long hours sped by with wingèd flight, as though I had been all the while engaged at faro in pleasant company; in truth, so utterly absorbed was I, that I knew not an instant of languor in which to reflect upon what was taking place about me.

Tonight's experience invites comparison with that evening which I spent *alla Scala*, upon the first day of my arrival in Milan. Then, a passionate delirium overflowed my soul and left it weary with exhaustion; my mind grew taut and strained

M

with the effort, lest the minutest shade of delight or of sensuality escape me. But tonight, all was content unlooked-for; it was the purest pleasure, attained without an effort, without anxiety, without a palpitation; the angel-host of Heaven knows such bliss. My advice to the traveller is this: when he visits the villages of Tuscany, he should pass himself off as a native of *Lombardy*. I have only to open my mouth for the Tuscans to realise that my accent is decidedly odd; but I command a certain fluency none the less; and therefore, so lofty are the heights of their disdain for any tongue which is not *la toscana favella* unalloyed, whenever I assert that I hail from Como, they take me at my word. I run a certain risk, I grant you: it would be dismaying to find that I had a *genuine* Lombard for my nearest neighbour. But *that*, however, *is one of the perils that attend my condition*, as Grillus, being changed into a swine by Circe,[1] did once remark to many-wiled Ulysses. On the other hand, the avowed presence of a *Frenchman* would immediately give a new twist entirely to the conversation.

The reader's *Patriotic Sentiment* will already have apprised him that I am suffering from a severe attack of *monomania*, and that my admiration for Italy is grown into a veritable *obsession*; yet I should play traitor to my conscience, if I failed to set down the truth *as I see it*. I have spent six years within the frontiers of this country, which (I suspect) the advocates of *Patriotic Sentiment* have never so much as visited. So much for a preface to what follows, for surely nothing less could suffice to render tolerable the abominable heresy which I am now about to utter: for I do verily believe that the Tuscan peasant is infinitely more intelligent than his French equivalent; and I believe further that the Italian peasant in general has been endowed by the bounty of Providence with a stronger and infinitely deeper capacity for emotional experience—or in other words, that he can weather infinitely more violent tempests of passion within his heart.

[1] In Fénelon's admirable *Dialogue*. [1826]

By contrast, the French peasant is gifted with a far greater store of *generosity*, and with a far richer supply of that *common-sense* which may prove so invaluable in the current happenings of daily life. A peasant from the uplands of Brie, having amassed capital to the tune of a thousand francs or so, which now lies either deposited in the bank, or else loaned out under mortgage, sleeps soundly in the comforting knowledge of his little fortune; the Italian peasant, on the contrary, knows no more tormenting source of anxiety than such a hoard, unless it be invested in *land*. (Certain provinces offer exceptions to this general rule: Piedmont; the immediate neighbourhood of Milan; Tuscany; and above all, Genoa, where, the land within its borders having proved insufficiently fertile to furnish corn enough for the subsistence of the population, every citizen is by tradition a merchant.) Without ever having stepped beyond the frontiers of France, any person who has travelled widely in the South will be aware that *generosity* is rare enough even among our own peasants in this area. The true headquarters of *generosity* is Paris, about which centre, within a radius of fifty leagues, extends the proper scope of her dominion.

SIENNA, *2nd February*. This morning, having driven back into Florence, how should I describe the joy I felt upon dis-covering, there in the coffee-house, one of my old acquaintance from Milan? He is off post-haste to Naples to witness the opening of the *teatro San-Carlo*, which has been rebuilt by Barbaja after having been destroyed by fire some two years since; but he is fated to arrive too late. He offered me a seat in his barouche: this proposal at one stroke sent flying all my sensibly-constructed schemes, and so I accepted; for after all, the object of my journey is not to discover the land of Italy, but to lay in a store of pleasure for myself. Yet I do honestly believe that the true reason for my acceptance lies in the fact that my acquaintance speaks *Milanese*; the Arab-fashioned gutturals of Florence are as a desert-wind that withers my heart; whereas, no sooner did I begin to speak with my acquaintance *delle nostre cose di Milan*, than my soul lay lapped in a kind of placid and tranquil serenity. This style of conversation, so steeped in candour, offers never so much as the shadow of a falsehood, never the least disquieting fear of ridicule. I doubt whether, in all my life, I have met this charming Milanese of mine so much as a dozen times; yet my heart goes out to him as to an intimate friend.

We halted no more than ten minutes in Sienna, just time enough to glance at the Cathedral, about which I shall not permit myself to say a word. I am writing in the barouche; we are proceeding without haste amid a wilderness of small volcanic outcrops carpeted with vineyards and stunted olive-trees: nothing could be uglier. Every now and then, lest we weary of these delights, we drive across a little plain infected with the vapours of some malodorous stream.

Nothing is so propitious to philosophising as the boredom of an unlovely journey. 'I could dearly wish', began my acquaintance, 'to see the establishment of an award for the best solution to the following problem: *What harm did Napoleon do to Italy?*'

One answer might be: 'He bestowed but two degrees of civilisation upon her, whereas he might easily have accorded her ten.'

Napoleon himself might have argued thus: '*You* chose to fling overboard one of the most vital of my edicts (the *Legal Stamp-Duty Act*, rejected in 1806 by the Legislative Assembly of Milan*); now *I*, being a Corsican, intuitively grasped the temperament of Italy, which never does things by fits and starts, but enjoys a grim consistency unknown in France; of this I was afraid. It was this uncertainty, just as much as the delusion of some monarchic whim, which counselled me to postpone all major reforms until the time of my journey to Rome—which journey I was fated never to achieve. I was destined to perish without ever beholding the *City of the*

Caesars, without ever dating from the *Capitol* a decree worthy
of that illustrious name.'

TORINIERI, *3rd February.*   Yesterday evening we halted for
supper at Buon-Convento. By a fortunate circumstance, the
barouche proved to be in need of some repair; consequently, I
abandoned my companion and installed myself in the nearest
barber's shop (this being a sacrifice which I, as a traveller, see
fit to lay upon the Altar of Duty). Here, by happy accident, I
chanced to fall in with a young priest from some neighbouring
parish, a most ingenious conversationalist, who, upon learning
that I was a foreigner, insisted upon doing me the honours of
the country and surrendering to me his rightful turn to occupy
the massive leather chair; which offer I accepted. We love none
so dearly as those we have obliged; consequently, in consideration of my *gallant sacrifice*, I was rewarded by a whole hour of
intimate conversation with my fledgling priest. At times,
remembering his cloth, he would launch out upon some harsh
tirade against the French; at others, recalling his own gift of
intelligence, with which he was plentifully endowed (a
thoroughgoing *Florentine* intelligence withal, compounded of
rationality and precision), he could find no praise too high for
that 'superlative French administration', at once so *rational*, so
firm and so *precise*, whose task it was to enlighten the slumbering,
sixteenth-century darkness of unhappy Italy with the luminous
consequences of eighteenth-century civilisation. Thanks to the
Napoleonic *régime*, Italy at one bound cleared three whole
centuries of progress. In those remote Pacific islands, which
the British are discovering in these latter days—islands whose
populations are ever and anon wiped out by small-pox—the
gift of conqueror to conquered is no longer *inoculation*, that
salutary panacea so harshly slandered by the powdered wigs of
1756, but rather *vaccination*, whose remedial properties so far
transcend those of the earlier discovery. Such was the rôle of
the French in Italy.

That same Imperial administration which, in France, too often curbed the thirst for rational knowledge, in Italy bore hard on nothing, save on what was utterly irrational and effete; hence the vast and justly-merited popularity of Napoleon in Italy, compared with his dark unpopularity in France. In France, Napoleon was busy liquidating the *Écoles centrales*, marring the *École polytechnique*, corrupting the whole system of state education, and sapping the very soul of the younger generation through the intermediary of his cherished minion, M. de Fontanes. Yet even that infinitesimal surviving modicum of common-sense and liberal culture which M. de Fontanes *dare* not confiscate from the Faculties of the *Imperial University* would have proved an invaluable benefit to Italy. In those provinces where men are born beneath the lodestar of *Imagination* (Bologna, for instance, or Brescia, or Reggio nell' Emilia), there was a multitude of young folk who, their hot heads stuffed to bursting-point with old Jean-Jacques' impossible utopias, and blithely unconscious of the manifold pricks and scourges which, in this imperfect world of ours, attend the birth of the least new institution, did loudly rail against Napoleon; yet never did they clearly grasp nor justly appreciate in what respect he had betrayed the country, nor yet for what offence he had deserved the hell of Saint-Helena. But in Florence, where the eye sees nothing but *reality*, all the positive advantages of the Napoleonic system shone forth with lustre undimmed. In course of conversation with this fledgling priest of mine, we touched on almost every branch of the Imperial Civil Service. The pettiness and the inexcusable vexations of the French administrative system were nowhere apparent south of the Alps, save in the matter of Excise and Revenue; whereas, to take the randomest example, our *Code Civil*— fruit of the luminous endeavours of men as wise as Treilhard, Merlin and Cambacérès—succeeded without a hint of intervening gradation to the inhuman laws of Charles V and Philip II.

The reader cannot have the remotest conception of the

fantastic anachronisms which plagued the life of Italy before the French arrived to sweep them away. 'For instance', remarked my young priest, 'in the high valleys of the Apennine, where lightning strikes the hills two or three times a month, it was still, as late as 1796, deemed *sacrilege* to affix a lightning-conductor to one's roof-top: *the Will of God shall brook no opposition*!' (In England, the *Methodists* once preached a similar doctrine.) Yet there is nothing in the world which affords an Italian greater pleasure than the architecture of his house. Among all the arts, excepting only music, architecture is that which speaks most nearly to his heart. An Italian will stop and idle away full fifteen minutes in contemplation of some fine doorway which is being built in a new house. This passion, moreover, has roots that I can easily appreciate: in Vicenza, for instance, not all the evil-minded imbecility of the Austrian Commandant, nor of his Chief of Police, can obliterate the masterpieces of Palladio, nor censure them as subjects of debate. It is, moreover, this same reverence for architecture which explains why Italians who arrive in Paris are so prodigiously shocked, and why their admiration for London is so boundless: 'Where', they exclaim, 'in all the world, shall you find a street so exquisite as *Regent Street*—or even remotely comparable?'

My young priest informed me that Cosimo I de' Medici, that baneful Prince who broke the character of Tuscany, was wont, regardless of the cost, to buy up every manuscript, whether of *History* or *Memoirs*, wherein allusion was made to his exalted House, *and burn it on the spot*.

In the distance, by the light of a lustrous moon, he pointed out to me the ruins of several of those cities of ancient Etruria, invariably perched on some hill-top eyrie; I meanwhile being filled with the serenity of this wondrous night, under the warm wind. On the homeward road, whither we turned our footsteps at two o'clock in the morning, my imagination devoured a span of one-and-twenty centuries, and I felt my heart within me swell (let the reader weigh well the full absurdity of this confession) in a fury of indignation against the Romans, who rose up, with no sounder justification than the ferocity of their own courage, to overturn the very foundations of those antique Etruscan commonwealths, so infinitely superior to themselves in art, in prosperity and in the secret skills of happiness. (The final conquest of Etruria took place in the year 280 B.C., after four centuries of intermittent warfare.) It is as though a score of Cossack regiments were to sack the *grands boulevards* and destroy the fair city of Paris: such vandalism would still count as a catastrophe for generations born ten centuries hence; the entire human race would have taken a step backwards, and with it, the art of human happiness.

Yesterday evening, at the *Golden Lion* where we were lodged, as we sat at supper with a party of some seven or eight travellers arrived from Florence, we were treated, on three or four occasions, to a display of the most exquisite courtesy. That nothing might be lacking to the pleasures of the evening, we were served at table by two lasses of uncommon beauty, one fair, the other most provocatively dark, who proved to be the landlord's own daughters. Observing them, one might truly have credited the belief that Bronzino had used them as models for the feminine figures in his famous painting of *Limbo*,[1] for which the pupils of the great David know no words strong enough to speak their scorn, yet which I venerate withal, as being so pre-eminently *Tuscan*. In Italy, a city is no less proud of the beauty of its women than of the genius of its poets. Our fellow-guests, after a chorus of praise for the truly noble features of this pair of peasant-girls, fell into a spirited debate

---

[1] At the time when I was writing, this painting used to hang in *Santa Croce*; since when, however, it has been transferred to the *Uffizi Gallery* in Florence, being deemed somewhat indelicate for a church. The *priests* were right; yet this same picture had hung for two whole centuries in *Santa Croce*, and had scandalised not a single pious soul. *Decency* is making mighty strides in these latter days: edifying, no doubt—but how *tiresome*! [1826]

concerning the respective merits of Milanese and Florentine beauty.

'What fairer objects could your heart desire', demanded a Florentine, 'than le signore Pazz***, Cors***, Nenci***, Mozz***?'

'The loveliest of all', retorted a Neapolitan, 'is signora Centol***, without a doubt.'

'Yet signora Florenz***', rejoined a Bolognese, 'is perhaps more perfect still than signora Agost***.'

Why, I cannot tell; but for some reason the remainder of the conversation would seem indelicate, were I to set it down in French. Yet, truth to tell, nothing was more reverently decent than our divers remarks; we spoke like sculptors.

Throughout the meal, from first to last, there was a steady stream of banter maintained between ourselves and the pair of handsome wenches who served us; and yet—strange to relate in such surroundings—not once did these remarks assume too suggestive or too free a character. They in their turn did frequently retort to the travellers' provocations by citing ancient Florentine proverbs, or else by apt quotations from the poets. There is far less of a dividing barrier here than in France between the daughters of a prosperous innkeeper and the scions of an ancient family; for no one in the whole of Italy has ever dreamed of aping the modes and manners of a glittering Court. When Ferdinand III appears in the midst of his subjects, there is nothing but his uncommon wealth—in consequence of which he may be conjectured to be uncommonly *happy*—to distinguish him from the rank and file of gentlemen among his subjects. The degree of content which he enjoys, the beauty of his wife, etc., are discussed openly and without restraint. No one would conceive of imitating his behaviour.

AQUAPENDENTE, 4th February. I have just been looking at some seven or eight remarkable paintings belonging to the older Florentine tradition. I confess that I am deeply moved by the steadfast *truth to nature* which is to be observed in Ghirlandaio and his contemporaries, who flourished too early to be submerged in the strong tide of *idealism*. It is this same outlandish *naïveté* which I love so well in Massinger, in Ford and in the other ancient English dramatists, those rugged contemporaries of Shakespeare. The *ideal* is a powerful nostrum which doubles the creative energy of a genius, and exterminates the weakling.

Near BOLSENA, 5th February, during a long uphill climb. My companion lies asleep on the seat beside me, having related to me divers anecdotes which are currently fashionable in Venice and Milan.

That well-known mountebank, the *marchese* Filorusso*, whose fame spreads far and wide, thanks no less to Buratti's satirical invention (in which, together with an *Elephant*, our *marchese* is the hero) than to his feat of arms upon the *piazza San-Fedele* in Milan, has recently fallen victim to one of the most memorable and stinging outrages which ever was inflicted upon a deserving pair of shoulders by muscular arms wielding flexible canes. Our Marquis, it appears, was strolling through the streets of Milan towards two o'clock in the morning, savouring the fragrance of that rich aroma which lingered in the wake of one of those municipal carts, locally known as *navach*, whose offices are but too indispensable in populous cities, when three young gentlemen, whom he recognised, received him in this unbecoming fashion. No sooner was daylight come, than our Marquis, despite the fever which, whether from fright or from pain, had fastened upon him, did hurry round to the constabulary post, at which the officer-in-charge, having heard his complaint, and following the idiotic procedure laid down by the Austrian Civil Administration, proceeded to demand:

'Your Excellency can produce *witnesses* to this occurrence?'

'My own back, sir!' retorted the *marchese*. 'Which is black and blue all over; doubtless also the three *bullies*, who will most probably confess.'

Now, the leader of this onslaught was none other than Vellicri, the celebrated *impresario*. In the old days, under the French *régime*, the police would have had a simple course to follow: they would have summoned Vellicri and asked him point-blank:

'Be good enough to inform us where you were at two o'clock this morning.'

But, according to the rules of Austrian procedure, this question is *illegal*; consequently, the outraged Marquis had no remedy but to return home to bed, and to receive expressions of sympathy and condolence. Every caller was secretly shaking with laughter—everyone, that is to say, except *la Gabrica*, that charming little singer who had, in fact, been the occasion of all this mighty disturbance. For our millionaire *marchese*, in flagrant defiance of his instincts, which were prodigiously avaricious, had styled himself the 'protector' of this winning little creature. Vellicri, who ruled his playhouse with a rod of iron, had refused to pay this same enchanting artist the sum of fifteen hundred francs, which there is strong evidence that he owed her, since the Tribunal, in response to due solicitation by the *marchese* Filorusso, subsequently condemned him, under pain of imprisonment, to make payment of the sum demanded. It was, in fact, in the heat of annoyance caused by this injunction to pay that Vellicri resolved to vent his spite against the Marquis. The latter, however, was scarcely recovered from the mortal fear which had possessed him at the sight of that grim trio of ruffians, when already he began to dream of Venice, that theatre of all his glory.

' 'Tis there', he mused, 'that I laid low the *Elephant*;[1] 'tis

---

[1] *Vide l'Elefanteide*, that admirable satire by signor Buratti*. Watch particularly for the description of the *tumbling figure*. Never was there any satirist to rival signor Buratti in the physical delineation of his heroes; when once you have read his poems, you can recognise his originals by

there that Vellicri plies his trade as *impresario*; I shall cause every opera he dare present to be hunted off the stage; I will *ruin* the fellow!'

And indeed, concluded my companion, he was as good as his word; during these latter months, every opera which has been staged at Vellicri's theatre has been remorselessly hounded off the boards, and our *impresario* is losing a fortune!

This tale gives some notion how the good folk of Italy spent their days before Napoleon assumed control of the country: by contrast, under his *régime*, Vellicri would have been hustled off to the galleys for two or three years, while the Marquis would have found himself in gaol, had he ventured to provoke a disturbance in the playhouse. Yet the cream of the jest is that no one played a greater part in restoring that state of affairs which permitted him to be set upon and outraged with impunity, than our *marchese* himself; for was he not strolling 'by chance' in the *piazza San-Fedele* while the mob was massacring Count Prina?

VELLETRI, 6th February. We spent no more than three hours in Rome. I caught a distant glimpse of the Dome of St Peter's, but, in accordance with a promise already made to my companion, I restrained my urge to visit. If I managed to glance at the Colosseum, it is simply that the highroad to Naples runs close by. The barouche halted, and we spent ten minutes exploring this noble monument, which, beyond question, is one of the most sublime objects that ever my eyes have had the fortune to rest upon. We penetrated into Rome by way of the celebrated *Porta del Popolo*. Ah! how easily we let ourselves be fooled! This famous approach is less impressive than the gateway to almost any other city I can think of; at all events, it never comes within a thousand miles of the approach to Paris by way of the *Arc de Triomphe*, arising in splendour

meeting them in the street. Byron's *Don Juan* contains not a few passages copied from Buratti. [1826]

from the circus of *l'Etoile*. The Brotherhood of *Pedants*, descrying hereabouts an unrivalled opportunity to display their *Latin*, have set about persuading us that modern Rome is beautiful: this is the mystery which underlies the reputation of the *Eternal City*. Our barouche was brought to a halt in the middle of the street, for the way was blocked by passing columns of troops, all marching off to some *Grand Review* held in honour of a very singular occasion: for the *Minister of War* has recently been elevated to the dignity of *Archbishop! Fabius, ubi es?* The streets of Rome are infected with an odour of rotten cabbage; and through the exquisite windows of the *palazzi* on the *Corso*, one can glimpse the creeping taint of poverty within. Lest the resplendent moral purity of his *Romish* subjects* be corrupted as by a foul pestilence, the Pope allows no living theatre to open its doors save only for the Carnival; during the entire remainder of the year, Rome must perforce make do with its wooden-limbed marionettes. A decree is imminent, forbidding women to appear upon the stage; instead, the public shall behold *castrati*. We dined at the *Armellino* (a tavern on the *Corso*, a proud and narrow thorough-fare lined with *palazzi*). Before our passports could be visaed, we were required to swear on oath that we had never seen service under *Murat*—precisely thus and not otherwise does the word appear in the printed text of the oath: not a sugges-tion of a *M. Murat*, or a *General Murat*. The unspeakable vulgarity of it!—like the crude and brutal *Capet* in the old days of the *Terror*.

We left the city* by the gate of *San Giovanni Laterano*. Magnificent view of the Appian Way, its course marked out across the landscape by a chain of crumbling antiquities; admirable solitude of the Roman *Campagna*; eerie effect of all these ruins in the midst of that boundless silence. How should I describe so strange an impression? During the space of three hours I experienced the weirdest of sensations, not the least ingredient of which was *awe*. For fear lest I be called upon to talk, I feigned sleep. I should have known a far greater sum of pleasure had I but been alone. The Campagna, traversed from end to end by those fragmented lengths of aqueducts, is to my eyes the sublimest tragedy that ever was conceived. It is a plain of magnificent proportions, without the faintest trace of cultivation. I halted the barouche at one or two points, to decipher an occasional Latin inscription. There is an element of wide-eyed *naïveté* in that impassioned sense of awe I bear towards a genuinely antique inscription; I imagine that I would gladly go down upon my knees, in order to allow my eyes to dwell with greater pleasure upon an inscription carved by Roman hands in that original spot, where, for the first time, after the battle of Lake Trasimene, the scattered legions halted in their flight; my mind would be so impregnated with the grandeur of it that for a week I should need no other substance to nourish my dreaming soul; the very cut of each letter would grow to be a thing that I should love. A *modern* inscription, on the other hand, is the most nauseating object under Heaven; nowhere (save in the rarest instances) does the unspeakable meanness of our present age ooze more hideously than through its armour of superlatives. I have spent today reflecting on my yesterday's emotion: my hurried journey through the streets of Rome, above all, that glimpse of the Campagna, have left me all on edge. Until these latter days, I sincerely believed in my remorseless loathing for *aristocracy* in any shape or form; and my reason enjoyed the consent and approval of my heart. On one occasion, when R***, the banker, observed to me: 'I discern in you, my friend, a touch of the *aristocrat*', I could have sworn that nothing lay further from the truth. Yet now, indeed, I have descried unmistakable symptoms of the disease within me: in seeking to cure the fault, I should succeed only in deluding my own perspicacity; instead, I have surrendered to the vice—surrendered with a wild song of ecstasy.

What is this *self*, this *I* that I am? I know not. One fine day, I awoke to find myself upon this earth; I discovered my fate to be forever linked with a certain body, character, estate. Am I to spend all my days, then, ineffectually seeking to alter that which cannot be altered, and so, meanwhile, forget to *live*? Rather do I propose to accept myself as I am, humbly submitting to my own defects. I submit most humbly, therefore, to these aristocratic tendencies of mine; notwithstanding that I have for the space of ten years, and in deep sincerity withal, denounced the very principle of aristocracy. Of all noses, I love the *Roman* species best; and yet, if fate decree that I am to be French, I must perforce resign myself to endure the variety allotted me by Heaven: *genus campaniensis*. What remedy? The Romans were for a scourge unto the human race, a noxious sickness which stunted the growth of civilisation in the world; had they never been, we in France might already have achieved a government not less advanced in reason than that of the United States of America. They it was who shattered the estimable republics of the old Etruscans; they it was again who came and sowed the seeds of turmoil among our ancestors, heirs to the inheritance of Gaul; never let it be said that we were mere barbarians—for, indeed, had we not the gift of *liberty*? They it was who, piece by piece, did build the countless ramifications of that machine called *Monarchy*—and why? To pave the way to infamy, to the reigns of a Nero, a Caligula, to the lunatic debates which reft the Lower Empire, touching the *uncreated* light upon Tabor.

And yet, in spite of so many grievances, my heart still sides with Rome. These old republics of Etruria, these Gaulish customs which were bastions of freedom—*I* see them not. On the other hand, in every page of history, I behold the deeds and see the life of Rome; and what the eye cannot see, the heart cannot love. Thus do I account to myself for my obsession with those vestiges of Roman grandeur, those ruins, those inscriptions. Nor is this the limit of my weakness: for I even detect in certain churches of remote antiquity the pale reflexion of still older pagan temples. Christianity, triumphant at the last after so many centuries of persecution, would fall with implacable rage upon a shrine of Jupiter, and rend it stone from stone; yet hard beside the old foundations, there would arise a new Church of St Paul.[1] Those same columns of the temple of Jupiter which had newly been torn down would now be made to serve a consecrated purpose; and since the Christian builders had not a notion of art, they would copy *all unawares* the pagan shrine.

Friars and feudalism—those twin cankers that eat out the heart of the body politic—were both excellent institutions in their time; in the olden days, nothing was set afoot at bidding of an empty theory; everything was a direct response to an immediate need. What is the policy of our privileged classes today? They propose to govern men of mature years and stature by bib, tucker and leading-strings! Could anything be more patently absurd?—yet in the beginning we have stood to profit one and all from such governance. Personally, I regard St Francis of Assissi as a very great man. And so it may well be by virtue of this argument—formulated all unconsciously in the dark recesses of my mind—that I surprise in myself a certain predilection for the Cathedral churches and the time-honoured ritual of the Christian Establishment; yet the antiquity of these things must be genuine and vouched for; the first faint flavour of St Dominic or of the Inquisition conjures up in my mind visions of the Extermination of the Albigensians, of the *Salutary Rigours* of the massacre of St Bartholomew, and thence, by a natural transition, of the massacres of Nîmes in 1815. Aristocratic leanings I may have; yet I confess that they desert me like a flash at the hideous sight of men such as Trestaillons and Trufémi.

Following the road out of Albano, and passing beside the

---

1 For example, the famous *San Paolo fuori le Mura* in Rome, which was burnt down in 1823. An attempt is being made (so rumour goes) to raise the money for rebuilding by founding a special *Order of Knighthood*, whose star and garter may be bought for *cash*. [1826]

tomb of the Horatii and the Curiatii, we chanced straightway upon a charming valley—indeed, the first attractive landscape since we turned our backs on Bologna and left behind our own beloved Lombardy. Singular elevation of the *palazzo Chigi*; fine trees; a broad glimpse of the sea; divine prospect; Italo-Hellenic architecture.

7th February. We halted in Terracina; and there, in that sumptuous hostelry erected by Pius VI—that same Pius VI 'who knew how to reign'*—we were invited to take supper with a party of travellers newly arrived out of Naples. Gathered about the table, I observed some seven or eight persons, amongst whom, in particular, my eyes lighted upon a fair-haired young man, of some five or six-and-twenty years of age, astonishingly handsome in spite of a slight touch of baldness. I pressed him for news of Naples, and in particular, of music in that city: he satisfied my curiosity with answers that were clear-cut, brilliant and humorous. I enquired of him whether, when I reached Naples, I might still hope to see Rossini's *Otello*, to which he replied with a smile. I pursued the topic, asserting that, in my opinion, Rossini was the bright hope of the Italian school; that he was the only living composer who had true genius as his birthright; and that his triumph rested, not upon the elaboration of his accompaniments, but upon the pure beauty of his melody. At this point I noticed that my man seemed faintly embarrassed, while his travelling-companions were grinning openly . . . to cut a long story short, this *was* Rossini in person*. Luckily—and by the merest stroke of good fortune—I alluded neither to that vice of *idleness* which mars the grandeur of his genius, nor to his numerous plagiarisms.

He told me that Naples will have no truck with the sort of music which is fashionable in Rome, while Rome demands a style of composition quite distinct from that which is popular in Milan. And how ill-rewarded is the poor composer's trade!

He must wear out his span of days in ceaseless journeying throughout the length and breadth of Italy; and his noblest opera will hardly bring him in two thousand francs. He told me that his *Otello* was no more than a qualified success, that he was on his way to Rome to compose a *Cenerentola*, and that from thence he was destined for Milan, to write a *Gazza ladra* for *la Scala*.

This impecunious *maestro* excites my liveliest interest; merry he is indeed, even to the point of hilarity, and contented enough in all conscience; yet is it not pitiful that, among all the Princes of Italy, there may not be found a single patron to set his name on the *Civil List* for a paltry couple of thousand crowns, and so set him free to await the dawn of inspiration before he must perforce put pen to paper? Who would be bold enough to reproach him for botching up a whole opera within a fortnight? He will sit down to work at a ricketty table, to the accompaniment of all the din and clatter from the inn-kitchen hard by; and he dips his pen in the muddy sludge of ink which the pot-boy brings him in an old ointment-jar. I have met with no man of more brilliant intellect within the furthest frontiers of Italy—yet assuredly he has not the least notion of his own quality, for Italy still lies and suffers beneath the grinding heel of *pedantry*. I spoke to him of my admiration for *l'Italiana in Algeri*, and asked him of which he thought most highly, *l'Italiana* or *Tancredi*. His answer snapped back at me forthwith: *il Matrimonio segreto*. The retort was both felicitous and disarming: for *il Matrimonio* is as forgotten in Italy as are the tragedies of poor Ducis in Paris. Why (I pressed him) should he not collect royalties from the divers companies which perform his twenty-odd operas? He showed me plainly, however, that, in the unsettled turmoil of present disorders, the very proposal was absurd.

We sat on, drinking tea, until well beyond the hour of midnight; this was the merriest evening I have yet spent in Italy; all seemed steeped in the boyish high spirits of a man who is happy at heart. Yet when, at long last, I took my leave of this great composer, I was possessed by melancholy. Canova and Rossini—none but these two (so intolerable is grown the government of Italy) are preserved to flower, alone and solitary, in the final devastation of this *Land of Genius*. With mournful delight, my lips repeated old Falstaff's lament:

There live not three great men in England; and one of them is poor and grows old*.

(*King Henry IV*, first part, Act II, scene iv.)

CAPUA, 8th February. I enquired whether there was opera tonight; and upon receiving a reply in the affirmative, I hastened round to the theatre. My eagerness was well rewarded. The opera on the programme—*le Nozze in Campagna**, an ingenious and facile composition by the somewhat frigid Guglielmi, son of a more famous father—was sung and acted with unimaginable verve and cohesion by a company of three or four poor devils who are paid the princely sum of eight francs for each appearance.

The *prima donna*, a big-boned creature of noble proportions, dark-haired, provocative and *disinvolta*, sang and acted her part in the very manner of perfection. Upon the instant, all the sullen rage of my heart against the degradation of Rome slipped from me like a garment; suddenly I was happy once more. The hero of the tale—according to the libretto, which was purchased for a generous thirty francs from the 'poet' who committed it—is a nobleman in love with one of his *serfs* (the term is perfectly appropriate in these regions); the maiden, meanwhile, is plighted to some village oaf, whose speech is pure Neapolitan dialect; and on every occasion when the nobleman arrives to declare his love, some wild imbroglio develops and drives him into concealment. The deep-felt, true and despairing jealousy which fills the heart of the poor peasant is genuinely dramatic; moreover, all dialects are more *natural*, and in consequence, more instantly moving, than any literary language—for all that I never understood two words together of this particular brogue. Two hours of intense delight: I fell into conversation with my nearest neighbours, extravagant partisans of Napoleon; they commented on various changes: judges, they said, were beginning no longer to demand bribes as a matter of course; out of ten robberies, one at least would be punished, etc., etc.

The final curtain fell at midnight; by one o'clock, we had already taken once more to the highroad. The Austrians have established watch-pickets every mile or so along the route; the local highwaymen are baffled, furious and half-dead of starvation.

NAPLES, 9th February. Grandiose approach to the city: for the space of an hour, we dropped down towards the sea, following a broad highway carved out of the same soft rock upon which Naples itself is built: thickness of the ramparts; first building—*l'Albergo de' Poveri*;* deeply impressive—no comparison with that over-rated bit of sham baroque, that chocolate-box effect that Rome is pleased to call the *Porta del Popolo.*

And so here we are at last, snugly established in the *Palazzo degli Studj*; step out of the door, turn left, and there before you lies the *via di Toledo*—one of the principal goals of all my journey, the busiest, most joyous thoroughfare in the entire universe. Yet would you believe it? For five mortal hours we trudged from inn to inn, vainly imploring shelter; there must be fully two or three thousand English tourists in the place; and when finally I ferreted out a lodging, it proved to be an eyrie perched up seven flights of stairs. Yet, for all its disadvantages, it faces the *San-Carlo*, and I can look out over Vesuvius and the sea.

Tonight, however, the doors of the *San-Carlo* remained implacably shut; instead, we set off hot-foot for the *teatro dei Fiorentini*, which is a tiny theatre in the form of an elongated horse-shoe, ideal for music—not unlike the *Salle Louvois* in Paris. Here, as in Rome, each ticket bears a number; all the first rows, I was told, were fully booked. The programme includes *Paolo e Virginia*, a popular opera by Guglielmi. By offering double, I managed to secure a seat in the second row. The auditorium was a glittering sight; every box was taken, crowded with women radiant in their finery; for here, unlike at *la Scala*, the whole well of the theatre is illuminated by a central chandelier.

Overture: complex, elaborate stuff, thirty or forty different themes in discordant juxtaposition, all too cramped for the listening ear to grasp, too crowded to awaken the slumbering sensibilities; an arduous, arid and wearisome piece of work, leaving the mind already surfeited with notes before the curtain rises.

Whereupon we behold *Paul* and *Virginia*, played by Margherita Chabran and Graciata Canonici; the latter, a simpering little minx, as *Paul*. The lovers have lost their way in the forest (same initial situation as in the French version of the opera)—a circumstance which calls imperiously for a duet. A duet we shall have, then, steeped in elegance and affectation. Enter the honest *Domingo*—in other words, Casaccia, the famous Casaccia, the idol of Naples much as Potier is the idol of Paris. His language is the dialect of the people; he is a veritable hippopotamus of a man, moreover—a circumstance which allows him to indulge in the broadest of farcical *lazzi*. For instance, being seated, he would resolve to cross his legs so as to seem more truly at his ease; the spirit was willing, but alas! the flesh was all too weak; straining in a final monstrous effort, he would overbalance upon his nearest neighbour, and send the whole assembly toppling headlong: general collapse (*cf.* the novels of Pigault-Lebrun). This actor, popularly known as Casacciello, is treated by the public like a demi-god; he intones his recitative through his nose, like some old capuchin Friar. (Here, at the *Fiorentini*, everyone sings with a sort of nasal drone.) But the repertoire of his antics soon struck me as repetitive; by the end, I was finding him less and less amusing. We from the North are fastidious, not easily satisfied by this southern sense of humour; our laughter is harder to release.

At all events, *Domingo*-Casacciello proceeds to guide the errant lovers back to the log-cabin. Now Virginia has a father, sung by Pellegrini, a first-rate *basso profundo*, whose rank in the Neapolitan hierarchy corresponds to that of Martin in our own: both actors command the same astonishing vocal flexibility, marred by the same frigidity of temperament. I have always found him extremely effective in arias which make no powerful call on the emotions. He is a mightily handsome fellow, by all Italian standards, with a great jutting nose and a fine black beard; the tally of his conquests (so I am told) is considerable; all I know for sure is that he is remarkably attractive.

The part of the *Ship's Captain* (tenor) was sung by a good-looking but disenchantingly wooden young man from Venezia Giulia, in which Province he is reported to have risen under Napoleon to the rank of *sous-préfet**. Signorina Chabran has a tolerable voice, but her interpretation was still more wooden and expressionless than that of la Canonici or Pellegrini; I found her infinitely less pleasing to watch than la Fabre, the little Milanese soprano whose strained and weary features seem sometimes to betray a hint of feeling. All in all, a passable performance, well-adapted to meet the tastes of the common-or-garden run of theatre-goers; yet not a note to appeal to the heart of him whose ambition it is to discover true portraits of that impassioned creature known as man.

The *teatro dei Fiorentini* is fresh and pretty; yet the proscenium arch is far too narrow, while the *décor* is as stale and as insipid as the music, for all that the latter is generally popular, and was greeted tonight with an awed and respectful silence. In fact, on two or three occasions, a prolonged and urgent *shushing* was heard to usher in the best-loved passages in the score.

And yet, when all is said and done, what lamentable stuff it was! All in the same, monotonous key—the echoes of an ice-cold disposition grimly resolved to utter 'sentiment'. The outcome was *vapid* beyond belief: but then, all fools adore *opera semi-seria*; their minds can grasp *melodrama*, whereas true comedy eludes their understanding. There are infinitely greater depths of human truth to be discovered in the traditional *opera buffa*—recall, for instance, the sample we saw at Capua. The popularity of Guglielmi's music (here, facts brook no denial) is phenomenal, and the applause comes deep from the heart; but no amount of applause can alter the plain, irrevocable truth of the matter, which is that such music is nothing but *ingenuity in vain pursuit of genius*; such, indeed, is the very theme-song of our century. Why, oh why does signor Guglielmi not make his home in Paris? There, by unanimous accord, he would be long and loud acclaimed a *great man*. Indeed, what is he else, but Grétry reborn into another age— a Grétry whose style is in part redeemed of its all-pervading *pettiness*. Mark also that his music still wears the semblance of a powdered wig (if the reader will forgive me so ill-judged and yet so picturesque a metaphor); while here and there, to give his tunes a touch of piquancy, this same *great man* will shame-lessly 'borrow' a dozen bars or so from Rossini—which 'borrowing' falls into the same category as Natoire or de Troye plundering a head from Guido Reni.

12th February. The long-awaited day at last: the gala-opening of the new *San-Carlo**. Farewell, sweet reason! What place has reason among such multitudes, amid such splendent tiers of boxes? There were not a few fists flying, not a few rude elbow-ings to be endured or given. . . . Indeed, I was resolved to keep my temper, and in that I was successful; but my triumph cost me both tails off my coat. My seat in the pit cost me two-and-thirty *carlins* (14 fr.); my tenth share in a third-tier box, no less than five whole *sequins*.

And in those first instants, I did verily believe myself borne away into the Palace of some Emperor of the East. My eyes were dazzled, my soul was transported. The loftiest imagination can conceive no scene more flower-like in its freshness, nor more impressive in its grandeur—two qualities which are not commonly met and reconciled. This first evening, I have surrendered utterly to pleasure; I have not strength enough to criticise. I am exhausted. Tomorrow will be time enough to describe those odd, those singular sensations which came to affright the assembled audience.

13th February. Standing once more within the theatre, I discovered anew that sense of awe and ecstasy. Search to the farthest boundaries of Europe, you will find nothing to rival it —what am I saying? Nothing to give so much as the haziest glimmering of the meaning of it. This mighty edifice, rebuilt in the space of three hundred days, is nothing less than a *coup d'état*: it binds the people in fealty and homage to their sovereign far more effectively than any *Constitution*, such as that which was granted to Sicily, and which a host of folk would dearly like to see extended to Naples, a realm which surely ranks as high. From Prince to pot-boy, all Naples is drunk with delight. . . .

And indeed, so delirious was I in contemplation of that noble building, that I found the music and the ballets no less enchanting than the rest. The auditorium is a symphony in silver and gold, while the boxes are blue as the deep sky. The ornamentation of the inner wall—which is cut away in front of each box to form a balcony—is moulded in high-relief. Indeed, it is this above all which sets the stamp of such magnificence—these golden torches artfully grouped and interspersed with massive *fleurs-de-lis*. At intervals, this frieze of ornament, which is of unimaginable richness, is cut by bands of low-relief in silver. Of these I counted, unless I am mistaken, in all some six-and-thirty.

The boxes, which have no curtains, are unusually spacious. I could generally observe some five or six persons seated at each balcony.

There is a wondrous chandelier, all shimmering with light which is mirrored and refracted on every hand as it falls upon the gold and silver of the reliefs—an effect which would be lost utterly if the ornaments were two-dimensional. I can conceive of nothing more majestic, nor more magnificent, than the sumptuous Royal Box, which is set astride the central doorway, raised aloft on two great golden palm-trees, each of natural size; the hangings are fashioned out of leaves of metal, tinted in palest red; even the crown, that superannuated emblem, seems scarcely too absurd. In startling contrast to the sumptuous grandeur of the Royal Box, I could picture nothing daintier nor more elegant than the tiny *incognito* boxes of the second tier, set hard against the proscenium of the stage. The hangings of blue satin, the mirrors and the gilt reliefs are apportioned with exquisite artistry and taste, the like of which I have not met in Italy. The darting light, which seeks out every corner of the building, reveals each minute detail to the eye of the beholder.

The ceiling* of painted canvas is a faultless mirror of that taste in art prescribed by the French school; it is one of the hugest paintings in existence. The same comments apply word for word to the drop-curtain. Both these works of art are notable monuments to a sterile inspiration.

I was forgetting to describe the panic which took possession of the feminine half of the audience on the night of the 12th. Towards the fifth or sixth scene of the gala-cantata, it was gradually remarked that the vast well of the auditorium was imperceptibly beginning to fill with a cloud of dark smoke. Soon, this billow began to thicken. At nine o'clock or thereabouts, I chanced to glance in the direction of the Duchess of C***, whose box lay next to our own; I had just observed her remarkable pallor, when she leaned towards me and whispered in accents of splendid terror: '*Ah! Santissima Madonna!* The theatre is on fire! They have tried once and failed; now they mean to try again. What will become of us?' In that instant, she was loveliness itself; her eyes, in particular, were of surpassing beauty. 'Signora', said I, 'if you can discover no worthier escort than an acquaintance of two days' standing, permit me to offer you my arm.' The great fire at the reception of Prince Schwarzenberg* flashed promptly into my mind; and even as I spoke with her, I recall that I was beginning to wrestle with a series of disquieting calculations; yet, in all honesty, more on her account than on my own. We were perched up in the third tier; the stairway was excessively narrow; there was destined to be a panic flight to safety. So absorbed was I in my search for some means to escape, that it was not until some two or three seconds had already elapsed that I grew suddenly aware of the distinctive smell of the 'smoke'. 'Why', said I to my fair neighbour, 'it is not smoke at all, but *fog* or condensation; the building, which is thoroughly damp, is drying out suddenly beneath the heat of such a multitude!' I realised then that everybody had arrived simultaneously at a similar conclusion, which, logical as it was, had none the less failed to save them from at least one unforgettable instant of panic; I realised further that, had it not been for the presence of the Court and the fear of adverse comment, those boxes would have been empty in a flash. Towards midnight, I made a round of visits: the women were perished with weariness, with dark rings round their eyes, their nerves on edge and never farther from the thought of pleasure, etc., etc.

14th February. The *San-Carlo* affords me a joy which seems well-nigh inexhaustible: the delights of great architecture are rare enough in all conscience! As for the delights of music, on the other hand, it would be unwise to seek them at the *San-Carlo*: whatever music there may be is inaudible. Of course, the Neapolitans themselves think quite differently;

they will swear their souls away that they can hear every note. My acquaintance from Milan has given me a footing in several boxes; tonight, on every side, I heard women complaining that they were *too visible*: not being able to believe my ears, I asked them to repeat this improbable piece of criticism. It seems that, thanks to the flood of illumination in the auditorium, the ladies find themselves perpetually 'on display'—an intolerable circumstance in any event, but here made four times as vexatious by the presence of a Court and royalty. Signora R*** was bitterly lamenting the curtained boxes of the *teatro alla Scala*. The central chandelier completely ruins the effect of any set on the stage; yet the *décor*, I suspect, is past praying for anyway, being almost as intolerable as the stuff one sees in Paris. All the theatres here fall under the responsibility of some great nobleman. The *décor* as a whole is spoilt by a common fault which shatters any dramatic illusion which it might otherwise produce; for the flats are constructed invariably some eight or ten inches *too short*, with the result that there is a constant procession of *feet* to be observed moving about below the pediments of the columns or among the roots of the trees. It is hard to conceive the absurdity of this perpetual distraction: the spectator's attention is held in hypnotic fascination by this shifting frieze of legs, and his fancy is constrained to guess at the purpose of each move.

Tonight, at the *San-Carlo*, I ran into an old acquaintance, Colonel Lange: he is the Town-Commandant of Naples under the Austrian administration; and during the course of the evening he introduced me to his remarkably handsome wife*. The day after tomorrow I am to dine with him, together with some eight or ten Austrian officers. Such patronage is worth decidedly more than the 'protection' of my so-called Ambassador.

The *Cantata**, which we endured at the gala-opening, is in the grossest vein of sixteenth-century flattery; the text has not a redeeming feature, no more than has the music. We in

France have learned that the most hypocritical flattery may be
tricked out in the ingenuous simplicity of a popular catch.
I should have thought that signor Lampredi might have had
sense enough to copy this notion.[1] In this field, the purest
genius is that of Metastasio. I know of no more brilliant handling of almost insuperable problems.

I have just been to the reading-rooms. The *Journal des
Débats*, I discover, has recently been deemed *too liberal*, and
banned!

20th February.   Naples, like Paris, is a great capital city; this,
perhaps, is the reason why I find so little to record. I pass my
days contentedly enough; but by bedtime (praise the Lord!)
I find that I have nothing new to write about; consequently,
I can retire to rest without sitting up half the night and working.
I am received 'at home' by the Princess Belmonte, likewise by
that most charming of men, the *marchese* Berio, and I am
treated with that same impeccable courtesy which has already
been accorded to some five hundred or so foreign visitors in the
past, and will doubtless be shown to a couple of hundred more
during the coming year. There is nothing save the rarest of
nuances to distinguish the tone which reigns in such company
from that of polite society in Paris. Conversation is livelier
here, perhaps, and assuredly *noisier*; now and then, the chatter
reaches to such a pitch of stridency that it gives me the ear-
ache. Naples, alone among Italian cities, has the true makings
of a capital; the rest are nothing but glorified provincial towns,
like Lyon.

1 Signor Lampredi is responsible for the only readable Literary Review
since the days of Baretti's *il Poligrafo* (Milan 1811). Other publications,
under the rubric: *Literature*, offer nothing but a series of ponderous
dissertations, not one of which would be admitted across the threshold of
the *Académie des Inscriptions et Belles-Lettres*, or else a species of poetic
lucubration worthy of M. Berthellemot. Just glance at the *Biblioteca
Italiana*, of Milan, a journal whose editor, signor Acerbi, is a salaried
minion of the Metternich government: nothing further need be said.
[1817]

23rd February. It was singularly *naïve* of me, at my age, ever to have imagined that a public institution could divide its attention between two different objects simultaneously. If the theatre is magnificent, the music must necessarily be abject; if the music is enchanting, the theatre must be shoddy beyond redemption.

The credit for having rebuilt the *San-Carlo* must go entirely to a gentleman by the name of Barbaja. Signor Barbaja, a Milanese by birth and a man of uncommonly handsome appearance, began his career as a waiter in a coffee-house; soon, by holding the bank at faro, he became a millionaire; and out of the anticipated profits of his monopoly of the bank, he built the *San-Carlo*. The old King wanted to engage signora Catalani: the notion was sensible enough; Galli, Crivelli and Tacchinardi should likewise have been invited to join the company; but there—signor Barbaja had a *protégée*, and that *protégée* was a signorina Colbran. As for Nozzari, who was so brilliant as Paolino* when we used to watch him in Paris (but alas! that was fourteen years ago)—I have no idea whose *protégé he* was. As things stand, the most impressive member of the company is the younger Davide; but it is really painful to witness the desperate efforts this poor young man is forced to make in order to pitch his brilliant but delicate voice into the cavernous immensity of this great vault. He has picked up from Nozzari the trick of producing a certain type of trill made with the head-voice. What he needs most urgently is a *small* theatre to sing in, together with a good teacher; even so, he is the finest tenor in Italy: Tacchinardi is losing his voice, and Crivelli is as perfect as a mechanical instrument, and is fast becoming just as soulless.

I was much struck by the orchestra. Its playing is precise and controlled; each instrument, when its turn comes to make an entry, attacks the note with open confidence. The execution as a whole is no less firm than that of the *Orchestre Favart*, while its tone is much lighter than is commonly met with

among Viennese orchestras; in consequence, its *piano* passages
are particularly impressive.

The *San-Carlo* is as far ahead of *la Scala* in the brilliance of
its orchestral performance as the Neapolitan theatre is inferior
to the Milanese in the poverty of its *décor* and the shoddiness of
its costumes. Tonight, we had a *bellissimo teatro*—in other
words, every seat in the house was taken. It was the Princess
Belmonte who observed that, amid such a rich profusion of
brilliant surfaces, all the women seemed to be dressed in *dirty
grey*, while their very cheeks seemed to bear the complexion of
lead. Ideally, the auditorium of a theatre should be decorated
in various shades of grey rather than in bright colours.

Italian audiences cherish a most singular passion for *premières*
(*prime sere*). Good, honest folk, who order their lives in strictest
economy from one year's end to the next, will nonchalantly
squander forty guineas on a box for the first night of a new
opera. Tonight, for instance, I observed, in the box of signora
Formigini*, a group of *dilettanti* who had travelled all the way
from Venice for the occasion, and who are due to start off
home again tomorrow. The people of Italy are close-fisted as
misers over the small things of life, yet reckless to the point of
prodigality over the things that really matter; in France, where
vanity occurs more commonly than passion, we abide by an
opposite principle.

King Ferdinand basks in a kind of effulgent glory reflected
from the magnificence of the *San-Carlo*; he can be seen in his
Royal Box *sharing* the ecstatic delight of the audience; and
indeed, this word *sharing* draws the veil of oblivion over a very
multitude of sins. (Anecdote concerning the cradle of the
newly-born *Infanta*, and the petition therein deposited,
humbly begging for the life of the beautiful *contessa* San-Felice,
who was hanged in 1799; I heard this tale from the lips of a
certain Neapolitan, who was much incensed at the sudden surge
of monarchistic fervour inspired in myself by the noble
architecture of the *San-Carlo*. 'This theatre', he concluded, 'is

here for all to behold; but what you do *not* see is the life of the smaller towns.' He had every right to offer me this sharp reproof. From what he was saying, I deduce that the Neapolitan peasant is little better than a savage, yet happy as were the natives of Tahiti before the advent of the *Methodist missionaries*.)

28th February. In the company of my sixteen-year-old *duchessa*, I visited the collection of paintings owned by *il cavaliere* Ghigi. My fair companion, I learned, was involved in a situation romantic enough in all conscience to form the plot of a novel, yet too delicate, perhaps, to be used as such within the framework of our present conventions. Prince Corvi, being in love with *la contessina* Carolina, the mother of my young *duchessa*, yet tasting all the bitterness of jealousy, for that he could find no means to loosen the tender bonds of her affection for the *cavaliere* P***, decided to reveal the secret of this *liaison* to the lady's husband, an amiable-tempered fellow, who refused to believe a word of this ill-timed denunciation. Baffled at the first attempt, the Prince resolved to go a step further, and repeated his denunciation to the *contessina*'s daughters, two charming and innocent creatures of fifteen or sixteen summers, who were most tenderly attached to their mother. These two unhappy children were so distressed by the discovery, that they privately resolved together to take the veil; they grew embarrassed in their mother's presence, and durst no longer speak a word to her. At long last, the elder of the two, falling upon her knees at her mother's feet, burst into tears and unburdened herself of all the tale of Prince Corvi's denunciation, together with the secret of their common resolution to enter a convent, lest they should suffer the contamination of a *woman taken in adultery*. Imagine the atrocious dilemma of the *contessina*—a mother torn between her adoration for her lover and her implacable sense of honour. By good fortune, she retained sufficient presence of mind to deny the whole story. This little narrative—which takes some twenty minutes in the telling—is perhaps one of the most beautiful and most moving episodes I have encountered in a year.

All Italy is no bigger than a cabbage-patch, and the wealthier families of one city are as well-acquainted with those of another as though they were next-door neighbours; were it not for this fact, there are two or three dozen episodes in similar vein which I could dearly wish to set down here, in place of all these abstract moral observations: for, in assessing the moral climate of a nation, any statement which is *vague* is *ipso facto* wrong. The reader whose boldest excursion has taken him no further than from Paris to Saint-Cloud, and who therefore is familiar with no manners other than those of his native land, will necessarily ascribe to such words as *decency, virtue, duplicity* and so on a significance materially different from that which *you*, my Italian friend, may have intended to convey by such expressions.

On one occasion, for instance, in Bologna, among the guests assembled at signora N***, I met a young woman, *la Ghita*, whose career might furnish the matter for the most fascinating, and indeed the most noble of romances, on condition that every detail were left intact and undisturbed. In my own *Journal*, this narrative fills up the space of some eleven pages: never was there a more vivid portrait of the manners of modern Europe and of that subtle shade of sensibility peculiar to Italy, nor a story which rises so many thousand leagues above the dutiful inventions of our novelists, nor yet a tale so full of incident, so alive with unexpected twists and turns, yet ever true to nature. It is the recurrent weakness of *comedy of character*, that the audience may easily foresee each separate eventuality which lies in wait to ensnare the hero; here likewise, the *hero* whom la Ghita so desperately adored (and still adores today, for all I know) is commonplace enough; the *jealous husband* is no less of a stock character; the *mother*, a caricature of inhuman ferocity; only the *leading lady* achieves a truly heroic stature*. But, once granting this, one might well scour the cities of London and of Paris, and gather up every woman of feeling in the two capitals, and pound them all together in a mortar, without ever extracting so rich a residue of sensibility as would endow a character of such unfathomable depth and energy. Yet all this wealth lies buried deep beneath a mask of plain simplicity, if not of coldness. I shall never cease to wonder at the inexhaustible store of energy which is seen to reside in the character of certain Italian women. A casual hint of coldness from their lover will rankle still within their hearts some six months after, and be treasured for sure retaliation or revenge; never will the memory of it, through weakness, be allowed to fade, or else be overlaid with other cares, as would occur in France. In Germany, a woman will forgive all, and, in the very devotion of her doting soul, forget. In England, among women of intelligence, some echo of this boundless sensibility may be found; but all too often it is vitiated by prudishness.

This *sensibility*, so characteristic of Italy, is plain absurdity in the estimation of the North. I have been pondering the problem for the last fifteen minutes, yet even now I have no notion, no conception even, how to explain, what terms to use to express this quality, to make it fit for northern understandings. The highest rational achievement of the finest intellects consists in grasping that certain matters lie beyond their power to grasp. In other words, the problem is, of its very nature, insoluble—like a tiger who would persuade a stag of the succulent joys of a carnivorous diet!

I am privately aware that these very words I have been writing are absurd; such mysteries belong to an arcane, esoteric doctrine, whose secrets should never be allowed to fall on vulgar ears.

2nd March.   Benefit-performance for Louis Duport*, the dancer. His last appearance on the stage. Such an occasion, in Naples, is truly momentous.

N

I was forgetting to mention the *décor* of his ballet, *Cinderella*. These sets were designed by an artist who is intimately acquainted with those laws which govern the *terrible* in art. The *Fairy's Palace*, with its funereal lamps, and that gigantic figure, sixty feet in height, whose stature dwarfs the very proscenium arch, while his finger points blindly towards the fatal star, stamps an enduring picture on the mind. But no mere words can make the thrill of such impressions comprehensible in Paris. The one defect of this noble set lay in its feeble colouring, together with a certain weakness in *chiaroscuro* (a lack of energy in the contrasting masses of light and shade).

This *Fairy's Palace* scene, together with another set from the same ballet which depicts a ballroom, faithfully modelled on *Stonehenge* and set in the depths of a forest, would be outstanding even in Milan. All in all, the Lombard designers have a far surer appreciation of the magic spell of *colour*; on the other hand, their actual designs are sometimes weak and ineffective—a fault which springs from a certain banality in the original conception. In Naples, trees are painted green, whereas, at *la Scala*, they appear *grey-blue*. Tonight's *la Cenerentola*, together with *Astolfo e Giocondo* (choreography by Vestris), are danced almost step for step as they might be in Paris; only the presence among the cast of Marianna Conti and Antonia Pallerini (an inspired mime, comparable with Giuditta Pasta) allows the programme to shed something of the frigidity of the French tradition; the cold technical perfection and the courtly graces of this latter school, however, are well represented by madame Duport, by Salvatore Taglioni and his niece Maria. As far as Duport himself is concerned, my admiration is a long-standing affair, dating back over many years; nor did I forsake my constancy tonight. I find his movements as fascinating as those of a kitten; I could sit for hours on end and watch him dance.

At tonight's performance, the audience could scarcely contain the wild tempests of its applause: indeed, the King in person gave the lead. From the box where I sat, I could hear the thunder of His Majesty's voice, and the enthusiasm grew rapidly to the proportions of a *furore*, which lasted fully three-quarters of an hour. Duport has lost none of the lightness which so delighted us in Paris in his interpretation of *Figaro*. Never is there the least suggestion of effort; step by step, the rhythm of his dancing grows fiercer, until, by the end, he is possessed by the very ecstasy and intoxication of that passion which animates his movements; indeed, the art of ballet itself can attain to no higher degree of expression; or at least, to be precise, *I* have never witnessed anything even comparable. By contrast, Vestris and Taglioni—in this, neither better nor worse than all mediocre dancers—can neither conceal the effort required, nor yet master the secret of *progression* in their dancing. In conse-quence, even the flavour of *sensuality* is missing from their interpretation; and sensuality, after all, is the primary aim of art. Here, at the *San-Carlo*, the women seem to be better dancers than the men; next to the voluptuous delights of sensuality, *admiration* is the chief emotion aroused by ballet—which two sensations, taken together, all but exhaust the compass of this, the narrowest of the arts. The eye, held in strange enchantment by the brilliance of the *décor* and the originality of the grouping, should, by coaxing the mind into a state of keen and tender receptivity, predispose it thus to appreciate the passions which the dance will illustrate.

I have been admirably placed to appreciate the difference between the two contrasting styles of ballet. Italian audiences are only too willing to admit the superiority of the French school, yet, all unsuspecting, are infinitely more susceptible to the peculiar genius of their own. Duport must indeed be satisfied, for there was no stinting in tonight's applause; yet the true, the heart-felt, the unbounded transports were reserved for Marianna Conti. My neighbour this evening was a French-man, a man of taste and breeding, who, at one point, being overwhelmed by the flood of emotions which possessed him, so far forgot himself as to address me a remark. '*Gross indecency!*' he kept repeating, over and over again. How right he was, indeed—and how much more so the audience in its ecstasy! For, after all, *indecency* is, by and large, a matter of convention; whereas ballet, as an art, relies almost wholly upon a positive degree of sensuality which is the sheer delight of Italy and the shocked despair of France. The Italian, caught up in that great provocative surge of rhythm and movement, will never once be visited by the slightest notion of indecency; in the pure perfection of art lies all his joy, much as a French audience may be held enthralled by the exquisite poetry of *Cinna*, yet never be shocked by the patent absurdity of the *unity of place*. In an art which is made up all of fleeting impressions, faults unperceived have no reality. A thing which is *charming* in Paris may be *indecent* in Geneva—such judgments are parochial affairs, depending wholly upon the degree of prudishness dictated by the local incumbent. Jesuitry is infinitely more propitious to art and human happiness than *Methodism*.

Whither should we turn to seek the *immutable ideal* of ballet? As yet, no such universal criterion of beauty has been discovered. Ballet, as an art, is too directly dependent upon climatic influences and upon the physical constitution of the human body. The *immutable ideal* would need to be fashioned anew every three hundred miles.

The French school has attained no higher than the height of *technical* perfection.

In the present age, what is needed is a genius to *use* these techniques, so painstakingly acquired. Ballet, in our time, is at the same stage as painting was when Masaccio appeared upon the scene. There *is* a genius alive today, and dwelling here in Naples; yet his art is despised and ill-considered—Viganò, the creator of *gli Zingari** (the *Gypsies*). The good folk of Naples were convinced that he was having a joke at their expense; for this particular ballet chanced to bring to light a most curious fact, whose truth had hitherto been unsuspected—

namely, that the general moral climate of the Kingdom of Naples is identical, custom for custom, with that of the Romany. (*Cf.* Cervantes' *Novelas*.) And thus it comes about that Viganò can point a moral for the legislators of the realm —so closely indeed is each art bound up part and parcel with the rest! Yet at the same time it is a major triumph, in the mastery of so recalcitrant an art, to have compelled it to express, portray —indeed, to portray so *well*—the manners of a society rather than the passions of a race (*i.e.*, habitual characteristics of behaviour in the pursuit of happiness, rather than violent humours and general moods). There was one episode in particular, where the dancers moved to an accompaniment of timpani, which shocked the poor Neapolitans to the very depths of their being; they were convinced that the whole thing was a deliberate hoax; and indeed yesterday, among the guests of Princess Belmonte, I met a young captain who would fret and storm himself into a very frenzy at the mere mention of Viganò. Naples today is in a decidedly curious frame of mind, nor may it hope to return to normal without a couple of resounding military victories in the style of Austerlitz or Marengo; until such time, the Neapolitans are fated to remain distinctly *touchy*. 'Yet', I might say to them without any sense of undue generosity, 'what mortal man had greater valour than signor di Rocca-Romana? Is it the fault of gentlemen of birth and breeding, if the tonsured hoards have eaten the heart out of the common people, who were rich in courage when they went by the name of Samnites, and yet are grown so crawling and contemptible since they took to worshipping San Gennaro?' The history of this ballet, and the subsequent tale of its repercussions, shed a sudden shower of light within my mind, and indeed set me finally on the proper path in my resolve to study this corner of the world. It was Noverre (so I am told) who discovered the *sensual* element in dancing; Viganò has widened its horizon of *expression* at every point. Yet this same unerring instinct for his art impelled him further, and led him to disclose the ultimate secret of the ballet, which is that ballet is *par excellence* the art of the *romantic*. The loftiest heights to which the spoken drama may attain have long since been scaled by Shakespeare; but *il Noce di Benevento* is not merely a feast of delight for the entranced imagination, but explores a realm of fancy unknown to *Imogen* in her *Cave*, or to the *melancholy Jacques* in the *Forest of Arden*. So vivid is the joy, so captivating the originality of it, that the soul, transported, knows no release from ecstasy from curtain-rise to curtain-fall —full five-and-seventy minutes; and although I never dare entrust to paper the fever-heat of such experience, for fear of earning ridicule beyond redemption, yet the memory of it lives on despite the years. No fleeting sketch in words can adequately convey the impressions of such an instant; only a boundless flood of talking, which should end by kindling the very depths of the listener's fancy. At home in France, in the Château de B***, I recall once how madame R*** held us all enraptured in the drawing-room until past three in the morning with her impressions of *il Noce di Benevento**. The secret of watching ballet is first to fill the imagination with pictures remembered from the old Spanish dramatists and from the *Novelas ejemplares*, so that fancy herself may embroider every predicament without external stimulus; furthermore, the mind should be already weary of words as a means for developing situations. Thus each individual fancy, fired to fever-heat by the music, may take wings and furnish forth speech of its own invention to set upon the lips of these ever-silent actors. Hence we may discover that ballet—ballet as Viganò has conceived it—may move with a speed which even Shakespeare could not emulate. Yet alas! it is to be feared that this inimitable art will soon vanish for ever; the peak of its achievement was reached in Milan, in the old, prosperous days of the Kingdom of Italy. Ballet demands vast financial resources, whereas *la Scala* is now so impoverished that I doubt whether it can survive above two or three years more: the present

Tyrant, unlike Lorenzo de' Medici, is in no way concerned to hide the chains of his oppression and the spiritual degradation of his subjects behind a glittering mask of art. Now that a squeamish piety has suppressed the gaming-rooms, from the profits of which the theatre proper used to be subsidised, the very memory of this art may well be fated to vanish from the mind of man; nothing will remain of it, save the name alone, like those of Roscius and Pylades. Paris never beheld its glory, and so it has remained but dimly known in all the rest of Europe.

Whenever the Milanese start talking to foreigners about *Coriolano* or *Prometeo*, about *il Noce di Benevento* or *Samandria liberata*, the listener*, unless he be endowed with the rarest gifts of a picturesque imagination, invariably finds his fancy chilled to freezing-point by the wild ecstasies of his companion. And since we in France are but most shabbily endowed with picturesque imaginations,[1] this medium of art would fall resoundingly flat. Our worthy Academicians—like La Harpe —are unable to grasp even so simple a phenomenon as Metastasio. I personally have seen no more than three or four ballets by Viganò. His imagination has about it a certain *Shakespearian* quality—yet the very name of Shakespeare, I suspect, would mean nothing to him*. Painting and music alike have a share in his genius. Frequently, when he cannot lay hands on a melody ready-fashioned to express his meaning, he will compose his own. I would be the last to deny that his *Prometeo* is entirely free from absurdities; yet, ten years after, the memory of it lives on as fresh as ever, and my mind is still astonished at its power. A further and most original characteristic of Viganò's genius is his *patience*. He will stand on the stage at *la Scala*, surrounded by eighty dancers, with a band of ten musicians in the orchestra-pit at his feet, there to spend a whole morning composing and implacably rehearsing, over

1 This quality, I suspect, may not uncommonly be found in Scotland. [1817]

and over again, ten bars of choreography which seem to him to fall short of final perfection. There is no stranger sight in all the world—yet I had vowed never to let myself speak of Viganò.

Memory is the sweet seductress who has tempted me astray. It is striking two o'clock in the morning: Vesuvius is erupting fire; I can see the lava streaming down the mountain-side, whose red mass stands out in sharp-cut contours against the indescribable dark beauty of the horizon. Three-quarters of an hour have I sat here at my window, perched high on the seventh floor, contemplating this sight, at once so new and so impressive.

5th March. 'In due course of time', remarked Monsignor R*** this evening, 'the *immutable ideal* of ballet will be established, and found to reside at some point between the far extremes of Duport and Marianna Conti. But first of all, some rich and pleasure-loving Prince must provide a *Court*—and that, alas! is a sight we ne'er shall see again. Each royal ruler is first and foremost concerned to set aside a sum of millions in the bank, that he may continue, should need arise and his Dynasty be overthrown, to live at least the life of a wealthy private citizen. The sovereigns of the present age, moreover, being resolved and adamant to oppose the wishes of their subjects, are fashioning for themselves one and all a life-long prospect of disquiet. This grave miscalculation may well result in the decay of art throughout the nineteenth century. In the twentieth century, the nations will know no better subject to discuss than politics; and folk will read the *Morning Chronicle* instead of clapping Marianna Conti.'

The chilly perfection which characterises the style of Mademoiselle Fanny Bias may in no wise be accommodated to this aesthetic ideal of ballet—at least, nowhere outside France. Were it given to me to make a choice between these two contrasting elements of *ideal beauty*, I confess freely that I should prefer the living, vivid *sensuality* of la Conti.[1] Some eight or ten years since, Mademoiselle Milière, equipped with all her faultless Parisian technique, appeared in Milan, danced— and was whistled off the stage forthwith. Whereupon she learned to breathe life into her rôles; and so, today, she is the very idol of *la Scala*—and doubtless would be hounded off the stage in Paris.

Yesterday, I climbed to the crater of Vesuvius; never in my life have I known such exhaustion. The devilish part of the ascent lay up the cone of ash which marks the summit. Yet, who knows? In a month's time, the whole landscape may have changed beyond recognition. *Hermits* (so-called) are as likely as not to be *robbers*, converted or otherwise: this resounding platitude I discovered in a book, duly signed by Bigot de Préameneu. I should need ten pages and the talents of Mrs Radcliffe, were I to describe the view which awaits the weary traveller's gaze as he sits down to consume his omelette, made to order for him by the Hermit of Vesuvius. Nor will I utter a word touching Pompeï, which is the most astounding, the most fascinating, the most entertaining spectacle I have ever encountered; no other sight on earth can furnish such *understanding* of antiquity. What endless speculations concerning the nature of art arise in the mind, as one contemplates the Fresco of the Minotaur, and indeed a score of others! Three times a week at least I pay a visit to Pompeï.

---

[1] The ballets of Gardel bear absolutely no relation to those of Viganò: the former is a dwarfish *Campistron* beside the latter's *Shakespeare*. Viganò, had he treated the same subject, would have made the onlookers tremble for his *Psyche*; Gardel, in the scene where he allows her to be tormented by the satanic host, falls into the same error as Shakespeare, when he allows a dethroned King to have his eyes gouged out on the stage, in full view of the audience. The spectator's imagination, being insufficiently stirred to feel this strong intensity of horror, is merely amused by the ugliness of the devil-brood, and laughs out loud at their green talons.
[1817]

14th March. I have just been to see *Astolfo e Giocondo*, by
Vestris III, grandson of him they called *le diou de la danse.*
Considered as ballet, this was miserable stuff. Duport's version
of the same tale is scarcely better: garlands *ad nauseam*, scarves
and favours for damsels to bestow upon their knights and
tender shepherdesses upon their swains in soft exchange of
tokens; followed by a *pas-de-deux* (with scarves or favours
aforementioned) in celebration of the solemn ritual! What
countless leagues from this to that scene in *la Samandria
liberata*, where the young bridegroom, his very soul consumed
with jealousy, sets foot once more within his Palace, and yet,
in spite of all, is swept up in that wondrous *pas-de-trois* with
his bride and the Negress who is his slave and mistress of the
music in his own seraglio. No one who watched it but was
bewitched heart and soul—yet none could tell why. This was
one of the greatest chapters in the *Anatomy of Love*: all past
offences shuffled off into oblivion by the presence of the
beloved object. Our taste in France might be compared with
that of some lovely woman who refuses to allow the artist to
use any *shadow* in the portrait of her he is making; it is like a
painting by Boucher beside Gros' masterpiece, the *Hospital at
Jaffa*. At long last, I have no doubt, this mincing, periwigged
nonsense will vanish from the face of the earth; but *we* shall
have vanished likewise some years before. We have not
enjoyed enough security for the great *Revolution* to make its
influence felt in the field of art. Art and letters still linger on
amid the sickly talents of the age of Louis XV: witness MM.
de Fontanes, Villemain, etc.

In normal circumstances, nothing can deepen the contempt
I feel for French music; however, my friends in France, by
the letters they had written, had almost caused me to waver
in my disdain. It needed but a little more persuasion, and I
might have conceded them a certain gift for lively tunes, a
talent for meaningless but pretty melody. But tonight's
experience of the ballet-music to *Giocondo* puts a final end to

all argument, as far as I am concerned. Never have I been made more vividly aware of the poverty, the barrenness, the gross, pretentious *impotence* of our music than through this score, into which have been poured pell-mell all those tunes by common consent avowed the prettiest, all those melodies which (once upon a time) could touch my heart. The awareness of true *Beauty* is stronger even than the haunting memories of youth. Such remarks as these are bound to seem absurd, outrageous, nay more, grotesque, *abominable*, to those whose minds are unacquainted with *Beauty* in her purest forms. But there! in any case, all *good and patriotic citizens* have assuredly cast this book into the fire a long while since, with horrified despair: 'The Author is not *French*!'

The vast size of both stage and auditorium at the *San-Carlo* is admirable for ballet. A squadron of eight-and-forty horse can manoeuvre with room and to spare in Duport's *Cinderella**, in which performance the cavalry aforementioned, and the various modes of combat in which they indulge, contribute a whole act to the drama—excessively boring, thoroughly unconvincing and exceptionally well-conceived to appeal to the vulgar taste of the multitude. The cavalry performs a charge at full gallop right to the very brink of the footlights. The riders are Germans—no Italian horseman could ever hope to keep in the stirrups under such circumstances. The ballet-school attached to the *San-Carlo* holds out the fairest promise for the future: signorina Mersi may, or may not, make a name for herself sooner or later, but in any case she is remarkably pretty. As a dancer, she has genuine originality of style.

Today—March 14th—I was seriously incommoded by the heat as I stood contemplating the *Farnese Bull*, set square in the middle of the delightful *riviera di Chiaja*, scarce twenty paces from the sea. In the country-side, all the apple-trees are flowering, and the almonds are covered with blossom; whereas in Paris, the winter has still another couple of months to go. Yet in Paris, a man may spend each evening in a different *salon*, nor ever fail to pick up two or three original ideas. So here indeed is a problem with no ready solution: *which of the two is preferable?*

15th March. A delightful ball given at the Royal Palace. Fancy-dress was the order of the evening, with masks in character; but soon enough the masks were set aside. I enjoyed myself hugely from eight at night until four in the morning. All *London* was present; and, in my opinion, it was the peerless beauties of Albion who carried off the prize. Yet there were not a few fair Neapolitans among the throng—among others, that unhappy little creature, *la contessa* N***, who, once a month, sets out for Terracina* to visit her lover. The *Master of the Household* is in no way deserving of all those resounding denunciations and slanderous diatribes in the manner of Tacitus which are hurled at him from every corner of Europe; he is just another *Squire Western*, straight out of *Tom Jones*—a sovereign who is far better versed in hunting boars than in hanging prisoners (1799-1822). . . . But hush! be silent, my tongue! For did I not promise that, wherever I might visit, unless I first had duly *paid* for my admission, I should observe discretion? Otherwise, the traveller's vocation lies dangerously near to that of *spy*.

16th March. Despite my profound contempt for modern architecture, I suffered myself this morning to be taken to visit signor Bianchi, of Lugano, sometime recipient of a pension from the Privy Purse of Napoleon. His designs are compara-tively free from that plague of arabesques, angles and offsets which are the very stuff of contemporary pettiness (*cf.* the Courtyard of the *Louvre*), and whose malign influence can be detected even in Michelangelo. The present age is too dwarfish to grasp the truth that the Ancients never employed *decoration for its own sake*; and that, in classical architecture, beauty was invariably a by-product of *utility*. How should this current generation of artists be expected to study the mirror of their own souls? Honourable men they may be, nor would I seek to deny it, and gifted with intelligence to boot; yet Mozart possessed a soul, and they do not. Never have they been swept headlong into the wild seas of extravagance by the strong surge of dreams and passions; in recognition of which sobriety they now sport the insignia of the *cordon noir* . . . which confers nobility!

Signor Bianchi has recently been commissioned to design the church of *San Francesco di Paola*, in Naples, facing the Royal Palace. The actual labour of building is to be entrusted by His Majesty to signor Barbaja, and doubtless we shall see the edifice completed in eight or ten years' time*. It would be hard to conceive a site less suitable for a church—indeed, rather than build, it were preferable to knock down two or three dozen houses hereabouts. The ideal place for a church would be the *largo di Castello*; but, throughout the length and breadth of Europe, the arid winds of vanity have withered every heart, and men have grown blind to the *eternal principles* of beauty. Bianchi's design is based on curvilinear forms, which is evidence at least that he has a true eye for classical architecture; yet he has failed to grasp the significant fact that the Ancients, when they built a temple, had in mind a purpose diametrically opposed to ours when *we* build a church: for the Greeks, religion was a festival and not a threat. The Attic temple, beneath those unblemished skies, was nothing but a theatre of sacrifice. There was no kneeling, no prostration, no beating of breasts; instead, there was the sacred ritual of dancing. It is indeed hard to conceive that mankind should have...............
....
....
But there! *novelty* is a primary desire and need of the human imagination*.

In the course of my visit to signor Bianchi, I met the two most remarkable individuals in the whole kingdom: General

Filangieri and signor Cuoco, the Councillor of State.

17th March. I need waste but few words on such music as I have heard at the *San-Carlo*. I arrived in Naples beside myself with expectation; yet the greatest sum of pleasure I have known —and that not excessive—was the opera I listened to in Capua.

My first experience at the *San-Carlo* was Rossini's *Otello*. I can conceive of nothing more *chilling*.[1] The wretched librettist must have needed something very close to genius to reduce the most powerful tragedy that ever was on any stage to such a tasteless mess of insipidity. On the other hand, Rossini has aided and abetted him in every way he knew. The overture, admittedly, is of an astonishing originality, entrancing, easy to grasp, and full of irresistible charms for the unmusical, yet never tending to banality. Yet, when the subject of the tragedy is Othello, the music may have all these qualities, and still be hopelessly, shamelessly inadequate*. Neither in the whole life's-work of Mozart, nor yet in Haydn's *Seven Last Words of Christ*, is there any music too profound for such a subject. Indeed, the most satanic discords, together with all the wealth and all the dissonance of enharmonic writing, would scarce suffice to portray the villainous Iago (*cf.* Pergolesi, *Orfeo*, first recitative). Rossini, so I suspect, is himself insufficiently master of his own idiom to describe such things. Furthermore, he is too good-humoured, too merry, too fond of his food.

One of the absurdest sights, yet one rarely met with outside Italy, is that of the father or of the husband of a famous *prima*

---

1 To punish myself for having entertained such unworthy thoughts in 1817, I am resolved to leave this epithet exactly as it stands. At the time, I was carried away, albeit unconsciously, by the tempest of my wrath against the *marchese* Berio, the author of that unspeakable *libretto* which turns Othello into a *Blue-Beard*! In the portrayal of the gentler emotions, Rossini (who has by now written himself out) never rose to within a thousand leagues of Mozart or Cimarosa; in compensation, however, he conceived a style so swift and glittering as these great masters never dreamed of. [1826]

donna: the term *dom Procolo** is commonly applied to designate such characters. On one occasion, Count Somaglia having chanced to offer his arm to the notorious Isabella Colbran, in order to show her round the premises of *la Scala*, her father, graver than a judge, proceeded to remark:

'You may deem yourself fortunate indeed, *signor conte*; are you aware that many a *Crowned Head* in Europe has thought it no dishonour to offer a royal arm to my daughter?'

'Sir!' retorted the Count, 'You forget that I am a married man!'

(The rejoinder has rather more spice in Italian.)

After *Otello*, I was obliged to sit through an opera called *Gabriele di Vergi*, by a young composer belonging to the Caraffa family. Stylistically, it was nothing but a slavish imitation of Rossini. However, the tenor Davide was nothing less than divine in the part of Coucy.[1]

I have also seen another performance of Paër's *Sargino*: Davide, inspired by signorina Chabran from the *teatro dei Fiorentini*, gave a most ingenious interpretation. And yet I found this famous opera not a whit less tedious here in Naples than in Dresden. Paër and M. de Chateaubriand are birds of a feather: however hard I try to appreciate the genius of either, my heart refuses to respond; the whole affair seems absurd. M. de Chateaubriand exasperates me: his is a brilliant mind which takes *me* for an oaf. Signor Paër, on the other hand, just bores me to tears; I find his vast and steady popularity astounding.

18th March. This evening, the *San-Carlo* company gave a performance of *Otello* at the *teatro del Fondo*. I picked out quite

1 Listening to the same opera today, I discover quite a number of deeply-moving passages. It is sufficient to hear one or two melodies by Caraffa or Perruchini interpreted by signorina Nina Viganò to realise that these two composers actually created the tradition of the *Italian song*—for instance, *il Travaso dell' Anima*. [1826]

a number of attractive themes, hitherto unsuspected: among others, the duet for two female voices in Act I.

These great, echoing caverns like the *San-Carlo* and *la Scala* are not the flowers of civilisation, but rather a brand of freakish and distorted excrescence. Each *nuance* must be magnified to monstrous size; but then, a *nuance* magnified is a *nuance* no more. Ideally, all aspiring singers should be reared in a *milieu* of unblemished chastity—yet nowadays, the very thought of such a thing is inconceivable. Cathedrals and choir-schools alone could have provided a suitable atmosphere. It is the common lament that Crivelli and Davide have no successors, Yet, since the great tradition of the old *castrati* declined and vanished, the deep secrets of music have vanished with them from the operatic stage. From sheer despair at their unnatural condition, these poor devils laboured to acquire the profoundest knowledge of their art. Invariably it was the *castrato* who, in *ensemble* passages, would bear the whole company upon his shoulders; he it was who alone could bring out latent genius in the *prima donna*, at once his pupil and his 'mistress'. Our present age owes surely two or three outstanding *prime donne* to Velluti.

Nowadays, as soon as the *tempo* offers the slightest difficulty, the singers give up in despair, and the poor listener might well be forgiven for imagining himself the victim of a crowd of *amateurs*. This curious phenomenon was well accounted for last night by Count Gallenberg, who explained it to the assembled guests of the *marchese* Berio. Italy and Germany are poles apart in this, for German music is harsh, bizarre and arid as the steppe, and would drive the wretched listener to despair and self-destruction, were not its creators the finest masters of the art of *tempo* that the world has ever known.

It is the established custom in Italy that the two hours' performance of an opera should be interrupted by an hour of ballet; and indeed, this tradition is based upon the feebleness of the human organism; it is, in point of fact, ridiculous to overwhelm an audience with two acts of operatic music in quick succession. Observe likewise that ballet, as conceived by Viganò, is both impossible and absurd in a small theatre. Now, there is an acoustical conundrum which I should like to set our present crop of learned geometers to rack their brains about, and which these illustrious gentlemen will doubtless treat with contempt unbounded, for the simple reason that it is too difficult for them. Here is the problem: is it not possible to devise a theatre with two separate stages of different dimensions? Or alternatively, to design one dual-purpose, adaptable stage, which, after a ballet, can be cut lengthwise by a partition resonant enough to project a singer's voice far out into the auditorium? Would it be possible, for instance, to lower a metallic curtain? Or else, perhaps, to construct a wall of hollow wooden blocks, faced with a drum-head on the audience's side? In Parma, at the *teatro Farnese*, the sound of a piece of paper being torn at the back of the stage will re-echo all over the building. Here you have a genuine acoustic phenomenon in conditions which should be meticulously reproduced; but of course, it is much less trouble simply to deny it. And another thing: Italian architects are well aware that nothing is better calculated to still the dreams and halt the wanderings of a vagabond imagination, than an atmosphere deficient in oxygen.

19th March. The *San-Carlo*, indisputably, has the status of a patriotic symbol for the good people of Naples: national pride, crushed by the campaign which ended in the death of Joachim Murat, has sought refuge within its portals. But here is the truth, plain and unvarnished: the *San-Carlo*, considered as an *instrument for making music*, bears absolutely no comparison with *la Scala*. Gradually, as the masonry dries out, its acoustics may grow less muffled; on the other hand, all the bright glitter of gilt-work which was applied too early to the still-damp surfaces of the rough-cast plaster ornamentation will soon grow hopelessly tarnished. The *décor* is the last word in banality, and moreover, offers no chance of improvement, since the effect is killed stone-dead by the central chandelier. This same chandelier has another disastrous result: it throws the actors' faces into shadow.

20th March. This evening, as I went to take my seat in the *San-Carlo,* a *gend'arme* came running after me and ordered me to remove my hat. The auditorium is a good four times the size of the *Grand Opéra* in Paris; yet I (*horribile dictu*!) had failed to notice the presence of God-knows-what insignificant princeling!

Paris is deservedly the capital of the universe, precisely because no man there knows his neighbour, while the Court is nothing but a sight to entertain the curious.

In Naples, the *San-Carlo* opens its doors but three times a week; consequently, as a *rendez-vous* for business transactions of every description, it offers none of the unfailing amenities of *la Scala*. If you explore the galleries, rows of *titles,* redolent of pomp and circumstance, and all writ large upon the doors of the private boxes, serve to remind you that you, poor worm, are but a zero, an atom, fit only to be blotted out for ever by an *Excellency.* Did you chance to cross the threshold in a *hat*? Then 'ware! for one of the heroic guard of Tolentino will soon be snapping at your heels. Does la Conti so enchant your eye and heart that you can scarce forbear to clap? Yet hold! for the presence of *His Majesty* turns all applause to guilt and sacrilege. Did you think to leave your seat among the benches of the pit? Tread warily, then, lest, as you pass among the crowd, you brush against some high-born *Nobleman,* his person draped in emblems, stars and orders, and by mischance, catch his *Chamberlain's Key* in your humble watch-chain loop (as it befell myself last night!)—for straightway, hark! the growl of '*disrespect*'! Wearied by such a surfeit of ceremony, would you resolve to leave the theatre and send for your hired carriage to take you home? Then be prepared to kick your heels and

wait, while some *Princess's* coach-and-six obstructs the door
for an hour, no less . . . wait, and catch your death of cold
meanwhile!

God be praised for great cities which have no Court! Not
because of Their glorious Majesties, who, by and large, are
egotistical, good-natured brutes, and who, by happy dispensa-
tion, have no leisure to turn their attentions towards the
affairs of private individuals; but rather on account of that host
of Ministers and Vice-Ministers of State, each one of whom is
pleased to constitute himself a source of police-interference and
molestation. This sort of nuisance, unknown in Paris, is the
constant bane of daily life in almost every capital city in the
continent of Europe. Yet what would you? Given eight or ten
Ministers-of-State, whose official duties between the lot would
scarcely occupy a single *préfet*, yet each and every one of whom
is dying to be administering *something*, how else are they to
pass the time away?

No sooner had I set foot in Naples than I learnt that the
Comptroller of the Opera was a *Duke*; as a matter of course,
therefore, I steeled myself well beforehand to walk into a
world of obscurantism and petty vexations. Those 'Gentlemen
of the Bedchamber' from the *Mémoires de Collé* peopled the
vision which promptly flashed across my mind.

Among the benches which fill the pit, every seat is numbered, and *rows one to eleven* are reserved unconditionally for
the military—Officers of the *Red Guards*, of the *Blue Guards*,
of the *Guards of the Gateway*, etc., etc.—or else are distributed
by special favour amongst the *élite* of permanent subscribers;
in consequence of which, the unhappy foreigner newly-arrived
in the city finds himself relegated to the twelfth row. Add to
this already considerable distance from the stage the vast area
occupied by the orchestra, and you will realise that the unlucky
tourist is mercilessly driven well back into the remoter half of
the auditorium, and installed willy-nilly in a position whence
he can neither see the stage nor hear the singers. No such

monstrous system prevails in Milan: at *la Scala*, first come, first served is the rule for every seat. In the fair and fortunate city of Milan, every man may know himself equal of his neighbour; but in Naples, the meanest threadbare *Duke* without a thousand crowns a year to bolster up his pretensions, may invoke the prestige of the best part of a dozen *stars* and *garters* to jab his insolent elbows in my ribs. By contrast, in Milan, an honest citizen with two or three millions to his name will courteously stand aside to let me pass, should I show signs of being in a hurry, expecting me to do the same for him should need arise; and you may study in vain to recognise the bearers of many a famous name, so simple is their aspect and so modest their demeanour. Tonight, exasperated by the insolence of the *gend'armes*, I abandoned the pit and made my way towards my box; and even then, as I climbed the staircase, my temper was scarcely improved by encountering, in descending phalanx, a dozen or fifteen star-spangled Lord-High-Whatnots and Generals, ambling majestically downwards beneath the accumulated weight and grandeur of their mightiness, their braided jackets and their monumental noses. I reflected upon the inscrutable necessity of all this rag-bag of hereditary nobility, stars, privilege, garters and insolence, without which mere *courage* could never be dreamed of in an army.

The final scene of Duport's ballet shows the apotheosis of Cinderella: she stands alone in the dark depths of a forest; then a back-cloth is lowered, and the audience beholds a wondrous palace riding high upon a hill-top, the summit of which is illuminated by the magical light of those incandescent white projectors, whose use is more or less understood at *la Scala*, but whose possibilities are far more effectively exploited here in Naples. As I sought to leave the theatre, I found the staircase blocked by a seething mass of people. To reach the exit, there are three steep flights of stairs to be negotiated, with each man crushed hard upon his neighbour's heels. The Neapolitans refer to this as one of the 'beauties' of the place. They have built the pit of their theatre a floor above the ground; this, in terms of modern architecture, is what is described as an 'ingenious improvement'; which means that, since there is but one general staircase to accommodate some two or three thousand spectators, and since this staircase is always cluttered up in any case with a host of footmen and bootblacks, the pleasures of this forced descent may best be left to the reader's own imagination.

To sum it up, then: the *San-Carlo* is a masterpiece of operatic architecture, provided that the curtain remains *down*! I feel in no wise inclined to eat my original words: the first sight of this theatre is indeed overwhelming; but as soon as the curtain goes up, then disappointment follows disappointment, each hard upon the heels of the last. Do you wish to sit in the pit? Then our friends the *gend'armes* will see you safe installed a dozen rows from the front, whence you cannot hear a note, nor yet so much as make out with your eyes whether the actor, whose frantic gestures you dimly perceive upon the distant stage, is young or old.[1] Do you decide to return to your box upstairs? Alas! this self-same dazzling, blinding light pursues you even here. Would you attempt to shut your ears against la Colbran's piercing ululations, by reading the paper until such time as the ballet shall begin? Impossible! Your box has no concealing curtains. Are you suffering from a cold, making it advisable to keep your hat upon your head? Inconceivable! The theatre is being *honoured* by the *presence* of Prince ***. Would you then take refuge in the coffee-house attached to the theatre? Poor comfort—it is nothing but a narrow and lugubrious corridor, of loathsome aspect. Or in the *foyer*? The staircase by which you must pass is so steep and so damnably awkward that, when you reach your goal at last, the breath is quite gone from your body.

1 At such a distance, all the genius of Madame Pasta would be completely lost. [1826]

21st March. This morning, I felt the fever of ambition upon me—a melancholy, atrabilious distemper which haunts me these two years. The ills of the mind, I knew from the Sages of the Orient, must be cured by the medicine of the body. I took a boat, therefore, and sailed four hours upon the sea; and landed finally at Ischia, armed with a letter of recommendation to don Fernando.

It was in the year 1806 (so he told me) that he had taken refuge in Ischia; nor had he once set eyes upon the city of Naples since the day the French, whom he abhors, usurped the dominion of the land. Ischia has no theatre; so, to console himself, he breeds vast quantities of nightingales in wondrous aviaries.

'Music', he argued, 'is an art which has no model in the natural universe, other than the song of birds; and, like the song of birds, music is a series of *interjections*. Now, an interjection is a cry of emotion, never an expression of thought. Thought may *produce* emotion; but the interjection itself is never anything but emotion pure and simple. Consequently, music is, of its very nature, incapable of expressing the dry and logical concepts of thought. Sometimes', added this most sensitive of *dilettanti*, 'my skylarks, singing in the morning, give voice to a strange *falsetto* note which reminds me of Marchesi and Pacchiarotti.'

I spent today four delightful hours in the company of don Fernando (who abominates all things French) and of the worthy islanders of Ischia. These islanders are pure African savages . . . good-natured simplicity of their dialect . . . they live off the produce of their vineyards. Scarcely a trace of civilisation—no small advantage, this, when 'civilisation' means wholly Popery and all its ritual. In Naples, a man of the people will inform you coldly: 'A year since, come August, there was a misfortune that I had', which, being translated into plainer language, means simply: 'In August last year, I murdered a man.' Yet, should you propose that he should accompany you up Vesuvius next Sunday, leaving at three o'clock in the morning, he will recoil in pious horror, exclaiming: 'Faith, *I*? And miss the Holy Mass?'

Ritual may be learnt by heart; but as soon as you admit the doctrine of *good works*, then such works may be good *to a greater or lesser degree*; hence it is but a step to an *Examination of Conscience*, and so, by relentless progression, on to the tenets of *Protestantism* and ultimately to the reckless merriment of an *English Methodist*.

22nd March.   I am truly distressed that I may not describe the delights of the ball given by Mr Lewis, author of *The Monk*, at the lodgings of Mrs Lushington, his sister. Amid the gross and philistine patterns of Neapolitan behaviour, the frank and upright moral character of England is a refreshing experience. When I danced an *écossaise*, I observed, among the other dancers, young Lord Chichester, but fourteen years of age and a plain midshipman aboard the frigate which dropped anchor yesterday in the roads. The English understand the miraculous effects of education—and as I read it, they are likely to need all the miracles they can muster, for I observed plainly in the faces of one or two Americans present that, thirty years from now, England will possess nothing in all the world, save her own happiness. Lord N[orth] agreed with me.

'Every nation in the world', I argued, 'detests the very name of England; yet this hatred is particularly violent among the rabble and the lower elements. Educated people draw a sharp distinction between Lord Grosvenor, Lord Holland—indeed, the bulk of the nation—and the present Ministry.'

'For all that', replied Lord N[orth], 'granted even that this general hatred among the nations were a score of times less temperate than it is, yet every state in Europe for a hundred years to come is destined to live through a mortal sickness, a revolutionary indigestion springing from its desperate resolve to win a constitution; and none can hope to command a Navy before the twentieth century.'

'Agreed', I answered, 'but the *Americans* detest you also, and will be lying in wait for you twenty years hence, armed with a commerce-raiding fleet five hundred strong. You are beginning to realise already—is it not true?—that France is no longer the "hereditary foe"; the escape of M. de Lavalette, followed by the *Loan**, has begun the work of reconciliation. So why not be generous with us?'[1]

Among the many biting epigrams, which I, as a Frenchman, was forced to swallow, the following in particular struck home:

'In some countries, when a score of persons are gathered together in one place to speak evil of the government, this is known as a *conspiracy.*'

One or two details that I have observed suggest to me that the art of conspiracy might well be better understood in Naples: here men at least would *act* instead of talking. This realm is destined without fail to achieve a bicameral government within the next two decades; despotism may crush the nation ten times running, and yet the nation will revolt an eleventh time against the despot. The present *régime*, with its obsessive resolve to put the clock back, is humiliating to the pride of the aristocracy.

Lord N[orth], one of the most enlightened men in England, agreed with me, albeit with a sigh.

(I caught sight once again of my beautiful *contessa*, who is wont to journey to Terracina to visit her lover. For sheer loveliness—the facts brook no denial—the women of Albion outdistance all their rivals: Lady Douglas, Lady Lansdowne.)

23rd March. A night of masked balls. I began the evening at *la Fenice*; later on, at half an hour past midnight I moved

---

[1] In the town of Troyes, in 1815, a party of Englishmen chanced to remark the well-appointed factory set up by M. Taissaire. Two days later, an Allied regiment appeared upon the scene, and smashed every loom in the shops. [1817]

across to the *San-Carlo*. I had looked to find a night of dazzling splendour—nothing of the sort. The stage of the theatre, transformed into a ball-room, enjoyed none of that lush magnificence which the scene-painters of *la Scala* are wont to lavish on such gala occasions; instead, all the decoration consisted of a plain white back-drop studded with huge *fleurs-de-lis* in gold leaf. Tickets can be had for as little as six *carlins* (about 2 fr. 50). The lowest brand of company imaginable—yet, in the *foyer*, where there were a score of gaming-tables stacked with gold, a gentleman might happen upon more suitable acquaintance. I derived great entertainment watching a certain lovely creature playing faro—a *duchessa* with whom I danced once, on the occasion of the party at the Royal Palace. Her chair stood some four paces from the tables; the task of placing and withdrawing her stakes was delegated to her lover; her own fair features showed not a trace of that hideous intoxication which stamps the face of the true gambler. The lover in question had been discussing art with me only a day or two before, and had talked to me of Paris. 'In Paris', he observed, 'no man alive will make a single gesture, unless it bear the stamp of *breeding*—in other words, of *imitation*; consequently, the art of painting is impossible in France. Genius in France, with the solitary exception of La Fontaine, is *sophisticated*; the least sophisticated artist can boast of no more genuine *naïveté* than can some pert but impoverished young lady of eighteen, who has already mismanaged three prospective wealthy marriages.'

24th March. The Countess of R***, that fair flower of Scotland, remarked to me this evening: 'Your compatriots, who are so irresistible during the first few hours of an acquaintance, have not the slightest notion how to inspire a truly *profound* passion. At first meeting, it must suffice to awaken curiosity; but your glittering, don-Juanesque Frenchman, who creates so dazzling an impression during the first instants, and thereafter loses ground progressively, can reign no more than for a fleeting moment over a woman's heart.'

'Here precisely', I rejoined, 'is the secret which explains the icy indifference with which I am about to bid farewell to the San-Carlo.'

Whereupon a Neapolitan prince, chancing to be present during this exchange, began to protest most energetically, and proceeded to refute our objections in the true manner of Italy —*i.e.*, by restating over and over again, on each occasion in more strident tones, the original claim to which objection had been made. I was busily engaged in staring about the room, hoping thus to bring his diatribe to a close for want of listeners to appreciate it, when I grew aware that he was insistently reiterating the outlandish word *Agadaneca*. This, apparently, is an opera of unimaginable splendour, which, encouraged by powerful ministerial patronage and dedicated in advance to His Majesty, has already been in rehearsal for some five months. 'At last', asserts the voice of public opinion, 'we shall behold an opera not unworthy of the San-Carlo.'

SALERNO, 1st April. Should you be curious to make first-hand acquaintance with the most degrading moral picture in the world, then I recommend that you should take a random peep behind the scenes at family life in Calabria ... incredible, the tales that I was told this morning! While I was in Bologna, I was reading the works of the *original* mediaeval historians, Capponi, Villani, Fiortifiocca, etc. Scarcely a page but contained anecdotes such as that of the massacre of Cesena by the Anti-Pope Clement VII.[1] And yet, when all is said and done, the imagination is left with a feeling of respect, or even of friendship, towards these colossal figures, the Castrucci, the Guglielmini, the Counts of Virtù*. There is no trace of such atrocities in the chronicles of the eighteenth century—so little,

1 Poggii, *Hist.*, lib. II, *la Cronaca sanese: 'E il Cardinale disse a messer Jovanni ...'* etc., etc. [1817]

indeed, that, in the long run, the reader must grow sick at heart from sheer contempt.[1] Yet the Calabrians—these I cannot despise, for all that they are *barbarians*, who profess an indivisible belief in Hell, indulgences and the *jettatura* (spell cast by a sorcerer).

2nd April. The strangest sight I saw in all my wanderings has been Pompei. Here, the traveller may feel himself transported bodily into the realms of antiquity; and he whose mind is trained, however ill, to believe nought but what is plain and proven, may discover in a flash more solid truth than the most ingenious of scholars. There is indescribable pleasure to be had from meeting face to face with this self-same antiquity, concerning which one has read such countless volumes. Today, I visited Pompei for the eleventh time; yet this is not the place to tell of what I saw. Two theatres have been excavated, together with a third at Herculanum; all so intact as scarcely to deserve the name of ruins. I wholly fail to see the need for that curious, *mystical* tone which Herr Schlegel has felt called upon to adopt in his recent treatises upon the antique theatre; yet I was forgetting that Herr Schlegel is a *German*, whereas I, apparently, *I*, ungifted Frenchman that I am, have no deep *innere Stimmung* concerning the meaning of the world. *Our* world having begun with the republics of antiquity, it is not wholly surprising to discover that the heroes of this epoch should seem such god-like creatures to later generations, whose souls—as in the case of Racine—are blanched to atrophy by the insipidity of kings and courtiers.

I have just been to see *Saulle* at the *teatro Nuovo*. I can only suppose that this tragedy (by Alfieri) touches some hidden spring in the subconscious national character of Italian audiences; at all events, it stirs them to wild outbursts of enthusiasm. In *Michal*, the daughter of Saul, they discover all the

---

[1] Lacretelle, Duclos, Bezenval, Saint-Simon, Rulhière, the Prince de Ligne, Mackintosh, Belsham, Hobhouse. [1817]

tender charms of *Imogen*. Yet I, for some reason, found myself impervious to all these qualities—so impervious, indeed, that I spent most of the evening in conversation with that young *marchese* of liberal sympathies who had lent me his box. Beside us, there sat a young girl, whose eyes, shining with all the joy and tenderness of love, flashed with a darting energy of passion, the like of which I never saw before. Three hours sped by us, swift as lightning. Next to her sat her betrothed, and her mother, relaxing her customary severity, allowed him to kiss his mistress' hand.

My *marchese* informed me that, here in Naples, only three of Alfieri's tragedies are permitted on the stage; in Rome, four; in Bologna, five; in Milan, seven; and in Turin, none at all. Consequent upon this censorship, applause becomes tantamount to waving a banner, whereas criticism is the stamp of a black obscurantist.

As a dramatist, Alfieri suffered from the absence of a wide enough audience. The groundlings are as vital to a genius as troops are to a general. Alfieri was fated to rage and fret against the tyranny of prejudice, only to finish by acknowledging his own surrender. Politically, and to the bitter end, his mind refused to grasp the incalculable benefits of a revolution which was destined to bestow, upon Europe and America alike, the advantages of parliamentary government, and to *make a clean sweep* of all the old abuses. Among the major poets of the world, Alfieri was perhaps second to none for the tempest of feeling which raged within him; but, in the first place, he never knew but *one* emotion; and in the second, his political viewpoint was always excessively narrow. He never grasped the elementary truth (see the concluding chapters of his *Autobiography*[1]) that no revolution can succeed without the

1 *Vita di Vittorio Alfieri, da Asti, scritta da esso*. . . . The reader should consult the original edition; the translation was badly chopped about by *Buonaparte's* police-censorship. Alfieri offers the typical portrait of every generous and noble spirit in Italy at the present juncture: more fury than intelligence. [1817]

creation of a new economic interest, *i.e.*, a new property-owning *élite*. To begin with, his mind never ran along those lines; while furthermore, he was an aristocrat, and a Piedmontese into the bargain.[1] The insolence of minor officialdom demanding his passport at the *barrière de Pantin**, together with the theft of some twelve or fifteen hundred volumes from his library, sowed seeds of rancour within his heart, which, falling in the fertile soil of his own aristocratical prejudices, decreed that he should forever fail to master the pure mechanics of liberty. This noblest of intellects never managed to realise that, in the field of politics, the *sine qua non* of tolerable writing is a careful act of *dissociation* from all the rubs and trifling personal vexations that the philosopher himself may have suffered in the course of his existence. In the closing phase of his life, he used to say that genius was the exclusive privilege of a *gentleman*; and when all was said and done, he, whose contempt for French literature verged close upon obsessive hatred, could offer nothing more than a grotesque exaggeration of the narrow conventions of Racine. To the Italian mind, it would be hard to conceive anything more consummately absurd than the cowardice of a *Britannicus* or the preciosity of a *Bajazet*. The average Italian, pursued night and day by the demon of mistrust, demands to *see*—and is constantly fobbed off with second-hand accounts. His vagabond fancy must perpetually be nourished by the visible splendour of action; otherwise his imagination rises up in passionate revolt, and bears him off to more fruitful regions. It is logical enough, therefore, to find that Alfieri's tragedies are greeted by many a smothered yawn. To date, I have discovered nothing better fitted to the temperament of Italy than *Richard III*, *Othello* or *Romeo and Juliet*.

---

[1] He never learned to appreciate the generosity of the Princes of the august House of Savoy. Sovereigns of the stamp of those who presently occupy the various thrones of Naples, Florence and Sardinia seem purposely to have been designed by nature to bring about a reconciliation between the monarchic principle and those whom pride has seduced into the wildest of excesses. [1817]

Signor Niccolini, current heir to the dramatic traditions of
Alfieri, is headed off on a false scent. *Cf. Ino e Temisto.*

3rd April.   Agadaneca, 'Grand Opera' . . . never in all my life
have I heard so much perilous rubbish decked out in so much
pretentious clap-trap; its 'two-hours' traffic' spanned moderately from seven in the evening until half an hour past midnight,
without a single instant's pause for breath, and without the
first faint sigh of melody in the music. I could almost have
thought myself at home in the *rue Lepeletier.* Long live opera
under Royal patronage! The master-stroke of the evening was
a scene in *Fingal's Cave* (for we are plunged deep in the realms
of Ossian!), luxuriously appointed with all the latest knick-
knacks straight from Paris. As a favour, I was granted permission to visit the stage. All the poor little creatures from the
ballet-school were moaning and lamenting: 'Five months'
rehearsal, and all for a flop like *that*!' I murmured a word or two
of polite sympathy to signorina Colbran: 'Indeed, sir', she
replied, 'the audience is more than generous; *I* was fully
prepared for them to tear up the very benches from the pit,
and hurl them at our heads!' I now realise, in fact, that the
librettists, to whom, previously, I had attributed nothing
worse than *banality*, are chronic *imbeciles* as well. Signorina
Colbran showed me their *Solemn Dedication to His Majesty*,
printed at the head of the libretto. It is their unassuming intention (so they claim) to 'revive the solemn awe and splendour
of Greek Tragedy.'..!

The music of Act III—a sort of ballet in the form of a
Pyrrhic dance—is by Gallenberg. Graf Wenzel von Gallenberg
is a German who has settled in Naples and who has a special
genius for composing ballet-music: this evening's sample was
worthless; but I have listened to passages from *Cesare in Egitto*
and from *il Cavaliere dei Templari*, where the music doubly
intensifies that state of indescribable intoxication produced by
the dancing. Ideally, music which is destined for the ballet

should have all the lightness of a brilliant sketch, in which *rhythm* assumes an unusual significance; it offers no field for that sort of complex orchestral scoring of which Haydn is such a master; but there is great scope for passages scored for the horn. The scene in *Cesare in Egitto*, where Caesar is allowed to cross the threshold of Cleopatra's bed-chamber, is scored in a style fit to incarnate the Houris of Mohammed himself. Not even the sighing and voluptuous genius of Tasso would have disowned the instant when the ghostly *Shade* appears before the affrighted eyes of the *Knight Templar*; for he, all unbeknownst, has slain his mistress; and now, wandering uncertainly after nightfall deep in some trackless forest of the Holy Land, chances to pass close beside the tomb where she lies buried; whereupon her spirit rises up before him, points heavenward in answer to his grief and questioning anguish, and melts into the immaterial air. The pale and noble countenance of la Bianchi, the tortured expression of Molinari, the sighing notes of Gallenberg's music—all these formed a scene whose memory will never fade within the recesses of my soul.

4th April.   A visit to the *teatro Nuovo*. The de' Marini company was giving its one hundred and ninety-seventh performance. Vestris, for all his stoutness, is the finest actor in Italy—indeed, in all the world; in *il Burbero benefico*, as in *l'Ajo nell' imbarazzo*, not to mention that host of worthless rhapsodies to which he alone gives shape and meaning, his skill is equal to that of Molé and Iffland. His performance will bear watching twenty times in succession without the slightest fear of boredom. If Mademoiselle Mars should be cast for the part of some dizzy or bird-witted flibbertigibbet, the slyest of secret glances, irresistibly seductive to the private vanity of the audience, will betray the fact that none is more sensitive than herself to the absurdity of her rôle, or to the idiocy of the gestures that she will presently allow herself to perform. This is a serious flaw, of which neither Vestris nor Madame Pasta is ever guilty.

In the eyes of Italian audiences (and more especially the feminine section thereof), none holds a higher place in the hierarchy than de' Marini, whose skill I have been admiring this evening in *li Baroni di Felsheim* (the translation of a play by Pigault-Lebrun) and in *i due Paggi*. In Italy, for a variety of reasons not wholly unknown to myself, natural simplicity is distinctly out of favour on the printed page; the average Italian must have his literature tricked out with all manner of high-flown and bombastic rhetoric. Our present fashion—those fulsome *Encomiums* by Antoine Thomas, *le Génie du Christianisme*, *la Gaule poétique*, and all the lush, poetical bag of tricks which, for ten years now, have made us the *envy of the civilised world* —such stuff would seem specifically devised to match the taste of Italy. The unpretentious prose of a Voltaire, a Hamilton or a Montesquieu leaves Italian readers patently unmoved. Here you have the principle which explains and underlies the boundless reputation of de' Marini. He fashions his art upon nature, yet distantly; indeed, nature may hardly be held to challenge the divine prerogative of *Rhetoric* within his heart. In days gone by, he was wont to steal away the very soul of Italy in his various *jeune premier* rôles; nowadays, he has turned to *Noble Father* parts; and since such parts admit a fair degree of bombast, I have often found entertainment watching his performance.

Naïveté is a virtue seldom met with in the Italian theatre; yet no Italian can tolerate *la Nouvelle Héloïse*. Such rare traces of *naïveté* as I have ever discovered dwell in the breast of signorina Marchioni, a young actress of desperately emotional temperament, who appears on the stage at least once, sometimes twice a day, beginning at four o'clock with an open-air matinée for the populace, and giving a second performance later, at eight o'clock, under the artificial glare of battens and footlights, for the gentry. Today I watched her twice—at four o'clock in *la Gazza Ladra*, and at eight o'clock in *Francesca da Rimini*— and on both occasions, she held me enthralled to the very brink of ecstasy. There is an actress in the de' Marini company, signora Tassari, who is not at all bad in parts of a similar character. Her husband, Tassari, is a first-class 'heavy', specialising in *Tyrants*.

Blanès, in the days before he went off and married a fortune, used to be the Talma of Italy. He was lacking neither in power nor in the gift of naturalism: as *Almachilde* in Alfieri's *Rosmunda*, he was the very incarnation of *terror*. In the same play, the title-rôle (poor Queen, unhappy victim of such tempestuous passions!) was played by signora Pelandi, whom I have never found anything but wearisome, but who, none the less, won herself a tempest of applause.

Pertica, whom I saw tonight, is a competent comic actor, more especially in heavy character parts. I found him boring beyond words in *il Poeta fanatico*, one of the dreariest plays ever perpetrated by Goldoni, yet one which is seldom long out of the repertoire. This may be realism, I grant you—yet how unspeakably *vulgar*! Besides which (as though this were not already sin enough!), it excites the contempt and derision of the brutal mob by dragging through the mud before its eyes that noblest work of nature: a great poet. Pertica was thunderously applauded in the part of *Brandt*, and indeed deserved his triumph, particularly in the final scene, when he speaks the line to Frederick II: '*I shall write you a letter.*'

But that which struck me most forcibly of all was the audience itself. I never beheld a sterner concentration, nor yet (miracle of miracles in this fair city of Naples!) a stiller silence. This morning, by eight o'clock, every seat in the house was sold; to get a ticket, I was forced to pay three times the proper price.

Backstairs patriotism, that besetting sin of Italy, admits, in my experience, two isolated exceptions: the readiness with which the average Italian audience will allow the superiority of French ballet; and the childish curiosity with which this same audience will open its mouth and swallow, whole and undigested, every tit-bit of drooling sentimentality ever translated from the German theatre.

o

To clap at French ballet implies that he who claps has been to Paris. The emotional responsiveness of Italy is so profound and so genuine, while reading is so rare an occupation, that nothing—not even the silliest of dramatised novelettes, provided only that it be bristling with incident and action—is too insipid to excite the unfailing compassion of these virgin sensibilities. For thirty years, not a single sentimental novel has seen the light of day in Italy. The logical deduction from this fact would seem to be, that when a man is exclusively pre-occupied with a single passion, no *portrait* of that passion, be it never so alluring, can leave him anything but stonily indifferent. The literary periodical is unknown in Italy. Bertolotti, that ingenious intellect, author of *Ines di Castro*, used to say to me: 'First furnish me with a castle-keep for refuge: *then* will I dare to speak a few home truths to the writers of Italy!'

Tonight's curtain-raiser consisted of a little comedy by Mercier, *la Jeunesse de Henri V*, in Duval's adapted version*. Pertica drew great bursts of laughter out of Prince don Leopold, who was present among the audience; but, dear God in Heaven! what dragging, desperate efforts he must make, compared with Michaut at the *Théâtre Français*! My nearest neighbour tonight turned out to be an Italian priest, who professed himself utterly bewildered by the success this play had had in Paris: 'Words!' he muttered. 'All you ever want is *words*! You never reach beyond, never grasp at the *character* underneath.' Count Giraùd, the Beaumarchais of Italy, has written two or three pretty comedies, including *l'Ajo nell' imbarazzo* and *il Disperato per eccesso di buon core*. Others—Nota, the lawyer, Sografi, Federici—are forever veering towards the abysses of melo-drama, and even their truly comical comedies are designed to appeal to a society far less cultured than our own. In this matter of sophistication, Picard is as far in advance of Goldoni as Molière is in advance of Picard. In the dramatic world of Goldoni, whenever a householder has guests for dinner, it is taken for granted that he must send out to borrow a set of cutlery for six, the family silver being presently in pawn. It must not be forgotten, however, that Goldoni was writing in Venice; and that the Venetian aristocracy would soon enough have furnished him with a cell (or coffin) in the *Leads*, had he proved rash enough to display a faithful portrait of *their* style of living before the eyes of their unhappy subjects. Consequently, Goldoni was obliged to confine his talent to the portrayal of dregs and outcasts, whose manners are so crude and so uncouth, that no others may fittingly serve for comparison. I find myself unable to laugh at their expense. As a dramatist, Goldoni was faithful as a mirror to the times in which he lived; yet he lacked even the dullest gleam of intelligence. Falstaff is the biggest coward the world ever saw; yet despite his cowardice (which is nothing less than astounding), he keeps his wits so razor-sharp about him that I am unable to feel contempt: he is an object worthy of my laughter. Falstaff rings truer still when he struts the boards before a morose and melancholy people who tremble at the very name of that relentless *Duty* whose voice the fat Knight so unfailingly disobeys. Suppose that Italy, in alliance with Hungary, should one day wrest the privilege of parliamentary government from the powers which hold her still in thrall: then, from that day forward, she will have neither time nor thought to spare for art. Aye, there's the rub—which Alfieri and all the rout of ranting phrasemongers after him quite failed to foresee. If ever Italy evolves a comic style of her own, it will have the *colour* of Fabre d'Eglantine's *Philinte* and the *grace* of Act IV of Shakespeare's *Merchant of Venice*: which quality, by the way, has no connection with the like-named virtue in Saint-Foix' comedy *les Grâces*.

5th April. I have just ridden thirty miles, and all to no purpose. Caserta is no better than a barracks set in a landscape as unpromising as that of Versailles. Because of the danger of earthquakes, all the walls of the palace are built five foot thick; in consequence—as at St Peter's—the apartments stay warm in winter and cool in summer. Murat attempted to complete this edifice: the paintings which adorn it are even drearier than those of Paris, but the general scheme of decoration is more grandiose.

To console my disappointed heart, I set off post-haste upon my return for Portici and Capo di Monte—elevations so enchanting that no Prince in all the earth may find the like. Nowhere under Heaven may the eye discover so wondrous a prospect of mountain, sea and civilisation. The traveller stands amidst the noblest manifestations of nature; yet, with all that, may, within a space of five-and-thirty minutes, sit listening to *il Matrimonio segreto*, sung by Davide and Lablache. Granting even that Naples may have rivals for natural beauty in Constantinople or Rio de Janeiro, yet can either city hope to emulate her in this? The citizens of Montreal or Torneaa are worthy folk, I allow; yet how should they ever conceive the notion of a fair Neapolitan, whose beauty is tempered by an implacable intelligence worthy of Voltaire? Such bewitching creatures are rarer even than a prospect of mountains or the entrancing panorama of a bay. Yet, were I to speak at greater length concerning signora C***, I should succeed in nothing save in goading the reader into a wry outbreak of laughter, whether from envy or from disbelief. Portici is to Naples what Monte Cavallo is to Rome. The average Italian is fully persuaded that we from the North are nothing better than barbarians in all matters relating to the arts—a conviction which is not merely ineradicable, but openly asserted on every possible occasion. Yet this same Italian is constantly agape with admiration at the originality and elegance of our *furniture*.

As I was leaving the *Museum of Antique Painting* at Portici, I met with a trio of English naval officers, who were on their way in. Now, this Museum contains no less than two-and-twenty rooms. On the road back into Naples, I kept up a steady gallop; yet before I reached the *ponte della Maddalena*, I was caught and overtaken by these same three English travellers, who, later in the evening, assured me that the paintings they had seen were positively *splendid*, and indeed one of the strangest sights in all the universe. The total time which they had spent inside the Museum amounted to somewhere between three and four minutes.

This collection, which affords such a treasure-house of curiosities for the true lover of art, consists of frescoes which have been removed from Pompei and Herculanum. They reveal a complete absence of *chiaroscuro*, a very limited range of colour, a passable feeling for design and considerable facility. Two items in particular I found pleasing: *Orestes recognised by Iphigenia in the Island of Tauris*, and *Theseus thanked by the young Athenians for having delivered them from the Minotaur*. Both contain a wealth of noble simplicity, without a single theatrical gesture. The general impression is of a series of bad works by Domenichino, albeit further still removed from greatness by the presence of numerous faults of draughtsmanship —errors which this fine artist would never have committed. There are to be observed at Portici, among a host of minor, half-obliterated frescoes, five or six major productions on the scale of Raphael's *Santa Cecilia*. Once upon a time, these frescoes served to ornament a bath-chamber at Herculanum. Yet no one save a scholar could be so asinine as to claim that such stuff outweighs the *quattrocento*; in point of fact, it is nothing but a highly-remarkable artistic curio; it serves to prove the existence *elsewhere* of a finely-developed style, much as those 'artistic wallpapers' manufactured in Mâcon serve to prove the existence of a painter such as David.

6th April. The *Giornale di Napoli* has taken up the cudgels on behalf of the *teatro San-Carlo* against the *Gazzetta di Genova*. I am firmly persuaded that every god and goddess in the whole of mythology, together with every Latin poet whose works are handed down to us, is invoked or quoted in this article, whose success has been phenomenal. In all other respects it is, from beginning to end, a tissue of shameless lies.

I am almost tempted to transcribe it *in toto*, simply to punish those among my readers (assuming such ignominious creatures to exist) who still refuse to grant unquestioning credence to all my anecdotes, and to the moral consequences which I draw therefrom.

Arbuthnot's *Martinus Scriblerus* is forgotten in London, as indeed is any satirist who has slain the *Monster* which he attacked. *Martinus Scriblerus* dates from 1741. Italy today (1817) is precisely ripe for such a satire.

The *abate* Taddei (editor of the *Giornale delle due Sicilie*) is infinitely more absurd than our learned friends MM. G*** and M*** in Paris*: but he is not *detested*, as they are. The Austrian commandant has forbidden him to designate anyone as a *bad citizen*. The honest Teutonic common-sense of these worthy Austrians has—on this occasion at least—prevented untold bloodshed in Naples.

7th April. Another evening with the de' Marini company. Their wardrobe is resplendent: all the cast-off finery of Napoleonic *senators* and *chamberlains*, which the sometime holders of these offices have been cowardly enough to sell. Half the success of the company may be traced directly to these costumes; my neighbours on every hand were gasping with admiration. I find myself entrusted with the strangest secrets. As things stand in Italy today, the strongest recommendation which any man may bear is to be French and to hold no official post of any kind.

Towards midnight, I proceeded to take tea with a party of Greek students, who are here to study medicine. If I had had the time, I would have left then and there for Corfù, where, as I suspect, the rigours of opposition put steel into the souls of men.

The factors which are essential if art is to flourish are often diametrically opposed to those which are indispensable if a nation is to be happy. Moreover, these factors can never exercise any *lasting* influence, for art demands a wealth of leisure, together with unbounded depths of passion; yet leisure leads inevitably to sophistication, while sophistication, no less inevitably, destroys the depths of passion. Logically, therefore, it is impossible to engender a nation of artists. No man with a spark of generosity in his nature but is racked with longing to see the resurgence of Greece; but what must fatally emerge from such a struggle is not the century of Pericles, but rather something resembling the United States of America. We are moving towards an era of universal suffrage; and universal suffrage, being wholly concerned with *government*, will have no leisure to dwell with impassioned fervour upon the subtleties of art. Yet what matter? Liberty is the necessity of necessities, while art is merely a *luxury*, whose lack can be endured without distress.

PAESTUM, 30th April. Any commentary upon the architecture of the temples at Paestum would require too long an exposition, and would involve concepts too hard to understand. My companion in the course of this excursion—a charming young man by the name of T***, who can point to relatives in both opposing parties, and who, in 1799, when the revolution broke out in Naples, was but fifteen years of age—has today related to me the following strange occurrence.

'In Naples, the sceptre of state was wielded by a woman of genius. Originally an enthusiastic partisan of the French Revolution (this, out of jealousy directed against a *Certain Person*), she soon came to realise the danger which threatened every throne in Europe, and took up arms against it with impassioned fury. *Were I not Queen of Naples*, she observed on one occasion, *I could dearly wish to be Robespierre*. And indeed, in one of the Royal Boudoirs there was to be seen a gigantic painting representing that fatal instrument by which her sister had perished*.

At the earliest rumour of the first Napoleonic victories, the Kingdom of the Two Sicilies was stricken with terror, and the government implored, and indeed obtained, conditions of peace. A republican Ambassador set foot in Naples; and in the timid breast of the Sovereign, humiliation poured oil upon the flames of hatred.

'One Friday night, the King of Naples chanced to pay a visit to the *teatro dei Fiorentini*, in order to see Pinotti, the celebrated comic actor. From his seat in the Royal Box, which was set hard against the stage, he could observe *citoyen* Trouvé who sat exactly facing him, at the opposite extreme of the proscenium arch. His Citizen Excellency the republican Ambassador was dressed in the uniform of the Court whose interests he represented: namely, in his own hair, unpowdered, and tight trousers. His Majesty, terror-stricken at the sight of *unpowdered hair*, promptly quitted the theatre, but not before he had had time to observe, among the spectators who thronged the pit, some fifteen or twenty heads of ominous darkness. Summoning the Officer of the Guard, His Majesty whispered a word in his ear; whereupon the Officer of the Guard in his turn proceeded to summon the notorious Cancelieri, the *factotum* of the military police. Quietly, the *teatro dei Fiorentini* was surrounded; and, as soon as the performance was ended, and the spectators began to emerge, each in turn was brought face to face with Cancelieri, who asked but one question: *Are you a Neapolitan?* As a result of this inquisition, seven young men, one and all scions of the noblest families in the Kingdom, one and all with hair unpowdered, were conducted to the Fortress of St Elmo. Upon the following morning, each was forced to put on a common military greatcoat; a horse-hair pigtail eighteen inches long was attached to the collar of his jacket; and all seven were promptly dispatched aboard an outward-bound troopship to serve as private soldiers in a regiment stationed in Sicily. One young Neapolitan of illustrious birth was sentenced to be put in irons, for the crime of having performed a violin concerto in the company of a French musician.

'Meanwhile, at home in France, the *Directoire* of the Republic had managed to dismiss the nation's finest troops, together with her greatest general, into exile in the land of Egypt. No sooner did the news of the defeat of Aboukir Bay reach the ear of the Court of Naples, than orders were given for the whole city to be illuminated; and shortly afterwards (12th September 1798), this same government decreed a levy of forty thousand men. Two-thirds of the available capital of the Kingdom was deposited in six banks, which issued a corresponding number of securities (*fedi di credito*). This trusting confidence—the height of absurdity under any despotic *régime* —was repaid as might have been expected. The King laid hands on all the capital funds thus deposited; the property of all the *luoghi pii* in the land was put up compulsorily for auction (to which sales, buyers came flocking in unprecedented numbers); and in a trice, behold a Neapolitan army, eighty thousand strong, drawn up along the frontiers of the Roman Republic, which, at that time, was held by no more than fifteen thousand French. The King, however, was reluctant to launch his assault until the Austrians had taken the first plunge. The news of this attack was brought from Vienna by an individual who claimed to be a royal courier; soon afterwards, however, it was discovered that this "courier" had been born, not in Austria, but in France; so dangerous a witness had of necessity to be disposed of, and in fact was murdered then and there beneath the eyes of the King himself, who, terror-stricken anew at the evidence of such subtle stratagems on the part of the *Jacobins*, forthwith gave orders for the assault. His army promptly captured the city of Rome; but, a few days later, this same army was routed neck and crop, and so, on the 24th of December 1798, King Ferdinand set sail for Sicily, leaving orders behind him in Naples for everything of military value—corn, ships, guns, powder, etc., etc.—to be relentlessly destroyed. In point of fact, however, the panic which had seized the Court was premature: General Mack capitulated to General Championnet, and so Naples was saved. But soon the city itself rose up in armed revolt; the mob of *lazzeroni* murdered the Duke of Torre and his brother, the scholar don Clemente Filomarino, and burned their bodies. Scared by visions of anarchy, the Neapolitan republicans appealed to Championnet, who replied that he would march into the city as soon as he saw the *tricolore* standard floating above the Castel Sant' Elmo. The patriot insurgents, under the leadership of signor di Montemiletto, gained possession of the designated fortress by means of a stratagem; and so, on the 21st of January 1799, the republican general launched his attack upon the city of Naples at the head of six thousand men. The *lazzaroni*, for their part, fought desperately and with indescribable courage. On the 23rd of January, Championnet rode into Naples, and nominated a provisional government of twenty-five chosen individuals, to whom he addressed the following words:

'*France, being made mistress of Naples by right of arms and by the desertion of her King, does hereby make a free gift of her conquest to the inhabitants of the city, thereby granting them, at one and the same time, both liberty and independence.*

'This sudden vision of freedom took full possession of many an unwary mind; the wild intoxication of the capital spread like wildfire to the provinces; the majority of the Bishops officially declared their allegiance to the Republic; while, in every town and village, the clergy in robe and surplice blessed with its presence the planting of the *Tree of Liberty*. But there remained one man still to be reckoned with; for Cardinal Ruffo, who alone among all the royalist faction possessed the will and character of a leader, had still not fled the soil of Italy. He had set up his headquarters at Reggio di Calabria, ever ready to take ship should the peril grow too imminent, yet never losing a moment to organise a dour, peasant resistance against the *Republic of Parthenope**. Cardinal Ruffo was a man whose fortune was still to be made; he transformed this *Vendée* into a *Crusade*, not merely by promising that the Gates of Paradise would fly open to every hero who met his death in such a righteous cause, but (and here indeed he showed his truest metal) by persuading all who listened *to believe that he spoke the truth*.

'Meanwhile, the English had occupied the Island of Procida, some six leagues from Naples, and were harassing the coastal regions by constant landings. Insurgent prisoners were dispatched to Procida, there to be condemned to death by a tribunal whose authority, by the desire of the Court, lay vested in the hands of its President, the abominable Speziale. The French troops, although scarcely more than a handful, made a number of sorties, in the course of which, despite the dire nature of the risks involved, they shot or dispersed each group of Ruffo's partisans whom they could run to earth. In actual fact, the republican authority had no real existence save within the walls of Naples itself, and in one or two provinces to a greater or lesser degree protected by the capital. Nevertheless, every man born who, be it but once in his life, had read a book, was a convinced republican, and the common enthusiasm knew no bounds.

'Yet it was the French themselves who gave orders that those arms should be destroyed, by which alone their republican allies might have been enabled to survive, and who further denied them the right to levy troops. Soon came the fatal news of Suvorov's victories in Lombardy; whereupon the French army, under the command of General Macdonald, having first—according to time-honoured custom—given a series of false pretexts for its manoeuvres, retired to Caserta, thus abandoning Naples, together with the newly-born republic, to the tender mercies of its enemies. The common laws of humanity, if nothing else, should have made it a sacred duty to the French to give the Neapolitan patriots a few hours warning, and to offer them means of escape. Yet the truth of the event was very different. The insurgents sent a deputation to *citoyen* Abrial, the representative of the *Directoire*, who, at that time, had established his headquarters in Capua.

'*For pity's sake*, implored the patriots, *if you intend to abandon us, tell us; tell us, and we too, one and all, will leave the city of Naples.*

'*Abandon good republicans, not I!* protested *citoyen* Abrial. *I would rather carry every man jack of you upon my own shoulders.* Whereupon he made the gesture of *Pious Aeneas*. The effect of this retort was to set back the clock of civilisation in the Kingdom of Naples by some thirty years.

'Six weeks after the retreat of the French, Naples fell into the hands of the allied armies, composed of Neapolitan royalists, British, Russians and Turks. The insurgents held their own for a while with commendable courage, but were soon forced to take refuge in the strongholds of the city. The first of these to surrender was the fortress of Avigliano, near the *ponte della Maddalena*, which was held by students from the Faculty of Medicine. The victors, as soon as they had forced the gates, began systematically to slaughter every patriot within the walls. Promptly, the insurgents resolved rather upon a more glorious form of death; a brand touched off the powder-magazine; and in the subsequent explosion, four hundred royalists perished together with the patriot defenders, among whom two alone survived.

'Meanwhile, the most singular and most gruesome horrors were being perpetrated in the streets of the city by the unbridled populace on the one hand, and by the royalists on the other. Women of the most illustrious birth and breeding were hauled naked to execution: the famous *duchessa* de' Popoli was fortunate to escape with no fate worse than a dungeon, whither she was dragged naked beneath her shift after enduring the coarsest and cruellest of indecencies. Yet the patriots still held out in two citadels within the city walls (the fortresses of Castel Nuovo and of Castel dell' Ovo), and likewise in the little stronghold of Castellamare, some six leagues distant from Naples. This latter fortress eventually surrendered to Commodore Foote, an officer whose name is still respected in Naples even today, some seventeen years after the event, and despite the crowded incidents of history. Foote used his authority to guarantee that the terms of the capitulation should be observed to the letter. It was the example of such scrupulous probity which finally swayed the resolve of the defenders of the two citadels within the walls; having exhausted their supplies of food and ammunition alike, they accepted their fate and agreed to submit *to the troops of the King of the Two Sicilies, of the King of England, of the Emperor of All the Russias, and of the Ottoman Porte*. Such is the exact wording of Article I of the *Terms of Surrender*, dated 3rd Messidor, Year VII, approved by the unhappily notorious brigade-commander Méjan, the French commandant of the fortress of St Elmo, and signed by Cardinal Ruffo, by Edward James Foote and by the Russian and Turkish generals. Here follow the terms of Article IV: *The person and the property of every individual member of the two garrisons (i.e.,* of Castel Nuovo and of Castel dell' Ovo) *shall be respected and guaranteed*. Article V is conceived in the following terms: *All the aforementioned individuals shall be offered the choice, whether to proceed aboard vessels flying the republican flag, which shall be provided for them, to convey them to Toulon; or whether to remain in Naples, and to continue to dwell therein without let or hindrance, either to themselves or to their families.*

'For many years, royalists have been wont to deny the existence of this treaty; unhappily for *Loyal Sentiment*, the original document has now finally been brought to light.

'Fifteen hundred patriots, comprising the garrisons of the two fortresses, declared their intention to leave the country; by an ill chance, however, while they still awaited the ships which were to carry them across the sea to Toulon, Lord Nelson appeared off Naples with all his fleet, including in his

retinue the English Ambassador and his wife, the notorious
Lady Hart Hamilton.

'On the evening of June 26th, the insurgents embarked
aboard the ships which were appointed for them; on the 27th,
under the watchful eye of a group of British naval officers,
each transport was moored under the guns of an English man-
of-war. On the following day, every individual of rank or
note among the insurgents was transferred aboard Lord Nelson's
flagship. Among this chosen band there was to be observed the
distinguished figure of Domenico Cerilli, who, for thirty years,
had been the personal friend and private physician of Sir
William Hamilton. Lady Hamilton deliberately went aboard
her paramour's flagship, the better to look at Cerilli and the
remainder of the insurgents, who had just suffered the new
indignity of being bound hand and foot. There, on the deck,
lay not merely the *élite* of a whole nation, but indeed—a factor
of considerably more weight and moment in the eyes of a
Peer of the Realm of England—the noblest heirs to the most
illustrious blood which graced His Majesty's Court. After the
illustrious victims had been duly inspected, they were
dispatched separately aboard the various vessels of the fleet.

'At long last, King Ferdinand III arrived out of his Sicilian
exile aboard an English frigate, and, without a moment's delay,
issued an edict by which he declared that never for an instant
had it been his purpose to agree to any terms of surrender
with the rebels. A second edict declared that all property
belonging to the insurgents was forthwith held to be confiscated. Commodore Foote, to the honour of his nation and of
humanity in general, observing this flagrant violation of a
treaty which he had guaranteed with his personal signature,
then and there handed in his resignation (an example which
was *not* imitated by Lord Bentinck* at Genoa).

'The patriots then addressed a petition to Lord Nelson,
written in French and full of doubtful spellings, in which they
demanded that the terms of the capitulation should be

observed. Lord Nelson returned this petition to its signatories, with the following words inscribed in his own hand at the foot of the concluding page:

'*I have shown your paper to your gracious King: who must be the best and only judge of the merits and demerits of his subjects**.

NELSON

'The epithet *gracious* accorded to the King of Naples under such circumstances is a flagrant instance of the ultimate depths of absurdity inherent in the British aristocracy. M. de Talley-rand, faced with such a rejoinder, might well have commented: *Whether or no it be a* crime, *I cannot judge; but most assuredly it is arrant nonsense.*

'The flagship of Admiral Nelson, aboard which vessel His Majesty King Ferdinand now had his stateroom, was surrounded on every hand by a fleet of feluccas, tartanes and other craft, which had been converted into prison-hulks for the insurgents. The patriots had been herded aboard pell-mell, like negroes; stripped of their apparel by the rabble of *lazzaroni* who had arrested them, crawling with vermin, sustained by draughts of foul, infected water, here they lay, exposed to the pitiless rays of the burning sun; indeed, the greatest torture that these poor wretches had to bear was the theft of their *hats*. Boat-loads of *lazzaroni*, appearing in ever-growing numbers as deputation after deputation from the mob rowed out to gaze upon the person of the King, would hurl the foulest insults at the rebels. Every morning, through the hatchways of their prisons, the patriots might catch a glimpse of Lady Hamilton setting forth upon Lord Nelson's arm, to while away the languid hours at Baja, Pozzuoli, Ischia, or in some other delicious nook set about the shores of the Bay of Naples; the sumptuous pinnace which conveyed her person was manned by four-and-twenty English ratings who hauled to the strains of *Rule, Britannia.* The libidinous behaviour of Lord Nelson, and the similarly abandoned tastes which attracted Lady

Hamilton to ***, finally decided the fate of the insurgents. Miss Hart, later destined to be known as Lady Hamilton, was renowned for her rare beauty, and had lived for many years in Rome, exercising the profession of *model*, in which capacity her services might be enjoyed by art-students for the sum of six francs precisely. When the axe fell, the first victim was the unhappy *San Gennaro*, who was accused of having protected the Republic. The King ordered the confiscation of all his property. St Januarius was dethroned, and St Anthony elevated in his stead; and the heretical guns of the British Navy thundered forth in honour of this hagiarchical promotion.

'Soon after, the most noteworthy individuals in the insurgent ranks were transferred to the dungeons of the citadels on shore. "Visits" aboard the improvised prison-hulks grew to be an almost daily occurrence, and each time, the incident took place under the benevolent eye of the English officers.

'As soon as he had dropped anchor in the bay, Admiral Nelson had caused a proclamation to be posted throughout the city, requiring that all those who had accepted office in any capacity under the Republic, or had signified their approval of the principles upon which it rested, should appear in person at the fortress of Castel Nuovo, where they were to leave a record of their name and address, together with full details of their manifold activities during the brief life of the Republic. Admiral Nelson gave his sworn word that any individual who freely made such a declaration should receive his personal protection and guarantee against pursuit or molestation *from any quarter whatsoever*. The number of poor, trusting fools who fell headlong into this booby-trap laid by the English was by no means inconsiderable. Three judges, distinguished no less for their upright virtue than for their learning, and respected by every faction alike, presented themselves for registration. Their names were Dragonetti, Gianotti and Colace. Ere many days had passed, the latter was hanged.

'On the 12th of August 1799, permission to set sail for Toulon was finally granted to the five hundred insurgents who still languished aboard the prison-hulks. Before their departure, however, they were required to sign a document of most curious import, yet legal for all that in the Kingdom of Naples: each patriot gave his individual oath, *that nevermore would he set foot within the domains of King Ferdinand, upon pain of forfeiting his life; and should he violate this promise, so did he grant and acknowledge unto every one among the King's subjects the right to slay him without fear or threat of retribution.*

'Until this time, the terror which dwelt in the breast of the Court of Naples at the thought of Joubert's army had prevented it from indulging in bloodshed. But gradually revenge grew bolder; the earliest victims were selected from among those insurgents who were unprotected by the treaty of surrender; and among the first sufferers was Prince Caraccioli. This brilliant intellect was the genius behind the Neapolitan navy; consequently, the good citizens of Naples will not easily be wooed away from their belief that, as in the case of the victims of Quiberon Bay, it was his precise talents in this direction which hastened his downfall. I will not tarry here to tell anew the tale, which all have heard, of the terror which was inspired by the sight of his corpse in the heart of a *Certain August Personage**.

'Soon after came the news that the French had been defeated at Novi. Now the final restraint was gone which hitherto alone had checked the furious wrath of Her Majesty Queen ***. Caution forbids me to publish details, at the hearing of which Suetonius himself might have turned pale. By the hand of her public executioner, Naples lost almost every single man of distinction among her citizens: Mario Pagano, who had drawn up the Constitution of the Republic; Scoti, Luogoteta, Buffa, Troisi, Pacifico; Generals Federici and Massa; Bishop Natali; Falconieri, Caputi, Baffi, Mantone, Pracelli, Conforti, Rossi, Bagni. The reactionaries experienced a peculiar thrill in the hanging of Eleonora Fonseca, a woman whose genius was as rare as her beauty; she had been editor of the *Monitore Repubblicano*, the first newspaper which had ever seen the light of day in Naples. Among the aristocracy who met their death (to the everlasting dishonour of *England*), we may recall the Duke of Andria, the Prince of Strongoli and his brother Mario Pignatelli; Colonna, Riario and the Marquis of Genzano. The two last-named, although neither was much above sixteen years of age, possessed a spirit which far transcended the prejudices of noble birth, and had loudly declared abroad their love of liberty. Genzano and the renowned Matera, both clad in French uniforms, had been handed over to the Court by brigade-commander Méjan. These illustrious heroes were hanged on the *largo del Mercato*—the very spot where Masaniello had once sparked off his older revolution.

'They died with a smile upon their lips, prophesying that, sooner or later, Naples would be free, and their death, *not avenged*, but *useful* to the enlightenment of their native country. Among this host of victims, the death of the enchanting *marchesa* San-Felice excited a special degree of curiosity. On one occasion, during the brief existence of the Republic, happening to spend the evening in a *salon* amid royalist company, she learned that, two days later, the brothers Bacri were proposing to organise an insurrection among the *lazzaroni*, and to murder all the officers of a certain post belonging to the *Republican Guard*. Among the officers attached to this unit was the lover of the *marchesa* San-Felice. Waiting until the very last moment, when the time came for him to take up his duties, she threw herself at his feet and implored him to remain in her apartments. *If there is danger*, declared her lover, *then the duty that forbids me desert my comrades is but the more compelling*. In the end he persuaded her (for such was the love she bore him) to reveal to him the secret of the plot; and when the day of reckoning came, not all the pleading of the Princess Royal herself could win a pardon for the *marchesa* San-Felice. I will not engage to add up how many thousands make the total count of victims in these tragic incidents. The executions continued; so likewise (and this constitutes a still more baleful reflection upon humanity) did the sentences of solitary confinement in dungeons, whose pestilential air was fatal to all who breathed it; nor did the *Terror* end until the events which were heralded by the treaty of Florence (1801).

'The philosophical spirit revealed by these Neapolitan patriots bears an extraordinary imprint: it is at once *sublime* and yet *serene*. By virtue of these twin qualities, it seems to transcend by infinite degrees all other philosophical systems propounded elsewhere in Italy or Germany. However, respecting the various documents which I have quoted, let me hasten to confess that one and all are drawn from printed sources: I have no knowledge of the originals*.'

I have been careful to suppress, during the course of this narrative, all the more gruesome details. Robespierre, whatever his faults, has this at least to be said in his favour: he did not count a majority of personal friends among the total number of his victims. Those whom he sacrificed, he sacrificed to a *system*, however ill-founded; not to his petty, personal spite.

OTRANTO, 15th May. I have journeyed hither by way of Potenza and Taranto. Were I to offer the reader a description of the little-known regions through which I have travelled, I should find myself in the unhappy state of running over into a *third* volume. I made the journey on horseback, armed with a sunshade, and accompanied by three of my new-found acquaintance. To escape the plague of insects, we slept by night on eight or ten occasion amid the straw in divers farms belonging to my companions or to their friends, and I had the pleasure of some entertaining conversation with the prosperous husbandmen of the region. This part of Italy has no more in common with Florence, than Florence has in common with le Havre.

The *marchese* Santapiro, a sometime acquaintance of Moscow

days, whom I have recently discovered anew here in Otranto, is a man who, being blessed with thirty thousand *livres* a year and two or three sabre-cuts received in duly honourable circumstances, has discovered in himself sufficient strength and independence never to flatter and never to tell a lie. Hitherto I was persuaded that so extreme a degree of eccentricity was inconceivable in Italy; Santapiro has afforded me proof of the contrary. For three whole years he paraded up and down the length of Italy this oddity or *quirk*; after which span of time, he had earned the universal reputation of a *monster*. This signal honour went promptly to his head; he began to cultivate a taste for paradox; he would maintain that music bored him stiff, that paintings turned a room into a catafalque, that he would gladly give any statue by Canova in exchange for some mechanical jumping-jack, such as are made in Paris, which rolled its eyes and stuck out its tongue; and indeed, in Naples, he offered concerts which cost him two or three times the normal price, simply for insisting that nothing should be heard save tunes by Grétry, Méhul and the like.

Santapiro is a man who goes through life with his character perched on stilts. Had he chosen rather to remain on a natural level, he had doubtless proved of unquestionably greater interest for *us*; yet, to the vulgar herd, his reputation as an *original mind* would have suffered beyond telling. He is a creature who is ever gay, ever unpredictable; he fills the horizon of the mind with a host of notions; and, listening to him, you may be moved to pass judgment upon certain of his ideas which, were it not for him, would never have so much as entered your head.

Yesterday, during the high heat of the day, we took siesta, each upon his leathern couch, installed in a vast shop-front which he has rented and sealed off from the street with curtains of green calico; and thus at ease, we lay consuming water-ices. I made irreverent remarks about the stilts he used to parade his taste for paradox; while he indulged in satirical comment concerning that squeamishness of mind which had forbidden me to make use of my letters of introduction in Florence. Santapiro has lived in this latter city for the past two years. Every creature born alive in Russia, he tells me, who, together with a tolerable fortune, possesses a modicum of intelligence, is persuaded that it is his bounden duty to see a winter out in Florence. There is also a host of wealthy English travellers, and, every evening without exception, four or five open *soirées*. Signor D*** maintains his own most excellently constituted company of actors within the town*, and employs them to perform the prettiest sketches from the charming pen of M. Scribe; signor D*** is the most philanthropic individual in all the realm of Italy; none, moreover, is proud possessor of better-authenticated *relics*. He owns some truly priceless bits of St Nicolas. There are two or three exclusive circles in which it is fashionable to perform comedies imported from France; this Gallic humour provides an entertaining contrast with the type of Italian mind which constitutes the audience, and which, with scrupulous attention straining at each line, is delighted if it grasps one sally in four.

'In Florence', pursued Santapiro, 'I used to keep a *palazzo*, eight horses and six lackeys, and I doubt if I spent a thousand guineas a year. . . . Many a fair creature from the North', he continued, 'has experienced a strange moral revolution at the passage of the Apennine; the further slopes are strewn with the abandoned *débris* of that prudish virtue which has condemned the *salons* of Paris to take refuge in *écarté*, and transformed all England into one vast mausoleum. A lover is all very well; but a *title*—ah! a title is a good deal better. One thing alone I fail to understand: how comes it that every *marquis* born within the boundaries of France, blessed with five-and-twenty summers, and fobbed off by fortune with a hundred guineas a year—how comes it, I ask, that every one such does not set off post-haste for Florence, armed with his family tree? There might he find a score of fledgling *misses*, pretty as pictures, wealthy too, and as good as gold for extra measure, ready to go down each upon her lovely knees and *beg* to be made a *marquise*. Every winter I have spent in Florence, I have watched some six thousand titled foreigners pass before my eyes. Each one brings as baggage from his own barbaric land one instructive anecdote and three grotesque prejudices. And all these aristocratic anecdotes have this in common: a derisive contempt for kings.'

'Are you a lover of the arts?' he enquired. 'Then I commend to your attention the recent rearrangement of the *Palazzo Pitti*. The Sovereign Prince of the city has learned to profit from the puritan foolishness of Rome, and has realised that Florence is destined to become the *Masked Ball* of Europe. Old Prince Neri, before he dies, is resolved to introduce some form of law and order; but signor Fossombroni will not have it so.' To finish, Santapiro retailed some seven or eight most entertaining anecdotes, which it would be infamous to print.

When the Princes of Lorraine landed on the coast of Tuscany (1738), the Florentines observed, arriving in their wake, a whole host of threadbare creatures, each with a staff or cane held in his hand: hence the word *cannajo*, which I had originally taken for a translation of the French *canaille*, particularly after hearing it pronounced in Florence with the guttural accent of the country—instead of *Santa Croce*, the Florentine says *Santha Hroce*.

Santapiro concluded by enunciating the strangest of calumnies, which will surely earn me the reputation of a *stivale*: which calumny consists in declaring that, in all Florence, there is but one man of letters who bears the stamp of true intelligence; but that this one unique intelligence is the intelligence of an angel, of a Talleyrand, of a Voltaire; and its possessor is the author of *il Disperato per eccesso di buon cuore*. Count Giraùd is descended from a Frenchman who came to Rome in the train of Cardinal Giraud.

CROTONE, 20th May. Imagine my surprise, here, in this furthest corner of the world, to have hit upon my old, brave comrade, Captain Joseph Renavans, who, in the days of our first acquaintance, in 1800, was a simple dragoon. He told me of his adventures, 'My regiment', he said, 'was the 34th of the line, always bearing the brunt, and through whose ranks I have watched some twenty thousand men appear and vanish. I was ever as you knew me: uncommunicative, unfriendly, always tempted to insolence towards my superiors; chance alone earned me the three steps of my promotion, and from the hand of Napoleon himself. My battalion was posted to Naples, and during the space of three whole years I fought a desperate campaign against the *banditti*. I was engaged in pursuit of the notorious Parella, who made no show of hiding his contempt for us. One day the Minister of State Salicetti summoned me to Naples. *Listen*, he said, *here is a sum of three hundred and fifty thousand francs; put a price on the head of the banditti; leave nothing unattempted; in short, this business must be finished and done with, for the politicians are beginning to stick a finger in the pie.* I issued a proclamation', pursued Captain Renavans, 'and had each parish priest announce it from his pulpit, to the effect that I would offer a reward of four hundred ducats for the head of Parella. Some three months later, as I lay in my billet, towards noon, half-dead of heat despite the darkness of my room, my sergeant gave me word that a stranger was waiting to see me. Some minutes later, in walked a peasant with a sack, which he prodeeded to untie, and drew therefrom, unblenchingly, the head of Parella, saying: *Give me my four hundred ducats*. I swear to you that never in my life did I start backwards in such a fright. I ran to the window, to open it for light. The peasant deposited the head upon my table, and, no sooner did my eyes fall upon it, than I knew beyond a doubt that this had been Parella. *How did you succeed?* I asked. *Signor Commandant, you must understand that, for the last twelve years, I have been Parella's barber, valet and trusted henchman; but three years since, at Whitsuntide, he chose to treat me with the haughtiest of insolence. In course of time, I chanced to hear our local priest proclaim in his sermon that you were prepared to offer four hundred ducats for the head of Parella. And so it came about that, this very morning, he happening to be alone with me while all our companions were abroad on the highroad, did say: "Now at last we have a moment's peace! My beard is grown abominably long; shave me, friend—I shall feel the fresher for it." Thus did I begin to shave that beard of his; and as my blade travelled round towards his moustache, I managed to snatch a glance behind his shoulders and saw that no one was approaching; whereupon, zick! I sliced his head off!'* At a later stage during this same conversation, Captain Renavans remarked: 'In France, all that I once had has been taken from me; so now I am here to discover whether the wife of a certain apothecary—a handsome creature once, in days gone by, and one that I did love—will perchance recall who I am; for she is a widow now, and faith! I am persuaded that I shall marry her, and even turn apothecary myself.'

'Do you know what surprises me above all else?' continued Renavans. 'This—that when Salicetti placed in my hands the sum of three hundred and fifty thousand francs, without demanding a receipt; and when, later, during the following six months, I used up every penny of this subsidy, doled out in trifling sums of fifty *louis* here and a hundred *louis* there, not a single *centime* of all that amount found its way into my own pocket. Rather did *I* contribute from my own small purse, to the tune of a couple of golden *louis* at least. Whereas today, in similar circumstances, I would gaily—if I could—feather my own nest to the tune of a hundred thousand francs, and never think twice about it.' (Here you have the difference between 1810 and 1826, and the explanation of the . . . . . .
. . . .*)

CATANZARO, 23rd May. My latest experience was to watch a peasant-woman in a fit of temper hurling her child against a wall not two paces distant, and using all the strength she had. I was certain that the child had received a fatal hurt; it is about four years old, and is rending the air with agonising screams beneath my very window; but apparently no serious damage has been done.

By degrees, as one penetrates ever deeper into Calabria, the racial features grow more and more distinctly Grecian. I have observed several men in their forties, whose countenance is an exact replica of the famous statue of Jupiter Mansuetus*. On the other hand, when one of these creatures veers to homeliness, the result, it must be confessed, is grotesque beyond description.

BRANCALEONE, 25th May. Today, before setting out on our excursion to the ruins of Locri, we hired the services of three armed peasants to accompany us. No brigands in the land did ever wear a more fearsome aspect; yet, for all that, these ferocious countenances held no trace of that which I most abominate—none of that hypocritical suavity, melting in appearance, yet flinty at heart, which characterises the Harlowe family (Richardson, *Clarissa*).

I know perhaps no sight in all the world more picturesque than that of some Calabrian peasant, surprised at the bend of a lane, or caught unawares at a clearing in the woods. The prolonged astonishment of these ruffians, one and all armed to the teeth, at the sight of ourselves, not isolated travellers but a solid phalanx, and no less desperately armed, was a comedy to behold. When the weather threatened thunder, their features, twitching as though with some foretaste of an electric charge, would seem almost to disintegrate. Such aspects as these, to a traveller accustomed only to the gentleness and urbanity of Gallic expressions, must fatally have produced a sensation of horror. It is our wont, at almost every such encounter, to seek to make some purchase from these strange Calabrian peasants, thus furnishing ourselves with the pretext for a moment's

conversation. It was near Gerace that we discovered the oddest
of all this peasant-clan, who astonished our ears with the most
fantastical of tales.

Near MELITO, 28th May.   Some few months since, a married
woman of this country, renowned for her unwavering piety
no less than for her uncommon beauty, did so far falter in the
path of virtue as to grant an assignation to her lover in a forest
remote among the mountains, some six miles distant from her
village. The lover was fortunate in the enjoyment of his mistress'
favours. Yet, no sooner had this instant of madness passed away,
than the full hideousness of her sin bore down upon her guilty
soul: motionless she remained, plunged in oppressive silence.
'Why so cold, so distant?' enquired the lover. 'I was dreaming',
replied his mistress, 'of the means we might employ to meet
again tomorrow; this woodman's hut, long since abandoned,
here where the forest is dark, is the most fitting spot.' The
lover took his leave; but the unhappy woman made no move
to return to her village; instead, she passed the night in the
heart of the forest, and whiled away the hours (as later she
confessed) partly in prayer, partly in digging two graves set
one against the other. The dawn broke; and ere long, with the
daylight, came her lover, only to meet his death at the hands of
his mistress, who, as he believed, did worship the very earth
on which he trod. Still prey to the same remorse, the poor,
tortured creature proceeded to bury her lover with the greatest
care and reverence; then, retracing her footsteps to the village,
she made her confession to the priest and embraced her
children. Lastly, she returned once more into the forest, where
she was later discovered, stretched lifeless in the hollow of the
trench which she had dug beside the grave which held her
lover.

REGGIO DI CALABRIA, 29th May.   There was a little girl,
a charming little lass, whose most precious possession of all

was a certain wax doll which she had been given as a present. The doll felt cold; so she put it out in the sun; the sun melted the wax, and the child was left weeping bitter tears over the loss of the thing she loved. This tale provides a perfect illustration of the deep-seeted national temperament of this furthest tip of Italy: *an impassioned childishness*. The local population lives a life of ease; never once does the idea of *duty* crop up inside a single head; the religion of the country lays no restraint upon the inclinations of its people, and in fact consists of nothing but a series of traditional rites and ceremonies, the like of which may be discovered nowhere else. The Calabrians do as their fancy takes them; and having done so, may then, on two or three occasions in the year, enjoy a little private conversation about their predominant passion, and thus convince themselves that Paradise is theirs.

Yesterday, in the street, I heard a woman saying: 'It was at midsummer that my son met his ill luck.' (To be interpreted: *It was on the 24th of June that my son struck down his enemy*.) 'But if that family won't be reasonable, and accept from don Vincenzo the best we have to offer, then the devil take them all! I want to see my son again.' The family, I should explain, was offering twenty golden ducats in compensation to the father of the young man who had been killed. Strength of character springs from one source only: a man must have known since earliest childhood the obligation to do distasteful things. Now, except in the *Terra di Lavoro* where agriculture is a meticulous art, and where square-bladed spades are used to till the soil, never save in the rarest of circumstances is a young fourteen-year-old Neapolitan obliged to face the lightest task he finds distasteful. In all his span of days, he would constantly prefer the discomfort of *going without* to the discomfort of *actually working*. Our imbecile travellers from the North are wont to hurl the epithet *barbarian* at the tatterdemalion populace of Calabria, for that it wears its threadbare clothes without a trace of shame ... nothing could seem more patently absurd to a native of Crotone than the suggestion that he should *fight* to win himself a red ribbon in his buttonhole or to decide whether his lord and master should be called Ferdinand or William. That sentiment of *loyalty*, of devotion to a given dynasty, which shines so brightly through the pages of Sir Walter Scott, and which should surely have earned him a Peerage, is as little known in these remoter parts as snow in May. And, truth to tell, I am not aware that the Calabrian is necessarily more clod-like on this account than many another I might name (this notion, let me confess, is in the worst possible taste). Sooner or later, your Calabrian *will* take up arms, and give a fair enough account of himself, in the cause of some *Secret Society* which has been at work on his imagination ten years or more. Already nineteen years have passed since Cardinal Ruffo discovered this salient truth; but, for aught I know, *societies* of this character may well have existed long before his time.

I once observed, upon the very shores of the ocean, hard by Dieppe, woods of high-standing timber which covered a considerable area. And I remember the peasants remarking: 'Those trees, sir, if ever we were unwise enough to cut them down, would never grow again. We can't replant, you see; it's the terrible sea-wind that burns up the young saplings.' For a similar reason, no strain of military valour can ever take root or flourish among the Neapolitans. At the first sign of growth, a sea-tempest of Gauls or Hungarians, hordes thirty thousand strong and skilled in battle since the beginning of time, will ride searing and scorching over this unhappy province. How would you have it, that a couple of thousand Calabrian peasants should dare stand up against such a furious array? New levies must be tempered in the fire of battle; but such a process demands a succession of petty skirmishes; and he who leads them to the first of these must do so with some confidence of victory. Never deigning to consider the workings of this mechanism, European diplomacy has made the most

nonsensical pronouncements about this people. The natives of
Calabria rejoice in two fixed beliefs: the rites of the Christian
religion and the *jettatura* (*i.e,,* the process of casting a spell upon
one's neighbour by means of the *evil eye*). Certain remote and
curious institutions, such as *justice* and *government*, are looked
upon as vexatious nuisances, to be sent hurtling to perdition
every eight or ten years, and to be constantly eluded in any
case in daily life. For the peasant, the vital thing is to have as
confessor, or else as godfather, a *fratone* (or influential monk);
or, failing this, to have a handsome woman in the family. In
more prosperous circles, it is the elder brother himself who
enters Holy Orders; proceeding then to arrange a careful
match between his younger brother and whatever pretty girl
may chance to be his mistress; such households are often
models of peace and harmony.

In many places—Taranto, Otranto, Squillace—we discovered
among this class of priests, one and all 'elder brothers' in the
family, an exhaustive knowledge of the Latin tongue and of the
relics of antiquity. Such folk as these are proud to dwell in
Magna Græcia. In this province, the staple reading of an educated man is Tacitus. Should a stranger excite suspicion by his
presence, it is customary to drop into Latin. A copy of Voltaire,
or of *le Compère Mathieu*, is valued as a treasure beyond price.
There was indeed one such in the boat which brought us from
Otranto to Crotone—being circulated thus from owner to
borrower over a distance of some forty leagues. On the other
hand, the Calabrians are ignorant of the first rudiments in the
art of conversation. *Eloquence* is often a different matter; and
woe betide you, should you set them on a subject that touches
them near to their heart; they will talk for an hour, neither
pausing for breath nor sparing your longsuffering ear the most
microscopic detail. Listening to such outbursts, I seemed to
catch an echo of that eloquence which pervades the harangues
of Livy. It was a priest from Brancaleone who spent two whole
hours in developing, for our especial benefit, this single theme:

'As a Christian and as a philosopher, I am distressed at the thought of all the cruelties soon to be perpetrated in Spain and Italy; yet on the other hand, *terror*—and in particular, terror inspired by the *Bishops*—is indispensable to both these peoples, whose conscience, roused to wakefulness by Napoleon, was still not stirred sufficiently to the depths. Murder and torture will strike home to them, knocking at the very portals of their souls; *then* alone will they understand that justice is not bought too dear at the price which must be paid to attain it. Take this unhappy land—take myself, who am speaking to you now— what should *justice* signify to me? Were it not that I had friends, together with a sufficiency of personal influence, I should be crushed to death. What profit have I ever known to come to me through *justice*? The most sacred, solemn oaths are daily violated, and the sight of it is there for all to see.' (The Archbishop, himself a son of a Minister of the Egyptian Pasha, was cast ashore here by a tempest at sea; with solemn promises, he was granted asylum; and, all oaths and swearings notwithstanding, was forthwith handed over to the Court of Rome. Rumour has it now that he languishes in the *Castel Sant' Angelo*; God knows what is being done to him*.) 'The fear of death', added don Francesco, 'being, among all passions, that which wields most constant dominion over mankind, not excepting even the most brutish among them, it follows that the only hope to bring enlightenment among the nations lies in the exploitation of this particular passion: by this argument you may perceive, within the framework of the Divine Plan, the *useful purpose* of the present inquisitions and massacres in Spain. Consider further how disastrous it had been, were it the *Good Faction*—the lovers of liberty—who had been forced to have recourse to such draconian measures!' etc., etc., etc. This part of Italy is never tired of talking about Spain.

The *idiomatic twists* of the Calabrian dialect would seem like lunatic extravagance in France. A young man whose aim it is to win the heart of every woman he meets is referred to currently as a *cascamorto* (*i.e.*, a man who pretends to *fall dead* upon the ground from sheer excess of passion every time he ogles a pretty wench).

If you would hit upon a symbol of all that lies at the furthest pole removed from the native spirit of Calabria, then think upon that languid and life-weary attitude which, among ourselves, is fullest incarnated in M. de Chateaubriand's *René* —itself both a copy and a model. Here, in this province, it is an accepted fact that, save in special circumstances, whose rare and unique singularity is so proclaimed by general outcry in every corner of the land, the common level of human happiness varies but to an infinitesimal degree in any walk, estate or condition of life. At the root of this philosophical attitude there lies an over-riding trust in *Destiny*, occasioned, perhaps, by reaction to the vicious spitefulness of human governments. These folk have countless figures of speech which reveal the one sensation which is never to be met with in Calabria: *despair*. If disaster is anticipated, the phrase comes pat: *Mancherebbe anche questa!* In the case of great good fortune, they say instead: *Ah, che consolazione!*

Don Francesco was telling me that in 1799, in the days of the Revolution, a young man, Prince Montemiletto, was despatched to London to negotiate a treaty in favour of the Republic. Mr Pitt for some while fobbed him off with empty words, and finally showed his open contempt for the young envoy by selecting a different individual altogether as Neapolitan ambassador, with whom he chose to conclude negotiations. The young Prince voiced his complaint. 'A beardless boy', retorted Pitt, 'is no ambassador!' Whereupon Montemiletto returned home to his lodgings and blew out his brains. A true Calabrian would either have cared not a fig for Pitt's retort, or else would have killed him dead. But alas! from one extreme of Europe to the other, in Naples not a whit less than in St Petersburg, the privileged classes are characterised by that same exquisite refinement of manners which robs them of the power of energetic action in an emergency.

And I, meanwhile, have disagreeable evidence that I do *not* belong to the aforementioned 'privileged classes': for want of the necessary passport, I may not cross the Straits into Messina, whose houses I can count, each one distinctly, from the window of my present lodgings. I could most dearly have wished to examine the ruins of Selinonte, and to look at certain specimens of sculpture, whose antiquity by far exceeds anything that I have met with hitherto.

At this point I would add from memory a few facts which I dared not commit to paper in Naples. On one occasion during this tour of Calabria, which is my present subject, chancing to spend the night upon an estate, whose bailiff was in the service of one of my travelling-companions, I caught allusions to the countless robberies committed by a gang of *banditti* known as the company *dell' Indipendenza*. The manner in which these depredations were carried out betrayed both skill and a truly *Turkish* bravado. At the time, I paid no attention to these tales; such escapades are daily occurrences in the district; I had neither time nor attention to spare from my study of the *manners* of the folk whom I was visiting. Later on, however, when I chanced to give alms to a poor beggar-woman—a soldier's widow left with child at her husband's death—I was told: '*She* has no claim on your charity, sir; she draws rations from the *banditti*.' It was on this occasion that I heard the tale which I here set down, omitting from my account many minor details of recklessness and courage.

'There exists in this region a *Company*, composed of thirty men and four women, one and all equipped with the noblest and swiftest horses in the land. The chieftain of this band is a sometime sergeant-at-arms *di Jachino** (in the service of Joachim Murat, King of Naples), who styles himself *Comandante dell' Indipendenza*. His practice is to send out warnings to the local landowners and *massari*, demanding that on such a day, such a sum be placed at the foot of such a tree—failing compliance with which demand, the house is consigned to the flames, and its inhabitants to torture and death. When the company is on the march, every farmer along the route is instructed to hold himself in readiness to serve food for so many persons at such a given hour; in each case, the tribute exacted is proportionate to the means of the victim. No Royal Progress enjoys a more meticulous commissariat.'

Some four weeks previous to the occasion on which I was given these details, a certain farmer, enraged by the imperious style of the command which he received to furnish a meal, sent word to the General commanding the Neapolitan army, and a numerous squadron of cavalry and infantry was brought up to surround the *indipendenti*. The latter, however, being apprised by a number of shots that the Neapolitan soldiery was firing wholly at random, cut their way out of the trap by means of a bold assault which left the landscape strewn with the bodies of their enemies, and allowed them to escape unharmed down to the last man. Immediately after this deliverance, they had word conveyed to the farmer, advising him to set his affairs in order. Three days later, the company took possession of the farm, and set up a solemn Tribunal; the farmer, put to the torture—as was indeed current judicial practice in Calabria before the French occupation—made full confession of his crime. The Tribunal then proceeded to deliberate *in camera*; after which, its members advanced with solemn step upon the farmer, picked him up and threw him into an enormous cauldron which was set upon the fire, and which was being used to boil milk for making cheese. As soon as the farmer was well and truly cooked, the company then obliged all the servants about the farm to make a meal of this infernal repast.

The chieftain might easily swell the ranks of his company to a thousand men or more; but he is wont to declare that he has no true talent to command above the number of thirty. He is

P

satisfied merely to maintain a steady complement. Scarcely a
day passes, but he receives new requests for employment;
however, he makes it a rule to insist upon proper qualifications
—*i.e., wounds received in battle, and not testimonials of good conduct*.
These are his very own words (2nd May 1817).

In the spring of this current year, the peasants of Apulia were
direly oppressed by famine; so the leader of the *banditti* made
it his business to distribute among the starving victims a series
of regular ration-vouchers, which the more prosperous citizens
were obliged to honour. This ration consisted of a pound and a
half of bread for a man, one pound for a woman and two pounds
for a woman with child. The woman who had first aroused
my curiosity had been receiving six two-pound vouchers a
week for the past month.

Moreover, no one can ever discover where the *indipendenti*
have their current headquarters. All the spies are on their side.
In Roman times, such a brigand would have been a Marcellus.

NAPLES, 16th June.   Returning from my Calabrian excursion,
I found myself subjected to a certain number of vexations; I
learned later that the authorities were 'uneasy' about me, while
I, for my part, was decidedly 'uneasy' lest I be expelled from
Naples. No other travellers, be they from Sweden, Saxony or
England, need live in fear of such a threat; but neither are they
welcomed with open arms by every person of distinction in the
land, upon no other credentials than the fact of being *French*
and *unprotected by the Embassy*. A certain noble and generous
citizen, whose name I shall never forget nor ever pronounce,
offered to find me sanctuary within his own house. Yet he had
met me but five or six times in all, and was himself in no little
disfavour with the authorities. This is the kind of incident from
which the strongest bonds of attachment towards a country
may be born. In Bologna, I have five or six acquaintance to
whom I might have turned with such a request; but then
Bologna never knew those two years of tyranny and murder

from 1799 to 1801. If divers police-officials *should* resolve to
make my life a misery, they could have, let me protest, none
but the flimsiest grounds for doing so; granted that there may
be a grain or two of contempt in my attitude towards themselves; yet even supposing that I were to cherish theoretical
approval for this or that stratagem aimed at their discomfiture,
I should none the less be of an opinion that, in this tricky
century of ours, subversive activities are strangely liable to be
found out; and further that, in case of failure, the wounded
pride of *Patriotic Sentiment* could hardly fail to attribute the
root and cause of all the evil to the presence of an *interfering
foreigner*.

However, leaving this aside, I have nothing but unqualified
admiration for the Neapolitan patriots. Naples may boast the
eloquence of Mirabeau and the bravery of Desaix. I am
privately convinced, beyond all doubt, that this country is
destined to achieve its parliamentary constitution before 1840.
However, since the gulf which separates a man of the merit of
signor Tocco from the primaeval brutality of the populace is
so immeasurably wide, the enlightened classes will of necessity
see their schemes founder more than once upon the rocks,
before they succeed in bestowing upon their native land the
gift of liberty. Consider the antiquated manners still prevailing
in *i promessi Sposi*, a novel by signor Manzoni.

19th June. Today, strolling along the *largo di Castello*, hard by
that most curious theatre built in a cellar underground, where,
by entering at street-level, you may discover yourself directly
among the seats of the gallery, I bought myself a book. My
purchase was entitled: *della Superiorità in ogni cosa del Sesso
amabilissimo* ... etc., 1504. Anyone who has given a moment's
passing study to the social history of women will remember
that it was François I who first invited them to Court in 1515.
Previously, every baron's castle had maintained the appearance
of a tyrant's stronghold, wherein friendship had no place, but

only slavish obedience: even she who was wife unto her Lord enjoyed no higher consideration than that of a slave, over whom her master might exercise the powers of life and death. She might be stabbed and killed: such accidents would pass for the lawful chastisement of broken vows. In some circumstances, the dagger-stroke would reflect the sudden wrath of a savage, ever jealous to assert his own moral superiority; in others, the death of the *châtelaine* might be requisite in order that her Lord might take unto himself another, whose favours were withheld until he should acknowledge her his wife. At the gallant courts of François I and Henri II, women began to prove *useful* to their husbands in the art of intrigue;[1] consequently their status rose rapidly towards equality, and ever more nearly so, as the fear of God began to lose the place of honour it had hitherto occupied in the heart of mankind. Yet in France during the sixteenth century women were still no better than domestic servants; whereas in Italy, one of the themes most constantly treated by those writers who, at the time, rode highest on the crest of fashion, was precisely the *Superiority of the Amiable Sex over that of Man*. The Italians, being more easily swayed towards the tender passions, having a lesser degree of coarseness in their nature, being less enamoured of physical prowess, less warlike and less feudal, were fully prepared to acknowledge this general principle.

The notions which women carried in their minds being in no way culled from books—since, in those far-off, fortunate

[1] Consider, in the library of monseigneur le duc d'Orléans, that most singular *Collection of Airs*, that were sung by the Maids of Honour to Queen Catherine de Medicis. Each volume, magnificently chased and bound with clasps of silver, bears in printed letters the name of the noble damsel whose office it was to sing such ballads. Their monstrous indecency is proof plain and incontrovertible of the utter falsity of the portrait of the manners of the age which may be discovered in *la Princesse de Clèves*. The *Mémoires de madame la duchesse d'Orléans*, mother of the Regent, are evidence that, even at the Court of Louis XIV, morals were cruder and coarser than those which reign today in 1826, in the household of the dreariest little calico cloth-maker; in compensation, however, there was infinitely greater wit. [1826]

days, they read but little—but rather founded upon the true and ascertainable nature of things, this reign of equality between the sexes introduced a phenomenal mass of plain and unpretentious *sense* into Italian heads. I could name a hundred principles of conduct, which elsewhere still call for proof and demonstration, yet which, in Rome, are taken as axiomatic. If ever women were to be admitted to a status of perfect equality, this would be the surest hallmark of *civilisation*; it would double the intellectual resources of the human race and proportionately multiply its eventual chances of happiness. Women are much closer to true equality in the United States of America than they are in England. In America, they are entitled by law to privileges which, in France, are granted to them only by favour of a sophisticated social tradition, or else for fear of ridicule. In any little English provincial township, the shopkeeper who takes two hundred pounds a year across his counter is in no lesser degree master of his wife than of his horse; whereas, among the merchants of Italy, a woman may enjoy consideration, liberty and happiness, one and all in exact proportion to her beauty. In Rome, a city where all *power* goes hand in hand with *celibacy*, you may chance to enter a shop and enquire after an engraving of Michelangelo's *Prophet Daniel*: 'Good sir, we have it—that I know; but it means searching through all the portfolios; would it trouble you to call again, when my husband is at home?' Here you have a new excess, the very opposite of that which prevails in England. Perfect equality, which must prove a source of happiness for both sexes alike, may be attained only upon one condition: namely, that the privilege of the *duel* should be extended to the other sex. And why not? The pistol calls for *skill*, not strength. In the ideal society, any woman, by voluntarily constituting herself prisoner for the term of two years, may, at the expiry of this statutory period, be granted a divorce. Such notions as these, in the year 2000 A.D. or thereabouts, will no longer seem fantastical*.

25th June. I heard today a jewel of repartee, which is the nine-days' wonder of the whole of Naples; unhappily, I cannot relate it here; perhaps, in any case, it would lose its savour in Paris. Everyone in France knows the story of the mother of many daughters, one of whom lay dying. In the frenzy of grief which seized her, the distracted mother called out: 'Dear God! Leave me *this* my daughter, and take unto Thyself all the others!' At which one of her sons-in-law, being present in the chamber, approached her, saying: 'Madam, are your daughters' husbands to be considered as one flesh and indivisible with your daughters in this matter?' This remark sent all those present into a fit of laughter, not excluding the dying girl.

This is a typical example of Gallic humour; the point is beautifully made. Yet, notwithstanding the solemnity of the hour, there is a manifest intent to please; the temptation to be amusing was well-nigh irresistible, nor was it resisted. In Italy, however, this same remark would have fired an outburst of indignation. The epigram, in Italy, is neither *light* nor *amusing*: rather is it pregnant with a boundless wealth of significance, as indeed among the Ancients. There was once a Florentine statesman, whose genius alone propped up the flagging strength of the republic, which, in that time, was threatened by the direst calamities. And in these circumstances, it fell out that an envoy must be found to fill an embassy of the utmost importance. Whereupon the Florentine cried out: *S' io vo, chi sta? S' io sto, chi va?* Among all the peoples of this modern era, none bears a closer resemblance to the Ancients than the people of Italy. Indeed, many customs and traditions may be observed, which have survived from an epoch *before* the Roman conquest. Compared with ourselves, Italy has received but a tolerably mild inoculation of feudalism; nor has she been grievously tainted with that sentiment which is the chief preoccupation of contemporary nations—indeed, their true and only religion— the false, monarchic cult of *honour*, which is a curious amalgam of *vanity* and *virtue* (that which is useful to the greatest number).

Some years ago it so befell that the most revered of scholars from the learned world of Paris was visiting the city of Naples. At that time, there was much discussion in polite society touching a certain Etruscan vase, of colossal dimensions and of wondrous craftmanship, that Prince Pignatelli had recently acquired by purchase. Our scholar, in the company of a certain Neapolitan gentleman, called to see the vase; but as it chanced, the Prince was absent from home, and it was an aged manservant who introduced the curious visitors into a low-ceilinged apartment, where, placed reverently upon a pedestal of wood, they discovered the ancient urn. The French antiquarian examined it minutely, admiring above all the exquisite subtlety of the design and the flowing elegance of the forms; and after a while, having taken out his note-book, he resolved to try and make copies of two or three groups of figures. For full three-quarters of an hour he stood there, plunged in a trance of admiration; eventually, however, he withdrew, not forgetting as he took his leave, to give the manservant an extremely generous tip. 'If Their Excellencies would be pleased to call again tomorrow, before the hour of noon', observed the retainer amid the profusion of his gratitude, 'the Prince himself will be at home, and Their Excellencies will be able to view the original.' In truth, the object which our scholar had so ecstatically been admiring was nothing but a copy made by some local craftsman. The *savant* begged his Neapolitan companion to say nothing of this misadventure, which, next day, was the talk of all the town. Were I so minded, I might even reveal the name of this illustrious man of learning*; for there are not a few persons who had direct acquaintance with the incident alive in Paris at the moment. Indeed, had I a truly malicious bent, I might quote further the 'discovery' (attributed to a Most Illustrious Personage*) of the pedestal of the famous *Column of Phocas* in Rome, which in point of fact already had been un-earthed in the year 1811 in course of the programme of restoration set afoot by the *Comptroller of Crown Property* in the city. But let us rather leave such anxious vanities in peace.

While I am on the subject of Etruscan vases, genuine or otherwise, I should mention that, being in Naples, I visited the *Museo degli Studj*, and saw the private collection which had once belonged to madame Murat. As soon as a vase shows traces of competent design, you may rest assured that it is a modern counterfeit . . . dear God! the *lies* that are published daily in the press! Some two years since, the Museum received an allocation of a thousand ducats to provide show-cases for the vases of this particular collection; to date, however, the Curator has managed to lay hands on no more than six hundred ducats of his allocation. The *abate* Taddei, of course, publishes this figure with a due number of noughts appended. Yet even so scrupulous a citizen as the *abate* Taddei *might* be lying . . . might he not? It is inexcusable of me, not to have mentioned earlier the draped figure of *Aristides* at the *Museo degli Studj*; but curiosity leads fatally to emotional exhaustion; and when finally the poor tourist returns to his lodgings, he is *dead*!

This *Aristides**, a truly admirable piece of sculpture, is an example of the revolt against idealism in art, like the bust of Vitellius which may be seen at Genoa. The hero has suspicions of a stomach; moreover, he is draped. Into the bargain, the poor fellow was so thoroughly roasted by the red-hot lava of Herculanum that his original marble is scarcely more than lime; he would crumble to dust at a touch. The statue is placed high up on a plinth. Now it was a recognised sport, among certain English tourists, after they had been well dined, to take a good run at the plinth, jump, and land on the top of it; yet the least slip in this exercise could have meant a hand placed on the statue to steady a failing balance . . . and there would have lain poor Aristides, all in powder. I learned later that this was a problem which much exercised the ingenuity of the Curators: for how should so delicate a matter of anxiety be broached in seemly fashion? Finally, someone had the happy inspiration to enquire at what hour these English gentlemen were wont to dine. Investigation revealed the fact that they were never drunk before two o'clock in the afternoon; consequently, the *Museo degli Studj* now shuts at two instead of four. I have fully satisfied myself of the truth of this curious circumstance; several keepers have shown me the edge of the plinth, some three foot off the ground, damaged by the impact of boots.

2nd July. It was chance, this morning, which led me into the society of don Nardo*, the most distinguished lawyer in Naples; as I was waiting in his antechamber, I observed a monstrous beeves'-horn, ten foot high if it was an inch, sticking perpendicularly out of the floor, like a gigantic nail. I can only suppose that it must have been put together out of three or four horns from less fabulous animals. Its purpose is to act as a sort of *lightning-conductor* against the *jettatura*—that is, against the 'evil eye'. 'I am perfectly well aware', said don Nardo, as I took my leave, 'of the absurdity of this superstition; yet what would you, all the same? Every lawyer is bound to make himself a pack of enemies; and so I find this object comforting.'

If there is one thing more fantastic still than this, it is surely the fact that there are people who actually believe that they possess the power to *cast* such spells. The Duke of Bisagno*— that *Great Poet*—was one day walking down the street. A peasant chanced to cross his path, bearing upon his head a large basket of strawberries. At the instant of meeting, the basket fell to the ground, and the strawberries began to roll about among the cobbles. The Duke, in great concern, ran over to the peasant: 'Good friend', he said, 'I swear to you I never looked at you!'

I was making a few irreverent remarks this very evening about the *jettatura* to a man of quite outstanding intellectual powers. 'Did you never read that book about the *jettatura* by Niccolò Volitta?' he enquired. 'Caesar, Cicero, Virgil . . . they all believed in it. Are such as these so greatly inferior in wisdom to ourselves?' Gradually, to my indescribable astonishment, it began to dawn upon me that this friend of mine *himself* believed in the *jettatura*. In fact, he presented me with a miniature beeves'-horn made of coral, which I now wear on my watch-chain. Whenever I find myself in fear of the evil eye, I am to twist it round and round between my fingers, taking care to point the sharp end in the direction of my enemy.

There was a merchant, a skeleton of a man with handsome, slightly Jewish eyes, who was recently come to Naples. Soon after his arrival, the Prince of *** invited him to dinner. Now, one of the Prince's sons saw fit to ask a certain *marchese* to sit beside our merchant at the table; and, when the meal was over, enquired of him:

'Well, and what did you make of your neighbour?'

'I?' asked the *marchese*, sorely puzzled. 'Why, nothing in particular.'

'I merely asked', said the Prince's son, 'because there are rumours that he is a bit of a *jettatore*.'

'Ah!' cried the *marchese*, growing pale upon the instant. 'What a disgraceful trick to play on me! But why couldn't you have warned me a moment earlier? I would have thrown my cup of coffee in his face!'

The secret consists in *breaking the column of air* which unites the eye of the necromancer to the object upon which it rests. This desired result may be obtained by throwing a quantity of liquid, although a gunshot is considered more effective still. It is by virtue of this same power of the *jettatura* that snakes and toads, merely by gazing fixedly at a bird singing away on the topmost branch of a tree, can cause it to fall from bough to bough, and so eventually to drop into the jaws of its waiting enemy. Take one large-sized toad and throw him into a jar filled with spirits of wine, where he will die, but with his eyes open. Now if, within the space of four-and-twenty hours following the creature's demise you look into these eyes, then the *jettatura* will be cast upon you, and you will fall to the ground in a dead faint. I offered to try out the experiment on myself, and was told for my pains that I was an *unbeliever*.

Here is a factual instance (*anno domini* 1824). Don Jo*, Curator of the Museum at P***, and moreover a man of considerable attainments, suffers from the imputation of being a *jettatore*. It was his longstanding desire to be granted an audience by the late King Ferdinand of Naples—an audience which this monarch, as may well be imagined, was a good deal more than loath to grant. At last, however, after some eight years of petitioning, the King yielded to the solicitations of don Jo's friends at Court, and agreed to receive the Curator of his own Royal Museum. The audience lasted some twenty minutes, during which time, from beginning to end, His Majesty was desperately ill at ease, incessantly manipulating between his fingers a miniature beeves'-horn made of coral. The following night, he was struck down by apoplexy.

I was told once, walking along the cliff-top at Dover, that a person of nervous temperament, standing on the very brink of a precipice, feels an irresistible temptation to jump into the abyss.

Belief in the *jettatura* is no less prevalent in Norway than in Naples. High praise for Francesco I, King of the Two Sicilies.

15th July. *Soirée* held by signora Tarchi-Sandrini at Portici. An enchanting drawing-room, not ten paces from the sea; between ourselves and the water, nothing but a little grove of orange-trees. Gentle lapping of the waves on the beach; view of Ischia across the bay; exquisite ices. I reached the house rather too early; consequently, witnessed the arrival of ten or a dozen women who appeared to be selected from among the most distinguished company of Naples. Signora Melfi has recently spent three years abroad, having followed her husband into exile; each year, she would pass the winter months in Paris; now she has returned, escorted by some twenty or thirty travelling-chests stuffed with the latest French fashions. Tonight, she soon found herself the centre of a ring of attentive listeners: 'A handsome young man', she was saying, 'and of the very *best* family, whispered this secret into my ear in Paris: *Since I ceased to dance, I find society less intolerably boring. The irksome weariness of inviting one's hostess to take the floor, of reserving a chair for sitting out, of manoeuvring for a partner—such vexing trifles would set my nerves on edge for a whole evening!*' How striking and how true a portrait of the web of civilisation in Paris: all genuine pleasure choked to death by the stifling restrictions of formality which society chooses to impose upon it.

'Whenever one of my acquaintance comes to call upon me', pursued signora *Melfi*, 'I can sense instantly whether his visit is dictated by *policy*, or whether simply by *brio*—in other words, because the notion chanced to jump into his head at the very instant when he was passing in the neighbourhood of my *palazzo*. Apparently this distinction—so vital, in all conscience —remains wholly invisible to those ladies who keep open house in Paris; no visitor ever crosses the threshold, save his presence is dictated by plan or policy. Formal visits, formal costume . . . behold the consequences of *severity*!'

'In England, education makes every man his neighbour's equal; the scion of a noble house has no resource, if he would set a distinction between himself and the son of plain Mr Coutts, save *affectation*. This unbecoming vice is shortly destined to overtake yourselves in France, for all that your asinine *liberal politicians* are so firmly persuaded that democratic government can breed naught but virtue and high-mindedness. I was saying one day to one of my more intimate acquaintance in Paris: *What a pretty sight, to be sure, are these boulevards of yours; and what extraordinary faces one may observe there!*

'*Yes indeed*, she replied, with an imperceptible echo of

the schoolma'am in her voice, *but of course it is not done to go walking there.*

'This remark was more than I could properly endure. *It is not done,* I burst out, *when what is done is done in imitation of someone else's doing. But you, my dear, are a daughter of a Peer of the Realm of France; you were born to the enjoyment of a splendid fortune; in you, therefore, I look to find that dauntless pride* which imitates no one. *If you are not the cynosure of the world, who then shall take your place? Some upstart creature with neither right nor title, save her own impertinence!*

'Dare one imagine, in days gone by, that the dashing duc de Bassompierre would have been concerned with the "slur" which might befall his noble reputation from walking in this direction rather than in that? To tell the truth, I seem to detect a touch of *parvenu* susceptibility about these modern proprieties. Bassompierre, faced with the doctrine that *it was not done* to go walking on the boulevard, would most assuredly have retorted: *I, sir, shall go where I please; and myself shall ennoble that place where I am!* It is fear of ridicule—*fear,* that ugliest of emotions —which steals away the youth of half the younger generation in Paris.

'I myself have seen a young man refuse to show himself at a concert—an admirable entertainment, given by all that was most fashionable in the operatic world that season, and in the programme of which, by a minor miracle, there was not a single thing of boredom—for no better reason than that he would be obliged to *be seen in company with all those appalling shopkeepers' wives from the rue Saint-Denis.* The very day following, I spoke to him: *Never dare pay your addresses to me again; in my eyes, you are ridiculous!* Queen Marie-Antoinette would drive out in a hired cab whenever the fancy took her; in those days', continued signora Melfi, turning on me, 'back in 1786, you used to know the meaning of laughter, and you had not yet learned to sell your souls. But six months ago, whenever I entered a drawing-room, and there discovered some two score gentlemen assembled, all from the very best families, I would say to myself: *Full six-and-thirty of those here present have sold their souls and consciences—or else are busy looking for a buyer. And these*, these *gentry, have the effrontery to sneer at us Italians and call us* vile! How admirable, how gentle and refined, is the tenor of life in Paris! The domestic *cat*, which, in London, is such a savage, spiteful brute, is a civilised and amiable creature when you meet her in the shops of Paris—a fact which speaks volumes in praise of your shop-girls. The mild and equable temper of the average Parisian *dog* is no less eloquent in respect of the *men* who are its masters.

'And what a fantastic deal of trouble you take to teach your sons the secrets of vanity, before you are so much as four years old! What affectation in their little dresses! In France, not twenty years from now, the *outward seeming* will have usurped the whole man. Already you are beginning to feel the harsh and frosty touch of *formality*: I foresee with deep dismay that you are destined to become as drab and melancholy as the English; even the simple act of blowing your nose will leave you constantly in *apprehension*, lest you be failing in some imperious *duty*.

'That above all which I admire in your *Jacobins* of the old stock, was precisely that they had minds above such trivialities; indeed, it was in order to uproot such unworthy preoccupations from the hearts of the younger generation that they invented the deliberately careless costume of a Marat. But your young men today appear forty before they are twenty. One might be led to suspect that they find all women hateful; their ambition, to judge by what they seem, lies towards the founding of a new religion. Similarly, I have the impression that your women, in the very flower of youth, experience a strange distaste for men: all of which would seem to herald a merry decade or so ahead!'

Signora B*** declared one day*: 'Music is incapable of portraying that sense of spiritual *aridity* which is the primary source of the prevailing atmosphere of *boredom* surrounding a Court. The only effective remedy for this distemper is *opera seria*, treated in the manner of Metastasio. The genius of Metastasio, no less than the music to which his words are set, endows the very cruellest of tyrants with feeling, and even with a touch of generosity. The courtier enjoys *opera seria*, because he is delighted that the public should be afforded a glimpse of his calling, seen in its most favourable light.'

'When first I arrived in Paris', asserted signora Melfi, 'one thing struck me most forcibly: whenever I was at a ball, I observed that *apprehension* caused the fingers of all the dancers to twitch convulsively. Never was there a sign, within a thousand miles, of those spontaneous high-spirits which are the natural prerogative of youth, nor even of simple enjoyment.'

'The irony of the situation', added Colonel T[ecco], 'is this: in French society, every individual consents to be a victim, in the hope that eventually others may lie at *his* mercy; for, after all, why else should a man abase himself before the fear of ridicule? Is ridicule a Minister of State, awarding honours, stars and decorations, and allotting pensions on the Civil List?'

'Nothing on earth', said don Francesco, 'is such anathema to the fashionable world of Paris as *energy*. This hatred hides its features behind a hundred different masks; none the less, you may rest assured that its presence is always felt, secretly dictating every movement of the heart.

'Energy may lead to unforeseeable situations; and in such emergencies, the man whose whole stock-in-trade is *vanity* may find himself left floundering. O shame unspeakable!'

'On one occasion', resumed signora Melfi, 'I was invited to make up a picnic excursion to the Spa at Enghien. One of the guests—a man of some intelligence, moreover—being piqued by jealousy, took a strange, perverted joy in deliberately throwing cold water over all the ingenious conversation and high spirits of his neighbours. Now that is something which we in Italy would never have endured. I was half-choked with fury; but in France, your women are such meek and mouse-like little creatures! They allowed this lunatic to have his own way; whereas I, at home, would have put him remorselessly in the place where he belonged, simply by picking upon one of his own inadmissible foibles and by taunting him without mercy until he fled the field. As it was, of course, our picnic went as merrily as a funeral bell.'

At this point, cutting short his wife's arraignment, don Francesco himself butted in on the conversation, exclaiming: 'And yet, in all the world, there is no *intellectual life*, save in Paris alone; only by living in Paris may a man enjoy the privilege of discovering, day in day out throughout the year, *some three or four completely new ideas;* and when at last I was forced to abandon Paris, I found that all else seemed stale and unprofitable. This special intellectual prerogative', he continued, turning to me, 'you owe, firstly to the fact of your geographical position, which is more central than that of London; and secondly, to the fact that you have no *Established Order* of things. What your ultimate destiny may be, I know not; Greeks or Helots? But such as you are in this present generation, never was there elsewhere under Heaven so rare and irresistible a mixture of reason, genius and generosity. Yet you are so easily swayed by circumstance, and so reverent in obeisance to the beck and call of fashion, that all this splendour of achievement hangs by a thread. It needs no more than that one of your legitimate sovereigns should prove to have inherited the genius of a Napoleon or the fascination of a François I, for you to resume that old condition of contented slavery, such as you accepted in 1680. Likewise it needs no more than that your younger generation should plunge a step or two deeper into the morasses of Teutonic mysticism, for France to fall headlong once more into that abyss of darkness which produced the *Colloquies of Poissy* and the *Massacre of St Bartholomew.*

'I have the impression', he continued, 'that you neglect your women, who endure and suffer all the miseries of boredom. But what would you, after all? *Such is the fashion!* It is *not done* to dream of overthrowing the tyranny of *écarté*; consequently, there they are, poor, lonely and unwanted creatures, and there they must stay, pining in solitude in a barren corner of the drawing-room.

'In 1785, when I was sent to Paris as ablegate of Pope Pius VI, I was desperately young. In those days, the life of a woman was a thing of wonder—a miracle of joy and vitality, of sweeping *élan* and ingenious delight; her whole existence seemed to me one constant round of madcap pleasures; and strangers came in crowds from Germany, from England, from every corner of the globe. Observe, however, that in 1785 the arts of amusement were still more grossly ill-developed in Germany and England than they are today.[1]

'But, ever since the days of Louis XIV, foreigners who know the land of France and ape its manners are invariably fifty years behind the times; and nowadays, when they sing the praises of fashionable Paris, their phrases still bear distant echoes of the eighteenth century, still reflect the admiration of the *marchese* Caraccioli, the Prince de Ligne or the *abbé* Galiani. Whereas, if the truth be told, your ancient gaiety is all undermined with *prudishness*; in 1785, the spirit of daring rode high above the fear of ridicule; but nowadays, from king to pastry-

---

1 No. This is untrue. London, having been cut off from the Continent of Europe for four-and-twenty years (1790-1814), has experienced during that time an intensification of the *principle of melancholy*. The aristocracy has learned the profoundest meaning of *fear*; it has both experienced and occasioned *hatred* (*cf.* the *Life of Bage*, by Sir Walter Scott). The superstition that Napoleon was an ogre who ate little children and who had never learned his alphabet has done serious damage to the cause of enlightenment, and consequently to the prospects of human happiness. Burke used to flatter the credulity of his aristocratic audience by declaring that in France, the narrow space left free between the guillotine and the populace was hired out to a mountebank, who used to entertain the mob with performing dogs on execution-days. [1826]

cook, the whole of France is *petrified*.'

Signora Melfi, who has left behind her some three or four intimate acquaintance in Paris, was determined to find an excuse for that drab spirit of *Methodism* which prevails in our present day and age among the younger women, and which deprives us of all that fabulous wealth of gallant anecdotes which used to be the common fashion in 1790.

'Madam', I replied, 'you seem to suppose that a woman is dismayed, lest some word uttered with over-much licence should shock the code of moral principles by which she would fain abide. Ah, how sadly you fall short of the mark! Her dismay springs rather from the duty which constrains her, after you have spoken, to sit in drab and melancholy silence, and so to give the impression—albeit momentarily—that she is too dull-witted to have grasped the point.'

'Paris', broke in don Francesco, 'is the only city in the world where a man may *live*. Elsewhere, he *vegetates*.'

'Precisely', retorted the Princess, 'a *man* may live—a *man*, whose staple fare is politics and intellectual novelty.'

'Nevertheless', protested Monsignor Cerbelli, 'in Italy, amongst ourselves, for all the fatal dearth of political opinion, you may yet discover the pure delights of art.'

'That is as though you should propose that I should dine off naught but coffee and water-ices', retorted don Francesco. 'The *essential* element of life is liberty and the security of the individual; art, in this nineteenth century of ours, is nothing but an inferior substitute. In Paris, the most reactionary book that was ever published finds readers, because the author is *forced* to accept certain general truths which, here in Italy, the most liberal and advanced of writers would scarcely dare envisage. If an author is to escape the gallows, he must enshroud these maxims in so thick a wrapping of dubitative forms that he has no chance to develop their subtler shades of meaning; consequently, I, the reader, am bored. The era of art and poetry has vanished for ever, because the habit of argument with an ideological opponent robs our imagination of the power to float away upon the airy currents of flattering illusion. If you would have proof of this assertion, do but consider the features —somewhat commonplace, no doubt, but comfortably re-assuring, of that hero of the nineteenth century, the Duke of Well***ton. We are no longer fortunate enough to afford to seek for *beauty*; for the present, we must confine our ambitions to *utility*. Society is destined henceforward to pass I know not how many centuries *in pursuit of the useful*.

'Paris is a generation ahead of every other community in Europe, touching the generosity and the sophistication of its inhabitants: all human thought must acknowledge Paris as its capital, for the philosophers who dwell within her gates have far outdistanced those of England—compare, for instance, two daily newspapers, *le Constitutionnel* in France and the *Morning Chronicle* in England. What, then, is missing from this fair city of Paris? Painters, poets, sculptors? And are *we* today in Italy any better provided?'

'None the less', protested Colonel T[ecco], 'those Paris *salons*, with their cheerless prudery, their eternal parties of *écarté* . . . !'

'Why then, my dear friend, we must take care ever to collect about us in Paris a sufficient number of Spaniards and Italians, that we may spend the evenings in our own company.'

'Should we not rather suppose this dispiriting cheerlessness', enquired signora Bel[monte], 'to be the necessary price and consequence of liberty? Consider the drawing-rooms of England or America . . .'

'Yet both those countries endure the hardships of a northern climate', replied don Francesco. 'Who knows, but that the *salons* of Mexico or Lima might be merry as fair-grounds?'

Here D***, that confirmed misanthropist, took up the thread of conversation with his habitual severity:

'The coddling, milk-and-water education which is given to children in France deprives the coming generation of every experience of *risk* or *suffering*. The science of rearing children, as it is conceived in Paris, is specifically calculated to annihilate the faintest trace of *will-power*; which, in the last resort, is nothing but the courage to expose one's person to the threat of danger. Indeed, whenever I call to mind the mildness of government in France, which, in Paris at least, is so moderate as to pass almost wholly unperceived, then I revere and venerate the persecutions to which young people are exposed in Milan or Modena; for it is tyrannies such as these which are destined to preserve our superiority in the field of *strength of character*. What prodigy of nature bestowed on us those great men of the fourteenth century, if not the dangers of the century preceding*?'

20th July. This evening, following a most solemn oath that I would forever hold my tongue, I was allowed to witness a performance of *satirical marionettes*. Since I have been here, I have renewed my acquaintance with a certain Neapolitan family—our friendship is a longstanding affair—whose members, despite their outward and apparent caution, are in reality highly intelligent individuals, ready with laughter to turn against all that deserves contempt, and bursting with merriment. As a consequence of the trust which is placed in my discretion, I was admitted to witness a satirical comedy, much after the taste of Machiavelli's *Mandragola*, performed by marionettes. The play reminded me, even in its opening scenes, of Collé's delicious 'Proverb', *la Vérité dans le Vin*. Yet this Italian version had qualities of dynamism, of dramatic intensity and of burlesque energy, together with a contempt for stylistic niceties and a deep respect for revealing and characteristic situations which far transcended those witty, ingenious, but somewhat frigid little comedies of Collé and Carmontelle.

Yesterday's farce* was entitled: *Si farà sì o no un segretario di stato?*

The leading part is filled by no less distinguished a personage than H*s H*l*n*ss himself, who entertains no excessive fondness for his Cardinal-Minister, one *don Cecchino**, an ancient dotard of eighty-two, who was, in former times, a most ingenious libertine and a mighty don Juan among the ladies. But now, in his senility, his wits are almost wholly gone a-wandering—a lapse from grace which leads to no dearth of singular imbroglios in the responsible office of Cardinal-Minister-of-State. There is one scene which is a delightful invention, a miracle of truth and comedy alike. Don Cecchino grants simultaneous audience to three suitors, a priest, a cattle-dealer and the brother of a *carbonaro*, each one of whom has presented a different petition: and the Minister, in his replies, persistently confounds the three. His embarrassment, when he realises full well that he has forgotten the ubstance of each request and yet is adamant to insist that he remembers perfectly, is truly comic. His Excellency speaks sternly to the cattle-dealer of his brother, who, having conspired against the safety of the state, now expiates his crime by merited confinement in a dungeon-cell; and expounds to the unhappy brother the objections which must be raised against the project of allowing into the Kingdom two hundred head of cattle imported from the Papal State. This is an invention which Molière himself might have acknowledged without misgivings; yet it possessed for us tonight an added merit, which even Molière cannot command. For, while we sat and watched this scene, and marvelled at the marionettes by which it was acted, there was not one among us but was fully aware that a similar circum-stance, not one whit less fantastic in its details, was being enacted in that very hour scarce two hundred paces distant from the drawing-room where we were assembled, the tears of laughter coursing down our cheeks. It is indeed a rigorous principle among my new-discovered friends of the marionette-theatre, never to stage a single situation unless it be modelled upon an actual event, witnessed and vouched for by the whole of society. In truth, as we sat and gazed at that little mannikin, no more than a dozen inches high, yet dressed exactly in the costume of His Excellency the Cardinal-Minister, to whom we, one and all, that very morning, had paid our due and humble respects, the laughter which possessed us welled up with such volcanic, subterranean force, that three times in succession there was no help for it but to stop the play. I am persuaded, moreover, that the very element of *danger* which attends this innocent diversion in no little degree contributed to its fascination. The whole audience numbered no more than eighteen persons, all of rank and quality: similarly, the marionette-parts are spoken by actors of no less elevated station.

The skeletal structure (*l'ossatura*) of this comedy was put together by a most ingenious little cleric, who, I suspected, is the *cavaliere servente* of one of the ladies of the household. Now, no cleric in Italy can ever forget, not so much as for an instant, that one day fortune may perform a miracle in his favour and bestow a Cardinal's Hat upon his humble person.

I discovered that the *ossatura* of the comedy proposed is always agreed upon in advance by the various actors among themselves, or rather, to be more precise, by the divers persons who are to lend their voices to the marionettes. This 'rough draft' of the action is written out on a sheet of paper, and affixed to a desk in the wings of the theatre, with a pair of candles to shed sufficient light. There are as many actors assembled in the wings, each one lending his voice to a given marionette, as there are characters in the drama. The actress who speaks the *ingénue* parts is always young herself. This improvised dialogue between the marionettes is delightfully natural, and rich with the most telling inflexions. Since the actors have no cause to concern themselves either with gesture or with facial expression, they speak their lines far more effectively than if they themselves were on the stage.

The value of this special quality of speech shows most clearly in the performance of satirical comedies, such as that which I have just now witnessed, whose cast included His Excellency the Cardinal-Minister; the noted banker Torlonia, Duke of Bracciano; the Ambassador of a Major Power; and divers other eminent personalities. The company of young actors who bestowed upon them their respective voices, and who, either that same morning or else the day before, had actually seen them in the flesh, contrived so perfect an imitation of their various accents and intellectual mannerisms that the spectator might well confess himself deceived and die with laughing. I further confirmed what I had already suspected: namely, that three or four among the audience had spent the earlier part of the evening actually in the presence of those same Eminent Personalities whom they were destined, by a most delicious twist of circumstances, to encounter once again upon the stage before the night was out. Might not this type of entertainment be imported into Paris? Provided that those responsible have wit enough to avoid the wearisome faults of gross libel and over-venomous satire, and to remain within the bounds of innocent merriment, natural probability, comic invention and good taste, this pastime (such, at least, is my private opinion) affords one of the most intoxicating pleasures that may be enjoyed in a despotic state.

MOLA DI GAETA, 25th July. Several young *signore* among my acquaintance are bound for Rome, to grace with their presence the magnificent ceremony of the *Assumption* which is due to be celebrated a few days from now. I have more or less seen what there is to see in Naples; not, however, without a few uneasy glances in the direction of the police. I am informed that a certain individual, bearing a name not unlike my own, once held office under Murat. In consequence of all this, yesterday evening, towards nine o'clock, I slipped out of the city. I would have preferred to follow the road through Aquino and Frosinone—a route which is extremely picturesque; but I will risk my footsteps in that direction some other time, when I am armed with a valid passport.

ROME, 1st August. I have just returned from the famous *Sistine Chapel* after hearing the Papal Mass, for which I had managed to secure myself the best place available, on the right, just behind Cardinal Consalvi; and I may now claim to have heard the celebrated *castrati* of the Sistine choir. No, forsooth! Never did I, in all my days, endure so dæmonic a caterwauling! This was the most excruciating cacophony I have encountered hese ten years. During the whole space of two hours that the Mass lasted, I spent full ninety minutes in unbelieving astonishment, feeling my pulse, examining whether I were not sick of some disease, enquiring of my neighbours' reactions. Unhappily, however, these neighbours of mine were English tourists—folk for whom *fashion* is a most implacable master: they replied to my puzzlement by quoting passages of Burney.

My mind being fully made up concerning the music, I found delight and compensation in the manly beauty of the ceiling and in Michelangelo's *Last Judgment**; meanwhile, I studied the features of divers Cardinals. One and all, they are simple-souled priests from country parishes: indeed, Cardinal Consalvi, the chiefest Officer of State, has been at some pains to exclude from his *entourage* any man capable of usurping his own position. Not a few show traces of ill-health; here and there I caught a hint of disdain in these ecclesiastical faces. No mortal man, at the age of fifty, could rejoice in a more handsome aspect than that of Cardinal Consalvi. From the evidence of his place in the Sistine Chapel, I concluded that he has never been ordained priest, but merely deacon. *Cf.* the excellent painting by M. Ingres.

8th August. Having scraped acquaintance with a pair of artists from Bologna, I persuaded them to escort me to the Sistine Chapel. I managed to convince them that it was they who were doing me the honours of the place. My reaction to that concert of saw-voiced capons was in no way improved. My companions, *with considerable reluctance*, were eventually brought to agree with me; but they begged me to reserve my final opinion until the ceremonies of Holy Week. But I, upon my honour, do verily begin to suspect that the adjourned hearing of the matter will perforce take place in my absence*. No mortal man who had an ear for music, or who, were it but once in all his life, had learned to hit a note, could endure the torture of listening to himself and others bellowing away at the top of their bent and stripping the lining off their own ear-drums. But Rome is a curious place: the Romans, having nothing under Heaven to occupy their minds, employ their idle hours in making art a thing of rivalries and petty factions. I have heard it seriously maintained, and by persons by no means devoid of intelligence, that such and such a miserable dauber, less competent even than our own variety of the species, is a *notable artist*—simply for his having been born in Rome. When art is bad, the critic cannot be too harsh; mediocrity deserves neither charity nor compassion, for nothing places our feeling for beauty in such immediate peril as the *second-rate*.

14th August. At last! I have unearthed some individuals with a scrap of sense! Not among the Romans, of course; but among the foreign envoys. *Their* opinion coincides exactly with my own. *Among any nation*, Herr M*** confided to me in German, *it is the mark of a fool to embroil himself beyond redemption in the cobweb-mesh of opinion spun by fashionable travellers, and to admire what others have admired before him.* He favoured me with a personal introduction to signor N***, the lawyer: in Rome, the *Gown* alone holds promise of a cultured mind, for the Roman aristocracy is moronic beyond reach of comparison. Here, at his apartments, I heard some excellent music; also I found a company assembled, conversing with a show of genuine erudition and right reason—at least until that fatal hour when *Patriotic Sentiment* seized them by the throat. In Italy, music is a topic accessible to the meanest intelligence; just as, in Paris, everyone has his opinions touching Racine and

Voltaire. Withdrawn into a corner of the room, I derived much pleasure from arguing with a great stout fellow, who taught me much that I did not know: later I discovered him to be a tailor who had made a fortune. Here in Rome, many young men are uncommonly fat.

15th August.   I have just been witness to the proud ceremony at St Peter's; everything a wealth of solemn splendour, save the music. The sight of that venerable Pontiff, clad all in white silk, borne upon a sedilia which was given him as an offering by the Genoese, and distributing blessings within the precincts of that Sublime Temple—this constitutes one of the most impressive spectacles I have ever seen. The seat I had procured lay at the foot of a stand or amphitheatre built of planks, rising up at the spectator's right hand, and occupied by some two hundred ladies. This number included two fair creatures from Rome itself, five from Germany and one hundred and ninety from England. In all the remaining area of the church, there was not a soul to be seen, save only some five or six score peasants, of horrifying aspect. I am indeed making an *English Journey*, without ever setting foot beyond the bounds of Italy. The larger proportion of these ladies were so overwhelmed by the beauty of the ceremony that their sensibility was only with difficulty made aware of the absurdity of that flock of *Sacred Capons* screeching their heads off in some hidden hen-house. A similar concealment is effected in the Sistine Chapel. In theory, I imagine, they are supposed to do no more than reinforce the chanting of the officiating priesthood.

18th August.   I have just beheld one of the most sublime, most moving sights that I have ever encountered in all my life. From the depths of St Peter's there emerged the Sovereign Pontiff, borne aloft upon an immense dais by his acolytes,

kneeling, that all might see, before the Blessed Sacrament. By
a stroke of fortune, the day was not too hot; we were favoured
by what is known locally as *una giornata ventillata*. From the
crack of dawn, the avenues leading to St Peter's Square had
been swept and sanded, the houses hung about with emblazoned
banners; such festive preparations may be seen in any city in
the world; but the sight which may be witnessed nowhere else,
save only here in Rome, is that obsessive multitude of faces,
stamped with the profound belief that the Pontiff who is
destined shortly to appear is the sovereign arbiter of their
eternal felicity or damnation. Seats and raised stands had been
set up, running the whole length of the two vast colonnaded
galleries which surrounded the *piazza*. From soon after sunrise,
there was a frenzied bargaining for the places of best vantage,
at which sport the most elegant of toilets might be observed in
contest with the most primitive apparel; for the untutored
peasant from the Abruzzi, provided that he can but muster the
sum of two *carlins* in his pocket, may find himself seated hard
beside some haughty and powerful Roman Prince; and indeed
here, in these native haunts of *equality*, money is the only
aristocracy whose privilege is recognised and valid. Whereas in
England once, watching the populace assemble to a meeting,
at which no less a man than Cobbett was to deliver an address,
I observed that the common folk had not the courage to climb
up and seat themselves aboard the farm-carts which had been
bringing produce in to market. It was an English cobbler who
explained to me, with profound respect: 'Those places, sir, are
reserved for the *gentry*.'

However, to return to myself, now seated most commod-
iously in the foremost row of all, here is the sight which I
beheld: upon a causeway, well-sanded and strewn with leaves
of laurel, there appeared first in solemn procession some five
or six *Orders* of Friars—grey Friars, white Friars, brown Friars,
black Friars, piebald, skewbald, particoloured Friars, Friars, in
a word, of every hue and complexion—their outstretched

hands equipped with monstrous torches, their downcast eyes fixed slantwise at the ground, their voices braying out unintelligible hymns. It was plainly their intent to catch the attention of the multitude by the abject humility of their gait; which purpose was constantly rendered null and void by the strong contempt which flashed out from their eyes. Next in order came the regular clergy of the seven great Basilicas, divided into seven distinct bodies by immense banners of scarlet and yellow, half-extended, borne aloft by acolytes clad in white; and each of these banners, of wholly oriental aspect, was preceded by a weird and wondrous instrument surmounted by a bell, from which, at regular minute-intervals, there was extracted a high and solitary note. Last of all appeared the highest dignitaries of the Church, together with the Cardinals, their heads enshrouded in their pointed albs. Then, all at once, the multitude made genuflexion; and there, mounted upon his advancing dais swathed in draperies fashioned of the richest and rarest stuffs, I beheld a figure, pale, inanimate and proud, likewise shrouded in vestments reaching high above the shoulders—a figure which seemed to me to merge into a single entity, a *Whole*, one and indivisible, together with the Altar, the swaying dais and the golden sun, before whose orb the figure was bowed down, as though in adoration. 'You never told me that the Pope was dead', complained a child who stood beside me to its mother. And no words can better convey the utter and motionless fixity of this unearthly apparition. At that instant, amongst the whole multitude which encompassed me on every side, there was not a single unbeliever; and even I was to be numbered among the faithful, if beauty may be counted a religion. The attitude adopted by the Pope is determined by tradition; nevertheless, since such a pose might prove distinctly uncomfortable for a man of advanced years and often of many infirmities, the draperies are so disposed that His Holiness may be seen to rest upon his knees, whilst in reality he is comfortably seated in an armchair.

25th August. An enchanting ball, held at the residence of an English lady in Rome. One of the most distinguished *Liberals* in the city drew me aside at one point during the evening, to observe:

'There is a book, sir, a book which is sublime, a book as I can judge, between whose pages there lies enfolded the ultimate happiness of all Princes and all peoples. The title of this book, sir? Why, *Chalmers' Dictionary*!*'

Such a remark is typical of the intellectual level I have met with at every turn, once south of Bologna. Yet genius— Alfieri, Canova—has the power to pierce the thickest walls, and even so gross a crust of ignorance as this. Not that even they are innocent, by any means, of a lingering taint of prejudice. In England, a man may be half a moron and still write a passable book. Here, a man of outstanding ability, such as Foscolo, can find no more profitable pastime than to compose a Latin pamphlet to confound his enemies.[1] Miss Julia G***: a striking pair of eyes.

26th August. Today I was taken to see the Church of the Company of Jesus, hard by the *Palazzo Venezia*. I am by no means insensitive to that feeling of *respect* to which the very sight of *power*, however unscrupulous, may give rise, when it has accomplished notable things. The church was filled with a most blackguardly set of cut-throats; as a precaution, we removed our watches, and had them carried back to the hotel. Doubtful taste shown by the Président de Brosses, in the passage where he contorts himself into ecstasies of admiration before the altar of St Ignatius Loyola. The bathos and the absurdity of this piece of stone-carving are unbelievable; indeed, it is the very incarnation of ignominy, carried to such a pitch of bad

---

1 *Didymi clerici Epistolæ*, Lugano 1816. Foscolo, the finest poetic talent in Italy after Monti and Manzoni, is the author of *i Sepolcri* and *Ajace*. Like Monti, his thought is paltry stuff, but his handling of the language of poetry is masterly. [1817]

taste, that I would not care to assert in what particulars its infamy resides; however, in France, in 1740 or thereabouts, taste in the arts had fallen into such a slough of barbarism that all things may be excused in an author who otherwise gave proof of such perceptive intelligence. Finally, the music began: divers organs, set in various corners of the church, made up a pattern of responses. The effect was decidedly agreeable; but here, as elsewhere, the performer abused the rich resources of his instrument. I have heard the same sort of thing a thousand times better done in Germany; yet, for all that, I spent two hours in a distinctly pleasurable frame of mind. Wonder of wonders! I observed two English visitors, who appeared to be *genuinely moved*! We watched the arrival of some eight or ten Cardinals who are well-disposed towards the Company of Jesus. Nowhere does this celebrated Order have more powerful enemies to contend with than here in Rome: Dominicans and Capuchins are implacable in the rage of their hearts. Cardinals welcomed with full military honours. Impressive bearing of the Roman soldiery. Convincing evidence of the intractable brutality of the mob, in that each side-chapel is guarded by a sentinel with fixed bayonet, while, in addition, further sentries patrol up and down the nave, among the kneeling congregation. A revealing touch, this last, here at the very source and centre of a religion whose claim it is to restrain mankind within the bounds of duty by spiritual laws alone, that one should be made conscious of the need for bayonets in spite of all—a need both more imperative and more apparent here than in Paris, where (so they tell us) we are *naught but pagan infidels*! I could hear these troops, newly-returned from France and still clad in the glorious uniform of the French army, intoning the Psalm *sotto voce* in unison with the populace. Would that Rome might but fashion herself a passable code of morals!—then should she be once again the metropolis of art. The singing of the congregation was excellent. Here in Rome, music and love are the staple topics of conversation, for a Duchess neither more nor less than for the wife of the humble barber who dresses her hair; nor—supposing the latter to be a creature of moderate intelligence—is the difference so great between the two extremes: the reason being, that while there may be *distinction of fortune*, there are no *distinctions of manners*. All Italians talk about the same things, each at the level of his own particular development: this is one of the most striking features of the prevailing moral climate south of the Alps—the conversation of His Highest and Mightiest Lordship in the land is fundamentally identical with that of the lackey who waits upon his person.

29th August. I am now the proud possessor of a box at the *teatro Argentina*. Yet all my machinations were so much wasted effort. The current production consists of Rossini's *Tancredi*. As a performance, it would have been hunted off the stage in Brescia or Bologna. The orchestra is even more dismal than the singers: but the dancing has to be seen to be believed! This same ballet-company which now affords the wonder and delight of Rome, was barely tolerated on the stage some six months since, in Varese, an insignificant little township in Lombardy.

It is the custom here for every patron to decorate his box according to his own peculiar fancy: one may observe curtains looped and tasselled as for a window in Paris, and balconies tricked out in silks, velvets or muslins; some of these inventions are absurd to a degree, but there is pleasure to be had in the very variety. In three or four instances, I perceived draperies so disposed as to suggest to the distant beholder the form of a *crown*; and upon enquiring, I received the explanation that this strange artifice affords a sort of consolation to the vanity of certain still-crowned but desperately impoverished heads, whose owners continue to eke out their declining years in Rome. Here, all is decadence, all is memory, all is dead. On days when the sweetness of nostalgia haunts my soul, then would I rather live my life in Rome: but the atmosphere of the city tends to steal away the strength of the spirit, plunging the mind into a sort of languid torpor; effort is unknown, energy is without purpose, nothing moves with haste. The most electrifying piece of news that Rome may hear is that Camuccini* has just put the finishing touches to a new painting. I called to inspect this *Morte de Cesare*: poor stuff, a feeble imitation of David. God in Heaven! I would rather choose the North with its vitality, despite the unspeakable horrors of its architecture.

Yet, truth to tell, the *ideal* existence would consist of an active daily life, alternating with intervals of leisure to enjoy that unique and wondrous richness of sensibility which is conjured into being beneath the peerless skies of Rome.

The straw which breaks the camel's back (as far as my own bad temper is concerned) is this: that on every occasion when I have ventured to call upon acquaintance in a nearby box, I have found my neighbours one and all in high delight with this nauseating performance. Roman vanity can scale quite unexpected heights of absurdity; this evening, for instance, I caught the phrase: *Quel cantar è degno di una Roma!*—which is the special, bombastic way a Roman loves to allude to his native city; no other form of speech is ever used. The aspect of such utter degradation caused me to grind my teeth, and I withdrew. Back at my inn, I began to hunt through my belongings to discover a volume of Montesquieu—finally I recalled that, only yesterday, I had had it confiscated at the customs, on the grounds that this was an author who was *most rigorously banned*. At length, from a hidden corner of my escritoire, I routed out a copy in 32° of the *Grandeur des Romains*. I read a few chapters; it was my pleasure deliberately to increase the foul and atrabiliar humour which possessed me. Towards two in the morning, I found myself in so abominably black a frame of mind that none could match my mood save Alfieri. I therefore read *Don Garcia* from cover to cover with the liveliest satisfaction: for there may scarce be four occasions in the year when I find Alfieri congenial to my temper.

Signor Nystrom, a man of penetrating mind and an architect of the highest promise, was good enough to accompany me on a visit to the *piazza* which encloses *Trajan's Column*. The Emperor Trajan raised this column in an extremely narrow kind of courtyard, hard by a basilica. The remarkable programme of public works, carried out between 1810 and 1814 by M[artial Daru], Comptroller of Crown Property in Rome, will have left traces more clearly visible to posterity than all the labours of a dozen pontificates, not excepting the most industrious. Napoleon set aside the sum of ten million francs for improving the beauties of the city. It was his eventual intention to have removed the whole of that twelve-foot layer of earth which ruins the appearance of the Forum.

30th August. Tonight, intent on visiting the *teatro Valle*, I arrived too early for the performance; there was no urgency, for all the seats in the pit are numbered; unless one is in the first few rows, not a word can be heard from the stage. To while away the time, I began to read the *Police Regulations*. How well this government understands the temper of its subjects; these regulations are *draconian*! A hundred strokes, to be administered forthwith upon the scaffold which stands in permanent readiness in the *piazza Navona*, with torch ever-burning and a guard on constant duty, for any spectator who wilfully usurps another's seat; *five years in the galleys* for any spectator who raises his voice against the usher (*la maschera*) of the playhouse—the official responsible for allotting the various places. All sentences to be passed *ex inquisitione*—i.e., according to those mild and magnanimous forms of procedure established by the Holy Inquisition. Everything that I myself have observed touching this audience—its total lack of any sense of politeness, honour or consideration, its haughty insolence contrasted with its cringing degradation once that insolence is rebuffed— all this affords me proof and confirmation of the statement made yesterday by signora R*** in my presence, to the effect that

Q

Tiberio Pacca, the present Governor of Rome, is an extremely capable official who needs no one to teach him his trade. I am resolved to have a copy of these *Regulations*, which are of his own devising: thus they may constitute part of the documentary evidence of this my *Journey*, in case I be accused of painting too libellously black a picture of the rule of ecclesiastical despotism.

After a seemingly endless delay, the music began: the opera in question was perpetrated by one Romani, who styles himself on the playbills: *Figlio di questa gran Roma*. As a composer, he is indeed worthy of the land which gave him birth: his music is nothing more than an undisguised *pastiche* of Cimarosa; and for this reason alone, despite its utter lack of inspiration, I found it not entirely disagreeable.

The *prima donna* of the *teatro Valle* turned out to be that same signora Giorgi whom I had already encountered in Florence; Rossini's music suited her better; here, she is nothing but a pale reflection of la Malanotte. The company includes a *buffo* of the old school, who disdains the current airs and graces of the trade, and who knows how to make his audience laugh; but alas! he is already getting on in years.

The libretto is a translation of Marivaux' *le Jeu de l'Amour et du Hasard*. The translator has added, of his own responsibility, a fine spate of slapstick cudgellings and a village bailiff, who, with the aid of a *Rhyming Dictionary*, composes a harangue for his master's delectation. We are all agreed, and have been so for some considerable while, that music cannot portray *wit;* for music is obliged to make her statements *slowly*, whereas the degree of speed with which a verbal retort is made in almost every instance *adds something to the literal meaning of the words*. The province of music is the portrayal of emotion; or rather, of one particular emotion, which is love.

Ever since the days of Mozart and Haydn, it has become fashionable for the melody to portray one shade of passion, while the orchestra depicts a wholly different set of sentimental *nuances*—*nuances* which, by some mysterious alchemy which I fail to understand, come imperceptibly within our souls to merge with the portrait of the dominant emotion. Composers such as Mayr, Winter, Weigl and Cherubini, having lost the art of handling the major element, have concentrated with exaggerated attention upon the accessory factor; yet even today, in spite of this discovery, music remains still obdurately hostile to *wit*.

1st September.   A second visit to the *teatro Valle*.

People who are perfectly happy, likewise people who are utterly insensitive, must of necessity find music an unendurable boredom: here we have the two reasons how it came about that the *salons* of Paris, in 1779, were so recalcitrant to this particular art. Mozart did well to shake the dust of France from off his heels; and indeed, were it not for *la Nouvelle Héloïse*, even Rousseau's *Devin du Village* was destined to be a catastrophic failure*.

Why is it, then, that he who is acquainted with sorrow may discover pleasure in the sound of music sung by the human voice? The answer is, that by some obscure process, and in a manner which offers no insult to the susceptibilities of pride, this art persuades us of the existence of *pity* among men: it transforms the sufferer's *arid despair* into the sweeter pangs of *regret*; it draws forth tears from his withered heart; but its powers of consolation extend no further than this. To gentler spirits, pining for the loss of some beloved object, it can bring nought but harm, hastening, by its insidious mockery, that slow consumption by which they are destroyed*.

21st September.   I have now spent fifty days in mingled awe and indignation. Why, what a thing of splendour were this site of Ancient Rome, had not her fatal star decreed, as crowning outrage, that the *Priests* should build their new metropolis upon the very ruins of the old! What glory might our eyes not still behold, were all those ancient stones—the *Colosseum*, the *Pantheon*, the *Antonine Basilica*, together with that fabulous wealth of monuments, now rased to the ground that *churches* might be built instead—still proudly standing within their ring of deserted hills, the *Aventine*, the *Quirinal*, the *Mons Palatinus*. O fortunate city of Palmyra!

With the solitary exception of St Peter's, nothing could be drearier than the architecture of modern Rome, unless it be the sculpture. This remark puts me in mind of Canova, who alone transcends the general mediocrity. He is at present engaged in peopling the Pantheon—that spot so dear to all those spirits who have hearkened to the call of Beauty, on account of the presence there of great Raphael's tomb—with the busts of divers artists of renown. Sooner or later, this edifice is destined to lose the name of *Church*, which title, in days gone by, preserved it from the destructive genius of Christianity; then it will become the sublimest of museums. The larger number of those busts which Canova has ordered for this purpose show little trace of art: one alone is the child of his own genius, and upon its base is carved the following inscription:

> A DOMENICO CIMAROSA
> ERCOLE CARDINALE CONSALVI,
> *1816*.[1]

In France, can you conceive the wailing and the lamentation with which our *Outraged Decency* would welcome such an

[1] Report of an incident which occurred in 1823 or thereabouts: a certain political party having gained the ascendancy, every one of these busts was exiled into a cluster of cramped and ill-lit chambers in the Capitol.

The tomb of Raphael, a monument which had been raised to the memory of this great man immediately after his death (1520), and upon which Cardinal Bembo had caused to be inscribed this noble couplet:

> *Ille hic est Raphael, timuit quo sospite vinci*
> *Rerum magna parens et moriente mori,*

was decorated with his effigy. This tomb was ruthlessly mutilated, and the bust relegated to the Capitol. [1826]

inscription? I am no longer at a loss to explain that secret
sympathy which has always warmed my heart towards
Cardinal Consalvi. He is the foremost statesman in Europe, for
the simple reason that he is the only honest man among the
pack of them. (It goes without saying that I make a formal
exception, covering all statesmen in all countries where this
volume may happen to appear.)

This rarest of individuals is roundly detested by every one of
his three-and-thirty colleagues-in-office. His projects are
ruthlessly cut about; he is constrained to abandon all the details
of execution to the eager grasp of incompetent fools: hence the
confiscation of my Montesquieu. The only way in which he
might effectively prepare to clean out the Augean stables is by
founding a *Polytechnic College*; and this means is denied him.

Glancing through my diary, I discover a score and more of
anecdotes concerning this remarkable statesman, not one of
which but redounds heartily to his credit. He is simple, sensible,
obliging; and to crown all—a virtue which must appear all but
incredible in France—*he is not a hypocrite*.

24th September.   Not in the healthy oyster, but rather in the
sick, does the fisherman seek for pearls. Ever since that day
when humanity turned its footsteps towards the goal of
democratic government, I have learned to despair of art; for in no
circumstances imaginable could it be deemed anything but a
rank absurdity to build so vain an edifice as St Peter's. Were
there not a score of ways, each a hundred times more *useful*, in
which to spend five hundred millions? Were there not two
hundred thousand starving wretches with needs to be satisfied,
was there not still full half of the Roman Campagna to be
brought under cultivation, were there not heirloom estates to
be purchased from eight or ten patrician families in Rome, and
subsequently to be shared out among two hundred thousand
peasants, for whom a single field would have proved inducement enough to make them husbandmen instead of brigands?

Towards the year 1730, the Papal Government, by what chance I no longer recall, found itself with a million to spend on what it pleased. Wherein lay the greater profit to mankind: to build the façade of *San Giovanni Laterano*, or to construct a set of quays beside the Tiber, from the *Porta del Popolo* to the *Ponte Sant' Angelo*?

The façade, as it stands, is a monstrous absurdity: but this is largely beside the point. The Pope voted for the façade; and Rome still lives in expectation of its river-front, which might perhaps help to stem the ravages of that malarial distemper which annually battens upon these sections of the city, from the first warm days of May until the first rains in October. Would you believe me, gentle reader, were I to tell you that, on the *Corso*, hard by *San Carlo Borromeo*, I was shown the very house, beyond which limit the fever has never been known to advance? This year, the drug *kinine* is working wonders. A distinguished apothecary, signor Manni, has learned to manufacture it as well as it is prepared in Paris.

A remark which was made to me yesterday: 'Is it not a monstrous shame, that François I did not oblige the Realm of France to turn Protestant?'

The answer which I made profoundly scandalised my would-be philosopher: 'Such an event had proved no less than a catastrophe for all mankind; we should have grown as melancholy and as reasonable as the worthy citizens of Geneva. Then farewell, *les Lettres persanes*! Farewell, Voltaire! Above all, farewell, Beaumarchais! Did you ever stop an instant to consider, what must be the total sum of happiness that dwells in a race, when high and low alike are busy from dawn to dusk with reading Beaumarchais' *Mémoires*? Is such a circumstance perhaps not more edifying than the sight of the Reverend Mr Irving setting forth to pawn his watch? Life is so full of disease and misery that laughter is patently *unreasonable*. All the baneful aspects of life in Italy as it was in 1650, with its Jesuits, its indulgences, its Catholic Christianity, were infinitely more propitious to art and human happiness than the most rational variety of protestantism. Indeed, the more downright rational it is, the more lethal it must prove to the fine arts and to the delights of living.'

(Here follows a list of items which, given the state of 'liberty' pertaining to the press in this year of grace 1826, it would be imprudent to send to the printer*:

(i)   A *Life of Pope Pius VII*, notwithstanding the fact that it shows that venerable Pontiff in a most favourable light.

(ii)   A *Life of Cardinal Consalvi*.

(iii)   A *Description of the Mechanism of Government in Rome*. With minor variations, affairs of state are managed precisely as in 1500: the whole thing is a most curious historical survival.

(iv)   A *History of the Conclave of 1823*, on which occasion I chanced to be myself in Rome. Night after night, in the *salon* of signora N***, we were privileged to hear a detailed account of each session of the Conclave, and to learn how each Cardinal had cast his vote.

(v)   A *History* of the secretary employed by Pope Pius VI, when engaged upon his *magnum opus* concerning the German Bishoprics: of the trick played upon this secretary by Cardinal Consalvi: and of the lovers of that remarkable lady, the wife of General Pfiffer*.)

CASTEL-GANDOLFO, 1st October. For a whole month now, I have been settled in Castel-Gandolfo; I while away my days on the shores of Lake Albano and at Frascati. I should be guilty of a flagrant injustice towards these enchanted spots, were I to describe them in less than twenty pages. . . . Anecdote concerning the young peasant-lad from Frascati, which I heard yesterday at the Villa Aldobrandini. . . . By some mysterious operation, the very climate of these regions excites a man to fall on his knees before the sacred altars of *Beauty*. However, I have already disserted at too great a length concerning beauty and all that touches it; if I were to add to what

I have written, I should end simply by wearying the unresponsive minds of the North. So here, instead, is a brief excursion into ethics. In Rome, barely a day passes but that I pay a call upon signor Tambroni at the *Palazzo Venezia*, where I am privileged to meet his charming wife (born in Chambéry), together with Canova, who is an intimate friend of the family, and two or three philosophers, the like of whom, for the impartiality of their views and the depth of their judgment, I have never encountered, nor even knew to exist.

Here, then, follows an extract from the notes which I jotted down last month. I still continue to pass my days in Rome; but fear of the malarial fever hunts me out to sleep in Castel-Gandolfo.

The races of the North are wont to grant this mortal life of ours a solemn, grave, and, if you will, *profound* consideration; whereas in Rome, where the level of human intelligence is perhaps not so vastly inferior to that of Edinburgh, men's attitude to life is passionate and vital, traversed with powerful and, if you will, *disordered* currents of sensation. In the former hypothesis, the ties of marriage and of family are governed by the most intransigent code of inviolability; whereas in Rome, a Prince Colonna—to pick one instance at random from the multitude—would normally consider marriage as an institution exclusively devised to determine the status of children and to control the division of property. Should you propose to a Roman that he should continue all his life to love the same woman, he would protest that, were she an angel pure and undefiled, you were none the less intent on robbing him of three-quarters of that element which makes the life of man worth living. Thus, in Edinburgh, the family is a *principal* consideration; in Rome, no more than an *accessory*. Allowing that the system which finds favour among the peoples of the North may sometimes breed monotony and boredom, it may also frequently afford a tranquil and enduring felicity. None the less, in my view, there is a more vital factor to be taken into account: for one is driven to suspect that the joyless system of the North may prove, in some secret fashion, to be bound up with *liberty*, and with all the wealth of happiness that it promises to mankind. The Roman system, on the other hand, makes no provision for this multiplicity of minute and independent kingdoms known as families; but in compensation, each individual is free to pursue his own private ideal of happiness.

Were it not that I feared to be stoned to death, I might be tempted to add that there is *one* country whose inhabitants have been at pains to import, for their own especial use and benefit, almost all the worst elements of the *ascetic* system of the Protestants, together with all the worst elements of the *voluptuous* traditions of Italy.

In England, except among those individuals who possess an income of £40,000 a year and upward, or else enjoy the privilege of noble birth, the marriage-bond is, to all intents and purposes, inviolable. Whereas in Rome, not a single member of the congregation, upon beholding the solemn celebration of a marriage before the altar, would dream of imagining this notion of inviolability and eternal vows. And after the first few years, since the husband has no illusions on this score, since indeed the whole matter was settled long ago by tradition and common consent—unless he chance himself to be in love with his own wife, in which case his status in no way differs from that of the more conventional lover in relation to his mistress—then he will most assuredly cease to concern himself with the propriety of his wife's behaviour.

There is, however, *one* land that I might name, where marriage is a purely financial transaction, and where the future bride and bridegroom are not so much as introduced to one another until the lawyers of their respective families have well and truly settled the terms of the contract. Yet *in spite of this*, the husband is wont to claim as his due no less a portion of inviolable fidelity than may be discovered in the marriage-vows of England; while at the same time he seeks to partake of all the pleasures that Italian society has to offer. In England, *a girl is free to choose her own husband*: to appreciate this vital fact, it is sufficient to observe the sitting-out rooms at an English ball.

I now intend to embark upon a topic which will certainly endanger the reputation of this *Journey*: and indeed, I have need of all the courage I can muster, for I propose to discuss the morals and manners of Rome. He who seeks to know Italy should turn to Rome; for Rome is a hundred times more *Italian* than Naples, which has already been contaminated by French influence, or than Bologna, which here and there shows traces of provincialism. In Rome, at ten-year intervals, it is the custom to elect a King; this *Royal Personage*, in the days of his youth, was perchance not wholly exempt from the passions of his kind; how vast a field is there here for the play of private ambition!

Rome knows nothing of that awkwardness and constraint, nothing of those rigid conventions, whose skilful exercise is elsewhere called a 'knowledge of the world'. When a man finds favour in a woman's eyes, she will seldom seek to conceal her pleasure. *Dite a* *** *che mi piace* is a phrase which, in Rome, a woman may readily employ, with neither shame nor scruple. If the man who is fortunate enough to inspire such tender feelings should chance to reciprocate them, he may enquire:

'*Mi volete bene?*'

'*Si.*'

'*Quando ci vedremo?*'

Such are the simple beginnings of a *liaison* which will normally endure for a considerable span of time, no less, perhaps, than eight or ten years. An attachment which is broken after a year or two brings little honour to the lady concerned; she will find herself spoken of as a 'sorry creature' one that is unsure, incapable of knowing her own mind. The perfect reciprocity of obligation which exists between the lover and his mistress plays no little part in strengthening the bonds of constancy. Another curious phenomenon, in this land of super-subtle political machinations, is that, in love, the art of dissimulation is steadfastly rejected. Only recently I had occasion to observe, at the sumptuous ball given by the banker Torlonia, Duke of Bracciano, that a woman will dance only with such partners as her lover may deem acceptable. Should you find in your heart sufficient impudence to enquire of some pretty woman the reason *why* she has refused your request, she will reply in all simplicity:

'*Il mio amico non lo vuole. Domandate al mio amico.*'

And each year you may expect to find one or two worthy Teutons blessed with sufficient *naïveté* to seek out the *amico* in question, and to sue for gracious permission to dance with his mistress.

The gentle sex, in Rome, is guilty of one most portentous injustice, which is to show high contempt for its sisters beyond the Alps. Were you to hearken to such opinions, you might form the notion that the women of France were better versed in flirtation than in love; and that, after a thousand pretexts and delays, they always come round eventually to the same point. I quote this opinion merely to given an instance of the *absurdity* of the judgments which a nation may sometimes make concerning its neighbours.

In Rome, on one occasion, a certain woman was asked what she would do if her lover should prove unfaithful to her—the lover being present in person at the time the question was voiced. Without a word, she rose from her seat, opened the door and vanished for an instant, then reappeared, groping blindly, as though feeling her way into a pitch-dark room. All the company stared at her in amazement, when suddenly, still with the same blind and groping gestures, she was seen to advance towards her lover—who was as fully mystified as all the rest—and deliberately to smash against his breast the fan which she carried in her hand.

This was all her reply. Conceive, if you can, what fine

and flowery phrases one of our own modish beauties must surely have employed in like circumstance!

4th October. Il marchese Ga[llo], the lover of signora Bo[na-corsi], one of the fairest women in all the city of Rome, did chance one day, together with his mistress, to be present among the guests assembled in the apartments of M. de Blacas. The *contessa* di Flores begged signor Ga[llo] to sing, adding, in a tone of voice apparently calculated to bring out the pun:

'*Cantate tanto bene, Galli!*'

At these words, la Bo[nacorsi] rose from her seat in a towering rage:

'*E che sapete voi se canta bene?*'

'*Sì, lo so benissimo*', retorted signora di Flores with icy self-possession: whereupon a deathly stillness took possession of the room, and there ensued a most terrible scene between the two women. The lover, an extremely handsome man, was witness of the engagement, but was daunted into silence. At length, divers mutual friends gave orders that the respective carriages of the two antagonists be called; and eventually, having represented to them how ill-becoming it was to engage in such disputes at the residence of a foreigner in Rome, did, with the utmost difficulty, persuade them to quit the ambas-sadorial drawing-room, each by a different door.

A Roman woman is always liable to inflict such scenes upon her lover; she may thrust a dagger to his heart; yet one thing she will never do, however grievously he may have wronged her—she will never repeat to others those secrets he entrusted to her in a moment of self-surrender. She may kill him, perhaps, and herself thereafter die of grief; but the secrets of his heart will perish with her. The dagger-thrust is extremely rare in polite society, but almost a daily occurrence among the populace, where a woman will seldom take consolation for the loss of her lover. I should be accused of flaunting the laws of decency, were I to relate some seven or eight anecdotes that I have gathered, one and all a matter of common scandal.

Every night in Rome may witness a different reception in society: whether at the residence of Their Excellencies the Austrian or French Ambassadors, or whether at the *palazzo* of some Roman Prince. The *secondo ceto* has no foothold in these exclusive *salons*, where the prevailing tone shows distinct traces of French influence. Rather let the enquiring traveller turn his attention to those receptions held by the wealthier merchants of the city—the acknowledged leaders of the *secondo ceto*—if he would study Roman manners and Roman customs in all their fullest spate of energy. An ambassadorial *soirée* is invariably attended by eight or ten Cardinals . . . but here, most aptly, there comes into my mind a recollection of the pleasant little spot which serves as an enforced retreat for that most charming and most witty of mankind, Count Santo-Domingo.

In spite of all that common gossip may allege against Italy, the individual who deliberately cultivates affectation is as rare a bird in Roman or in Milanese society as the man who behaves with natural simplicity in Paris. In Rome, however, it is not the practice to rail against religion: much as, in Paris, it is not the custom for a man of breeding to utter coarse obscenities in a drawing-room. *You* are persuaded that the Italian is a hypocrite through and through, forever lying and dissembling; yet, if the truth be known, he is the least artificial creature in all the Continent of Europe, and the least concerned with his neighbour's opinion. *You* would have him be the craftiest of schemers, a model of consummate prudence, a very Machiavelli incarnate: yet do but consider that childlike innocence, that simple trust in virtue reminiscent of the *Girondins*, which characterises the conspirators of Piedmont or Naples. In every respect, I believe the Roman to deserve the crown above all the other peoples of Italy: he is endowed with greater strength of character, with deeper simplicity, with incomparably more intelligence. Do but grant him a Napoleon for the space of twenty years, and you will see him rise, beyond question, to be the foremost race in Europe. Had I but space enough, I should not find it hard to furnish proof of this assertion. If ever this pamphlet deserves the honour of a second edition, I propose to append a dozen anecdotes in support of the foregoing contention.

10th October. Last night, I chose to sleep in Rome. It was close to striking nine as I forsook those splendid halls, set in the proximity of a grove of orange-trees, which are known by the title of the *caffè Ruspoli*: opposite the entrance to this coffee-house stands the *Palazzo Fiano*. As I emerged, there was a man standing by the entrance to a sort of cellar, calling out: *Entrate, o signori!* ... (*Take your seats, gentlemen! The show is just about to start!*) And so, in effect, I took my seat in this tiny theatre, for which I paid the sum of 28 *centimes*. At such a price, I was mightily apprehensive of ill-company and fleas. Before long, however, I was reassured. From the tone of the conversation about me, I perceived that my neighbours were honest tradesfolk of the city; for in Rome, the price of 28 *centimes* is high enough to ward off the baser elements of the mob. I doubt whether there be any race in Europe with a greater fondness for the bite and ingenuity of satire than the worthy citizens of Rome; so acute and subtle are their minds, that they will pounce with eager delight even upon the remotest of allusions. The element which raises the level of their happiness so infinitely far above that which commonly prevails, say, in London, is their acquaintance with *despair*. Accustomed now for three whole centuries to regard the evils which it endures as inevitable and eternal, the Roman *bourgeoisie* feels no desire to pour forth the seething rage within its heart against the Minister; it has no wish to bring about his death; it knows full well that *this* particular incarnation of authority will merely be replaced by another, not a whit less evil-minded. Consequently, what the people of Rome desire above all else is a chance to show their strong contempt for the powers that control their destiny, and to laugh at their expense: hence the dialogues between *Pasquino* and *Marforio*. But, here in Rome, the censorship is more meticulous than in Paris; consequently, comedy in the live theatre is nothing but a string of unspeakable platitudes. True laughter has sought refuge among the *marionettes*, whose performances are, to all intents and purposes, improvised.

My evening spent in the company of the marionettes of the *Palazzo Fiano* was a most agreeable experience, for all that the actors stood scarcely a dozen inches off the ground; the stage upon which they strutted, parading their miniature and brightly-painted persons, was perhaps some ten foot wide by four foot high. The factor which contributes hugely to the pleasure and, I would make so bold as to claim, to the *illusion* of the performance, is the *décor* of this tiny theatre, which is admirable. Every door and every window of the houses which form the stage-set is meticulously designed to conform to the perspective of actors who, instead of standing five feet high, stand no more than twelve inches.

The popular hero with the Roman public, the character whose various adventures it follows with the most passionate interest, is christened *Cassandrino*. Cassandrino is a spruce old gentleman of some fifty-five or sixty summers, alert and nimble in his movements, white-haired, scrupulously powdered and exceedingly *soigné*—a man, in short, who bears a singular likeness to a *Cardinal*. This Cassandrino, moreover, is a man of the world; he is never known to lose his temper—for indeed, what good purpose should he serve by doing so, in a land unacquainted with military insolence? His *forte* is a most exquisite tact in the appreciation of social niceties; above all, none shows finer craftsmanship than he in manipulating the passions of the hour. All these qualities are essential to his popularity, for, without them, the worthy citizens of Rome would dub him a *villano* (peasant), at whose antics they would hardly condescend to laugh. In a word, then, Cassandrino possesses more or less all the virtues of the perfect gentleman, and would rank as a sort of sexagenarian *Grandison*, were it not his weakness to fall regularly in love with every pretty wench who may chance to stray across his path; and being a creature of the South, with small inclination to sit and *dream* of love, his thoughts soon veer towards seduction. Now, you will surely grant me this, that such a character is by no means ill-conceived to appeal to a nation which is governed by an oligarchic Court—a Court composed entirely of *celibate priests*, amongst whom, as indeed elsewhere, power tends to accumulate in the hands of old age. And who would dream of taking offence at Cassandrino? Cassandrino has retained his popularity for over a century now. I scarcely need to mention that he is a *layman*; yet, take any audience that comes to laugh at Cassandrino, I would be prepared to wager that there is not a single person present who can see him without his Cardinal's *zucchetto*, or at least without the violet stockings of a *monsignore*. The *monsignori*, incidentally, are the junior officials of the Papal Court, the *Auditors-in-Council* of the Realm: this is the first rung on the great ladder of preferment. Cardinal Consalvi, for instance, began as a *monsignore*, and wore violet stockings for full thirty years of his life. Rome is swarming with *monsignori* of Cassandrino's age, upon whom fortune has omitted to smile so early as she did on Cardinal Consalvi, and who, having resigned themselves to wait in patience for the coming of the *Hat*, seek other consolations in the meantime.

This evening's performance was entitled: *Cassandrino allievo di un pittore*. A distinguished painter has many pupils and a sister of surpassing beauty. Cassandrino, a dapper little old fellow of sixty, resolves to call upon her in her drawing-room, and, from the instant he crosses the threshold, contrives to give himself all the modest airs and graces of a young Cardinal.

The first entry of Cassandrino upon the stage of the

marionette-theatre, and the three or four turns he finds time to take about the room while awaiting the arrival of his mistress, whom the *cameriera di casa*, suitably mollified by the gift of a *paoletto*, has gone to warn of her suitor's arrival, are alone sufficient—so faithfully do the gestures of our little mannikin reflect the peculiarities of gait and style affected by the typical young *monsignore*—to put the audience into a ripe good humour. At long last, the painter's pretty sister condescends to appear; and Cassandrino, who, on account of his age, has not yet screwed up courage enough to risk making his intentions too patently plain, begs her to grant him leave to sing a *cavatina*, which he has recently heard at a concert, and by which his heart is still entranced. The whole ingenuity of the character lies precisely in the contrast between this sense of timid circum-spection, bred of his years, and the multiplicity of shrewd and minutely-calculated devices which he employs to blind the feminine eye to the snowy whiteness of his hair. This *cavatina* was a thing of unqualified delight: it was, in fact, one of Paisiello's most charming compositions. The audience ap-plauded in a wild transport of enthusiasm—indeed, the dramatic illusion suffered not a little in consequence; for, the melody having been sung off-stage by the daughter of a certain shoemaker, who is gifted with a most wondrous voice, ever and anon the onlookers would call out: *brava la ciabattina!*

This impassioned *aria* serves in good stead of a declaration by the love-lorn Cassandrino. The painter's pretty sister responds with an avalanche of compliments touching the daintiness of his appearance and the robustness of his health—compliments which this elderly bachelor snaps up with fatuous avidity. Promptly, he snatches at the pretext to relate to her the detailed history of his tail-coat, of which the cloth was specially imported from France. Next, he begins to dissert upon his trousers, newly-arrived from England, upon the noble mysteries of his repeater watch (he draws it forth from his pocket, causes it to strike), which cost him a hundred guineas from the most fashionable watchmaker in London ... to be brief, Cassandrino one by one displays all the current foibles and absurdities of an elderly celibate; it tickles him to allude to all the fashionable shopkeepers in Rome by their pet nicknames, to pick out each distinguished foreign dandy, to point at him with his finger in the street—and you may be sure that there are always one or two such creatures, who, by the outrageous lengths to which they carry their own absurdities, will not escape unnoticed by the malicious eye of Rome. To emphasise each word, he moves his chair a few inches closer to that upon which the object of his heart's-desire is seated. Of a sudden, however, the soft delights of this *tête-à-tête* are disturbed by the irruption of the lady's brother, the young painter, who appears in a pair of gigantic side-whiskers, with his hair falling in long and curling locks about his neck. (Such is the compulsory uniform of *genius*!)

The young artist requests Cassandrino, somewhat brusquely, that he should forbear to honour his sister with any further visits, and returns a certain miniature which our hero had earlier given him to have restored.

Cassandrino, far from raging and ranting, showers endless compliments and flattering commendations upon the irate young man who is forcibly showing him the door. The latter, now left alone with his sister, turns to her in indignation: 'How can you be so careless of your reputation as to receive in private the visit of a man who can never marry you?' At this remark, unmistakable in its implications, I verily did believe that the applause would carry off the roof. There followed a pleasantly droll monologue by Cassandrino alone in the street. Nothing will serve to console him for the ban which forbids him to call upon his mistress. One by one he airs his grievances, alternately railing against some minor distemper that springs from his age and lamenting the torment of his over-heated passion. The audience listened with profoundest concentration, wrapped in a silence that was broken at each new phrase by sudden bursts of laughter. The subtle arguments which he advances to persuade his reason to connive at that venerable accumulation of years which time has heaped upon him are the richer in comedy, in that Cassandrino is by no means a fool; on the contrary, he is a man of wide experience, and even of some considerable intellectual power, who commits such indiscretions only because he is in love. After much deliberation, he resolves at length to trick himself out as a young man, and so, disguised as a youth of eighteen desirous to learn the secrets of painting, to seek out the artist in his apartment.

In Act II, we witness his arrival at the painter's house. His disguise consists of a pair of enormous black side-whiskers; however, in his hurry, he has forgotten to remove the curling locks, all white with rice-powder, which nestle about his ear. By devious stratagems, he manages to secure an interview with his mistress; and the love-scene between Cassandrino and the damsel is a thing of wondrous absurdity: he worships the very ground she walks upon, and his infatuation is the perfect caricature of an elderly bachelor in love. He is forever harping upon the theme of his fortune, and finally brings himself to the point when he proposes to share it with her. 'We shall live happily ever after', he declares, *and none shall know of our happiness!*' At this last remark, the audience interrupted the performance for fully two minutes on end with its laughter and its transports of delight. Poor Cassandrino still drags beseeching at his mistress' knees, when he is surprised in this posture by an ancient aunt belonging to the girl, who had known him well some forty years before, in Ferrara, where he was then employed; she reminds him that he had once spoken to *her* of love, and forces him to endure such persecution that he, in despair, takes refuge in the painter's studio. But soon enough, like some reincarnated Pourceaugnac, he is with us again, with all the rabble of young men in hot pursuit, laughing and jeering at this new 'fellow-student' of theirs, with his jet-black side-whiskers and his snow-white hair. At this point, the painter himself appears upon the scene, sends his pupils about their business, and embarks upon a lengthy and decidedly humourless dialogue with Cassandrino. Unlucky Cassandrino begins to suspect that there is a dagger unsheathing for him not too far away; and soon he is half-dead with fright, not at the prospect of being set upon and killed, but rather at the prospect of *causing a scandal*—yet another characteristic touch, which that Roman audience, in its deep sagacity, greeted with a joy that was almost delirious.

At long last, the young painter, having had his fill of entertainment at the expense of poor Cassandrino, whom he insists upon mistaking for a robber, deigns to recognise him. 'Your declared intention in coming here', he says, 'was to beg a lesson in painting. Very well, then: a lesson you shall have. The theme of our first period of instruction is to be *colour*. My pupils will begin by removing your clothes; next, they will proceed to paint your skin from head to foot in noblest hues of scarlet (allusion to a certain *Eminent* costume); finally, having thus elevated you to the very peak of your ambition, they will be pleased to walk you up and down the *Corso*.' So terror-struck is Cassandrino that he agrees to marry the ancient aunt whose favours, in days gone by, he had once courted in Ferrara. The aunt promptly flings her arms about his neck. Finally, however, Cassandrino steps down towards the footlights and takes the audience into his confidence: 'If ever I cherished ambitions to assume the scarlet, I hereby renounce them for ever: instead, I shall become the uncle of the adored object of my desires; and *then* . . .'. At this point, he pretends to hear the noise of someone calling and turns away his head, while the audience drowns his voice in their applause.

As soon as the performance was over, a small child stepped upon the stage to trim the lights: immediately there were cries of alarm from two or three strangers in the audience. And indeed, this child seemed nothing less than a *giant*, so perfectly had the illusion been maintained until that instant, and so little had we been aware of the miniature stature or of the wooden heads of the actors who, for fully three-quarters of an hour, had had us rocking in our seats with laughter.

Immediately afterwards, we were favoured with a ballet, the *Enchanted Well*, a tale drawn from the *Arabian Nights*; more astounding, if such a thing were possible, than even the comedy that had gone before, for the natural and unstilted grace which informed the movements of the dancers. I made enquiries among my neighbours, to discover something of the *mechanism* of these fascinating little wooden puppets. The feet, it seems, are made of lead; the threads which control them pass through the centre of the body and emerge from the crown of the head, concealed all together in a black tube, which further hides the individual threads which are used to animate the head itself; thus the only threads which are at all visible are those which are used to control the movements of the arms. This is why the best places in the theatre are those which are some five or six paces distant from the stage. The *eyes* are likewise movable, but cannot be controlled; the movement depends merely on the angle of the head, varying as it inclines more to the left or to the right.

But what I despair of portraying for you is the wondrous skill with which these puppets ape the very forms of nature, employing means which, to judge by my description in this letter, seem even to myself so crude and primitive.

18th October. This evening, in the midst of the conversation which reigned in the drawing-room of signora Crescenzi, a stranger suddenly began to speak. He was a man of some six-and-thirty years, unusually handsome in appearance, with eyes even darker than those which are commonly met with in Rome. For fully five minutes he spoke; no one thought to interrupt his monologue, which was delivered with some elegance; and thereafter he relapsed into a sullen silence. Not a soul replied to what he had said; and soon the conversation was resumed, as though the interruption had been due to some natural accident.

Here is the history of the *principessa* di Santa Valle—a history which, in any case, has already been published in numerous accounts, and which I earnestly entreat the reader to pass over, if he should already be acquainted with the substance of it.

There was once a woman of rare beauty, a Countess, whose birthplace lay in distant Germany—one of those cosmopolitan creatures so cossetted by our nineteenth-century diplomacy—and who lived in Naples in the lap of luxury, where her house was open to receive the finest flower of Neapolitan society. Upon her knees, the visitor might frequently observe a charming little girl, no more than eight or ten years old; the Countess, who was still young, seemed content to spend all her days, either in kissing her, with a love that seemed to verge on ecstasy, or else in kicking her and biting her with her teeth. The child, near to desperation, obtained the consent of her protectress, through the good offices of a young priest, a friend of the family, that she might be placed in a convent at Sorrento —that same region from whose soil there sprang the genius of Tasso, and which is still the loveliest spot on earth. In this retreat, her beauty burgeoned no less rapidly than her mind. She had scarcely passed her sixteenth year, when already her name was on every tongue as the most peerless being in all the city of Naples. Now there was a vain and foppish creature, by name Prince Santa-Valle, who at that period possessed all the finest horses and all the smartest barouches most recently brought from London; and he was persuaded that it needed nothing but the most beautiful woman in Naples to complete the luxury of his establishment. Poor Emma, dwelling in no little terror of the unpredictable temper of the Countess, her guardian, who claimed to have found her an orphan at a way-side inn, and to have adopted her, was only too delighted to marry a creature who could tell her, better than whomsoever you might choose to name in all Italy, by how many hair's-breadths the cuff of a shirt should extend beyond the sleeve of a coat. She took the title of *principessa*. The marriage-negotiations were handled with consummate skill by the cosmopolitan Countess; but it was not until the Prince was entangled beyond hope of escape that she confessed to him that Emma was her own daughter, and that the father was that young priest of Roman blood who was frequently to be seen in her apartments. Here at last was the explanation of the startling beauty of this child born of a union between an uncommonly lovely woman of northern stock and one of the handsomest men in all the South. Not many months had elapsed since Emma's wedding, when political circumstances obliged the Prince of Santa-Valle to abandon Naples. The young Princess moved to Rome, where she was accorded a sumptuous reception by the renowned Prince Antonio Borghese, a man of many deserts. She had been lodged for a considerable length of time beneath the roof of the *Palazzo Borghese*, when suddenly rumours of her husband's death began to circulate in Roman society. The young widow hastened to assume the cloak of mourning; and the world was the richer for two hearts over-flowing with happiness. For Emma had developed a passionate attachment for a young nobleman of Rome; yet, until that day, had never spoken with him, save in the presence of an ancient duenna of the Borghese household, whom she had taken into her service as soon as she had succumbed to the temptation of receiving her lover in her own apartments. Scarcely had she put on her weeds, when the forthcoming marriage of the noble young Roman became an open secret in aristocratic circles. After the lapse of a full year—the happiest year that poor Emma had known in all her life—all seemed set for the instant when she was to be united with her lover, and when she might at last enjoy his society free of the presence of the ancient duenna, when out of the blue came the news that she was not a widow after all. Ere long, Prince Santa Valle

made his entry into Rome. A few days later, his young wife
was discovered lying lifeless beneath a bower of blossom in
the beautiful Farnese gardens, which overhang the Forum.
Never a breath of suspicion attached to the husband, who was
a charmingly complaisant fellow and quite ignorant of jealousy.
It was concluded that the young Princess had surrendered to
some transcendental notion, engendered in her by her Germanic
origins.

'Her lover has all but lost his reason', added the acquaintance
who had been talking to me. 'You have the evidence of your
own ears. It is none other than that unhappy mortal whom
you saw but a few moments since. When he is alone, you may
overhear him conversing with the Princess Santa Valle; he is
persuaded that she answers his words, and he will speak to her
of the preparations for their forthcoming marriage.'

ROME, NAPLES AND FLORENCE

THE END

NOTES

p. v. CONTENTS. The majority of titles in this Table of Contents are taken from the 1826 edition. Each title served originally as a page-heading: hence their somewhat arbitrary character.

p. 1. PREFACE. The original (1817) edition of *Rome, Naples et Florence* had been introduced by a much shorter preface. In 1824, when a new edition was under discussion, Stendhal wrote the present preface, and submitted it to V. Jacquemont for approval. Jacquemont found it 'détestable'; in consequence of this verdict, Stendhal abandoned it, and the 1826 edition appeared without any preface at all. A few sentences were incorporated in the text of the work (see below, p. 471); but the bulk remained in manuscript until it was finally published by Daniel Muller in the Champion edition of 1919.

p. 1 ... *a second edition.* ... The first edition of *Rome, Naples et Florence* appeared in Paris in the late summer of 1817. Only a few weeks later, a second edition appeared *in French* in London (October 1817): *Rome, Naples et Florence en 1817, ou Esquisses sur l'état actuel de la société, des moeurs, des arts, de la littérature, etc. de ces villes célèbres.* Paris, chez Delaunay, libraire au Palais-Royal. Londres, chez Colburn, libraire, 1817.

p. 1 ... Fashionable Society. This sentence is an adapted quotation from a personal letter which Stendhal received from Byron (29 May 1823), and which was subsequently published in *le Globe* (2 November 1824).

p. 3 BOOKSELLER. *De l'Amour*, a work to which Stendhal was particularly attached, since it was directly inspired by Mathilde Viscontini, was dogged by ill-success from the first. It was published in the summer of 1822 by Mongie in his *Librairie Universelle*, and proved a dismal failure. Mongie's letter, here quoted, and Stendhal's reply have by now become almost proverbial—the very symbol of a man of genius unrecognised in his own generation.

p. 5 ... *three weeks from now?* This first paragraph, with its concluding quotation from Beaumarchais (*Barbier de Séville*, Act III, scene v), sets the tone of the whole book. The *Edinburgh Review* (November 1817) quoted it *in extenso*, and accused the author of being 'flippant'—an epithet which has stuck. Although much of *Rome, Naples et Florence* is, of course, directly autobiographical, the reader should beware of accepting everything at its face value. Stendhal's 'hero'—an army officer on leave—is fictional.

In 1817, Stendhal had been living in Italy more or less continuously for three years: he was, moreover, thirty-four years of age, not twenty-six, as he would like the reader to believe. On the other hand, in 1811, and again in 1813, he *had* made not dissimilar journeys to Italy, having first obtained leave from his superior in the Napoleonic civil service, Pierre Daru. In particular, when he returned from the journey of 1811, he found himself in strong disfavour with Daru. The disgrace was short-lived, but the memory of it still rankled, and it is this which explains the otherwise obscure reference to 'His Excellency' and the 'Eunuchs'.

The opening pages of this 'diary', up to and including 6th October, are copied, with minor alterations, from the 1817 edition. The remainder of the description of Milan, and the whole description of Bologna, are new, and we do not find any considerable borrowings from the earlier text until 23rd January (the opera in Florence).

p. 6   ... *the common gaol.* This anecdote concerning Madame Catalani is taken from the *Journal des Débats*, 13th November 1816.

p. 7   ... *I drove out to Desio....* Stendhal's particular attachment to Desio is explained by the fact that it was associated with Mathilde Visconti. Her cousin, signora Traversi, owned a villa there, and Mathilde was a frequent visitor.

p. 8   ... *a canvas by Guido Reni....* Cf. *Histoire de la Peinture en Italie* ch. cxxx, note.

p. 10   ... *It is genius!* Stendhal's admiration for Solliva was short-lived, and he later admitted his mistake, both in *Rome, Naples et Florence* (see below, p. 309), and in the *Vie de Rossini*: 'Style sévère dans la bouche des artistes charlatans ... veut presque toujours dire emploi des lieux communs de l'harmonie, emploi qui fait souvent illusion aux ignorants, et dont, par exemple, je fus tout à fait dupe en 1817, dans la *Testa di Bronzo*, de, Soliva, à Milan' (*V.R.*, ch. ii).

p. 10   ... *joined his drama-class....* Stendhal and Martial Daru had jointly taken lessons in dramatic declamation, first from La Rive (Aug. 1804), and later from Dugazon (Dec. 1804-May 1805). It was here that he met his early love, Mélanie Guilbert.

p. 11   ... *ruthlessly abridged....* Here, as elsewhere, Stendhal uses the verb *syncoper*, whose correct meaning he seems to have misunderstood.

p. 11   ... *an Upper and a Lower House.... Rome, Naples et Florence* is full of allusions to Stendhal's political theory. In common with the majority of French liberal reformers at the time, he cherished the ideal of a constitutional government with a Patrician and a

Plebeian House, modelled upon a not entirely realistic vision of the English parliamentary system. Bicameral government of this type seemed to him to offer a panacea for all political evils: no other system allowed for the simultaneous coexistence of those two mutually incompatible qualities which he believed essential to the good life and to human happiness: democratic *liberty* and aristocratic *sensibility*.

p. 14 ... *the poet Malaspina*. In another fragment (*R.N.F.*, ed. Muller, vol. 2, pp. 319-320), Stendhal gives this character his true name: Radaelli, with whom the novelist was personally acquainted. In a letter to Mareste, Stendhal identifies 'Zilietti' as the banker Soreri, and mentions that 'Gina' came from Novara.

p. 17 ... *the widow of Marshal Ney*. ... The lady in question stayed in Milan from 21st-29th October 1816: Stendhal notes elsewhere: 'Mme la Maréchale Ney était au spectacle. On parvient à la faire sortir à temps. Grande discussion politique dans la loge de Milady D.' (*R.N.F.* 1817, ed. Martineau, p. 220).

p. 20 ... *concealed spouts and fountains*. ... *Cf*. more detailed description of this fashionable entertainment in de Brosses, *Lettres d'Italie* (ed. Colomb, 1836), vol. II, pp. 313-316.

p. 20 ... *the* Rezegon di Lek. Milanese dialectal form of the *Resegone di Lecco* (the *Saw* of Lecco).

p. 21 ... *the Sextet in Act II*. Stendhal refers again to this sextet in the *Vie de Rossini* (ed. le Divan, vol. I, p. 32). In a marginal note, he remarks: 'Lord Byron avait les plus beaux yeux du monde en écoutant ce sestetto'.

p. 23 ... *better-planned streets*. ... In the original, 'les rues les plus commodes', to which, in a footnote, Stendhal adds, in his own inimitable brand of English: '*The most comfortable streets*'.

p.25 ... *one of its greatest advantages*. On several occasions, Stendhal returns to this description of *la Scala*: *cf. L'Italie en* 1818 (8th Aug. 1818) and *Vie de Rossini* (vol. II, pp. 261-263).

p. 25 ... has *eventually taken place*. The details are fairly exact. Signora Catalani was in Milan in 1816, and gave her first concert, with the programme described, on 23rd November. Stendhal had already heard her sing in Paris in 1806.

p. 32 ... *the gentle art of playing tarocchi*. De Brosses (vol. II, pp. 207-210) gives a detailed description of the game as then played. According to him, the game needed ninety-seven cards—an ordinary pack with four court-cards in each suit instead of three, forty special cards, and a jester (*il matto*). Muller, however, asserts that the present-day game needs merely seventy-eight cards.

p. 33 ... *this age of cant.* ... In English in the original. The quotation is taken from the Preface to Cantos vi, vii and viii of *Don Juan*.

p. 34 ... *merely affected and absurd?* Muller has pointed out the striking resemblance between Stendhal's caricature of 'M. Mal***', and Mme de Staël's *comte d'Erfeuil* in *Corinne*. Both writers were exasperated to the point of frenzy by the reactions of the average brash and philistine Frenchman travelling abroad in Italy.

p. 46 ... *a drawling, nasal type of speech*. The remainder of the paragraph, which depends for its sense on a complex cross-pun in French and Italian, I am regretfully forced to declare untranslatable; here is the original: '. . . les femmes de la haute noblesse affectent de parler du nez. J'ai entendu l'une d'elles dire d'une autre femme: *A-t-elle du sang bleu?* ce qui veut dire: *Est-elle vraiment noble?* et j'ai eu la sottise de rire aux éclats (*sang bleu* se prononce de même en milanais et en français).'

p. 49 ... *the column-counting statisticians.* ... Osbert Sitwell (*Left Hand, Right Hand*, pp. 32-40) quotes from the diaries of his great-grand-father, Colonel Hely-Hutchinson, who likewise made an 'Italian journey' in 1817-1818 .The Colonel was a fine specimen of a 'column-counter': 'The palace [of Caserta] has 746 feet in length by 576 in breadth, and is rectangular. It is 113 feet in height with two *grands étages* and three smaller. Vanvitelli was the architect . . .'.

p. 49 ... *da Vinci's wondrous Herodias.* ... Signora M*** V*** is plainly Mathilde Viscontini. Stendhal frequently identified her with a painting which he referred to as 'da Vinci's *Herodias*', but which is in fact Luini's *Salome with the Head of John the Baptist*, which he had seen in Florence, and of which there is a copy in the Louvre.

p. 51 ... backstairs patriotism. ... In the original, *patriotisme d'antichambre* —a favourite phrase with Stendhal which he attributes originally to Turgot. *Vide: Le Divan*, 1957, No. 1, pp. 22-25.

p. 60 ... *frozen portions of human corpses*. Stendhal was justifiably proud of his part in the Retreat from Moscow. He left the city on 16th October 1812 as Director-General of the Reserve Commissariat, avoided the disaster of the Berezina by his own initiative and foresight, and reached Vilna on 7th December. He finally reached Paris on 31st January 1813, 'gelé au moral comme au physique'.

p. 61 ... *unsuited to musical treatment*. Stendhal develops this idea at length in the *Vie de Rossini* (vol. II, pp. 34-60).

p. 61 . . . *scandal about a man of genius.* . . . Stendhal himself is not above spreading the grossest forms of scandal about Rossini. See letters to Mareste of 12th and 18th July, 30th Aug. and 22nd Dec. 1820.

p. 65 . . . L'Esprit des Lois de la Société. A parody of the title of Montesquieu's celebrated masterpiece. Stendhal's hostility to Mme de Staël was deep-rooted and persistent. Above all, he objected to her *style*, which seemed to him to embody all the 'false' aspects of romanticism.

p. 66 *Silvio Pellico.* . . . Pellico, Ludovico di Breme, Guasco, Ermes Visconti, and in fact the majority of Stendhal's Milanese acquaintance here referred to, formed the intellectual vanguard of the *carbonari.* In 1820, the majority of these liberal reformers were arrested, and Stendhal himself fell directly under suspicion. In order to discredit him without compromising themselves, the Milanese authorities spread the rumour that Stendhal was a secret agent in the pay of Louis XVIII. By 1821, his position had become untenable, and he was forced to leave the country. It is essential to keep in mind this political background, in order to understand many of the allusions in *Rome, Naples et Florence.*

p. 68 la Nina. . . . Nina Viganò, daughter of the choreographer, would appear to have been one of the earliest professional singers of Italian folk-songs. Stendhal admired her unrestrainedly (*Corresp.* vol. V, pp. 113-4; 136; 155-6; 157-60; 177-8; 285; 290; 335; 344-5; etc.). Partly at Stendhal's instigation, la Nina attempted a professional season in Paris, but failed lamentably.

p. 70 . . . *at the* Cascina di Pom'. . . . In current Milanese dialect, to spend one's holidays 'alla cascina di Pom'' means simply to have no holidays at all.

p. 71 . . . *a certain Count Vitelleschi.* . . . The original hero of this tale was one of the Counts Lechi—a Brescia family with whom Stendhal was well acquainted.

p. 74 . . . *invites your gaze this very evening.* Obviously an extract from a much earlier draft of the book—a typical example of Stendhal's deliberately 'unstudied' style of writing. The passage probably dates from 1813 or 1814, and is interesting as a memorial to Stendhal's first contact with Rossini—the composer who was later to preoccupy him so intensely. The passion for ballet-slippers 'in white satin' is characteristically romantic: *cf.* Pushkin *Evgenyi Onyegin.*

p. 75 . . . *which* love *has afforded it by day.* An essential part of Stendhal's theory of music. Music, he insists, can create no emotion by itself; but it can re-create, or reflect, or intensify *emotions already present in the listener.*

p. 76 ... *neither imitated.* Stendhal is one of the founders of the romantic theory of *genius.* A genius (an 'artist') is *different* from other members of society; he lives on a higher plane; above all, he is *original,* a law unto himself; if he imitates others, he is *ipso facto* a craftsman, not an 'artist'.

p. 77 ... *the personal character of M. David.* .... David had been a fervent Jacobin, and was exiled by the Restoration government. In his attitude towards David, Stendhal's political and aesthetic ideals come into violent collision. He detested him as a *classic*; yet he revered him as a *jacobin,* and reviled those who had persecuted him. This dilemma tends to blind him to many significant artistic trends in his own period.

p. 79 ... *the mask of affectation is stripped away.* Stendhal's reading of mediaeval and renaissance Italian history profoundly affected his outlook. It served to reinforce his native 'espagnolisme', and contributed markedly to that passion for violent deeds and flamboyant characters which is so fundamental to his greatest novels.

p. 81 ... *a prospect which I find less attractive still.* Here, it is decidedly the 'fictitious hero' speaking, not Stendhal. Game-shooting was the most enduring passion of Stendhal's life.

p. 89 ... *la Simonetta.* .... Cf. *Journal,* 19th Sept. 1811.

p. 90 ... *a ballet by Salvatore Viganò.* In general, the objects of Stendhal's admiration have shown themselves worthy of his faith in them, and their works have stood up to the passage of time. If Viganò seems to offer an exception to this rule, that is perhaps due more to the ephemeral nature of his art than to any inherent weakness in his own creative gifts. The reader is referred to an article by H. Prunières in the *Revue Musicale* (1st Dec. 1921) and to the biography by Carlo Ritorni, *Commentario della Vita e delle Opere coreodrammatiche di Salvatore Viganò* (Milan 1838).

p. 90 ... *and saw Kean in* Othello. .... Stendhal saw Kean in *Othello* and *Richard III* in London in October 1821, and was deeply (but by no means uncritically) impressed.

p. 90 ... *Madame Pasta.* Giuditta Pasta was the prop and pillar of the *Théâtre Italien* in Paris from 1821 to 1826. Stendhal considered her the greatest living *prima donna,* and was at least partially in love with her. He took rooms in the same house where she lived in the rue de Richelieu, and there wrote the *Vie de Rossini,* where he dedicated a whole chapter to her and her art (vol. II, pp. 171-193).

p. 92 ... *Beccaria.* Much of Stendhal's information on Beccaria is borrowed from Pietro Custodi, *Vita di Cesare Beccaria* (Padua 1815), and from the *Biographie Michaud.* His enthusiasm, however, is genuine, and his judgments are original and personal.

p. 97 ... *vengo adesso di Cosmopoli.* A quotation from Giuseppe Mosca's *opera buffa: I pretendenti Delusi.* Stendhal uses the quotation again in the *Promenades dans Rome* (15th Nov. 1828).

p. 97 ... *some of the more pointed passages.* For the full text, see the *Poesie edite, inedite e rare di Carlo Porta* (Florence 1884); also the *Poesie milanesi di Carlo Porta e Tommaso Grossi* (Milan 1903). The latter edition gives the full text of Grossi's *El dì d'Incœu,* which, in Stendhal's opinion, was the finest poem ever written in Milanese dialect.

p. 100 ... *I took pleasure in the writing of them.* There is not a single painting described in detail in *Rome, Naples and Florence.* This is because Stendhal had already used the descriptions he had written of his favourite paintings for the *Histoire de la Peinture en Italie.*

p. 102 ... *the organisers had selected Vieillard.* . . . A very celebrated Milanese caterer. Daniel Muller has published an interesting extract from the carbonarist journal, *il Conciliatore* (6th Dec. 1818), by Ermes Visconti, which contains a number of references to Vieillard (*R.N.F.,* vol. II, pp. 416-418).

p. 109 ... *its pure perfection.* Once again, an allusion to Mathilde Viscontini.

p. 113 ... persona grata *with the government.* A reference to the malicious rumours that Stendhal was an agent of Louis XVIII (see above, note to p. 66).

p. 115 ... *Ebrea di Toledo.* Despite Stendhal's assertion, Viganò *did* succeed in producing a ballet of this title. *Cf.* Carlo Ritorni, *op. cit.*

p. 117 ... *Johann von Müller used to tell us in Cassel.* . . . Stendhal was in Cassel in 1806; it is therefore not unlikely that he may have had contact with the Swiss historian, Johann von Müller, who died in that same town in 1809.

p. 120 ... *the big industrialists.* . . . An allusion to one of Stendhal's most curious minor writings: *D'un nouveau Complot contre les Industriels,* published in December 1825. The theme is one which is hinted at in certain passages of *Rome, Naples et Florence*: Stendhal is one of the earliest philosophers to discover that the new industrial bourgeoisie, with its cult of utilitarian materialism, was fundamentally hostile to the higher ideals of art.

p. 124 *Montesquieu,* Oeuvres Diverses. The exact quotation is as follows: 'Il y a aujourd'hui à Naples cinquante mille hommes qui ne vivent que d'herbe, et n'ont pour tout bien que la moitié d'un habit de toile; ces gens-là, les plus malheureux de la terre, tombent dans un abattement affreux à la moindre fumée du Vésuve: ils ont la sottise de craindre de devenir malheureux' (*De la Grandeur des Romains et de leur Décadence*, ch. xiv).

p. 126 . . . *the most wondrous experience that the game can offer*. . . . Stendhal spent many evenings playing faro in the company of Giuditta Pasta: on which occasions, her lover, le chevalier de Micheroux, was invariably present.

p. 130 . . . *the Jesuits of Modena*. It is not hard to fill in the blanks, when we remember that it was one of Stendhal's favourite anti-clerical paradoxes, to argue that the Church could do no greater service to the heretic than to burn him alive. In a marginal note, written at a much later date, Stendhal adds: 'J'ai oublié ceci . . . Cela prouvait qu'on a raison de brûler un hérétique et de lui infliger une douleur de deux heures avec un feu *mortel*, pour lui éviter une douleur de deux cents ans avec un feu plus chaud, car il est divin.'

p. 139 . . . *da on asen come lù*. The poems from which this quotation and the previous one are taken (*i.e.*, *la Preghiera* and the sonnet *Sissignor*) may be read in the *Poesie edite, inedite e rare di Carlo Porta*.

p. 139 . . . *là in d'on canton*. . . . Quoted from Tommaso Grossi's *Vision of Count Prina* (*El dì d'incœu*).

p. 141 . . . *Hugues Capet*. See Dante, *Purgatorio*, canto xx.

p. 142 . . . *an ingenious young man*. . . . Undoubtedly, Eugène Scribe—the first post-revolutionary dramatist to win a major and lasting success in the theatre. It was he who first perfected the genre of the *historical comedy*.

p. 147 . . . *in the face of the advancing Cossacks*. . . . During the winter of 1813-14, Stendhal was attached to the staff of the comte de Saint-Vallier, and was concerned with organising the defence of the Dauphiné. In March, he was back in Paris, fighting desperately against the atmosphere of defeatism to have the art-treasures of the Musée Napoléon stored in safety; and a few days later, he witnessed the Cossack regiments storm the heights of Montmartre.

p. 148 . . . *ever since* 1820. . . . Here, the fictitious 'hero' takes over. Stendhal had lived in Italy fairly continuously from 1814 until 1821; but from 1821 until 1830, he made his home largely in or near Paris.

p. 150 . . . *such a multitude of academies*. Stendhal's epithet is not unjustified. M. Millin (on the cover of the *Magasin Encyclopédique*, for which he was responsible) chose to style himself: 'Membre de l'Institut,

Chevalier de la Légion d'Honneur, Conservateur des Médailles, des Pierres gravées et des Antiquités de la Bibliothèque du Roi, professeur d'archéologie; des Académies impériales de Moscou, de Vilna, de Corfou; des Curieux de la Nature à Erlang; des Sociétés Royales de Dublin, de Munich, de Turin, de Goettingue, de Berlin; des Sociétés Linnéenne de Londres, Minéralogique d'Iéna, des Sciences Physiques de Zurich, Pontanienne et d'Encouragement de Naples, d'Agriculture de Tréja; des Beaux-Arts, Colombaire et de celle d'Agriculture de Florence; de celles de Pistoïa et du Valdarno; de celles des Antiquités de Copenhague, d'Archéologie de Rome; de celles de Lyon, Rouen, Abbeville, Boulogne, Poitiers, Niort, Nîmes, Marseille, Avignon, Alençon, Caen, Grenoble, Colmar, Nancy, Gap, Strasbourg, Mayence, Trèves, Francfort, Nantes, Soissons, Lille, Evreux et Mâcon'.

p. 151 ... *I have dated this letter of mine from Pavia*. . . . Everything suggests that *Rome, Naples et Florence*, in its original draft was intended to be in letter rather than in diary form. The same is probably true of the *Vie de Rossini*.

p. 158 ... *and with naked legs*. Stendhal was not the only one who was profoundly shocked by Bosio's statue of Louis XIV, which was erected in 1822. A correspondent in *Le Miroir* (27th Aug. 1822) refers to 'la terrible perruque': 'Ne serait-il pas temps qu'on fît trêve à ces anachronismes qui constituent en Grecs ou en Romains des compatriotes dont le nom a besoin d'être inscrit au-dessous de leurs images pour les faire reconnaître, tant le travestissement est ridicule!'

p. 159 (*Rome, 1814, C. Alb.*) An allusion to Cardinal Albano and to the return to Rome of Pope Pius VII in May 1814. Stendhal gives the story in greater detail in the *Promenades dans Rome*, at the dates 4th June and 16th Oct. 1828.

p. 161 ... *the tragedy of Annibal*. . . . Stendhal had already told the tale of the printer's somewhat specialised admiration for M. Firmin-Didot's tragedy in *Racine et Shakespeare*.

p. 166 ... *of transmuting famous scientists into Barons*. . . . An allusion to *Baron Cuvier*, with whom Stendhal was personally acquainted, although he never wholly forgave him his passion for titles.

p. 166 ... *the evidence of the Président de Brosses*. . . . *Lettres d'Italie*, xxi. Stendhal had already quoted (or rather *mis*quoted) this letter in the *Vie de Haydn* (ed. Champion, p. 352), deliberately twisting de Brosses' statement to mean that Cardinal Lambertini had a primary duty to visit the opera three times a week. This also explains the allusion below (see p. 176), to the 'priesthood which

R

once upon a time, in 1740 or thereabouts, was so unstinting in its patronage of music'.

p. 166 . . . *the* Catholic among Catholics. St Dominic, who, as the instigator of the Crusade against the Albigensians, was one of the great villains of history for Stendhal.

p. 169 *Mr Bysshe-Shelley.* . . . Stendhal certainly met Byron, but there is no confirmatory evidence that he met Shelley. None the less, this would seem to be the first reference to the great English poet from the pen of a French writer.

p. 176 . . . *something* pretentious *about concerts.* . . . Another essential element in Stendhal's musical appreciation. For him, music meant exclusively *vocal* music. 'The dreariest thing in all the world', he writes in the *Vie de Rossini*, 'is a violin concerto.'

p. 188 . . . *as little shame as I.* A pun, which is inadequate in translation. Here is the original: 'Le duc d'Ayen se moquant un jour de cette tragédie: "Vous n'êtes donc pas bon Français?" lui dit le roi Louis XV. "Plût à Dieu, sire, que les vers de la tragédie le fussent autant que moi!"' Stendhal alludes to this same pun in the *Vie de Rossini* (vol. II, p. 82).

p. 188 . . . *I made a first attempt.* . . . In the *Nouveau Complot contre les Industriels.*

p. 188 . . . *and a Rossarol.* Another MS version substitutes the name Confalonieri for that of Rossarol.

p. 189 . . . backstairs patriotism. . . . See above, note to page 51.

p. 189 . . . *any* prima donna. . . . This is one of Stendhal's most persistent complaints, not only against the administration of the *Théâtre Italien*, but against the critics of the French press in general. According to him, there was, from 1817 onwards, a deliberate conspiracy organised by Paër, Berton, etc., in order to ruin the reputation of any singer not born or trained in France. In point of fact, Stendhal exaggerates considerably, and there is little or no evidence to support his allegations.

p. 191 . . . *not a stranger to this fault.* Once again, an allusion to Mathilde Viscontini, who, it should be added, was patriotic in a good as well as a bad sense, and was closely allied with the carbonarist movement.

p. 193 . . . *a sight of this my letter.* . . . More evidence of an earlier draft in letter-form.

p. 196 . . . *of général de Narbonne.* Stendhal is very fond of this anecdote (*cf. Vie de Rossini*, vol. II, p. 79; *Vie de Napoléon*, ch. xxii).

To some extent, it symbolised his own ambiguous attitude towards Napoleon.

p. 198 . . . *the opening duet of* il Matrimonio segreto. . . . This duet (*Cara, non dubitar* . . .) was, according to Stendhal, one of the supreme achievements in all music; it had the two essential qualities of great music: it was supremely melodious, and it embodied the vital characteristics of love: 'la pudeur', 'la tendresse', and 'une tristesse regrettante'.

p. 200 . . . *a certain acquaintance of mine*. . . . Stendhal himself, returning to Paris in 1821, after seven years in Italy.

p. 202 . . . (*Grimm, Part III, vol. II, p.* 102). The hero of this anecdote (which Stendhal had already related in *De l'Amour*) was le comte de Chabriant.

p. 204 . . . *la duchesse de Poitiers*. . . . The real names of the characters in this anecdote were the duchesse de Polignac, the comte de Coigny (=the comte de Canaples), and madame de la Suze (=madame de Luz). The same tale provides the dénouement of Scribe's *le Roi de carreau*.

p. 205 . . . *le duc de Sône*. . . . In real life, the duc de Chaulnes. Stendhal refers to this anecdote again in *Promenades dans Rome* (5th June 1828).

p. 209 . . . *a maximum of two score readers*. . . . Stendhal's desire that his books should be read by the 'Happy Few' alone is highly characteristic, and recurs constantly throughout his life. He believed that the public at large was fated to misunderstand him, at least until the year 1890; but he had hopes of the twentieth century.

p. 210 . . . *the Ministry of M. Pasquier*. Stendhal himself explains this allusion in a marginal note: 'Un M. Renamont de Brivasac, espion de Pasquier, dupa la plupart des patriotes italiens refugiés en Suisse. Il les créait chevaliers de la Régénération universelle, et puis leur disait: 'De vrais frères n'ont pas de secrets les uns pour les autres: dites-moi tout! Et ils disaient.'

p. 212 . . . *pockets an insult in public*. Stendhal indicates in the margin that the real name of Count Radichi was *Scotti*, and that the incident took place in 1769. This same tale is referred to again in the *Vie de Rossini*, where the town is again Bergamo.

p. 215 . . . *if ever the Malvasia episode*. . . . Probably Cardinal Malvasia. Cf. *Promenades dans Rome*.

p. 215 *Carlo Verri*. . . . Stendhal writes Carlo for *Pietro* Verri.

p. 217 . . . *whom we nicknamed jokingly Camilla*. . . . An allusion to Paër's popular opera, *Camilla, ossia il Sotterraneo*—a gruesomely melodramatic or 'gothic' work, inspired by Mrs Radcliffe.

p. 217 (De l'Amour, *vol. I, p. 129*). This tale, in fact, had been told in detail by Stendhal in the earlier work. In a manuscript addition, Stendhal notes of 'Camilla': 'Elle ressemblait à la statue de Marie Stuart couchée sur son tombeau, qui est à Westminster.'

p. 222 . . . *tax deducted. Cf.* letter to Mareste of 28th March 1820.

p. 223 . . . *a good* 150 *miles distant from Paris*. . . . The issue of the *Journal des Débats*, as indicated, does in fact contain a long article concerning the tendency for country land-owners to abandon their estates, and to migrate towards Paris.

p. 226 *Prim-faced women*. In English in the original.

p. 227 . . . *e di più v' è il gusto*. In the original edition, this sentence marked the end of the first volume.

p. 229 . . . *To give vent to his passions*. In English in the original.

p. 231 . . . *Lettres d'Italie* (p. 350). The reference is to the first edition (Paris, Ponthieu, 1800, 3 vols.). In the Colomb edition (Paris 1833), the description of Bologna is to be found in vol. I, pp. 231-265.

p. 235 . . . *the native* raciness *of Italy*. The word *raciness* is in English in the original; Stendhal's editor, Colomb, failed to spot this, and insisted on printing the French word *racines* instead, regardless of the fact that it made nonsense of the text.

p. 251 . . . *the* Société de la Vierge. . . . After the fall of Napoleon, the Church made a frantic effort to regain its hold over the working classes by the organisation of various 'societies' of Christian Action. Innocent as these may have been in intention, they rapidly acquired political influence, and gained an evil reputation for hypocrisy, social obscurantism and espionage. Stendhal considered them to be unmitigated evils: *cf. Le Rouge et le Noir*, ch. xvii.

p. 256 . . . *from Paris to Saint-Cloud*. A proverbial phrase, to which Stendhal is particularly attached. It originates in a brochure entitled: *Le Voyage de Paris à St.-Cloud par mer et le retour de St.-Cloud à Paris par terre*, by Néel and Lottin, and was taken up by L.-S. Mercier in his *Tableau de Paris* (ch. xxvi: *Des Parfaits Badauds*).

p. 257 . . . *the tyrant in* Télémaque. This is an interesting link in the development of Stendhal's ideas: for, as the reader will remember, the notion of sleeping every night in a different room is one which is suggested by Count Mosca to his pusillanimous sovereign in the *Chartreuse de Parme*.

p. 257 . . . *some repulsive incidents*. Stendhal has noted in the margin that this alludes to the activities and eventual murder of Giulio Besini, the chief of police to the Duke of Modena. The story of his murder is told in detail in the *Promenades dans Rome* (20th November 1827).

p. 259 . . . *M. Courier.* . . . Allusion to Paul-Louis Courier and his pamphlet: *Lettre à M. Renouard, libraire, sur une tache faite à un manuscrit de Florence* (1810). Also (two paragraphs further on) to his *Lettre à Messieurs de l'Académie des Inscriptions et Belles-Lettres* (1819). Stendhal was a great admirer of Courier, and in 1821, when Courier was in prison, had sent him a signed copy of his *Histoire de la Peinture en Italie*.

p. 260 . . . *but that a man should wallow.* . . . A marginal note suggests that this refers to the duc de Rivière, the personal friend of King Charles X.

p. 264 . . . *the fearful name of* Romanticism. . . . Both *Racine et Shakespeare*, and, in a less obvious way, the *Vie de Rossini*, were polemical pamphlets written in the heat of the 'grande bataille romantique'; and echoes of the battle may still be heard in *Rome, Naples et Florence*. This whole passage on Florentine prose may be taken as an elaboration of Stendhal's famous definition: 'Classicism is what used to please our great-grandfathers; Romanticism is what pleases *us*.'

p. 264 . . . *il Conciliatore.* . . . *Il Conciliatore, foglio scientifico-letterario,* the famous carbonarist news-sheet of Milan, which appeared twice weekly from 3rd Sept. 1818 until 17th Oct. 1819, when it was suspended by the Austrian authorities. Its contributors included all Stendhal's carbonarist circle: Count Porro (on agriculture); Ludovico di Breme (history of civilisation); Silvio Pellico (foreign literature); Berchetti ('letters to the Canon, his uncle'); Borsieri; Romagnosi; Rasori; Ressi; and in particular, Ermes Visconti (romanticism). The authorities attempted to counter its influence with a broadsheet of their own (*L'Accattabrighe*), but without success.

p. 267 . . . *discoursing upon its merits.* The tone of this passage suggests that literary self-advertisement is something that Stendhal would *never* stoop to. The truth is notoriously different, and scholars are still busy identifying all the various articles written by Stendhal, anonymously puffing his own books. The extreme example is, of course, his public quarrel with Carpani over the *Vies de Haydn, Mozart et Métastase*.

p. 272 . . . *and begging for more.* A quotation from Beaumarchais' *Mariage de Figaro*:

Figaro: . . . j'étais né pour être courtisan.
Suzanne: On dit que c'est un métier si difficile!

Figaro: Recevoir, prendre et demander: voilà le secret en trois mots!

p. 273 . . . *can never seem more than thirty.* All this section, together with the 'theory of crystallisation' which follows, is nothing but a rapid précis of Stendhal's celebrated analysis of love, as set out in *De l'Amour,* and as exemplified in *le Rouge et le Noir.*

p. 280 . . . *fabric of your position.* The moral dilemma, here merely sketched, of the young man who is both a *liberal* and a *Marquis,* is worked out in detail in Stendhal's first novel, *Armance,* which was published in 1827, only a year after this edition of *Rome, Naples et Florence.*

p. 280 . . . *baggage-master to* Royal-Cravate. . . . According to Chuquet (*Stendhal-Beyle,* p. 324, note), this statement is incorrect.

p. 287 . . . *between the poets and the philosophers.* This is one of the most fundamental dilemmas in Stendhal's thought, and it recurs in one form or another in almost everything he ever wrote. On the one hand, man cannot exist without liberty, and liberty can only be guaranteed by universal suffrage in a parliamentary democracy. On the other hand, parliamentary democracy, if it is to work efficiently, makes intellectual demands upon the citizen which rob him of the *leisure* necessary to art and graceful living; and without art, existence is not woth enduring. As far as Stendhal is concerned, there is no solution; art is ultimately doomed, and mankind is condemned to a drab and cheerless future of endless political debate.

p. 290 . . . *Giovanni Auguto.* . . . Both these anecdotes concerning Auguto are borrowed from Pignotti, *Storia di Toscana,* bk iv, pp. 211-212.

p. 295 . . . *the sham 'culture' of our Academies.* It may be doubted whether Stendhal's historical erudition was quite as deep and far-reaching as he would sometimes like to suggest. He probably discovered most of the 'original sources' referred to in one or two of the larger compendia of historical writings—in this case, in Muratori, *Rerum italicarum scriptores* (Milan, 27 vols., 1723-51).

p. 304 Fremono amor di patria. . . . Quoted from Ugo Foscolo's poem *I Sepolcri,* written in 1807, on the occasion of a new law concerning cemeteries. *Cf.* letter to Mareste, 9th April 1819: 'Six cents vers, qui sont ce qu'il y a de mieux depuis vingt ans.'

p. 308 *I flew like the wind to the* Hhohhomero. . . . At this point, Stendhal once more takes up the original text of 1817, with minor variations; but only for a few pages. The borrowings end with the quotation from the *Vicar of Wakefield.* Concerning the Florentine pronunciation, *cf. Journal d'Italie,* 27th Sept. 1811.

p. 308 . . . *about that same* libretto. . . . This is inaccurate. Rossini's libretto was specially written for him by Sterbini, and was not the same as that which had been used previously by Paisiello. The signora Giorgi-Righetti, referred to in the same paragraph, was the original *Rosina* at the *première* in Rome (20th Feb. 1816). A few years later, this same lady was so incensed by the number of inaccuracies and unfavourable criticisms contained in Stendhal's first article on Rossini (1822) that she published a vigorous reply (*Cenni di una donna già cantante. . .*, Bologna 1823).

p. 309 . . . primo buffo *parts*. The tale of this army officer turned amateur comedian was deemed profoundly shocking by the *Edinburgh Review* (November 1817).

p. 309 . . . *the trio of the second-act* finale. . . . Stendhal returns to a more detailed analysis of this trio in the *Vie de Rossini* (vol. I, pp. 276-7). Here, his comments refer only to the concluding section of this trio (*zitti, zitti, piano, piano!*); the earlier sections he dismisses (quite unjustifiably) as mediocre.

p. 310 . . . profoundly shocked *by Rossini's temerity*. Not only this anonymous 'young Englishman', but likewise the austere *Edinburgh Review*, was shocked by Rossini's 'impudence'.

p. 310 . . . *an historical pageant*. This piece of musical gossip is only partly true. Garcia was probably responsible for the guitar *accompaniment* to Almaviva's aria; the tune itself was partly adapted from an earlier chorus in *Aureliano in Palmira*. Nor should it be forgotten that Garcia was, in any case, a reputable and successful composer in his own right.

p. 310 . . . simple and inoffensive. The quotation comes from ch. i of Goldsmith's *Vicar of Wakefield*—a book which Stendhal had long admired. With the reference to the *Habeas Corpus Act* a few lines later, we reach the end of this section of Stendhal's borrowings from the 1817 edition.

p. 312 . . . sempre zitelle. The quotation is from Count Giraùd's *La Cetra Spermaceutica*. *Cf. Corresp.*, 3rd March 1820.

p. 319 . . . *never ceases to amaze me*. Stendhal's admiration for de Brosses was constant and unwavering; more than any other single book, the *Lettres d'Italie* may be said to have 'inspired' *Rome, Naples et Florence*. The reference, again, is to the first edition; in the 1836 edition, the passage alluded to occurs in vol. I, p. 265 *et seq*.

p. 329 . . . à la sauce piquante. Quotation from Berchoux, *La Gastronomie*, canto I. In its context, it alludes to the culinary debates which occupied the reign of the Emperor Domitian:

> *Le sénat mitaux voix cette affaire importante,*
> *Et le turbot fut mis à la sauce piquante.*

p. 334 . . . *by the Legislative Assembly of Milan.* . . . This stamp-tax was originally passed by the Government of the Cisalpine Republic in the Year VII, but the disturbances of the period made it impossible to enforce. In 1805, during Napoleon's journey to Italy, it was put formally before the Legislative Assembly of the Republic of Italy, which promptly rejected it. Consequently, one of Napoleon's first acts, upon the establishment of the Kingdom of Italy, was to re-enact it by decree.

p. 340 . . . *the* marchese *Filorusso.* . . . The hero of this caricature was the *marchese* Marucci, by origin a Greek, later a spy in the service of Russia, and among the blackest reactionaries of the period. His *campaign* on the *piazza San Fedele* refers to the murder of Count Prina by the mob (20th April 1814), while Marucci stood by, shouting for blood.

p. 341 . . . *by signor Buratti.* Stendhal not merely admired Buratti, but actually contributed an article on him to the *Biographie Universelle de Furne* (6 vols, Paris 1832).

p. 343 . . . *his* Romish *subjects.* . . . Stendhal uses the curious phrase 'le Italiens de Rome'. Similarly, Duclos, in his *Considérations sur l'Italie* (1791), uses the same paraphrase 'pour ne pas profaner le nom de Romain, en parlant des Romains modernes'.

p. 343 . . . *we left the city.* . . . The 'hero's' itinerary, which takes him directly from Florence to Naples *without stopping in Rome* is a deliberate device (borrowed by Stendhal from de Brosses) to avoid the obvious.

p. 347 . . . *'who knew how to reign'.* See above, p. 170.

p. 347 . . . *this* was *Rossini in person.* This chance meeting between two of the greatest geniuses of their age in a wayside inn offers fascinating material for the imagination. Unfortunately, the incident is imaginary in the first place. Admittedly, Rossini was travelling from Naples (*Otello, teatro del Fondo*, 4th Dec. 1816) to Rome (*La Cenerentola, teatro Valle*, 25th Jan. 1817) at about this period; but Stendhal was elsewhere. In fact, Stendhal only met Rossini in Milan in the latter months of 1819.

p. 349 . . . is poor and grows old. The correct version of this quotation is: '*There live not three good men unhanged in England and one of them is fat and grows old*'. Stendhal's misquotation (for once!) is deliberate.

p. 349 . . . le Nozze in Campagna. . . . The attribution by Stendhal of this opera to Pietro Carlo Guglielmi, rather than to his father, Pietro Alessandro, directly contradicts the standard authorities, Fétis, Larousse, etc. None the less, M. Martineau (*R.N.F.* 1817, p. 373, note 96) has shown that Stendhal was perfectly correct.

p. 350 ... Albergo de' Poveri. ... The *Albergo reale de' Poveri* was a huge orphanage built round a church. The *Palazzo degli Studj* referred to a few lines below included the Royal Museum, a Library and the Academy of Fine Arts.

p. 352 ... *to the rank of* sous-préfet. The singer in question was Alberico Curioni (1785-1875), a distinguished tenor, reputed to have been the handsomest man on the Italian stage. He sang at the *San-Carlo*, later in Barcelona and London, and appeared in several Rossinian operas, notably *Otello*, *la Donna del Lago* and *Pietro l'Eremita* (*Mosè*). There is no confirmation of his administrative activities.

p. 353 ... *the new* San-Carlo. The *teatro San-Carlo*, opened in 1737, was destroyed by fire on 13th Feb. 1816. But the reconstruction, under the impulsive direction of Barbaja, the impresario, and Bianchi, the architect, took place so rapidly, that the re-opening was held on 12th Jan. 1817. Stendhal was in Rome at the time.

p. 355 *The ceiling.* ... This painted ceiling was the work of Giuseppe and Anselmo Cammarano, Frantz Sulle and Gaspare Magnai. The curtain was painted by Giuseppe Cammarano.

p. 356 ... *at the reception of Prince Schwarzenberg.* ... A reference to the terrible fire which broke out on 1st July 1810, at a reception held by Prince Schwarzenberg in honour of Napoleon.

p. 357 ... *his remarkably handsome wife.* All Stendhal's feminine acquaintance are, *ipso facto*, both impeccably aristocratic and peerlessly beautiful. To dismiss this notorious 'ducomanie' as simple snobbery would be to oversimplify the problem. In this case, the evidence strongly suggests that Stendhal's romantic imagination was hard at work. An anonymous contemporary describes the same lady as follows: 'Une grande poupée mince, sans grâce, blanche comme un satin neuf, physionomie aussi bête que l'était le colonel corse échappé du service français depuis l'abdication de Bon. .... Elle était fille d'une maîtresse de pension de Milan ayant été femme de chambre française émigrée.'

p. 357 *The cantata.* ... The work used on this auspicious occasion had been specially written by Simone Mayr: *Il Sogno di Partenope* (libretto by Lampredi).

p. 359 ... *so brilliant as* Paolino. ... Paolino is the hero of Cimarosa's *Matrimonio segreto*. Stendhal had seen Nozzari in the part in Paris in 1804.

p. 360 ... *signora Formigini.* ... The larger part of this description of Naples is adapted from the 1817 edition; but Stendhal adds or alters names to suit his fancy. In 1817, for instance, both 'signora Formigini' and 'la princesse Belmonte' of the preceding paragraph had been lumped together as 'la duchesse de C***'.

p. 362 . . . *achieves a truly heroic stature.* In this anecdote, the heroine, 'la Ghita', is probably a portrait of Francesca Lechi (see *Index*).

p. 363 . . . *Louis Duport.* . . . Stendhal had often watched Duport dancing in Paris. The 'Madame Duport' referred to a few lines further on was his sister. At this date, they were in fact in Naples, producing a ballet entitled *La Virtù premiata*, with music by Gallenberg.

p. 366 . . . gli Zingari. . . . This little ballet formed an interlude in a larger work, a mime-drama entitled *Clotilde duchessa di Salerno*, composed by Antonio Capuzzi. The subject of the ballet was borrowed from *la Gitanilla*, one of Cervantes' *Novelas Ejemplares*.

p. 368 . . . *il Noce di Benevento.* . . . A ballet by Viganò, originally composed in 1801, revived in Milan in 1812. The theme was borrowed from Gozzi: the tree in question was popularly supposed to be the site of the great witches' sabbaths. Martineau suggests, among other possibilities, that 'Madame R***' is Madame de Staël, who had in fact been a guest at the Château de Vizille (for thus is designated, in 1817, the 'Château de B***').

p. 369 . . . *the listener.* . . . This unsympathetic listener is by no means imaginary; specifically, it is Stendhal's friend, the baron de Mareste, who not merely refused to be converted by Stendhal's enthusiasm, but actively jeered at it.

p. 369 . . . *would mean nothing to him.* Viganò's ignorance of Shakespeare was probably less profound than Stendhal imagines—at all events, he produced a highly successful ballet entitled *Otello*. But in any case, Stendhal was determined that he should be enlightened, and on 9th Feb. 1818 wrote him a detailed letter suggesting suitable choreographic themes in Shakespeare's plays —particularly in *Cymbeline*.

p. 373 . . . *in Duport's Cinderella.* . . . This is, in fact, the ballet alluded to above: *La Virtù premiata.* Duport played the King; Mme Duport, Cinderella. Other parts were danced by Salvatore and Maria Taglioni, Adelaïda Mersi, Marianna Conti, etc.

p. 374 . . . *sets out for Terracina.* . . . Terracina is only some sixty miles north-west of Naples; but at the time it lay within the Papal States, and so provided a convenient refuge for persecuted political refugees.

p. 375 . . . *in eight or ten years' time.* In fact, the church was not finished until 1846.

p. 375 . . . *of the human imagination.* Stendhal's blank lines may be filled in without too much effort: 'It is indeed hard to conceive that mankind should have seen fit to abandon so admirable a religion in favour of one which is in all respects so abominable. But there! *Novelty* is a primary desire and need of the human imagination.'

p. 376 . . . *shamelessly inadequate.* In the *Vie de Rossini*, Stendhal gives a detailed analysis of *Otello*, in which he allows himself to have been converted to the music, after having seen Madame Pasta in the part of Desdemona. But he never forgives Berio his libretto.

p. 377 . . . *the term* dom Procolo. . . . Strictly speaking, the term was applied to the 'protector' or platonic lover of any great *prima donna*. It originates in a satire by Benedetto Marcello (1686-1739): *Il Teatro di Musica alla moda.*

p. 386 . . . *the* Loan. . . . In 1817, France was enabled to negotiate a loan from the great banking-houses of London, thanks to the support of the British Government.

p. 388 . . . *the Counts of Virtù.* Here again, most of Stendhal's historical material is drawn, not from original sources, but most probably from Lorenzo Pignotti, *Storia della Toscana fino al Principato, con diversi saggi sulle scienze, lettere ed arti* (10 vols, 1813-1816).

p. 391 . . . *at the* barrière de Pantin. . . . According to Alfieri himself (*Vita*, epoch iv, ch. xxii), the incident took place in Aug. 1792, at the *barrière Blanche*, as he was setting out from Paris.

p. 396 . . . *in Duval's adapted version.* The original play, of doubtful propriety, was entitled *Charles II, Roi d'Angleterre, en certain lieu.* . . . It appeared anonymously in 1789, and was popularly attributed to Mercier. The *Jeunesse de Henri V* had enjoyed a popular run at the *Théâtre Français*, with Michaut as Captain Copp.

p. 400 . . . *MM. G*** and M*** in Paris.* . . . Probably Michaud and Geoffroy. The 1817 edition substitutes 'F***' for 'G***' (=Féletz).

p. 401 . . . *by which her sister had perished.* Queen Caroline of Naples (originally Princess Maria-Carolina of Austria) was the sister of Queen Marie-Antoinette of France.

p. 404 . . . *the* Republic of Parthenope. The French invasion of Italy in 1799 transformed the Kingdom of Naples into *la République parthénopienne.*

p. 408 . . . not *imitated by Lord Bentinck at Genoa.* In 1814, Lord Bentinck commanded a successful expedition against Genoa, where he issued two proclamations which anticipated by nearly half a century the proclamation of Italian unity, and thereby 'caused some embarrassment to his government'.

p. 409 . . . merits and demerits of his subjects. In English (mis-spelt) in the original.

p. 411 . . . *a Certain August Personage.* King Ferdinand III, King of the Two Sicilies. The 'anecdote du cadavre debout sur la mer' is alluded to again in the *Vie de Rossini* (vol. II, p. 223, note). Admiral Caraccioli was hanged from the yard-arm of the ship, and then cut down so as to fall into the sea. Two days later, by a freak of chance, the corpse appeared, floating bolt upright and with its head above the waves, heading straight for Naples. Much superstitious terror ensued among the population.

p. 413 . . . *I have no knowledge of the originals.* Most of this history of the Neapolitan revolution was probably drawn by Stendhal from Vincenzo Cuoco's *Essay upon the Revolution in Naples.* See also J. Turquan and J. d'Auriac, *Lady Hamilton, Ambassadrice d'Angleterre, et la Révolution de Naples*; H. Acton, *The Bourbons of Naples* (London 1956).

p. 415 . . . *actors within the town.* . . . 'Signor D***' is undoubtedly Prince Demidoff (*cf. Promenades dans Rome*, 15th Jan. 1828). Juliette Drouet, the celebrated friend of Victor Hugo, was a member of the troupe.

p. 418 . . . *explanation of the.* . . . Once again, it is not difficult to guess at the missing passage: 'the explanation of those remarkable fortunes amassed by certain members of the government in 1826'. However, a marginal note also refers to the 'millions perdus en Espagne'.

p. 419 . . . *the famous statue of Jupiter Mansuetus.* Cf. *Histoire de la Peinture en Italie*, ch. lxxxvi, note.

p. 424 . . . *God knows what is being done to him.* This extremely obscure reference is slightly illuminated by the *Promenades dans Rome*: 'La présence d'un prisonnier d'importance n'a pas permis qu'on nous montrât [les fresques de Jules Romain au Château de Saint-Ange]. C'est un archevêque égyptien qui a, dit-on, mystifié la Cour de Rome, et, à son tour, a été pipé par le gouvernement napolitain; l'archevêque avait pris pour confident un jésuite.' (*P.R.*, 1st June 1828.)

p. 426 . . . *a sometime sergeant-at-arms di Jachino.* . . . Stendhal's anecdote here is historically exact. The robber-band in question was that known as the Meomartino band, led by Gaetano Vardarelli, who was born jn Apulia in 1780, and had in fact seen service under Murat. In 1817, a truce was concluded between Vardarelli and the Neapolitan authorities, and the remaining members of his band were formally enrolled in the police. Soon after, however, they were all murdered one by one.

p. 431 . . . *will no longer seem fantastical.* Cf. *De l'Amour*, chs. liv-lvi. Certain of these ideas were borrowed by Stendhal from the *Edinburgh Review*. It is worth noting, however, that Stendhal's ideas concerning emancipation, divorce, etc., are decidedly unenlightened, even for his own time. The Utopian Socialists of the eighteenth century (not to mention exceptional writers, such as de Sade on the one hand, or Mary Wollstonecraft on the other) had put forward far more advanced views concerning the position of woman in society.

p. 433 ... *this illustrious man of learning*. ... The Count de Clarac, according to a marginal note.

p. 433 ... *a Most Illustrious Personage*. ... Marginal note: 'Voyage de M. le Comte de Forbin. [Découverte] attribuée à M. de Blacas par M. de Forbin. La gloire, si gloire [il] y a, est à M. le Baron M[arti]al Daru.' De Blacas was the French Ambassador in Rome; Martial Daru was Stendhal's second cousin and intimate friend, who was nominated Comptroller of Crown Property in Rome on 12th March 1811. The discovery of the inscribed pedestal of the column (13th March 1813) is related in the *Promenades* (24th Jan. 1828).

p. 434 *This* Aristides. ... This statue (now labelled *Aeschines*) may still be seen in the National Museum of Naples.

p. 435 ... *the society of don Nardo*. ... Don Bernardo, according to a marginal note.

p. 435 *The Duke of Bisagno*. ... 'Ventignano, le Baour de Naples', according to a marginal note. Baour-Lormian (1770–1854), the translator of Ossian, was a poet whom Stendhal particularly detested.

p. 437 *Don Jo*. ... Don Jorre, Curator of the Museum at Portici, according to a marginal note.

p. 440 *Signora B*** declared one day*. ... Signora B*** = signora Aresi, according to a marginal note.

p. 446 ... *of the century preceding*. The whole of this long discussion, to which Stendhal gives the title: *Paris vu de Portici*, takes the place of a curious section headed *Paris d'autrefois* in the 1817 edition, in which Stendhal had undertaken a paradoxical apologia for the *Ancien Régime*.

p. 446 ... *Yesterday's farce*. ... This paragraph seems to have been written a day later than the paragraph preceding it, and Stendhal has forgotten to make the necessary adjustment in time.

p. 447 ... *one* don Cecchino. ... According to a marginal note, H*s H*l*n*ss = Pope Leo XII; don Cecchino = the Cardinal della Somaglia.

p. 450 . . . *Michelangelo's* Last Judgment. . . . Stendhal's famous description
of this painting will be found in the *Histoire de la Peinture en
Italie*. Delacroix thought it a masterpiece of descriptive writing.

p. 451 . . . *will perforce take place in my absence*. In the *Vie de Henry Brulard*
(ch. xxxviii), Stendhal tells how he did eventually grant the
'sacred capons' a second hearing (in January 1836), and found
them not a whit more agreeable.

p. 455 Chalmers' Dictionary. The 1817 edition and the English translation
of 1818 give *Chalmers'*; the 1826 and 1854 editions give *Chambers'*.
It is still not clear which is meant. Alexander Chalmers' *General
Biographical Dictionary* (32 vols., London 1812-1817) was an
important contemporary work, and we know that on 3rd Dec.
1818, Stendhal was copying out passages from it for an article on
Shakespeare. On the other hand, it was still unknown in Italy,
whereas Ephraim Chambers' *Cyclopaedia, or Dictionary of Arts
and Sciences* (2 vols, London, 1728) had been thrice translated
into Italian. All in all, the evidence seems to be in favour of
Chalmers'.

p. 458 . . . Camuccini. . . . It is somewhat unexpected, judging by Stendhal's
text, to discover that the *Morte di Cesare* was by no means one
of Camuccini's recent works. It was painted in 1793, when the
artist was twenty-two years old, and in fact made his reputation.
Stendhal again refers disparagingly to Camuccini in the *Promenades* (14th June 1828).

p. 461 . . . *a catastrophic failure*. Stendhal has got his dates inverted. *Le
Devin du Village* was performed in 1753, while *La Nouvelle
Héloïse* was published only in 1761.

p. 461 . . . *by which they are destroyed*. Another essential passage in the
complex pattern of thought which goes to make Stendhal's
theory of musical sensibility.

p. 465 . . . *it would be imprudent to send to the printer*. It was certainly *not*
political cautiousness which prevented Stendhal from handing
these various passages to the printer, but the printer, who, for
financial reasons, refused to accept them. Delaunay had signed
a contract with Stendhal for *one* volume of thirty sheets; already
Stendhal was well on with vol. II, and had reached sheet thirty-
nine! Plainly, Delaunay was imperiously demanding that the
inexhaustible writer should stop. From this point onward, we
are constantly aware that Stendhal has given up trying to finish
the book as he would have wished: this explains the curious
ending, the total lack of any conclusion. Of the 'omitted'
passages, all found their way eventually into the *Promenades dans
Rome*; but then the same thing happened again: Delaunay

called a halt, and the *Description of the Mechanism of Government in Rome* once again had to be eliminated. It was finally published by Colomb in his *Journal d'un Voyage en Italie* (Paris 1833).

p. 465 . . . *the wife of General Pfiffer.* Marginal note: 'Jardin de St.-Georges, et le tour qu'il joua à Mgr. della Genga, depuis Léon XII. Cette histoire de Léon XII sous le nom du Cardinal Banti aurait remplacé vingt pages sur la danse.' *Cf.* Chuquet, in *la Revue*, 1st Jan. 1913.

BIOGRAPHICAL INDEX

NOTE: *where more than one spelling is common, that used in the text is given first, and the alternative in brackets. An asterisk (*) against a page-reference indicates that, although the person concerned is clearly alluded to on the page shown, he or she is not actually mentioned by name.*

Aeneas, 'pious'. Hero of virgil's epic; 406.

Aeneid (epic poem). See Virgil.

Affò, Father Ireneo, s.j. (b. Busseto 1741; d. 1797). Italian scholar, who worked mainly in Parma and Ferrara in the eighteenth century. His works include a *Storia di Parma* (1797), a *Ragionamento sopra una stanza dipinta del celeberrimo Antonio Allegri da Correggio nel monistero di S. Paolo in Parma*, and a number of writings on Parmengianino, on dialect poetry, etc.; 77.

Agadaneca (musical drama). See Saccente; also Gallenberg.

Agar (painting). See Guercino.

Agost***, signora, of Bologna; 339.

Agosti, contessa (*née* Barral), of Milan. A relative of one of Stendhal's closest friends of his younger days, Louis-Joseph-François Barral (1783-1859); 46.

Aïssé, mademoiselle d' (b. 1695; d. Paris 1733). A Circassian slave, originally purchased at the age of four by the French Ambassador to Constantinople, the comte de Ferriol, and brought to France in 1700. She fell in love with the chevalier d'Aydie (1692-1768) and wrote him a series of remarkable *Letters*, which were published in 1787; 263.

Ajace (tragedy). See Foscolo.

Ajo nell' imbarazzo, l' (comedy). See Giraùd, Giovanni.

Alari, Count. Art-patron in Milan; 80.

Albano, Cardinal Guiseppe (b. 1750; d. Rome 1834). Italian churchman, head of the most reactionary group in the College of Cardinals, and strong supporter of the Austrian domination; 159, 171, 296.

Albany, Louise-Maximilienne-Caroline of Stolberg-Gedern, Countess of (b. 1752; d. Florence 1824). In 1774, she was married to Charles-Edward Stuart, the 'Young Pretender', self-styled 'Count of Albany'. Soon after, she met Alfieri, and became his mistress. In 1783, she was officially separated from Charles-Edward; in 1788, she was secretly married to Alfieri, and lived with him until his death (1803). From 1803-1824, she was the most noted hostess in Florence; 317.

Albareze, Count, of Bologna; 255, 256.

Albergati-Capacelli, Francesco (b.

Bologna 1728; d. Venice 1804). Italian dramatist, friend of Goldoni and Voltaire. He specialised in comedies, but was among the first to introduce the *comédie larmoyante* into Italy. He also translated Voltaire. His best-known work is *il Ciarlatore maldicente*. *Il Pomo* was written about 1780; 264.

Albigensians. A religious sect, influential in southern France 1150-1200. In 1209, a crusade against them was preached by Pope Innocent III and St Dominic (*q.v.*), and the heretics were exterminated with a cruelty which has become legendary; 346.

Alcaforada, Marianna. Author of the celebrated *Lettres d'Amour d'une Religieuse portugaise, écrites au Chevalier de C***, officier français en Portugal. . . .* First translated into French in 1669; 130.

Alembert, Jean le Rond d' (1717-1783). French writer, philosopher and mathematician, illegitimate son of Madame de Tencin. Founder-collaborator of the *Encyclopédie*, and author of the famous *Discours Préliminaire*; 92.

Alessi, Galeazzo (b. Perugia 1512; d. 1572). Major Italian architect of the Renaissance, whose main works are to be seen in Genoa. Towards the end of his career, he worked also in Milan, where he designed the church of the Madonna di San-Celso (1568), and was consulted on the plans for il Duomo; 99.

Alexander VI Borgia, Pope from 1492 to 1503. Politician and statesman, with perhaps an exaggerated reputation for treachery; 238.

Alexander the Great (B.C. 356-323). King of Macedon and pupil of Aristotle; conqueror of Greece and of Persia as far as the Indus; 131.

Alfieri, Vittorio (b. Asti 1749; d. Florence 1803). Poet and political figure, and Italy's greatest tragic dramatist. Stendhal was at first a great admirer of A.; later, his enthusiasm cooled; 11, 12, 112, 142, 143, 146, 218, 220, 258, 272, 301, 317, 389, 390, 391, 392, 395, 397, 455, 458.
Works referred to:
   Agide (tragedy, *c.* 1785); 112.
   Don Garzia (tragedy, *c.* 1784); 458.

Principe (il) e le Lettere (treatise, 1778–1786); 218.

Rosmunda (tragedy, *c.* 1780); 395.

Saulle (tragedy, *c.* 1784); 389, 390.

Vita di Vittorio Alfieri, da Asti, scritta da esso . . . (autobiography). Published in two parts, 1790 and 1803; 390.

Almachilde. Character in Alfieri's *Rosmunda*; 395.

Ambrose, St (b. Trèves, A.D. 340; d. 397). One of the Fathers of the Latin Church. Archbishop of Milan. Following the massacre of Thessalonika, he imposed penance upon the Emperor Theodosius; 81.

Ammirato, Scipione (b. Lecce 1531; d. Florence 1601). Italian historian, best known for his *Storie Fiorentine* (Florence, 1600-1641). A. was proclaimed the greatest historian of his age; 295.

Amour, De l' (Psychological analysis). See Stendhal.

Amours de Psyche, les (poetic novel). See La Fontaine.

Ancillo, signor. Minor Venetian poet; 70.

Anderloni, Faustino (b. Brescia 1766; d. Pavia 1847). Perhaps the best of the nineteenth-century classic engravers. Professor of Art in the University of Pavia from 1801; 106, 236.

Anderloni, Pietro (b. Brescia 1785; d. Lecco 1849). Brother of the above, with less talent but a wider range. His works include the illustrations to a treatise on *Aneurisms* by Dr Scarpa (*q.v.*); 106, 236.

Andria, Duke of (=Ettore Carafa, Count of Ruvo, son of the Duke of Andria: b. Naples 1763; executed Naples 1799). Neapolitan insurgent. After escaping from the Castel Sant' Elmo, he became the leader of the Republican forces against Cardinal Ruffo's royalist levies; 412.

Angelico, fra Giovanni da Fiesole, known as (b. Fiesole 1387; d. Florence 1455). Dominican friar, and major Italian painter of the Tuscan school; 30.

Angeloni, Luigi (b. Frosinone 1759; d. London 1842). Italian writer and liberal politician, a disciple of Rousseau and the *Encyclopédistes*. From 1801-1823, A. spent much of his time in exile in France, where he wrote for the émigré journal *l'Esule*, and composed his major political treatises, including: *Sopra l'ordinamento che aver dovrebbono i governi d'Italia* (1814), and *Dell' Italia uscente il settembre* 1818 (2 vols., 1818). He died in great poverty; 250.

Annal. Mediol.; 289.

Annals of Pistoia (chronicle). See Tronci.

Annibal (tragedy). See Didot, F.

Annoni, signora, of Milan; 85.

Annunciation, the (painting). See Carracci, Lodovico.

Anthony, St, of Padua (b. Lisbon 1195; d. 1231). Missionary friar who preached the Gospel among the Moorish tribes of Africa; 410.

Antonj, signor degli, of Bologna; 169, 246, 247, 291.

Apocalypse, the. Last book of the New Testament, written by St John the Evangelist on the Island of Patmos in the reign of the Emperor Domitian; 239.

Apostoli, Francesco (b. 1755). An unsuccessful Italian official, repeatedly victim of the political troubles of his time. He was imprisoned in Corfù (1794-7); later in Sebenico and Petervaradino. Turned towards literature at the end of his career; his most successful work, the *Lettere sirmiensi per servire alla storia della deportazione de' cittandini cisalpini in Dalmazia ed Ungheria*, deals with the second period of his imprisonment; 57.

Apotheosis of Napoleon (painting). See Appiani.

Appert, Benjamin-Nicolas-Marie (b. 1797). French philanthropist and educational reformer. In 1822, he was himself imprisoned for having helped two political prisoners to escape. The work referred to by Stendhal is the *Rapport sur l'état actuel des prisons, des hospices et des écoles des départements de l'Aisne, du Pas de Calais et de la Somme* (1824). His major work is *Bagnes, Prisons et Criminels*, 4 vols., 1836; 149.

Appiani, Andrea (b. Milan 1754; d. Milan 1817). Milanese painter greatly favoured by Napoleon, who, in 1796, made him 'commissario superiore' for procuring works of art for Paris. He was a competent fresco-painter; but is best known for his portraits, and for his vast symbolical canvases glorifying Napoleon; 52, 57, 65, 77, 107.

Arabian Nights, the (oriental tales); 330, 479.

Arbuthnot, Dr John (b. Kincardine 1667; d. Hampstead 1735). Scots physician, philosopher and writer, the friend of Swift, Pope, Gay, etc. As a physician, he attended Queen Anne during her last illness. His literary satire, the *Memoirs of Martin Scriblerus*, was composed during the first years of the century, but remained unpublished until 1741; 400.

Aresi, contessa Antonia Barbara Giulia Faustina Angiola Lucia, *née* Fagnani (b. Milan 1778; d. 1847). One of the most celebrated coquettes of Milan; her lovers (including Foscolo) were innumerable; and she had been the toast of the French army of occupation; 108, 440*, 441*.

Argentina, teatro (Rome). See *Theatres*.

Ariosto, Ludovico (b. Reggio d'Emilia 1474; d. Ferrara 1533). Major Italian poet, employed by the House of Este. His *Orlando Furioso* was begun in 1506, published in 1516, and considerably revised in 1532; 142, 245, 265, 267.

Aristides the Just (B.C. 540-468). Athenian general and statesman, the opponent of Themistocles. In B.C. 490 he fought with distinction at the battle of Marathon, and in 477 was entrusted with drawing up the laws of the maritime confederacy; 434.

Aristodemo (tragedy). See Monti.

Aristotle (B.C. 384-322). Greek philosopher; 253.

As You Like It (comedy). See Shakespeare.

Astley, Mr. Bootmaker of Bond Street, London; 189.

Astolfo e Giocondo (ballet). See Isouard; also Vestris III.

Astore, Count. A victim of Cesare Borgia; 238.

Augustus, Emperor (Caesar Octavius: b. Rome B.C. 63; d. Nola A.D. 14). The first and most magnificent of all the Roman Emperors; 301.

Augustus III, Elector of Saxony and King of Poland (b. Dresden 1696; d. Dresden 1763). An ineffective monarch,

bested at all points by Frederick the Great. His only real interests lay in painting and music, and he added vastly to the collection of art treasures at Dresden; 162.

Auguto, Giovanni. Mediaeval *condottiere* of English origins. His portrait on horseback, by Paolo Uccello, may still be seen in Santa Maria del Fiore, Florence; 290.

Ayen, duc de. One of the many titles of Louis, duc de Noailles (1713-1793). French soldier and administrator, created maréchal de France in 1775. Famous for his witty and sarcastic tongue; 188.

Azaïs, Pierre-Hyacinthe (b. Sorèze 1766; d. St Emilion 1845). French philosopher of a woolly and optimistic persuasion, who taught a system of 'providential justice'. His main work, *Des Compensations dans les Destinées humaines*, appeared in 1809. He also wrote many tales for children; 254.

Azario, Pietro (b. Novara 1312; d. *c.* 1364). Italian historian at the Court of the Visconti of Milan. His major work, *Liber Gestorum in Lombardia per e contra Vicecomites*, is a mine of information on early Renaissance manners and customs; 157.

B***, Château de (1817 edition: Château de Vizille). Mansion owned by Claude Périer, whose son, Alphonse, was a life-long friend of Stendhal. Madame de Staël is known to have been a visitor here; 368.

B***, contessa, of Milan. Presumed mistress of Rossini; 61.

B***, madame. Blind Frenchwoman in Bologna; 225.

B***, marchese, of Milan; 129.

B***, signora, of Naples; 440.

Bacri (Baccheri) brothers. The four sons of a Neapolitan merchant of English origins, Vincenzo Baccher, of whom the leaders, Gennaro and Gerardo, were shot by the republican insurgents in 1799. See also under *San Felice*; 412.

Baffi, signor. Neapolitan insurgent, executed in 1799; 411.

Baffò, Giorgio (b. Venice 1694; d. Venice 1768). Venetian dialect poet, who was happiest describing in detail the joys of carnal love. See the

Raccolta universale delle opere di Giorgio Baffò, 4 vols., Cosmopoli, 1789; 139.

Bagni, signor. Neapolitan insurgent, executed in 1799; 411.

Bajazet (tragedy). See Racine.

Banti, Brigitta Giorgi (b. Crema 1759; d. Bologna 1806). A street-singer, engaged by de Vismes for the *Opéra* (1778). A pupil of Sacchini, Piozzi and Abel, she is reputed to have learnt nothing at any time. A brilliant natural soprano, who sang in many operas by Gluck, Paisiello, Nasolini, Bianchi, etc. On her death, she bequeathed her larynx to the Municipality of Bologna; 25.

Barbaja, Domenico (b. Milan 1778; d. Posilipo, 1841). One of the greatest *impresari* of all time. His 'discoveries' include Rossini, Bellini, Donizetti, and the dancer Maria Taglioni, besides many others. After managing the San-Carlo, he went to Vienna as manager of the Kärthner-Thor and Auf dem Wien theatres. He himself figures in an opera, *La Sirène*, by Auber and Scribe; 333, 359, 375.

Barbiere di Siviglia (opera). See Paisiello.

Barbiere di Siviglia (opera). See Rossini.

Baretti, Guiseppe (b. Turin 1719; d. London 1789). Italian poet and journalist, who lived much of his life in London. His works include the satirical *Account of the Manners and Customs of Italy* (London 1768-9), and a number of dictionaries; 358.

Baroni di Felsheim, i. Play, author unknown, based on a popular novel by Pigault-Lebrun (*q.v.*); 394.

Bartholomew, St. Martyr, one of the Twelve Apostles. (*Massacre of:*) Murder of the Huguenot leaders in France on the night of 23 August 1572, at the instigation of Marie de Médicis and the Princes of the House of Guise; 51, 346, 442.

Bartolomeo, fra, di San Marco (b. Savignano 1469; d. Florence 1517). Dominican friar, and major Italian painter of the Tuscan school; 266, 302, 317, 319.

Bassi, Luigi (b. Pesaro 1766; d. 1825). An eminent Italian *buffo* baritone, who spent the better part of his career in Prague, where he was most successful in operas by Paisiello. Mozart's *Don Giovanni* was written for his voice. Later manager of the Dresden operahouse; 17, 18, 22, 60.

Bassompierre, François, duc de (b. Lorraine 1579; d. Provins 1646). French general and statesman with a striking personality and most ingenious wit. For the sin of conspiring against Richelieu, he spent twelve years in the Bastille (1631-1643), where he wrote a *Journal de ma Vie*, which gives a valuable portrait of his age; 439.

Bassville, Nicolas Hugou de (b. Abbeville 1753; killed Rome 1793). French adventurer and diplomat. The son of a dyer, B. had been successively priest, tutor and sub-editor of the *Mercure Politique*. In 1792, he was sent with Mackau as French representative to Naples, whence he soon moved to Rome; and in January 1793 he was murdered by the Roman populace, which was rioting in protest against the seizure of Avignon from the Pope. See also *Monti*; 140, 141.

Bassvilliana, la (epic poem, dedicated to Pope Pius VI). See Monti.

Bathurst, Miss. English visitor to Rome, accidentally drowned in the Tiber, near the Ponte Molle, in January 1828. (*Cf. le Globe*, 30 January 1828); 41.

Bayle, Pierre (b. Ariège 1647; d. Rotterdam 1706). Notable French philosopher and polemist, champion of the Protestant faction and the greatest advocate of religious toleration; 252.

Beaumarchais, Pierre-Augustin Caron, Sieur de (b. Paris 1732; d. 1799). French watchmaker, inventor, musician, diplomat, intriguer, poet, playright, financier, etc. His *Mémoires contre Goezmann* (1773-1774) are a series of brilliant satirical pamphlets directed against a High Court judge and his incautious wife; they created a vast public scandal, and contributed greatly to discredit the judicial authority of the *Ancien Régime*; 157, 190, 252, 396, 464.

Beccaria, Count Cesare di (b. Milan 1738; d. Milan 1794). Italian philosopher, writer and reformer; one of the leading figures in European penal reform. In 1768, B. was appointed professor at the *Scuole Palatine* in

Milan; 78, 92, 93, 94, 95, 110, 111, 220.
His major works are:

Il Caffè (periodical, edited by B. and
Pietro Verri, 1764-1766); 92.

Dei Delitti e delle Pene (Livorno
1764); 92, 110.

Beethoven, Ludwig van (1770-1827).
German composer, whom Stendhal,
at this period, knew mainly from
hearsay; 309.

Belintani, signora, of Milan; 127.

Bellegarde, Field-Marshal Henri, comte
de (b. Dresden 1756; d. Vienna 1845).
Austrian general of Savoyard origins,
who fought against Napoleon in Italy
and Austria. In 1814, he was appointed
Governor-General of all Austrian
possessions in Italy, until his retirement
in 1825; 96, 97.

Belmonte, Lucrezia Pignatelli, Princess of
(fl. 1740-1820). Originally an intimate
friend and dissolute confidante of
Queen Caroline of Naples, she later
became an ardent republican. In 1817
(when she was well into her seventies)
she had recently made peace with
Ferdinand and returned from exile.
She had literary pretensions, and
painted abominably; 67, 358, 360, 367,
445.

Belsham, William (b. Bedford 1752; d.
Hammersmith 1827). English political
writer and historian, of strong whig
sympathies. His chief work is the
Memoirs of the Reign of George III to
the Session of Parliament 1793 (6 vols.,
1795-1801). B. was one of the more
liberal-minded historians of his time;
389.

Bembo, Cardinal Pietro (1470-1547). A
celebrated renaissance humanist and
latinist, with a European reputation.
Bembo was secretary to Pope Leo X.
His best-known work is his Storia di
Venezia (1487-1537); 462.

Bentinck, Lord William Cavendish
(1774-1839). English general and
administrator. Served under Welling-
ton during the Napoleonic campaigns,
and was dictator of Sicily; governor-
general of Bengal (1828); later first
governor-general of India. In 1814,
Bentinck commanded a successful
expedition against Genoa, where he
issued two proclamations which,
'anticipating by nearly half a century

the proclamation of Italian unity,
caused some embarrassment to his
government'; 241, 409.

Bentivoglio dynasty (Bologna); 165, 277,
282, 283, 288.

Giovanni I (reigned 1401-1402); 283.
Anton-Galeazzo (1416-1435); 283.
Annibale (1438-1445); 283, 284, 285.
Ercole (father of Santi); 285.
Santi (1446-1462); 285, 287, 288.
Giovanni II (1462-1506); 285, 286.
Annibale II (1511-1512); 286, 287.
Ermes (1511-1512); 286, 287.

Bentivoglio, Ippolito. (Stendhal is in
error, either with the name, or with
the date. An Ippolito Bentivoglio,
author of a number of 'dramatic fables',
flourished c. 1660-1680; on the other
hand, the scholar, dramatist and friend
of Ariosto was Ercole Bentivoglio
(1506-1573).); 287.

Bentivoglio, don Tommaso, of Bologna:
latter-day descendant of the above;
276-283.

Benvenuti, Pietro (b. Arezzo 1769; d.
Florence 1844). Italian painter who
studied in Florence and Rome; friend
of Camuccini (q.v.). Director of the
Florentine Academy of Fine Arts,
1803. None of the paintings mentioned
by Stendhal (la Morte di Cesare; le
Fatiche d'Ercole; la Giuditta) is among
his better-known works; 319.

Benzoni dynasty, of Crema; 271.

Benzoni, contessa (b. Corfù 1756; d.
Venice 1833). A friend of Stendhal,
one of the most celebrated coquettes of
Venice at the end of the eighteenth
century. Famous for her wit, beauty
and eccentricity, she had been the
heroine of the famous romance, la
Biondina in Gondoletta. When the
French entered Venice, she had danced
the Carmagnole in a Grecian tunic on
the Piazza San-Marco; 69.

Béranger, Pierre-Jean de (1780-1857).
French poet and song-writer. His early
work is light and epicurean; his later
songs biting and satirical. He was also
a competent librettist; 32.

Berchetti, Giovanni (pseud. Grisostomo
Berchet) (b. Milan 1783; d. Turin
1851). Italian novelist and translator,
of Swiss origins. His translations
include Gray, Goldsmith and Schiller.
In 1816, he published Sul Cacciatore

feroce e sulla Eleonora di G. A. Burger: Lettera semiseria di Grisostomo, and this gave him his pseudonym for his articles to *il Conciliatore* (1818-1819). In later years, he worked in an Italian bank in London and wrote novels; 67, 264.

Berchoux, Joseph (b. St-Symphorien-en-Laye 1765; d. Marsigny 1838). French satirical poet, whose whole reputation now rests upon one work: *La Gastronomie* (Paris 1800); 329.

Bergerie, Madame Rougier de la. Wife of a *préfet* of the Yonne, with whom Stendhal became acquainted through his friend Crozet in Paris in 1810; 65.

Berio di Salsa, marchese Francesco. Celebrated social figure in Naples, and patron of Canova. Librettist of Rossini's *Otello* and *Ricciardo e Zoraïde*. In Naples, his libretto for *Otello* was much appreciated: he was congratulated on 'toning down the tremendous catastrophes of the ferocious Shakespeare'; 358, 376, 378.

Bernardin de Saint-Pierre, Jacques-Henri (b. Le Havre 1737; d. 1814). French writer, best known for his exotic and sentimental novel *Paul et Virginie*. He was also a popular philosopher, who specialised in optimistic proofs of the existence of God by the argument from final causes; 254.

Berthellemot, Pontus-Gaspard. Bad French versifier, official of the Paris Municipality under Napoleon; 358.

Bertoletti, Antonio (b. Milan 1775; d. 1846). Italian general who had served under Napoleon from 1796. He took part in the ill-fated Egyptian expedition, and served with honour in the Peninsular War, at the defence of Tarragona; 213.

Bertolotti, Davide (b. Turin 1784; d. 1860). Italian dramatist, poet, historian and journalist. In Milan, he edited *il Spettatore*, to which Stendhal sent contributions. A facile writer in the early romantic tradition. His works include three tragedies: *Tancredi* (1826); *Ines di Castro* (1826) and *i Crociati a Damasco* (1829); 396.

Berton, Henri Montan (1767-1844). Son of the well-known composer and conductor, Pierre Montan Berton (1727-1780). As a violinist, Berton was

an infant prodigy; he was a pupil of Rey and Sacchini. His best-known work was *Montano et Stéphanie* (1798); 16.

Besenval, Pierre-Victor, baron de (1742-1794). French soldier and writer, in command of the Swiss regiments in 1789; withdrew his troops without orders when the Bastille was attacked. Author of the *Mémoires de M. le Baron de Besenval* (3 vols., 1805), and of tales; 389.

Besini, Giulio. Chief of Police to the Duke of Modena; 130, 257*.

Bettoni, Nicolò Zanon (b. Padua 1770; d. Paris 1842). Italian printer and publisher, who, in 1807, brought out the first edition of Foscolo's *Sepolcri*. Later, however, the business failed; in 1832, B. tried to start again in Paris, failed once more, and died in debt and poverty; 111, 146.

Bianca, signor della, of Milan; 74.

Bianchi, Margherita. Popular *prima ballerina* at the San Carlo, Naples; 393.

Bianchi, Pietro. Minor Italian architect, formerly held in great esteem by Napoleon. Architect of the San Carlo in Naples, and of S. Francesco di Paola, which is modelled on the Pantheon in Rome; 374, 375.

Bias, Fanny (1785-1825). A pupil of Coulon, she became *prima ballerina* of the *Grand Opéra*, Paris, in 1817. She created the rôle of Elise in the famous Aumer-Gyrowetz ballet, *Les Pages du Duc de Vendôme*; 370.

Biblioteca Italiana, la (periodical). See Acerbi.

Bignami, Maddalena (*fl.* 1780-1830). Wife of a Milanese banker, and cousin of Mathilde Viscontini (*q.v.*). Mistress of Ugo Foscolo. Stendhal had met her through a letter of introduction from Bianca Milesi (*q.v.*); 37.

Bigot de Préameneu, Félix-Julien-Jean (b. Rennes 1747; d. Paris 1825). French lawyer and politician: deputy to the National Assembly; imprisoned under the Terror. Under Napoleon, he had a hand in drawing up the *Code Civil*, and was made a peer of France during the Hundred Days. His writings are wholly political; 371.

Billington, Elizabeth (b. Soho, 1768; d. Treviso 1818). Great English soprano,

Reggio and Parma, and later throughout Italy, but failed in Paris (1823).
Retired 1828; 9, 10, 22.

Bonténard, Madame de. French *émigrée*;
102.

Borda, Dr. Milanese physician of liberal
sympathies; 101.

Borghese, Prince Marcantonio IV (1730-
1800). One of the most resplendent
and sumptuous Roman aristocrats of
the eighteenth century, who spent
lavishly on paintings, buildings and
gardens. His son Camillo (1775-1832)
was a noted liberal, and married
Pauline Bonaparte (*q.v.*); 481.

Borghese, Princess. See Bonaparte,
Marie-Pauline.

Borgia, Cesare, Duke of Valentino, son
of Pope Alexander VI (*q.v.*) A skilful
politician and diplomat, but with an
evil reputation for cruelty, treachery
and debauched amusements; 238.

Boroni, Captain (*note*: Boroni was the
maiden name of Stendhal's mistress,
Angela Pietragrua); 216-217.

Borromeo, St Charles (1538-1584);
Archbishop of Milan and patron saint
of that city: one of the leaders of the
great reform within the Catholic
church; 51, 53, 62, 63, 146, 156, 202.

Borsieri, Pietro (b. Milan 1786; d.
Belgirate 1852). Milanese civil servant,
carbonaro and writer, one of the
founders of *il Conciliatore*. Imprisoned
in the Spielberg 1820-1836; later
deported to America. Author of *Le
Avventure letterarie di un Giorno, o
Consigli di un galant'uomo a vari
scrittori*—from which a number of
ideas in *Rome, Naples et Florence* are
borrowed; 66, 264.

Bosio, Francois-Joseph (b. Monaco 1768;
d. Paris 1845). Sculptor, known as the
'French Canova'. He had all the faults
and none of the virtues of the illustrious Italian. His statue of Louis XIV
may still be seen in the Place des
Victoires; 158*.

Bossi, Giuseppe (b. Busto Arsizio 1777;
d. 1815). Painter and poet in Milanese
dialect. 1807-9 (with Appiani) reorganised the Brera. As an art-critic,
his *Cenacolo di Leonardo da Vinci* (1810)
had considerable influence on Stendhal.
See also Porta, Carlo; 138, 232.

Botta, Count Carlo (b. San-Giorgio

1766; d. 1837). Italian historian and
poet, imprisoned for his republican
ideals. After release, he fled to France:
governor of Piedmont under Napoleon, rector of the Universities of
Nancy and Rouen. Disgraced in 1822.
His works include *Histoire d'Italie de
1789 à 1814* (5 vols., Paris 1824); 162.

Botta, Count, of Milan; 44.

Boucher, François (b. Paris 1703; d.
Paris 1770). French painter, typical of
the grace and delicacy of the school of
Watteau and Fragonard; 372.

Boufflers, Stanislas-Jean, chevalier de (b.
Nancy 1738; d. 1815). French soldier
and administrator, Governor of Sene-
gal. He was also a poet of considerable
charm, and enjoyed an international
reputation as a teller of anecdotes; 204.

Bourbon dynasty: Kings of France from
Henri IV (1589) to Charles X (1830).
King Ferdinand of Naples was also a
Bourbon; 230.

Bragadin family, of Venice. One of the
oldest and most celebrated patrician
clans of that city; the best-known
representative of the clan was Marcantonio B. (1523-1571), Governor of
Cyprus when the island was captured
by the Turks; 71.

Bramante (Donato d'Angelo Lazzari,
known as: b. Fermignano 1444; d.
Rome 1514). Major Italian architect,
uncle of Raphael. Responsible for the
plan of St Peter's Square in Rome; 99.

Brandt. Character in Goldoni's *il Poeta
fanatico*; 395.

Braschi (Romualdo Braschi-Onesti,
known as Prince B.). Son of the sister
of Pope Pius VI, who granted him the
reversion of his own titles in 1778 and
made him cardinal in 1786. He was
major-domo of the Vatican; 173, 207.

Bréguet, Abraham-Louis (b. Neuchatel
1747; d. Paris 1823). Celebrated Swiss
watch-maker. Besides his special trade,
he also invented a wide range of
precision instruments for physics and
astronomy. His son, Louis Bréguet (b.
Paris 1803), was also a distinguished
instrument-maker; 150.

Breislak, Scipione (b. Rome 1768; d.
Milan 1826). Well-known Italian
geologist, who had been Inspector of
Manufacturers of Saltpetre and Gun-
powder under Napoleon. His opponent

was the Englishman James Hutton (1726-1797), whose *Theory of the Earth* (translated into French 1815) caused much speculation; 297.

Breme, Ludovico Arborio Gattinara di (b. Turin 1780; d. Turin 1820). Sometime Warden of the House of Pages at the Court of Prince Eugène; State Councillor of the Kingdom of Italy, Knight of the Iron Crown, etc. Leader of the romantic-carbonarist group which so attracted Stendhal, and original founder of *il Conciliatore*; 28, 64, 65, 66, 67, 68, 142, 264.

Britannicus (tragedy). See Racine.

Bronzino, Angiolo (b. Florence 1502; d. Florence 1572). Italian painter, most celebrated of the Tuscan portraitists. His painting, *la Discesa del Salvatore al Limbo* is now in the Museo di Santa Croce; 338.

Brosses, le Président Charles de (1709-1777). One of the wittiest minor writers of the eighteenth century. Best known for his *Lettres historiques et critiques sur l'Italie* (Paris, 3 vols., 1799), and his *Histoire des Navigations aux Terres Australes* (1756); 91, 166, 231, 246, 318, 455, 456.

Brunelleschi, Filippo (b. Florence 1377; d. Florence 1446). The greatest architect of the early Italian renaissance. He was responsible for the great dome of Santa Maria del Fiore, and also for the Palazzo Pitti; 300.

Bruni, Leonardo (known as *l'Aretino*) (b. Arezzo 1369; d. Florence 1444). Italian statesman, scholar and historian. Chancellor of the Republic of Florence in 1411. His two major works are the *Commentarius rerum suo tempore gestarum* (1475) and the *Historiae Florentini Populi* (publ. Strasburg 1610); 295.

Bubna von Littitz, Ferdinand Anton, Count (b. Zàmrsk 1768; d. Milan 1825). Austrian field-marshal, ambassador to Paris in 1813; governor-general of Lombardy after the fall of Napoleon. In 1821, he put down the Piedmontese insurrection; 43.

Buffa, signor. Neapolitan insurgent, executed in 1799; 411.

Buonaccorsi, Filippo (b. San Gimignano 1437; d. Cracow 1496). Italian statesman, poet and historian. His major historical work is the *Historia de his*

quae a Venetis tentata sunt, Persis ac Tartaris contra Turcos movendis (publ. Hagenau 1533); 295.

Buoninsegni, Pietro. Mediaeval Italian chronicler, author of the *Historia Florentina* (publ. Florence 1580); 295.

Buratti, Pietro (b. Venice 1772; d. Treviso 1832). Venetian dialect-poet, songwriter, satirist and patriot. Arrested in 1813 for a violent protest against the blockade of Venice. Among his satires, the best-known are *l'Elefante* (1819), which earned him three months in prison, *la Streffeìde* and *l'Uomo*; 70, 139, 340, 341, 342.

Burbero Benefico, il (comedy). See Goldoni.

Bürger, Gottfried-August (b. Molmerswende 1747; d. Göttingen 1794). Major German lyric poet, one of the heralds of romanticism, and the direct precursor of Goethe; 67.

Burke, Edmund (b. Dublin 1728; d. London 1794). English statesman, philosopher and orator, best remembered for his merciless attacks upon Jacobinism: *Reflexions on the Revolution in France, and on the Proceedings in certain Societies in London relative to that event*; 443.

Burney, Charles, *Mus. Doc.* (1726-1814). English organist, composer and writer, and a pupil of Dr Arne. Apart from his *General History of Music* (1776-1789), two other works of Burney concern Italy: the *Present State of Music in France and Italy* (1771: known as the *Musical Tour*); and *La Musica che si canta annualmente nelle funzioni della settimana santa nella cappella ponteficia* (1784); 450.

Byron, George Gordon, Lord (1788-1824). English poet, who together with Walter Scott, was one of the greatest heroes of the romantic revolutionaries; 33, 47, 116, 141, 215, 247, 248, 269, 273, 325, 342.

Poems referred to include:
Childe Harold's Pilgrimage (1810-1818); 269.
Corsair, The (1814); 269, 273.
Don Juan (1819-1824); 215, 342.
Parisina (1816); 247-248, 273.

C***, contessa, mistress of Beccaria; 110.
C***, contessa, of Mantua; 46.

C***, duchessa, of Naples; 355-356.

C***, signor, of Milan; 136.

C***, signor, of Portici; 398.

C***, signora Fulvia, of Milan; 133-134.

C***lo, Prince, of Lucera; 178-187.

C***lo, Lauretta, of Lucera; 178-187.

Cabanis, Pierre-Jean-Georges (1757-1808). French physician and philosopher, disciple of Condillac and friend of Mirabeau. Cabanis (with Tracy) was the leader of the physiological-materialist group which styled itself *les Idéologues*. His major work is a treatise entitled *Des Rapports du Physique et du Moral de l'Homme* (2 vols., Paris 1802); 97, 254.

Caesar, Julius. Roman general and dictator; 436.

Caffè, il. Periodical of encyclopaedist inspiration edited by Beccaria and P. Verri (1764-1766); 92.

Cagliostro (Giuseppe Balsamo, known as Count Alessandro C.) (b. Palermo 1743; d. Fortress of San Leo, 1795). Celebrated mountebank, who practised spiritualism in masonic circles and at the court of Louis XVI, where he was involved in the affair of the Queen's Necklace. In 1789, he was arrested and condemned to death in Rome; the Pope commuted his sentence to life-imprisonment in San Leo, where he died five years later; 243.

Cagnola, Luigi (b. Milan 1762; d. Inverigo 1833). Milanese architect, an admirer of Palladio, who executed many public monuments in Milan under Napoleon. His major works include the Porta Marengo in Milan and the Rotonda at Inverigo; 38, 52*.

Caligula (b. Antium A.D. 12; d. Rome 41). Roman Emperor, A.D. 37-41; 345.

Cambacérès, Jean-Jacques, duc de (b. Montpellier 1753; d. Paris 1824). One of the finest intellects thrown up by the French Revolution. Member of the *Convention*; Second Consul during the Consulate; Arch-Chancellor under the Empire. His greatest work, however, was done in the background, and includes the major part of the *Code Napoléon*; 336.

Camilla. Heroine of opera of this title by Paër (*q.v.*); 216-217.

Campan, Jeanne-Louise-Henriette, *née* Genest (1752-1822). Lady-in-waiting to Marie-Antoinette. Later in life, she became a well-known educationalist and principal of an Academy at Ecouen. Author of the *Mémoires sur la Vie privée de Marie-Antoinette* (3 vols., Paris 1822); 86, 104.

Campistron, Jean Galbert de (b. Toulouse 1656; d. Toulouse 1723) French poet and tragic dramatist, whose plays, conceived in emulation of Racine, did much to debase the idiom of the classical theatre; 371.

Camuccini, Vincenzo (b. Rome 1771; d. Rome 1839). Italian painter, a pupil of Corvi and friend of Benvenuti (*q.v.*), Bossi, Monti and Ermes Visconti. 1804, appointed director of the Vatican mosaics. His *Morte di Cesare* is an early work (1793); 458.

Canaples, comte de (=Auguste-Gabriel de Franquetot, comte de Coigny: b. 1740; d. 1817). French soldier and courtier, chevalier d'honneur to Madame Elisabeth; Lieutenant-General under the Restoration; 203-204.

Cancellieri. Chief of Police in Naples in 1799; 402.

Candide (satirical novel). See Voltaire.

Canedoli, Baldassare. Murderer of Annibale Bentivoglio, of Bologna (1455); 284.

Canning, George (b. London 1770; d. Chiswick 1827). English statesman, one of the most notorious anti-Jacobins of the Revolutionary period. Secretary of State for Foreign Affairs, 1807; Leader of the House, 1822; Prime Minister, 1827. His policy was primarily one of non-intervention, while at the same time he encouraged the emergence of minority national groups in Europe; 131, 242.

Canonica, Luigi (b. Tesserete 1762; d. Milan 1844). Italian architect, a pupil of Piermarini. His main work was in Milan, where he built the Great Arena, the Royal Palace, the Villa Bonaparte and the Teatro Carcano. He specialised in theatre-design; 38.

Canonici, Graciata (? Giacinta). Italian soprano, a leading light of the teatro dei Fiorentini, Naples. Member of the original cast of Rossini's *Occasione fa il Ladro* (1812); 351, 352.

Canova, Antonio (1757-1822). Italian sculptor, born at Possagno. His reputation today is perhaps less exalted than Stendhal would have wished; his works, none the less, are of entrancing grace and sweetness; 2, 12, 20, 75, 76, 77, 138, 173, 258, 301, 349, 414, 455, 462, 466.

Works referred to:

Statue of *Alfieri* (1810: in Santa Croce, Florence); 301.

Statue of Pope *Clement XIII* (Rezzonico) (1787-1792: in the Vatican); 75.

Statue of Pope *Pius VI* (Braschi); 173.

Statue of *Cimarosa* (1816: Pantheon); 462.

Cantata: il Sogno di Partenope. See Mayr.

Canzoniere (sonnet-cycle). See Petrarch.

Capet, Hugues. First King of the 'third dynasty' of the Kings of France. The name *Capet* was used as the official designation of Louis XVI after his deposition; after his death, Marie-Antoinette was known as *veuve Capet*. See also Dante, *Purgatorio*, canto xx; 141, 343.

Capponi, Neri (b. Florence 1388; d. Florence 1457). Florentine writer, statesman, diplomat and soldier. In 1441, C. negotiated the Treaty of Cremona between Florence and Milan. As a historian, he is known for his *Commentari delle cose seguite in Italia tra il 1419 e il 1456*, and the *Cacciata del conte Poppi ed acquisto di quello stato per il popolo fiorentino*; 269, 285, 295, 388.

Caputi, signor. Neapolitan insurgent, executed in 1799; 411.

Caracciolo, Domenico (b. Naples 1715; d. Naples 1789). Italian economist, diplomat and statesman. In 1771, Caracciolo was appointed Neapolitan ambassador to Paris in succession to the abbé Galiani (*q.v.*), and his wit was no less appreciated in the *salons* than that of his predecessor; 443.

Caracciolo, Francesco. Italian admiral, descendant of an ancient Neapolitan family which originated with Giovanni Caracciolo, favourite of Giovanna II, queen of Naples. Admiral Caracciolo was hanged by Nelson in cruel and degrading circumstances on 29 June 1799; 411.

Caraffa (Carafa), Michele Enrico C. di Colobrano (b. Naples 1787; d. 1872).

Italian composer who lived mainly in Paris and studied under Cherubini. Like Stendhal, he had experienced the Retreat from Moscow. At the height of his fame (1822-35), his popularity rivalled that of Rossini and Auber. His opera *Gabriele di Vergy* had its *première* at the *teatro del Fondo*, Naples, on 3rd July 1816; 68, 377.

Caravaggio, Michelangelo Amerighi or Merisi, known as *il C.* (b. Caravaggio 1569; d. 1609). Major Italian painter, who marks the transition, in Italy, from the traditions of the Renaissance to that of later centuries; 270.

Carcano, teatro. See *Theatres*.

Cardano, Gerolamo (b. Pavia 1501; d. Rome 1576). Italian scholar, humanist philosopher and mathematician. A doctor by training, C. preached a confused doctrine of medicine and astrology; his fame rests upon his discoveries in the field of mathematical equations, chemistry and practical physics; 266.

Carloni, signor. Milanese portrait-painter, descendant of a famous family of Lombard artists, including Carlo-Innocenzo(1686-1775); Carlo-Antonio (1650-1708) and Diego (1674-1750); 107, 108.

Carmagnola (Francesco Bussone, known as Count C.: b. Carmagnola 1380; executed Venice 1432). Italian *condottiere*. He entered the service of Filippo-Maria Visconti in 1416, and served him with such success that this Prince took fright and attempted to get rid of him. C. fled to Venice, and was given command of all Venetian forces in the field against Milan. In 1432, however, he was accused of treason, and beheaded. See also under *Hayez*; 100.

Carmontelle (Louis Carragis, known as: b. Paris 1717; d. Paris 1806). French painter, draughtsman and dramatist, master of the Revels to the duc d'Orléans. In this latter capacity, C. created for his entertainment a new kind of light comedy, the 'proverbe', later perfected by Musset. (Collected edition, 8 vols., 1768-1781); 446.

Carnot, Lazare-Nicolas-Marguérite (1753-1823). Mathematician, War-Minister under Robespierre in the

Committee of Public Safety, known as the 'organisateur de la Victoire'. It was Carnot who built up the military machine which Napoleon was to exploit; 146, 220.

Caroline, Queen: Maria-Carolina of Austria, wife of Ferdinando di Borbone, King of the Two Sicilies. A strong-willed, tyrannical and unbalanced princess who completely dominated her *fainéant* husband. Sister of Marie-Antoinette, and grandmother of Napoleon's consort, Marie-Louise; 401, 411.

Carracci, the. Famous family of Bolognese artists; 19, 64, 166-168, 288.

Lodovico Carracci (b. 1555, d. 1619), who painted the *Angel of the Annunciation*; 166, 167.

Agostino Carracci (b. Bologna 1557; d. Parma 1602); 167.

Annibale Carracci (b. Bologna 1560; d. Rome 1618); 167.

Casaccia (Casacciello). Popular Neapolitan singer and actor, descendant of a long line of artists; 351, 352.

Casanova de Seingalt, Giovanni Giacomo (b. Venice 1725; d. Dux 1798). Famous eighteenth-century adventurer and hero of many romantic escapades. His *Memoirs* were written between 1791 and 1798, and published in part by Brockhaus in German in 1822; 135.

Cascese, Agnolo da. Florentine clothmerchant, adoptive father of Santi Bentivoglio (*q.v.*); 285.

Cassandrino. Popular hero of the Roman puppet-theatres; 473-479.

Cassandrino allievo di un pittore. Marionette-play, of anonymous authorship; 474.

Cassera, contessa Luigia, *née* Ferrari (b. Cremona 1796). A brisk young widow of Milan, whom Stendhal met in 1816, and whose box at la Scala he frequented assiduously. In 1822, she remarried, and thereafter became 'disquietingly virtuous'; 45*, 53*, 70*, 126*.

Castiglione, Baldassare (b. Casatico 1478; d. Toledo 1529).Soldier-scholarstatesman of the Renaissance, best remembered for his classical treatise on Renaissance manners, *il Cortegiano*. As a, diplomat he gave his services chiefly to the sovereigns of Mantua and Urbino; 62.

Castrucci family; 388.

Castruccio Castracani degli Antelminelli, Duke of Lucca (b. Lucca 1281; d. 1328). Italian *condottiere*, leader of the Ghibelline faction in Lucca. In 1316, C. overthrew the reigning Duke of Lucca, Uguccioni, captured Pisa and Pistoia, and was likely to make Lucca the dominant power in central Italy when he died; 71, 305.

Catalani, Angelica (1780-1849). Italian soprano, one of the most flamboyant operatic tyrants of all time. Trained under Marchesi and Crescentini; *début* in Mayr's *Lodoïska*, La Fenice, 1795. In 1815, she became directress of the Italian opera in Paris, and ruined a fine tradition within the space of four years by her domineering avarice; 5, 6, 24, 25, 26, 27, 28, 29, 359.

Catena, signora Bibin, of Milan. This lady, to whom Stendhal refers so often and with such enthusiasm, has so far eluded identification; 14, 32, 45, 108.

Cattaneo, Gaetano (b. 1771; d. 1841). Curator of the Numismatical Collection of the Brera. C. was a close friend of Carline Porta; 77.

Catullus, Caius Valerius (b. Verona B.C. 84; d. *c.* B.C. 47). Latin poet, whose lyrical verses, at once scholarly, elegant and libertine, were inspired by the immortal Lesbia; 265-267.

Cavaletti, baron Francesco. Italian army officer with an estate at Monticello. C. had served with distinction in Napoleon's armies in the Peninsular War, was a *Chevalier de la Légion d'Honneur*, and had won the *Iron Crown*; 43, 44, 121-126, 209.

Cavaliere dei Templari (ballet). See Gallenberg.

Cecchino, don (=Cardinal della Somaglia, *q.v.*); 447-448.

Cellini, Benvenuto (1500-1571). Italian sculptor, engraver and goldsmith, born in Florence. His famous *Autobiography* remained in MS until 1728; the translation referred to is by Saint-Marcel, Paris (Le Normant) 1822. C.'s *Perseus* (whose casting is described in the *Memoirs*) still stands in the *Loggia de' Lanzi* in Florence; 233, 246, 269, 306.

Cenerentola, la (opera buffa). See Rossini.

Centola, signora, of Naples. Descendant of a powerful Neapolitan family. In 1734, it was a Prince of Centola who was deputed to offer the official welcome to King Charles III; 339.

Cerbelli, monsignor, of Naples; 444.

Cerilli (Cirillo), Domenico (b. Grumo Nevano 1739; d. 1799). Distinguished physician and naturalist, whose main work lay in the field of botany and entomology (*Entomologiae Neapolitanae specimen primum,* Naples 1787, etc.). President of the Legislative Council of the Parthenopean Republic in succession to F.-M. Pagano. Executed 1799; 408.

Cervantes Saavedra, Miguel de (b. Alcala de Henares 1547; d. Madrid 1616). Spanish writer. Besides the celebrated *Don Quixote,* he also composed plays and short stories (*Novelas*), of which the best-known are the *Novelas Ejemplares* (publ. 1613); 159, 367, 368.

Cesare in Egitto (ballet). See Gallenberg.

Cesena, Massacre of. February 1377: the city was sacked and 6,000 inhabitants massacred by Cardinal Robert de Genève, under the orders of Pope Gregory XI; 388.

Cetra Spermaceutica, la (satirical epic). See Giraùd.

Chabran, Margherita. Italian soprano, a pupil of Pellegrini, who was singing in Naples *c.* 1815-1818. She sang in the *première* of Rossini's *la Gazzetta*; 351, 352, 377.

Chabriant, comte de. Hereditary Captain of the Gardes de Monsieur. *Fl.* 1750-1800; 201-202.

Chabrol de Volvic, Gilbert-Joseph-Gaspard, comte de (b. Riom 1773; d. Paris 1843). French scientist, statistician and administrator. Member of the scientific survey of Egypt. *Préfet* of Montenotte (Italy), 1806. *Préfet* de la Seine, 1812; one of the greatest civil administrators of the City of Paris. The work referred to is the *Statistique des Provinces de Savone, d'Oneille, d'Acqui, et de partie de la Province de Mondovi, formant l'ancien département de Montenotte,* Paris (Didot), 2 vols., 1824; 91.

Chalmers, Alexander (b. Aberdeen 1759; d. London 1834). Scots man of letters and biographer, who edited Shakespeare, Pope, Gibbon, etc. His main works are the *British Essayists* (45 vols., 1803), and the *General Biographical Dictionary* (32 vols., 1812-1817); 455.

Chamfort, Nicolas-Sébastien Roch, known as de C. (b. Clermont-Ferrand 1741; d. Paris 1794). French dramatist, critic and moralist, celebrated for his concise and witty style. His ingenuity is embodied in his *Maximes, Caractères et Anecdotes.* He committed suicide under the Terror; 57.

Championnet, Jean-Antoine-Etienne (b. 1762, Valence; d. Antibes 1800). French general with the revolutionary armies. Defeated the Neapolitans under Mack outside Rome in December 1798, occupied Naples on 23 January 1799. Recalled 27 February, replaced by Macdonald. C. left a noble reputation for bravery, incorruptibility and human justice; 404.

Chantrey, Sir Francis Leggatt (b. Jordanthorpe 1781; d. London 1841). English sculptor, renowned for his portraits (William Pitt, George III, James Watt, etc.). Founder of the Chantrey Bequest; 42.

Charles, Archduke of Austria, Duke of Teschen (b. 1771; d. 1847). Third son of Leopold II. Austrian soldier and strategist, field-marshal 1796. Leading figure in the anti-Napoleonic coalition. He fought so well at Wagram that Napoleon contemplated offering him the Crown of Hungary; 175, 215.

Charles V (b. 1500; King of Spain 1516; Emperor of Germany 1519; abdicated 1555; d. 1558, in the monastery of Yuste). One of the greatest of Renaissance sovereigns, and life-long enemy of François I; 336.

Charles VIII (b. Amboise 1470; King of France 1483; d. 1498). An ambitious monarch, fond of flamboyant but not always successful military ventures; 80.

Chateaubriand, vicomte François-René de (1768-1848). One of the greatest French prose-writers of the Romantic period; also a major political figure in his time. Best known today for his *Mémoires d'Outre-Tombe*; 76, 167, 377, 394, 425.

Works referred to:

René (ultra-romantic novel) (1805); 425.

Génie du Christianisme, le (1802: a treatise proving that Christianity is the most poetic of all religions); 76, 112, 167, 394.

Châtelet, Gabrielle-Emilie le Tonnelier de Breteuil, marquise du (b. Paris 1706; d. Lunéville 1749). French blue-stocking and letter-writer, now remembered mainly for her liaison with Voltaire, who wrote metaphysical disquisitions for her pleasure; 32.

Chaulnes, Michel-Ferdinand d'Albert d'Ailly, duc de (b. 1714; d. 1769). French soldier and amateur scientist of repute, who spent most of his fortune on his collection of scientific instruments; 273*.

Chaulnes, duchesse de. Wife of above; 273*.

Cherubini, Maria Luigi Carlo Zenobio Salvatore (b. Florence 1760; d. Paris 1842). Italian composer, later naturalised French. Director of the Conservatoire from 1822, and one of the greatest teachers of his time; 461.

Chiaramonte, Cardinal. See Pius VI, Pope.

Chiari, abate Pietro (b. Brescia 1711; d. Brescia 1785). Italian novelist and dramatist, rival of Goldoni. Of his forty novels, the best-known are la Francese in Italia (1759) and la Donna che non si trova (1762)—an imitation of the Nouvelle Héloïse; 128.

Chichester, Sir Charles (b. Devon 1795; d. Toronto 1847). British officer in the 14th Regiment of Foot, who was stationed in Naples in 1817. Later he served in India, Spain, the West Indies and America, and was Lieutenant-Governor of Trinidad. Stendhal seems to have confused him with Stephen Lushington (q.v.); 385.

Childe Harold's Pilgrimage (poem). See Byron.

Chronicles of Bologna; 295.

Chronicles of Pisa; 295.

Chronicles of Sienna; 295.

Chronicon Petri Azarii (history). See Azario.

Cicero, Marcus Tullius (106-43 B.C.) Roman poet, philosopher and stylist; 24, 218, 259, 268, 436.

Works referred to:

De Legibus (Dialogue, founded on the Laws of Plato); 268, 269.

Pro Scauro (Speech in defence of M. Aemilius Scaurus, B.C. 54, accused of the mismanagement of Sicily); 259.

Cimabue (Cenno de Pepe, known as: b. Florence 1240; d. Florence 1302). Italian painter, father of the Tuscan school and master of Giotto; greatest of the 'primitives'; 313.

Cimarosa, Domenico (b. Aversa 1749; d. Venice 1801). Major Italian composer of the eighteenth century. Stendhal placed him second only to Mozart in the hierarchy of genius; 10, 12, 19, 26, 163, 186, 198, 309, 348, 376, 398, 460, 462.

Il Matrimonio segreto (opera buffa in 2 acts, libretto by G. Bertati based on comedy by G. Colman and D. Garrick; Vienna, Burg Theatre, 7 Feb. 1792); 198, 359*, 398.

Cinderella (Cenerentola) (ballet). See Gallenberg, la Virtù premiata.

Cinna (tragedy). See Corneille.

Cinti (Laure-Cinthie Damoreau, née Montalant, known as Mlle C.: 1801-1863). Famous French soprano; début, Théâtre Favart, 1816; later, as Madame Cinti-Damoreau, she was the reigning queen of the Opéra-Comique. Rossini wrote Le Siège de Corinthe and Moïse for her voice; 17.

Circe. Enchantress in the Odyssey, who transformed the companions of Ulysses into swine; 332.

Clarissa Harlowe (novel). See Richardson.

Clement VII, Anti-Pope from 1378 to 1394. Cardinal Robert de Genève, elected Pope in opposition to Urban VIII; recognised by France, Spain, Scotland and Sicily; resided at Avignon; the first Pope of the great western schism. See also Cesena; 388.

Cobbett, William (b. Farnham 1762; d. 1835). Celebrated English journalist, writer and political agitator, who began life as an extreme tory and ended as an extreme radical. Founder of the first 'popular' newspaper, the Twopenny Tract (1816); 453.

Cocomero, teatro del. See Theatres.

Codronchi, Antonio (1748-1826). Italian churchman; Grand Almoner of the

Kingdom of Italy under Napoleon. After 1815, he rallied to the monarchy, and became Archbishop of Ravenna; 214-215.

Coffee-Houses:

Accademia, caffè dell' (Milan); 34, 53, 61, 137, 141.

Battistino, caffè (Milan, *la Scala*); 145.

Nobili, casin dei (Milan); 134.

Padua, caffè di (Milan); 57.

Ruspoli, caffè (Rome); 472.

Servi, corsia dei (Milan); 98, 105, 107.

Colace, signor. Neapolitan judge, hanged in 1799 for his participation in the Republic; 410.

Colbran, Isabella Angiola (1785-1845). Italian soprano, for whose voice Rossini wrote most of his Neapolitan operas. A pupil of Marinelli and Crescentini, she was the finest coloratura soprano in Europe. Stendhal is notoriously unfair to her abilities. In 1822, she married Rossini; 359, 377, 383, 392.

Collé, Charles (1709-1783). French songwriter and dramatist of some repute; 381, 446.

Works referred to:

Journal Historique, ou Mémoires critiques et littéraires sur les Ouvrages dramatiques et sur les Evénements les plus mémorables, depuis 1748 *jusqu'en* 1751 (Paris, 3 vols., 1805-7); 381.

La Vérité dans le Vin, ou les Désagréments de la Galanterie (1-Act 'proverbe' in prose, Paris 1789); 446.

Colonna, Giuliano. Neapolitan aristocrat, youngest son of the Prince of Stigliano; arrested in 1786 for his part in the 'Giordano Plot'; executed in 1799 for having served under the Republic; 412.

Colonna di Paliano, Prince Filippo III (d. 1818). A latter-day representative of the great house of Colonna. During the French occupation of Italy, C. had received the King of Sardinia in his *palazzo* in Rome; 466.

Commentaire sur l'Esprit des Lois (treatise). See Tracy.

Commines, Philippe de la Clyte, Sire de (b. Hazebrouck 1447; d. Argenton 1511). The greatest of the French chroniclers, who saw service under four successive monarchs. Author of the *Mémoires de messire Ph. de Comynes sur les principaux faicts et gestes de Louis onzième et de Charles huictième son fils, roys de France;* 279.

Compagnoni, Giuseppe (b. Lugo 1754; d. Milan 1833). Italian philosopher and publicist, professor of constitutional law at Ferrara. Editor of divers periodicals, *le Memorie enciclopediche; il Mercurio d'Italia,* etc. Translator of Destutt de Tracy's *Logique;* 230, 232.

Compère Mathieu, le. Satirical novel (1765) by the abbé Henri-Joseph Dulaurens—an anti-clerical publication for many years attributed to Voltaire; 225, 423.

Conciliatore, il: Foglio scientifico-letterario. Celebrated carbonarist newspaper, appearing in Milan twice weekly (3 September 1818-17 October 1819) until it was suspended by the Austrians. Its 'platform' included political liberalism, unification of Italy, and literary romanticism; 264.

Conclavi de' Pontefici romani (history). See Leti.

Condillac, Etienne Bonnot, abbé de (b. Grenoble 1715; d. Beaugency 1780). French philosopher, leading figure of the 'sensualist' movement. Condillac was the master of Cabanis and Destutt de Tracy, and therefore indirectly of Stendhal himself; 311.

Confalonieri, Count Federico (b. Milan 1785; d. Hospenthal 1846). One of the leading members of the Milanese carbonarist *élite,* and founder of the *Conciliatore.* In December 1820, he was arrested, and confined for thirteen years in the Spielberg; 67.

Conforti, Francesco (b. Calvanico 1743; executed Naples 1799). Italian theologian and philosopher, author of the *Anti-Grozio;* Professor of history, head of the Censorship under the Bourbons, arrested 1796 for 'excessive liberalism'. Minister of the Interior under the Parthenopian Republic; 411.

Congrès de Vienne, le (pamphlet). See Pradt.

Consalvi, Cardinal Ercole (1757-1824). Roman politician and administrator, chief minister to Pope Pius VII. A skilled and subtle diplomat, who was largely responsible for negotiating the

Concordat of 1801. See also *Ingres*; 103, 122, 123, 169, 170, 174, 210, 256, 257, 291, 292, 450, 462, 463, 465, 474.

Conservatoire (Milan); 9, 25-26, 28.

Constant de Rebecque, Benjamin (1767-1830). French politician and writer, a *protégé* of Mme de Staël. After the fall of Napoleon, he became leader of the liberal opposition. His best-known novel, *Adolphe*, appeared in 1815; 263.

Constitutionnel, le (Journal de Commerce politique et littéraire). Originally founded by the ex-Jacobin Gémond (1815) as *l'Indépendant*, it took its famous title *le Constitutionnel* in 1819; later it was to serve as vehicle for Sainte-Beuve's *Causeries du Lundi*; 3, 445.

Constitutions des Jésuites, les (manual of religious discipline); See Loyola.

Conti, Marianna (b. Milan 1790). Italian *prima ballerina*, celebrated no less for her multitudinous love-affairs than for her talent; 364, 365, 370, 371, 380.

Coray (Koraïs), Diamantis (b. Smyrna 1748; d. Paris 1833). Celebrated Greek scholar, philologist and patriot. As a hellenist, his work was voluminous and valuable; today, however, he is remembered as the foremost propagandist in western Europe of the cause of Greek independence; 261.

Cori (Corri), Frances (b. Edinburgh 1795). Mezzo-soprano, niece of the composer Domenico Corri. She made her career chiefly in Italy, where she married the tenor Paltoni; 26.

Corinne (novel). See Staël, madame de.

Corio, Bernardino (b. Milan 1459; d. *c.* 1510). Italian historian in the service of Ludovico il Moro, who commissioned him to write the history of Milan: *la Patria Historia* (Milan 1503); 295.

Coriolano (ballet). See Viganò, Salvatore.

Corneille, Pierre (1606-1684). The noblest French dramatist, and the true father of French classical tragedy. His *Cinna, ou la Clémence d'Auguste* was performed in 1640; 19, 90, 366.

Cornelius, Peter von (b. Düsseldorf 1783; d. 1867). German painter, who specialised in academic frescoes of gigantic and of monstrous frigidity and size dullness; 30.

Corner (Cornaro), Count. Governor of

Bergamo *c.* 1760. Off-shoot of the famous Venetian family of this name; 212.

Corner (Cornaro), Count Andrea. A colonel in the Napoleonic army, a notorious dandy and rake who got through a fortune of five millions in a few years. The very *immensity* of the sum impressed Stendhal (*Cf. Souvenirs d'Egotisme*, ch. ix); 70.

Correa, Lorenza (b. Lisbon 1771). Portuguese soprano, pupil of Pareja. *Début*, Madrid 1790; Venice 1792. She sang mainly in Naples and Paris; 25.

Correggio, Antonio Allegri da (1494-1534). Italian painter vastly admired by Stendhal; 11, 12, 19, 77, 101, 107, 141, 160, 161, 162, 163, 266, 302.

Works referred to:

Maddalena, la (Dresden); 163.

Madonna adorante il figliletto (Uffizi); 160.

Madonna detta di San Giorgio (Dresden); 163.

Santa Notte, la (Dresden); 162, 163.

Vergine del S. Girolamo (Parma); 141, 161.

Corsair, the (poem). See Byron.

Cors***, signora, of Florence; 339.

Corsini, Prince Neri (1771-1845). Florentine statesman and ambassador. Plenipotentiary at the Congress of Vienna. Tuscan Foreign Minister and President of the Council; 324, 416.

Corvi, Prince, of Naples; 361.

Cosimo. Corsican domestic in Florence; 323.

Coucy, Raoul de. Semi-legendary French hero, who was killed at the siege of Acre in 1191, during the 3rd Crusade. Hero of Carafa's *Gabriele di Vergy*; 377.

Courier de Méré, Paul-Louis (1772-1825). French classical scholar and satirist, author of brilliant and witty pamphlets against the government of the Restoration. C. was murdered by his gamekeeper in 1825; 259, 260, 272.

Works referred to:

Lettre à M. Renouard, libraire, sur une tache faite à un manuscrit de Florence (1810); 259.

Lettre à MM. de l'Académie des Inscriptions et Belles-Lettres (1819); 260.

Coutts, Thomas (b. Edinburgh 1735; d. London 1822). Founder of the celebrated banking-house; personal banker to George III. C. moved in the highest social circles, despite the fact that his first wife had been a chamber-maid, and his second an actress; 438.

Crabbe, George (1754-1832). English poet, whose greatest works are inspired by the sufferings and degradation of the poorest classes; 269.

Cranach, Lucas (1472-1553). German painter and engraver, whose figures (*e.g.*, his *Adam and Eve*) have a curiously touching *naïveté* and grace. Friend of Martin Luther; 239.

Crébillon, Claude ('Crébillon *fils*') (1707-1777). French novelist and master of prose style, with a lasting reputation for licentiousness; 273.

Crescentini, Girolamo (b. Urbania 1766; d. 1846). One of the greatest Italian male mezzo-soprani, and the last representative of the old tradition. *Début*, Rome 1783. Cimarosa composed *gli Orazii e Curiazii* for his voice; 26, 282.

Crescenzi, signora, of Rome; 479.

Crespi, Daniele (b. Busto Arsizio 1600; d. Milan 1630). Minor Lombard painter, whose only important work is the series of frescoes in the Certosa di Garegnano; 19.

Creuzé de Lesser, baron Auguste (b. Paris 1771; d. 1839). French poet, dramatist, traveller and administrator; appointed *préfet* in 1815 and baron in 1818. His works include a *Voyage en Italie et en Sicile fait en 1801-1802* (Paris 1806), besides a miscellaneous output of satirical epics, Spanish romances and comedy-vaudevilles; 157.

Cristoforis, Giovanni-Battista de' (b. Milan 1785; d. Milan 1838). Lawyer and administrator under the Kingdom of Italy. 1815, Professor of History in Milan. An ardent admirer of romanticism and contributor to *il Conciliatore*; 232.

Critique of Pure Reason (philosophical discourse). See Kant.

Crivelli, Gaetano (b. Bergamo 1774; d. 1836). Well-known tenor, who had been a pupil of Aprile. *Début*, Brescia 1793. His talents as an actor matched the quality of his voice; 25, 359, 378.

Cronaca Sanese, la (chronicle). See Dei.

Cruscati, don Tiberio. Character in *il Pomo*, by Albergati (*q.v.*).

Cujas, Jacques (1522-1590). Outstanding French scholar, jurist and latinist of the Renaissance. He edited many works on law (in particular, the *Codex Justinianus*), and was concerned with the reinterpretation of Roman jurisprudence in terms of the society for which it was originally devised; 268, 269.

Cuoco, Vincenzo (b. Civitacampomarana 1770; d. Naples 1823). Neapolitan statesman, writer and historian. State-Councillor under the Bourbons. Under the republic, C. played a discreet part, but later became the most fervent apologist of *Parthenopia*. His *Saggio storico sulla Rivoluzione napoletana del 1799* (Milan 1806) is the chief source of Stendhal's account; 376.

Curiatii. The heroes of Alba who fought the brothers Horatii in single-handed combat and were slain. As a result of their defeat, Alba became subject to Rome; 347.

Curioni, Alberico (b. Milan 1785). A distinguished tenor, reputed to have been the handsomest man on the Italian stage. He sang at the San-Carlo, later in Barcelona and London, and appeared in several of Rossini's operas; 352*.

Cusani, marchese Francesco (b. Milan 1802; d. Carate Brianza 1879). Italian historian, author of the *Storia di Milano* (1861-73). In 1826, he was still very young, but had begun to make a name for himself as translator of W. Scott and Victor Hugo; 21.

Cymbeline (play). See Shakespeare.

D***, marchesina, of Milan; 75.

D***, signora, of Naples; 445.

D***, signora, of Bologna; 213, 214, 215.

Danneker (Dannecker), Johann Heinrich von (b. Waldenbuch 1758; d. Waldenbuch 1841). German sculptor, best-known for his *Ariadne with a Panther* His portraits include those of Schiller and Lavater; 42.

Dante Alighieri (1265-1321). The greatest Italian poet, born in Florence, but by

S

no means wholly devoted to poetry, for he figured largely in the political life of his time, and was finally exiled in 1302, living the rest of his life in Verona and Ravenna. The section on Hugues Capet occurs in *Purgatorio*, canto xx; 12, 65, 76, 141, 169, 260, 262, 263, 300, 301, 305, 313, 318.

Danton, Georges-Jacques (b. Arcis-sur-Aube 1759; executed Paris 1794). One of the greatest, and certainly the most attractive, of the leaders of *la Montagne*; 146, 220, 291.

Daru, Martial-Noël-Pierre (b. Montpellier 1775; d. Paris 1827). Stendhal's cousin, and one of his closest friends. Daru was a capable administrator who, in 1811, was appointed *Intendant des Biens de la Couronne* in Italy, and who was responsible for a number of major public works in Rome; 434*, 459.

Daru, comte Pierre-Antoine-Noël-Bruno (b. Montpellier 1767; d. Paris 1829) Brother of the above. Administrator, civil servant and writer, and one of Napoleon's most efficient *Intendants*. From 1800 to 1814, Daru was Stendhal's protector and superior in the service; 5*.

David (sculpture). See Michelangelo.

David, Louis (1748-1825). French painter, politician and revolutionary. Under Robespierre, D. was Minister of Fine Arts; later he became Court painter to Napoleon; but at the Restoration he was exiled and died in Brussels; 64, 76, 77*, 164, 319, 338, 399, 458.

Davide, Giovanni (1789-1851). A prodigious tenor with a range of three octaves. *Début* Brescia 1810. Rossini wrote parts for him in *il Turco in Italia*, *Otello* and *la Donna del Lago*. He died as manager of the opera-house in St Petersburg; 359, 377, 378, 398.

Davoust (Davoût), Louis-Nicolas, Duke of Auerstaedt, Prince of Eckmühl, Marshal of France (b. Annoux 1770; d. Paris 1823). One of Napoleon's most valued and efficient lieutenants. His campaigns included Wagram and Moscow; 37, 125.

Davy, Sir Humphry (b. Penzance 1778; d. Geneva 1829). English chemist and inventor, best-known for his invention of the miners' safety-lamp. Among his many other writings is an Italian

Journey, under the title of *Salmonia* (1827-8); 131.

Death of St Peter Martyr (painting). See Reni.

Decazes, Elie, Duke of (b. 1780 at S.-Martin-du-Laye; d. Decazeville 1860). French statesman, *Président du Conseil* under Louis XVIII. In spite of Stendhal's criticism, D.'s policy was comparatively liberal; his object was 'de royaliser la nation, de nationaliser le royalisme'; 257.

Dei, Andrea (XIIIth-XIVth c.). Italian chronicler who wrote the first part of the *Cronaca sanese* (Muratori, *Rerum Ital. Script.*, vol. xv); 295.

Delandine, Antoine-François (b. Lyon 1756; d. Lyon 1820). French lawyer, writer and historian, appointed librarian to the city of Lyon in 1803. The bulk of his writings concern the regional history of the Lyonnais. D. is rumoured to have died 'of sheer fright and exhaustion' as a result of the upheavals of the years 1814-1815; 169.

Delille, abbé Jacques (b. Aigueperse 1738; d. 1813). French poet, one of the leading figures of the pre-romantic period. Best known for his horticultural epic, *Les Jardins, ou l'art d'embellir les Paysages* (1782) and for his astounding ingenuity in periphrasis; 191.

Delitti (dei) e delle Pene (philosophical treatise). See Beccaria.

Della Superiorità in ogni cosa del Sesso amabilissimo (1504); 429.

Delort, madame. A pupil of madame Campan (*q.v.*); headmistress of an Academy for young ladies, Milan; 86.

Demidoff, Prince Nikolai Nikitich (b. St Petersburg 1773; d. Florence 1828). Resplendent Russian aristocrat and art-patron. Besides his private theatre in the *palazzo Ruspoli*, he formed a world-famous collection of paintings and a natural history museum which he left to the University of Moscow; 415*.

Denon, Dominique-Vincent, baron (b. Chalon-sur-Saône 1747; d. 1825). French engraver, who, under Napoleon, became Director-General of the National Museums of France. Stendhal worked under his orders in 1811 and again in 1814; 49, 76.

Desaix de Veygoux, Louis (b. Riom 1768; killed Marengo, 1800). French general who was largely responsible for Napoleon's victories in Egypt, and who was instrumental in winning the battle in which he met his death; 429.

Descartes, René (b. La Haye 1596; d. Stockholm 1650). French philosopher, author of the *Discours de la Méthode* (1637); 252.

Devin du Village, le ('intermède'). See Rousseau.

Dialogues des Morts (philosophical-moral treatise in dialogue form). See Fénelon.

Diderot, Denis (b. Langres 1713; d. Paris 1784). One of the greatest French thinkers of the eighteenth century, and responsible for editing the *Encyclopédie*; 253.

Didymi Clerici Epistolae (polemical satire in Latin). See Foscolo; 455.

Didon et Enée (painting). See Guérin.

Didot, Firmin (b. Paris 1764; d. Paris 1836). French scholar, poet and publisher, member of one of the best-known of all French publishing families. As an author, his reputation rests upon his work as a latinist; his play *La Mort d'Annibal* was published by himself in 1817; 130, 161.

Didot, Pierre (l'aîné) (b. 1760; d. 1853). Founder of the great publishing-house, together with his brother Firmin and his sons Jules and Ambroise-Firmin; 157.

Di Flores, contessa, of Rome; 470.

Directoire, le. Name given to the government of France between the fall of Robespierre and Napoleon's *coup d'état* (27 October 1795-9 November 1799). Its leader, prop and mainstay was Barras; 403, 406.

Disperato per Eccesso di buon Core (comedy). See Giraùd.

Dominic, St (b. Caleruega 1170; d. Bologna 1221). Castilian preacher, founder of the Dominican Order of Friars, and one of the leading figures in the Crusade against the Albigensians; 166*, 346.

Domenichino (Domenico Zampieri, known as). Italian painter (b. Bologna 1581; d. Naples 1641). A notable draughtsman and colourist; 164, 167, 169, 288, 295, 399.

His works include:
Saint Agnes; 295.
Saint Andrew; 164.

Don Garcia (tragedy). See Alfieri.

Don Juan (satirical epic). See Byron.

Dorat, Claude-Joseph (b. Paris 1734; d. Paris 1780). French poet of the preromantic period, best-known for a species of short narrative poem called the *héroïde*, which he perfected; 64.

Douglas, Lady. See Glandervie.

Dragonetti, signor. Neapolitan judge and patriot, compromised in the revolution of 1799. Father of the celebrated Luigi Dragonetti (1791-1871), one of the leaders of the *Risorgimento*; 410.

Du Bellay, Martin (b. *c.* 1490; d. 1559). French historian, whose *Mémoires* (together with those of his brother Guillaume) cover the period 1515-1547, and deal with the wars between François I and Charles V; 156.

Du Belloy (Pierre-Laurent Buyrette, known as Dormont du B.: b. Saint-Flour 1727; d. Paris 1775).French actor, poet and dramatist. His 'historical tragedy', *le Siège de Calais*, was performed on 13 February 1765; 188, 189.

Ducis, Jean-François (b. Versailles 1733; d. Versailles 1816). French dramatist who contributed to the rise of the Melodrama as a dramatic form. His 'translations' of Shakespeare have to be read to be believed; 348.

Duclos, Charles Pinot (b. Dinan 1704; d. Paris 1772). French novelist, wit, scholar and philosopher, author of a number of gossipy histories (*Mémoires secrets sur le Règne de Louis XIV, la Régence et le Règne de Louis XV*, 1790; *Mémoires pour servir à l'histoire des moeurs du XVIIIe siècle*, 1751; etc.); and of a *Voyage en Italie* (1791); 232, 273, 325, 389.

Du Deffand, Marie de Vichy-Chamrond, marquise du D. (b. Château de Chamrond 1697; d. Paris 1780). Eighteenth-century *femme d'esprit*, whose *salon* was frequented by Montesquieu, Voltaire, etc. In 1765, when she had been blind for twelve years, she developed a passion for Horace Walpole, from which resulted an amazing correspondence; 92.

Due Muri, contrada de'. Street in Milan,

near *il Duomo*, where Stendhal had had a room in 1811. Here, he received his mistress Angela Pietragrua; here also he began to write his first book, the *Histoire de la Peinture en Italie*; 120.

Due Paggi, i. Comedy, author unidentified; 393.

Dugazon (Jean-Baptiste-Henri Gourgaud, known as: b. Marseille 1746; d. Sandillon 1809). French actor, *début* 1771. At the Comédie Française, D. specialised in comic valets. Professor of dramatic declamation at the *Conservatoire*; 10.

Dumouriez, Charles-François (b. Cambrai 1739; d. 1823). French general in the service of the early revolutionary armies. Victor at Valmy and Jemappes; conqueror of Belgium. His sympathies, however, lay with the *Girondins*; he was relieved of his command by the Jacobins and, to escape the guillotine, fled from Paris and deserted to the enemy; 280.

Duport, Louis (1781-1853). French dancer and choreographer; *début* at the Opéra, 1801; 1808, leading dancer at St Petersburg; 1816, director of the Carinthian Gate theatre, Vienna. His ballet, *la Cenerentola, ossia la Virtù premiata*, was set to music by Gallenberg (*q.v.*); 363, 364, 365, 370, 372, 373, 382.

Duport, madame. French dancer, sister of the preceding; 364.

Duval, Alexandre-Vincent Pineux-D (b. Rennes 1767; d. Paris 1842). French dramatist, sailor, engineer, politician, etc. A fierce opponent of the romantic innovators. Director of the Théâtre de l'Odéon in Paris in the time of Angelina Bereyter. His play, *la Jeunesse de Henri V* is based on an obscene comedy attributed to L. S. Mercier, *Charles II, Roi d'Angleterre, en certain lieu.* (Paris 1789.); 396.

Ebrea di Toledo, la (ballet). See Viganò.
Eclogues. See Virgil.
Egisto (tragedy). See Alfieri, *Agide*.
Elefanteïde, l' (satirical poem). See Buratti.
Elena (opera). See Mayr.
Elisa, Princess. See Bonaparte, Marie-Anne-Elisa.
Eloisa (b. Paris 1101; d. Nogent-sur-

Seine 1164). The niece of Canon Fulbert, celebrated on account of her ill-fated love for Abelard; 273.

Enchanted Well, The. Marionette-ballet, details unknown; 479.

Epimenides (b. Phaestus B.C. 650) Cretan poet and prophet, a semi-legendary hero of Cnossus, who is reputed to have taken shelter from the sun in a deep cave, and there to have slept for fifty-seven years; 171.

Epinay, Louise-Florence-Pétronille Tardieu d'Esclavelles, marquise d'E. (b. Valenciennes 1726; d. Paris 1783). One of the great patrons of the *philosophes*, and particularly of Rousseau; lover of the baron Grimm. Her *Mémoires et Correspondance* were published in 1818; 273.

Erasmus, Didier (b. Rotterdam 1467; d. Basle 1536). Dutch scholar, perhaps the greatest of the Renaissance humanists. Best-remembered for his *Colloquies* and his satirical essay: *In praise of madness*; 131.

Ercolani, Princess, of Bologna; 196.
Erostrate (novel). See Verri, Alessandro.
Esprit de l'Eglise, de l' (historical treatise). See Potter.
Esprit des Lois, l' (philosophical treatise). See Montesquieu.
Essai sur l'Indifférence en matière de Religion (philosophical treatise). See Lamennais.
Etange, Julie d'. Heroine of Rousseau's *Nouvelle Héloïse* (*q.v.*).

Eugène de Beauharnais, duc de Leuchtenberg, Prince d'Eichstadt, Viceroy of Italy (b. Paris 1781; d. Munich 1824). Son of the ill-fated General de Beauharnais (guillotined 1794) and of Joséphine Tascher de la Pagerie, later wife of Napoleon. As a soldier, he had seen service in Egypt and at Acre; his administration of Italy was of the highest order; 9, 37, 59, 131.

Eugenio IV, Pope (Constantio-Gabriele Condolmer: b. Venice 1383; Pope 1431; d. Rome 1447). A pontiff whose whole career was absorbed in trying to mend schisms within the church; 283.

Euripides (b. Salamnia B.C. 480; d. B.C. 405). Greek tragic dramatist. His *Iphigenia in Aulis* (B.C. 405) served as a model for Racine's *Iphigénie*; 39.

Eustace, Rev. John Chetwode (b. 1762; d. 1815). An Irish Catholic priest, author of *A classical Tour through Italy, exhibiting a view of its scenery, its antiquities and its monuments . . . with an account of the present state of its cities . . . and an account of the recent spoliations of the French* (London, 2 vols., 1813); 209.

F***, monsignor, of Bologna; 206.
F***, signor, of Milan; 88.
F***, signora, of Milan; 51.

Fabius Cunctator (d. B.C. 203). Illustrious Roman soldier, appointed pro-dictator after the defeat of Lake Trasimene; by skilful delaying tactics, he brought about the eventual defeat of Hannibal; 343.

Fabre, Giuseppina (*fl.* 1810-1830). French soprano, brought up in Milan. She sang at la Scala, 1814-16; at Venice, 1817; at Palermo, 1819. An excellent *prima-donna*, whose reputation, however, spread little outside Italy; 7, 16, 17, 21, 352.

Fabre, Xavier-Pascal (b. Montpellier 1766; d. 1837). French portrait-painter who spent much of his career in Florence; 317.

Fabre d'Eglantine, Philippe-François-Nazaire Fabre, known as d'E. (b. Carcassonne 1750; guillotined Paris 1794). French actor, dramatic poet and anarchistic revolutionary. Known as *le chef des pourris*, he fell with Danton and Desmoulins. His masterpiece, *Philinte de Molière, ou la Suite du Misanthrope*, was performed at the Theatre de la Nation, 22 February 1790; 397.

Falconieri, signor. Neapolitan insurgent, executed 1799; 411.

Falstaff, Sir John. Character in Shakespeare's *Henry IV, Pt. I (q.v.)*.

Famiglie celebri italiane (history). See Litta, P.

Famille du Jura, la (tale). See Lemontey.

Fantozzi, Count, of Milan; 127.

Farina, monsignor, Bishop of Padua; 95.

Farina, Girolamo Donato, known as *il F.* (*fl.* 1530-1570). Friar of the Order of the *Umiliati*, who shot an arquebus at St Charles Borromeo while he was praying in the Cathedral of Milan (26 October 1569). F. was incensed at the proposed abolition of his Order,

which took place on 7 February 1571; 63.

Farnese, teatro (Parma). See *Theatres*.

Fatiche d'Ercole, le (painting). See Benvenuti.

Favart, théâtre (Paris). See *Theatres*.

Federici, Camillo (Giovanni-Battista Viassolo, known as: b. Garessio 1749; d. Padua 1802). Italian comic dramatist, influenced by Iffland and Kotzebue, author of a vast number of plays, translations and adaptations; 396.

Federici, Francesco. An officer in the royal Neapolitan army, who joined the republicans in 1799. F. led the republican armies against Ruffo's guerrillas, but was routed in the Terra di Lavoro, and retreated to Naples, abandoning all his artillery. Executed 1799; 411.

Fellenberg, Philipp Emanuel von (b. Bern 1771; d. Hofwyl 1844). Swiss pedagogue of international repute, a disciple of Pestalozzi. His school was situated on his own estate at Hofwyl. His numerous writings had a profound effect on Swiss education; 84, 293.

Felsina Pittrice (art history). See Malvasia.

Fénelon, François de Salignac de la Mothe (b. Périgord 1651; d. Cambrai 1715). French divine, preacher, educationist and writer. In 1689, he was appointed tutor to the Duc de Bourgogne, for whom he wrote his famous allegorical novel, *les Aventures de Télémaque* (1699), and later the *Dialogues des Morts* (1712); 111, 161, 257, 332.

Fenice, teatro della (Naples). See *Theatres*.

Ferdinand III of Lorraine (b. 1769; Grand-Duke of Tuscany, 1791; dethroned by the *Directoire*, 1799; restored, 1814; d. 1824). His consort referred to was his second wife, Maria-Fernanda, daughter of Maximilian I, King of Saxony, whom he had married in 1821; his successor was Leopold II (1797-1870); 313, 323, 324, 325, 339, 416*.

Ferdinando I di Borbone, King of the Two Sicilies (Ferdinand III of Sicily, Ferdinand IV of Naples: b. Naples 1751; King, 1759; deposed 1798; restored, 1799; deposed again, 1806; restored, 1815; d. 1825). An appalling monarch, totally under the thumb of

Girondins, the. Political party in the French Revolution, representing the progressive bourgeoisie. Equally opposed to royalists and jacobins, they conspired to bring about the death of Louis XVI; but they themselves were annihilated by Robespierre; 220, 471.

Giuditta, la (painting). See Benvenuti.

Glandervie, Lady Sarah. Daughter of Frederick North, 5th Earl of Guilford; husband of the Irish Lord Douglas Glandervie. Visitor to Naples in 1817; 386.

Goethe, Johann Wolfgang von (1749-1832). German poet, etc. His romantic novel, Die Leiden des jungen Werthers, appeared in 1774. Cf. Foscolo; 128, 315.

Gohorry (Gohory), Jacques (b. Paris c. 1500; d. Paris 1576). French poet, historian, alchemist and translator from Latin, Italian and Spanish. His poetry is little known; his major contribution to his time was the translation of Machiavelli; 265-266.

Goldoni, Carlo (b. Venice 1707; d. Paris 1793). Italian dramatist, who began to write for the theatre in 1747. G. introduced the new, 'realist' comedy into Italy, to replace the traditional Commedia dell' arte; 395, 396, 397.
Works referred to:
Burbero benefico, il (comedy, originally written in French: 1771); 393.
Nozze in Campagna, le (basis of Guglielmi's opera: 1768); 349.
Poeta fanatico, il (comedy: c. 1756); 395.

Goldsmith, Oliver (1728-1774). Poet, novelist and dramatist. The Vicar of Wakefield was written in 1766; 310.

Gorani, Count Giuseppe (b. Milan 1740; d. Geneva 1819). Italian adventurer, writer and politician. Took part in the insurrection of the Corsicans against Genoa; later was associated with the Encyclopédistes and the Girondins. His Mémoires secrets et critiques des Cours, des Gouvernemens et des Moeurs des principaux Etats d'Italie (3 vols., Paris 1793) is a bitterly anti-monarchic pamphlet; 122.

Goury, M. de. Character from the 'proverbe', Le Château de Cartes, by Michel-Théodore Leclercq (1777-

1851): publ. in Proverbes dramatiques, 7 vols., 1823-26; 80.

Grâces, les (comedy). See Saint-Foix.

Grand Opéra (Paris). See Theatres.

Grandeur des Romains (de la), et de leur Décadence (history). See Montesquieu.

Grandison (novel). See Richardson.

Grèce en 1825, la (description). See Lauvergne.

Grétry, André-Ernest-Modeste (b. Liége 1741; d. Montmorency 1813). French composer, best known for his opera Richard Coeur-de-Lion. Founder of the tradition of the Opéra-Comique, so heartly despised by Stendhal; 353, 414.

Greuze, Jean-Baptiste (b. Tournus 1725; d. 1805). French painter, founder of the sentimental-realist-domestic school. Diderot, in particular, was impressed by his 'pathetic interiors'; 270.

Grillus (Gryllus). Elder son of Xenophon, who fell at the battle of Mantinea; 332.

Grimm, baron Frédéric-Melchior (b. Ratisbon 1723; d. 1807). French critic of German origins, a leading figure in the Encyclopaedist movement. His Correspondence (with Raynal, Diderot, Meister, etc.) is one of the major sources of eighteenth-century literary history; 84, 201-202.

Gros, Antoine-Jean, baron (b. Paris 1771; d. 1835). French painter of the early romantic period, who specialised in historical paintings: e.g., le Champ de Bataille d'Eylau (1808, Louvre) and Les Pestiférés de Jaffa (1804, Louvre); 319, 372.

Grossi, Tommaso (b. Bellamo 1790; d. Milan 1853). Italian novelist and satirist, best remembered today for his 'historical romance', Marco Visconti (1831). His early satire, el di d'incoeu (la Prineïde) was directed against the mob who murdered Count Prina; 46, 139, 140, 142.

Grosvenor, Robert, 2nd Earl G., 1st Marquis of Westminster (b. London 1767; d. 1845). English art-patron; as Viscount Belgrave, he built the area known as Belgravia. Added considerably to the Grosvenor Collection; 385.

Guarnacci, marchese, of Volterra; 328.

Guasco, Carlo, of Milan. Lawyer, later assistant prosecutor, Turin. A minor

and Spanish claims, but who was forced to abandon French claims in Italy; 430.

Henri IV (b. 1553; King of France 1589; assassinated 1610). The founder of the modern state of France; 260.

Herodias. Painting attributed by Stendhal to Leonardo da Vinci: it is in fact *Salome with the Head of John the Baptist*, by Luini (*q.v.*); 49, 107.

History of Milan. See Verri, P.

Hobhouse, John Cam, Baron Broughton (b. 1786; d. London 1869). English scholar and statesman, friend of Byron. His works include the *Historical Illustrations of the Fourth Canto of Childe Harold*, and an *Essay on Italian Literature*; 389.

Hohenlohe-Waldenburg-Schillingsfurst, Leopold Alexander, Prince von (b. Waldenburg 1794; d. 1849). German faith-healer; member of the Society of the Heart of Jesus. In 1821, he acquired a reputation for miracles, particularly in Bamberg; 241,

Holbach, Paul-Henri, baron d' (b. Edesheim 1723; d. 1789). French philosopher of German origins. His major treatises, *Système de la Nature* and *Système social*, carry the Lockeian sensualism of the *philosophes* to its logical atheistical conclusion; 92.

Holland, Henry Richard Vassall Fox, 3rd Lord H. (b. 1773; d. 1840). English whig statesman. As a pro-French liberal, he spent most of his career in opposition, and canvassed for the abolition of the slave-trade; 385.

Homer. Greek epic poet; 109, 131.

Horace (Quintus Horatius Flaccus). Latin poet; 93.

Horatii, the Roman brothers of noble birth who fought single-handed against the Curiatii in the Alban wars; 347.

Hume, David (b. Edinburgh 1711; d. Edinburgh 1776). Scots philosopher. In 1763-1766, Hume visited Paris, and was welcomed with frantic enthusiasm; 92.

Iffland, August Wilhelm (b. Hanover 1759; d. Berlin 1814). German actor and dramatist, one of the outstanding character-actors of the *drame bourgeois*. As a dramatist, he was chief rival to Kotzebue; 393.

Imbert, signora. Stendhal's landlady in Florence; 311.

Imogen. Heroine of Shakespeare's *Cymbeline* (*q.v.*); 368, 390.

Indipendenti. Calabrian bandits. See note to p. 426; 426-428.

Ines di Castro (tragedy). See Bertolotti.

Ingres, Jean-Auguste-Dominique (b. Montauban 1780; d. Paris 1867). French painter, a pupil of David. His famous painting of the *Sistine Chapel* (1814) includes a portrait of Cardinal Consalvi; 450.

Innocent IV, Pope (Etienne Aubert, b. Beyssac, *c.* 1300; Pope 1352; d. Avignon 1362). A friend of Petrarch, and patron of the arts. Re-established the papal authority in Rome through Cardinal Albornoz; 288, 289.

Ino e Temisto (tragedy). See Niccolini.

Institut Français. Centralised organisation, founded under the *Constitution de l'An III*, embracing the five major academies of France; 260.

Invito a Lesbia, l' (poem). See Mascheroni.

Iphigenia (tragedy). See Euripides.

Iphigénie en Aulide (tragedy). See Racine.

Irving, Edward (b. Annan 1792; d. Glasgow 1834). Scots divine and evanglising preacher (*c.* 1822). Founder of the sect known as the *Irvingites*, he established a Holy Catholic Apostolic Church, whose present centre of worship is in Gordon Square, London; 147, 464.

Isouard, Nicolo (b. Malta 1775; d. Paris 1818). Operatic composer, *protégé* of the Princess Belmonte. *Début*, Naples 1795. His *Joconde* had had a great success in Paris, and formed the basis of the ballet-pantomime *Astolfo e Giocondo*, with Armando Vestris as the Shepherd and Bernardo Vestris as Astolfo (Naples, 1816); 364, 372-373.

Italia (l') avanti il Dominio dei Romani (history). See Micali.

Italiana in Algeri, l' (opera). See Rossini.

Itinerario Italiano, edizione accresciuta da Giuseppe Vallardi (Milan, Vallardi, 1818); 232.

Izimbardi, signor, of Milan. Master of the Mint, according to Stendhal; 46, 53, 136-138, 141, 202, 215.

Jeu de l'Amour et du Hasard, le (comedy). See Marivaux.

Jeunesse de Henri V, la (comedy). See Duval.

Jo, don, of Portici (=Jorre?); 437.

Jobez, Emmanuel (b. Morez 1775; d. Lons-le-Saulnier 1828). French writer, poet and politician. Member of the Chamber of Deputies during the Hundred Days; liberal deputy under the Restoration; 229.

Joseph II (b. Vienna 1741; Emperor of Austria, 1765; d. 1790). A comparatively liberal sovereign, who showed all the characteristics of the ideal 'benevolent despot'; 94, 122, 237.

Joubert, Barthélemy (b. Pont-de-Vaux 1769; killed 1799). French general in the revolutionary armies, who won renown in the Italian campaign. Killed at the battle of Novi; 411.

Journal. See Stendhal.

Journal des Débats politiques et littéraires. One of the great periodicals of the nineteenth century. Originally the *Journal des Débats et Décrets* (1789), it changed title in 1814. Its early editors included Fiévée, Geoffroy, Dussault, Hoffmann, Chateaubriand, Villemain, etc.; 223, 358.

Julius II (Giuliano della Rovere: b. Abbissola 1443; Pope 1503; d. Rome 1513). A military pontiff who recovered most of the lost papal territories, organised the Holy League, and drove the French out of Italy; 286.

Jupiter Mansuetus; 419.

Juvenal (A.D. 60-110). Latin poet and satirist; 93.

K***, Count, of Poland; 192.

Kabale und Liebe (drama). See Schiller.

Kant, Immanuel (b. Königsberg 1724; d. Königsberg 1804). German philosopher of Scottish origin, author of the *Critique of Pure Reason* (1781); 66, 89, 254, 311.

Kean, Edmund (b. London 1787; d. Richmond 1833). English actor; *début* as Shylock, Drury Lane 1814. The greatest interpreter of romantic intensity in acting; in 1818, K. went as Talma's guest to Paris, and in 1828, produced *Richard III* there, to the enthusiasm of the younger generation of revolutionaries; 90.

Keller, graf von. German officer, Milan occupational force; 133-135.

King Henry IV, Part I (play). See Shakespeare.

Klenau (Kleinau), Johann, baron von Janowitz, Count of (b. Bohemia 1760; d. 1819). German general in the Napoleonic wars; surrendered with Mack at Ulm, but had his revenge at Leipzig and Dresden. Governor-General of Moravia, 1814-1818; 96.

Koenigsfeld, baron. German visitor to Milan; 18.

Kotzebue, August-Friedrich-Ferdinand von (b. Weimar 1761; assassinated Mannheim 1819). German dramatist who perfected the *Schicksalstragödie* (e.g., *Menschenhass und Reue*, 1790). Intriguer, traitor and Russian spy; 116.

Krammer (Kramer). Family of German industrialists settled in Milan. Teresa Kramer was the friend of Monti and Grossi, and the patron of the carbonarist *élite*; 103.

L***, signora, of Milan; 127, 145.

L***, signorina, of Milan *(aet.* 15); 127.

Lablache, Luigi (b. Naples 1794; d. Naples 1858). Italian *basso buffo cantante* of French descent. *Début*, Naples 1812. His reputation reached its peak after 1830, when he was appointed singing-master to Queen Victoria; he was one of the torch-bearers appointed to guard the coffin of Beethoven; 398.

La Bruyère, Jean de (b. Paris 1645; d. Versailles 1696). French writer and moralist. His major work, *les Caractères*, appeared between 1688 and 1696; 270.

Lacretelle, Charles-Jean-Dominique de (b. Metz 1766; d. Macon 1855). French historian and journalist, assistant editor of the *Journal des Débats*, 1790. Leader of the *jeunesse dorée*, exiled by Napoleon. His historical works are voluminous and tendentious: *e.g.*, *Histoire de France pendant le XVIIIe siècle* (14 vols., Paris, 1808-1826); 389.

Lacuée, Jean-Girard (b. La Massas 1752; d. Paris 1841). French general and military administrator, a pillar of the War Office under the Convention, the *Directoire* and the Empire. He was involved in the massacre of Toulon, but escaped: Stendhal's reference is none the less obscure; 154.

1825, *ou Mémoires historiques et biographiques sur Ibrahim, son Armée, Khourchid, Sève, Mari et autres Généraux de l'Expédition d'Egypte en Morée* (Paris 1826). An Appendix (pp. 232-240) contains a *Note sur Lord Byron*, based on a conversation with Father Paul, of the Franciscan Convent of Athens. *Cf. le Globe*, 6 and 9 May 1826; 325.

Lavalette, Antoine-Marie-Chamans, comte de (b. Paris 1769; d. 1830). French administrator, postmaster-general under Napoleon, condemned to death for his activities during the Hundred Days. Escaped from prison in romantic circumstances, aided by his wife, Emilie de Beauharnais, and three English officers; 386.

Lavater, Jean-Gaspard (b. Zürich 1741; d. 1801). Swiss poet, philosopher and Protestant theologian, who gained an international reputation through his discovery of the 'physiognomical science'—the science of determining human character by analysing the lineaments of the face; 259.

Lechi family. A vast and noted clan from Brescia. Stendhal, on his journey to Italy in 1811, had shared a coach with Count Giacomo Lechi (1768-1845), and subsequently met many of the tribe:

Lechi, Count***. An eighteenth-century representative, whose exploits are depicted in the tale of 'Vitelleschi'; 71-74.

Lechi, señora Carmelita. See Lamberti.

Lechi, signora Francesca (Fanny). See Gherardi: Ghita.

Lechi, Giuseppe (1766-1836). Italian general of carbonarist proclivities, who had fought with the Cisalpine Legion at Varallo (8 May 1800) and Raab; 213.

Lemercier, Louis-Jean-Népomucène (b. Paris 1771; d. Paris 1840). French critic and dramatist of the Revolution and Empire. His play, *Pinto, ou la Journée d'une Conspiration* (5 acts, prose, 1801) is the first 'historical comedy' on the French stage; 291.

Lemontey, Pierre-Edouard (b. Lyon 1762; d. 1826). French politician and novelist: appointed controller of the Censorship by Fouché. His novel, *Irons-nous à Paris, ou la Famille du Jura*, was a polite tribute, written for the coronation of the Emperor Napoleon I; 196.

Leo X, Pope (Giovanni de' Medici: b. Florence 1475; Pope 1513; d. 1521) The most magnificent of pontiffs, and an unstinting patron of art, literature and science; 111, 230, 266.

Leo XII, Pope (Annibale della Genga: b. Genga 1760; Pope 1823; d. Rome 1829). Leo XII improved the papal treasury and set his house in order; but his decrees of 1825 mark him out as the enemy of liberalism and of Italian aspirations to liberty; 296, 446*.

Leopold II (b. Vienna 1747; Grand-Duke of Tuscany, 1763; Emperor of Austria, 1790; d. Vienna, 1792). Brother of Marie-Antoinette and of Queen Caroline of Naples. A comparatively intelligent despot; 123, 145, 250, 321, 325.

Leopold, Prince of Salerno (b. Naples 1790). Youngest surviving and favourite son of Ferdinand of Naples; 396.

Lepeletier, rue (Paris). See *Theatres* (Grand Opéra).

Lepri family, of Bologna; 170-173, 235.

Leti, Gregorio (b. Milan 1630; d. Amsterdam 1701). Seventeenth-century Italian scholar-adventurer at the courts of Louis XIV and Charles II, constantly on the border-line of diplomacy and espionage. His *Conclavi de' Pontefici romani, quali si sono potuti trovare fin a questo giorno* was published in 1667; 206.

Lettere di Iacopo Ortiz (novel). See Foscolo.

Lettre à MM. de l'Académie des Inscriptions (satirical pamphlet). See Courier.

Lettre à M. Renouard, libraire ... (satirical pamphlet). See Courier; Furia.

Lettres de Madame Du Deffand (correspondence). See Du Deffand.

Lettres d'Italie (travel book). See Brosses, Ch. de.

Lettres d'Italie (travel book). See Roland de la Platière.

Lettres d'une Religieuse Portugaise. See Alcaforada.

Lettres persanes (philosophical satire). See Montesquieu.

of Leonardo da Vinci. His finest work is in fresco, notably at Saronno and in the chapel at Lugano. His *Salome with the Head of John the Baptist* is now in the Uffizi; 19, 49, 64, 315.

Lullin de Châteauvieux, Jacob-Frédéric (b. Geneva 1772; d. 1842). Swiss economist, writer and traveller, author of the economic survey: *Lettres écrites d'Italie en 1812 et 1813, à M. Charles Pictet* (Geneva 1815); 327.

Luogoteta, signor. Neapolitan insurgent, executed 1799; 411.

Lushington, Fanny Maria, *née* Lewis. Sister of 'Monk' Lewis (*q.v.*), she had married Sir Henry Lushington. Her son (later Admiral Sir Stephen Lushington) was a midshipman in the Mediterranean fleet off Naples in 1817, and was fourteen years of age. Stendhal seems to have confused him with Charles Chichester, who was then twenty-two, and an officer in the army; 385.

Luz, madame de (=madame de la Suze, of a family descended from the Counts of Champagne); 204.

M***, Herr, Austrian Ambassador in Rome; 451.

M***, signora, of Milan; 44.

M***, signora, of Milan (*aet.* 55); 127.

Macdonald, Alexandre, Duke of Taranto (b. Sedan 1765; d. 1840) French field-marshal, who distinguished himself at Wagram. In February 1799, he succeeded to Championnet in command of the French army of occupation in Naples, and in April carried out the withdrawal to Salerno; 405.

Machiavelli, Niccolò (b. Florence 1469; d. Florence 1527). Italian statesman and writer, secretary to the Florentine Government. Besides the *Prince*, M. wrote a notable satirical comedy, *la Mandragola* (1513); 4, 118, 146, 266, 272, 301, 313, 320, 446, 471.

Mack, baron Karl von (b. Nennslingen 1752; d. 1828). Austrian field-marshal, remembered as 'le malheureux Mack', after he had allowed himself to be surrounded by Napoleon at Ulm, and had surrendered with 30,000 men. He was scarcely less unfortunate in the service of Naples, and was totally outmanoeuvred by Championnet in the battle of Rome (December 7-9, 1798); 404.

Mackintosh, Sir James (b. Alldourie 1765; d. London 1832). Scots historian, philosopher and M.P. Stendhal knew him mainly from his contributions to the *Edinburgh Review*; 389.

MacPherson, James (b. Ruthven 1738; d. Belleville House, 1796). Scots scholar, perpetrator of the most famous literary fraud of all time, when (1760-1763) he published a series of 'ancient bardic poems', which he claimed to be the work of the ancient Scottish poet 'Ossian'. These poems, the exquisite distillation of pre-romanticism, took Europe by storm; 392.

Madonna, la (painting). See Reni.

Madonna blessed by Jesus, The (painting). See Correggio.

Maïno. A 'notorious robber' of Alessandria. Stendhal saw him after his capture in 1802; 159.

Maïnoni, signora, of Milan; 46.

Maintenon, Françoise d'Aubigné, marquise de (b. Niort 1635; d. Saint-Cyr 1719). Grand-daughter of the poet Agrippa d'Aubigné; wife, later widow of the satirist Scarron; mistress, later wife of Louis XIV; 192-193.

Maio (Maj), Angelo (b. Schilpario 1782; d. Castelgandolfo 1854). Italian philologist who discovered the art of deciphering palimpsests. 1810, Clerk of the Ambrosiana; 1819-1838, Librarian of the Vatican; 1838, Cardinal. One of the greatest scholars of his age; 259.

Mal***, monsieur. French visitor to Milan; 33-34.

Malanotte, Adelaïda (b. Verona 1785; d. 1832). Italian contralto of aristocratic birth. *Début*, Verona 1806. Rossini made her reputation when he wrote *Tancredi* for her voice. Retired 1821; 460.

Malaspina, signor (=Radaelli, *q.v.*).

Malatesta dynasty, of Ravenna. Italian noble family of Guelf sympathies, founded by Duke Verrucchio (1212-1312), who left his nickname as a legacy to his descendants; 271.

Malclerc, Colonel (imaginary character); 82-84.

Malespini, Ricordano (thirteenth century). Tuscan chronicler, author of a

organist, lawyer and historian; head of the Censorship (1762), director of the *Gazette de France* (1771). M. was accused of persecuting the *Encyclopédistes*, and was bitterly attacked by Beaumarchais in the *Mémoires contre Goezmann*; 190.

Marini, Giuseppe de' (b. Milan 1772; d. Santa Maria di Papua 1829). Italian actor who specialised in character parts, either in straight comedy or in the *drame bourgeois*; 393, 394, 400.

Marini, signora, of Milan. Wife of a Milanese physician, and close friend of Antonia Aresi (*q.v.*). Stendhal had met her in 1800-1, when her gallantries were notorious; 35, 108.

Marivaux, Pierre Carlet de Chamblain de (b. Paris 1688; d. Paris 1763). French dramatist, novelist and journalist, creator of the sentimental-realist novel in France (*La Vie de Marianne*, 1731-1741). Of his numerous and witty comedies, the best known is *le Jeu de l'Amour et du Hasard* (1730); 195, 263, 273, 460.

Marliani, signor Rocco, of Milan; 91, 93, 94.

Marmont, Auguste-Frédéric-Louis de M., duc de Raguse (b. Châtillon-sur-Seine 1774; d. 1852). French field-marshal, who served with distinction at Austerlitz, Leipzig, etc., but finally betrayed Napoleon after the fall of Paris. His *Mémoires* were published in 1857; 253.

Marmontel, Jean-François (b. Bort 1723; d. Abloville 1799). French moralist, dramatist and librettist, who worked in conjunction with Piccini. Best known for his *Contes Moraux*, his *Bélisaire* and his *Mémoires* (1792-1804); 19, 195, 252.

Marriage of the Virgin (painting). See Raphael.

Mars, Mlle. (Anne-Françoise-Hippolyte Boutet, known as: b. Paris 1779; d. Paris 1847). French actress, *début* at the Théâtre Feydeau, 1794. Finest interpreter of the early romantic dramatists; 393.

Martin, Jean-Blaise (b. Paris 1769; d. La Roncière 1837). Famous French comic baritone, *début* 1788. A fine natural voice, but lacking in style. Administrator of the *Opéra-Comique* (1801-1823); 352.

Martinetti, Cornelia, *née* Rossi (1781-1867). Italian *femme d'esprit*, poetess and novelist, famous in Bologna for her *salon* and her beauty. She had written a novel (*Amélie*) in French. Stendhal met her in Bologna in 1817, and again in Rome 1823-4; 247, 298.

Martinus Scriblerus (satire). See Arbuthnot.

Masaccio, Tommaso (b. Florence 1401; d. Florence 1428). Italian painter of the Tuscan school, responsible for the frescoes at Santa-Maria del Carmine, Florence; 304, 315, 366.

Masaniello (Tommaso Aniello, known as: b. Amalfi 1623; assassinated 1647). Neapolitan patriot, leader of an ill-fated revolt against the Spaniards in 1647. Symbolic figure, national hero of the *lazzaroni*; 412.

Mascheroni, Lorenzo (b. Castagneta 1750; d. Paris 1800). Italian mathematician, scholar and poet; an ardent liberal, Deputy of the Cisalpine Republic, and member of the international commission for drawing up the metric system; 140, 150-151.

Mascheroniana, la (poem). See Monti.

Massa, Orazio. Neapolitan officer, general under the Republic; as Commandant of the Castel Nuovo, it was M. who persuaded his fellow-revolutionaries to accept Ruffo's terms of surrender. Executed 1799; 411.

Masséna, André, duc de Rivoli, prince d'Essling (b. Nice 1756; d. 1817). French field-marshal, who served with distinction at Rivoli, Zürich, Wagram, etc. Napoleon referred to him as *l'enfant chéri de la Victoire*; 98.

Massinger, Philip (b. Salisbury 1583; d. London 1640). English dramatist of great power and originality. Best known for the comedy, *A New Way to Pay Old Debts*, and the tragedy, *The Renegado*; 340.

Matera, signor. Neapolitan insurgent, for many years an officer in the French army. When Macdonald ordered his evacuation, M., legitimately wearing his French uniform, attempted to leave likewise, but was arrested by Méjean, and handed over to Ruffo; 412.

Matilda (novel). See Normanby.

Matrimonio segreto, il (opera buffa). See Cimarosa.

Mattei, Alessandro. Italian churchman and diplomat, of Roman patrician stock. Intermediary between Pius VI and Napoleon (1797). Archbishop of Ferrara; Cardinal-Bishop of Porto; 171.

Maximilian I (b. Mannheim 1756; King of Bavaria 1806; d. Nymphenberg 1825). An intelligent monarch, who had served in the French army (1777-1789), and who always changed sides at the right moment; 5, 6.

Mayr, Johann Simon (b. Mendorf 1763; d. Bergamo 1845). Italian composer of German origins. A prolific composer of operas, whose influence on Rossini was not inconsiderable; 19, 21, 137-138, 461.
Works referred to:
Elena e Costantino (opera seria: la Scala, 1816); 21.
Sogno di Partenope, il (cantata, libretto by Lampredi: San Carlo, 1817); 357-358.

Mazzocchi. Bandit-chieftain; 180.

Medici dynasty (Florence); Guelf family which rose to power in the early fourteenth century, and died out in 1737:
Cosimo I (Duke of Florence 1537-1574); 115, 285, 305, 337.
Cosimo III (1670-1723); 321.
Lorenzo il Magnifico (1469-1492); 286, 300, 369.
Giovanni delle bande nere (Captain of the Papal forces: 1498-1526); 266.

Medici di Marignano, Gian-Giacomo de', known as il Medeghino (1495-1555). Rival of the Sforza dynasty in N. Italy; 50.

Médicis, Catherine de (b. Florence 1519; d. 1589). Queen of France by her marriage to Henri II; Regent of France during the minority of Charles X. Largely responsible for the Massacre of St Bartholomew; 430.

Méhul, Etienne-Nicolas (b. Givet 1763; d. Paris 1817). French composer of serious and comic operas, heartily despised by Stendhal. His best-known work is Joseph (1817); 414.

Meister, Jakob Heinrich (b. Zürich 1744; d. Zürich 1826). Swiss philosopher and critic, who lived in Paris 1762-1789, and was a close friend of Grimm, Raynal and the Encyclopaedists. His

Voyage de Zürich à Zürich par un vieil habitant de cette ville appeared in Zürich in 1818; 84.

Méjan (Méjean), Colonel. French officer in Gen. Macdonald's army of occupation. When Macdonald withdrew from Naples, M. was left in command of a garrison in the Castel Sant' Elmo to cover the retreat. Although not specifically responsible for the safety of the Republicans, his total disregard of their interests has left a stain on the French army; 407, 412.

Melfi, don Francesco, of Naples; 441, 442, 443, 444, 445.

Melfi, signora, of Naples; 438, 439, 440, 441, 442, 444.

Mellerio, Count Giacomo (1777-1847). Leader of the militant reactionary faction in Milan; celebrated for his excessive piety; 20.

Melzi d'Eril, Francesco, Duke of Lodi (b. Milan 1753; d. Bellagio 1816). Sometime vice-president of the Cisalpine Republic; Lord Chancellor of the Kingdom of Italy. Greatest Italian statesman of the Napoleonic period. In 1815, he negotiated unsuccessfully to grant the throne of Italy to Prince Eugène; 103.

Mémoires contre Goezmann (polemical satire). See Beaumarchais.

Mémoires de Madame Campan. See Campan.

Mémoires de Collé. See Collé.

Mémoires de Madame la Duchesse d'Orléans. See Orléans.

Mémoires secrets des Cours d'Italie (history). See Gorani.

Memoirs of Benvenuto Cellini. See Cellini.

Memoirs of Casanova. See Casanova de Seingalt.

Memoirs of Correggio (art-history). See Affò, Ragionamento . . .

Memoirs of Harriette Wilson. See Wilson.

Mengs, Raphael (b. Bohemia 1728; d. 1779). German artist, Court-Painter to King Ferdinand of Naples. Uninspired artist in the neo-classical tradition; 173.

Merchant of Venice, The (play). See Shakespeare.

Merci (Mersi), signorina. Ballet-dancer at the San-Carlo; 373.

Mercier, Louis-Sebastien (b. Paris 1740; d. 1814). French writer of the revolutionary period, one of the founders of the 'melodrama'. Best known today for his *Tableau de Paris*—a Stendhal-like day-to-day account of Paris under the revolution. See also under *Duval*; 396.

Mercure du Rhin, le (der Rheinische Merkur). German periodical, publ. Coblenz 1814-1818. Banned finally for liberalism, and its editor, Josef von Gorres (1776-1848) exiled; 251.

Merlin, Philippe-Auguste (b. Arleux 1754; d. 1838). French jurist, philosopher and statesman; sometime President of the *Convention Nationale*; one of the five members of the *Directoire*; important contributor to the *Code Napoléon*; 336.

Mesdames de France. The aunts of Louis XVI, who received guitar and harp tuition from Beaumarchais; 104.

Metastasio (Pietro Antonio Domenico Bonaventura Trapassi, known as M.: b. Rome 1698; d. Vienna 1782). Italian poet, dramatist and librettist, who lived in Vienna from 1730. By far the most popular source of opera-libretti in the eighteenth century. His *Achille in Sciro* dates from 1735; 113, 358, 369, 441.

Metternich-Winneberg, Prince Klemens Wenzel Lothar von (b. Coblenz 1773; d. 1859). Austrian minister, greatest European statesman of the early nineteenth century. General arbiter of the destiny of Europe after 1815; unwavering supporter of the principle of absolute monarchy; 95, 215, 220, 358.

Mezzofante (Mezzofanti), Giuseppe Gaspare, Cardinal (b. Bologna 1774; d. Rome 1849). Italian scholar, bibliophile and linguist; Professor of Arabic at the University of Bologna. In 1838, M. succeeded to Maio (*q.v.*) as librarian to the Vatican; 168-169.

Micali, Giuseppe (b. Livorno 1769; d. Florence 1844). Italian historian and archaeologist; a pioneer in the rediscovery and revaluation of Etruscan art. Author of *l'Italia avanti il dominio dei Romani* (2 vols., Florence, 1810: translated by Raoul-Rochette, Paris, 4 vols., 1824); 328.

Michal, daughter of Saul (I *Samuel* xviii); 389.

Michaud, Joseph-François (b. Albens

1767; d. Passy 1839). French historian, journalist and biographer, today remembered as the founder of the celebrated *Biographie Universelle*. Chief editor of *la Quotidienne*, one of the leading newspapers of the day; 400*.

Michaut, Antoine (b. Paris 1768; d. Paris 1826). French actor, who enjoyed great popularity at the Comédie Française under the name of Michot. *Début*, 1781. Specialised in the portrayal of artisans, *bourgeois* and sailors; 396.

Michelangelo Buonarroti (1475-1564). Italian painter, etc.; 32, 50, 75, 76, 77, 166, 266, 272, 300, 301, 304, 306, 313, 314, 328, 374, 431, 450.
    Works referred to:
        David (sculpture: Florence, Bargello); 306.
        Last Judgment (roof-painting: Sistine Chapel); 450.
        Moses (tomb of Pope Julius II, San Pietro in Vincoli, Rome); 76.
        Prophet Daniel; 431.

Milesi, Bianca (b. Milan 1790; d. Paris 1849). Close friend of Stendhal and aunt of Mathilde Visconti. Fervent supporter of the carbonarist *élite*; 61, 141.

Milière (Millière), Antonia. French ballerina, born in Paris. A pupil of Gardel. After 1814, she danced with notable success at la Scala; 371.

Millico, Giuseppe (b. Terlizzi 1739; d. Naples 1802). Italian male soprano, one of the greatest *bel-canto* singers of the eighteenth century, and a friend of Gluck; 26.

Millin, Antoine-Louis (b. Paris 1759; d. 1818). French archaeologist of distinction; Curator of Antiquities in the *Bibliothèque Nationale*; editor of *le Magazin Encyclopédique*. Author of a *Voyage dans le Milanais* (Paris 1817); 49, 150.

Mirabeau, Honoré-Gabriel-Victor Riquetti, comte de (b. Bignon 1749; d. Paris 1791). French statesman, greatest orator of the Revolution, whose course was seriously affected by his untimely death; 220, 291, 429.

Mirra (ballet). See Viganò.

Misson, François-Maximilien (b. Lyon 1650; d. London 1722). French author and traveller, of Protestant stock. As Tutor to the Earl of Arran, he made a

'Grand Tour', which resulted in the *Nouveau Voyage d'Italie* (The Hague, 1691); 232.

Modena, Francesco IV, Duke of (b. Milan 1779; Duke, 1806; d. 1846). In 1831, Duke F. lost his crown for the second time, and was restored by Austrian arms. Symbol of all the worst aspects of the anti-liberal reaction; 130*.

Molé, François-René (b. Paris 1834; d. 1802). French actor, unrivalled king of comedy, 1778-1795. Enthusiastic partisan of the Revolution. His greatest success was in Fabre d'Eglantine's *Philinte* (q.v.); 393.

Molière (Jean-Baptiste Poquelin, known as: 1622-1673). French comic dramatist. His *Monsieur de Pourceaugnac* (comedy-ballet, three acts, prose) dates from 1669; 19, 190, 396, 447, 477.

Molinari, Nicola. Celebrated Italian dancer and mime, engaged at the San-Carlo in 1817, at la Scala in 1820; 393.

Molini, Giuseppe. Owner of a popular public reading-room in Florence, where Stendhal, in 1819, had spent many hours devouring the novels of Walter Scott; 322.

Mongie, P. Parisian publisher and bookseller, who had undertaken to produce Stendhal's *De l'Amour* (1822); 3.

Monitore Repubblicano (*Monitore Napoletano*). Periodical, Naples, February-July 1799. Edited by Eleonora Fonseca-Pimentel (q.v.); 412.

Monk, The (Gothic novel). See Lewis.

Montaigne, Michel de (c. Château de Montaigne 1533; d. 1592). French moralist, author of the *Essais* (1580-1588). He also wrote a private *Journal de Voyage en Italie*, composed in 1580, published in 1774; 232.

Montemiletto, Prince of (=Girolamo Pignatelli, Prince of Moliterno; b. Naples 1774: d. Naples 1848). Hero of the stratagem which captured the fortress of Sant' Elmo in 1799; Neapolitan ambassador in Paris, 1799-1800; Ambassador to England (appealing for help against Murat); 1808, 404, 425.

Montesquieu, Charles de Secondat, baron de (1689-1755). French philosopher, wit and historian; 101, 110, 124,

126, 164, 272, 273, 394, 458, 462, 464. *Esprit des Lois* (1748); 164*.

Grandeur des Romains (de la) et de leur Décadence (1734); 124*, 458.

Lettres persanes (1721); 110, 273, 464.

Monti, Vincenzo (b. Alphonsine 1754; d. Milan 1828). Italian poet, recognized leader of the neo-classic revival; 46, 65, 66, 112, 139, 140, 141, 143, 151, 258, 265, 325, 326, 455.

Works referred to:

Aristodemo (tragedy: 1786-7); 112.

Bassvilliana, la (In Morte di Ugo Bassville: 4 cantos, 1793); 140, 141.

Mascheroniana, la (In Morte di Lorenzo Mascheroni; 4 cantos, terza rima, 1802); 140, 143, 151.

Morte, la (sonnet); 325-326.

Monti, Teresa, *née* Pichler (b. Rome 1769; d. 1834). Milanese actress, wife of above (1791); notorious for her infidelity. Mistress of Stendhal's cousin, Martial Daru; 112.

Monvel (Jacques-Marie Boutet, known as M.: b. Lunéville 1745; d. Paris 1812). French actor, *début* 1770; also dramatist and librettist. Closely associated with Talma. Father of Mlle Mars; 90.

Moore, Thomas (b. Dublin 1779; d. Sloperton 1852). Irish poet, musician and singer, who owed his early successes more to his magnificent voice than to his poetic talent. Remembered today chiefly for the *Irish Melodies* (1807-1834); 269.

Morellet, abbé André (b. Lyon 1727; d. Paris 1819). French philosopher and writer, friend of Diderot and of Mme Geoffrin. His *Mémoires sur le XVIIIe siècle et la Révolution* (1821) are a valuable contemporary document; 110.

Morning Chronicle, The. Leading whig periodical of the early nineteenth century. Founded 1793; 370, 445.

Morris, Commodore Richard Valentine (b. Morrisania 1768; d. 1815). American diplomat and naval officer, who was in command of the U.S. naval detachment in the Mediterranean 1798-1803; 211.

Morte, la (sonnet). See Monti.
Morte di Cesare, la (painting). See Benvenuti.

Morte di Cesare, la (painting). See Camuccini.

Moruzzi, cavaliere. Master of the Mint in Milan under Napoleon; 120.

Moscati, Count Pietro (b. Milan 1739; d. Milan 1824). Celebrated Milanese physician and statesman, sometime member of the Supreme Council of the Cisalpine Republic, later Senator of the Kingdom of Italy. Stendhal had met him in 1811; 101.

Moses (sculpture). See Michelangelo.

Mozart, Wolfgang Amadeus (b. Salzburg 1756; d. Vienna 1791). Austrian composer; 9, 10, 16, 19, 26, 61, 74, 163, 375, 376, 460, 461.

Mozz***, signora, of Florence; 311, 339.

Müller, Jean de (b. Schaffhausen 1752; d. Cassel 1809). Swiss historian, celebrated for his *Histoires de la Confédération Suisse* (5 vols., 1786-1808); 117.

Murat, Joachim (b. La Bastide-Murat 1767; executed Palermo 1815). Brother-in-law of Napoleon, and a notable soldier. King of Naples, 1808-1815; 188, 189, 280-281, 343, 379, 398, 426, 449.

Murat, Madame. See Bonaparte, Caroline.

Muratori, Lodovico Antonio (b. Vignola 1672; d. Modena 1750). Italian scholar, archaeologist and historian, whose *magnum opus* consisted in collecting, transcribing and re-editing the texts and MSS of Italian mediaeval chroniclers: *Rerum Italicarum Scriptores*, Milan, 27 vols., 1723-1751. This work is the major source of Stendhal's knowledge of mediaeval Italian history; 216.

N***, contessa, of Naples; 374, 386.

N***, Count, of Milan; 45.

N***, marchese, of Milan; 132-135.

N***, Princess, of Milan; 83.

N***, signor: a lawyer in Rome; 451.

N***, signora, of Bologna; 362.

N***, signora, of Milan; 97, 108.

N***, signora, of Rome; 465.

Napoleone legislatore, panegirico (pamphlet). See Giordani.

Narbonne-Lara, Louis-Marie-Jacques Amalric, comte de (b. Colorno 1755; d. Paris 1813). French soldier and courtier, Minister of War 1791-1792. Reputed lover of Mme de Staël.

Used by Napoleon as confidential ambassador; 45, 196, 223.

Nardi, Iacopo (b. Florence 1476; d. Venice 1563). Italian chronicler and dramatist, exiled in 1530 for his activities in defence of the Florentine republic. Author of the *Istorie della Citta di Firenze*, 1494-1538 (publ. Lyon 1582); 295.

Nardo, don (=? Bernardo), lawyer in Naples; 435.

Natali, Bishop. Neapolitan insurgent, executed 1799; 411.

Nathan. Jewish goldsmith on the Ponte Vecchio, Florence; 319, 320, 326, 327.

Natoire, Charles-Joseph (b. Nîmes 1700; d. 1777). French painter and engraver, given to academic mannerisms; his work has a certain faded prettiness; 353.

Nella, marchesina, of Bologna; 233, 234.

Nelson, Lord Horatio (b. Burnham-Thorpe 1758; killed Trafalgar 1805). English admiral, whose victories alone served to redeem his inglorious intervention in the Neapolitan revolution; 67, 407, 408, 409, 410.

Nencini, marchesina, of Florence. A famous beauty. Many years later (1841) we find Stendhal at a ball given in her house; 339.

Nerli, Filippo (b, Florence 1485; d. Florence 1556). Italian administrator and chronicler, a friend of Machiavelli. Governor of Modena; ambassador to Rome; Captain of Pistoia. Author of the *Commentari de' fatti civili occorsi dentro la città di Firenze dall' anno 1215 al 1537* (publ. 1728); 295.

Nero (Lucius Domitio Nero Claudius: A.D. 37-68). Roman Emperor; 206, 345.

Ney, Michel, duc d'Elchingen, prince de la Moskowa (b. Sarrelouis 1769; executed 1815). French field-marshal, the greatest of Napoleon's lieutenants. Made a peer of France by Louis XVIII in 1814; returned to his old allegiance during the Hundred Days; shot as a traitor at the second restoration; 17, 203, 230.

Ney, Aglaé-Louise, *née* Auguié de Lascans. Daughter of a sometime postmaster-general, and wife of above; 17.

Niccolini, Giambattista (b. Tuscany

1782; d. Florence 1861). Italian poet, historian, dramatist and patriot. Librarian to Princess Elisa; ardent republican. His tragedy, *Ino e Temisto*, appeared *c.* 1812; 322, 392.

Niccolò III, Duke of Este (1393-1441). Sovereign who begins the aggrandisement of Parma at the expense of Milan and Venice. Parisina Malatesta was his second wife; the murder took place in 1425; 248.

Nicolas, St. Bishop of Myra, persecuted in the reign of Diocletian; 415.

Niebuhr, Barthold Georg (b. Copenhagen 1776; d. Bonn 1831). Danish historian of German origins; statesman and economist who, in 1806-10, reorganised the finances of Prussia. Author of the *Römische Geschichte* (1811-12 and 1827-28); 329.

Night (painting). See Correggio.

Niobe. Mythological figure, symbol of tragic motherhood; 108.

Noce di Benevento (ballet). See Viganò.

Nomina dell Capellan (Milanese dialect poem). See Porta.

Normanby: Constantine Henry Phipps, 1st Marquis of N., Earl of Mulgrave (1797-1863). English liberal statesman, Governor of Jamaica (1832): Ambassador to Paris (1846-52). In his youth, he wrote romantic novels, including *The English in Italy* (1825) and *Matilda* (1825); 148.

Nota, Alberto (b. Turin 1775; d. Turin 1847). Italian comic dramatist and lawyer. Tutor and librarian to the Royal House of Savoy. His early works are melodramas; later he turned to comedies of manners (*la Sposa novella*, 1827, etc.); 396.

North, Frederick, 5th Earl of Guilford (1766-1827). Scholar, statesman and philhellene. 1798, Governor of Ceylon. A brilliant linguist, a great traveller, best remembered for his ardent championing of the Greek cause. Chancellor of the 'University of Corfù'; 385, 386.

Notti romane al Sepolcro degli Scipione (poetic novel). See Verri, A.

Nouvelle Héloïse, la (novel). See Rousseau.

Novelas Ejemplares (tales). See Cervantes.

Noverre, Jean-Georges (1727-1810). French dancer, choreographer and theorist; pupil of Dupré. Noverre worked in most European capitals (esp. Stuttgart), and laid the foundations of modern classical ballet with his *Lettres sur la Danse* (1760). His methods were popularised in France by Gardel, in Italy by Viganò; 367.

Nozzari, Andrea (b. Bergamo 1775; d. 1832). Italian tenor, pupil of Davide the elder and Aprile. His voice improved greatly in middle age, and he was at the height of his powers 1815-20, during his collaboration with Rossini; 359.

Nozze in Campagna, le (opera buffa). See Guglielmi, P. C.

Nunziata, la (painting). See Sarto.

Nuovo, teatro (Naples). See *Theatres*.

Nystrom, Per Axel (b. Stockholm 1793; d. 1868). Swedish architect who studied in Rome. Later secretary of the Academy of Fine Arts in Stockholm. Stendhal met him in 1823-4; 459.

Octavie, marquise. Name invented by the satirist Béranger (*q.v.*) to designate madame du Cayla, the mistress of King Louis XVIII. Madame du Cayla was notorious for the 'scandalous' sexual practices with which she used to entertain the elderly monarch; 128.

Old Mortality (novel). See Scott, W.

Orestes recognized by Iphigenia in the Island of Taurus. Fresco at Pompeii; 399.

Orfeo (cantata). See Pergolesi.

Orléans, Philippe, duc d' (b. Saint-Germain-en-Laye 1640; d. 1701). An unintelligent and boorish Prince, ancesor of the last king of France (Louis-Philippe); 430.

Orléans, Anne-Marie-Louise-Henriette d'O., duchesse de Montpensier, known as 'La Grande Mademoiselle' (1627-1693). A niece of Louis XIII, and a 'Cornelian heroine' who, after her activities during the Fronde, retired prudently to her estates for five years to compose her *Memoirs* (publ. 1729); 430.

Ossian (pseudo-epic). See MacPherson.

Otello (opera seria). See Rossini: Beria di Salsa.

Othello (tragedy). See Shakespeare.

Ottofredi, signora, of Bologna; 177.

Oxford, Lady; 276.

P***, cavaliere, of Naples; 361.

P***, signor, of Milan: a notorious don-Juan; 136.

P***, signor, of Milan: a serious individual; 84.

P***, signora, of Milan (?=Pietragrua); 80.

Pacca, Tiberio (b. Benevento 1786; d. Naples 1837). Nephew of Cardinal Bartolomeo P. (1756-1844); Governor of Rome, 1816. P. 'amava il gioco e le donne', forged the signature of Card. Consalvi, was detected and dismissed from office, 1820. A corrupt and incompetent administrator; a similar scandal occasioned his downfall in Turin, 1835; 460.

Pacchiarotti, Gasparo (b. Fabricano 1740; d. Padua 1821). Italian male soprano, a pupil of Bertoni. P. rapidly gained an international reputation which lasted until his retirement in 1792; 27, 384.

Paccini, Giovanni (b. Catania 1796; d. Pescia 1867). Italian composer, pupil of Marchesi and Furlanetto. One of Rossini's most successful imitators. Left some forty-three operas, including il Barone di Dolsheim (La Scala 1818); 98.

Pacifico, signor. Neapolitan insurgent, executed 1799; 411.

Paër, Ferdinando (b. Parma 1771; d. Paris 1839). Italian composer who worked in Paris from 1807, and became director of the Théâtre Italien in 1812. Collaborated with Rossini, 1824-6. One of the most popular bread-and-butter composers of his age: his operas include Camilla, ossia il Sotterraneo (Vienna 1799) and Sargino (Dresden 1803); 216*-217*, 377.

Pagani, don Giulio, of Milan; 106.

Pagano, Francesco Mario (b. Brienza 1748; executed Naples 1799). Italian lawyer, dramatist, philosopher and republican patriot, one of the great heroes of the early Risorgimento. President of the Legislative Council of the Parthenopian Republic, and author of the Constitution; 411.

Paisiello, Giovanni (b. Taranto 1740; d. Naples 1816). Italian composer, pupil of Durante; 'Director of National Music' under Napoleon. A major composer of the pre-Rossinian era: his version of the Barbiere di Siviglia appeared in St Petersburg, 1782; his

Rè Teodoro in Venezia in Vienna, 1784; 19, 26, 98, 131, 308, 310, 475.

Palagi, Pelagio (b. Bologna 1775; d. Turin 1860). Bolognese scholar, painter, sculptor and architect, who opened a studio in Milan in 1815. His portraits include one of Angelo Maio (Ambrosiana); 80.

Palazzo Fiano (marionette theatre). See Theatres.

Paletta, Giambattista (b. Montecrestese 1748; d. Milan 1832). Italian physician. Head surgeon of the Ospedale Maggiore; Professor of Anatomy (1795); Professor of Clinical Surgery (1816); 101.

Palladio, Andrea (b. Padua 1508; d. Vicenza 1580). Italian architect, pupil and successor of Bramante. Most of his work is to be seen in Venice and Vicenza; 38, 337.

Pallerini, Antonia. Prima ballerina at la Scala, finest interpreter of Viganò. Her love-affairs were as famous as her other talents; 90, 364.

Palmieri, Matteo (b. Florence 1406; d. Florence 1475). Italian statesman and chronicler; gonfalonier of justice, and ambassador in the service of Florence. P. left a Life of Niccolò Acciaiuoli in Latin, a Storia della guerra pisana; a Historia Florentina, etc.; 295.

Pandolfi, monsignor. Vice-Legate of Bologna; 174.

Paolo, fra (= Alexander Farnese, Pope Paul III, elected 1534: by summoning the Council of Trent, P. put an end to many abuses within the Catholic Church); 237.

Paolo e Virginia (opera semi-seria). See Guglielmi, P. C.

Paradisi, Count Giovanni (b. Reggio nell' Emilia 1760; d. 1826). Italian poet and statesman; sometime member of the Directoire of the Cisalpine Republic; President of the Senate of the Kingdom of Italy. Retired into private life, 1815; 162.

Parella. Notorious Calabrian bandit; 417-418.

Parini, abate Giuseppe (b. Bosisio 1729; d. 1799). Major Italian poet and critic of the eighteenth century. His masterpiece is the satirical-didactic poem, il Giorno, published in four parts, 1763-1801; 93, 94.

Perrucchini, signor. Minor Italian composer; 68, 377.

Perseus (sculpture). See Cellini.

Pertica, Nicola (b. Rome 1769; d. Naples 1821). Italian character-actor, who had belonged to Prince Eugène's company in Milan. After 1815, he returned to Naples, and became the idol of the public and the court; 395, 396.

Perticari, Count Giulio (b. Savignano 1790; d. Pesaro 1822). Italian writer who had married the daughter of the poet Monti, Costanza, later accused of poisoning him. In 1818, he became a patron of Rossini. A sound patriot, but a staunch bulwark of anti-romanticism; 268-269.

Pestiférés de Jaffa, les (painting). See Gros.

Peter Martyr, Saint; 169.

Petrarch, Francesco (b. Arezzo 1304; d. Padua 1374). The first modern Italian poet, best known for his *Sonnets*; 153-154, 255, 301, 313.

Pfiffer, François-Louis (b. Luzerne 1716; d. 1802). Swiss soldier and geographer, Lieutenant-General in the service of France; 465.

Philinte (comedy). See Fabre d'Eglantine.

Philip II (b. 1527; King of Spain 1556; d. 1698). An ambitious tyrant, who laid claim to the thrones of France, England and the Low Countries; 36, 106, 123, 181, 192, 200, 336.

Philippe-Auguste (b. Gonesse 1165; King of France 1180; d. 1223). A great administrator, rival of Henry II and Richard Coeur-de-Lion in England; 307.

Picard, Louis-Benoît (b. Paris 1769; d. Paris 1828). French actor, dramatist and novelist; director of the Théâtre de l'Odéon, and for a short while, of the Italian Opera in Paris; 233, 396.

Pickler (Pichler, Piccheri), Antonio (1697-1779); his sons Giovanni (1734-1791), Luigi and Giuseppe; and his grandson Antonio. Famous family of Italian artists who specialised in the engraving of precious stones; 320.

Piermarini, Giuseppe (b. Foligno 1734; d. Foligno 1808). Italian architect, a pupil of Vanvitelli, whose works include the drab façade of la Scala, the *palazzo reale* and the *palazzo Belgioioso* (all in Milan); 37, 306.

Pigault-Lebrun (Charles-Antoine-Guillaume Pigault de l'Epinoy, known as: b. Calais 1753; d. La Celle Saint-Cloud 1835). French novelist and playwright, extremely popular in his own time. His novels are licentious but witty, and include *les Barons de Felsheim* (4 vols., 1798-9); 351, 393.

Pignatelli di Strongoli, Prince Ferdinando. Neapolitan aristocrat of republican sympathies. In 1793, he and his brother Mario were involved in the famous 'jacobin plot'. Both brothers were arrested, and turned king's-evidence against their fellow 'freemasons', after which they escaped from the country. In 1799, both returned with Championnet's army 'to wipe out their shame in blood'; and both were executed in 1799; 412.

Pignatelli di Strongoli, Prince Mario. Brother of above; 412.

Pignatelli, Prince Giuseppe. Art-collector in Naples; 433.

Pignotti, Lorenzo (b. Figline nel Valdarno 1739; d. Pisa 1812). Italian poet, fabulist and historian. His historical compendium, *Storia della Toscana sino al principato, con diversi saggi sulle scienze, lettere e arti* . . . (9 vols., Pisa, 1813-14) is, together with Muratori, Stendhal's chief source of information about mediaeval Italy; 76, 215.

Pin, signor. Milanese municipal councillor; 98.

Pinalverde, signora, of Bologna; 243.

Pino, Domenico (b. Milan 1767; d. Cernobbio 1828). Italian soldier who volunteered under Napoleon in 1796. General in command of the Cisalpine Brigade; War Minister under the Kingdom of Italy. Served in the Peninsular War and the retreat from Moscow. Retired 1815; 213.

Pinotti, signor. Neapolitan comic actor. Fl. 1790-1800; 402.

Pinto (historical comedy). See Lemercier.

Pistoia, Bishop of (=Scipione Ricci, 1741-1810. R. ardently supported the plans of Leopold II of Tuscany for subordinating the ecclesiastical to the civil authorities; the *Synod* of Pistoia (1786) led to rioting and to the eventual flight and disgrace of the Bishop). See *Potter, L. J. A. de*; 238.

Pitt, William, 'the Younger' (b. Hayes

the Jacobins during the French Revolution; 401, 413.

Rocca-Romana, Ludovico Caracciolo, Duke of. Neapolitan officer, who first distinguished himself in Mack's disastrous campaign against Championnet. Elected General of the People against his will in 1799; later transferred his allegiance to Ruffo. Well-known social figure, 1820-1830; 367.

Rochefort, madame la maréchale de (*fl.* 1740-60); 325.

Roland de la Platière, Jean-Marie (b. Thizy 1734; died Paris 1793). French writer and statesman, Minister of the Interior in 1792. Friend of the Girondins; committed suicide on hearing the news of his wife's execution. His works include the *Lettres écrites de Suisse, de Sicile, d'Italie et de Malte, par M.*** à Mlle *** à Paris en* 1776, 1777 *et* 1778 (Amsterdam 1780, 6 vols.) ; 83, 280.

Roland de la Platière, Manon, *née* Philipon (b. Paris 1754; guillotined Paris 1793). Wife of the preceding, whose marked sympathy for the Girondins brought about her downfall. Her *Mémoires* (1797) were written during her final imprisonment; 209.

Rolla, Alessandro (b. Pavia 1757; d. Milan 1841). Italian violinist, composer and conductor. His pupils included Paganini. 1802, leader and conductor of the orchestra of la Scala; 1805, professor at the Milan *conservatoire*; 19.

Romagnosi, Gian-Domenico (b. Salso Maggiore 1761; d. Milan 1835). Italian jurisconsult, philosopher and liberal politician. Professor of Civil Law, Pavia, 1807. Contributor to *il Conciliatore*; editor of the *Giornale di Giurisprudenza universale*. Arrested 1821; 46.

Romani, Pietro (1791-1841). Roman composer of no distinction whatsoever; 460.

Romano, Giulio (Giulio Pippi de' Giannuzzi, known as: b. Rome 1482; d. 1546). Italian architect, and painter in the Roman tradition; a pupil of Raphael; 266.

Romeo and Juliet (play). See Shakespeare.

Ronchetti, signor. Bolognese bootmaker and patriot; 189, 236.

Ronconi, Domenico (b. Lendinara 1772;

d. Milan 1839). Italian singer; *début*, Venice 1797. Sang largely in Vienna, St Petersburg and Munich. Founded a school of singing in Milan, 1829; 98.

Roscius, Quintus (*fl.* first century A.D.). A freed slave who became the greatest actor in the Roman Empire; 369.

Roscoe, William (b. Liverpool 1753; d. Liverpool 1831). English historian and M.P., author of a *Life of Lorenzo de, Medici* (1796) and a *Life of Leo X* (1805), 325.

Rosenfeld. Pseudo-Messiah (*fl.* 1760-1770); 239-240.

Rosmunda (tragedy). See Alfieri.

Rossarol (Rosaroll), Giuseppe (b. Naples 1775; d. Nauplia 1825). Italian general and patriot of Swiss origins; exiled to Marseille for his share in the 1799 Neapolitan revolution; officer in the Cisalpine Brigade, then under Murat; involved in the carbonarist uprising in Naples (1820-21); escaped to Spain, and took part in the Greek war of liberation; 188.

Rossi, signor. Neapolitan insurgent, executed 1799; 411.

Rossini, Gioacchino (b. Pesaro 1792; d. Paris 1868). Italian composer; 2, 60, 61, 63, 74, 258, 268, 308, 309, 310, 312, 347, 348, 349, 353, 376, 377, 378, 457, 460.

Works referred to:

Barbiere di Siviglia, il (libr. by Sterbini: Rome, teatro Argentina, 20 Feb. 1816); 308, 309, 310, 312.

Cenerentola, la (libr. by Ferretti: Rome, teatro Valle, 25 Jan. 1817); 348.

Gazza ladra, la (libr. Gherardini; Milan, la Scala, 31 May 1817); 60, 61, 348.

Italiana in Algeri, l' (libr. Anelli; Venice, teatro San-Benedetto, 22 May 1813); 309, 348.

Otello (libr. Berio di Salsa; Naples, San Carlo, 4 December 1816); 347, 348, 376, 378.

Tancredi (libr. Rossi; Venice, teatro Fenice, 6 February 1813); 63, 309, 348, 457.

Rousseau, Jean-Jacques (b. Geneva 1712, d. Ermenonville, 1778). French philosopher, novelist, musicologist, etc. His novel, *la Nouvelle Héloïse*, appeared in 1761; his operetta, *le Devin du Village*,

Santa Valle, Princess Emma; 480-482.

Santo-Domingo, Giuseppe-Ippolito. Franco-Italian writer, author of numerous political pamphlets. In 1824, S.-D. published his *Tablettes Romaines, contenant des faits, des anecdotes et des observations sur les moeurs et les usages, les cérémonies, le gouvernment à Rome,* which was seized by the censorship and publicly condemned; 471.

Sanuto (Sanudo), Marin (b. Venice 1466; d. Venice 1536). Venetian administrator and chronicler, who held various offices of state. He left a series of remarkable *Diaries*; also a *Vite dei Dogi* and a *Storia della guerra dei Veneziani contra il duca di Ferrara* (publ. 1829); 295.

Sargino (opera). See Paër.

Sarto, Andrea del (b. Florence 1486; d. 1531). Major Italian painter of the Florentine school; the *Nunziata* referred to may be that by Albertinelli (Uffizi); 107, 266, 215.

Sassoferrato (Giovanni-Battista Salvi, known as *il S.*: b. Sassoferrato 1609; d. Florence 1685). Italian painter, whose works in the Brera include a *Madonna col Bambino*; 108.

Saulle (tragedy). See Alfieri.

Saurau, Count Franz von (b. Vienna 1760; d. Vienna 1832). Austrian soldier and administrator; Governor-General of the united provinces of Venice and Lombardy, 1815-1817; 70, 96, 195.

Scala, la (Milan). See *Theatres*.

Scarpa, Antonio (b. Motta di Livenza 1747; d. Pavia 1832). Milanese surgeon and anatomist of international renown. Professor of anatomy and clinical surgery in the University of Pavia; 101, 150.

Schiller, Johann-Christoph-Friedrich (b. Marbach 1759; d. Weimar 1805). German poet and dramatist. His *tragédie bourgeoise, Kabale und Liebe,* appeared in 1784; 112.

Schlegel, August-Wilhelm von (b. Hanover 1767; d. 1845). German philosopher, critic, poet and dramatist, one of the founders of German romanticism. His chief work on the theatre is the *Vorlesungen über dramatische Kunst und Literatur* (1808); 389.

Schwarzenberg, Karl-Philipp, prince of S., duke of Krumau (b. Vienna 1771; d. 1820). Austrian field-marshal and diplomat. On 2 July 1810, he held a ball at the Austrian Embassy in Paris, in honour of the marriage of Napoleon and Marie-Louise, which he had negotiated. A fire broke out, and caused numerous casualties; 356.

Scoti, signor. Neapolitan insurgent, executed 1799; 411.

Scott, John (b. Aberdeen 1783; d. 1821). Well-known Scottish journalist, editor of the *London Magazine,* and one of the most popular travel-writers of the period. His *Sketches of Manners and Scenery in the French Provinces, Switzerland and Italy* were published in 1821, a few months after S. had been killed in a duel; 48.

Scott, Walter (b. Edinburgh 1771; d. 1832). Scottish novelist, whose *Old Mortality* had appeared in 1816. The *Life of Bage* was written in 1821, as an introduction to vol. ix of the *Novelists' Library*; 78, 180, 322, 422, 443.

Scribe, Eugène (b. Paris 1791; d. 1861). French dramatist and librettist, whose immense output of perfectly-constructed plays earned him vast popularity; 114, 143*, 415.

Senator of Bologna, The; 254.

Sepolcri, i (poem). See Foscolo.

Seven last Words of Christ (quartet). See Haydn.

Sforza dynasty, Milan. A powerful Lombard family, founded by Muzio Attendolo, known as Sforza (1369-1424), which succeeded to the Visconti as Dukes of Milan:
Francesco Alessandro (1401-1466); 79-80.
Galeazzo-Maria (1444-1476); 80.
Lodovico il Moro (1452-1508); 80.

Shakespeare, William (1564-1616). English dramatic poet; 90, 340, 349, 368, 369, 371, 376, 390, 391, 397.
Works referred to:
As You Like It (1600); 368.
Cymbeline (1609-10); 368, 390.
Henry IV part I (1597); 349, 397.
Merchant of Venice (1595); 397.
Othello (1604-5); 90, 376, 391.
Richard III (1593); 90, 391.
Romeo and Juliet (1593); 391.

Shelley, Percy Bysshe (b. Horsham 1792; drowned, la Spezia 1822). English

T

the 'tour' described. Later, of course, the pseudonymn was retained.
De l'Amour (psychological treatise, 1822); 3, 217.
Journal (from which the 'tour' is deemed to be extracted; *not* the same as Stendhal's published *Journal*); 1, 90, 91, 148, 207, 362.
Storia di Toscana (history). See Pignotti.
Storia Padovana (chronicle). See Gattari.
Strongoli, Prince Ferdinand. See Pignatelli di Strongoli.
Suetonius (C. Suetonius Tranquillus: *fl.* A.D. 70-141). Roman historian, author of the *Vitae Duodecim Caesarum*, a 'prodigious compendium of scandalous anecdotes'; 411.
Suvorov, Alexander (b. Moscow 1729; d. 1800). Russian general of great efficiency. By a series of forced marches, he chased the French out of N. Italy; but was finally held by Masséna at Zürich; 405.
Sybils, the (fresco). See Volterrano.

T***, signor, of Naples; 401.
T***, signora, of Bologna; 231.
Tacchinardi, Nicola (b. Leghorn 1772; d. Florence 1859). Italian tenor of remarkable ugliness. Engaged at the *Théâtre Italien*, Paris, 1811-1814, where Stendhal had heard him frequently; 359.
Tacco, Ghino di. Italian robber-chieftain; 160.
Tacitus, C. Cornelius (A.D. 55-120). Roman historian of noted bitterness and pessimism; author of the *Annals*; 24, 374.
Taddei, abate Emmanuele (1771-1839). Italian journalist, editor of the *Monitore* in Naples under Murat. In 1815, the obliging *abate* reversed his principles, changed the name of his paper to the *Giornale delle due Sicilie*, and scribbled on; 400, 434.
Taglioni, Maria (1804-1884). The greatest dancer of the golden age of romantic ballet. Pupil of her father, the choreographer Filippo T. Still comparatively unknown in 1817; 364.
Taglioni, Salvatore (1790-1868). Italian dancer, brother of the better-known Filippo, and uncle of Maria. Resident choreographer at the San-Carlo, where he worked in association with

Gallenberg; 364, 365.
Taissaire (Teisseire), monsieur. Son of Camille Teisseire and Marine Périer, and grandson of that 'ancien jacobin de Grenoble' who so impressed Stendhal in his childhood; 386.
Talma, François-Joseph (b. Paris 1763; d. Paris 1826). French tragic actor. *Début*, Comédie Française 1787. One of the great reformers of the French theatre, T. completed the break with the classical tradition, and inaugurated the phase of romantic realism; 10, 90, 395.
Talleyrand-Périgord, Charles-Maurice de, Prince of Benevento (b. Paris 1754; d. 1838). French diplomat, originally Bishop of Autun. Foreign Minister under the *Directoire*, Consulate and Empire; dominating figure at the Congress of Vienna; Ambassador to England under Louis-Philippe; 409, 416.
Tambroni, cavaliere Giuseppe (b. Bologna 1773; d. Rome 1824). Italian politician and writer; administrator under the Kingdom of Italy. His works include a *Life of Canova* and a *Treatise on Painting*; 171, 238, 281, 466.
Tambroni, signora. Wife of the preceding; 466.
Tamburini, Pietro (b. Brescia 1737; d. Pavia 1827). Italian scholar, historian, philosopher and jurist. Professor of Theology at Pavia, 1778. Despite his ecclesiastical calling, T. was pro-French, even pro-jacobin, and held office under the Cisalpine republic. His *Vera Idea della Santa Sede* appeared in Pavia in 1784; 76, 95.
Tancredi (opera seria). See Rossini.
Tarchi-Sandrini, signora, of Portici; 437.
Tassari (Tessari), Alberto (b. Verona 1780). Italian actor of some repute in Naples, who specialised in tragic tyrants and noble fathers.
Tassari (Tessari), Carolina, *née* Cavaletti (b. Gorizia 1794; retired 1845). Famous Italian actress, wife of the preceding. Originally a member of the company maintained by Prince Eugène. Played in works by Nota, Alfieri, Giraud, Ventignano, etc.; 395, 395.
Tasso, Torquato (b. Sorrento 1544; d. Rome 1595). Italian poet, author of

Vellicri, signor. Impresario in Venice; 341, 342.

Velluti, Donato (b. Florence 1313; d. Florence 1370). Florentine diplomat and chronicler. Ambassador to Bologna, 1350; etc. Author of the *Cronica domestica* (publ. Florence 1731); 295.

Velluti, Giambattista (b. Montolmo 1780; d. Bruson 1861). Italian male soprano; *début* Forli 1800. The only major *castrato* of the period 1812-1825; 16, 378.

Vera Idea della Santa Sede (history). See Tamburini.

Vérité dans le Vin, la ('proverbe'). See Collé.

Veronese, signor. Coffee-house owner, Milan; 236.

Veronese (Paolo Caliari, known as *il V.*: b. Verona 1528; d. Venice 1588). Italian painter, one of Stendhal's most admired artists; 7, 315.

Verri, Alessandro (b. Milan 1741; d. Rome 1816). Italian novelist and encyclopaedist, brother of Pietro V., who contributed more than thirty article to *il Caffè*. Later, V. turned to writing novels of an emphatic, pre-romantic, post-*Werther* type: *e.g.*, the *Notti romane al Sepolcro degli Scipione* (1792-1804; inspired by Young); *Vita d'Erostrate* (Rome 1815; an anti-Napoleonic allegory); 111-112.

Verri, Pietro (b. Milan 1728; d, Milan 1797). Brother of the preceding. Economist and historian, close friend of Beccaria; one of the leaders of the Italian enlightenment, co-founder of *il Caffè*. His *Storia di Milano* appeared 1783-1799; 78, 92, 93, 94, 111, 112, 194, 215, 289.

Vestale, la (ballet). See Viganò.

Vestris I, Gaetano-Appolino-Baldassare (b. Florence 1729; d. Paris 1808). Celebrated dancer, 'star' of the *Grand Opéra*, 'le diou de la danse'. Founder of a famous family; 372.

Vestris III, Auguste-Armand (*fl.* 1790-1850). Dancer and choreographer, grandson of the preceding, whose career was mainly made in Italy. His ballet *Astolfo e Giocondo* was based on Isouard's *Joconde* (Paris 1814); 364, 365, 372.

Vestris (Luigi Vestri, known as *le gros V.*:

Florence 1781; d. Bologna 1841). Italian actor, no relation of the preceding. The greatest character-actor of his age; particularly successful as interpreter of Goldoni; 393.

Vicar of Wakefield, The (novel). See Goldsmith.

Vie de Scipion Ricci (history). See Potter, L.-J.-A. de.

Vieillard (Veillard), M. et Mme. Milanese caterers; 102.

Viganò, Elena (Nina) (*fl.* 1810-1830) Daughter of Salvatore. Singer of Italian popular songs, with whom Stendhal became emotionally involved *c.* 1818; 68, 69, 70, 377.

Viganò, Salvatore (b. Naples 1769; d. Milan 1821). Major Italian choreographer; also composer; 68, 71, 115, 128, 258, 366, 367, 368, 369, 370, 371, 372, 379.

Works referred to:

C. *Marzio Coriolano* (La Scala, 1811); 71, 369.

Ebrea di Toledo, l'; 115.

Mirra, ossia la Vendetta di Venere (la Scala, 11 June 1817, music by Gioja); 68, 90.

Noce di Benevento, il (composed 1801, based on Carlo Gozzi; revived la Scala, 26 April 1812); 368, 369.

Samandria Liberata, ossia I Serviani (composed 1798; revived la Scala 21 August 1813); 369, 372.

Uomini di Prometeo (gli), ossia la Forza della Musica e della Danza (la Scala, 22 May 1813); 369.

Vestale, la (text by de Jouy; music by Spontini and Gioja; la Scala, spring 1818); 128.

Zingari, gli (composed Vienna 1799 for insertion in *Clotilde Duchessa di Salerno*; music by Capuzzi; revived la Scala, 30 March 1812); 366.

Villa, signor. Milanese commissioner of Police; 56.

Villani, Giovanni (b. Florence *c.* 1275; d. 1348). Greatest of the Florentine chroniclers, of strong Guelf sympathies. Author of the *Nuova Cronica*, which deals with the history of Florence down to the year 1346; 295, 388.

Villani, Matteo. Florentine chronicler,